ASIA

IN THE MAKING OF EUROPE

ASIA

IN THE MAKING OF EUROPE

DONALD F. LACH

VOLUME

II

*A
Century of
Wonder*

BOOK THREE: THE SCHOLARLY DISCIPLINES

THE UNIVERSITY OF CHICAGO PRESS

CHICAGO AND LONDON

THE UNIVERSITY OF CHICAGO PRESS, CHICAGO 60637
The University of Chicago Press, Ltd., London

Library of Congress Cataloging in Publication Data

Lach, Donald Frederick, 1917–
    Asia in the making of Europe.

    Includes bibliographies.
    CONTENTS: v. 1. The century of discovery. 2 v.—
v. 2. A century of wonder. Book 1. The visual arts.
Book 2. The literary arts. Book 3. The scholarly
disciplines. 3 v.
    1. Asia—Discovery and exploration. 2. Europe—
Civilization—Oriental influences. I. Title.
DS5.95.L3   901.93   64-19848

International Standard Book Number: Vol. 2: Book 1: 0-226-46750-3
                                    Books 2 and 3: 0-226-46751-1

Endpaper: "Transporting Chinese Women in Public" from Theodor de Bry's
Indiae orientalis (Frankfurt, 1599). Courtesy of the University of Chicago
Libraries.

Contents

[v]

Contents

The National Literatures

Contents

BOOK THREE

PART III

The Scholarly Disciplines

[vii]

Contents

Illustrations

[ix]

The Scholarly Disciplines

Introduction

An analytical ordering of scholarship, consonant with the intellectual activities of the sixteenth century, cannot be made successfully within the framework of modern learning, divided as it is into separate disciplines well insulated one from the other by differences of subject matter and methodology. In an era when cosmography combined the studies of geography, history, mathematics, astronomy, and navigation the stress in scholarship was upon the interrelatedness of disciplines rather than upon their individual internal arrangement and development. Renaissance intellectuals showed no hesitation in pursuing universal topics, often preferring them to critical inquiry within a narrowly defined field of study. They were more deeply concerned about the relationships of God and man to nature and about the correlations between the arts and sciences than they were about discovering the intellectual approaches most suitable to the various sciences. In the course of their investigations they searched the classical and religious authorities, compared those findings with contemporary observations and conclusions, and sought to reconcile the conflicts discovered between traditional and recent learning, both within and among what we call separate disciplines.

Secular Humanists worked to recover the best of the Ancients, but prevailing beliefs often required them to blend classical learning with Christian traditions. Orthodox scholars and theologians also looked backward, but what they saw was a pristine past in which a sinless mankind spoke one universal tongue and lived contentedly doing the bidding of the one true God. Tension between the secular and the Christian had long existed in many speculative fields of scholarship and was exacerbated in all branches of learning by the Reformation and its aftermath. Over the course of the century the knowledge of both the classical and religious authorities was challenged and sometimes openly derided as inadequate or inaccurate by the proponents of a newer learning which upheld the primacy of empirical observation and demanded, though unavailingly, new syntheses of universal dimension and applicability.

It was quite apparent to many contemporaries that neither classical nor Christian learning, nor a combination of the two, could explain or encompass what was being discovered overseas. The very existence of the Protestants, as well as the multitudes of heathens found in America and Asia, belied the church's claim to universality and undermined the credibility of much of its traditional learning. Efforts were made in all aspects of scholarship to stretch established boundaries or to reinterpret conventional doctrine in an effort to accomodate the new information without destroying the traditional structures of learning. In some cases the accommodation was adequate; in others it failed. Basic changes soon came, even in the sixteenth century, to those disciplines whose theoretical limits would stretch no further.

The reactions in scholarly Europe to the opening of the East were conditioned by the character of the disciplines involved as well as by the reigning intellectual conflicts. Speculative scholarship was touched last, and perhaps least obviously, by the new geographical revelations. The practitioners of each discipline were the first to absorb the shock of the new discoveries: artisans rather than artists, alchemists rather than chemists, cartographers rather than geographers, lexicographers rather than linguists were the ones first exposed. As a group the practitioners were more receptive than the theoreticians to the new products and information of Asia and found little trouble in accommodating them. The scholars learned in the canons of Antiquity and the church were less willing to admit the inadequacy or error of traditional learning and consequently were slow to adjust their intellectual perspectives.

Among the natural sciences the newly independent discipline of botany was the most deeply influenced by the broadening of Europe's scientific horizons. Geography, long the handmaiden of cosmography, reasserted independence as its domain suddenly became enlarged and more clearly defined as earthbound. Students of language and geography were quicker than most others to grasp the idea that the theories of the past governing their disciplines were too narrow to contain the flood of new scientific information that poured into Europe. They were also quicker to incorporate the Asian materials, as they became available, into new technical literature and hypotheses. The botanists, even more than the geographers and linguists, impatiently brushed aside the authorities of the past and under the pressure of new knowledge began to reevaluate general concepts and to experiment with novel organizing principles for their discipline. While the opening of the overseas world helped to erode the prestige of the established authorities, it would be a long time before new syntheses emerged to replace those of the past and to accommodate fully the new knowledge.

CHAPTER IX

Technology and the Natural Sciences

Modern science originated in Europe during the sixteenth century as an amal-
gam of medieval technology, Greek learning, medicine, and mathematics. The
inherited technology was the product of the unflagging efforts of a multitude of
craftsmen in Europe and Asia to harness nature to the uses of man.[1] Artisans of
China, India, Mesopotamia, and Greece faced similar practical problems for
whose solutions they often invented similar devices independently, sometimes
simultaneously. Increased intercourse through trade and warfare helped to
diffuse some of the inventions or the ideas for inventions from one cultural
region of Eurasia to the others. The general flow of techniques before 1500 was
from east to west, from China and India to Europe. In the Islamic cultural
region, which after A.D. 750 stretched from Spain to Turkestan, the ideas,
stories, inventions, and techniques of the older civilizations met and commingled
one with the other. From here they were conveyed from the Crusading era

---

[1] The following brief account of medieval technology is based generally on the admirable works
by Lynn White, Jr.: *Medieval Technology and Social Change* (Oxford, 1962); "Tibet, India, and Malaya
as Sources of Western Medieval Technology," *American Historical Review*, LXV (1960), 515–26;
"The Act of Invention: Causes, Contexts, Continuities and Consequences," *Technology and Culture*,
III (1962), 486–97; "Medieval Borrowings from Further Asia," in O. B. Hardison (ed.), *Medieval and
Renaissance Studies*, No. 5 (1974), pp. 3–26; "Cultural Climates and Technological Advance," *Viator*,
II (1971), 171–201; "Indic Elements in the Iconography of Petrarch's *Trionfo della Morte*," *Speculum*,
XLIX (1974), 201–21. Also valuable in this context are Joseph Needham, *Science and Civilization in
China* (6 vols.; Cambridge, 1965–74), especially Vol. I; and the same author's essay "Science and
China's Influence on the World," in R. Dawson (ed.), *The Legacy of China* (Oxford, 1964), pp. 234–
308. See also C. M. Cipolla, "The Diffusion of Innovations in Early Modern Europe," *Comparative
Studies in Society and History*, XIV (1972), 46–53; C. Singer, "East and West in Retrospect," in
C. Singer *et al.* (eds.), *A History of Western Technology* (5 vols.; Oxford, 1956), II, 753–76; A. C.
Graham, "China, Europe, and the Origins of Modern Science," in S. Nakayama and N. Sivin (eds.),
Chinese Science. Explorations of an Ancient Tradition (Cambridge, Mass., 1973), pp. 45–69; and A. R.
Hall, "The Changing Technical Act," *Technology and Culture*, III (1962), 501–15.

(eleventh to fourteenth centuries) onward to Europe where they were rapidly and ingeniously incorporated into medieval technology. By 1500 most of the basic inventions of Asia were well established in the technology of Europe.[2]

To the time of the Crusades the medieval West had few direct and almost no permanent relations with the regions east of Byzantium and the Islamic world. Europe was therefore unconscious of the remarkable civilizations then flourishing in China and India. China was more isolated than India from westward intellectual or scientific intercourse because of its ideographic language. By contrast many of the literary and scientific achievements of India's Classical Age (fourth to twelfth centuries) passed gradually into Persian, Arabic, Hebrew, and Latin texts. As a consequence of these literary transmissions, India was constantly associated in medieval Europe with the conquests of Alexander, inexhaustible wealth, magic, mathematics, and saintlike Brahmans. China, before it was reintroduced to Europe as the "Cathay" of the medieval travelers, continued to be almost unknown and was certainly unrecognized as the source from which the medieval West received many of its most innovative technological ideas.

A multitude of inventions now attributed to China were received in Europe by people who had no clear idea where they had originated or by what routes they had come. Specifically, Europeans were certainly aware that silk, spices, and gems came from somewhere in the East. But they did not associate the group of inventions relating to horses which appeared in eighth-century Europe with India or China, even though the arrival of the Chinese form of the Indic stirrup might have ultimately been as important to military development as gunpowder later became. While the fiddle bow of Java and the pointed arch and vault of Indian Buddhist architecture had appeared in Europe before 1100, the twelfth century was the first to see a significant cluster of borrowings from China: the traction trebuchet,[3] the magnetic needle for navigation, and paper. Gunpowder, known in China by 1040, did not appear in Europe until the mid-thirteenth century.[4] Along with these importations the Europeans of the late thirteenth century became increasingly conscious of their ability through invention to make nature work for human ends.

"The invention of invention" received a mighty stimulus in the twelfth and thirteenth centuries by the arrival in Europe of Hindu-Arabic mathematics.[5] The transmission to Latin Europe of Indian methods of arithmetical notation and enumeration came through the translation of Arabic writings, as did trig-

---

[2] The only important basic machine not known to the Chinese before 1500 was the continuous screw; it seems to have been invented in Europe independently.

[3] See D. R. Hill, "Trebuchets," *Viator*, IV (1973), 101–2.

[4] On the confused history of gunpowder and cannon see the massive collection of data in James R. Partington, *A History of Greek Fire and Gunpowder* (Cambridge, 1960), *passim*. For further discussion see H. Nambo, "Who Invented the Explosives?" *Japanese Studies in the History of Science*, IX (1970), 53, 82–84.

[5] For a study of the unique role of intuition in the formation of Indian mathematical concepts and symbols see D. Uvanovič, "The Indian Prelude to European Mathematics," *Osiris*, I (1936), 652–57.

onometry and its related concepts. The decimal system of "Arabic" numbers, each numeral being given a value according to position, and a special cipher being assigned to the concept zero, had been in use in India by A.D. 270. While certain components of the Indian system were probably derived from Babylonian and possibly from Chinese sources,[6] the European borrowers usually associated algorism with India rather than Babylonia, China, or the Arabic intermediaries. Leonardo Fibonacci of Pisa in his *Liber abaci* (1202) produced the first text to show Europeans how to calculate "after the manner of the Indians." The first chapter opens with a discussion of how any number can be written using the nine figures and the zero. And throughout the remainder of the book Leonardo continues to explore for his readers the possibilities of the decimal position system. Thereafter Indian algorism gradually replaced the abacus in the calculations made for commerce, government, and technology.

Since transmissions of innovation exhibit a fascinating tendency to cluster in time and space, it is not surprising to find Fibonacci's contemporaries experimenting with other Indian concepts. Through Arabic writings and similar channels the Europeans became fascinated with the Indian idea of perpetual motion, a scientific will o' the wisp that has ever since stirred the minds of curious men. In their designs of perpetual motion machines, the Europeans turned to magnetism, the force most efficiently exploited by the Chinese to rotate automatically their armillary spheres and clocks. Gravity and magnetism, forces more constant than wind and water, led Europeans to think of the energy of the universe itself as the primary source of the vast supplies of power required to drive mechanical devices.

Not directly important to science, except perhaps in the new appreciations of nature they exhibited, were the customs and practices adopted by the mendicant orders of the Catholic Church, especially the Dominicans and the Franciscans. Their versions of mendicant asceticism were highly reminiscent of Buddhist and Hindu practices: the knotted cord around the Franciscan's waist, the joined and pointed hands in prayer, and the counting of prayers by means of beads. The Franciscan reverence for birds and animals might also be related to Hindu antecedents as well as a generally responsive and open-minded attitude toward nature which can best be appreciated by reading the accounts of their overland missions to Asia.

Remarkably few new ideas, devices, or techniques of Asian origin showed up in Europe during the fourteenth century, the appearance of playing cards being an exception. It is possible, but certainly not established, that Chinese techniques of anatomical dissection were employed at Bologna in 1316.[7] The Malay blowgun (*sumpitan*) arrived in Italy before 1425, probably by way of Venice and the spice routes of the East. An influx of Tartar slaves in the period before

---

[6] For the Babylonian contribution see O. Neugebauer, *The Exact Sciences in Antiquity* (2d ed.; Providence, 1957), chaps. i and ii; on the East Asian priority see Needham, *loc. cit.* (n. 1), 237.

[7] See S. Miyasita, "A Link in the Westward Transmission of Chinese Anatomy in the Later Middle Ages," *Isis*, LVIII (1967), 486–90.

and after 1400 was accompanied by the appearance of several new items borrowed from the East: the Chinese helicopter top, the Chinese water-powered trip-hammer, and the ball and chain governor for mills which imitates in principle the hand-operated prayer cylinder of the Tibetans. Whether or not movable-type printing came at this time from China or Korea to Europe is a question still being debated.

From the thirteenth to the fifteenth centuries the belief had become firmly rooted in Europe that technological progress was possible and that men could forward it by their own efforts. While Europe remained inferior to the East in subtle handicrafts—sericulture, textile weaving, and porcelain production—it began to run ahead during the early Renaissance in methods of basic production. On the eve of the great overseas discoveries the Europeans had reached a point where they had at their command more diversified sources of power and the means for utilizing them skillfully than any other civilization, ancient or contemporary. The West, unlike the East, fostered those basic machines—clocks, screws, levers, pulleys—essential to mechanization and quantity production. At the same time the aim of European invention began to be directed more and more toward comprehension of the ordered cohesion of the universe. Europe's technological preparation, scientific attitude, and control of energy yielded the productivity, organizational skill, and naval and military superiority that made possible its successful overseas expansion. To a degree this technological superiority of Renaissance Europe over Greco-Roman antiquity and the great civilizations of Asia resulted from the earlier borrowings of Europe from the East.[8]

I

TECHNOLOGY AND ENGINEERING

Today the field of technology is confined to the applications made by engineers and inventors of the basic discoveries of theoretical science. To the mechanics and artisans of the sixteenth century technology remained, as it had to their forebears, the empirical attempt to use nature without the guidance of that orderly body of knowledge called science. To a society in which nine-tenths of the population was still engaged in tilling the soil, the mechanical invention was much more novel and its impact more profound than similar innovations are today. Since continuity and gradualness rather than sharp breaks characterize the process of technological change, the history of technology, more than most histories, resists narrow time divisions; innovations and inventions are ordinarily more important in their potential for future development than for any imme-

---

[8] Cf. A. G. Keller, "The Scientific and Technological Sages of Ancient China," *Ambix*, XVIII (1971), 49.

diate advantage they may bring. It is extremely difficult to assess the impact of inventions upon sixteenth-century society because the time span under consideration is so short when compared to the thousand years of the Middle Ages. A survey of the technical borrowings of Europe from Asia in the sixteenth century is nonetheless possible, primarily because the efforts at imitation stand out sharply from the slow internal genetic developments. Any assessment of the long-range impact of imitative adaptation can be only suggestive and provisional at best. In the most generalized sense the borrowings, like other sixteenth-century technological innovations, certainly contributed to the growth of the primitive sciences of mechanics and dynamics.[9]

New stimuli to technological advance were provided in the sixteenth century by the overseas discoveries, the rise of the national state and its patronage of technology and science, the publication of increased numbers of books on technological and related subjects, and the application of mathematics to the traditional arts and crafts.

But specifically what were the products and ideas brought to Europe in the sixteenth century which possessed immediate or potential influence on technology? The relevant imports from Asia included, sometimes in samples and at other times in quantity, a wide variety of ceramics, lacquerware, wooden furniture, textiles, and musical instruments as well as wax, resin, caulking, tung-oil varnish, elephant hooks and bells, folding screens, parasols, bamboos and reeds for water carrying, maps, charts, books, and paintings.[10] In European books and in the legends and pictures on Western maps information could also be found about printing, paper, manufacture of palm leaf books, architecture, textile weaving, the compass, measuring devices, weapons, gunpowder, ships, pumps, watermills, hammocks, palanquins, bells, speaking tubes, and sailing chariots.[11] As can be observed from these lists, no new basic tools or inventions appear. These imports are primarily curious devices and products that appealed to the sailors, merchants, and missionaries in their travels about the East, and commodities like porcelains and textiles which enjoyed a good market in Europe. The many omissions from these lists may also be accounted for by the tendency on the part of the early collectors and writers to concern themselves with Asian humanity, flora, and fauna rather than with devices.[12] Such an observation leads to the conclusion that the Europeans, while standing in awe of Chinese craftsmanship, felt that they had little left to learn from the East about basic tools and contrivances.

The only European invention of the century for which there is a firm genetic relationship to an Asian prototype is the sailing chariot of Simon Stevin (1548–1620). Escalante, Barros, Mendoza, and Linschoten were the sixteenth-century

[9] See E. J. Dijksterhuis, *The Mechanization of the World Picture* (Oxford, 1961), p. 243.

[10] See the table of imports in *Asia*, II, Bk. 1, 55.

[11] See *ibid.*, Vols. I and II, *passim*.

[12] Cf. the discussion of the response to America in I. B. Cohen, "La découverte du nouveau monde et la transformation de l'idée de la nature," in A. Koyré (ed.), *La science au seizième siècle* (Paris, 1960), pp. 191–210.

writers who first reported on the use of sailing carriages in China.[13] European engravers, possibly on the basis of such literary materials, prepared portraits of these land yachts for maps and books, the details of which they certainly derived from their own fertile imaginations. The separate map of China prepared by Luis Jorge de Barbuda published in the 1584 version of Ortelius' atlas is one of the first extant examples to depict land ships.[14] They are placed in the blank spaces outside China proper to the north and west of the Great Wall. Information on technical details about the construction of sailing chariots was apparently limited to what might be garnered from these portraits and from Linschoten's remark that the Chinese "make and use chariots of such excellent construction that they are propelled by the wind on a flat plain as if they were in the water."[15]

Simon Stevin, a highly reputable Dutch engineer and scientist, probably was urged by Prince Maurice of Nassau to undertake the construction of a land yacht or even a fleet of them. The ancient Egyptians had transported their gods on sailing chariots, but it is unlikely that Stevin or his contemporaries knew anything of this feat.[16] Botero reported in 1588 that "not many years since" sailing chariots were tried out in Spain.[17] But no evidence exists to show that Stevin knew of these Spanish experiments. From the available evidence, both literary and pictorial, it seems probable that Stevin constructed his chariots along lines suggested by the engravings of the Chinese land yachts. The general idea was after all more important than the details of construction; all that was needed was to put together the carriage and the sail, both well-known devices, and construct a sensitive steering mechanism.

Much of what is known about the first trial run of Stevin's yacht in 1600 was related by Hugo de Groot (1583–1645), better known as Grotius, who was then but seventeen years of age. Grotius' remarks on the incredible speed and maneuverability of the sailing carriage are supported by the testimony of a number of his contemporaries and by later witnesses.[18] They are unanimous in asserting that it carried as many as twenty-eight persons along the beach for a distance of nearly sixty miles in less than two hours. Such a speed in land transit was certainly impossible for any other vehicle of 1600; so the importance of Stevin's experiment lay, whether he himself realized it or not, in letting Europeans know that men are capable of traveling overland at speeds previously not

---

[13] See *Asia*, I, 741, 770–71. Also see pls. 32, 33, 34.

[14] See *ibid.*, p. 819. For a reproduction of the map see *ibid.*, in illustrations following p. 752, as well as the independent land ship engraving from Theodor de Bry, *Indiae orientalis* (Frankfurt, 1599). Another independent engraving appears in the lower right-hand corner of the map of China in Gerard de Jode, *Speculum orbis terrarum* (Antwerp, 1593).

[15] See H. Kern (ed.), *J. Huygen van Linschoten, Itinerario . . .* ('s-Gravenhage, 1910), Pt. 1, p. 65.

[16] See R. J. Forbes, "The Sailing Chariot," in E. J. Dijksterhuis (ed.), *The Principal Works of Simon Stevin* (6 vols.; Amsterdam, 1955–66), V, 3–4.

[17] From the *Greatness of Cities* (1588) as translated in P. J. Waley and D. P. Waley (eds.), *Giovanni Botero, The Reason of State* (London, 1956), p. 226.

[18] See Forbes, *loc. cit.* (n. 16), pp. 5–7.

attained.[19] Although others did not immediately follow Stevin's lead by constructing sailing carriages of their own, the idea he fostered was never lost to succeeding generations. Sailing chariots of this type ply the beaches of Belgium today and modifications of them are extremely popular at many beachside resorts throughout the world.

The other European inventions of the sixteenth century which may owe a debt to Chinese prototypes cannot be so clearly documented as the land ships. Most of the suspected cases rest on the ground of priority, and on the probability that the invention itself or the idea for it was more likely diffused than independently discovered. The Chinese helicopter top, known as early as the fourth century A.D., made its earliest appearances in Renaissance European paintings and in the drawings of Leonardo da Vinci.[20] The kite, like the helicopter top, was one of the precursors of aerodynamics and aviation. In China the kite dates perhaps as far back as the fourth century B.C. and by the time of Marco Polo man-lifting kites were in use in the Mongol empire.[21] In Europe Giambattista della Porta in his *Magia naturalis* (1589) was perhaps the first to refer to the kite. He probably saw Asian kites that the curious had brought back to Europe, and he calls them "flying sails." [22] Paddle-wheel boats were known in China as early as the eighth century A.D. No practical paddle-wheel vessel appeared in Europe until 1543. In that year Blasco de Garay in Spain constructed boats for harbor use that were manned by forty men working treadmills.[23] The Portuguese experimented with caulking their vessels in the Chinese manner and the Dutch probably added leeboards to their craft that were copied from Chinese models.[24] The wheelchair, known in China since the sixth century A.D., also evidently first appeared in Europe at this time.[25] The case for the borrowing of these contrivances from Asia is strengthened by the fact that they all occur during the relatively short period of the sixteenth century, and form a technological cluster relating to transportation (cf. Pls. 30, 31, 35). It hardly needs to be pointed out that efficient human transport was one of the thorniest problems confronting the armies, navies, and business travelers of an expanding and internally mobile Europe.

---

[19] Also emphasized by Needham, *op. cit.* (n. 1), IV, Pt. 2, 280–81. It should be observed that Stevin himself never mentions the land yacht in his extant books or notes. Even though he possibly thought of it as a toy designed to please his patron, it should be recalled that toys have often anticipated in principle many major inventions: helicopter, balloon, etc. Though I have not seen it, the Amsterdam publisher Claes Jansz.Visscher evidently issued a report in 1652 in Dutch, Latin, and French on Maurice's "Windt-wagen." See under Stevin in *A Short Title Catalogue of French Books, 1601–1700, in the British Museum* (London, 1973).

[20] Needham, *op. cit.* (n. 1), IV, Pt. 2, 583.

[21] *Ibid.*, pp. 577, 589.

[22] *Ibid.*, p. 580. Also see B. Laufer, *The Prehistory of Aviation* (Chicago, 1928), pp. 31–38.

[23] See Needham, *op. cit.* (n. 1), IV, Pt. 2, 414.

[24] On caulking see below, p. 418; for the leeboards see E. Doran, Jr., "The Origin of Leeboards," *Mariner's Mirror*, LIII (1967), 51.

[25] It may be seen in several engravings by Hans Burgkmair, the artist of the "Triumph of Maximilian" and the "King of Cochin" series (see *Asia*, II, Bk. 1, 79–81). For detail see H. L. Kamenetz, "A Brief History of the Wheelchair," *Journal of the History of Medicine*, XXIV (1969), 205–6.

Internal migration stimulated by repressive state policies, disruptions of war, religious persecution, and the desire for quick riches was one of the most characteristic features of life in sixteenth-century Europe. The consequent diffusion of artisans, perhaps more than the publication of books, had the effect of spreading technical knowledge quickly from one European center to the other. Portuguese cartographers, pilots, and navigators carried what had been classified as state secrets to Spain, Italy, France, and Holland. Rulers vied for the services of knowledgeable craftsmen as they sought to achieve a greater degree of self-sufficiency, particularly in expensive luxury items. The Medicis of Florence, for example, sought far and wide for artisans who might quickly find for them the secret of porcelain manufacture.[26] Constantly at war, or confronted with the threat of war, the rulers of Europe patronized gunsmiths and devoted large sums to the building and improvement of cannon, arsenals, and artillery trains.[27] Arms and other essentials were often admitted duty free when it was impossible to develop competitive home industries. Guido Panciroli (1523–99), the Paduan professor who composed the *Nova reperta* (Amberg, 1599), raised a question which has ever since troubled students of the origins of cannons. He asked:

Guns as well as *Printing* were found out by the *Chinese* many Ages ago. . . . But how is it possible or credible that an Instrument so necessary for the besieged to repel the Attacks of their Enemies should lie dormant so long? Whereas, as soon as ever the Use of Guns was known to the Venetians in 1380 . . ., it was presently communicated to the other Peoples so that now nothing is more common throughout the World.[28]

The answer to this and several other problems relating to the diffusion of techniques may be found, in some part at least, in the fact that Europe, unlike China, was composed of competing states and nationalities involved in intense religious and cultural hostilities that China did not experience. Rapid progress in technological advancement has more often occurred in a context of tension and war than in the quiet of isolation and peace.

Many contemporary writers, including Polydore Vergil, Cardano, Bodin, and Panciroli, considered the compass, printing, and gunpowder to be inventions of such fundamental importance that "the whole of antiquity has nothing equal to show."[29] A number of commentators, like Panciroli himself, credited

---

[26] See *Asia*, II, Bk. 1, 107–8.

[27] See C. Cipolla, *Guns, Sails, and Empire* (New York, 1965), p. 26.

[28] From the English translation of 1715, *The History of Many Memorable Things Lost* . . . (2 vols. in 1; London, 1715), p. 385; this is an epitomized translation from G. Panciroli, *Nova reperta*, second edition of 1608, p. 68. Buonaiuto Lorini avers that firearms were brought into Europe via Turkey by German merchants; Raleigh in his *History of the World* (see above, p. 386) credits the Chinese. Since many Christians abhorred firearms, the theories of outside invention had the advantage of placing the responsibility on infidels. See J. R. Hale, "Gunpowder and the Renaissance: An Essay in the History of Ideas," in C. H. Carter (ed.), *From the Renaissance to the Counter-Reformation: Essays in Honor of Garrett Mattingly* (New York, 1965), pp. 116–17. The earliest reference to Chinese influence on European fireworks is in G. B. della Porta, *Magia naturalis* (Naples, 1589), Bk. XX, chap. x. For further commentary see Cipolla, *op. cit.* (n. 27), pp. 21–22 n. 2, 104–5.

[29] From Cardano, *De subtilitate* (Lyons, 1550), Bk. III.

the Chinese with one or more of these key inventions. While many of the authors remain content merely to record a Chinese origin for printing, others assert that it was brought from China to Germany by travelers over the land routes. Panciroli, who actually "saw some few pages printed at China," realized that Gutenberg's movable-type printing differed in technique from xylographic printing and concludes therefrom that "typography is old in China, but as found out in Mentz, it is a modern thing."[30] He recognizes that the magnetic compass was unknown to Antiquity, asserts that it was discovered at Amalfi three hundred years earlier, reports that others believe it was brought back to Europe by Marco Polo, and notices that Osório claims Vasco da Gama took it "from certain barbarous Pyrates roving about the Cape of Good Hope."[31] From these and numerous similar observations, it becomes clear that the intellectual world of the sixteenth century was aware that Europe of the past owed a heavy technological debt to China. While curious Asian inventions, techniques, and devices continue to be regularly noted in contemporary travel accounts, no writers of the sixteenth century identify specific Asian devices that should be copied for the immediate benefit of Europe. They seem content to speculate about the origins of key inventions and to assume that Asia no longer has anything to contribute to Europe other than porcelains, lacquers, and textiles.

Many Chinese textile weaves and decorative motifs had been successfully copied before 1500 by European makers of figured fabrics. During the sixteenth century the Europeans nonetheless continued to import Asian textiles, especially the Indo-Portuguese and Sino-Portuguese works prepared especially to appeal to European tastes.[32] No marketable European copies of Chinese porcelain or Asian lacquerware appeared before the last quarter of the century. Porcelains continued to be imported in quantity, even after the Italians had managed to produce a marketable faïence. The vogue for lacquer in Europe was met by the efforts of Venetian craftsmen to prepare recipes for lacquer varnish and to master the technique of applying it to traditional boxes and other art objects. The process which they finally developed at the end of the century was based on Near Eastern rather than Far Eastern techniques.[33] The demand for Chinese, Japanese, and Indian creations continued to mount, however, perhaps because the inferiority of European products had the effect of highlighting the superior quality of the Asian imports. From literary evidence, such as notes in inventories and comments in books, it is clear that the Europeans still generally

[30] For these comments see *The History of Many Memorable Things Lost* (n. 28), pp. 342–43; for the discussion in full see the Latin original, *Nova reperta* (n. 28), pp. 589–602.

[31] *Ibid.*, p. 337; for Latin discussion see *ibid.*, pp. 564–89.

[32] See *Asia*, II, Bk. 1, 95–99. Also see J. F. Flanagan, "Figured Fabrics," in Singer *et al.* (eds.), *op. cit.* (n. 1), III, 199–202; and G. F. Wingfield Digby, "Some Silks Woven under Portuguese Influence in the Far East," *Burlington Magazine*, LXXVII (1940), 52–61.

[33] See H. Huth, *Lacquer of the West: The History of a Craft and an Industry* (Chicago, 1971), chap. i. Huth discerns two waves in the European craze for lacquer: from *ca.* 1550 to 1630 when the Near Eastern technique was copied and after 1660 when the Far Eastern technique was imitated.

associated all imported porcelains and lacquers with further Asia rather than the Near East.

The regular availability of certain Asian manufactured products, and the flexibility exhibited by Asian artisans in designing their products to appeal to the European buyer, certainly had an inhibiting effect upon technological experiment in Europe. A dearth of key Asian products—teak, bamboo, products of the coco palm, zinc, tin—as well as a shortage of artisans also inhibited practical experiment in Europe. The first Portuguese to arrive in Malaya found a tin coinage already in use; their successors soon adopted a tin coinage of their own at Malacca. But in Europe it was only in England, where the metal was locally available, that a few tin coins were minted during the sixteenth century.[34] When the requisite materials were on hand, imitation was more successful. Curved roofs on the town halls of Padua (1306) and Vicenza (1560) could easily have been modeled on drawings of a palace in India.[35] Sulphur matches, which were sold in Hangchow when Marco Polo was there, appear in Europe for the first time around 1530;[36] probably because sulphur and wood were cheap and universally available matches soon became relatively common. But the nonexistence in Europe of certain dyes and clays prevented experimenters from producing successful imitations of Asian colors, varnishes, and porcelains. Many years passed before European technicians could provide adequate substitutes for the raw materials they lacked, and before they began to understand how to combine the materials they did have in the proper proportions to produce satisfactory imitations.

Europe possessed an advanced technology in scientific instruments at the beginning of the sixteenth century. Public clocks driven by weights were then commonplace; over the course of the century domestic clocks driven by springs became popular in the cities.[37] The clockmakers, especially those of Augsburg and Nuremberg, were among the most innovative and ingenious of Europe's craftsmen. But they, like other instrument makers, concentrated upon improving and perfecting existing creations rather than experimenting with the manufacture of new devices. Technical advance slowed down in the second half of the sixteenth century in all branches of mechanical endeavor.[38] This deceleration in innovation may have been connected with advances in communication. The migration of artisans from place to place contributed to the education of others while inhibiting independent creative effort. The multiplication of printed books dealing with mathematical methods and illustrated with numerous mechanical contrivances had the effect of forcing the conscientious craftsman to read about the works of his colleagues elsewhere before undertaking experiments on his own.[39] To make the task of the artisan easier, books called

---

[34] See E. S. Hedges, *Tin in Social and Economic History* (New York, 1964), p. 6.
[35] See M. S. Briggs, "Building Construction," in Singer *et al.* (eds.), *op. cit.* (n. 1), III, 249.
[36] See Needham, *op. cit.* (n. 1), IV, Pt. 1, 71.
[37] See C. M. Cipolla, *Clocks and Culture (1300–1700)* (London, 1967), p. 49.
[38] See B. Gille, *Engineers of the Renaissance* (Cambridge, Mass., 1966), p. 199.
[39] See D. de Solla Price, *Science since Babylon* (New Haven and London, 1961), pp. 51–52.

"theaters," comparable in their encyclopedism to the cosmographies and atlases of the period, began to appear in many languages. They purported to show through their texts, diagrams, and illustrations what had so far been accomplished in various technical fields. Further advances in European technology therefore had to wait for the artisan to understand, digest, and adapt this stock of new information to his own ends. This period of stock-taking occurred contemporaneously with the publication of new information on China. Ironically, the failure of Chinese invention to exert a more significant and immediate influence on sixteenth-century technology may perhaps be attributed to the general conservatism of the European artisans themselves.

2

MATHEMATICS AND ASTRONOMY

From the time of primitive man to today a close relationship has existed between the observation of the heavens and the reckoning of time on earth. Mathematics in the advanced civilizations of China, India, and Europe was studied in early times more for the needs of astronomers in making calendars than for the mundane requirements of farmers and merchants. In China and India, as opposed to Greece, the preoccupation was with arithmetic and algebra rather than geometry.[40] Certain of the algebraic conceptions of Pythagoras, such as irrational numbers and the theorem named for him, may have been derived in ancient times from Indian mathematics.[41] During the twelfth and thirteenth centuries the Hindu-Arabic numerical and computational system as well as elements of Indian astronomy certainly passed through the Islamic world into Europe, possibly by means of Spanish intermediaries.[42] Information on the decimal position and on linear and quadratic equations entered Europe through the translations of the arithmetic and algebra of al-Khwārizmī, a ninth-century mathematician of Baghdad from whom algorism takes its name. The sine of trigonometry, which had first appeared in Indian astronomical works, was introduced to Europe through the translations of the Arabic works.[43] In Europe

[40] For a general statement on the characteristics of Chinese mathematics see U. Libbrecht, *Chinese Mathematics in the Thirteenth Century* (Cambridge, Mass., 1973), pp. 1–18.

[41] Other Pythagorean ideas which are sometimes credited to his knowledge of India: the doctrines of transmigration and metempsychosis, abstention from animal flesh, and the division of the natural world into the five elements of fire, water, earth, air, and empty space (ether). See S. Sen, "Transmissions of Scientific Ideas between India and Foreign Countries . . .," *Bulletin of the National Institute of Sciences of India* XXI (1963), 209.

[42] The problem of the literary transmission of Indian numerals to Europe was complicated by the prior existence of the *ghubar* numerals used in Spain by the western Arabs. For a convenient survey see S. R. Benedict, *A Comparative Study of the Early Treatises Introducing into Europe the Hindu Art of Reckoning* (Concord, N.H., 1916).

[43] See J. Filliozat, "Ancient Relations between Indian and Foreign Astronomical Systems," *Journal of Oriental Research* (Madras), XXV (1957), 7–8. For further discussion consult L. Hogben, *Mathematics in the Making* (London, 1960), p. 149.

trigonometry and the Indian numerals were at first taken up by astronomers; they helped to introduce them to others by using them in the folk calendars they prepared. The Hindu-Arabic numerals were nonetheless slow in coming into use because computation with them was too advanced for the merchants to grasp easily and too novel for the universities to accept readily.[44]

In the sixteenth century European mathematics underwent a reorientation in a practical direction to meet the new requirements of bankers and businessmen who had to deal with a vastly increased supply of money and a rapid rise in the numbers of transactions they completed. The mounting requirements of technicians in navigation, gunnery, astronomy, military architecture, and art also increased the demand for improvement of calculation techniques. To meet these demands more effectively the writers of arithmetic books and other practical manuals quickly turned to the Hindu-Arabic system of reckoning. In time they also algebraized most of the more common methods of computation and developed trigonometry into a homogeneous system.[45] A few algebras continued to be translated into the vernacular from Greek and Latin versions of Arabic texts. Some of the Portuguese arithmetic books included problems on nautics, shipping, and the merchandizing of spices. A German arithmetic dated about 1525 brought into usage in Europe the words "positive" and "negative," possibly translations through Arabic of the Chinese words *chang* and *fu*.[46]

The cosmographers with their varied interests in practical astronomy, mathematics, and cartography were among the first to introduce this new system of reckoning to a larger public.[47] Peter Apian (1495–1552), the popularizer of Ptolemaic astronomical and cartographical ideas, published a vernacular text for the instruction of merchants in computation by the new method. In his remarkable *Eyn neue und wolgegründete Underweisung aller Kauffmans Rechnung* (Ingolstadt, 1527) he taught the use of all the elementary operations from addition to multiplication, explained how to abstract square and cube roots, and began his arithmetical progressions with zero and linked them to a variety of geometrical progressions with which his readers presumably already had some acquaintance. The extraction of roots of lower degrees was highly developed in China as early as the first century B.C.; and the treatment of roots of higher degrees seems to have traveled westward to the Arabic world in the fifteenth century and quickly thereafter into Europe.[48] Most striking both for the history of European mathematics and for the diffusion of ideas is Apian's description for the first time in a Western text of the arithmetical triangle of binomial coefficients, later called the Pascal triangle. Known to Chinese mathematics from around A.D.

[44] See B. Datta and A. N. Singh, *History of Hindu Mathematics* (Bombay, 1962), p. 95.

[45] Based on H. L. Wussing, "European Mathematics during the Evolutionary Period of Early Capitalistic Conditions (15th and 16th Centuries)," *Organon*, IV (1967), 89–93.

[46] See B. A. Rosenfeld and M. L. Cernova, "Algebraic Exponents and Their Geometric Interpretations," *Organon*, IV (1967), 111–12.

[47] For a listing of arithmetic books see D. E. Smith, *Rara arithmetica: A Catalogue of the Arithmetics Written before the Year MDCI . . .* (Boston and London, 1908). For Apian's portrait see pl. 27.

[48] Needham, *op. cit.* (n. 1), III, 146–47.

1100, this triangle shortly traveled westward. It was so important to Apian that he had it depicted on the cover of his book.[49] Toward the end of the seventeenth century, the Pascal triangle facilitated the study of infinite series, the calculus of finite differences, and the theory of probability.

The many other books of commercial or applied arithmetic published during the sixteenth century contributed only slightly to the development of pure mathematics. Most of the practical changes they effected had a delayed theoretical impact. The adoption by printers of the common symbols $+$, $-$, and $=$ contributed to the Western system of notation in algebra.[50] A growing appreciation of algebra in Europe led to its application to geometry, and to the technique of using geometrical and algebraic solutions as checks on each other.[51] Trigonometry was freed of its geometrical elements by Rheticus and Viète, thus increasing the ease and rapidity of manipulation by which new mathematical relationships could be discovered. In the universities mathematics, previously the monopoly of cosmographers and astronomers, began to be taught as an independent discipline.

Many of the earliest professors of mathematics were individuals with navigational or cartographic interests. The first occupant of the chair founded at Nuremberg in 1526 was Johann Schöner, the globe maker who was inspired by Magellan's voyage as well as by the mathematical and astronomical ideas of Regiomontanus.[52] The chair of mathematics at Coimbra was first held by Pedro Nunes, the royal cosmographer and foremost Iberian mathematician of the sixteenth century.[53] University teachers of mathematics still retained an interest in the relationship of their subject to cosmography as is illustrated by an examination of the private library of Johann Scheubel (1494–1570), professor at Tübingen, who kept many cosmographies in his collection of mathematical treatises.[54] The mathematics they taught started with the most elementary subject matter contained in the arithmetic books and cosmographies and advanced only slowly to higher mathematics. Even in the universities therefore the emphasis for most students was still on application rather than on mathematics itself. The scientific training of Matteo Ricci, the founder of the Jesuit mission in China, at the Collegio Romano between 1572 and 1578 was limited "to the principles of the whole of mathematics" and to its applications to a variety of disciplines, including astronomy.[55]

---

[49] For further discussion see A. Koyré, "Mathematics," in R. Taton (ed.), *History of Science: The Beginnings of Modern Science from 1450 to 1800*, trans. A. J. Pomerans (2 vols; London, 1964), II, 32–33. Also see pl. 28 for his title page.

[50] See Hogben, *op. cit.* (n. 43), pp. 174–75.

[51] See Graham, *loc. cit.* (n. 1), p. 59.

[52] See Koyré, *loc. cit.* (n. 12), p. 28. On his other activities see above, pp. 328–29, and below, pp. 456, 459.

[53] For his navigational ideas and influences see above, p. 277, and below, p. 462.

[54] See the listing in B. B. Hughes, "The Private Library of Johann Scheubel, Sixteenth-Century Mathematician," *Viator*, III (1972), 417–32.

[55] For the three-year curriculum he followed in mathematics see H. Bernard, *Matteo Ricci's Scientific Contribution to China* (Peking, 1935), pp. 26–27.

Scholars were generally satisfied by mathematical demonstrations on paper. Artisans on the contrary found arithmetic and geometry indispensable to the practical tasks of measuring distances and angles as well as calculating lengths, areas, and volumes. Artists and cartographers were led by the needs of their crafts to tackle unresolved problems in projective geometry. The astronomers, who stood between scholars and artisans in terms of their functions, were involved in speculative and practical mathematics as well as instrument making. Long devoted to calendar making, timekeeping, and astrological prediction, the astronomers of the sixteenth century also became key figures in the development of scientific navigation and innovators in the use of algebra. They were likewise leaders in the development of scientific procedure and methods, for their discipline, even when confined to the primitive tasks of making calendars and astrological charts, combined mathematization with testing by observation. While much of their scientific activity still remained fundamentally empirical and traditional, the astronomers led the way in the search for satisfying causal explanations and more disciplined working methods.[56]

The astronomers of China, India, Islam, and Europe had all sought since ancient times to discover or invent a system by which the apparent motions of the heavenly bodies could be accounted for rationally and their past and future positions determined accurately. They also searched similarly for an understanding of stellar and other extraterrestrial influences on mankind, thus making astrology one of the more practical aspects of the astronomer's endeavor. Each of the several astronomies as it evolved naturally reflected the world view and the religious and scientific predispositions of the society in which it arose. In China the astronomers were part of the government service and intimate advisers of the emperor. Their single most important task was to reckon the calendar and to keep records of the movements of the heavens. For a period of about fifteen centuries (fifth century B.C. to A.D. 1000) the Chinese records of celestial phenomena are the most complete and reliable available. In the early centuries of the Christian era, Indian astronomy, under Greek influence, turned from its previous preoccupation with charting the heavens for purposes of calendar making to a greater emphasis on astrological prognostication. In the Islamic world a fusion occurred of the Greek and Indian systems to which innovations were added based primarily on systematic and careful observations. But all of this knowledge was shown to be lacking and incomplete when the returning Portuguese revealed new stars as well as new lands to the scientific community of Europe.[57]

Elements of Hindu astronomy had passed into medieval Europe through al-Khwārizmī's astronomical tables. During the twelfth century Spanish Moors and Jews, as well as foreign scholars, worked at translations of numerous Arabic

---

[56] See Dijksterhuis, *op. cit.* (n. 9), p. 243; E. G. R. Taylor, *The Mathematical Practitioners of Tudor and Stuart England* (Cambridge, 1954), p. 7; and Graham, *loc. cit.* (n. 1), p. 60.

[57] See R. Hooykaas, "The Impact of the Voyages of Discovery on Portuguese Humanist Literature," *Revista da universidade de Coimbra*, XXIV (1971), 552. Cf. pl. 24.

astronomical texts at Barcelona, Tarragona, and Toledo.[58] Their translations rapidly circulated to the rest of Europe, where the interest in them sprang initially from a growing fascination for astrology. A parallel vogue for the construction of astrolabes and quadrants modeled on Arabic examples was similarly inspired. In the fourteenth century the Catalans, as their Mediterranean empire expanded eastward, began systematically to collect all the available information on the known world, both geographical and astronomical. For example, in 1379 Mossen Bernat d'Anglesola met an Indian woman on Cyprus "who told him many things about the marvels of her land of India." [59] Through the Catalans and through astrology in the fourteenth and fifteenth centuries the Portuguese acquired the requisite tools—tables, charts, quadrants, and astrolabes—necessary to establish latitude and to advance the infant science of navigation. Sometime after the death of Prince Henry the Navigator in 1460, astronomical studies were instituted at the university of Salamanca. The astronomers of Salamanca and later those of Coimbra played an important role in preparing the materials used by the navigators of Portugal and Spain.[60]

Every student of astronomy was introduced to the subject through the *Tractus de Sphaera* (*ca.* 1230) of Sacrobosco (John of Holywood), a concise description of the fundamental circles of the celestial sphere as seen from the earth; it contained little on planetary theory. In northern Europe the translated Arabic text of al-Fargani was more commonly studied before 1450 than was Ptolemy's *Almagest*, probably because it was a clear and simple textbook.[61] By the fifteenth century a new *Sphaera* was needed that would explain at a more sophisticated level the whole Ptolemaic system of heavenly bodies. To fill this need the Humanist astronomers led by Georg Peuerbach (1423–61) inaugurated a return to Ptolemy and his *Almagest*. Though Peuerbach and his pupil Regiomontanus prepared an excellent abridgment of the *Almagest*, it was not printed for general use until 1515.[62] The published *Almagest* appeared in time to provide Nicholas Copernicus (1473–1543) with the materials he required to "prove" his speculative cosmology. Regiomontanus' *De triangulis omnimodis* (completed *ca.* 1464; first printed at Nuremberg in 1533), a comprehensive textbook, established trigonometry in Europe as an independent branch of mathematics.[63] The trigonometrical methods of Regiomontanus became valuable astronomical tools in the skillful hands of Copernicus, Rheticus, and Viète.

While the theoretical and mathematical underpinnings of a new cosmology were being set in place, the heavens themselves were becoming broader and

[58] See G. Beaujouan, *La science en Espagne aux XVᵉ et XVIᵉ siècles* (Paris, 1967), pp. 9–10.

[59] As quoted *ibid.*, p. 18.

[60] See *ibid.*, pp. 33, 44.

[61] See W. P. D. Wightman, *Science in the Renaissance* (2 vols.; Edinburgh and London, 1962), I, 106–7; also O. Neugebauer, "Hindu Astronomy at Westminster in 1428," *Annals of Science*, VIII (1952), 221–28.

[62] See Wightman, *op. cit.* (n. 61), I, 109.

[63] See D. J. Struik, *A Source Book in Mathematics, 1200–1800* (Cambridge, Mass., 1969), pp. 97, 133; also see Wightman, *op. cit.* (n. 61), I, 96.

more complex. Vague references to southern constellations and stars had appeared in the ancient works of Ptolemy and others. Allusions to the Southern Cross and related celestial phenomena invisible from northern latitudes were discerned by some sixteenth-century observers in passages of Dante's *Divine Comedy*.[64] But the constellations of the southern skies began to be described at first hand only in the sixteenth century. Like practically all stargazers, the early voyagers tried to find terrestrial objects in the configurations of the stars. Vespucci on his American voyages and Corsali in connection with his travels in Asia first noticed and described a constellation that came to be called Apus, or the bird of paradise,[65] the mythical bird of the Moluccas which also stirred the imaginations of contemporary collectors, naturalists, and emblem makers. In *The Decades of the newe worlde . . .* (1555) Richard Eden conveyed to the English public what Vespucci and Corsali had reported "Of the Pole Antartike and the Starres about the same." The Southern Cross, a brilliant constellation which lies within the Milky Way, was noticed by most of the voyagers and referred to in the *Lusiads* as "a group quite new in the new hemisphere."[66] Cristobal de Acosta, the Spanish naturalist, called it the "Southern Celestial Clock" in deference to its importance for tropical navigation.[67] The shiny clouds which could be seen as the ship approached the tip of Africa became known as "Magellanic clouds."[68] After a time the new phenomena of the south began to appear on the celestial globes of Mercator and others; Mollineux's globe of 1592 shows clearly the Southern Cross and other new astral discoveries.[69] Thomas Blundeville describes Mollineux's celestial sphere

as touching the map of stars which covereth the celestial Globe certain Southerne images, as the Crosse, the southerne Triangle, and certain other stars, whereof some do signifie Noes Doue, & others do signifie the image called Polophilax. . . . He setteth downe also two cloudes nigh unto the South pole, but not the use thereof.[70]

Johann Bayer, a Protestant lawyer of Augsburg and a follower of Tycho Brahe, brought the discoveries into general astronomical literature by listing and describing twelve of the new southern asterisms in his celebrated catalog called *Uranometria* (1603).[71]

Occurring at the same time as the new astral revelations were speculations about the heavens and their relationship to the expanding world. The classical conception of a closed and hierarchical universe had first been clearly challenged by Nicholas of Cusa in his metaphysical tract *De docta ignorantia* (1440). Here he postulates an indivisible universe with the earth as but one of many celestial

---

[64] For the precise references see R. H. Allen, *Star Names: Their Lore and Meaning* (New York, 1963), pp. 186–87.

[65] *Ibid.*, pp. 43–45.

[66] Speech of Vasco da Gama (Canto V).

[67] Allen, *op. cit.* (n. 64), p. 189.

[68] *Ibid.*, pp. 294–95.

[69] See pl. 25.

[70] Blundeville, *His Exercises, containing eight treatices . . .* (London, 1597), pp. 247^v–248^r.

[71] See Allen, *op. cit.* (n. 64), p. 13.

bodies possessing its own motion. Copernicus held that the earth was in fact one of the planets. But he was also well aware that the inherited conception of the earth was being radically transformed by the overseas explorations. In his famous *De revolutionibus orbium coelestium*, completed around 1530 but not published until 1543, he observes:

Ptolemy in his Cosmography extends inhabitable land as far as the median circle, and he leaves that part of the world unknown, where the moderns have added Cathay and other vast regions as far as 60° longitude, so that inhabited land extends in longitude farther than the rest of the ocean does. And if you add to these the islands discovered in our time under the princes of Spain and Portugal and especially America—named after the ship's captain who discovered her—which they consider a second *orbis terrarum* on account of her so far unmeasured magnitude, we would not be greatly surprised if there were antipodes or antichthones. For reasons of geometry compel us to believe that America is situated directly opposite to the India of the Ganges.[72]

Copernicus went even further in his cosmology; he placed the sun at the center of the universe. His immeasurable universe was larger than Aristotle's, for he had to account for the absence of stellar parallax as the earth moved around the sun. But his universe was not infinite; it was limited by the sphere of fixed stars.[73]

Copernicus' major work was published in 1543, the year the Portuguese first arrived in Japan. Neither of these portentous events could be fully understood by contemporaries or quickly assimilated into the prevailing cosmological and geographical conceptions. Very few contemporaries embraced the doctrines of Copernicus or even commented on their implications. The churches and the universities remained passive and unresponsive to the end of the century. No basic textbooks of astronomy adopted the Copernican theory.[74] Gemma Frisius in a letter of 1556 was one of the first to write approvingly of it. Thomas Digges in England welcomed it as an advance over the system of the Ancients but cautioned that further observations were needed to test its detail.[75] Other English astronomers expressed similar views. Clavius, the Jesuit astronomer and calendar reformer, was openly hostile to the Copernican cosmology. Tycho Brahe, the father of observational astronomy, was equally critical of it. Johannes Kepler completed the revolutionary transformation of the traditional cosmology and provided the Copernican idea with the mathematical underpinnings so vital to its ultimate triumph.

[72] From Bk. I, chap. iii, pp. 1–2, as translated in *Great Books of the Western World* (Chicago, 1965), XVI, 513.

[73] See A. Koyré, *From the Closed World to the Infinite Universe* (New York, 1958), chap. 1; and the same author's "The Copernican Revolution," in Taton (ed.), *op. cit.* (n. 49), II, 52–53, 61–66; for the general implications of Copernican thought see T. S. Kuhn, *The Copernican Revolution* (Cambridge, Mass., 1957), especially chaps. v and vi; and H. Dingle, "Astronomy in the Sixteenth and Seventeenth Centuries," in E. A. Underwood (ed.), *Science, Medicine, and History* . . . (London, 1953), I, 455–68.

[74] See F. R. Johnson, "Astronomical Text-Books in the Sixteenth Century," in Underwood (ed.), *op. cit.* (n. 73), I, 285.

[75] See Wightman, *op. cit.* (n. 61), I, 116–17.

Simon Stevin and Tycho Brahe made their greatest contributions to scientific knowledge during the last years of the sixteenth and the first years of the seventeenth century. By that time the decimal position of Hindu-Arabic numerals was in common use throughout Europe, but decimal fractions were not. Although decimal fractions were known to some of Stevin's predecessors, their use was far more ancient in China than in Europe. Stevin, the builder of the sailing carriage of Chinese origin, may have been inspired in the *Tenth* (1585), his most notable mathematical work, to employ the Chinese-derived system of decimal fractions as well as the decimal point from what he had learned about them through intermediary sources. Likewise, it is conceivable that he was influenced by Chinese mathematical and astronomical ideas to work out his method for the calculation of an equally tempered musical scale. Further research may indeed reveal that Stevin was himself subject to a cluster of intellectual stimuli from China.[76]

Some of these conjectures about the interest of Europeans in Asian mathematics and astronomy are supported by an examination of the history of calendar reform in sixteenth-century Europe. The need for coordinating the civil and ecclesiastical years of the Julian calendar with the astronomical events themselves had made calendar reform a goal for centuries. From the Christian viewpoint a rectification of the Julian calendar was necessary in order to fix the date of Easter on which the dates for other church festivals depend. In 1582 Pope Gregory XIII finally introduced a new calendar that modified the one in use. The task was not completed by this pronouncement, however, because Clavius and his associates had to make an immense number of ancillary calculations over the next twenty years before the official compilation of the Gregorian calendar (Rome, 1603) could be issued. In the interim much discussion took place in Europe about the wisdom, accuracy, and acceptability of the modifications. The Protestants were particularly vocal in challenging the pope's authority to determine the reckoning of time.

One of the first responses, long in preparation, came from the pen of the erudite Joseph Justus Scaliger, the French Huguenot (see pl. 36). The father of the discipline of historical chronology was moved to undertake his *De emendatione temporum* (1583) by his study of Eastern languages and history. His major object in this work was to divorce the discussion of chronology from theological and metaphysical speculation and to establish a scientific ordering for world history. In his study of calendars and calendrical cycles, as well as in his parallel study of historical epochs, he combed the ancient, medieval, and Oriental writings as well as the travel accounts of his own day.[77] His information on the "Ten Stems" and "Twelve Branches" of Chinese chronological reckoning may have come from a 1437 compendium of Persian calendars and

---

[75] See Needham, *op. cit.* (n. 1), III, 89; IV, 226–28.

[77] The best recent study is A. T. Grafton, "Joseph Scaliger (1510–1609) and the Humanism of the Later Renaissance" (Ph.D. diss., Department of History, University of Chicago, 1975), especially pp. 174–75, 181–82.

chronologies.[78] He includes among his sources many of the references in European writings to the calendars of Asia. From Nicolò de' Conti he comments on the Hindu method of reckoning by eras.[79] He quotes a letter of 1565 from Luis Fróis, the Jesuit leader in Japan, on the antiquity of the lunar calendar in the East and refers to Marco Polo's remarks on the same subject.[80] In his revised edition of 1598, much of which was prepared at Leyden, he added other materials on Asian calendars and epochs.

From Scaliger's comments and from the Jesuit letters it is clear that the educated public of Europe was aware of the existence in Asia of calendars of great antiquity that had been reckoned without the direct benefit of Greek and Roman learning. Also it was generally conceded that the Julian calendar was imperfect and there was widespread dissatisfaction with the Gregorian modifications. But the Europeans overseas still believed in the superiority of their calendar, their astronomy, and their methods of reckoning. When Ricci entered China, he was permitted to go to Peking because the authorities hoped that he might be able to correct the Chinese calendar which had long been at variance, like the Julian in Europe, with astronomical events. While Clavius, Ricci's instructor in Europe, was making the calculations for the new Roman calendar, Ricci was calling for astronomers and mathematicians to be sent to Peking where there was a shortage of competent calendar makers.[81] When the requested scientists finally arrived in the imperial Chinese capital, the "Western learning" they introduced was an arithmetic, algebra, and trigonometry heavily indebted to India, and an astronomy that possessed elements earlier derived from the Hindu, Chinese, and Arabic cosmologies.

3

NAUTICS AND NAVIGATION

Jean Fernel (1497–1558), the eminent French physician and mathematician, issued a Renaissance *blason* around 1530. It celebrates the new spirit sweeping Europe inspired by a growing conviction that the enterprises of the Moderns surpassed those of the Ancients, particularly in navigation:

This age of ours sees art and science gloriously rerisen after twelve centuries of swoon. Art and science now equal their ancient splendor, or surpass it. . . . Our age today is doing things of which antiquity did not dream. . . . The Ocean has been crossed by the prowess of our navigations and new islands found. The far recesses of India lie revealed. The Continent of the West, the so-called New World, unknown to our forefathers, has

[78] See J. J. L. Duyvendak, *Holland's Contributions to Chinese Studies* (London, 1950), pp. 7–8.

[79] J. J. Scaliger, *De emendatione temporum* (Paris, 1583), pp. 231–32.

[80] *Ibid.*, pp. 112–13. On Scaliger's general interest in Asia see above, pp. 358–59.

[81] See Ho Peng-yoke, "The Astronomical Bureau in Ming China," *Journal of Asian History*, III (1969), 148.

in great part become known. In all this, and in what pertains to astronomy, Plato, Aristotle, and the old philosophers made progress, and Ptolemy added a great deal more. Yet, were one of them to return today, he would find geography changed past recognition. A new globe has been given us by the navigators of our time.[82]

Unhistorical as this quotation is with respect to the achievements of the Middle Ages, it exhibits one brand of enthusiasm current in Europe about the successful breaching of the chaos of the seas and the discovery of the new islands (including continents in this conception) within them. To answer questions about why so much of the world had so long remained hidden, orthodox Christian writers like Barros and Galvão expressed the belief that a veil had been lowered over the original creation, as over the original language, to punish man for his sins. The navigators, in the words of Simon Grynaeus in the preface to the *Novus orbis*, were "invincible and truly divine souls . . . who have reclaimed the empire of the earth and of the sea as the heritage of their first parents."[83] The conquest of the sea was thus a victory for man which appeared to have the divine blessing.

One of the most profound and influential discoveries of the Iberian navigators was the simple fact that there are things worth discovering on the sea, in distant lands, and at home. The transmission through Iberia of Arabic texts and instruments reached its apogee in the thirteenth century. Thereafter the abstract sciences went into decline in Iberia and reached their nadir in the fifteenth century. Only cosmography and nautical science, particularly as exemplified by the Majorcan school, remained alive and stimulating.[84] The cosmographers, who were typically landlubbers, were the custodians of most of the information brought back to Spain relating to exploration and navigation. They were also the first to cope with the unsettling task of reconciling the scientific hypotheses of the past with the new information on the natural world.[85] The seagoing navigators before 1480 were unaware of most of the complexities involved in sailing with charts, tables, and instruments. They continued, as their forerunners had, to navigate vessels by a kind of primitive marine sense that was based on nautical lore and on an empirical knowledge of the seas, winds, tides, landmarks, and other visible signs. They confined their literary activities to recording in the rutters the coastal configurations, landmarks, and wind directions.[86] This traditional art of pilotage continued to be practiced even in oceanic navigation, such as fishing off the Grand Banks, throughout the sixteenth century.

Eastern navigation, when Vasco da Gama first met with it, was likewise an

---

[82] From his *Dialogue* (*ca.* 1530) as quoted in J. D. Bernal, *Science in History* (4th ed., 4 vols.; London, 1969), II, 404–6.

[83] Analysis based on M. W. G. L. Randles, "Sur l'idée de la découverte," in M. Mollat and P. Adam (eds.), *Les aspects internationaux de la découverte océanique aux XVe et XVIe siècles* (Paris, 1966), pp. 17–21.

[84] See J. M. Millás Vallicrosa, "Nautique et cartographie de l'Espagne au XVIe siècle," in A. Koyré (ed.), *op. cit.* (n. 12), pp. 31–34.

[85] For a general discussion of cosmography see U. Lamb, *A Navigator's Universe: The "Libro de Cosmographia" of 1538 by Pedro de Medina* (Chicago, 1972), pp. 3–4.

[86] See P. Adam, "Navigation primitive et navigation astronomique," in Mollat and Adam (eds.), *op. cit.* (n. 83), pp. 91–105.

essentially empirical art. In the Indian Ocean, maritime intercourse had since its beginning concentrated in the northern reaches. Sailing in this region was greatly facilitated by the contiguity of the coasts and by the proximity of numerous islands. Under clear tropical skies, the Arab pilots normally enjoyed good visibility of sea, land, and heavens. They were not troubled, as Atlantic navigators were, with storms, currents, shifting winds, deadly calms, and floating icebergs. The directional regularity of the monsoons (Arabic for "the season for sailing") was enough to give the Eastern pilot an orientation that was more reliable that that derived from a compass. Many of the extant Arabic navigational charts are simply lists of the best dates for leaving the main ports with each monsoon. The most scientific of the techniques developed by the Arabs was that of fixing latitude by means of stellar altitudes, especially by reference to the Southern Cross.[87] Chinese junks also crossed the Indian Ocean about 1420 without charts of any kind and may even have attempted rounding the Cape of Good Hope about sixty-five years before the Portuguese successfully turned that corner. The great fleets of Ming China probably used compasses as direction finders and carrier pigeons as communicators.[88] But in no sense were the junks of China or the fragile ships of the Arabs prepared to cope with the difficulties of traversing the Atlantic Ocean.

A revolution in ship construction occurred in Europe, especially in Iberia, during the last generation of the fifteenth century. But that it not to say that the European development was utterly independent. Nicolò de' Conti had noted early in the century that Chinese ships were larger than European vessels and that they boasted multiple masts and sails. Over the previous fifteen hundred years a few inventions fundamental to the evolution of the sailing craft were possibly transmitted to Europe from the East: the sprit sail from India (A.D. second century); the lateen sail of the Arabs (eighth century); the mariner's compass and the axial sternpost rudder from China (late twelfth century); and the principle of multiple masts from a number of possible Asian sources (fifteenth century).[89] The one-masted European ship of 1350 had evolved rapidly into the

[87] See A. Teixeira da Mota, "Méthodes de navigation et cartographie nautique dans l'Océan Indien avant le XVIᵉ siècle," *Studia* (Lisbon), No. 11 (1963), 49–50; G. R. Tibbetts, "The Navigational Theory of the Arabs in the Fifteenth and Sixteenth Centuries," *Revista da universidade de Coimbra*, XXIV (1971), 323, 341; and F. C. Lane, "The Economic Meaning of the Compass," *American Historical Review*, LXVIII (1963), 610–11. The best general discussion of ships, seamanship, and navigation is in J. H. Parry, *The Age of Reconnaissance* (New York, 1964), chaps. iii–v.

[88] See G. R. D. Worcester, *Sail and Sweep in China* (London, 1960), p. 5; on the archaeological research in East Africa relating to the Chinese voyages see Needham, *op. cit.* (n. 1), IV, Pt. 3, 497; on Chinese use of the magnetic compass at sea see *ibid.*, p. 562. Also see Chang Kuei-sheng, "The Maritime Scene in China at the Dawn of Great European Discoveries," *Journal of the American Oriental Society*, XCIV (1974), 347–59.

[89] See Needham, *op. cit.* (n. 1), IV, Pt. 3, 653, 698; other authorities reject attribution to China of the mariner's compass and the axial sternpost rudder. On the "true compass" see *inter alia* Teixeira da Mota, "Méthodes de navigation . . ." (n. 87), pp. 88–89; for the argument against the sternpost rudder based on the differences between the steering problems of junks and keeled ships see P. Adam and L. Denoix, "Essai sur les raisons de l'apparition du goûvernail d étambot," *Revue d'histoire économique et sociale*, XL (1962), 98–100.

three- or four-masted ships of 1500, a development of the first magnitude in the history of sailing. The full-rigged ship was a prerequisite for the lengthy voyages of discovery for it was handier than a ship with a single mast in contending with adverse winds. Its heavier and larger hull was better able to stand the buffeting of the seas and to accommodate a larger number of people and a vaster tonnage of cargo.[90] Early in the sixteenth century the Portuguese learned to protect the hull by applying additional strake layers both above and below the waterline, a technique which they had learned after observing the treatment given Chinese junks.[91]

In Portugal the great change from pilotage to positional navigation and from the construction of one-masted vessels to full-rigged ships and fleets preceded and accompanied the fundamental navigational endeavors of the reigns of John II (1481–95) and Manuel I (1495–1520).[92] Information was requested from noted foreign cosmographers—for example, Torricelli and Hieronymus Münzer—on the possibilities of a western navigation to Asia. By 1485 the cosmographers and astronomers employed by the Portuguese had simplified the noon solar declination tables for computing polar altitude when finding latitude both north and south of the equator.[93] Pilots had to be taught to apply declination to their open-sight observations of the sun in order to determine latitude in any part of the world. The voyage around Africa to India and back required the use of declination tables, even though the navigator was able by these means to fix his latitude only approximately. Pilot books and other hydrographic works began to appear in small numbers around 1490.[94] If navigators were to use their books, instruments, tables, and charts effectively, the astronomers would have to provide more accurate predictions of the apparent motion of the heavenly bodies. Astronomy and astrology quite suddenly became as influential on life at sea as they had long been to life on land. In an age when most Europeans believed in astrology, the rule of the stars probably contributed to a feeling of safety at sea. The ability of the Portuguese in opening and maintaining the sea road to the East rested on their success in welding the astronomers, cosmographers, cartographers, shipbuilders, and navigators into an effectively working team.[95]

The route to India around the Cape was much more difficult than the route

[90] See Needham, *op. cit.* (n. 1), IV, Pt. 3, 474; and G. P. B. Naish, "Ships and Shipbuilding," in Singer *et al.* (eds.), *op. cit.* (n. 1), III, 474–77.

[91] See Needham, *op. cit.* (n. 1), IV, Pt. 3, 664, 698. Marco Polo had observed the Chinese process of caulking; the Portuguese developed a similar caulking made of coir from India and tung oil from China. The first Portuguese to visit China, Jorge Alvarez, sent samples of tung oil back to Lisbon. See *Asia*, I, 732. Also see H. Hart, *Sea Road to the Indies* (New York, 1950), p. 87n.

[92] For general discussion see L. Gallois, "Les portugais et l'astronomie nautique à l'époque des grandes découvertes," *Annales de géographie*, XXIII (1914), 289–302.

[93] See D. W. Waters, *The Art of Navigation in England in Elizabethan and Early Stuart Times* (London, 1958), pp. 47–48.

[94] Consult R. A. Skelton, "The Seaman and the Printer," *Revista da universidade de Coimbra*, XXIV, (1971), 493–94.

[95] See A. Cortesão, "Nautical Science and the Renaissance," in E. A. Underwood (ed.), *op. cit.* (n. 73), I, 309–16.

to America and produced many more shipwrecks as well as a genre of tragic literature.[96] The navigator of the route to India, as Vasco da Gama quickly learned, had to be able to contend with the vagaries of both the Atlantic and the Indian oceans. When he first landed at Melinde, Da Gama and his aides learned new techniques from Ahmad Ibn-Majid, the eminent Arab navigator who piloted them across the Indian Ocean to Calicut. On his return to Portugal, Da Gama brought back several *kamals*, instruments used in the East for observing the altitude of the stars.[97] The Portuguese experimented with these on Cabral's voyage and later ones, and the *kamal* may have inspired the adoption of the mariner's cross-staff by European seamen early in the sixteenth century. Information from Ibn-Majid and Arabic nautical texts appears on the Cantino map (1502) and those planispheres modeled on it.[98] Without question Da Gama himself inaugurated the Portuguese policy of learning as much as possible about navigation and shipbuilding from the Easterners. From their own observations, and probably from Arab charts as well, the Portuguese had prepared their own tables of the Southern Cross by 1505. Albuquerque, as he pushed east of India, also collected Javanese maps and seacharts, particularly those relating to regions that still remained unknown to Portuguese navigation.[99]

The rutters prepared in Portugal itself became ever more detailed on Eastern navigation. Latitude charts with graduated meridians were also developed for the use of pilots and cosmographers.[100] In 1509 cosmographers published at Lisbon the navigational manual called *Regimento do estrolabio do quadrante* which included Sacrobosco's *Sphaera* supplemented by the *Almanach perpetuum* (ca. 1475) of Abraham Zacuto. With its calculations for finding latitude at night, its tables of latitudes of known places, and its explanation of dead reckoning (deductive reckoning), the *Regimento* became indispensable to both pilot and cosmographer. Most of the navigational manuals subsequently prepared were little more than enlargements and modifications of this fundamental treatise.

Pedro Nunes (1502–57), the chief cosmographer of King John III of Portugal, produced possibly the most comprehensive and influential cosmography of the sixteenth century, the *Tratado da sphera* (see pl. 29). It includes a Portuguese translation of Sacrobosco, a commentary on Peuerbach's *Theoricae novae planetarum*, the first book of Ptolemy's *Geographia*, and a sophisticated discussion of the nautical chart. Nunes abandoned Zacuto's tables and replaced them with Regiomontanus' more accurate calculations of the sun's declination.

---

96 On the *Histórico tragico-maritima* see above, pp. 131–35.

97 For a description see Waters, *op. cit.* (n. 93), p. 53.

98 See below, pp. 452–53, for the Portuguese maps.

99 See below, p. 483.

100 The earliest dated and signed Portuguese portolan extant is of 1492 and it shows the Atlantic, the Mediterranean, and the coastline of Africa as far south as Sierra Leone. It is preserved at the Yale University library. For a reproduction see O. Vietor, "A Portuguese Chart of 1492 by Jorge Aguinar," *Revista da universidade de Coimbra*, XXIV (1971), 515–16. For the later rutters see C. R. Boxer, "Portuguese Roteiros, 1500–1700," *Mariner's Mirror*, XX (1934), 172–76; and A. Teixeira da Mota, "Evolução dos roteiros portugueses durante o século XVI," *Revista da universidade de Coimbra*, XXIV (1971), 5–32.

He described for the first time the loxodromic curve so vital to map projection, and explained the method of great-circle sailing. Like other astronomers, Nunes was impressed by the mariners' accounts of the Southern Cross and wanted better data on it and the other celestial phenomena of the tropics. João de Castro experimented in 1539 at sea and on the island of Chaul off the west coast of India with Nunes' astronomical instruments and tested his ideas about magnetism. Using the "shadow instrument" of Nunes, Castro recorded systematically the variations in declination between Portugal and India. He investigated the boulders of Chaul to determine why they attracted his needle as if they were lodestone.[101] Many of his observations as well as his tables had a profound influence on subsequent Portuguese and general European navigational and cartographical endeavor. For all of this, wrote the Jesuit historian G. B. Maffei in 1588, "the whole of Europe owes no small debt to the Portuguese."[102]

Cosmography meanwhile was also developing rapidly in Spain. Enciso's *Suma de geographia* (1519) was comparable in its navigational aspects to the Portuguese *Regimento* of a decade earlier.[103] Among those who welcomed back the survivors of Magellan's expedition was the young Pedro de Medina (1493–1567) who later recorded the reaction of his contemporaries to the first circumnavigation of the earth.[104] Around 1548 Medina became cosmographer to Emperor Charles V and acted as one of the teachers, examiners, and navigational experts employed at the Casa de Contratación at Seville. Although he wrote works in a number of fields, his most famous were his textbooks on navigation: the *Arte de navegar* (1545) and the two entitled *Regimiento de navegacion* (1552 and 1563). Many of Medina's observations and conclusions were based on those advanced by Nunes. Nonetheless Medina was better known in Europe than Nunes because he wrote his manuals in Spanish rather than Portuguese and also was more generally translated. The first of five French editions was a translation (1554) by Nicolas de Nicolay, later the cosmographer of King Henry II. Three Italian editions were published in Venice.[105] Michael Coignet, the printer and cosmographer of Antwerp, published in 1581 the first of four Flemish editions. In that same year John Frampton produced the first of two English editions. Copies of Medina's works were taken to sea by Frobisher and Drake.[106] The more comprehensive compendium on navigation (1551) by Martin Cortes was also popular in England in the translation (1561) of Richard Eden.[107] It advanced the suggestion that the magnetic pole and the

---

[101] The effect was probably from the heat radiating from the rocks. See Needham, *op. cit.* (n. 1), IV, Pt. 1, 314 note b.

[102] *Le istorie . . .* (Florence, 1599), p. 11.

[103] On its general importance in Spain see above, p. 169.

[104] See Lamb, *op. cit.* (n. 85), p. 11.

[105] It was probably one of those editions which inspired Bernardino Baldi in his didactic poem called *Nautica.* See above, pp. 217–18.

[106] See Lamb, *op. cit.* (n. 85), pp. 4–5.

[107] *Breve compendio de la sphera y de la arte de navegar* (Seville).

24. Magellan as navigator. From A. Thevet, *Les vrais pourtraits* . . . (Paris, 1584), p. 528^r. Courtesy of the Newberry Library.

fort, as when the former guarde is Eaſt, you ſhall find this ſtar, counting from the North ſtarre, to be Northweſt, and almoſt 45. degrees diſtant from the Pole, with which ſtarre if you worke, as you did before with the head of Meduſa, ſauing that you ſhall not neede to turne the inner into the oppoſite point, but onely to rebate from the point on which it falleth 9. houres and ½. you ſhall know all the thinges laſt mentioned. And this rule (as hee ſaith) is ſo generall as you may haue your deſire by working in like manner with any other ſtarre that is to you certainly knowne, and is at that time aboue the horizon.

What ſtarres are obſerued by thoſe that ſayle beyonde the Equinoctiall line vnder the South Pole.

Chapter 43.

The ancient Aſtronomers, as Ptolomey, Timochares, Hipparchus and others did neuer deſcribe any Starre to be more nigh vnto the South pole, then that which is called Canopus, which is a faire bright ſtarre of the firſt bigneſſe, and according to the Tables of Copernicus, is diſtant from the South pole 38 degrees, and ⅔. But thoſe that haue ſayled in the South ſeas of later dayes, haue found out other ſtarres vnknowne to the ancient Aſtronomers, which are much nearer vnto the ſaid Pole. For Albericus Veſputius whiteth of thoſe ſtarres, making together a Triangle Orthogonall, that is to ſay, hauing one right angle, now called the ſoutherne Triangle, the middle Star whereof is diſtant from the South Pole 9. degrees, ½.

There be alſo lately founde out diuers images of other ſtarres nigh vnto ye South pole, as that which is called Noah his Doue, or Pigeon, and another called Polophilax, made in the ſhape of a man, whoſe longitude and latitude hath not as yet bene rightly ſet downe by any that I haue read.

But the ſea men of theſe preſent dayes doe moſt commonly obſerue foure great ſtars, which according to the ſhape and forme ther of they call the Croſſe, imagining the greateſt ſtarre of the foure to be the foot, & that which ſtandeth right ouer him, to be the head of the croſſe, & the other two to be the 2. armes: and when they

hi that the head doeth directlie anſwere the foote, then they ſaye that the foote of the ſaide croſſe is right aboue the Pole, and diſtant from the ſame 30. degrees. Therfore hauing taken the altitude or height of that ſtar aboue ye Horizon with their Aſtrolabe they ſubtract 30. degrees from that altitude, and the remainder is the eleuation of the Pole. Medina in his ſixt booke & eleuenth chapter ſetteth downe the ſhape of the foreſaine croſſe in this manner.

The head.
The croſſe.
the foote.

And he ſaith that theſe ſtarres are neither anie of thoſe ſtarres that are appointed to the twelue Signes in the Zodiaque, nor yet any of the 36. Images or conſtellations that bee in heauen. Moreouer he ſaith, that in taking the altitude of the great ſtarre called the foote being in his right place, and that you finde his altitude to be 30. degrees, then you may aſſure your ſelfe that you are right vpon the Equinoctiall. And if you find his altitude to be more than 30. degrees, then you are paſt the Equinoctiall towardes the South Pole. But if you finde it to be leſſe than 30. degrees, then you are ſtill on the North ſide of the Equinoctiall.

Beſides the ſtarres aboue mentioned, our Mariners in theſe North partes of the worlde are woont to obſerue diuers other ſtars, to the number of 32. whoſe longitude and declination together with their bigneſſe and alſo when they riſe and ſet, and when they are mounted to the Meridian, that is to ſay, are iuſt South, is plainely ſet forth by Tables collected of purpoſe out of the Aſtronomicall Tables by William Boorne, which Tables you ſhall finde in the 20. Chapter of his booke called the regiment of the ſea. And Robert Norman doeth alſo ſet downe the like tables in his booke called the Attractiue, & therefore I thinke it ſuperfluous to repeat the ſame againe here, & ſpecially ſith I haue deſcribed vnto you all the ſtarres that be in the firmament that were knowne to the ancient Aſtronomers, and haue ſhewed you how to find out by the Globe their longitudes, their latitudes, their declinations,

25. Discussion and depiction of the Southern Cross. From T. Blundevile, *His Exercises* . . . (London, 1597). Based on the work of Pedro de Medina, the Spanish cosmographer. Courtesy of the Newberry Library.

26. Woodcut of the combat between Magellan and the natives of Mactan in the Philippines. Notice nudity of the natives and their primitive weapons and surroundings. From A. Thevet, *La cosmographie universelle* . . . (Paris, 1575), p. 462[r]. Courtesy of the Newberry Library.

PETRVS APIANVS LEISNICENSIS.
Divi Imp. CAROLI V. Mathematicus et Comes Palat. Caes. Equestr. dignit. et in Academia Ingol. stadiana Mathes. Profess. Publ.
Nat. A. cıɔ cccc xcv. ·Denat· *A. cıɔıɔL ıı.*

27. Peter Apian (1495–1552), mathematician and cosmographer. Reproduced from O. Muris and G. Saarmann, *Der Globus im Wandel der Zeiten* (Berlin, 1961), pl. 20.

28. Pascal's Triangle, an Asian invention (?), on the title page of the first edition of P. Apian's book on practical reckoning. Reproduced from D. E. Smith, *Rara arithmetica* (Boston and London, 1908), fig. 78. Courtesy of the Newberry Library.

29. Frontispiece of the Portuguese *Tractado da sphera* (1537) by Pedro Nunes. Reproduced from A. Cortez-Pinto, *Da famosa arte da impressão* (Lisbon, 1948), facing p. 202.

30. Woodcut of juggernaut in Hindu religious festivals. Notice the believers who have thrown themselves beneath its wheels. From A. Thevet, *La cosmographie universelle* . . . (Paris, 1575), p. 384ʳ. Courtesy of the Newberry Library.

31. An East Indian vessel, a coracora. From B. Gomes de Brito, comp., *História tragica maritima*, ed. A. Sergio (Lisbon, 1955).

32. A sailing chariot from the lower right corner of the map of China in Gerard de Jode's *Speculum Orbis Terrarum* (Antwerp, 1593). Reproduced from *The Principal Works of Simon Stevin* (6 vols.; Amsterdam, 1955–66), Vol. V, fig. 3.

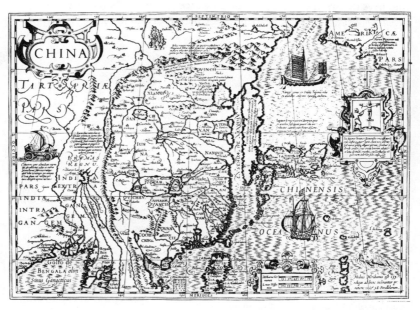

33. China in the Mercator-Hondius Atlas (Amsterdam, 1606). Notice the landship at left and the vessel above Japan. Reproduced from R. A. Skelton, *Decorative Printed Maps of the Fifteenth to Eighteenth Centuries* (London, 1952).

34. Landships constructed for Prince Maurice of Holland by Simon Stevin. Engraving by Swanenburgh, after a drawing by De Gheyn (Rijksmuseum, Amsterdam). Reproduced from *The Principal Works of Simon Stevin* (6 vols.; Amsterdam, 1955–66), Vol. V, fig. 2.

XXIV.

QVOMODO primores in China super sellis circumferantur, &
de nauibus genialibus.

Vnt varij dignitatum gradus in China, quorum Man-
dorini sunt præcipui, qui in sellis serico auroque obuelatis
magnifice circumferuntur. Hi sunt qui regnum admi-
nistrant, quorum opera si quis vti velit, atque eo nomine eos compellare, necesse est, vt procumbens in genua co-
ram illis compareat. Sūt proximi à rege, nec præter eos alij per regnū principes habentur, nec ad ea fastigia præter doctos & literatos, vlti euehun-
tur, inter quos quisque eminentior est, prout eruditione fuerit præstan-
tior. Ceteroquin illi ipsi sunt aeque gulæ dediti atque vulgus Chinensium,
deliciantur, genioque indulgent terra mariq; in quem vsum naues splen-
dide apparatas habent, serico auroque intectas, apposita in medio mensa
opipare instructa.

G   MODVS

35. Chinese mandarins on houseboat. Notice the porcelain
bowls and the chopsticks held by the Chinese on the barge.
From T. De Bry, *India Orientalis* (Frankfurt-am-Main, 1598),
Vol. II, pl. xxiv.

36. Portrait of J. J. Scaliger (1540–1609) at work. Reproduced from T. H. L. Scheurleer and G. H. M. Posthumus, eds., *Leiden University in the Seventeenth Century* (Leyden, 1975), pl. 2.

37. Library of the University of Leyden (1610). Engraving by J. C. Woudanus. Notice the maps on the wall and the globes. Reproduced from T. H. L. Scheurleer and G. H. M. Posthumus, eds., *Leiden University in the Seventeenth Century* (Leyden, 1975), pl. 1.

true pole of the earth were not identical. Most later mariners' handbooks in Dutch and English were limited to detailing the seas and coasts of Europe.

The discovery of the maritime route to India brought in its wake the quick disappearance of European oared trading vessels and warships and their replacement by sailing craft.[108] The naval successes of Portugal in the Indian Ocean were due in part to the superiority in maneuverability of these European gun-equipped sailing vessels over the Turkish galleys dependent on human energy and on the old tactic of ramming and boarding.[109] Although the great Chinese junks once rivaled in size the Portuguese caravels, the navy of the Ming empire had almost totally disintegrated by the sixteenth century. But European seamen still had lessons to learn from Asian shipbuilders. The lug sails adopted in Europe around 1586 were possibly derived from Asian prototypes as were the chain pumps for emptying the vessel of bilge water.[110] In Asian waters the Portuguese rigged their *lorchas* with mat-and-batten sails, though these were not exported to Europe, probably because the bamboo for the battens was not readily available.[111] The rations on shipboard for the return voyage were supplemented by Asian products, especially by coconuts and other fruits. The navigators of the latter half of the century had nothing to gain, however, from studying Eastern navigational techniques. The instruments and charts at their disposal were far more advanced than any materials of Eastern provenance. European navigation and nautics, whatever they had borrowed in previous times from Asia, had by 1600 outstripped all Asian knowledge about ship construction, instrument making, and sailing. Nautical transmissions in the future would almost all flow from Europe to Asia.

4

ALCHEMY AND CHEMISTRY

Centers of alchemical—that is, early chemical—research existed in Antiquity in China, India, and Egypt. Chinese alchemy antedates Indian and Western alchemy. The workers in all three ancient centers concentrated on metallurgy and the transmutation of metals. In China and India, in contrast to Hellenistic society, the search for an elixir of life was a dynamic element in early research. The alchemy of medieval Europe and the Islamic countries was derived primarily from the Hellenistic tradition. Like so many other matters, the alchemical ideas of the East were eventually transmitted to Europe through the medium of Arabic writings undertaken in the later Middle Ages. The Sino-Indian concept of the elixir of life first appeared in Western texts of the twelfth century.

[108] See L. Denoix, "Charactéristiques des navires de l'époque des grandes découvertes," in Mollat and Adam (eds.), *op. cit.* (n. 83), p. 147.
[109] See Cipolla, *Guns, Sails, and Empire* (n. 27), pp. 101–2.
[110] Based on Needham, *op. cit.* (n. 1), IV, Pt. 2, 610, 613, 667.
[111] See *ibid.*, p. 599.

But in Christian Europe the quest was subsequently directed to finding preparations to lengthen life rather than, as in the case of certain Chinese practitioners, seeking for elixirs that would guarantee physical immortality. Fundamental to the production of the elixir was an alloy of copper, zinc, and nickel known to the Chinese as *pai-t'ung* or "white copper," and to the Indians, Arabs, and Europeans by a variety of other names. Whatever else might be said about the influence of Eastern upon European alchemy, it is clear that the search for an elixir of life, emphatically enunciated in the thirteenth century by Roger Bacon and concurred in by other medieval scientists, was a concept that the Europeans learned about from the East. It was also one which helped to change the direction of European chemical research from the transmutation of metals to the preparation of medicines.[112]

"The task of alchemy is not to make gold, but medicines," proclaimed Paracelsus (1493?–1544) in his *Paragranum* (1529–30).[113] With this declaration, the German physician and egocentric father of modern alchemy, T. B. von Hohenheim (Paracelsus), boldly challenged the chemical traditionalists as well as the followers of Aristotle, Galen, Dioscorides, and Celsus. Paracelsus spent his early years in travel and in learning whatever he could from all possible sources about alchemy, medicine, and metallurgy as well as about the latest trends in speculative thought. From 1513 to 1515 he studied medicine in Italy, especially at Ferrara, and was on hand when a wave of interest swept the peninsula about the elephant of India received by Pope Leo X in 1514.[114] In 1517 and 1518 Paracelsus traveled to Iberia, visited Lisbon, and toured other parts of Portugal.[115] While he commented adversely on most foreign medical practices, he seems to have observed curiously and without criticism the Arab-Spanish techniques—possibly because they represented a fusion of alchemy and medicine.

From Iberia Paracelsus went north to England and the Netherlands. Of Antwerp, the great entrepôt of the spice trade, he remarked: "There you can learn more at the marketplace than in German or foreign schools."[116] He then went by sea to Hamburg and to the Baltic region where he took service as a

---

[112] For the most recent scholarly conclusions on this subject see H. J. Sheppard, "Alchemy: Origin or Origins," *Ambix*, XVII (1970), 69–84; Needham, *op. cit.* (n. 1), V, Pt. 2, 1–8; A. G. Debus, "The Significance of Early Chemistry," *Journal of World History*, IX (1965–66), 39–58; and the same author's excellent article on "Alchemy" in the *Dictionary of the History of Ideas* (New York, 1968).

[113] K. Sudhoff (ed.), *Paracelsus, Sämtliche Werke* (14 vols.; Munich, 1929), VIII, 185.

[114] On the elephant of Rome see *Asia*, II, Bk. 1, 135–42.

[115] On other Germans in Portugal see above, pp. 327–29. Since Paracelsus visited Spain before Magellan's departure, it has been suggested, though without supporting evidence, that the Paracel Islands north of the Philippines might have been named for the German physician. For this suggestion see B. de Telepnef, "Wanderwege des Paracelsus von 1512–1525," *Jahrbuch der schweizerischen Paracelsus-Gesellschaft*, III (1946), 151–52. It is sufficient to point out that T. B. von Hohenheim was evidently not known as Paracelsus at such an early date. Paracelsus' own account of his European travels appears in the preface to *Das erste Buch der grossen Wundarznei* (1536) in which he refers to the places here mentioned and notes that he had visited "as well a variety of other countries on which there is no need to comment." See Sudhoff (ed.), *op. cit.* (n. 113), X, 19–21.

[116] As quoted in Telepnef, *loc. cit.* (n. 115), p. 156.

military surgeon. He pushed eastward in 1521 to Moscow and was possibly a prisoner of the Tartars for a brief time. He returned to Venice by way of Poland, took a ship to Alexandria, and eventually wandered as far eastward as Jerusalem. While he was certainly welcome everywhere in his capacity as an army surgeon, he was probably not so widely traveled as some commentators allege. The stories about his visits to China and India are probably the pious fabrications of disciples who wanted to account for lacunae in his biography by crediting their teacher in the occult sciences with enjoying direct access to hermetic and Eastern thought.[117]

Paracelsus was probably introduced to the occult sciences by his father and by his friend, Heinrich Cornelius Agrippa van Netterheim (1486–1535). Both Agrippa and Paracelsus had traveled widely in Europe at a time when excitement about the overseas discoveries was at a high pitch. Agrippa worked for a while as court astrologer to King Francis I of France before becoming librarian to Margaret of Austria, regent of the Netherlands. At Antwerp he was in touch with Maximilian of Transylvania, the reporter on Magellan's circumnavigation and councillor to Emperor Charles V. In the markets of Antwerp Agrippa was able to obtain the stones and herbs from all over the world that were so essential to the study and practice of the black arts. In 1530 he published his two major works, one on the occult sciences and the other on the uncertainty and vanity of the sciences.[118] While he criticizes the learned of Europe for their baleful ignorance about the overseas world, he himself turned eastward for inspiration in the occult arts. "For," he writes, "the Indians, Aethiopians, and Persians always had the pre-eminence in Magick."[119]

In his own writings Paracelsus makes but very few direct references to the distant East. His medical preparations, of course, include numerous Eastern products: "Indian myrobolani," "oil of nutmeg," "oil of cloves." The pre-occupation with "tartar" in his nosological theories cannot be related on the basis of available materials to his supposed imprisonment by the Tartars.[120] In his

---

[117] See commentary in A. E. Waite (trans.), *The Hermetic and Alchemical Writings of Paracelsus...* (2 vols.; London, 1894), I, xii. Leonhart Thurneiser in the next generation after Paracelsus also supposedly made journeys to the East. His writings reinforce the Eastern connection, for they include passages in various Oriental languages. J. B. van Helmont, one of the more renowned seventeenth-century followers of Paracelsus, asserted that Paracelsus was a prisoner of the Tartars from 1513 to 1521 and that he became during that time a convert to Buddhism. See F. Oesterle, *Die Anthropologie des Paracelsus* (Berlin, 1937), p. 12.

[118] He started writing the *De occulta philosophis libri tres* around 1509, and the *De incertitudene et vanitate scientiarum* around 1526.

[119] From the English version called *The Vanity of Arts and Sciences* (London, 1684), p. 110.

[120] In chemistry the word "tartar" refers to the residue of acid potassium tartrate or argol which is deposited during the process of fermentation on the interior of wine casks. From etymological studies it is not possible to establish a relationship between the Tartar peoples and the chemical term. It is not too far fetched to suggest the possibility of such a relationship, however, when it is noticed that both words appear in European languages for the first time in the thirteenth century and that "Tartar" soon came to have a variety of ancillary and figurative meanings: "silk cloth," "savage," and "hell." But in the present state of our knowledge, it is not possible to show with any precision that the chemical term was derived from the name of the Eastern people, or that Paracelsus had any such connection in mind when he evolved his conception of tartaric disease.

Buch von den tartarischen Krankheiten (1537–38) he does, however, stress a point also made elsewhere, that the prescriptions of Asia and Africa are not effective in Europe. At the same time he is also not certain that his own remedies will work outside of Europe.[121] This view is related to his belief that every region of the world—even distant Calicut—has its own diseases, cures, and physicians and that diseases and treatment differ in all climes from one chronological period to another.[122] Although Paracelsus was one of the first to use metals systematically in the preparations of medicines, he does not indicate any awareness of the debt owed by European alchemy to the East for this practice. In addressing himself to the main medical problem of his era—the control of syphilis—Paracelsus rejected the American guaiac treatment in favor of inunction with mercury. If Paracelsus may be credited with intellectual consistency, it appears from this decision that he rejected the prevailing idea that syphilis originated in America. And this despite the fact that a pandemic of syphilis raged in Europe and that Varthema in his popular travel book published in 1510 noticed that people were even dying in India of the "French disease."[123] The Paracelsians recognized, however, that a new medicine was required for the new age both in theory and in *materia medica* to cope with its more debilitating diseases.[124]

Although direct connections between Paracelsian and Oriental medicine cannot be established by specific references, it is clear that European iatro-chemical teachings were derived ultimately from Chinese, Indian, and Arabian practices that had earlier been transmitted to Europe. Much easier to document from his writing is Paracelsus' heavy debt to aspects of Hellenistic thought, particularly as expressed in Neo-Platonism, Gnosticism, the Kabbala, alchemy, astrology, and magic.[125] In Italy and Germany the Humanists of Paracelsus' era were translating numerous Greek and Hebrew sources into Latin and the vernacular languages. From these diverse materials Paracelsus peopled his special world with a multitude of "spirits" which migrate in a Pythagorean (Indian ?) manner from body to body.[126] From the medieval alchemists—Arnold of Villanova, the Lullists, and John of Rupescissa—Paracelsus derived his aversion to the supremacy of the reasoning intellect and his preference for experience and experiment as tools of learning and as means of penetrating natural mysteries.[127] From a plethora of ancient and medieval sources, Paracelsus created an occult

[121] Sudhoff (ed.), *op. cit.* (n. 113), XI, 26–27.
[122] Most clearly expressed in a document in the Breslau city library quoted in Oesterle, *op. cit.* (n. 117), p. 138.
[123] See L. D. Hammond (trans. and ed.), *Travelers in Disguise* . . . (Cambridge, Mass., 1963), p. 214. Varthema observed also: "You must know that I have seen this disease three thousand miles beyond Calicut, and it is called *pua* and they say it is about seventeen years since it began, and it is much worse than ours." On the popularity of Varthema in Germany see above, p. 332.
[124] Johannes Guintherius of Andernach in his *De medicina veteri et nova* (1571) pointed out that Islamic and Indian authors had introduced new medicines as they were required. See A. G. Debus, "The Paracelsians and the Chemists . . .," *Clio Medica*, VII (1972), 191.
[125] See W. Pagel, *Paracelsus: An Introduction to Philosophical Medicine in the Era of the Renaissance* (Basel and New York, 1958), p. 39.
[126] See *ibid.*, p. 216.
[127] *Ibid.*, pp. 258–59.

world view which excited both the admiration and the antagonism of contemporaries.

The strange world of Paracelsus with its astral bodies, demons, and semina,
has led many scholars to look for parallels in the thought of Paracelsus, the
Hellenes, and the Indians.[128] When it is considered how heavily Paracelsus
drew upon Hellenistic thought, it is perhaps natural, for those who see parallels
or even influences of India in Pythagorean and Hellenistic thought, to look
likewise for parallels between Paracelsian and Indian ideas. The most promising
of these approaches are those which seek specificity and are not content to show
vague similarities about such matters as how body and soul are connected in the
Vedanta, in Neo-Platonism, and in Paracelsus. Far more rewarding intellectually are the efforts·being made to establish identities in the recurrent use of
"eight" or "eightnesses" in the classical *Sāṅkhya* philosophy of India (post
fourth century A.D.) and the cosmology of Paracelsus.[129]

The cosmic and the occult in Paracelsus' thought was supplemented at a
practical level by his experiments with metals, particularly in the preparation
of medicines. Most of the important drugs of the sixteenth-century pharma-
copoeia were inorganic substances whose attributes were not always well
understood.[130] Paracelsus worked in mines where he studied at first hand the
attributes of metals.[131] In his *Von Mineralien* he was the first to remark on
metallic zinc as "another metal generally unknown."[132] Metallic zinc first
became available in Europe during the sixteenth century as an import from
China and India. The metallurgical process of extracting zinc from calamine
(zinc silicate) was well known in the East long before the sixteenth century.
Sanskrit texts dating from the eleventh to fourteenth centuries give recipes for
its manufacture.[133] But it appears that most of the zinc imported from Asia
really came from China rather than India during the sixteenth century.[134]

---

[128] On the parallels between Indian and Greek medicine see J. Filliozat, *La doctrine classique de la
médecine indienne: Ses origines et ses parallèles grecs* (Paris, 1949), chap. ix.

[129] The literature on Paracelsian-Indian parallels is more suggestive than convincing. It ranges
from the popular occult suppositions of nineteenth-century scholars like Franz Hartmann in which
Indian thought is made to appear a major source for Paracelsus to the disciplined efforts of Walter
Pagel and his associates. For the most interesting of the recent endeavors see J. Strebel (ed.), *Paracelsus,
Sämtliche Werke* (St. Gall, 1947), III, 1–59; J. Wunderly, "Zum Problem des feinstofflichen Leibes in
der indischen Philosophie, im Neuplatonismus und in Paracelsus," *Episteme* (Milan), III, (1969) 3–15;
W. Pagel, "The Eightness of Adam and Related Gnostic Ideas in the Paracelsian Corpus," *Ambix*,
XVI (1969), 119–39; W. Pagel and M. Winder, "The Higher Elements and Prime Matter in Renaissance Naturalism and in Paracelsus," *Ambix*, XXI (1974), 93–127. These and other references were
furnished me through the courtesy of Walter Pagel in a letter of April 22, 1975. For a few references
to "eightness" in Indian thought see G. J. Larson, *Classical Sāṃkhya: An Interpretation of Its Meaning*
(Delhi, 1969), pp. 173 n. 17, 209–10, 212.

[130] For a discussion of the present status of the controversy over the sixteenth-century interest in
"chemical drugs" see R. P. Multhauf, "Old Drugs in New Bottles," *Isis*, LXIII (1972), 408–12.

[131] See O. Zekert, *Paracelsus: Europäer im 16. Jahrhundert* (Stuttgart, 1968), p. 139.

[132] (Strassburg, 1582), p. 425.

[133] For examples, see P. C. Ray, *History of Hindu Chemistry* (2 vols.; London, 1902), II, 17, 19, 22.

[134] See H. C. Hoover and L. H. Hoover (trans. and eds.), *Georgius Agricola, De re metallica, Translated from the First Latin Edition of 1556* (New York, 1950), p. 409n.

Georg Agricola (1490?–1555), the father of mineralogy, remarked in his *De natura fossilium* that he enlisted scholars, merchants, and miners to bring him samples of unknown minerals and metals from all parts of the world, even Africa and Asia.[135] He recognized zinc as a metal shortly before his death and he comments on it in two of his writings published posthumously.[136] In Europe metallic zinc was sometimes called "tutenag" and was often confused with *pai-t'ung* (Eng. "paktong") or the "white copper" of China.[137] Garcia da Orta in his *Colloquies* (1563) identifies three forms of "tutia" ("tutenag") known in India and reports that "tutia" is taken to Portugal where the druggists sell it.[138] Then, as if to validate his acceptance of the metal as a drug, he remarks: "The Indian doctors know the use of mineral substances in medicine. I have seen them melting and pulverizing metals such as steel, iron, and mercury."[139] Zinc was also used in Europe in the fabrication of brass.[140]

In the earliest reports from the field, and in the writings of the Portuguese chroniclers, "calay" (from Hindi *kala'i* or Malay *kalang*), Indian tin, is mentioned as both a metal and a form of coinage. Most of the writers, including Barros, judge it to be finer than European tin, note that it is mined in the Malay peninsula, and observe that it can readily be purchased at Malacca.[141] Linschoten's remarks on "calay" introduced this metal of the East Indies into the mainstream of European chemical literature. Andreas Libavius (*ca.* 1560–1616), a founder of modern chemistry, noted Linschoten's observations in his *Commentariorum alchemiae* (1606).[142] He also obtained a sample of what he calls "calay," possibly zinc in this case, from a cargo that the Dutch had captured in 1596 from the Portuguese. He describes a number of its properties, including its combustibility, and remarks that it was not known how the Indians extracted the mineral. Later he told a friend that the mineral called zinc in Carinthia and the Tyrol was the same as the "calay" of Malabar![143] "Tutenag," once it had come to mean metal in general rather than the name for a specific metal, was also confused in Europe with "calay."

While Agricola had called early in the century for the careful identification

---

[135] For a German translation and evaluation of this remark see E. Herlitzins, *Georgius Agricola (1494–1555)* . . . (Berlin, 1960), pp. 62, 194.

[136] See Hoover and Hoover (eds. and trans.), *op. cit.* (n. 134), p. 112n.

[137] On this confusion see H. Yule and A. C. Burnell, *Hobson-Jobson* (2d ed.; Delhi, 1968), pp. 932–33. The word itself is possibly a Portuguese rendition of Sanskrit *tuttha*, an oxide of zinc. In the modern Portuguese dictionary the word *tutanaga* still appears in various spellings and with the general meaning of "metal." Also see Needham, *op. cit.* (n. 1), V, Pt. 2, 212. For its derivation from the Persian word for "smoke" see D. Goltz, *Studien zur Geschichte der Mineralnamen* . . . (Wiesbaden, 1972), p. 259. In Latin it became the name for zinc oxide.

[138] According to Lonicerus (Lonitzer, Adam) and others, "tutia" was used by European physicians to clean and heal flesh wounds. See his *Kräuterbuch* (Frankfurt, 1598), p. 709.

[139] C. Markham (trans.), *Garcia da Orta, Colloquies on the Simples and Drugs of India* (London, 1913), pp. 408n., 451–52.

[140] See R. P. Multhauf, *The Origins of Chemistry* (New York, 1967), p. 314.

[141] See S. R. Dalgado, *Glossário Luso-asiático* (2 vols.; Coimbra, 1919–21), I, 179. "Calaim" is still the Portuguese word for "fine tin."

[142] Pt. II, Bk. 1, chap. 8.

[143] See J. R. Partington, *History of Chemistry* (3 vols.; London and New York, 1961–62), II, 258–59.

of unknown minerals and metals, his successors were possibly confused in their cataloging efforts by the appearance in Europe of *pai-t'ung*, the Chinese "white copper" of trade. Uncertainty about the nature of this cupro–nickel alloy that resembles silver was not confined to European scientists. The Islamic alchemist Jabir Ibn Hayyan (Latinized as Geber), included *khar sini* (Chinese iron) in his list of seven known metals, apparently not recognizing it as an alloy.[144] Although objects and ingots of *pai-t'ung* were imported from China, the European chemists of the sixteenth century never comprehended its nature. The Arabs, and probably the Europeans as well, often used *pai-t'ung*, possibly because of its mysterious character, in preparing the elixir of life. Libavius in his *De natura metallorum* (1599) describes it as a new metal from the East Indies, "not zinc but a special kind of sonorous tin."[145] Despite all the confusion about the names and attributes of Eastern metals, the chemists and metallurgists of the sixteenth century sought to bring them, however unsuccessfully, into their own repertory, to understand their properties, and to relate them to known substances.

5

BOTANY

The recovery and publication in the fifteenth century of the writings of the ancient Greek and Roman naturalists provided a firm foundation for the modern edifice of the biological sciences. During the Renaissance the most respected of the ancient commentators on plants were Aristotle, Theophrastus, Pliny the Elder, Dioscorides, and Galen. Pliny's *Historia naturalis*, previously popular in manuscript copies, was first printed in 1469 and reprinted before 1500 in fifteen Latin and three Italian versions. Manuscript copies of Dioscorides' *Materia medica* were also widely circulated before it was printed in Latin in 1478 and in the original Greek in 1499. The Greek versions of Theophrastus' texts on plants were included in the first printed edition of Aristotle's works which appeared at Venice in 1497. Interest in Galen was apparently more limited, but some of his writings appeared in Latin manuscript books before the end of the fifteenth century. Both Galen and Dioscorides were physicians; their main concern therefore was to describe those plants deemed most valuable as drugs.

The influence of the ancient writers on fifteenth-century botany was at first limited by the continuing dominance of Salneritan medicine, preoccupation with Arabic writings on science, and the persistence of the herbal traditions inherited from the Middle Ages. A number of the anonymous medieval herbals which for centuries had circulated widely in manuscript were put into print late in the fifteenth century. In the sixteenth century the herbals continued to

---

[144] See E. J. Holmyard, *Alchemy* (London, 1968), p. 80. While there was a Jabir of the eighth century, the source of this statement is probably from a work of the fourteenth century.

[145] As quoted in Needham, *op. cit.* (n. 1), V, Pt. 2, 227.

compete with the writings of Antiquity for the attention of students of plant life, physicians, and pharmacists.[146] The founding of the science of botany from these commingling traditions was one of the greatest synthetic scientific achievements of the sixteenth century. The movement toward botanical synthesis was accelerated by the discovery of a whole New World of plants in the Americas and insular Asia and by the study at first hand of exotic specimens from Africa and continental Asia.

The plants and drugs of Asia had awakened the interest of European naturalists, merchants, and travelers long before the opening of the sea route to India. The great collectors and catalogers of Antiquity carried out many of their studies in the Levant where spices and drugs of more distant Asia could be readily found in the market cities at the western end of the caravan routes.[147] Many of the six hundred different plants, animals, and minerals described by Dioscorides originated in India and China. The descriptions of exotic plants by the Greek physician were necessarily limited to dried specimens, fruits, seeds, and leaves, and to a few living specimens of the sort Galen grew in his garden. Pliny, who was usually attracted by the fabulous, was certainly fascinated by the exotica of the plant world.

Most of the medieval naturalists followed Pliny blindly and were not even inclined to study in their natural surroundings the plants native to Europe. Marco Polo, who was more interested in the fauna than in the flora of Asia, remarks with keen interest nonetheless on the forests and plants of the parts of Asia he visited. More than any previous commentator he sought to locate precisely the places of origin of the valuable spices of commerce.[148] The Florentine merchant F. B. Pegolotti appended to his handbook for merchants, *La practica della mercatura* (*ca.* 1340), a list of 288 marketable spices and drugs most of which originated in the East.[149] In the fifteenth century Poggio Bracciolini, who summarized the travels of Nicolò de' Conti in the East, described in some detail the cinnamon tree of Ceylon and the cultivation of ginger in India. He also commented briefly on durians, bananas, coconuts, mangos, and a number of other edible fruits.[150] Clearly many of the plants of the East, unlike those of the Americas, were already firmly established in the plant world known to Europeans before the discovery of the water route to India.

Certain of the descriptions of Asian plants prepared before 1500 were repeated or amplified by on-the-spot observers, chroniclers, and poets of the sixteenth century. Varthema's *Itinerario* (1510), probably the most popular of the Eastern

---

[146] On the early printed herbals see W. Blunt, *The Art of Botanical Illustration* (London, 1950), chap. iv; and A. Arber, *Herbals: Their Origin and Evolution* (2d rev. ed.; Cambridge, 1938), chap. ii.

[147] See F. Guerra, "Drugs from the Indies . . .," in M. Florkin (ed.), *Analecta medico-historica* (Oxford, 1966), p. 29.

[148] See L. Olschki, *Marco Polo's Asia* (Berkeley, 1960), pp. 155–57.

[149] On Pegolotti see *Asia*, I, 45.

[150] For the botanical references in Poggio's *India recognita* (1492) see L. D. Hammond, *op. cit.* (n. 123), pp. 9, 11, 12–13, 16, 18, 21. Cf. pls. 38, 39.

travel accounts, provided more detail than its predecessors on the familiar pepper plant, coco palm, cinnamon, and ginger root. Most original were Varthema's discussions of three kinds of aloes wood and his descriptions of the cultivation of nutmegs, mace, and cloves in the Moluccas.[151] In recounting the riches of Ceylon he remarks that it produces "sweet oranges, the best, I believe, in the world."[152] Balthasar Springer, the Augsburger who visited India in 1505–6, extols the luxuriant vegetation of Malabar and declares that "pepper grows on vines like wine grapes do."[153] The Portuguese themselves had meanwhile begun to feel a need for a more thorough survey of the drug traffic and the sources of the spices. Tomé Pires, a pharmacist by training, sent a letter from Malacca around 1515 to King Manuel on the plants of the East.[154] But this, and the nearly contemporary travel account of Duarte Barbosa, were long left unpublished.[155] Another pharmacist, Simão Alvares, wrote a report in India between 1546 and 1548 on the origins and attributes of the drugs being sent to Portugal at that time; it also remained unpublished.[156] The surgeon Luís de Almeida arrived in India around 1548, but he evidently left no report at all on botanicals.[157] The botanists of Europe thus remained quite uninformed about the plants of the East newly seen during the first half of the sixteenth century. Throughout the first two generations of the Portuguese expansion into Asia, they were forced to rely, as they had before, on traditional descriptions, on the Asian products that appeared in European markets, and on whatever second-hand reports they heard or read.

Serious botanical study in Europe was meanwhile undergoing a reorientation stimulated by the revival of the classical texts, the establishment of botanical gardens, the printing of illustrations, and the neo-Aristotelian demand for classification. The *Materia medica* of Dioscorides which appeared in at least seventy-eight editions during the sixteenth century was the starting point for botanical organization and discussion.[158] The work of the Greek physician, in which the plants were usually arranged in alphabetical order, was the object of both unreserved acclaim and vituperative denunciation. One of the main

[151] For precise references see *ibid.*, pp. 148, 150, 152–54, 166, 186–87, 191–92. Dioscorides had described but two kinds of aloes wood.

[152] *Ibid.*, p. 165. For the importance of this remark to the history of the "sweet orange" see below, pp. 441–42.

[153] See F. Schulze, *Balthasar Springers Indienfahrt, 1505/06 . . .* (Strassburg, 1902), pp. 54–55; also see *Asia*, I, 162–63.

[154] For his list of thirty plants and their botanical names see M. Lemos, *História da medicina em Portugal* (2 vols.; Lisbon, 1899), II, 217–74.

[155] Barbosa's account circulated clandestinely in manuscript (see above, p. 58) and was published in part by Ramusio at mid-century. Its main importance, however, was for the drug trade. See Guerra, *loc. cit.* (n. 147), p. 50.

[156] It was finally published by Jaime Walter in "Simão Alvares e o seu rol das drogas da India," *Studia* (Lisbon), X (1962), pp. 117–49.

[157] See L. Bourdon, "Luís de Almeida, chirurgien et marchand . . .," in *Mélanges d'études portugaises offerts à M. Georges Le Gentil* (Lisbon, 1949), pp. 69–85; and J. Z. Bowers, *Western Medical Pioneers in Feudal Japan* (Baltimore, 1970), pp. 11–14.

[158] See J. Stannard, "Dioscorides and Renaissance *Materia medica*," in M. Florkin (ed.), *op. cit.* (n. 147), pp. 1–3.

objects of the botanists was to identify the plants described by Dioscorides with living or dried specimens. Since Dioscorides wrote mainly of Mediterranean and Levantine plants, the German botanists in particular became confused by descriptions which could not be applied to the plants native to northern Europe. The early scholar-naturalists of Germany—Otto Brunfels, Hieronymus Bock, and Leonhart Fuchs—consequently contented themselves with compiling illustrated herbals designed primarily for the book trade and for the use of physicians and pharmacists.[159] Brunfels failed even to understand the simple fact, well known to Theophrastus, that different geographical regions have their own characteristic plants.[160] Bock, a more sophisticated botanist, included in his herbal descriptions a few overseas plants.[161] Fuchs acknowledged the opening of Asia by calling the capsicums of his garden the "peppers of Calicut."[162] The Paracelsians in their aversion to the use of foreign drugs were forthrightly opposed to the inclusion of exotic specimens in the herbals.[163]

Some Italian scholars, especially those located in the vicinity of Venice, were much more aware than the Germans of the exotic plants of Asia. The Humanists of the circle of Pietro Bembo were amateurs of gardens and plants. Next to his magnificent villa in Padua, Bembo had a garden in which he experimented with lemons, oranges, and the "rarest simples."[164] Andrea Navagero, who had a splendid garden of his own on the island of Murano, gathered information on exotic plants while on his embassy to Spain from 1524 to 1528. He relayed his news to Ramusio, who had a garden in Venice, and through him it was circulated to other interested persons.[165] In neighboring Ferrara, Antonio (called Musa) Brasavola (1500–1555), physician and herbalist, was one of the first botanists to grow exotic plants and to criticize Dioscorides roundly. After 1536 he began to grow plants from Greece and Asia Minor in a garden on an island in the Po River. In his writings he explicitly challenged his colleagues who continued to rely on the texts of Antiquity and the herbals. He claimed in his *Examen omnium simplicium medicamentorum* that the Ancients were ignorant of 99 percent of the world of plants.[166] He received support for his position when Amato Lusitano (1511–68), a Portuguese physician, arrived at Ferrara in 1540 to teach medicine. The author of a commentary on the first two books of Dioscorides, published at Antwerp in 1536, Amato from his experiences in Portugal and the Netherlands brought with him valuable knowledge about

159 For discussion of the illustrated herbals see *Asia*, II, Bk. 1, 81–82.

160 But Brunfels outstripped the ancients by recognizing ferns, mosses, and conifers as separate groups of plants. See J. von Sachs, *Geschichte der Botanik* (Leipzig, 1875), pp. 3–5.

161 See B. Hoppe (ed.), *Die Kräuterbuch des Hieronymus Bock . . .* (Stuttgart, 1969), p. 80.

162 See pls. 40, 41, 42.

163 See Arber, *op. cit.* (n. 146), p. 255. On Paracelsus' ideas on foreign medicaments see above, p. 424.

164 See V. Cian, *Un decennio della vita di M. Pietro Bembo (1521–31)* (Turin, 1885), pp. 37n, 123.

165 For a survey of Navagero's activities and his correspondence with Ramusio see M. Cermenati, "Un diplomatico naturalista del Rinascimento, Andrea Navagero," *Nuovo archivio veneto*, N.S., XXIV (1912), 164–205. Also see above, p. 200.

166 (Rome, 1537), pp. 65–66.

Asian plants as well as a highly skeptical attitude toward Dioscorides and traditional botany.[167]

The question most hotly debated with regard to exotic plants was whether they were truly "new" or whether they had previously been described under other names.[168] The first sixteenth-century translation and commentary of Dioscorides' work was published in 1516 by Jean Ruel (1474–1537) of Paris. It was superseded in 1553 by Amato's complete commentary called *In Dioscorides Anazarbei de medica materia libros quinque enarrationes . . .* (Venice).[169] Amato, a Marrano refugee from Portugal, was supremely conscious of the impact on botany of his countrymen's discoveries. He sought everywhere for specimens of Eastern plants and for recent information on their habitats. For example, he acquired a China root brought directly from China by Portuguese sailors in 1549; he waxed enthusiastic in his writings about its efficacy in the treatment of syphilis. From Franciscus Barbosieus, a Marrano physician of Ancona who had practiced in India for eighteen years, he acquired other specimens from the East.[170] In his commentaries he seeks, somewhat erratically, to provide the native names for Indian plants. He never ceases to praise "our Portuguese" for revealing so much of the unknown world of plants and for providing him with materials to challenge the knowledge of the Ancients and his contemporaries.[171] Despite the adverse reactions of some of his colleagues, Amato's commentary went through six editions between 1553 and 1565.

Amato's most prominent adversary was Pietro Andrea Gregorio Mattioli (1501–77), a graduate of Padua and one of the leading naturalists of the day. He had published at Venice in 1544 the Italian *Commentarii a Dioscoridi* which Amato severely criticized in his Latin commentary. Employed as a physician by Archduke Ferdinand, Mattioli carried out his botanical researches under Habsburg patronage at Gorizia (1539–54) and at Prague (1554–70). With his time rather free to follow his own interests, Mattioli continually revised and amplified his commentaries with new materials and illustrations. He also found time to publish at Venice in 1548 an Italian translation of Ptolemy's *Geography*. His *chef d'oeuvre*, however, was a Latin commentary on Dioscorides published in 1554 and lavishly illustrated by Giorgio Liberale of Udine and Wolfgang Meyerpeck of Freiberg in Saxony, who were likewise retainers of the Habsburgs.[172] The Latin edition with its detailed commentary was shortly translated into German, French, and Czech. The success of this book is apparent from the

---

[167] While in Ferrara, Amato possibly corresponded with Hieronymus Dias, a Portuguese physician of Goa whom he had known earlier in Antwerp. On the early career of Amato see H. Friedenwald, *The Jews and Medicine: Essays* (2 vols.; Baltimore, 1944), I, 336–48; II, 433–34. Also see pl. 44.

[168] See Stannard, *loc. cit.* (n. 158), pp. 12–13.

[169] I have used the 1588 edition published at Lyons. It includes a fair number of woodcut illustrations.

[170] See Friedenwald, *op. cit.* (n. 167), II, 435.

[171] For example, see *In Dioscorides*, pp. 33, 39; a full discussion of his knowledge of the spices and simples of India is to be found in R. Jorge, *Amato Lusitano* (Lisbon, 1962), pp. 215–78.

[172] *Commentarii in sex libros Pedacii Dioscorides*. On the portraiture of plants in the botanical books see *Asia*, II, Bk. 1, 81–84.

large number of editions and printings it went through until well into the eighteenth century.

Mattioli's title is misleading in the sense that his work contains far more than Dioscorides' catalog of plants with comments. The Italian botanist spent most of his leisure hours over a quarter of a century in augmenting and correcting his work. He personally supervised the production of most of the editions which appeared before his death in 1577. Thus they include references to all the plants known to him. Although Mattioli did field work himself in the Tirol, most of his information on exotic plants was communicated to him by others. One of his main informants was Wilhelm Quackelbeen (*ca.* 1526–61), a physician to Auger de Busbecq, the imperial emissary (1554–55, 1555–62) to Constantinople. From these legates Mattioli received more than fifty specimens and at least thirty descriptions prepared on the spot by Quackelbeen. Included among the descriptions were several of fruits and plants from the distant East, such as camphor and ginger.[173]

A perusal of a German translation (1563) and a French translation (1572) of Mattioli's work reveals that he sought through informants both in India and Europe to obtain better descriptions and clearer portraits of the Asian plants.[174] He complains that he is unable to find a picture of the cinnamon tree because it cannot be grown in Europe, only in India.[175] He was more fortunate, however, in obtaining from a Portuguese a first-hand drawing of the common round pepper plant which grows in Calicut.[176] His researches on pepper were also aided by Francesco Calzolari (1522–1609), physician and naturalist of Verona, who sent him a whole cluster of pepper corns. He personally saw pepper growing at Naples and at Venice "in the garden of Maphei de Mapheo where one may see several other rare and exquisite plants."[177] From these observations he concludes that because different types of pepper and pepper trees grow in Italy, there must be many more varieties of them in India. But most of his other comments relate to the physical characteristics and economic uses of the exotic products available in Europe. Of ebony he writes that it is more like stone than wood for it sinks in water. The Indians, he reports, make from ebony drinking vessels, boxes, cases, writing instruments, and nails, which they send to Europe.[178] He also remarks that the "ginger of Calicut" is imported into Italy both in dried form and preserved in sugar.[179] Mattioli also lets his readers know

---

[173] See the article in *Biographie nationale de Belgique*.

[174] References here are to the German translation by Dr. Georg Handsch, *New Kreüterbuch mit den allerschönsten und artlichsten Figuren aller Gewechss . . .* (Prague, 1563), and the French translation by Dr. Jean de Moulines, revised and augmented by the author himself in more than 1,000 places, called *Commentaires . . . sur les six livres de Ped. Dioscoride . . .* (Lyons, 1572). See pls. 45–50, and compare to pls. 40–42.

[175] *New Kreüterbuch* (n. 174), pp. 13^r–13^v.

[176] *Ibid.*, pp. 217^v–218^r.

[177] *Commentaires* (n. 174), p. 342.

[178] *New Kreüterbuch* (n. 174), p. 59^v. Cf. the collections of curiosities discussed in *Asia*, II, Bk. 1, 29–30, 46–54.

[179] *Commentaires* (n. 174), p. 344.

that the best aloes wood comes from Calicut and that the Portuguese import whole trunks of this tree.[180]

In Portugal itself experimentation with Asian plants was limited to the owners of a few private gardens. João de Castro, the great viceroy of India (1545–48), is credited traditionally with introducing the sweet orange in 1548 by successfully bringing a living tree to Lisbon. At his county seat called Pehna Verde, near Sintra, Castro built a terraced garden in which he grew a number of rare Indian trees. After 1528, Braz de Albuquerque possibly constructed a similar garden of botanical rarities at the Quinta da Bacalhoa near Sétubal.[181] But the greatest Portuguese gardener of the sixteenth century did not live in either Portugal or Europe. Serious experimentation with the plants of tropical Asia took place mainly in the gardens at Goa and on Bombay Island planted by Garcia da Orta, a physician who lived for over thirty years in India.

Orta arrived in India during 1534. Twenty-nine years later, in 1563, he published at Goa his *Coloquios dos simples e drogas e cousas mediçinais da India.*[182] Here he discusses in dialogue form fifty-seven drugs and simples commonly found in Eastern markets for use as spice, food, or medicine. Most of his information about the botanical characteristics of the plants he learned from personal observation or through informants. He evidently knew no Sanskrit and was consequently unable to consult Indian pharmaceutical and botanical materials. Orta, probably the most learned Portuguese to reside in India for a long period, was caustic about the lack of scientific curiosity displayed by his countrymen as they voyaged from one Asian port to the other:

They are not desirous of knowing anything about the things in the countries they visit. If they know a product, they do not seek to learn from what tree it comes, and if they see it they do not compare it with one of our trees, nor ask about the fruit, nor what it is like.[183]

Although his task was obviously difficult, Orta succeeded in writing a book that was to become basic to the allied sciences of tropical medicine and botany.[184]

Orta's aim in his book, like the earlier reports of the Portuguese pharmacists, was to study the herbal products vital to trade. Consequently the text has a strong utilitarian bent and even occasionally contains references to matters of purely political or military interest. It is not as important for new observations and descriptions as for the confirmation, correction, and amplification of those

[180] *Ibid.*, p. 51. The wood itself is aromatic; a purgative was usually made in India from its leaves.
[181] See R. S. Nichols, *Spanish and Portuguese Gardens* (New York, 1902), pp. 225–28.
[182] For a biographical and bibliographical sketch see *Asia*, I, 192–94. Following p. 164 in *ibid.* there is reprinted the title-page of Orta's *Coloquios.*
[183] As translated in C. Markham (ed.), *Colloquies on the Simples and Drugs of India by Garcia da Orta* (London, 1913), pp. 86–87.
[184] For an evaluation of Orta and a comparison of his work with that of Nicholas Monardes, the druggist of Seville and student of American drugs and simples, see C. R. Boxer, *Two Pioneers of Tropical Medicine: Garcia d'Orta and Nicholas Monardes* (London, 1963).

previously made and for establishing botanical connections not seen before.[185] Orta's descriptions, though not always in this order, give the common names of the plants in as many languages as possible, their place of origin, and their geographical distribution along with their characteristics as simple or drug, their medicinal use, and the best method of administering them. His botanical descriptions, as opposed to his pharmaceutical and medical comments, are succinct and rudimentary, comparable to the descriptions in most contemporary herbals. He generally gives more attention to the vegetal parts than to the fruit or to the flower organization. In the case of those plants, fruits, or flowers of alimentary importance his descriptions are naturally more detailed. On flowers he generally comments on numbers or abundance, the color, the aroma, and at times on the similarity to Portuguese flowers. He treats fruits in a similar fashion. His best botanical descriptions are of the floral structure and leaf patterns of the leguminous plants, such as "bangue" (*Cannabis indica*, or Indian hemp) and "galanga" (*Alpinia galanga*), which possess close taxonomic affinities.[186]

The influence of Orta on contemporary thought was profound, despite his distance from Europe and despite the fact that very few copies of his Goa publication ever reached there. At Goa he entertained and instructed the poet Camoëns and printed an ode dedicated to Viceroy Francisco Coutinho, Count of Redondo. Near the end of the ode Camoëns added a paean in praise of Orta:

The lore which Achilles once valued I studied with thee, you opened my eyes to its charm. In your garden of herbs each flower, each tree, were seen in your time by your friend. The fruits of that garden collected from far were unknown to the learned of old.[187]

In the *Lusiads* the poet celebrates the flowering plants of Asia, identifies them as native to particular places or regions, and almost never mentions their economic uses. All but one or two of Camoëns' plants can be identified as tropical.[188]

Orta's book also produced a significant impact upon botanical writing in Europe. Charles de L'écluse (1526–1609), the Flemish botanist known also as Clusius, was among the first to recognize the importance of the *Colloquies* to the systematic study of plants. While escorting Jakob Fugger on a visit to Portugal in 1564–65, he acquired a copy of Orta's book. Immediately upon his return to the Netherlands, he began to translate it into Latin. L'écluse's copy of the *Colloquies*, annotated in a microscopic but readable Latin script, is extant. His epitomized Latin version published by Christopher Plantin is far different

185 He does apparently notice for the first time an oxalid, *Biophytum sensitivum*, and is original in describing the sleeping position of tamarind leaves. See Arber, *op. cit.* (n. 146), p. 105.

186 Analysis based on C. das Neves Tavares, "A botânica nos *Colóquios* de Garcia de Orta," in *Garcia de Orta* (commemorative vol.), XI, No. 4 (1963), 684–88. João de Loureiro in *Flora Cochinchinensis* (Lisbon, 1790) commemorated Orta's contribution by giving the name Garciana to one of his genera. It is retained in the International Code of Botanical Nomenclature only as a synonym of *Philydrum Banks*. Linnaeus also commemorated Orta in his *Garcinia Mangostama*.

187 This very unliteral translation is from Markham (ed.), *op. cit.* (n. 183), p. xii. For other stanzas in English translation see above, p. 151 n.

188 Aside from Orta, Camoëns used Barros as a source for Asian vegetation and adopted the historian's characterization of Ceylon as "the mother of cinnamon." See Conde de Ficalho, *Flora dos Lusiadas* (Lisbon, 1880), pp. 13–14. Also see above, pp. 156–57.

from Orta's original in organization and style.[189] The dialogue form is abandoned in favor of straightforward descriptions of the best-known simples and
drugs of commerce. Orta's work had been published without illustrations; the
careful Clusius added a few portraits but only of those vegetable products from
afar that could be purchased in Antwerp markets.[190] The epitomizer is also
more inclined than Orta to refer without comment to the disagreements
between the writers of Antiquity and the gardener of Goa.

The Spanish, who controlled the Netherlands until about 1567 or the year of
Clusius' epitome, had long been anxious to find out more about the intricacies
of the spice trade in the East. In Spain an interest in the exotic plants of America
and insular Asia can be traced back to Peter Martyr and to the writings of
Oviedo in the first generation of the sixteenth century.[191] Andrés Laguna
(1499–1560), a Spanish physician who lived longer in northern Europe and
Italy than in Spain, published at Antwerp in 1555 a Spanish commentary on
Dioscorides that became a standard reference book in the Iberian pensinsula.[192]
Like Mattioli he based his Dioscorides upon the earlier commentary (1516) of
Jean Ruel; he also embellished it with numerous engravings that had been cut
in Venice during 1554. The renown of Laguna, who had been physician for a
time to Charles V and later to Pope Julius III, helped to establish his work as the
last word in *materia medica*.[193] The great pharmacist Nicholas Monardes of
Seville furnished him with materials on exotic plants, and his acquaintance with
the leading botanists of northern Europe, such as Mattioli, led him to follow
their example in organizing experimental gardens. It was Laguna who convinced Philip II in 1555 to establish a botanical garden at Aranjuez.[194] Cervantes
is the best witness to Laguna's fame: Don Quixote says, "At this time I would
rather have a slice of bread and a couple of heads of salt pilchards than all the
herbs described by Dioscorides, though commented upon by Dr. Laguna
himself."[195]

Laguna's commentaries, like those of Mattioli, dwell mainly on the economic
value of the exotic plants. For a time at least his information was enough to

---

[189] Entitled *Aromatum et simplicium aliquot medicamentorum apud indos nascentium historia* (Antwerp,
1567). In commemoration of the four-hundredth anniversary of the *Colloquies* a modern reprint of
this work along with a Portuguese translation was published at Lisbon in 1964 by *Junta de Investigaçoẽs
do Ultramar*.

[190] I have previously stated incorrectly (*Asia*, II, Bk. 1, 82) that Clusius' epitome was not illustrated.
I meant to say that it was not illustrated, as his later works were, with the engravings of the plants
themselves.

[191] See above, pp. 170–71.

[192] Entitled *Pedacio Dioscórides Anazarbeo, acerca de la materia medicinal y de los venenos mortiferos . . .*
(Antwerp, 1555). Later editions were issued at Madrid (1560) and Salamanca (1570, 1586). A reprint
of the Salamanca edition of 1570 is included as Vol. III in C. E. Dubler, *La 'Materia Medica' de
Dioscorides . . .* (5 vols.: Barcelona, 1953–55).

[193] For an appreciation of his commentary and its influence in Spain see J. Olmedilla y Puig,
Estudio histórico de la vida y escritos del Sabio español Andrés Laguna . . . (Madrid, 1887), chap. vi.

[194] See M. Colmeiro, *Ensayo historico sobre los progresos de la botánica, . . . especialmente con relacion a
España* (Barcelona, 1842), p. 10.

[195] Translated from M. de Cervantes Saavedra and F. R. Marin (eds.), *El ingenioso hidalgo, Don
Quijote de la Mancha* (10 vols.; Madrid, 1947–49), II, 56–57.

satisfy the Spanish crown, scholars, and merchants. But with the establishment of the Spanish in the Philippines around 1565, the need for detail on the spices and on the vegetable resources of the East became more pressing. The reopening at this period of the controversy over the ownership of the Spiceries was accompanied by the publication in Spain of two books which purportedly contained the most recent information on Asian simples and drugs.

Juan Fragoso, physician to Philip II, published in 1572 the *Discoursos de las cosas aromaticas arboles y frutales . . . de la India Oriental* (Madrid).[196] While it is based in part on Orta's *Colloquies*, the number of plants on which Fragoso comments are fewer and more carefully selected. They are arranged alphabetically and the discourses are more succinctly written than Orta's rambling colloquies. Following the table of contents, Fragoso lists the authorities, including Orta, who are named in the book. He includes practically every one of his predecessors who had anything at all to contribute to the study of Asian flora, from the writers of Antiquity to Laguna. In addition to botanists, he lists among his authorities the writings of Polo, Varthema, Barros, and Ramusio. The work itself is much more original than bibliographers usually indicate, for Fragoso compares Orta's work to the other sources and points up discrepancies.[197] A Latin translation by Israel Spach of Fragoso's book was published at Strassburg in 1600.

Even more original and important was the book prepared in Spain by Cristobal de Acosta (*ca.* 1525–*ca.* 1594), a Portuguese physician with many years of personal experience in the East.[198] Before 1550 he was in maritime Asia as a soldier in the service of Portugal. During his first tour of duty he met Orta in Goa. He returned to Portugal but soon rejoined a former captain, Luís de Ataide, who was to embark for India as viceroy. Acosta landed at Goa in 1568, a few months after Orta's death. While in India with Ataide, he acted as physician to the royal hospital in Cochin and collected botanical specimens at various places along India's west coast. He returned to Portugal with Ataide in 1572 and soon left for Burgos in Spain where he acted as municipal physician from 1576 to 1587. Here, and perhaps in the last years of his retirement at a hermitage near Huelva, he wrote three texts on Eastern matters. Two of his manuscripts have never been located;[199] the third, printed at Burgos in 1578 under the title

---

[196] A copy of this rare book on microfilm is in the National Library of Medicine at Washington. The full title page reads: *Discoursos delascosas aromaticas, arboles y frutales, y de otras muchas medicinas simples que se traen de la India Oriental, y sirven al uso de medicina, autor el licencia do Iuan Fragoso medico, y cyrugiano de su Magestad. Con privilegio. Impresso en Madrid en Casa de Francisco Sanchez. Año 1572. Vendese en casa de Sebastian Yuañez librero en Corte.*

[197] It is incorrectly cataloged as an unacknowledged and unauthorized translation of Orta's book to which Fragoso adds remarks on American products in D. M. Colmeiro, *La botánica y los botánicos de la peninsula hispano-lusitania* (Madrid, 1858), pp. 152–53.

[198] Much misinformation about Acosta and his career has long been circulated in bibliographies and monographs. The most accurate account of his activities is the article by Francisco Guerra in the *Dictionary of Scientific Biography*. Also see pl. 53.

[199] For the titles of the unpublished manuscripts, one on the voyage to the East Indies and the other on the flora and fauna of the region from Persia to China, see *ibid.*

Tractado de las drogas y medicinas de las Indias Orientalis, rivaled Orta's book in authority and influence.[200]

A number of scholars of the past have unjustly asserted that Acosta's *Tractado* is little more than a translation or an epitome of Orta's *Colloquies*.[201] That Acosta knew Orta's work and used it in the preparation of his own he freely acknowledges. Textual comparison reveals, however, that the two books differ markedly in form, arrangement, and subject matter. Acosta eschewed the dialogue form adopted by Orta in favor of a straightforward, concise, and systematic description of the plants, an approach more acceptable to botanists. To his text Acosta added twenty full-page woodcuts, the sketches for some of which he had made in the field.[202] When Acosta deals with the plants discussed in Orta's book his remarks generally amplify those found there. The corresponding chapters dealing with identical plants vary greatly in length. Of the forty-seven plants described by Acosta, Orta does not even mention fourteen of them; nine of Orta's plants do not appear in Acosta's book. Most of Acosta's descriptions are clearer and more precise than those which can be extrapolated from Orta's *Colloquies*.[203]

For new information on Asian plants most of the Italian botanists from the middle to the end of the century had to depend upon the translations of Orta, Acosta, and Clusius that were published at Venice and elsewhere in Italian and Latin.[204] Like Brasavola and the earlier botanists, the later Italian students of plant life also scoured the travelers' accounts for descriptions of Asian flora.[205] Girolamo Cardano, the Milanese polyscientist, depended almost entirely upon Ramusio's travel collection for his knowledge of foreign plants and was flattered when his name was cited by botanists.[206] Even Andrea Cesalpino (1519–1603), the eminent professor of Pisa and botanical systematizer, relied in 1583 on Varthema, the traveler from Bologna, for his descriptions of aloes wood, pepper, and ginger.[207] Cesalpino is also aware of Orta's work, probably from the epitome of L'écluse, for he mentions the Portuguese naturalist in his

[200] Translated into Italian by F. Ziletti (Venice, 1585); French by A. Colin (Lyons, 1602, 1619); Latin by L'écluse (Antwerp, 1582, 1593, 1605). See pl. 54.

[201] See Arber, *op. cit.* (n. 146), p. 105; Markham (ed.), *op. cit.* (n. 183), p. xiv.

[202] For one of his woodcuts not sketched in the field see *Asia*, II, Bk. 1, 154. Also see pl. 52.

[203] See J. Seide, "The Relationship of Garcia da Orta's and Cristóbal Acosta's Botanical Works," *Actes du X⁰ congrès international d'histoire des sciences*, VII (1953), 564–67. See also the Portuguese translation of the *Tractado* prepared by Dr. Jaime Walter (Lisbon, 1964) for the four-hundredth anniversary of Orta's book. In the notes Walter indicates specifically how much or how little Acosta depended upon Orta for each of his chapters.

[204] Orta was published in Latin epitome in 1567 and in numerous revised versions issued at Antwerp thereafter. Annibal Briganti published an Italian translation of Orta at Venice in 1576. F. Ziletti translated Acosta into Italian at Venice in 1585. Clusius published Acosta in Latin at Antwerp in 1582 and 1593.

[205] For example, Brasavola quotes Marco Polo and the Portuguese to the effect that Borneo is the source of camphor. See his *Examen omnium*, p. 465; also see pp. 420–24.

[206] See *De subtilitate* (Lyons, 1580), pp. 303–5; in *The Book of My Life* (New York, 1962) Cardáno recalls (pp. 250–52) being cited by Amato Lusitano, H. Bock, L. Fuchs, and L'écluse.

[207] *De plantis libri XVI* (Florence, 1583), pp. 53, 62, 426.

dedication to Francesco de' Medici as one who has seen many things in the East that were unknown to the writers of Antiquity.[208]

Grand Duke Francesco of Tuscany (reigned 1574–87) possessed more than a passing interest in the plants of the East. Early in his reign he tried unsuccessfully to buy the contract for marketing the spices from India.[209] He was also eager to learn the secret of porcelain manufacture and was responsible for the production of the Medici porcelain.[210] It was Francesco who commissioned Filippo Sassetti (1540–88) to buy exotic plants in Lisbon and Goa for his experimental Boboli gardens.[211] In India Sassetti, at the urging of Cesalpino and the grand duke, sought to learn whether or not "cinnamon" and "cannella" were but different names for the same product; in this effort Sassetti was not successful. Grand Duke Francesco corresponded with Ulisse Aldrovandi (1522–1605), the eminent naturalist of Bologna, and helped to finance his collecting activities.[212] He sponsored Jacopo Ligozzi (1547–1626) and encouraged him to paint naturalistic representations of exotic plants.[213] Aldrovandi also worked through Florence's representative in Spain to obtain accurate drawings of overseas plants. The library of the University of Bologna today preserves ten volumes of the plant drawings collected by Aldrovandi.[214]

For Francesco and other Italians interested in Asia, the year 1585 was memorable. The grand duke was the first among the dignitaries of Italy to greet and entertain the young legates from Japan.[215] Mendoza's famous book on China first appeared in this year at Rome.[216] News of the successful penetration of China by the Jesuits was also circulating in Rome when the Japanese converts arrived there. Nor was botany far behind in cultivating enthusiasm for the East; in that year Castor Durante (1529–90) published at Rome a lavish edition of his *Herbario nuovo* with 874 woodcuts.[217]

Durante, a native of Gualdo, was an amateur of Latin poetry and a professional in medicine. He was the personal physician of Sixtus V, who ascended the papal throne in 1585. The title page of Durante's Roman edition carries an insignia (IHS) of the church and the patent of the pope. Like the Catholic Church

---

[208] For his specific references to Orta's descriptions see *ibid.*, pp. 83, 116, 190, 426.

[209] See *Asia*, I, 133.

[210] *Ibid.*, II, Bk. 1, 108.

[211] *Ibid.*, I, 476; II, Bk. 1, 40–41.

[212] See especially O. Mattirolo (ed.), "Le lettere di Ulisse Aldrovandi a Francesco I . . .," *Memorie della Reale Accademia delle scienze di Torino*, 2d ser., LIV (1904), 359, 364–65, 383.

[213] For his painting of the entire plant of *Datura stramonium* see *Asia*, II, Bk. 1, pl. 36.

[214] See O. H. Giglioli, "Jacopo Ligozzi disegnatore e pittore di piante e di animali," *Dedalo*, IV (1923–24), 556.

[215] See *Asia*, I, 694.

[216] *Ibid.*, pp. 743–44.

[217] The full title page reads: *Herbario nuovo di Castore Durante, Medico, e Cittadino Romano. Con figure, che rappresentano le vive Piante, che nascono in tutta Europa, e nell' Indie Orientali, e Occidentali. Con versi Latini, che comprendono le facoltà de i semplici medicamenti . . . In Roma, Appresso Bartholomeo Bonfadino, e Tito Diani, MD LXXXV.* Earlier editions were printed at Venice in 1583 and 1584. Apparently there was also another Roman edition of 1585 by Iacomo Bericchia and Iacomo Turnieri (see Arber, *op. cit.* [n. 146], p. 280).

itself, the *Herbario nuovo* claims universality. The preface contains a long list of the authorities consulted, including Amato, Clusius, Acosta, Mattioli, Monardes, and Orta. Durante's book, like other herbals, is organized alphabetically and almost every plant is pictured; sometimes the entire plant is shown and sometimes only the product. Durante probably worked closely with the printers and engravers of Venice and Rome, for many of his illustrations are identical to those found in the works of Acosta and L'écluse.[218] Perhaps the printers even borrowed the original woodcut blocks. Some of the plates are imaginary or indistinguishable representations, as in the case of the cinnamon tree.[219] Durante's texts describing exotic plants and their uses are heavily dependent upon L'écluse. The Latin poems describing the qualities of the plants appear to be from Durante's own pen. Despite its somewhat chaotic organization, the *Herbario nuovo* continued to be reprinted and translated into the eighteenth century. Later biologists, including Linnaeus, commemorated Durante by giving his name to a plant in the family Agnuscastus.

The Italian contemporaries and successors of Durante continued to enlarge their botanical horizons through the importation and cultivation of exotic plants and through the collection of dried plants from all over the world. The more enterprising, like Aldrovandi, increasingly began to examine the plants from afar for their botanical as well as their therapeutic interest. Prospero Alpini (1553–1616) was the first Italian physician to study tropical plants in their native surroundings. He went to Egypt in 1580 as physician to the Venetian consul at Cairo. After three years he returned to Venice where he prepared two books based on his Egyptian experiences. In the *De medicina Aegyptiorum* (1591), which ranks as one of the earliest efforts to understand non-European medicine, he points out how the simples and woods of India and China are employed medicinally in Egypt.[220] His *De plantis Aegypti* (1592) describes fifty-seven plants, including the opium poppy, the coffee bush, and the banana tree. Alpini was thereafter engaged to teach botany at Padua and in 1603 became director of its famous botanical garden. Here he, like L'écluse at Leyden, began systematically to cultivate exotic plants, mainly for their botanical interest. His scientific preoccupation with exotic plants contrasts sharply with the kind of interest in plants as curiosa represented by Ferrante Imperato (1550?–1625?), the famous collector of Naples.[221]

In northern Europe the most active and influential student of exotic plants

[218] Cf. pl. 52.

[219] Mattioli, it should be recalled, would not try to illustrate the cinnamon tree because he had been unable to find an accurate depiction of it. See above, p. 175.

[220] As evidence for the importance of this relationship, it should be noted that the 1645 edition of Alpini's work was bound with Jakob de Bondt's *De medicina Indorum*. His discussion of the products of Asia may be found on pp. 117ᵛ–118ʳ.

[221] Imperato had a small garden of his own and he corresponded with many of the leading botanists of Europe. But that collection rather than science was his major concern is revealed by an examination of his *Historia naturale* (Naples, 1599). The best study of his career is A. Neviani, "Ferrante Imperato speziale e naturalista napoletana," *Atti e memorie dell'Academia di Storia dell'Arte Sanitaria* (Rome), 2d ser. II, No. 2 (1936), 57–74, 124–45, 191–210, 243–67.

was L'écluse. His Latin adaptations and translations of the books of Orta and Acosta were published separately by Plantin and were reissued in his collected works published in 1593 and 1601.[222] Translations of L'écluse's versions appeared in Italian, and the influence of the various editions of his works rapidly became apparent in the botanical writings of others. The great compendium called *Historia generalis plantarum* (2 vols.; Lyons, 1586–87) put together by Jacques d'Aléchamps and his associates included as a final class (No. XVIII) a section called "Of Foreign Plants." Both its woodcuts and its descriptions of Asian plants derive ultimately from Orta and Acosta, and immediately from the epitomes of L'écluse.[223]

In 1573, three years after Mattioli left Prague, L'écluse became prefect of the imperial botanical garden in Vienna. During his several years in Vienna he came to know the young Netherlandish physician Bernardus Paludanus, who was later to be associated with Linschoten in the preparation of the latter's travel account. As the wars of religion tore the Low Countries apart, L'écluse, a Protestant, traveled over northern Europe from Hungary to England to learn as much as he could from others about exotic flora while studying at first hand the plants of Europe's frontiers. In his book on the plants of Austria and Hungary published in 1583 he included descriptions of the various Eastern plants that had been brought to these places from Constantinople, especially the tulip.[224] L'écluse paid more than one visit to England before and after 1580 where he became acquainted with Sir Philip Sidney and Sir Francis Drake. From the great navigator he received specimens of "New World" flora, including items from the East Indies.[225] In England he also found, in 1581, the copies of Monardes and Acosta in Spanish which he epitomized and translated into Latin and published at Antwerp in the following year.

After 1582 L'écluse wandered from place to place in northwestern France, Austria, and western Germany seeking a tranquility which he finally found in Frankfurt around 1587. As things gradually settled down in the Netherlands again, his relations with the Calvinists of the northern provinces became closer. In 1593 he went to Leyden to take up a post at the university's botanical gardens, one that he retained for the rest of his life. In the comparative calm of the university he also had time to renew his friendship with Ortelius in Antwerp and to become an intimate of J. J. Scaliger.[226] He experimented in the university

222 On his publications of Orta and Acosta see *Asia*, I, 194–95; II, Bk. 1, 82–83.

223 "In the year 1587 came forth the great Historie of Plants printed at Lyons. . . . And at the end thereof there is an Appendix containing some Indian plants, for the most part out of Acosta." See "To the Reader" in Thomas Johnson's 1633 edition of Gerard's *Herball* (1597).

224 *Rariorum aliquot stirpium, per Pannoniam, Austriam, et vicinas quasdam Provincias observatarum historia* . . . (Antwerp, 1583), especially pp. 122–211.

225 See the engraving of sago bread as reproduced in *Asia*, II, Bk. 1, pl. 45. Drake's botanical cargoes have never been inspected thoroughly, but it is obvious from the writings of L'écluse that they stirred widespread interest. See J. Ewan, "Traffic in Seeds and Plants between North America, England, and the Continent during the 16th and 17th Centuries," *Actes du XIIᵉ Congrès international d'histoire des sciences*, VIII (1968), 47.

226 On Scaliger see above, pp. 358–59; on Ortelius see below, pp. 467–69.

gardens with the cultivation of exotic plants. In 1599 he built an enclosed winter house, a conservatory, in which he grew tropical plants. He kept abreast of the maritime activities of the Dutch as he inquired of Linschoten and others about the plants of the East. In 1601 he published the first of his complete works with revisions called *Rariorum plantarum historia* (Antwerp). In its preface he speaks in moving language about the great pleasure he got from studying the flora of all parts of the earth and of his wonder at their infinite variety.[227]

The Europeans of the sixteenth century were the first to cultivate the exotic plants for the purpose of studying them systematically. The common pre-Renaissance gardens were the private convent plots used for cultivating herbs for the table and for drugs. The development of the palace with its decorative gardens was accompanied in the fifteenth century by an interest in exotica. Private experimental gardens of the kind that so entranced Navagero and Bembo became more common in the sixteenth century. Most important for the advance of scientific gardening was the founding of royal, noble, municipal, and university gardens. In the generation of 1540 to 1570 botanical gardens were established in most of Europes' important political, commercial, and educational centers. A number of these—for example, Padua (1545), Zurich (1561), and Lyons (1564)—were supervised by eminent botanists who experimented self-consciously with exotic plants. At Padua and in several of the gardens of northern Europe conservatories were built to house the tropical plants.[228]

Good evidence exists to show that a number of Asian plants began to be generally cultivated in Europe during the sixteenth century. Rice, which Theophrastus had originally described, became a European economic crop of importance only in the late fifteenth and early sixteenth century.[229] In 1585 Durante noted that rice, a plant native to maritime Asia, was being cultivated "in many places of Italy where the earth is moist and marshy."[230] A more direct and dramatic introduction occurred in connection with the sweet orange of China. The bitter Seville orange, citron, lemon, and lime had reached Europe via the overland route long before 1500. A strong tradition exists to the effect that João de Castro returned to Portugal in 1548 with a living tree, *Citrus sinensis*, which was presumably still on view at Lisbon in 1697.[231] Ten years after its successful transplanting to Lisbon, the China sweet orange was being cultivated in the Vatican gardens where it was called the "Lisbon orange."[232]

---

[227] Details of his career and a complete list of his writings may be found in J. Theunisz, *Carolus Clusius: Het merkwaardige Leven van een Pioneer der Wetenschap* (Amsterdam, 1939).

[228] For a list of the plants first cultivated at Padua and Pisa in the sixteenth century, including therein the coco palm, bamboos, and *cinnamoenum camphora*, see E. Hayms, *A History of Gardens and Gardening* (New York, 1971), p. 128.

[229] See V. Hehn, *Kulturpflanzen und Hausthiere in ihrem Übergang aus Asien nach Griechenland und Italien sowie in das übrigen Europa* (rev. ed.; Hildesheim, 1963), pp. 504–7.

[230] *Op. cit.* (n. 217), p. 392.

[231] The authority of 1697 was the Jesuit Louis Le Comte in his *Nouveaux mémoires sur l état présent de la Chine* (Paris, 1701), p. 172.

[232] See Hehn, *op. cit.* (n. 229), p. 454.

Some doubt has been expressed about the veracity of this tradition. It had been pointed out that sweet oranges were being cultivated in southern Spain in 1525 and that some of the early travelers expressed no surprise at finding sweet oranges in Asia.[233] But this last assertion is not entirely true, for Varthema in 1510 celebrated the sweet oranges of Ceylon as the best in the world.[234] Whatever the truth may be about priority it is certain that cultivation of the sweet orange in Europe was associated at the time with its introduction by the Portuguese. Other sixteenth-century introductions of Asian plants cannot be dated with equal precision. Ginger was grown as far north as Paris and in 1530 the Spanish introduced it to Mexico. In America it grew so copiously that by the end of the century ten times more ginger was imported into Europe from Mexico than from the East.[235] Mattioli saw the pepper plant growing in gardens in Naples and Venice.[236] Valerius Cordus (1515–44), a learned botanist, reports that solanaceous plants were being grown in German gardens, including the capsicum and datura native to India.[237]

Europeans held the plants of the East in great esteem for their medicinal qualities. The Chinese rhubarb (see pl. 50) sold by pharmacists was ordinarily one of three or four species of *Rheum*. Its root had a substantial market as a cathartic. In France during 1542 it sold for ten times the price of cinnamon, a drug also common in the pharmacies.[238] The China root (*Smilax glabra*) enjoyed a great reputation after Charles V in 1535 was reportedly cured of the gout by this drug, and it vied with guaicum and mercury as a cure for syphilis.[239] A glance at Brasavola's *De medicamentis . . .* (Venice, 1552) reveals that Indian myrobalan, ginger, and camphor were highly regarded as purges.[240] Cordus in his preparations relies also on other spices from the East, including mace, sandalwood, pepper, cardamom, and cubeb.[241] Opium imported from India was prescribed frequently as a sedative or anesthetic. Henry VIII recommended ginger as a specific against the plague, and gingerbread men were popular at Elizabeth's court for their gustatory qualities.[242] Coconuts in various forms were also sold in pharmacies and were prescribed for a variety of ailments.[243]

[233] This view was first expressed by G. Gallesio, *Traité du citrus* (3 vols.; Pisa, 1917), II, 297–98.

[234] For a similar conclusion see E. S. Hayms, *Plants in the Service of Man* (Philadelphia, 1972), p. 148.

[235] See F. Guerra, "Drugs from the Indies . . .," *loc. cit.* (n. 147), p. 38.

[236] See above, p. 432.

[237] See E. L. Greene, *Landmarks of Botanical History* (Washington, D.C., 1909), p. 285. Paludanus and Linschoten also comment on the cultivation and use of the datura in Europe. See A. G. Camus, *Mémoire sur la collection des grands et petits voyages . . .* (Paris, 1802), pp. 196–97.

[238] F. A. Flückiger and D. Hanbury, *Pharmacographia: A History of the Principal Drugs of Vegetable Origin, Met with in Great Britain and British India* (London, 1874).

[239] See G. Capivaccio, *Opera omnia . . .* (Frankfurt, 1603), p. 816, and pl. 51.

[240] P. 146ʳ.

[241] Also see his *Dispensatorium, hoc est, pharmacorum conficiendorum ratio* (Venice, 1556), especially pp. 1–53.

[242] See F. Perry, *Flowers of the World* (London, 1972), p. 309. Shakespeare writes in *Love's Labour's Lost* (V, i): "And I had but one penny in the wourld, thou should'st have it to buy ginger-bread." Also see pl. 52.

[243] See A. Lonitzer, *Kreüterbuch . . .* (Frankfurt, 1598), p. lxxxi. This book is filled with colored woodcuts.

38. Cinnamon cultivation. Notice the inaccurate depiction of the trees and, by contrast, the faithful depiction of the twills—the latter undoubtedly observed by the artist in the markets of Europe. From A. Thevet, *La cosmographie universelle* . . . (Paris, 1575), p. 436^v. Courtesy of the Newberry Library.

39. Pepper gathering. Notice accurate depiction of the corns and leaves, probably observed by the artist in the marts of Europe. From A. Thevet, *La cosmographie universelle* . . . (Paris, 1575), p. 425^v. Courtesy of the Newberry Library.

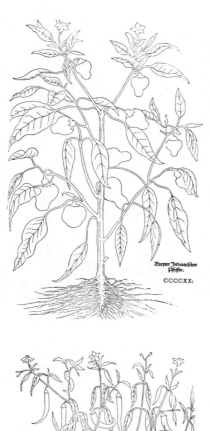

40. Broad Indian pepper. From L. Fuchs, *New Kreüterbuch* . . . (Basel, 1543), p. ccccxx.

41. Calicut pepper. From L. Fuchs, *New Kreüterbuch* . . . (Basel, 1543), p. ccccxviii.

42. Long Indian pepper. From L. Fuchs, *New Kreüterbuch* . . . (Basel, 1543), p. ccccxix.

43. Portrait of Andrea Navagero, the Venetian Humanist. Reproduced from M. Cermenati, "Un diplomatico naturalista del rinascimento, Andrea Navagero," *Archivio veneto*, 3d ser., Vol. XXIV.

44. Portrait of Amato Lusitano, Portuguese botanist and physician. Reproduced from R. Jorge, *Amato Lusitano* (Lisbon, 1962), frontis. Courtesy of the Newberry Library.

New Kreüterbuch

Mit den allerschönsten vnd artlich-
sten Figuren aller Gewechß/ dergleichen vormals in keiner sprach nie an tag kommen.

Von dem Hochgelerten vnd weit-
berümbten Herrn Doctor *Petro Andrea Matthiolo,* Rö: Kay:
May: Rath/ auch derselben/ vnd Fürstlicher Durchleuchtigkeit Ertz-
hertzog Ferdinanden ꝛc. Leibdoctor. Erstlich in Latein
gestellt. Folgendts durch Georgium Handsch/ der
Artzney Doctorem verdeutscht/ vnnd endtlich
zu gemeinem nutz vnd wolfart Deutscher Nation in druck
verfertigt.

Geieret mit bilen feinen newen experimenten/ künstlichen
Distillieröfen/dreyen wolgeordneten Registern/vnd andrer
nutzbarkeit/wie auß der Vorred zuersehen.

Getruckt zu Prag/ durch Georgen Melantrich von Aventin/ auff
sein vnd Vincenti Valgriß Buchdruckers zu Venedig vncosten.

M. D. LXIII.

Mit Röm: Kay: May: Freyheit vnd Priuilegien.

45. Title page of Pietro Mattioli's *New Kreüterbuch* . . . (Prague, 1563).

Indianiſcher oder Chalecutiſcher Pfeffer.   Siliquaſtrum ſiue Piper Indicum. A

¶ Dieſe Indianiſchen Pfeffers ſinde noch andere zwey geſchlecht/ nemlich/ das kleine/ vnd mehr. Das kleine iſt nidriger/ bringet auch kleiner ſchoten. Das ander tregt runde ſchoten.

Natur/Krafft/vnd Würckung.

¶ Der Indianiſche Pfeffer hitzet vnd trückenet im letzten grad. So man jhn auſſerwendig des leibs auff der haut legt/ beiſſt er ſie auff. Hat ſonſt eben die krafft/ wie der gemeine Pfeffer/ damit wir ſonſt würetzen/ dauon wir im volgenden Capitel handlen wöllen.

¶ Den Indianiſche Pfeffer heſſt im Latein Siliquaſtrum, Piper Indicum ſiue Chalecuticum. Teütſch/ Pſpt Indyaniſch oder Türcky.   o   Von gemei-

46. Indian or calicut pepper. From P. Mattioli, *New Kreüterbuch . . .* (Prague, 1563), p. 217ʳ.

Muſcatnuß.   Nux Myriſtica, ſiue Moſchata. A

Solch iſt gantz zu den wenigern der glieder/ vnd Gensabern/ ſo ſich von Blütt erregen. Auch hilfft es zu Vawtzhandel/ſo manє anſchmieret.

Muſcaten blüet.

Die Muſcaten blüet hat gleich dieſe krafft/ wie die Muſcat ſelbs/aber dieweil ſie an der ſubſtantz ſubteiler/iſt ſie auch krefftiger zu allen obgenandten gebreſten/ zerteylet eher die ſäfte/vnd winde.

¶ Für das Hertz zittern nütze Muſcaten blüet/es hilfft.

¶ Die Muſcaten nüßt heiſſen Griechiſch μοσχοκάρυον. Lateiniſch Nux Moſchata, Myriſtica. Italiſch Inſbaguer. Welſch Noce moſchada. Spaniſch Nuez de eſpecie. Frantzöſiſch Nois muſcaden. Behmiſch Ballty Moſſtácowé.   T iij   Von Haſel-

47. Nutmeg. From P. Mattioli, *New Kreüterbuch . . .* (Prague, 1563), p. 111ʳ.

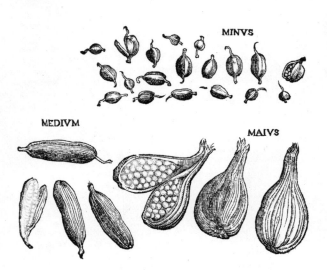

Cardamömle vnd Parißkörner.   Cardamomum.

Kramerneglen.   Caryophy

CARDAMOMI SPECIES

MINVS

MEDIVM

MAIVS

der gleichet mit seinem stamm vnd holtz dem Buchbaum/ mit den blettern dem Zimmet/
genommen das sie ein wenig runder vnd kürtzer sindt. Die frucht oder Neglen schwitzt
Sommer/ so sie zeitig worden. Die besten Neglen findt oben an den knöpfflen breyt/ so
schen den fingern zerdruckt/ geben sie ein kleine ölige feuchtigkeit.

¶ Die gegenwartige contrafactur ist genommen worden von einem zweigle so
zweigle der wolerfarne Franciscus Calzolarius Apotecker zu Veron mir gesendet hat.
auch die Mußcatlen/ das findt die grobra/ vngeratenen Neglen/ die man im Latein
nennet. Item die stile/ daran die Neglen hangen/ Fusti genandt. Die bletter aber/ welch
zweige abgemalet ligen/ hab ich von den Portugalesern bekommen.

Natur/ Krafft/ vnd Würckung.

48. Cardamon. From P. Mattioli, *New
Kreüterbuch* . . . (Prague, 1563), p. 220ʳ.

49. Cloves. From P. Mattioli, *New
Kreüterbuch* . . . (Prague, 1563), p. 222ᵛ.

Rhabarbarum.

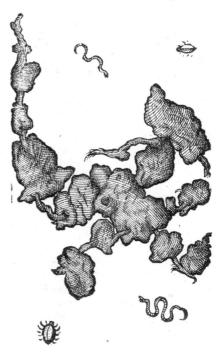

50. Rhubarb. From P. Mattioli, *New Kreüterbuch* . . . (Prague, 1563), p. 253ʳ.

51. China root, compared in size to beetles and worms. From French version of Garcia da Orta called *Histoire des drogues* . . . (Lyons, 1619). Courtesy of the Newberry Library.

52. Woodcut of ginger plant and root. From the *Tractado* (1578) of C. de Acosta.

TRACTADO

Delas Drogas, y medicinas de las Indias
Orientales, con sus Plantas debuxadas al
biuo por Christoual Acosta medico y cirujano que las vio
ocularmente.

En el qual se verifica mucho de lo que escriuio el Doctor Garcia de Orta.

Dirigido a la muy noble y muy mas leal ciudad de
Burgos cabeça de Castilla y camara de
su Magestad.

EN BVRGOS.
Por Martin de Victoria impressor de su Magestad.
M. D. LXXVIII.
Con Priuilegio.

Esta tasado en ciento ynouenta y dos marauedis.

53. Portrait of Cristobal de Acosta, physician and botanist. From C. de Acosta, *Tractado* . . . (Lisbon, 1964), frontis.

54. Title page of Cristobal de Acosta's treatise on the drugs and medicinals of the East Indies (Burgos, 1578).

Such a profound interest in the curative properties of plants gradually led to study of the plants themselves and to their relationships to one another.

Representatives from Asia of at least twelve different botanical families were known in sixteenth-century Europe.[244] While considerable difference of opinion existed as to their exact place of origin within Asia, most of the authorities agreed generally on whether a particular botanical specimen came from the region of China, India, or Malaysia. The influx of plants from Asia and the Americas led the more imaginative of the botanists to begin studying natural affinities as a new basis for classification. Fuchs recognized that the narcotic odor exhaled by the herbage of the datura was characteristic of the nightshade and its solanaceous relations. The capsicum, like the datura, was new to botany, but Fuchs failed to locate it along with datura because it lacked the characteristic narcotic odor. Bock likewise failed to place the capsicum correctly, but he did observe that its leaves and flowers resemble the solanaceous plants in form.[245] From such simple beginnings the science of plant taxonomy took root.

While the German and Netherlandish botanists stressed similarities in their plant analyses, Cesalpino and the Italians centered their attention on differences—for example, between cinnamon and canella. Systematic groupings, in which both similarities and differences were noticed, began to appear in the works of Matthias de l'Obel (1538–1616), often called Lobelius, and Gaspard Bauhin (1566–1624).[246] The latter collected an herbarium of 4,000 dried plants, including exotic species, which is preserved at the University of Basel.[247] Brunfels had described 240 plants in 1562; the Lyons *Historia* of 1587 reached 3,000; Bauhin's *Pinax* (1633) contained 6,000. In Book XI, Section III of the *Pinax*, Bauhin assembled a group he called *Aromata*, or those plants which are connected one to the other only by their economic usefulness to man. In his descriptions of Asian plants Bauhin borrowed freely from Orta, Acosta, and Clusius and added remarks of his own. Linnaeus in the *Species plantarum* (1753) cites Bauhin as an authority for his descriptions of the common mango, betel palm, mangosteen, calamus or sweet flag, and the tamarind.[248] By 1952, 600,000 varieties of plants (a hundred times as many as Bauhin wrote about) had been described, a process begun in the sixteenth century as botanists began increasingly to study, relate, and classify plants according to their natural affinities.[249] Comparisons and efforts to establish the geographical origins and distribution of plants also inspired the botanists to begin looking for an *ordo*

---

[244] See R. M. Newcomb, "Botanical Source-Areas for Some Oriental Spices," *Economic Botany*, XVII (1963), 127–32.

[245] Greene, *op. cit.* (n. 237), pp. 208–10, 252.

[246] See Sachs, *op. cit.* (n. 160), pp. 6–7.

[247] See Arber, *op. cit.* (n. 147), p. 114.

[248] See S. Bobroff, "Exotic Plants in Linnaeus' *Species Plantarum* (1753)" (Ph.D. diss., Department of History, University of Chicago, 1973), p. 41.

[249] See A. Cailleux, "Progression du nombre d'espèces de plantes décrites de 1500 à nos jours," *Revue d'histoire des sciences*, VI (1953), 42–44.

universalis in "which things which are far and widely different become, as it were, one thing." [250]

Asia, unlike America, had ancient connections, both direct and indirect, with Europe. For many centuries before 1500, technological devices and ideas, mathematical and astronomical conceptions, and nautical and navigational techniques had traveled in both directions, but mainly from East to West. Over the course of the sixteenth century this flow was gradually reversed. The superiority of Europe in mechanization, in military and naval power, and in navigation was eventually established and generally recognized. In Europe confidence grew with the passage of time that Europeans were braver, more efficient, and better organized than the observed peoples of Asia. As Europeans often freely sailed the seas of the East and battered and captured strategic ports, the conclusion became inescapable that Europeans had little to learn from Asia of practical importance to commerce and empire. While they admired, imported, and imitated the subtle handicrafts of China and India, the Europeans saw nothing practical to borrow from Asia but minor technical devices—sailing chariots and caulking techniques!

Since most of Asia's fundamental tools and mathematical conceptions were familiar to Europe before 1500, the Europeans of the sixteenth century concentrated upon products rather than devices or ideas. While they already knew many of the animals, plants, and minerals of commerce, the Europeans of the discovery era, motivated as they were by a strong desire for economic gain, generally brought back with them those Eastern items for which they were assured a market. Metallic zinc, "the white copper of China," and fine Indian tin were added to their cargoes as a demand grew in Europe for these foreign metals. New plants were also brought to Europe to stock the pharmacies and markets with medicinals and foods for which a demand was constantly growing. It was the rare traveler to the East—a Garcia da Orta or a Francesco Sassetti— who bothered to inquire about unusual scientific phenomena or to carry out experiments.

The scientists of Europe, as they often complained, received but few new insights from travel accounts or other sources about the similarities and differences between the vegetable, animal, and mineral kingdoms of Europe and Asia. The initiative in scientific study was generally taken by the scientist at home, such as Pedro de Medina, rather than by the residents in Asia—Orta, Acosta, and Sassetti being the exceptions who prove the rule. Paracelsus, who had traveled widely in Europe, was only slightly aware of how dependent he was upon the minerals of Asia for his alchemical experiments with the elixir of life. The botanists, on the other hand, with their great need to know about the environments of the new plants and vegetable products of Asia were deeply interested in learning everything possible about habitats. As a consequence it

---

[250] From the preface to De l'Obel's *Stirpium adversaria nova* (1570–71) as quoted in Arber, *op. cit.* (n. 147), p. 177.

was the botanists, aided by the cosmographers and navigators, who persisted in their efforts to obtain specific details on the world of nature in Asia.

The botanists and chemists had the distinct advantage, not enjoyed by many other scientists, of dealing with easily portable objects that could be brought to them in quantity and variety. Minerals, plants, and vegetable products were also marketable, or potentially so; consequently, they were eagerly sought for in the field and quickly brought to public sale and to the attention of curious scientists. Exotic minerals, as well as seeds, plants, and fruits, were examined to determine whether they were really *new* and unknown to the authorities of Antiquity. Scholarly debates soon arose centering on questions connected with the identification, description, and classification of the new products of the East. In the process skepticism about the adequacy of the older authorities increased, as scientists were forced to modify, amplify, or discard ancient descriptions and classifications.

The science of botany reacted much more positively than any of the other sciences to the "New World" of plants and their products. The authority of Dioscorides was gradually eroded as new species were described on which he had incorrect information or none at all. His predominance was completely undermined by the new herbals of tropical plants prepared by Orta and Acosta which were popularized in Europe at large by L'écluse in his Latin epitomes. Experiments with exotic plants in European gardens also enabled the botanists to describe the living plants, as well as the dried specimens, and to examine them in a natural habitat. Description of the plants, without so much as a glance at Dioscorides, was followed by study of their medicinal qualities and their economic uses. With the increase in both the number and availability of the exotic plants and their scientific descriptions, botanists began to study taxonomic affinities and to classify the plants. While the desire was strong to discover a universal system of classification, the time was not yet ripe. Many known plants were still without scientific descriptions when Bauhin compiled his *Pinax* (1623). Botany had to wait until the *Species plantarum* (1753) of Linnaeus to receive its first ordering on a universal scale.

CHAPTER X

Cartography and Geography

The Greek and Hellenistic geographers, beginning with Eratosthenes (276–196 B.C.) and concluding with Ptolemy (*fl.* A.D. 127–151), laid the foundations in the West for the scientific study of the earth. In their works cartographic representation was accorded a prominent place. The *Geography* of Strabo (*ca.* 63 B.C.–post A.D. 21) included directions for drawing a map scientifically on either a globe or a plane surface. Ptolemy ordained that the most important points in the known world should be placed on the map according to their latitudes and longitudes. In the Middle Ages the classical science of geography was transformed into a religiously oriented cosmography which sought to reconcile biblical history and myth with more recent empirical and conventional observations.

Most of the studies which fall today in the province of geography were before 1500 included in the definition of cosmography, a branch of learning that described and mapped both the heavens and the earth. The Greek word "geography," as well as the scientific study of the earth, was revived and incorporated into the corpus of modern learning by 1600. By the sixteenth century geography's object had gradually come to be the depiction of the terrestrial sphere alone. Over the following two centuries the ancient association between cartography and geography was retained, for "to know the map" remained the fundamental work of the geographer. The word "cartographer," as an identification separate from geographer, first appeared in the European vocabulary only in the nineteenth century.[1]

[1] The general history of geography as a scientific discipline and as a branch of learning has still to be written. In his standard analysis of *The Nature of Geography* (Lancaster, Pa., 1946), Richard Hartshorne ignores the developments of the sixteenth century; for a tentative effort to treat early developments see H. Beck, "Entdeckungsgeschichte und geographische Diziplinhistorie," *Erdkunde*, IX (1955), 197. For a discussion of the vocabulary of geography see F. de Dainville, *Le langage des géographes: Termes, signes, couleurs des cartes anciennes, 1500–1800* (Paris, 1964), especially pp. vii–x, 1–2.

The history of Renaissance geography divides into two interrelated parts: the topographical descriptions of Europe and the depiction of the overseas world as it was gradually revealed. The regional geographers and Humanists of Europe concentrated upon producing complete and accurate maps as well as literary descriptions of local landforms, products, and peoples. Their materials were painstakingly gathered through surveys in the field and from neighborhood informants. As a result of these researches they soon learned to distrust the Ptolemaic placements of European cities and regions. In their establishment of more accurate latitudes and longitudes the chorographers, or regional geographers, used the most advanced technical equipment and the most sophisticated mathematical procedures then available. The cosmographers, like Sebastian Münster, compiled the earlier chorographic studies and produced more generalized maps and descriptions from them. The empirical, scientific materials of the local geographers were then integrated into the cosmographical works along with the more fanciful descriptions of overseas places and peoples derived from the writers of Antiquity and the trained and untrained recorders of contemporary events. It was only in the latter half of the century that the humanistic and empirical methods of local and regional geography began to be applied to the earth's entire surface.

The reconnaissance of the world beyond Europe was certainly the most dramatic geographical event of the Renaissance. The learned in society had been prepared by earlier disclosures to appraise the reports of distant discoveries with a critical mind and a skeptical eye. The descriptions of Asia by the Franciscan missionaries, Marco Polo, and Mandeville had stimulated both wonder and disbelief at all levels of quattrocentro society. To the learned the accounts of the medieval travelers, especially that of Marco Polo, began to assume greater credibility with the rediscovery of the geographies and maps of Antiquity and with the appearance in manuscript and printed editions of Poggio Bracciolini's fifteenth-century version of the travels to India of Nicolò de' Conti.[2] Those who were nautically minded were also able to learn from the reports of the Portuguese and Spanish voyages of the fifteenth century that maritime excursions over the ocean-sea were revealing at a rapid pace the existence of new places and peoples unknown to the ancient world. The realization dawned, especially in Spain and Portugal, that "discovery" requires putting the new places on a map with the idea of reaching them again. But recording the discoveries on the official maps at Lisbon and Seville was a huge task. For in the century from 1475 to 1575 Europe's perception of the world, particularly in land and water relationships, underwent its greatest change in history.

World maps of the pre-printing era, whether wall decorations or pictures of the known world on canvas, vellum, or parchment, had quickly included materials gathered by the late medieval travelers in their overland trips to Asia.[3]

---

[2] For details see *Asia*, I, 59–71.

[3] See R. A. Skelton, *Explorers' Maps: The Cartographic Record of Geographical Discovery* (London, 1958), p. 3.

Usually these lavish productions, such as the Catalan map (1375), existed only in unique examples. The world charts of the fourteenth and fifteenth centuries, though few in number, introduced a new realism to graphic depiction as a result of the efforts designers made to locate correctly the known mountains and other obvious dramatic physical features.[4] In his world map of 1459 Fra Mauro even records, possibly from Arab sources, the presence of Chinese naval junks off Aden in East Africa, and, on the authority of Marco Polo he shows a single "Ixola de cimpagu" (Japan) off the coast of Asia.[5] Still these beautiful and informative charts were fundamentally only improved versions of the medieval world pictures. It was not until the Ptolemaic maps were issued in printed form from 1477 onward that the scientific map became available to a broad public. Ptolemy's concept of plotting positions on a grid of parallels and meridians taught the learned community how essential accuracy and precision are in determining geographical location, extent, and direction.

I

THE ECLIPSE OF PTOLEMY

Ptolemy's geographical treatise introduced mathematical cartography to Renaissance Europe. It was translated from Greek into Latin about 1406, and this original version, with emendations and corrections, remained the reigning text for the next century. One of the remarkable aspects of Ptolemy's work was his elucidation of several methods of map projection first discovered by Marinus of Tyre. The first method, with straight meridians and curved parallels, was favored by Ptolemy for its ease of construction. Most maps prepared after 1450 adopted this Ptolemaic projection but often with modifications of the author's own devising. The first printed edition of Ptolemy to include the twenty-seven original maps, or the Ptolemaic atlas, was issued at Bologna in 1477. A modified projection, or an equal area projection with curved parallels and curved meridians, was created for the maps included in the edition of Ptolemy's geography by Francesco Berlinghieri published at Florence around 1480. This metrical version in Italian was also the first edition to include "modern maps" along with those which conventionally belonged to the Ptolemaic portfolio.[6]

The popularity of Ptolemy's geography peaked in the period from 1475 to

---

[4] See M. Eckert, *Die Kartenwissenschaft: Forschungen und Grundlagen zu einer Kartographie als Wissenschaft* (2 vols.; Berlin, 1924–25), I, 419–20.

[5] Skelton, *op. cit.* (n. 3), p. 23; also, George Kish, "Two Fifteenth-Century Maps of 'Zipangu': Notes on the Early Cartography of Japan," *Yale University Library Gazette*, XL (1966), 206. Cf. pl. 58.

[6] See G. R. Crone, *Maps and Their Makers: An Introduction to the History of Cartography* (4th rev. ed.; London, 1968), pp. 68–76.

1513. His major competition from Antiquity was Strabo, whose *Geography* first appeared in Latin translation in 1472. Ptolemy' geographical authority nonetheless remained supreme. Between 1475 and 1490 seven printed editions of his geographical treatise, most with maps, appeared in Europe. No new edition was issued between 1490 and 1507, probably because of a flood of new geographical materials on regions and continents not known to Ptolemy. In the thirty-four printings of Ptolemy in Latin, Portuguese, and Italian which appeared from 1507 to 1599 the editors concentrated on modifying the original Ptolemaic maps and on adding "modern" maps to the conventional series.[7] Its text was retranslated, or partially retranslated, by a number of leading sixteenth-century scholars: Pirckheimer (1525), Erasmus (1533), and Servetus (1535).[8] The great Mercator himself published his own modified version of the text and maps in 1578.

The recovery, translation, copying, and publication of Ptolemy stimulated the development of both printing and the profession of mapmaking. Cartography developed in Italy during the fifteenth century in conjunction with the printing trade. A similar evolution occurred in the other European printing centers over the course of the sixteenth century. The importance of printing to cartography is not confined to reduction in cost and to ease of distribution in quantity.[9] In fact, the incunabula printed before 1500 were expensive to produce and only circulated like the manuscript books in very limited editions. What is more significant for scientific purposes is the ability of the printer to produce virtually *identical* copies.[10] Earlier generations were able to reproduce verbal materials exactly, but not visual materials. With the coming of the age of printing, as well as woodcut and copper engraving, it became possible to convey unvaryingly the visual materials which lay beyond description or definition by words. Printed maps, as exactly repeatable pictorial statements, were, like other engravings printed both in books and separately, the fundamental means for relaying to a broad public a new sense of world geographical relationships and configurations. European printed maps, the first of which appeared only several centuries after the Chinese had printed the earliest of their world pictures, were usually drawn following the astronomical system of locating devised by the

[7] For a table listing the extant versions of Ptolemy's *Geography* from 1475 to 1599 see C. Sanz, *La geographia de Ptolomeo* . . . (Madrid, 1959), pp. 272–78; for an explanation of the hiatus in publication between 1490 and 1507 see A. Cortesão, *History of Portuguese Cartography* (2 vols. of 3 projected; Coimbra, 1969–71), I, 112–13.

[8] For an English translation of the prefatory remarks to the Servetus edition, see C. D. O'Malley (trans. and ed.), *Michael Servetus: A Translation of His Geographical, Medical, and Astrological Writings* . . . (Philadelphia, 1953), pp. 15–37. It is his comparison here of the French and Spanish national characters that Münster depended upon when making his derogatory statements about Spain. See above, p. 24.

[9] See R. A. Skelton, *Maps: A Historical Survey of Their Study and Collecting* (Chicago, 1972), p. 10.

[10] For further discussion of this point see N. J. W. Thrower, *Maps and Man* (Englewood Cliffs, N.J., 1972), pp. 43–44; W. M. Ivins, Jr., *Prints and Visual Communication* (Cambridge, Mass., 1953), pp. 23–24; and R. A. Skelton, *Decorative Printed Maps of the 15th to 18th Centuries* (London, 1952; reprinted 1965), pp. 1–5.

Greeks.[11] The European public therefore possessed from the inception of printing a cartographic tradition that was secular, scientific, and cosmopolitan in its orientation and prepared to alter its geographical ideas and maps to accommodate the latest information.[12] For scholars the production of reliable maps by a variety of authors opened the door to the study of comparative cartography and classification.[13]

The Italians and Portuguese of the fifteenth century learned about geography from each other. The Portuguese had inherited from the Genoese and Venetian navigators the technique of preparing portolans of the coasts they visited. These were passed down from one seagoing generation to the next but were not generally distributed abroad. All that survive directly recording Portuguese explorations of the fifteenth century are the Venetian charts that included information gathered at Lisbon by the sailors making the run to Flanders.[14] The high reputation of the Italians as geographical experts led King Alfonso of Portugal in 1474 to consult Paolo da Pozzo Toscanelli (1397–1482), the celebrated Florentine cosmographer, about the shortest way to India.[15] Evidence that information on the Portuguese voyages was being regularly received in Florence can readily be found in the maps of Henricus Martellus (*fl.* 1480–96) published in 1490. He amended Ptolemy's map of Asia and in the process produced the traditional base map to which the later discoveries in Asia would be added. Martellus' world map takes into account Marco Polo's description of the East, Toscanelli's mistaken view that the shortest route to India is across the Atlantic Ocean, and the entry of the Portuguese into the Indian Ocean in 1488.[16]

The enlargement of the Mediterranean portolan charts into the Atlantic map was made possible by the development of new navigational techniques. In oceanic navigation dead reckoning was gradually replaced by astronomical navigation. Longitude had still to be estimated from the distance run and the compass course followed. But it now became possible on board ship to determine an approximate latitude by instrumental observation of a heavenly body, and to determine the ship's position closely enough for practical purposes. In the final quarter of the fifteenth century the scale of latitudes was introduced by the

---

[11] The first printed map known is a map of west China included in an encyclopedia published around A.D. 1155; the earliest printed European map first appeared in 1472. See J. Needham, *Science and Civilization in China* (Cambridge, 1965–75), III, 549, and figs. 227–28. The traditional Chinese maps were far more ethnocentric than the European, for they make little reference to the rest of the world or even to their Asian neighbors. For the appearance of the Western world on traditional Chinese maps see Kuei-sheng Chang, "Africa and the Indian Ocean in Chinese Maps of the Fourteenth and Fifteenth Centuries," *Imago mundi*, XXIV (1970), 21–30. Modern maps of East Asia follow European cartographic practices. See H. Nakamura, *East Asia in Old Maps* (Honolulu, *ca.*, 1964), p. 1.

[12] This is true of the "modern" maps; a number of pre-Ptolemaic maps were naturally reproduced in the printed editions of ancient and medieval classics. See Skelton, *Decorative Printed Maps* (n. 10), p. 2.

[13] See Skelton, *Maps: A Historical Survey* (n. 9), pp. 12–13.

[14] *Ibid.*, pp. 40–41.

[15] For further discussion consult L. Bagrow and R. A. Skelton, *History of Cartography* (Cambridge, Mass., 1964), p. 72.

[16] See Skelton, *Maps: A Historical Survey* (n. 9), pp. 10–12.

Portuguese to sea charts and this then became a factor in the preparation of maps, which could now be graduated into latitudes with greater precision than ever before.[17] The Portuguese representations of coasts and placements of coastal cities were adopted universally by the makers of portolans and maps during the sixteenth century.

The "Storm and Stress" period in Europe's changing conception of the world occurred in the first generation of the sixteenth century. John Cabot (d. 1498) and Columbus (d. 1506) both died firm in the conviction that they had arrived off eastern Asia by sailing westward.[18] The return of Vasco da Gama in 1499 was followed by the gradual adoption in Portugal of a policy of strict control over the dissemination of information about everything relating to the route to India.[19] So effective was the control over information concerning the discoveries of the 1490's that but one original chart (1492) showing them has been preserved. Even for the first decade of the sixteenth century the known survivals are very few.[20] This scarcity of original charts enhances the importance of the extant planispheres and other materials dating from the opening of the sixteenth century.[21]

The Cantino planisphere of 1502 was the first of the world maps to modify significantly the Ptolemaic depiction of Asia. Probably the work of a Portuguese cartographer, it appears to be adapted from the *padrão*, or official map, housed in the hydrographic office of Lisbon. While Ptolemaic influence remains on the Cantino map, the representation of the southern coasts of Asia seems to be based on materials from Arabic navigational charts. The pointed peninsula of India is clearly represented, though in an abbreviated depiction. The Malay peninsula extends much too far to the south, Sumatra and Madagascar are misplaced, and everything to the east of Malacca is still in the realm of fantasy.[22] But what is most surprising is the great reduction in the longitudinal extent of Asia, its eastern extremities lying approximately, as they really do, about 160° east of the line of demarcation. Like many of the medieval maps (and it was possibly modeled in part on the Catalan atlas), the Cantino planisphere includes a number of informative legends relating what was known about the places, products, and peoples of the East and the exploits of the Portuguese there. This planisphere,

[17] See A. Cortesão and A. Teixeira da Mota, *Portugaliae monumenta cartographica* (6 vols.; Lisbon, 1960–62), I, xvii–xviii; and A. Teixeira da Mota, "A evolucão da ciência nautica durante os séculos XV–XVI na cartografia portuguesa da época," *Memórias de Academia das ciências de Lisboa, Classe de letras*, VII (1962), 247–66; A. Teixeira da Mota, "Influence de la cartographie portugaise sur la cartographie européenne à l'époque des découvertes," in M. Mollat and P. Adam (eds.), *Les aspects internationaux de la découverte océanique aux XVe et XVIe siècles* (Paris, 1966), pp. 224–28.

[18] Cf. S. E. Morison, *The European Discovery of America: The Southern Voyages, A.D. 1492–1616* (New York, 1974), p. 297. Also see W. E. Washburn, "The Meaning of Discovery," *American Historical Review*, LXIX (1962), 10. The globe depicting Cabot's voyage of 1497 indicates that he thought he had reached Asia. See H. Wallis, "The Use of Terrestrial and Celestial Globes in England," *Actes du XIe Congrès international d'histoire des sciences*, IV (1965), 204.

[19] For a more general discussion consult *Asia*, I, 151–54.

[20] Crone, *op. cit.* (n. 6), p. 81.

[21] A planisphere is a map formed by the projection of a sphere, or part of one, on a plane surface.

[22] For more detail consult *Asia*, I, 219.

unlike the Pedro Reinel maps of the period, does not include the scale of latitudes, but it does show the equator and the tropics.[23] A number of similar maps were apparently produced in Portugal around 1502 and, like the Cantino map, were either smuggled out of the country or sold abroad. Most of these world maps ended up in Italy and Germany where they were adopted as prototypes by the cartographers of those countries.[24]

Although the authority of Ptolemy was particularly profound in Italy, it was most seriously challenged by the new planispheres prepared there in the early sixteenth century. The so-called King-Hamy planisphere (1504?), the world chart (*ca.* 1505) of Nicolay de Canerio, and the *mappamondo* (1506) of G. M. Contarini, as well as a few woodcuts in travel books, were among the first Italian maps to follow Portuguese prototypes.[25] Italian cartographers of the fifteenth century—especially in the anonymous world map of 1457 preserved in Florence and in the world chart of Fra Mauro—had not been at all slow to include new names and information in their essentially Ptolemaic maps; in the sixteenth-century planispheres the Ptolemaic outline of Asia, as well as its place names and coast lines, likewise began to be adjusted in deference to new knowledge.

The Italian maps are, in general, less accurate and far more Ptolemaic than the Cantino planisphere. For example, in the Contarini map, a unique copy of which is preserved in the British Museum, the cartographer endeavors to show the India of Vasco da Gama by inserting a narrow peninsula between the Persian Gulf and the Indus River of Ptolemy. The publication at Rome in 1507 and 1508 of the revised edition of Ptolemy's *Geography* added six "modern" maps to the traditional collection in which basic changes of the Ptolemaic world outline are portended (see pls. 61–63 and compare pls. 64–66). Some of its editions included also a world map attributed to Johannes Ruysch which is similar to Contarini's map.[26] The Venetian edition (1511) of Ptolemy states frankly that the cartographer realizes the Ptolemaic maps must be modified and corrected in the light of new geographical knowledge then being acquired. While the world map prepared for this edition by Bernardus Sylvanus represents a break with the Ptolemaic tradition, the eastern part of Asia remains Ptolemaic and China is still called "Sina."[27]

Knowledge of Ptolemy's works spread from Italy to Germany in the latter half of the fifteenth century. At Nuremberg the brilliant astronomer and mathe-

---

[23] It was probably based on a prototype graduated into latitudes. See Teixeira da Mota, *loc. cit.* in Mollat and Adam (eds.), *op. cit.* (n. 17), pp. 239–40.

[24] See Cortesão, *op. cit.* (n. 7), I, 113.

[25] *Ibid.*, p. 122.

[26] See Crone, *op. cit.* (n. 6), pp. 96–98. Contemporaneously Benedetto Bordone (*fl.* 1490–1515) of Padua published in 1508 a world map in both Ptolemaic and non-Ptolemaic projections. See R. Almagià, "Padova e l'Ateneo padovano nella storia della scienza geografica," *Revista geografica italiana*, XIX (1912), 471–72.

[27] See Cortesão, *op. cit.* (n. 7), I, 120–23; G. Kish, "The Cosmographic Heart: Cordiform Maps of, the Sixteenth Century," *Imago mundi*, XIX (1965), 17; and Skelton, *Maps: A Historical Survey* (n. 9), p. 66.

matician, Regiomontanus (1436–76), first undertook the explanation, simplification, and criticism of Ptolemy's *Almagest*. From study of Ptolemy's astronomy Regiomontanus and his associates were led to an investigation of the Alexandrian's *Geography*. In the process they applied algebra and trigonometry to the study of topography and shortly began to point out the mistakes and shortcomings in Ptolemy's map of Germany and to suspect his accuracy on places even less well known to him. After the death of Regiomontanus his followers began to prepare new maps of Germany and to develop new instruments for making astronomical and topographical observations and calculations. Bernhard Walther, pupil and patron of Regiomontanus, published the *Ephemerides* of 1474–1506 at the printing press he established for the publication of scientific studies. It was to this early group of scholars that the German school of geography owes its mathematical bent.[28]

The predilection of the Nurembergers for innovation, particularly the invention and construction of mechanical instruments, aided the economy and enhanced the scientific reputation of the city. Their willingness to sponsor new projects is well illustrated by the story of Martin Behaim's globe (1492). The traveler Behaim took to Portugal some of the findings of German science and was entrusted by King John II with a post in his navigational service; in 1490 he returned to Nuremberg to attend to family business. While there he was asked by the city fathers to supervise the construction of a globe. The magistrates also provided a subvention for its execution by Jörg Holzschuler; the painter Georg Glockendon was engaged to decorate the gores and to inscribe the legends.[29] Behaim's famous globe still provides a picture of the world as it was envisaged on the eve of Columbus' first voyage. In constructing a globe Behaim and his associates had to make a determination about the width of the ocean between Europe and Asia, a distance that Toscanelli had grossly underestimated. The Nurembergers also retained a traditional view of the great extent of the Eurasiatic continent. The outlines on the globe of the land masses, probably derived from a printed map, are generally Ptolemaic except for the African coast. Behaim's outlines were followed by a host of later cartographers who sought to force the discoveries into his slightly modified Ptolemaic view of the world.[30] Others were even more conservative. The woodcut of the world map that appears in Georg Reisch's encyclopedic *Margarita philosophica* (Freiburg, 1503) retained a projection that is purely Ptolemaic.[31]

The geographical Renaissance in Germany began in Alsace, the trade corridor through which easy connections ran to Italy and France. Its capital, Strassburg,

[28] See L. Gallois, *Les géographes allemands de la Renaissance* (Paris, 1890), pp. xvii–xix; Bagrow-Skelton, *op. cit.* (n. 15), p. 125; and G. Strauss, *Nuremberg in the Sixteenth Century* (Bloomington, Ind., 1967), chap. vi. Also see above, pp. 408–9.

[29] Behaim probably saw the globe as a means of persuading the patrician merchants of Nuremberg to participate in overseas activities. See Graf Freiherr von Pölnitz, "Martin Behaim," in K. Rüdinger (ed.), *Gemeinsames Erbe: Perspektiven europäischer Geschichte* (Munich, 1959), p. 135.

[30] See Crone, *op. cit.* (n. 6), pp. 64–67.

[31] For a reproduction see Bagrow-Skelton, *op. cit.* (n. 15), p. 100.

was at the crossroads of the printing and wood-engraving trades which flourished in the surrounding cities of Nuremberg, Augsburg, Freiburg, and Basel. The idea of preparing and publishing a new translation of Ptolemy with "modern maps" was advanced as early as 1505 by Johann and Gauthier Lud of Lorraine. Natives of St. Dié, the Lud brothers were printers who were sponsored in their geographical interests by Duke René II of Lorraine. The Alsatian poet and geographer Matthias Ringmann (1482–1511) was soon recruited to aid with the St. Dié project. He had obtained one of the first editions of Vespucci's letter of 1503 reporting on his third voyage (1501–2) and had published it at Strassburg in 1505. From this and other materials he had read, Ringmann himself had arrived independently at the conclusion that Ptolemy was badly in need of revision.[32] When he arrived at St. Dié in 1507, he met Martin Waldseemüller (1470–1518), the famous German cartographer.

The first production of St. Dié was the *Cosmographiae introductio* of 1507.[33] It is divided into two distinct parts: a general discussion of cosmography, and a reproduction of the letters of Amerigo Vespucci to which are appended a plane projection wall map of the world and the gores for a globe.[34] A massive woodcut in twelve sheets, the world map in a single cordiform projection was based on Ptolemy with modifications derived from Vespucci's texts and the Canerio world chart. Asia, as in most Ptolemaic maps, is vastly overextended eastward. The popularity of this map with the next two generations of cartographers may be attributed to its inclusion of America rather than to any of its other innovations.[35]

While the *Cosmographiae* was mainly the work of Waldseemüller, the *Geography* of Ptolemy published at Strassburg in 1513 was a fully collaborative effort of the group at St. Dié. The text was retranslated by Ringmann from Greek into Latin. Included, as in previous editions, are the twenty-seven maps of Ptolemy and a supplement of "modern maps." The Ptolemaic maps themselves are but slightly altered, though the longitudinal extension of Asia is reduced markedly. Of the twenty new maps, five show the Portuguese and Spanish discoveries of the previous century. The work of Waldseemüller, the new maps of the overseas world are based on Portuguese prototypes or adaptations of them. It was probably the separate map of southern Asia from this collection, or one modeled on it, that Sir Thomas More consulted while preparing his *Utopia*.[36] All the "modern maps" were reprinted in the later editions

---

[32] Cf. above, pp. 334–35; and see Gallois, *op. cit.* (n. 28), pp. 40–42.

[33] For an English version see C. G. Herbermann (ed.), *The Cosmographiae introductio of Martin Waldseemüller in Facsimile* (New York, 1907).

[34] For a discussion of the text see above, p. 335.

[35] See Crone, *op. cit.* (n. 6), pp. 99–100. Carlos Sanz, the eminent Spanish historian of cartography, questions the attribution of this map to Waldseemüller in "The Discovery of America: The Three Maps Which Determined It, Promoted Knowledge of Its Form, and Fixed Its Name," *Terrae incognitae*, VI (1974), 82. The idea has also been advanced that Johann Grüninger of Strassburg, the publisher of the 1509 edition, actually printed the woodcuts for the St. Dié edition. See H. B. Johnson, *Carta Marina: World Geography in Strassburg, 1525* (Minneapolis, 1963), pp. 21–24.

[36] See above, p. 364, and pl. 56.

of Ptolemy published at Strassburg in 1520, 1522, and 1525. The 1522 edition also includes two additional maps of India and the East.[37]

Waldseemüller and his followers were the first to break completely with the Ptolemaic tradition by preparing a world map based entirely on the Portuguese discoveries. The *Carta marina* of 1516, a woodcut in twelve sheets, is a marine and navigation chart which, according to its title, shows the "navigations of the Portuguese and the form and nature of all the known world and sea, places and limits which became known in our time and do not agree with old traditions, and also those of which the ancient authors did not know."[38] This new map with its declaration of independence never enjoyed the popularity of Waldseemüller's more conventional world maps. Lorenz Fries (*ca.* 1490–1531), a cosmographer, and Martin Grüninger, a Strassburg publisher, were among the few who showed a profound and continuing interest in the *Carta marina*. In his 1522 edition of Ptolemy, Fries brought materials from the *Carta marina* into the atlas through the maps he added.[39] Unfortunately these were badly drawn and poorly printed. Three years later Fries published his own *Carta marina* (1525), a reduction and copy of Waldseemüller's original. Along with the marine chart he published in German a guide, with instructions for its use, based on Waldseemüller's notes and on the available travel accounts, such as Varthema's. Fries' work, like the original, is rich in legends and illustrations. But both the author and the printer eschewed sensationalism for commercial gain; they based their materials on recent travel accounts rather than on Mandeville and the monstrosities of the East associated with that book and its illustrations. Fancy is not similarly outlawed, for King Manuel is shown riding around the Cape of Good Hope seated on a sea lion. Fries' book was reissued in 1527 and 1530.[40]

The Alsatian school died with Ringmann and Waldseemüller but not before it had brought home to the Germans and their neighbors the importance of the overseas discoveries to changing geographical conceptions. Its productions, especially the Ptolemy of 1513, helped to revitalize geography at Nuremberg and to stimulate its development at Augsburg.[41] Mathematically minded Nurembergers were especially fascinated by the problem of devising new projections which would more adequately represent the known world in all of its dimensions. Johann Werner (1468–1528) and his associates proposed three cordiform projections. Study of these projections reveals that in his representations Werner correctly emphasized the prevalence of land masses in the Northern Hemisphere.[42] His contemporary, Johann Stabius of Nuremberg, sketched a

---

[37] See Cortesão, *op. cit.* (n. 7), I, 124.

[38] As translated *ibid.*, p. 132.

[39] See Bagrow-Skelton, *op. cit.* (n. 15), pp. 114–15.

[40] Entitled *Uslegung der Mercarthen* . . . , a single copy of the last edition is preserved in the state library of Bavaria at Munich. Though designed to appeal to the public, it appeared at a time when religious tensions were high and when most German readers were buying polemical tracts. See Johnson, *op. cit.* (n. 35), pp. 3–5, 43, 51–78, 114.

[41] See F. Grenacher, "Guide to the Cartographic History of the Imperial City of Augsburg," *Imago mundi*, XXII (1968), 87.

[42] See Kish, "The Cosmographic Heart" (n. 27), p. 21.

globular map which was finished and decorated by Albrecht Dürer and issued as a woodcut in 1515.[43] In this same year, Johann Schöner, a Nuremberg priest and professor, produced his first globe and accompanied it with a descriptive text entitled *Luculentissima terrae descriptio* (Bamberg, 1515) in which he criticizes Ptolemy's latitudes and longitudes, provides a new table for Europe, Asia, Africa, and the newly discovered places, and urges all princes to obtain more precise determinations for the geography of their own countries.[44] But Schöner's gores were still modeled on the modified Ptolemaic map of Waldseemüller printed in 1507. The Ptolemaic tradition was also preserved at Nuremberg by the efforts of Werner and Willibald Pirckheimer to provide more understandable translations of the *Geography*. Pirckheimer's translation, printed in 1525, was adopted by Mercator for his edition of 1584.

The Ptolemaic world map was stretched and strained by early sixteenth-century cartographers to accommodate the existence of the "New World," *or those regions not known to Ptolemy.*[45] Ptolemy's land area covered fully one-half of the circumference of his earth, running continuously from the Canaries through China. What is more, his earth, based on ideas inherited from the Arabs, possessed a circumference only about three-fourths of its actual size. As a consequence of these errors, the space left for the New World and the vast Pacific Ocean—or the distance of 130° from Panama to the coast of China—was limited to a mere 70°.[46] The Cantino world chart (1502) sought to correct this error by reducing the longitudinal extent of the Eurasiatic continent, implying thereby that a vaster distance separated America from Asia than Columbus and most European cartographers believed.[47] Ptolemy's authority, however, was so imposing in Spain, Italy, and Germany that his fundamental errors were corrected only slowly. The estimates available to Magellan in 1519 on the extent of the Pacific Ocean fell about eighty percent short of the truth. For a full century after the return of the "Victoria" the width of the Pacific continued to be underestimated by as much as forty percent.[48] The maps prepared before 1570 also regularly presented widely divergent views on the relations between the two Americas, on the placement of insular Southeast Asia and Japan, and on the configuration of the east coast of continental Asia.

The Spanish, who presumably knew more about the Atlantic, the Americas,

[43] Bagrow-Skelton, *op. cit.* (n. 15), p. 127 and fig. 39.

[44] See Gallois, *op. cit.* (n. 28), pp. 111–14. For his tables compared to true latitudes and longitudes see *ibid.*, appendix, pp. 246–47.

[45] On the meaning of "mundus novus" see Morison, *op. cit.* (n. 18), p. 155; on the persistence of the idea that the "New World" included the insular Pacific region, as well as the two Americas, see above, pp. 339–40, and below, pp. 516–17. The word "America" was first placed on both North and South America by Mercator in his world map of 1538. Thereafter the Americas began more frequently to be equated with the New World. The older definition persisted, however, in many maps, cosmographies, and histories to the century's end.

[46] Based on E. Heawood, "The World Map before and after Magellan," *Geographical Journal*, LVII (1921), 432.

[47] See Crone, *op. cit.* (n. 6), pp. 87–88.

[48] See Morison, *op. cit.* (n. 18), p. 403.

and the western shores of the Pacific than any other Europeans, were extremely slow about producing maps. Juan de la Cosa, Columbus' pilot, prepared a world map (probably between 1500 and 1508) which shows for America a continuous continental coastline, running from north to south but without any indication that America is separate from Asia. The map of Asia is decorated on the interior with a portrait of the Three Kings and its southern coasts are inscribed as lands discovered by Manuel of Portugal.[49] The Contarini map of 1506 is the earliest printed map to show a sea passage dividing Cuba from Cipangu, and Cipangu from the coast of Cathay.[50] Cartographic conceptions were not improved by the appointment of Vespucci in 1508 as pilot-major of Spain. In this post he had the responsibility for preparing and keeping up to date the *padron réal*, the official map of the world at Seville. Vespucci, whatever his qualifications were, apparently did little during his tenure beyond organizing an administration. The Spanish, far behind the Portuguese in establishing a central organization for trade and navigation, continued to depend throughout the pre-Magellan period upon the cartographic information relayed to Seville by spies, renegade Portuguese seamen, and smuggled maps and charts.[51] They also garnered information from maps and globes imported from Italy and Germany. It is even possible that Magellan convinced the king to back his circumnavigation by showing him Schöner's globe of 1515, or one like it.[52] Since no copies of the *padron réal* are extant for the period before 1527, it is impossible to know how much information on the Pacific the Spanish had in their possession before the departure of Magellan.[53]

The return of the "Victoria" should have produced much more of a revolution in Europe's view of the world than it actually did. The Magellan adventure did serve to remove all remaining doubts about the sphericity of the earth. It corrected the Ptolemaic proportions of water to land on the earth's surface and proved that the land far exceeded the water area. The vast width of the Pacific Ocean was established and the knowledge began to spread that Asia and America, at least in their southern reaches, were very far apart (see pl. 80). The Magellan voyage contributed also to a growing belief in the unity and independence of the Americas as the New World. It dispelled forever all the ideas that Asia could be reached by a relatively brief westward voyage. Magellan's passage around America secured an access to the Pacific by sea; this feat revived interest in Spanish voyages to the Spice Islands. But it still left open the question of a land connection between North America and northeastern Asia, an issue that would not be resolved until the time of Bering in the eighteenth century. Nor did it

[49] See J. M. Millás Vallicrosa, "Nautique et cartographie de l'Espagne au XVIᵉ siècle," in A. Koyré (ed.), *La science au seizième siècle* (Paris, 1960), pp. 34–37.
[50] Consult Skelton, *Explorer's Maps* (n. 3), p. 59.
[51] See Teixeira da Mota, *loc. cit.*, in Mollat and Adams (eds.), *op. cit.* (n. 17), pp. 240–41.
[52] See Morison, *op. cit.* (n. 18), pp. 381–82.
[53] For further discussion of the hypothetical Pacific see *Asia*, I, 221. Also see L. C. Wroth, "The Early Cartography of the Pacific," *Papers of the Bibliographical Society of America*, XXXVIII (1944), 137–51.

change the traditional belief in the southern continent postulated by earlier cartographers; if anything it seemed to confirm the existence of a land mass to the south of Magellan's strait. Finally it left unsettled the question of the position in longitude of the Spice Islands and whether they legally belonged within the Portuguese or the Spanish demarcation.[54]

The conflict over the location and ownership of the Moluccas between 1519 and 1529 had a stimulating effect upon the study of cosmography and cartography, especially in Spain.[55] Balboa's discovery of "the South Sea" in 1513 and the assertions in the *Suma de geographia* (Seville, 1519) of Enciso had inspired some Spaniards to claim before the return of the "Victoria" that everything east of Malacca lay within the Spanish demarcation.[56] Peter Martyr was one of the first publicists to claim the Moluccas for Spain after the return of Magellan's men. A serious review of the Portuguese conquests in the East also began in Spain at this time.[57] In the middle of this new activity was Diogo Ribeiro (d. 1533), an expellee from Portugal who arrived opportunely at Seville in 1519. He was at once employed in making charts, compasses, quadrants, and spheres for Magellan's fleet. In 1523 Charles V elevated him to the post of royal cosmographer, and he represented Spain and its claims at the discussions with Portugal over the ownership of the Moluccas. He helped to prepare materials for the Spanish fleets leaving from Coruña and experimented with making metal pumps for ships and mines. He worked with Martin Centurione, Charles' ambassador to Genoa, in preparing a translation of the *Book* of Duarte Barbosa.[58] In the meantime he constructed a number of planispheres, probably using the *padron réal* as his authority. In 1526 Charles V wrote to Ferdinand Columbus asking him to work with Ribeiro and others to prepare a world map "on which are located all the islands and continents discovered up to now and that will be discovered from now on[!]"[59]

From 1525 to 1532 Ribeiro prepared, or is credited with preparing, five planispheres. The most finished of these is the world chart of 1529 now preserved in the Vatican. It is both a marvelous synthesis of what was then known about the world and an obvious effort to validate the Spanish claim to the Moluccas. The planisphere of 1529 comprehends the whole circuit of the globe between the polar circles; the archipelago of the East Indies is placed in both the eastern and western margins. The placement of the continents in terms of latitude and longitude is relatively accurate, but Asia is still overextended to the east by about twenty degrees. The Moluccas are located too close to the Asian mainland and, possibly because of the overly eastward prolongation of Asia, they are

[54] The Portuguese maps, beginning around 1510, locate the Moluccas quite accurately, or about 6° within the Portuguese demarcation. See Crone, *op. cit.* (n. 6), pp. 90–92. But see Ribeiro's Asia, pl. 67.

[55] For details of the conflict see *Asia*, I, 114–19.

[56] See above, p. 169.

[57] See above, pp. 170–71.

[58] Two manuscript copies of translations of Barbosa are extant in the state library of Bavaria in Munich (cod. Hisp. 8). But it seems unlikely that they are copies of this translation. See above, p. 58.

[59] As quoted in Cortesão and Teixeira da Mota, *op. cit.* (n. 17), I, 88.

represented as being within the Spanish demarcation. It is quite likely that a semi-Ptolemaic Asia was retained to make possible this favorable placement of the Moluccas.[60]

News of the successful circumnavigation of the globe was quickly relayed to the rest of Europe by several participants in the voyage, by excited Spanish writers, and by foreign diplomats in Spain.[61] The Latin report by Maximilian of Transylvania was the first to be published; it appeared at Cologne and Rome in 1523. Johann Schöner at Nuremberg was one of the first to bring the information obtained from Spain into the mainstream of German cartography. He constructed a new globe (not extant) in 1523 that was based on the sketchy geographical information contained in the account of Maximilian and on a map which had been sent from Spain to an anonymous man of "high station." To accompany his globe Schöner prepared a short tract on the discoveries of the Spanish and the Portuguese. But on the globe itself, while he evidently showed America as a separate continent, he divided it from Asia by only a narrow ribbon of water. The Moluccas he placed within the Spanish demarcation. He evidently continued to receive maps from Spain after he assumed the chair of mathematics at Nuremberg in 1526, for in his *Opusculum geographicum* (Nuremberg, 1533), a geographical treatise prepared as a guide to another of his globes, he seems again to follow uncritically the newer maps being prepared in Spain.[62]

Pirckheimer, the Nuremberg Humanist, like his colleague Peutinger of Augsburg, did his best to keep abreast of the latest discoveries. Both men also reexamined thoroughly the writings of Antiquity to determine whether or not the Ancients had known about the sea route around Africa to India.[63] In his 1525 translation of Ptolemy, Pirckheimer was concerned exclusively with producing a worthy Latin translation of the Greek text. But in his *Germania* (1530), he takes off on an excursion to other parts of the world, at least with respect to place names. In the first appendix to this little book he lists in tabular form the Ptolemaic names of Asian places and their "modern" equivalents: Alambater = Diu; Monglossum = Goa; Sinyla = Calecut or Chossin; Sinae = Schin.[64] An examination of Pirckheimer's unpublished papers reveals that he also collected extracts of geographical materials from both classical and contemporary travel accounts. Since he was an advocate of teaching geography at the secondary level (*Mittelschule*), it may be surmised that he intended these extracts to be used as instructional materials.[65]

Much more was done for popular education by the publications of Peter Apian (1495–1552), a geographer who republished the maps of others and constructed

---

[60] Based on the analysis by Crone, *op. cit.* (n. 6), pp. 93–95. See pl. 47.

[61] For details see *Asia*, I, 171–77.

[62] Based on Gallois, *op. cit.* (n. 28), pp. 90–91.

[63] Cf. above, p. 335.

[64] Cf. the maps in A. Berthelot, *L'Asie ancienne centrale et sud-Orientale d'après Ptolomée* (Paris, 1930).

[65] See M. Weyrauther, *Konrad Peutinger und Wilibald Pirckheimer in ihren Beziehungen zur Geographie: Eine geschichtliche Parallele* (Munich, 1907), p. 40. He examined the Pirckheimer papers then housed in the Nuremberg library.

several globes and maps of his own (see pl. 27). What is most important about his maps and writings is his expressed determination to bring new materials on the overseas world into geography (see pl. 59). He outspokenly derides those who clung to the authority of Ptolemy and asserts that in a conflict between ancient and modern sources the student should always give greater credence to the eyewitness testimony of contemporary travelers and to those works based on their accounts.[66] He deplored his own lack of opportunity to travel widely and to make observations of his own.[67] Throughout his life he remained a firm Catholic and spent most of his mature years in Bavaria. It was probably because of his religious orthodoxy that his cosmographical works circulated so widely in Europe. His most original cartographic work was his cordiform world map published in 1530.[68] While his outline of Asia remains basically Ptolemaic, he shows a relatively large Pacific Ocean as well as an insular Southeast Asia. The map's margin is decorated with facing portraits of Ptolemy and Vespucci. Each figure is holding a heart-shaped map. On the one Ptolemy holds the Ptolemaic map of the world is super-imposed as an illustration of how much of the world was unknown to him; on Vespucci's map the Ptolemaic projection is left blank and the rest of the world revealed by the discoveries is sketched in around its outline (see pls. 65–66).

2

THE NEW CARTOGRAPHY

While others adapted the Portuguese works to their own ends, the Portuguese themselves continued to produce basic new maps and rutters. For the period from 1500 to 1600 the works of twenty-eight Portuguese cartographers are extant. References in textual materials reveal the existence of nineteen others for whom no authenticated work survives. No other country in sixteenth-century Europe could equal in number this total of forty-seven cartographers. Most of the maps they prepared concentrated on the oceanic rather than on the Mediterranean world. Their creations were ordinarily not portolan charts but planispheres, world charts, and maps of the Atlantic and Indian oceans. By 1559 the Portuguese had traced onto their maps more than sixty thousand kilometers of new coastlines, almost half of which were of Asia and Malaysian islands.[69] Because of their close association with oceanic navigation, the Portuguese cartographers

---

[66] For details of his cosmography see above, p. 354.

[67] See W. Näf, *Vadian und seine Stadt St. Gallen* (St. Gall, 1944), p. 268.

[68] The original is preserved in the map room of the British Museum. For a technical analysis see D. Woodward, "Some Evidence for the Use of Stereotyping on Peter Apian's World Map of 1530," *Imago mundi*, XXIV (1970), 43–48. For a reproduction see pl. 64.

[69] See Teixeira da Mota, *loc. cit.*, in Mollat and Adam (eds.), *op. cit.* (n. 17), pp. 233–35. Also see the same author's article, "Evolução dos roteiros portugueses durante o século XVI," *Revista da universidade de Coimbra*, XXIV (1971), 5–32.

and cosmographers were highly critical of plane charts which ignored the earth's curvature and the convergence of meridians. Many of their earliest planispheres include tables of latitudes. In 1534 Pedro Nunes determined the true character of rhumb lines or the line along which the compass maintains a constant bearing. The Portuguese were also inclined to record on their charts and maps many rules of navigation as well as materials of hydrographical and cosmographical interest. Currents, tides, flotsam, fish, birds, trees, or fruits that the seamen saw in the sea or on islands and coasts often appear as illustrations or are described in legends.

The Portuguese nautical and oceanic maps were particularly important after 1530 as models for the French cartographers. The French were at first only mildly curious about the discoveries that they had learned about at second hand, primarily through Latin writings and translations.[70] Their theologians continued to be absorbed for a long time with sacred geography and particularly with exact descriptions and mappings of the Holy Land.[71] The sailors of Normandy and Brittany were the first Frenchman to respond positively to the discovery of America. Oronce Finé (1494–1555), a Paris professor of mathematics, was the only French intellectual of the first generation of the sixteenth century to possess more than a passing interest in the cartographic revolution sweeping Italy and Germany (see pl. 68). Through his friends at the College of Sainte-Barbe he learned directly about the overseas victories of the Portuguese and Spanish.[72] Possibly he also knew the Lopo Homem-Reinels world atlas (1519) which King Manuel commissioned, it is believed, for dispatch to King Francis.[73] It was not until the 1530's that Finé or the members of the Dieppe school of hydrography and cartography began to issue maps.[74] Most of the maps produced at Dieppe were modeled on Portuguese charts until the French began about 1540 to record the Atlantic voyages of their fellow countrymen. Around 1546 Jean Roze of Dieppe was commissioned by King Henry VIII of England to prepare maps of the Atlantic for the use of his navigators.[75] The French maps were among the earliest to stress the complete separation of North America from northeastern Asia. French cartographers, including Finé, also devoutly believed in a great southern continent (Antarctica) to which they attached Brazil. Thevet and other French cosmographers helped to keep this notion alive for quite a while.[76] Despite all this cartographical activity, Jacques Signot was able to publish and sell *La division du monde* (Paris), which appeared in five editions from 1539 to 1560 without ever mentioning the two Americas or the new discoveries in Asia.

---

[70] See above, pp. 255–56.

[71] See F. de Dainville, *La géographie des humanistes* (Paris, 1940), pp. 89–90.

[72] For his life and works see L. Gallois, *De Orontio Finaeo gallico geographo* (Paris, 1890), chap. i.

[73] See Cortesão and Teixeira da Mota, *op. cit.* (n. 17), I, 61.

[74] See Bagrow-Skelton, *op. cit.* (n. 15), pp. 132, 244. Finé's world map in a double-heart projection was published in the *Novus orbis* of 1532. See pl. 69.

[75] See A. Anthiaume, *Cartes marines, constructions, navales; . . . chez les normands, 1500–1650* (2 vols.; Paris, 1916), I, 51–52, 61–71.

[76] See above, pp. 302–5.

In the middle years of the century the Portuguese at home and overseas continued to correct and amend their earlier charts. D. João de Castro, disciple of the cosmographer Nunes, deliberately tested some of the navigational instruments, methods, and ideas of his teacher on his voyage to India of 1538–41.[77] A series of three new rutters was produced as the result of this voyage and the master chart of the world in Lisbon was altered accordingly. About 1545 an anonymous planisphere was executed in Lisbon on the basis of the modified master chart—the first planisphere definitely prepared in Portugal since the Cantino map. This elaborate world chart is decorated with clothed and unclothed portraits of the rulers of Asia, including even the emperor of China (see pl. 14). Its new information was transmitted to France, Italy, England, and the Netherlands through the subsequent cartographic creations of Diogo and André Homem and Bartolomeu Velho. The works of Velho dating from around 1560 are particularly novel in the detail they give on interior physical features and places. It is possible that La Popelinière obtained some of his information on Asia from Velho's maps.[78]

In Germany, where cosmography reached its apogee at mid-century, the newer Portuguese maps apparently made almost no impression.[79] Like Apian, the German cosmographers, as subjects of an emperor who was also king of Spain, continued to rely heavily on the 1529 map of Ribeiro (pl. 67) and on Spanish reports about America. It is upon this tradition, rather than upon the more recent Portuguese maps, that the descriptions and maps of Asia are based which appeared in German popular travel accounts and cosmographies. The German cosmographers were also inclined to depend upon literary sources— Marco Polo, Poggio, and Varthema—rather than the Portuguese maps. The printers, who were so influential in preparing the cosmographies, probably preferred to reproduce the older woodcut maps and illustrations rather than to incur the expense of new engravings. Certainly the religious wars and the disruptions attending them had a deleterious effect upon cartographic development in Germany. Whatever the reasons, it is clear that by 1550 innovation in German cartography consisted only of additions to descriptive regional geography.

The Italians, like the French, were more responsive than the Germans to the newer Portuguese cartographic representations. Giacomo Gastaldi (*ca.* 1500– *ca.* 1565), the cosmographer of Venice, was the most prolific and influential of the Italian cartographers. From 1544 to his death twenty-one years later Gastaldi constructed over one hundred maps. He prepared the "modern maps" for the Italian edition (Venice, 1547–48) of Ptolemy and followed that by producing ten maps for inclusion in Ramusio's great travel collection. But his most original creation was his separate map of Asia prepared between 1559 and 1561 in three parts on six sheets. For his materials on the interior of Asia he relied heavily on

---

[77] See Cortesão and Teixeira da Mota, *op. cit.* (n. 17), I, 127.
[78] See *ibid.*, II, 67–68, 89–92. On La Popelinière see above, pp. 315–16.
[79] For a general discussion of the cosmography of Münster see above, pp. 340–41.

the version of Marco Polo published by Ramusio.[80] A study of his Asian place names reveals that he depended, as in his earlier maps, on the Portuguese planispheres and possibly on the Italian translations of Castanheda (1556) and Barros (1561). He certainly uses place names, particularly for the interior of India (especially "Cospetir" and "Pale"), which can be found only in the Portuguese chronicles. On the third part of his map Gastaldi tries to set the record straight by giving a list of the Ptolemaic place names and their "modern" counterparts.[81] Gastaldi's maps were widely circulated through the numerous engravings of them published by Antonio Lafreri of Rome and his associates.[82]

The Italians of the Renaissance were more inclined than other Europeans to decorate their palaces with wall maps.[83] At Venice a fresco map of the world painted about 1400 had graced the wall of a special room in the ducal palace until it was destroyed by fire in 1483. In 1553 the Council of Ten concluded a contract with Gastaldi to prepare wall maps of Asia and America.[84] The map of Asia was to be based on Marco Polo for Cathay and Barros for China, presumably from their writings in Ramusio's collection. These were to be added to a map of Africa prepared in 1549 by Gastaldi. The projected map of America, because of an insufficiency of information, was never finished. The two completed maps later vanished and in their place there are now eight maps drawn in the eighteenth century by Grisellini.[85]

Duke Cosimo de' Medici of Florence was evidently inspired by the Venetian example to keep his fresco maps in a room of their own. He first acquired Lopo Homem's planisphere of 1554 with its recent detail on the East Indian archipelago, China, the Liu-ch'iu islands, and Japan.[86] Later he received a book from Portugal on the voyage from Lisbon to the Moluccas that was written by a Portuguese pilot who had himself made the voyage fourteen times.[87] Cosimo then summoned Ignazio Danti (1536–86), a Dominican, to design a unique atlas that would be painted on the wooden panels of the cupboards in the room now called the Sala della Guardaroba.[88] Between 1563 and 1575 Danti completed fifty-three mural maps for the duke's wardrobe room. They included maps of

[80] See A. H. Nordenskiöld, "Intorno alla influenza dei 'Viaggi di Marco Polo' sulle carte dell' Asia di Giacomo Gastaldo," *Revista geografica italiana*, VIII (1901), 496–505.

[81] For a reproduction of the part on East Asia as copied by Gerard de Jode (1578) see Bagrow-Skelton, *op. cit.* (n. 15), p. lxviii. Also see pls. 74, 75.

[82] See *ibid.*, pp. 137–38.

[83] For a brief history of cartographic representations in Italy see R. Almagià, *Monumenta cartographica Vaticana* (4 vols.; Vatican City, 1944–55). III, 11–14.

[84] See R. Gallo, "Le mappe geografiche del Palazzo ducale di Venezia," *Archivio veneto*, 5th ser. XXXII (1943), 62–63.

[85] See Bagrow-Skelton, *op. cit.* (n. 15), pp. 216–17.

[86] See Cortesão and Teixeira da Mota, *op. cit.* (n. 17), I, 67–69.

[87] He gave this book to Danti to help him in the preparation of his maps. See the letter of Danti to Ortelius from Rome (December 24, 1580) in J. H. Hessels (ed.), *Abraham Ortelii . . . epistulae* (Cambridge, 1887), p. 242.

[88] For a portion of this collection see the photographs in Bagrow-Skelton, *op. cit.* (n. 15), pl. CXIII, and in G. Kish, "The Japan on the 'Mural Atlas' of the Palazzo Vecchio, Florence," *Imago mundi*, VIII (1951), 52–54.

the Spiceries (1563) (see pl. 76), the other East Indian islands (1573), China (1575), and parts of Japan (undated). On a map of East Asia Japan is shown off the coast of China and on another it is depicted as the farthest away from Europe of the West Indies. Danti shows Japan as one island, probably because he depended more on Marco Polo than on the Jesuit letterbooks. In 1569 while working on the mural maps, Danti published his treatises on the construction and use of the astrolabe and the sphere.

Danti was summoned to Rome in 1580 by Pope Gregory XIII to supervise the decoration of the newly constructed Galleria del Belvedere. As pontifical cosmographer Danti was aided in his work by two artists, Girolamo Muziano and Cesare Nabbia. While completing a series of Italian maps for the Belvedere Gallery, Danti and his staff began to work on wall maps for the cosmographic loggia, the third story of the Raphael loggias in the Vatican palace. In the northern wing they constructed a wall atlas which included the world map in two hemispheres as well as maps of the continents and of many parts of the overseas world. Included among them were decorative maps of Ceylon, India, Malacca, China, and Tartary; Japan was shown on a map of New Spain. All these maps have since perished, but the general map of Asia was almost certainly based on Gastaldi's map of the continent with modifications inserted from other maps.[89] The later map of Asia (1597) by Fausto Rughesi in the Vatican library is similarly based on Gastaldi though with major changes in the delineation of East Asia (see pl. 77). The library map is certainly the first mural painting to give Korea a peninsular configuration.[90] This depiction can only be accounted for by reference to the artist's knowledge of the materials then available in the Jesuit letters.[91]

New centers of cartographic industry arose about mid-century in the cities of the Netherlands and in the Rhine valley. The maritime position of the Flemish cities, especially Antwerp, required the Netherlanders to learn as much as possible about the lore of the sea. It is therefore not surprising to find that their geographers were originally more skilled in navigation and in the allied sciences of hydrography and oceanic cartography than in regional land survey or map-making. Johannes Ruysch (*ca.* 1460–1533), the first Netherlander to produce a world map, worked in Rome at the papal palace about 1508. Based either on the Cantino or the Canerio maps, Ruysch's creation for the Ptolemy of 1507–8 had shown clearly that he was well acquainted with the discoveries of the Portuguese in Asia.[92] The printers of Antwerp were meanwhile issuing books and pamphlets in which the public could learn of the overseas voyages and be

[89] See F. Banfi, "The Cosmographic Loggia of the Vatican Palace," *Imago mundi,* IX (1952), 23–30; and for a contemporary reference to the map of Asia which shows "Quinsay" (Hangchow) in China see A. Merens (ed.), "De reis van Jan Martenez. Merens door Frankrijk, Italie en Duitschland, anno 1600," *Mededeelingen van het Nederlandsche Historisch Instituut te Rome,* 2d ser. VII (1937), 138–39.
[90] See Almagià, *op. cit.* (n. 83), II, 69–71.
[91] On Korea in the Jesuit letters see *Asia,* I, 720–21.
[92] Consult J. Keuning, "Sixteenth-Century Cartography in the Netherlands," *Imago mundi,* IX (1952), 38–39; also cf. the discussion of Dutch literature, above, pp. 353–54, and pl. 61.

entertained by the primitive woodcuts with which they were illustrated. A comparison of Ruysch's excellent map with these northern woodcuts exhibits clearly the wide scientific gap which separated Italian from Dutch geographical knowledge in the early sixteenth century.

Scientific geography originated in the Netherlands through the activities of Gemma Frisius and his pupils. A professor at Louvain from 1525 to his death thirty years later, Gemma was at the university in those years when it played host to a number of Portuguese students and when Damião de Góis was publishing there his Latin books on the overseas discoveries.[93] Gemma, also a student of the German cosmographies, in 1529 published at Antwerp Apian's work that had been first issued at Landshut five years before. To the 1544 edition of this cosmography he added a small woodcut, the only one of his world maps which still survives.[94] He also constructed globes, astrolabes, and armillary spheres. A terrestrial globe of around 1535, discovered only in 1951, includes on it the most important cities of Asia and refers to Maximilian of Transylvania as the one who inspired the globe.[95] In 1536 Emperor Charles V granted a license for four years to Gemma "Phrisius" and Gaspar à Myrica "to issue for the general use of those interested, a Globe or a Sphere, enlarged, augmented and more splendid than that previously issued (together with a Celestial Globe) with the addition of Countries and Islands recently discovered . . . not a few of which are fortunately being imbued with the Christian religion."[96] The following year he completed a pair of large globes; he was assisted in the construction of the terrestrial globe by his pupil, Gerard Mercator (1512–94).[97]

Ptolemy's shackles were cut off cartography permanently by the works of Mercator and his associates in the Low Countries. Franciscus Monachus, Mercator's friend and a Franciscan monk, had sought in *De orbis situ ac descriptione* (Antwerp, *ca.* 1530), a book in the form of a public letter, to exorcise the "hallucination of Ptolemy" by refuting his *Geography*. While Mercator was not so flamboyant, it can readily be gathered from his globes, maps, and correspondence that he was likewise convinced that the Ptolemaic illusion had to be dispelled. Among his earliest independent works was his world map of 1538 in a double cordiform projection adapted from Finé's earlier map.[98] Here the continental land mass of Eurasia remains basically Ptolemaic with several additions to the interiors from the medieval travelers and with a few modifications of Asia's coastlines. His Pacific is still a narrow band of water, but he shows clearly the many islands of the East Indian archipelago. Like the French school

[93] See above, p. 21.

[94] See Bagrow-Skelton, *op. cit.* (n. 15), p. 133.

[95] It is now in the Globusmuseum of Vienna. For discussion see R. Haardt, "The Globe of Gemma Frisius," *Imago mundi*, IX (1952), 109–10.

[96] As quoted *ibid.*, p. 109.

[97] See Bagrow-Skelton, *op. cit.* (n. 15), p. 133. For a portrait (1557) of Gemma Frisius with globe and instruments of cartography engraved by Jan van Stalburch see A. S. Osley, *Mercator* (London and New York, 1969), pl. 41.

[98] For a reproduction see Bagrow-Skelton, *op. cit.* (n. 15), fig. 42. Cf. pl. 69.

he posits a large Antarctica to the south of Magellan's strait, though he does place Brazil in South America. He followed his world map with a terrestrial globe, completed in 1541, on which he drew the rhumb lines correctly as spirals. Around 1552 he left Louvain for Duisburg, an ancient city and inland port of the Hansa at the junction of the Ruhr and Rhine rivers.

In his Duisburg workshop Mercator compiled geographical data and drew and engraved his own maps. He also taught mathematics and cosmography at the local Latin school from 1559 to 1563. It was possibly this experience that convinced him a new atlas was badly needed to replace the antiquated Ptolemaic collections.[99] Visitors from near and far appeared at Mercator's workshop as his maps became more famous. In the Netherlands the house of Plantin held a monopoly of the sale of his maps from 1566 to 1576. The Antwerp printer also sold them through his shop in Paris and at the Frankfurt book fairs.[100] Plantin's accounts testify to an increasing demand in England for world maps and globes. After Mercator published his celebrated world map in 1569, his son, Rumold, went to London as an agent for a Cologne bookseller who marketed maps.[101]

Mercator's world chart of 1569 was the first of his creations to be drawn according to the projection that has ever since carried his name. He evidently derived his projection empirically, since Edward Wright (1558?–1615) was the first to analyze its properties mathematically.[102] Mercator devised a cylindrical projection in which all meridians are straight lines perpendicular to the equator and the lines of latitude run parallel to it. This projection proved to be a boon to navigators for they could now for the first time lay down a compass course as a straight line. But it was also revolutionary in the sense that in his depiction of the continents Mercator broke completely with the cartography of Ptolemy. Still he continues mistakenly to postulate a great southern continent. Possibly he perpetuated the myth of the Antipodes by following a common misreading of Marco Polo and Varthema from which some contemporaries concluded that a continent lay to the south of Java Major. Southeastern Asia is based, according to Mercator's own statement in the legend, on the Portuguese maps. However, he still confuses the river of Canton in China with the classical Ganges. He persists also in showing North America as being separated from northeastern Asia by a narrow Strait of Anian. In other words his map left open many hotly debated geographical issues regarding the continuity of the New World, its relationship to Asia, the possibility of a northern passage, and the existence of a huge southern continent.[103]

The English, in particular, were perplexed after their own navigational ex-

---

[99] Consult J. Keuning, "The History of an Atlas, Mercator-Hondius," *Imago mundi*, IV (1947), 37.

[100] See L. Voet, "Les relations commericales entre Gerard Mercator et la maison Plantinienne," *Duisburger Forschungen*, VI (1962), 231–32.

[101] See R. A. Skelton, "Mercator and English Cartography in the Sixteenth Century," *Duisburger Forschungen*, VI (1962), 160–61.

[102] Suggestion of Thrower, *op. cit.* (n. 10), p. 53. For a poor reproduction of the map see Bagrow-Skelton, *op. cit.* (n. 15), pl. LXX.

[103] Based on Crone, *op. cit.* (n. 6), pp. 116–18. Cf. pl. 80.

periences to find Mercator showing an open polar sea that could presumably be used for a northeastern passage to Cathay.[104] In what remains of his correspondence it is clear that Mercator himself continued to fret about the easiest route to Asia. He was still willing in 1577 to believe in the possibility of sailing from Mexico to Asia across a narrow strait.[105] Three years later he wrote to Hakluyt expressing astonishment on learning that the English had decided to give up sailing to Cathay by the "convenient and easy" northeastern route.[106] In writing to Ortelius six months later about Drake's expedition through the Strait of Magellan, he tells of receiving a secret letter informing him that Arthur Pet had been sent to Asia by the northeastern passage with the idea of meeting Drake in Java.[107] Drake's successful circumnavigation evidently stimulated Mercator to learn whatever he could about the southern routes to Asia. He conducted a long-distance epistolary debate on navigation and other subjects with Filippo Sassetti, the Florentine Humanist who resided at Goa from 1583 to his death in 1588. Mercator's biographer, Walter Ghim, wrote in 1595, that "a sizeable bundle of these and similar letters can be readily found in the house of his heir."[108] One year later his heir, Rumold, wrote to Ortelius that in looking for a manuscript among his father's books and papers he had vainly "searched through the authors of Indian travels and epistles."[109] Though nothing remains but these references, they clearly indicate that Mercator continued to collect materials on the East until the time of his death in 1594.

The cartographic works of Mercator's later years also testify to his determined curiosity about the overseas world, especially those related to the ambitious composite works he projected. Contemporaneously with the publication of his world map in 1569, he began planning an atlas which was to give a complete, illustrated account of the genesis and growth of the universe. In connection with this project he corrected Ptolemy's maps in two publications of the *Geography* of 1578 and 1584.[110] Work on the maps for the atlas went slowly, partly because of his lengthy, painstaking researches and partly because of a shortage of trained engravers. The maps of the overseas world were left after his death for Hondius to complete and to add to the famed Mercator-Hondius *Atlas* finally printed in its entirety in 1606.[111]

Mercator's close friend, Abraham Ortelius (1527–98) of Antwerp, was a

---

104 See Skelton, "Mercator and English Cartography" (n. 101), VI (1962), 165–66.

105 See the letters of Johannes Metellus of 1577 in M. van Durme (ed.), *Correspondance mercatorienne* (Antwerp, 1959), p. 31.

106 From Duisburg, July 28, 1580, *ibid.*, pp. 158–59.

107 December 12, 1580, *ibid.*, pp. 162–63. For a translation see H. P. Kraus, *Sir Francis Drake* (Amsterdam, 1970), pp. 86–87.

108 Ghim's brief biography was originally printed in the first Duisburg edition of Mercator's *Atlas* of 1595. For this quotation see the English translation in Osley, *op. cit.* (n. 97), p. 193.

109 See above, p. 65.

110 For a reproduction of a part of his map of Asia in the Ptolemy of 1578 published at Cologne see Skelton, *Decorative Printed Maps* (n. 10), pl. 13.

111 See Bagrow-Skelton, *op. cit.* (n. 15), p. 180. For a portrait (1614) of Mercator and Hondius see J. Keuning, "The History of an Atlas" (n. 99), facing p. 37.

cartographer, publisher, and collector of distinction. In his early years he worked as an illuminator of maps; it was perhaps through this activity that he met Mercator at the Frankfurt book fair in 1554. Ortelius traveled in Germany and Italy before making a tour of France with Mercator in 1560. At this time Mercator possibly inspired the young Ortelius to take a more scientific interest in cartography. Plantin's records for these years show that Ortelius was a regular purchaser of maps and other sources of geographical information.[112] He also began at this point to try learning more about the geography of the East from his correspondents in Lisbon.[113] His original maps began to appear in 1564, the first being a large world map in eight sheets. Three years later he published a map of Asia in two sheets, the map that became the model in format for those he included in his atlas. His map of Asia is largely based on the Gastaldi map.[114]

As in the case of his map of Asia, Ortelius sought everywhere for the best available models. He then drew his own maps after these models before handing his manuscript over for engraving to Franz Hogenberg and his assistants. At the suggestion of his friend Aegidius Hooftman, Ortelius began to think in terms of standardizing the size and format of his maps with the idea of producing an up-to-date atlas. He worked rapidly and before long had reduced the best available modern maps to a uniform format for publication as a book. The first edition (1570) of *Theatrum orbis terrarum* consisted of seventy maps on fifty-three sheets with accompanying texts. Whenever possible Ortelius mentions the name of the original author of the maps and cites other sources that he used. He prefixed to the atlas a list of the cartographers known to him and itemized their works which had come to his attention. In short, he produced an encyclopedia of cartography that was to become the model for the numerous "Theaters of the World" produced in the following century.

The *Theatrum* was an immediate scholarly and financial success. Over the last third of the sixteenth century twenty-five separate printings were issued: twelve in Latin, four each in German and French, three in Dutch, and two in Spanish.[115] Five of these were completely new editions called *Additamenta*. In the later editions the number of maps grew steadily from 70 to 101 and the list of cartographers was extended from 87 to 183. The first edition included a general map of Asia (map 3), and separate maps of Tartary (47) and the East Indian archipelago (48). The map of Asia was thoroughly revised for the edition of 1579 and a separate of China (97) was inserted into the *Additamenta* of 1584 between Tartary and the East Indies. Five years later a map of the Pacific Ocean was added, and in 1595 a separate of the Japanese islands.[116] Beginning in 1579

---

[112] For his biography see C. Koeman, *The History of Abraham Ortelius and His Theatrum Orbis Terrarum* (Lausanne, 1964); and the same author's bibliographical work, *Atlantes Neerlandica* (5 vols.; Amsterdam, 1969), III, 25–27.

[113] See J. H. Hessels (ed.), *op. cit.* (n. 87), p. 24.

[114] See above, p. 462.

[115] Based on the table of editions in Koeman, *Atlantes Neerlandica* (n. 112), III, 31. The first edition in English appeared only in 1606.

[116] Based on analysis in *ibid.*, pp. 34–68.

he introduced a new section of historical maps called the *Parergon*. These maps of ancient geography were primarily of his own creation and there were 38 of them by 1598, the year of his death.[117] In 1577 the engraver Philippe Galle and his associates began producing pocket atlases or "Epitomes" of the *Theatrum* in the vernacular. Their epitomized maps were crude, but the pocket atlases were a great commercial success.[118]

Ortelius' personal fame rose with the popularity of the *Theatrum*. In 1573 the duke of Alba, acting on behalf of King Philip II, presented him with a royal diploma naming him "Geographer of His Majesty." But Ortelius was not to enjoy the rewards of his work. When the "Spanish Fury" struck Antwerp in 1576, he fled to England. He returned a year or so later to the quiet city of Liége, his native place. Beginning with the edition of 1579 Plantin took over the technical responsibility of publishing the *Theatrum*, and Ortelius was thereafter able to devote himself to a study of ancient archaeology and numismatics while continuing to revise and amplify the atlas. From 1581 to the end of his life he lived in Antwerp where he spent his time adding to his museum, receiving visitors, and carrying on an extensive correspondence.

Mercator and Ortelius remained friends and regularly wrote letters in which they exchanged information relating to geography and cartography. The Spanish prelate and royal adviser Benito Arias Montano was one of Ortelius' most ardent admirers and regular informants. He had originally arranged for Ortelius' appointment as royal geographer. In his travels about Europe he often sent news to Ortelius about the globes and maps he saw in distant places, arranging in some cases for copies or descriptions to be sent to Antwerp.[119] Ortelius reciprocated by sending his own works and other geographical materials to Spain[120] and acted as an intermediary when Arias Montano sent books and specimens to Clusius.[121] Ortelius also corresponded with other cartographers, Ignazio Danti in Rome and Luís Teixeira in Lisbon.[122] From England he received letters relating to the rising British determination to challenge the overseas monopoly of Philip II.[123] He corresponded with Paludanus of Enkhuizen about Dutch hopes for a northeast passage to China and encouraged the navigational and publication activities of J. H. van Linschoten (see pls. 72, 73).[124]

Dutch interest in the cartography of the East received a sharp stimulus when the United Provinces, still technically in revolt against Spain, decided to open direct and independent maritime relations with the Spiceries. Linschoten, who

[117] See *ibid.*, p. 69.

[118] See *ibid.*, p. 71.

[119] See especially his letter to Ortelius from Rome, February 28, 1576, in Hessels (ed.), *op. cit.* (n. 87), p. 141.

[120] See *ibid.*, p. 471.

[121] *Ibid.*, pp. 498–99, 684–85. On Clusius see above, pp. 439–41.

[122] *Ibid.*, pp. 242, 505–6.

[123] See especially the letter of Emanuel van Meteren, of November, 1592, itemizing the booty obtained from the capture of the Spanish carrack, "Madre de Dios," *ibid.*, p. 541.

[124] *Ibid.*, pp. 677–78, 705, 911. See pls. 72, 73.

had spent five years (1583–88) in the Portuguese service at Goa, returned to Enkhuizen in 1592 with sailing directions, rutters, and maps of the East prepared in Portugal. Dirck Gerritz and other Dutch sailors returned from the East with additional data on navigation and geography. Cornelis and Frederick de Houtman were sent to Lisbon in 1592 where they were able to obtain copies of twenty-five nautical charts prepared by the Portuguese cartographer Bartolomeu Lasso (*fl.* 1575–90). The Estates General of Holland then ordered that the Lasso maps should be printed and that a standard map of the world should be constructed on which future discoveries might be recorded.[125] Petrus Plancius (1552–1622), the Reformed theologian and cartographer, prepared such a world map in 1592. He also constructed a separate map of the Moluccas. These were published in Amsterdam by Cornelis Claesz between 1592 and 1594 in time for the first Dutch voyages to the East by the Cape route.[126]

The Dutch had long been exploring the possibility of sailing directly to the Spiceries and China via a northern passage. They had been assured by Gemma, Mercator, and other eminent cartographers that such a passage would be shorter and easier than the southern routes, especially the one by way of the northeast. But the Amsterdam merchants led by Plancius, a preacher turned promoter, finally gave up this hopeless project. They then began to organize themselves and their fleets for a direct attack upon the Iberian monopoly. Plancius, like Hakluyt in England, saw an opportunity for his countrymen to supplant the Portuguese in the East Indies. And he carried over his boldness to cartography. His large world map of 1592 in eighteen sheets was based upon Mercator's world map of 1569 and a manuscript map of the Portuguese cartographer Pedro de Lemos. But Plancius cavalierly abandoned Mercator's projection in favor of the simple cylindrical projection of Lemos' map.[127] Contemporaries connected with the trading voyages evidently favored the Portuguese projection for it continued to be popular in England and Holland until well into the seventeenth century. Plancius' map was apparently used as the standard by pilots and navigators, thus making it comparable to the *padrão* of the *Casa* in Lisbon. But the more scientific Dutch geographers—Jodocus Hondius (1563–1612) and William J. Blaeu (1571–1638)—continued to follow the Mercator tradition.

The English, like the Dutch, dreamed throughout most of the sixteenth century about sailing to wealthy Cathay and the fabulous Spiceries through a northern passage.[128] Before 1550 only a few Englishmen knew anything about world geography (see pl. 60). In *The Cosmographical Glasse* (1559) William

---

[125] See R. Bonaparte, "Les premiers voyages des Neerlandais dans l'Insulinde, 1595–1602," *Revue de géographie*, XIV (1884), Pt. 1, 448.

[126] The engravings were done by Jan à Deutecum. For a clear reproduction of the surviving Molucca map see A. de Smet, *La cartographie hollandaise* (Brussels, 1971), p. 27, pl. III. On Plancius' career see J. Keuning, *Petrus Plancius, theolog en geograaf* (Amsterdam, 1946).

[127] See Crone, *op. cit.* (n. 6), pp. 124–25. Also see Keuning, "Sixteenth Century Cartography in the Netherlands" (n. 92), pp. 59–60.

[128] See above, pp. 368–70; also see E. G. R. Taylor, *Tudor Geography 1495–1583* (London, 1930), chap. 1.

Cunningham divides geography from cosmography but without providing the reader with any satisfying geographical sustenance. The learned John Dee (1527–1608) was the first of his countrymen to undertake the study of scientific geography. When but twenty years of age, Dee enrolled at the University of Louvain and remained there from 1547 to 1550. Here he studied navigation and other geographically related subjects with Gemma Frisius and struck up a close friendship with Mercator. The probability is that he first became acquainted with Ortelius while visiting Antwerp in 1550. On his way back to England in that year he stopped in Paris where he encountered Finé and Postel.[129] In his baggage he carried the cosmographical books and the world map of his teacher, the gores for a globe, and cartographic instruments. Gemma's views, inherited both by Mercator and Dee, of the feasibility of polar passages to Cathay lent the weighty support of Charles V's cosmographer to the case of those in England who had long been pressing for northern voyages.[130]

Dee himself had an urgent desire to see the way to Cathay opened. An amateur of magic, alchemy, and Hermeticism, he firmly believed the ancient tradition that the East was the home of the most advanced adepts in the occult arts. In his eagerness to penetrate the secrets of the universe, Dee continued, after his return to England, to correspond with his friends abroad and to study the latest of their works on nautical science and cosmography. He established a friendship by correspondence with Pedro Nunes, the mathematician and cosmographer of Coimbra who had earlier published a number of practical manuals on the sphere. He cultivated figures close to the court and worked with Richard Chancellor, the practical seaman and navigator. Through Chancellor, he probably came to know Sebastian Cabot, the navigator, and Richard Eden, the collector of travel literature.

The Marian period (1553–59), when Eden became prominent through his publications,[131] was an epoch of difficulty for Dee. Chancellor died in 1556, and this was followed for a period by the practical abandonment of the search for Cathay. Dee himself was suspected of heresy by a Catholic government which had about as much sympathy for his religious ideas as the Catholic Church had for Postel's.[132] Dee unavailingly addressed a supplication to Queen Mary to save and recover the ancient writers and the monuments that had been dispersed in Henry's time, for "many of them in the unlearned mens hande, do still yet (in this tyme of Reconciliation) daily perish."[133] The advent of Queen Elizabeth quickly brought a change in Dee's fortunes and influence. Between 1562 and 1564 he traveled on the Continent again. From Antwerp he went to Zurich, Urbino, Rome, and as far east as Pressburg in Hungary. He met in his peregrinations many new persons of high social station as well as fellow intellectuals.

---

[129] Based on P. J. French, *John Dee: The World of an Elizabethan Magus* (London, 1972), pp. 28–32.
[130] See Taylor, *op. cit.* (n. 128), pp. 77–83.
[131] On these publications see *Asia*, I, 209–11.
[132] On Postel see above, pp. 268–69.
[133] Ms. Ashmolean, 1788, p. 5.

Through their common interest in the occult, he learned to know the leading Habsburg princes of the day. On his return to England in 1564, Dee settled down at Mortlake where he lived for the next two decades. Here he housed his collections and library, as Mortlake became a veritable academy for the study of navigation and geography.[134]

Both English and foreign visitors descended upon Dee, and Dee opened his library and his mind to them. The Elizabethan public became absorbed again after 1566 with renewed efforts to find a northern route to Cathay. The maps of Mercator and Ortelius were then selling at London in quantity.[135] Daniel Rogers, the diplomat and antiquary, probably brought his uncle, Abraham Ortelius, to Mortlake in the spring of 1577. Adrian and Humphrey Gilbert, half-brothers to Sir Walter Raleigh, were often Dee's guests. In 1581 "yong Mr. [John] Hawkings, who had byn with Sir Francis Drake" appeared at Mortlake.[136] John Leonard Hall of Worms spent the summer of this year with Dee learning the variation of the compass preparatory to an overland journey to "Quinsay" (Hangchow) that he was presumably making at Dee's suggestion.[137] Sir Francis Walsingham and Sir Edward Dyer, particularly the latter, consulted Dee on navigational matters.[138] At Mortlake Sir Philip Sidney pored over maps in his efforts to follow the voyages of Frobisher. Sidney was a close student of the voyages and of natural history; Hakluyt dedicated his *Divers Voyages* (1582) to Sidney.[139]

Dee, while entertaining and instructing his visitors, was also an active propagandist for the scientific study of geography. In a preface to the English translation (1570) of Euclid, Dee made a strong case for the study of mathematics as an essential tool in the learning of surveying, navigation, hydrography, and cosmography.[140] Dee and Dyer, despite all setbacks, continued to urge more exploration, particularly of the northern routes to Cathay. They avidly sought information from all sources and Dyer patronized John Frampton and his translations of Spanish materials on Asia.[141] In the spring and summer of 1577 Dee hastily prepared a book which was designed to point up how easily Englishmen, if only they would work together, could tap the fabled wealth of Cathay and the riches of Ophir besides.

Dee's *Famous and Rich Discoveries* was never published, and there remains today only a badly mutilated copy of it.[142] While this book is full of contem-

---

[134] On his library see above, pp. 69–70.

[135] See Taylor, *op. cit.* (n. 128), p. 99.

[136] J. O. Halliwell (ed.), *The Private Diary of John Dee and the Catalogue of His Library of Manuscripts* (London, 1842), p. 11.

[137] See *ibid.*, pp. 11, 17.

[138] See French, *op. cit.* (n. 129), p. 62.

[139] See W. A. Ringler, Jr. (ed.), *The Poems of Sir Philip Sidney* (Oxford, 1962), p. xxvii. Clusius dedicated his translation (1581) of Monardes to Sidney.

[140] See Taylor, *op. cit.* (n. 128), pp. 103–5.

[141] Consult *ibid.*, pp. 11, 17.

[142] Brit. Mus., Vitellius, C. vii, Cotton Mss. For its table of contents see Ms. Ashmolean, 1788. For a few quotations from the remaining manuscript see Taylor, *op. cit.* (n. 128), pp. 114–17.

porary information and misinformation it may safely be concluded that Dee was trying to advise those in government and elsewhere who were planning Drake's circumnavigation as to what the expedition should look for in the Pacific region. In its opening chapters he ordains that Solomon's navy had found the land of Ophir in the Pacific beyond New Guinea and to the south of the East Indies in the great Southern Continent. Presumably Drake would be wise to look for it. Since Dee himself hoped to take an overland voyage to Cathay, or to instruct others on how best to do it, this book contains numerous chapters on the interior reaches of Asia and of the maritime East based on the ancient writers and Marco Polo. He was evidently inspired by references in Polo to posit the great southern land "rich in gold" which he identifies with the biblical land of Ophir.[143] Dee, like Mercator, remained convinced that Cathay itself could be most easily reached by a northeastern passage. The failure of the northern voyages, as well as his personal concern to find the philosophers' stone, led Dee to abandon geographical studies in 1583. His library and laboratory were shortly afterwards destroyed by an outraged mob who believed that Dee had been holding communion with evil spirits.[144]

Dee's motives for studying geography and encouraging navigation and exploration were closely related to his philosophical and religious beliefs. He might be called "the English Postel," for Dee was fundamentally much more inspired by ideas of *Concordia mundi* than by the establishment of new trade routes. He was fascinated by the occult and he thought of Asia as the source and repository of mystical knowledge. Wisdom, true faith, and material wealth were all to be found in his Orient. Mathematics and cosmography were the keys by which men are enabled to unlock its secrets. An eager collector of data, Dee was inclined to use it primarily to substantiate his personal cosmic beliefs. The Bible he accepts literally as a book of divine wisdom; so he seeks to reconstruct Solomon's voyages to Ophir by reference to the latest navigational and geographical data available. He was never greatly interested in the idea of establishing plantations in America; the new continents were but obstacles on the sea road to Asia. In his formula for world concord he posited an "incomparable Brytish Impire" that would bring to the world a common religion and eternal political harmony. His queen, like Postel's French king, would employ the material wealth of Cathay and Ophir and the wisdom of the Orient to give reality to his apocalyptic vision.[145]

Dee's younger contemporaries, like the mob at Mortlake, were disturbed by his vision and more dedicated to winning immediate practical goals. The dream of empire for them was limited to the establishment of Britain as a real contender in the race for overseas trade and colonies. Richard Willes, the continuator of Eden, quoted approvingly Ptolemy's dictum that "the first principle and

---

[143] On Sir Walter Raleigh and Ophir see above, p. 386.

[144] On his last years at Mortlake see Taylor, *op. cit.* (n. 128), chap. vii.

[145] Based on the analysis in French, *op. cit.* (n. 129), pp. 180–82, 195. For Postel's ideas see above, pp. 268–69.

chiefe grounde in all geographie . . . is the historie of travel." [146] This idea was reiterated by Richard Hakluyt the younger, who elevated it to an axiom for later Elizabethan geographical study. For both Willes and Hakluyt the modern study of geography began with the discoveries of the Portuguese and the reports about them. "Through the discovery of the fare Indies, the Moluccaes and new founde landes, of late to be wondered at, as no other faculty more, I dare to be bold to say, that generally all Christians, Jewes, Turkes, Moores, Infidels, and Barbares be this day in love with Geographie." [147]

While this was certainly a rhetorical exaggeration, Willes here reflects the enthusiasm of many of his contemporaries for overseas navigation and the study of the earth. Others were similarly inspired by Drake's circumnavigation (1580) and the defeat of the Spanish Armada (1588). The "Epistle Dedicatorie" to the first edition (1589) of *The principale navigations* tells in Hakluyt's own words about his hopes for the overseas world. But Hakluyt had no time for theoretical geography or the manufacture of maps and globes. He illustrated his works with the maps of others. He dismisses cosmography as "those wearie volumes . . . most truly and unprofitablie ramassed and hurled together." Few statements appear in his work that relate to causation or to other concerns of scientific geography. He comments on the monsoons and on the advantage of islands as bases and other matters primarily of practical concern to mariners, explorers, and traders. His aim is to convince his contemporaries of the feasibility and necessity of embarking upon a systematic program of navigation, exploration, colonization, and trade. [148] To help in implementing this program he compiled, translated (or had translated), and published (or had published) the most important travel accounts available. [149]

By his zeal in publication Hakluyt provided others with the raw materials for geographical analysis and generalization. English cartography was spurred at the same time by the presence in London from 1583 to 1593 of Jodocus Hondius, the Flemish cartographer and engraver. He engraved in 1592, and possibly provided help in the construction of, the first English globes that were prepared by Hakluyt's friend Emery Molyneux, a Lambeth mathematician. They recorded England's overseas activities, including the circumnavigations of Drake and Cavendish. [150] New conclusions about the world's hydrography were possibly derived therefrom, including John Davy's assertion of 1595 about the Pacific: "America is further separated from Asia, then from any the sea coastes either of Europe or Africa." [151] In *A Briefe Description of the Whole World*

[146] From *The History of Traveyle* (London, 1577), p. iv^r. On this collection of travel literature see *Asia*, I, 211–12.

[147] See *ibid.*, p. iii^v.

[148] Based on G. R. Crone, "Richard Hakluyt, Geographer," in D. B. Quinn (ed.), *The Hakluyt Handbook* (2 vols.; London, 1974), I, 8–14, and R. A. Skelton, "Hakluyt's Maps," *ibid.*, pp. 48–69.

[149] See F. M. Rogers, "Hakluyt as Translator," *ibid.*, pp. 37–47, and D. B. Quinn *et al.*, "The Primary Hakluyt Bibliography," *ibid.*, II, 461–97.

[150] See H. Wallis, *loc. cit.* (n. 18), p. 205.

[151] *The Worldes Hydrographical Description* . . . (London, 1595), unpaginated. Cf. pl. 80.

(1599) George Abbot, the learned Archbishop of Canterbury, incorporated whatever he could learn about the places and peoples of East Asia from the recent Iberian sources.[152] The world chart added to Hakluyt's *Navigations* of 1599 was constructed in England, probably by Edward Wright.[153] The following year Hakluyt also published information on China derived from the large Chinese map brought back by Cavendish in 1588 along with notes on the eastern navigation "such as hath not bene heard of in these parts."[154] But it was not until after 1600 that a world atlas would be published in England or even in the English language.

The production of atlases implies the existence of a brisk map trade, competent engravers, and an entrepreneurial printing industry. In England the importation of maps and geographical works was sporadic and the collections few.[155] The printers and engravers of London were also relatively few and much less skilled than those who flourished in the great Continental printing centers. The booksellers of the Continent sold the English their publications, but they bought almost no books or maps from England. Map preparation and printing, as well as most other forms of geographical publishing, remained a Continental monopoly until the last decade of the sixteenth century.

3

ATLASES, PATRONAGE, AND GEOGRAPHICAL LEARNING

The world atlas, as it evolved in the sixteenth century, derived directly from the twenty-seven maps of Ptolemy's *Geography*. The "modern maps" added over the course of the sixteenth century were essentially little more than revisions of the Ptolemaic portfolio provided by contemporary geographical knowledge. It was mainly in the printing shops that the idea for a new atlas began to take shape. Francesco Rosselli (*ca.* 1445–*ca.* 1513), the Florentine map engraver and printer, was the first publisher on record to specialize in the selling of maps. He and his fellow Italian map dealers sold separates of everything from town plans to world charts, some of their own devising.[156] About 1533 Antonio Lafreri and Antonio Salamanca began to sell their prints and maps in Rome. They also acquired maps from abroad which they copied and sold, sometimes without

---

[152] Pp. C1–C2, G3.

[153] See H. Wallis, "Edward Wright and the 1599 World Map," in D. B. Quinn *et al., op. cit.* (n. 149), I, 69–73.

[154] As quoted in Skelton, *Explorers' Maps* (n. 3), p. 165.

[155] See Taylor, *op. cit.* (n. 128), p. 25.

[156] See R. Almagià, "On the Cartographic Work of Francesco Rosselli," *Imago mundi*, VIII (1951), 27–52. For the inventory of Rosselli's shop see A. M. Hind, *Early Italian Engraving* (7 vols.; London, 1938–48), I, Pt. 1, 304–9.

credit to the cartographer.[157] Lafreri and his associates also sold collections of maps to their customers, and in 1570 they engraved a special title page for them showing Atlas, the Greek god, standing with the universe on his shoulders.[158] These collections, arranged in Ptolemy's order, differ from modern atlases in that they were not standardized in terms of contents or size.

The commerce in maps during the first half of the century was most highly developed at Venice. But Venice's period of greatest cartographic originality and influence came only at mid-century when Gastaldi reached his apogee. This great cartographer is credited with producing 109 separate maps, including 2 world maps and a separate of Asia. Before 1570 his works were put together as an atlas.[159] At Rome, Ignazio Danti and his associates were shortly going to paint their murals in the Vatican and in so doing create a veritable atlas of wall maps.[160]

Separate maps were sold by book dealers in northern Europe too. Hieronymous Gourmont of Paris produced a catalog of his offerings as early as 1536.[161] Every March and September throughout the century maps were put on sale at the Frankfurt book fair. Georg Willer, the leading book dealer of Augsburg, listed for sale in 1573 a host of Venetian sheet maps including Gastaldi's world map in two different editions and Camocio's map of Asia.[162] Other great wholesalers from Antwerp, Cologne, and Nuremberg attended the Frankfurt fair to buy and sell maps as well as books. Plantin's records indicate that he exported maps, atlases, and globes to retailers in the Netherlands, France, England, Germany, Spain, and Italy. Mercator and Ortelius themselves were frequent visitors to the fair to augment their collections and to oversee the sale of their own maps.[163]

In northern Europe the vogue for composite works, especially the cosmographies, probably contributed to the idea of the atlas. Mercator, the first of the northern cartographers to plan an atlas, was certainly delayed in his efforts to complete the maps by his preoccupation with cosmography. Ortelius was successful in completing the *Theatrum* because he was content merely to assemble, reduce to a uniform size, engrave, and publish the best available maps. With the publication of the *Theatrum* (1570) the Ptolemaic atlas was separated completely from the modern atlas; Ortelius even began in 1579 to add a historical atlas (the *Parergon*) of his own creation to the revisions of his compendium. Others were quick to produce competing atlases, and more specialized collec-

---

[157] Salamanca faithfully copied Mercator's world map (1538) except for the name; some issues of it carry Lafreri's name. See R. Almagià, "La diffusion des produits cartographiques flamand en Italie au XVIᵉ siècle," *Archives internationales d'histoire des sciences*, XXXIII (1954), 46–48; also see R. Tooley, "Maps in Italian Atlases of the Sixteenth Century," *Imago mundi*, III (1939), 12.

[158] See Bagrow-Skelton, *op. cit.* (n. 15), pp. 138–39, 179.

[159] See Tooley, *loc. cit.* (n. 157), pp. 16–47.

[160] See above, pp. 463–64.

[161] Consult Bagrow-Skelton, *op. cit.* (n. 15), p. 247.

[162] See L. Bagrow, "A Page from the History of the Distribution of Maps," *Imago mundi*, V (1948), 57–59.

[163] See Bagrow-Skelton, *op. cit.* (n. 15), p. 45.

tions of maps. Gerard de Jode in 1578 published a two-volume world atlas of eighty-four maps on sixty-five sheets (cf. pls. 74, 75). Matthias Quad, a Cologne engraver, published in 1600 a geographical handbook with maps of the overseas world derived from Ortelius' works (see pl. 81). The famous atlas of cities (produced between 1572 and 1617) was a direct imitation in title and form of the *Theatrum* of Ortelius.[164] A Cologne publisher produced small, specialized atlases, including a separate one on Asia (1600).[165]

While the public at large bought sheet maps and atlases in quantity, the high-born and wealthy assembled decorative maps for their collections. The Este rulers of Ferrara, whose geographical interests are well known, collected printed and manuscript maps, one of the most important being the Cantino map of 1502. Most of the great book collectors were also connoisseurs of maps and globes.[166] In explaining the craze for map collecting, John Dee wrote in 1570:

Some to beautify their Halls, Parlers, Chambers, Galeries, Studies, or Libraries with; other some, for things past, as battles fought, earthquakes, heavenly firings, and such occurrences in histories mentioned: thereby lively as it were to view the place, the region adjoining, the distance from us, and such other circumstances: some other, presently to view the large dominion of the Turk: the wide Empire of the Muscovite: and the little morcel of ground where Christiandom (by profession) is certainly known little I say in respect of the rest, etc.: some other for their own journeys directing into far lands, or to understand other mens travels . . . liketh, loveth, getteth and useth Maps, Charts, and Geographical Globes.[167]

King Philip II of Spain must have felt similarly, for he had his agents constantly on the lookout in Venice and Antwerp for maps to add to his collection.[168] Lesser lights too, like Viglius de Ziuchem, president of the Privy Council of Louvain, possessed an impressive collection of printed and manuscript maps.[169]

Maps and globes were more than mere decorative objects to the collectors of all social and economic levels. Increasingly over the century they were used as aids to historical and contemporary studies. The newly rising national state of the Renaissance encouraged the collection of cartographical and geographical materials and the preparation of other technical instruments and books essential to navigation. In Portugal, Spain, and the Low Countries the state extended its patronage and control to cartography. The kings of Portugal in the fifteenth century had looked to Italy for maps and other aids to navigation.[170] Even before 1500 a royal hydrographic office was created at Lisbon charged with the responsibility for the custody and correction of the sea charts and for the maintenance

---

[164] Georg Braun and Franz Hogenberg, *Civitates orbis terrarum* . . . (6 vols. in 3; Cleveland, 1966).

[165] See Bagrow-Skelton, *op. cit.* (n. 15), p. 186.

[166] On book collectors see above, pp. 71–73.

[167] From *The Elements of Geometrie* . . . (London, 1570), as quoted in Skelton, *Maps: A Historical Survey* (n. 9), pp. 27–8.

[168] See Skelton, *Decorative Printed Maps* (n. 10), p. 27.

[169] See the map inventory dated 1575 reprinted in Anon., "Old Inventories of Maps," *Imago mundi*, V (1948), 18–20.

[170] See Crone, *op. cit.* (n. 6), pp. 54–64.

of the standard map.[171] A similar organization existed at Seville after 1508.[172] A chair of geography and navigation was established at Seville in 1552 whose incumbent gave courses to candidates for a pilot's license. At the end of the century the Dutch created a state-supported mercantile organization that eventually became the Dutch East India Company (1600); the British were but two years in following suit.

Elsewhere in Europe geography and cartography relied upon the sporadic patronage of rulers, governments, and the church. The papacy lent its encouragement and financial support to the revision of Ptolemy produced at Rome in 1507–8.[173] Duke René II of Lorraine was meanwhile sponsoring the activities of Waldseemüller and his associates at St. Dié and Strassburg. In Nuremberg the city government encouraged the making of instruments and globes. Tensions between Portugal and Spain over the ownership of the Moluccas brought more state patronage and control to geography. Diogo Ribeiro, the Portuguese refugee, was appointed royal cosmographer in 1523 by order of Charles V and served Spain as a cartographic expert in the international discussions over the location of the Spiceries.[174] Other Portuguese cartographers entered the service of the French kings.[175] The office of cosmographer or geographer of the king came into being in France in 1560.[176] At Venice the Council of Ten contracted in 1553 to have new wall maps prepared for the ducal palace. Cosimo de' Medici and two popes employed Ignazio Danti to decorate their palaces with wall maps. Ortelius was appointed royal geographer to Philip II in 1573. In England John Dee's activities were followed closely by court circles and the queen. Both Dee and Hakluyt contributed heavily to the queen's growing interest in challenging Spain and in setting England upon a new course in overseas exploration and trade. Geography was certainly in the service of the state in most western European countries by the end of the century.

Popular education in geography advanced swiftly in the latter half of the century through the huge production of printed maps, atlases, cosmographies, and travel collections. But geography as an academic discipline distinct from cosmography was far from being universally established. At the dawn of the sixteenth century the major text required for student reading was the thirteenth-century treatise of Sacrobosco entitled *De sphaera*. It is a lucid but brief exposition of the Ptolemaic analysis of the material universe, both celestial and terrestrial. While it did not contain ignorant nonsense about the people of the antipodes standing on their heads, it preserved the Aristotelian and Ptolemaic illusions of

[171] For the few details available on the Portuguese offices see J. Denucé, *Les origines de la cartographie portugaise* . . . (Ghent, 1908), pp. 1–6.

[172] See Cortesão and Teixeira da Mota, *op. cit.* (n. 17), I, 90.

[173] Johannes Ruysch, for example, was employed in the papal palace while he prepared his famous world map. See Keuning, "Sixteenth-Century Cartography" (n. 127), p. 38. Also see W. Roscoe, *The Life and Pontificate of Leo X* (4 vols.; London, 1827), II, 257.

[174] See Cortesão and Teixeira da Mota, *op. cit.* (n. 17), I, 87–88. See pl. 67.

[175] On Bartholomeu Velho see *ibid.*, II, 89–92.

[176] Thevet was the first appointee. For a list of the "geographes du roi" see *Bulletin de la société géographique d'Anvers*, I (1877), 477–84.

the relative proximity of the coasts of Europe and Asia; that is, the elongated Eurasiatic continent. The recovery of Ptolemy's *Geography* in the fifteenth century reinforced the assertions of Sacrobosco about the earth. Since the authority of the ancient writers went almost unquestioned in Renaissance universities and academies, the intellectuals were particularly slow to grasp how revolutionary the overseas voyages were for cartography and geography. Sacred geography in its preoccupation with the Holy Land and the pilgrim literature did nothing to shake the supreme confidence generally felt about the conclusions of the Greeks and the Romans.

The Germans were less inclined than others to accept uncritically the prevailing geographical dogma. In the fifteenth century Regiomontanus and his associates at Nuremberg began to question Ptolemy's authority in both astronomy and geography. It was perhaps as a reaction to the mathematical orientation of the Nuremberg school that a few descriptive geographers were led to talk about geography as something independent of mathematics and cosmography. Conrad Celtis (1459–1508), the classicist, taught geography at Vienna with the visual aids of globes and ancient maps. He, like many Viennese geographers, was more concerned with chorography, or regional mapping and description, than with faraway places. The Wittenberg professor Bartel Stein (1476–1522) specifically asserted that he did not want to teach cosmography since it involved training in mathematics and astronomy. He preferred to teach "the conditions of the inhabited regions of the earth, or geography as the Greeks called it." [177] In his lectures he stressed the value of geographical knowledge for understanding the physical relationships of one people to the other, for finding the shortest routes for commercial and military movements, and for following the peregrinations in the *Aeneid*. Like Celtis, he based most of his interpretations upon the *De situ orbis* (1471) of Pomponius Mela (*fl. ca.* A.D. 50) and paid no attention to newer information (see pl. 55). Others were forthrightly hostile to the study of geography. In his *Vanity* (1530), H. C. Agrippa van Netterheim (1486–1535) wrote:

Now this Art that undertakes to teach us to Describe and Measure so large a World, such unsearchable Seas, and discover to us the Scituation of all Islands and Regions, Bounds, and Remarkable Places; together with the Originals, Customs, Manners, and different Dispositions of innumerable Nations, what fruit doth it further yield us? but Only that it makes us covetous to pry into the Concernments of other people while we forget ourselves. [178]

By contrast, his contemporary Apian did all he could to encourage the study of geography (see pl. 59). He was also among the first of the academic commentators to prefer the contemporary writers to the ancient authorities when their testimonies conflicted. Pirckheimer went one step further when he advocated teaching geography in the secondary schools from both classical and

---

[177] As quoted in H. Beck, *Geographie* (Munich, 1973), p. 105.
[178] *The Vanity of Arts and Sciences* (London, 1684), pp. 76–77. Also see above, p. 423.

contemporary sources. By this time, however, the Reformation was turning German attention away from geographical studies.

Gemma Frisius, a follower of Apian, began to teach scientific geography at Louvain in 1525. He, like most Netherlandish geographers, was less interested in land survey than the Germans and more concerned with navigation and the ancillary sciences of hydrography and cartography. The most influential of Gemma's students were Mercator, Jacob van Deventer, and John Dee. Though Mercator was mainly an independent cartographer, he taught mathematics, cosmography, and geography at the Latin school of Duisburg for four years. Dee, on his return to England in 1551 with maps and globes, probably stimulated the study of cosmography at Cambridge and perhaps inspired William Cunningham's *The Cosmographical Glasse* (1559), the first original work on the subject in English.[179] On the Continent meanwhile the editions of Münster kept rolling off the press in large numbers. His associate, Achilles P. Gasser (1505–77) of Augsburg, collected a library of historical, geographical, and medical books which his neighbors were free to consult.[180] Apian and Frisius, and Cunningham following them, were beginning at mid-century to write of geography as a branch of learning differing from cosmography by making the description of the earth its exclusive object.[181]

A fundamental impetus was given to geographical learning and cartography by the activities and publications of the Jesuits. From its inception at the Collège of Sainte-Barbe in Paris, the Society of Jesus was connected with the Portuguese expansion in the East. The first Jesuits to travel in Asia were overwhelmed by the vast distances separating one place from the other and by the difficulties of communication. Xavier urged that geographical reconnaissances should be undertaken to determine the shortest routes. At Coimbra technical courses in mathematics and geography were taught by Portuguese cosmographers to the Jesuits being prepared for foreign missions.[182] The letters from missionaries in the field were required reading in the Jesuit colleges and the students often wrote themes or orations on subjects inspired by the epistles from the East. The students of rhetoric at the Roman college, founded in 1551, were assigned as homework the task of translating the Jesuit letters into Latin.[183] Following the pattern prevailing in the secular Italian universities, the Jesuits taught geography as part of mathematics. Cristoforo Clavius (1538–1612), the teacher of Matteo Ricci, was trained in the German mathematical tradition and was a leading figure in reforming the calendar.[184] He taught mathematical cartography and the manufacture of scientific instruments at Rome from 1551 to his death. This

---

[179] See Taylor, *op. cit.* (n. 128), p. 26; and above, p. 370.

[180] Many books from his valuable library are still preserved in the Vatican library. See K. H. Burmeister, "Achilles Pirmin Gasser (1505–77) as Geographer and Cartographer," *Imago mundi*, XXIV (1970), 57–62. On the publication of Münster see above, pp. 339–41.

[181] For a fuller comment see Dainville, *Le Langage* (n. 1), pp. 1–2.

[182] *Ibid.*, pp. 106–7.

[183] *Ibid.*, pp. 134–35.

[184] See above, p. 414.

type of practical curriculum was generally followed also at the Jesuit colleges of
Coimbra, Ingolstadt, Vienna, Cologne, and Würzburg.[185]

The students of the Jesuit schools in France were expected to own and read
works on the missions. An examination of the personal effects of entrants to the
College of Toulouse from 1574 to 1587 reveals that most of the students possessed copies of Jesuit letterbooks and Maffei's history of Jesuit activities in the
East.[186] Both these books are also listed in Michel Coyssard's *Mémoire* on
the spiritual and worldly books that students should own and read often. The
question remains how these readings affected the teaching and study of geography. In some French colleges geography was taught by having the teachers
read contemporary materials into dictations (*dictées*) based on the work of
Pomponius Mela (pl. 55). An examination of five notebooks (*cahiers*) dictated
at the famous college of Clermont in Paris between 1584 and 1588 reveals that
the three young teachers there amended their comments on Pomponius Mela
with references to the works of A. Schott on Spain and of Osório on Portugal
and its empire in the East.[187] Fronton du Duc, one of the young teachers, was
possibly inspired by the presence in 1584–85 of the Japanese legates in Europe
to dictate an exercise on Japan, probably based on his own reading of the Jesuit
letters:

The writings of the Moderns also extol, to the East, the [country of] Japan about which
Paul the Venetian [Marco Polo] has related so many things. But assuredly, some Moderns
have imprudently applied to Japan what he said about Zipangu, what he relates of Gotoo
[Buddha?] and Goxo [ruling shōguns] matters which we have found to be completely
otherwise in Japan, which is not one single island but includes three principal islands. In
the first is located the city of Meaco [Miyako], whose king Nobunanga [Oda Nobunaga]
rules over many other kingdoms. The second is called Ximo [Kyushu]; the third Xicocu
[Shikoku]. Herein there are numerous kingdoms which, by virtue of the diverse kinds
of continuous wars that convulse these regions, fall into the hands of whatever princes
are most powerful.[188]

The other two instructors of Clermont discoursed similarly on Vasco da Gama's
voyage to India and on the geography of China. In the meanwhile commentaries
and syllabuses on cosmography and geography were being prepared at Coimbra
by order of the Jesuit General so that the professors might not be tempted to
teach a geography of their individual invention.[189] The Coimbra publication
was quickly translated into French by Father Louis Richeome; the geographical
curriculum in the French colleges thereafter became more mathematical and
less rhetorical.

[185] *Ibid.*, pp. 38–41.
[186] See F. de Dainville, "Libraires d'écoliers toulousains à la fin du XVIe siècle," *Bibliothèque
d'humanisme et renaissance*, IX (1947), 138–39.
[187] See F. de Dainville, "Les découvertes portugaises à travers des cahiers d'écoliers parisiens . . .,"
in Mollat and Adam, *Les aspects internationaux* (n. 17), pp. 39–41.
[188] *Ibid.*, p. 42. For the identification of "Gotoo" as Buddha, or the five Buddhas (*Go-chi*) of the
Shingon sect, see *Asia*, I, 662 n.
[189] See F. de Dainville, *La géographie des Humanistes* (n. 71), pp. 25–26.

Richard Willes, the onetime Jesuit, returned around 1573 to Elizabethan England in "love with geographie." He soon found a sponsor in the countess of Bedford through whom he was introduced to a circle ardently interested in geography and exploration. In his student days at Winchester and Oxford Willes had studied the maps in the cosmographies of Johannes Honter (1498– 1549) and Münster.[190] Training in geography was certainly a part of his education at Louvain, where he prepared for entering the Society of Jesus. Like the novices of Toulouse, at Louvain he probably had to study the Jesuit books on the missions. Later in Italy he became personally acquainted with Maffei, the historian of the missions in Asia. His most complete comment on the state of geographical studies in England is found in the dedication, addressed to the countess of Bedford, of *The History of Travelye* (1577). Here he bemoans the fact that there is "no place, no permanent, no publicke chayre, no ordinarie lecture, no commune stipende, no special reward due unto the studentes in Geography." He notes that "Geometry is first and than Geography." Finally he queries:

Who but Geographers doe teach us what partes of the earth be cold, warme, or temperate. Of whom doe we learne howe to divyde the world into partes, the partes onto provinces, the provinces into shyres. . . . Set Geographie asyde, you shall neyther be able to get intelligences of the situation and strength of any cities, not the limites and boundes of any countrey, not the rule and government of any kingdome. . . . Wil you see what wise and experte traveylers, skilful in Geometry and Astronomy, (for that is to bee a Geographer indeede) be able to doe.

While Dee and Willes had both obtained their geographical training on the Continent, the younger Richard Hakluyt was evidently introduced to geography by his cousin, the elder Richard Hakluyt. He broadened his horizons by independent study, but never gained the mathematical grasp enjoyed by Dee, Willes, or Edward Wright. While geography was not included in the normal curriculum of Oxford, Hakluyt and a number of his contemporaries gave public lectures in which they pointed out how maps, spheres, and globes were being reformed in deference to the opening of the overseas world.[191] Hakluyt did little thereafter to promote geography as an academic subject, and with the departure of Dee in 1583 for the Continent, the thrust of English geographical interests turned to accumulating materials essential to navigation and overseas trade. Much new information came to the English through their Dutch associates. But the Protestant English were virtually cut off from access to the flood of new materials on the East being sent to Europe by the Jesuits. In 1599 George Abbot exhibits the British attitude in a brief note on Japan in which he remarks: "This country was first discovered by the Iesuits, who in blinde zeale have traveled unto the farthest partes of the worlde, to winne men to their religion."[192]

---

[190] See A. D. S. Fowler (ed. and trans.), *"De re poetica"* by *Wills* [*Willes*] (Oxford, 1958), p. 18.
[191] See Crone, *loc. cit.* (n. 148), pp. 8–9.
[192] See G. Abbot, *A Briefe Description of the Whole Worlde* (London, 1600), p. G3.

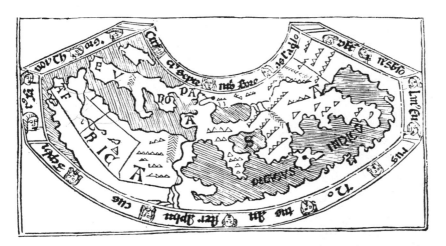

55. World map from Pomponius Mela's *Cosmographia*, a Spanish incunabulum of 1471.
Reproduced from T. Bowie *et al.*, *East–West in Art* (Bloomington, Ind., 1966), fig. 234.

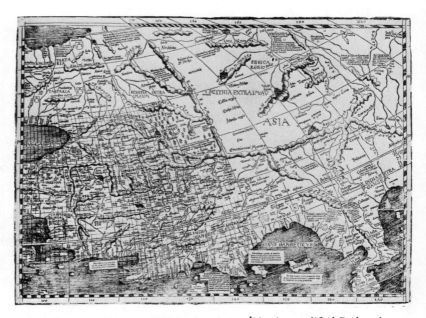

56. From the Waldseemüller *Cosmographia* (1507). Possibly the modified Ptolemaic map used by Sir Thomas More and his contemporaries. Calicut is spelled "Calliqut." Reproduced from Yūsuf Kāmal, *Monumenta Cartographica Africae et Aegypti* (5 vols.; Cairo, 1926–51), Vol. V, Fasc. 1, No. 1514.

57. From the Waldseemüller, *Cosmographia* (1507). Highly approximate map of Southeast Asia in a Ptolemaic projection with materials added from traditional reports and letters of Amerigo Vespucci. Reproduced from Yūsuf Kāmal, *Monumenta Cartographica Africae et Aegypti* (5 vols., Cairo, 1926–51), Vol. V., Fasc, 1, No. 1514.

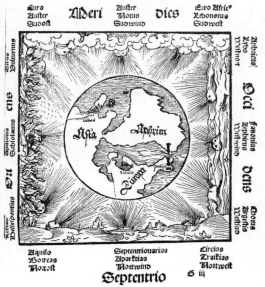

58. "Cipangu" (Japan) in the fifteenth-century Florence codex of Heinrich Martellus, *Insularium* (No. 12). Reproduced from G. Kish, "Two Fifteenth-Century Maps of 'Zipangu': Notes on the Early Cartography of Japan," *Yale University Library Gazette*, XL (1966), *ca.* p. 206.

59. World picture from the *Cosmographicus* ... (1524) of Peter Apian. Notice that the only places named are Venice, Portugal, and Calicut (Callicüt). Courtesy of the Newberry Library.

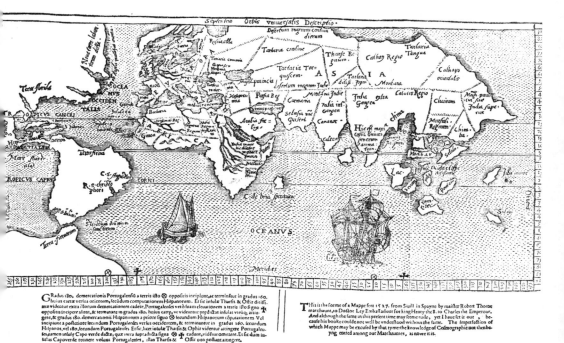

60. First English world map (1527) sent from Seville to London by the merchant Robert Thorne. Reproduced from a Carlos Sanz reproduction.

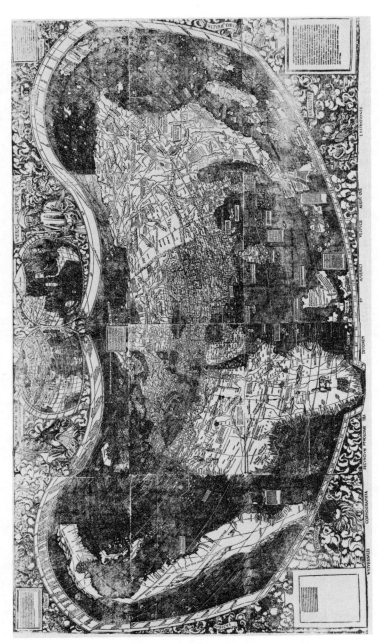

61, 62, 63. A cordiform world map of 1507 based on Ptolemy and incorporating materials from the letters of Amergio Vespucci. Notice the vignettes above the map with Ptolemy and his world map facing Vespucci and a picture of the new discoveries. Compare to Apian's cordiform map of 1530 (pl. 64). Entire map and vignettes reproduced from a Carlos Sanz reproduction.

64, 65, 66. Peter Apian's cordiform map of the world (1530). Vignettes of the map of the "old world" of Ptolemy and the "new world" of Vespucci placed in cordiform outline. Original in the British Museum. Reproduced from a copy supplied by David Woodward.

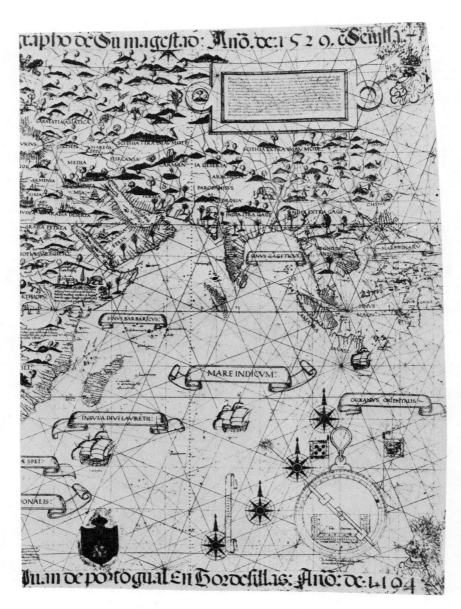

67. Asia on the planisphere of Diego Ribeiro (1529?). Reproduced from A. Cortesão and A. Teixeira da Mota, *Portugaliae monumenta cartographica* (6 vols.; Lisbon, 1960–62), Vol. I, pl. xxxix.

68. Oronce Finé, French geographer and cartographer. Reproduced from A. Thevet, *Les vrais pourtraits* . . . (Paris, 1584), p. 564ʳ. Courtesy of the Newberry Library.

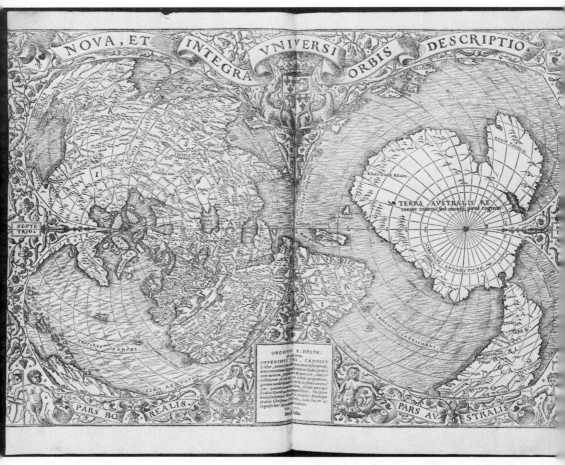

69. World in double cordiform projection showing the Austral continent by Oronce Finé from *Novus Orbis* . . . (Paris, 1532). Includes newer geographical data on India and Southeast Asia. This was possibly a source for Rabelais' voyage to the *Dive Bouteille*. Courtesy of the Newberry Library.

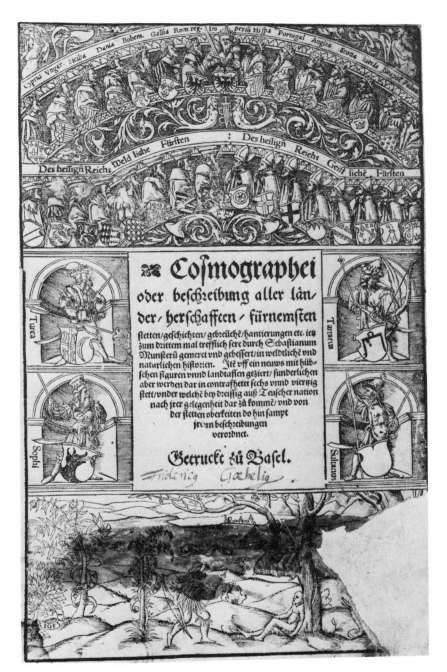

70. Title page of the first edition of Sebastian Münster's *Cosmographei* (Basel, 1550).

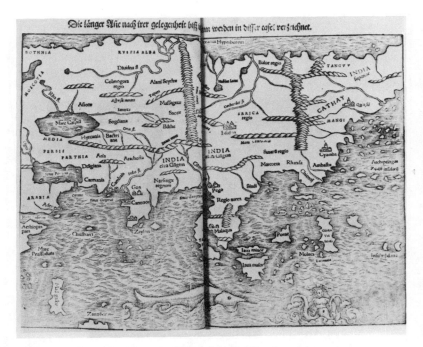

71. Woodcut map of Asia from Münster's *Cosmographei* (Basel, 1550).

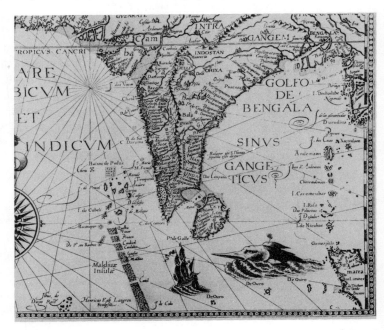

72. One of the better maps of south India, based on a combination of printed and oral sources and printed in Linschoten's *Itinerarium* (1596). Reproduced in Yūsuf Kāmal, *Monumenta Cartographica Africae et Aegypti* (5 vols.; Cairo, 1926–51), Vol. V, Fasc. 1, No. 1546.

73. Eastern hemisphere from Linschoten, *Itinerarium* (1596), based on Plancius' world map of 1594. Notice the open passage, the symbols of Asia in the upper right-hand corner, and the placement of Korea and Japan.

74. Western half of C. De Jode's map of China (1593) with vignettes of a Chinese cormorant catching a fish and of a three-headed Japanese idol. Vignettes based on literary descriptions of Mendoza and Maffei. Courtesy of the Newberry Library.

75. Eastern half of C. De Jode's map of China (1593) with vignettes of a Chinese houseboat and landship. Courtesy of the Newberry Library.

76. Wardrobe map of the Medici showing the Spice Islands. Reproduced from L. Berti, *Il principe dello studiolo* (Florence, 1967).

77. The Indian peninsula on a mural in the Vatican. Based on Gastaldi's general map of Asia. Reproduced from R. Almagià, *Monumenta cartographica vaticana* (4 vols.; Vatican City, 1944–55), Vol. IV, pl. XX.

78. Map of China from Mendoza's *Il gran regno della Cina* (Bologna, 1589). Notice that the cities of South China mentioned in Mendoza's text are shown here. Also observe the turtle-back shape of Japan. Reproduced from N. Nordenskiöld, *Periplus* (Stockholm, 1897), p. 145.

79. Map of the Jesuit mission stations in Japan. Outlines of the islands and their placement based possibly on a Japanese map. Reproduced from A. Cortesão and A. Teixeira da Mota, *Portugaliae monumenta cartographica* (6 vols.; Lisbon, 1960–62), Vol. II, 127, pl. 239 B.

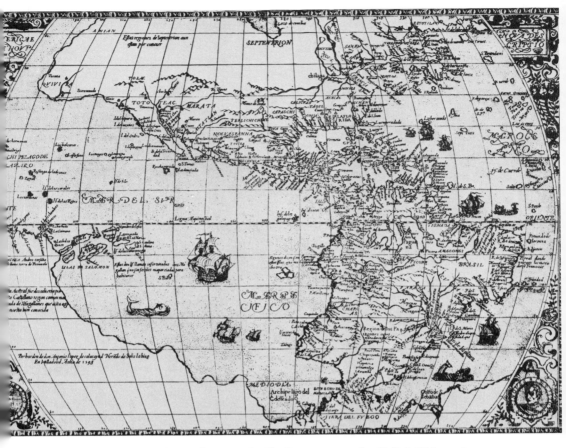

80. Map of America and the South Sea, or Pacific Ocean, prepared at Valladolid in 1598. Notice the proximity of North America to northeastern Asia, the Austral continent with New Guinea on its northern coast, and the numerous islands groups. Reproduced from a Carlos Sanz reproduction.

81. Title page of the *Geographisch Handtbuch* (1600) by the engraver Matthias Quad. Notice that the figures representing Europe and Asia are clothed while the figures of Africa and America are not. As in other symbolic representations of Asia, the figure here wears a turban and carries a censer in which exotic woods burn. Courtesy of the Newberry Library.

82. Imperial globe (*Reichsapfel*) of King Erik XIV of Sweden. Insular parts of Asia possibly based on a Gastaldi map or an adaptation of one. Reproduced from O. Muris and G. Saarmann, *Der Globus im Wandel der Zeiten* (Berlin, 1961), pl. 4.

83. Quentin Massys' painting in celebration of the visit to Antwerp of Lucas Rem, the German voyager to India. St. Luke, the patron of Lucas Rem, holds a crucifix atop a globe. The cross stands to the right, above India. The portrait may suggest that Rem had utilized Behaim's globe. Reproduced from H. Freiherr von Welser, "Der Globus des Lukas Rem," *Mitteilungen des Vereins für Geschichte der Stadt Nürnberg*, XLVIII (1958), facing p. 112.

The Jesuits certainly went deeply into the fields of geography and cartography in winning men to their religion. They collected a vast amount of data on the physical and human geography of Asia and even acquired literary and cartographic materials in Japanese and Chinese which were used in Europe to reform maps, globes, and cosmographies. When the Portuguese first arrived in South Asia, they quickly learned that the local sailors had their own nautical charts and navigational instruments.[193] Very few such maps are extant today, because most of these Eastern charts were incised on fragile palm leaves. In 1511 Albuquerque acquired a map drawn by a Javanese pilot which showed the Cape of Good Hope, Portugal, Brazil, the Red Sea, the Persian Gulf, the Spiceries, and the navigations of the Chinese and Japanese. This map never got back to Portugal because it was lost in a shipwreck. A portion of it, however, was copied by the Portuguese navigator Francisco Rodrigues, who probably included materials from it on his other charts. The portion actually copied and sent to King Manuel in 1512 gave the Javanese names in transliteration.[194] The great historian João de Barros included in the third decade (1563) of his *Asia* materials translated from Chinese geographical texts. Since Barros' *Geography* has never been found, it is not possible to determine whether he had a Chinese map in his collection. In 1588 Cavendish certainly brought a Chinese map back to England which he had acquired in the Philippines, and in 1590 the Jesuit Michele Ruggiero brought a map of China to Rome which he had obtained in Macao.[195]

Most revealing, however, on the use made by Europeans of Asian maps, is the history of the appearance of Japan in European cartography. From their unique knowledge of Japan the Jesuits contributed substantially to the depiction of that island kingdom.[196] Japan, as one island, began to appear on European maps around mid-century. The Portuguese maps of East Asia of the latter half of the century can be divided into four types according to their depiction of Japan, whether as one island or as several. The Mercator type shows Japan in the shape of an oval; this depiction was possibly copied from Chinese maps on which islands are usually represented as ovals.[197] Such a conclusion is reinforced by the appearance on these maps of the names "Lequio" major and minor, names that were used in the Ming dynasty with reference to the Liu-ch'iu islands and Formosa. The Homem-type maps, on the other hand, show Japan as a peninsula protruding southward into the sea from the eastern coast of Asia. This configuration appears to be based on a Japanese map of the *Gyogi* type, a traditional schematic map popular at the time. The Ortelius-type maps copy the

[193] Bagrow-Skelton, *op. cit.* (n. 15), p. 208.

[194] For commentary see Crone, *op. cit.* (n. 6), pp. 91–92; also Cortesão and Teixeira da Mota, *op. cit.* (n. 17), I, 80–83.

[195] See P. M. D'Elia, *Storia dell' introduzione del Christianismo in Cina* . . . (3 vols.; Rome, 1942–49), I, 251, n. 2. This map is no longer extant.

[196] See *Asia*, I, 709–10. See pl. 79.

[197] For example, see the Chinese world map from a Chinese encyclopedia (1562–77) reproduced in Bagrow-Skelton, *op. cit.* (n. 15), p. 198, fig. 67.

Homem maps in terms of Japan's extension but switch its principal axis from a north-south to a more correct east-west direction. The Dourado-type maps which began to appear around 1563 resemble the *Gyogi* maps but no evidence exists to establish a relationship.[198] The Dourado map shows Japan in a crescent-shaped or turtle-back outline, probably because the Europeans knew nothing of northern Honshu. On all European maps, even the best, Honshu is oriented east-west instead of northeast-southwest and Kyushu extends too far to the south by two degrees.[199]

Some of the other European maps, especially the sketches for wall maps and the woodcuts in printed books, appear to be based on the Jesuit letters and on maps of the *Gyogi* type actually available in Europe, China, India, and the Philippines.[200] On most of the maps based on Jesuit sources a cross indicates the presence of a Christian mission station, or perhaps where one once was.[201] The separate map of Japan by Luís Teixeira which first appeared in the 1595 edition of Ortelius' *Theatrum* is the best representation of Honshu and Kyushu printed in the sixteenth century. It also shows Korea, but portrays it as a long slender island between China and Japan. No indication of Yezo (Hokkaido) appears on this map except in a legend, though the Jesuits had been reporting on its existence periodically throughout the latter half of the century.[202] Inacio Moreira, a Portuguese Jesuit cartographer who first went to Japan in 1584, returned to Miyako early in 1591 as a member of Valignano's entourage. On this occasion and later, the Jesuits learned that Korea was attached to the continent and that it bordered southeastern Manchuria.[203] Moreira prepared a map of Yezo in 1591, but it was evidently not immediately available to cartographers. In the map of China published in the Mercator-Hondius atlas of 1606, however, Korea is correctly divided from northeastern Asia by nothing more than a river. But its extension remains directly southward and is much too great. On the Japan map in the same atlas, Korea is still depicted as an island.[204]

The willingness of cartographers and geographers to accept information from Asian sources and to modify and revise the Ptolemaic view of the world on the basis of them was a distinct contribution to the rise of a new spirit of naturalism, experimentalism, and scientific investigation. A new love of nature had been discovered in the thirteenth century by the Franciscans. That the love of nature was followed by a curiosity about all its forms is exemplified in the observations of the friars and other travelers who made the overland trek to China and back

---

[198] Analysis based on Nakamura, *op. cit.* (n. 11), pp. 51–55, and on the same author's *Maps of Japan Made by the Portuguese before the Closure of Japan* [in Japanese; see Bibliography] (3 vols.; Tokyo, 1966–67). Fernão Vaz Dourado actually worked in Goa about 1568.

[199] See Bagrow-Skelton, *op. cit.* (n. 15), p. 178.

[200] See *Asia*, I, 710.

[201] See maps *ibid.*, following p. 656.

[202] For details see *ibid.*, pp. 723–25.

[203] See O. Yoshitomo, "Desenvolvimento cartográfico da parte Extrema Oriente da Asia pelos Jesuitas Portugueses em fim do século XVI," *Studia* (Lisbon), XIII (1964), 17–19.

[204] For reproduction of the two maps from the Mercator-Hondius atlas see Skelton, *Decorative Printed Maps* (n. 10), pls. 44 and 45.

again. The maritime adventurers of the following centuries made contributions to natural scientific inquiry, perhaps because they were not governed by the heavy hand of literary authority. Their traditions were confined to practical seamanship, a few instruments of navigation, and the rutters. The development of a schedule of regular voyages to the East was governed more by the monsoons and other natural phenomena than by economic considerations. Rules of navigation were soon developed and some of these, such as the scale of latitudes, began to appear on Portuguese maps. The Portuguese warn soberly that many of the elaborate plane charts are misleading because their makers ignored the earth's curvature and the convergence of meridians.[205] The ideas of the cartographers and cosmographers, unlike those of many other scientists, were tested constantly in the crucible of experience, were challenged repeatedly by the authorities of the expanding states, and were regularly revised.[206] A more critical scientific attitude toward geography was thus quickly transmitted to the rest of Europe along with the maps of the Iberians.

Early maps were often far more than a representation of the earth's surface, or part of it, with place names. With their legends and decorations, some of them were brief cosmographies. They gave the careful and critical viewer much more than configuration and spatial relationships. That the map was thought of as art form is best established by reference to the number of famous engravers—for example, Albrecht Dürer and Philippe Galle—who worked on maps and globes. In the maps prepared by lesser artists a tendency grew to decorate the map or to insert legends in all the open spaces, a practice that sometimes was so profuse as to detract from the cartographic message. Ships were among the favorite decorative devices used to fill in the open spaces of the seas. The ships on early Portuguese maps tend to be more realistic than those in the printed books.[207] One map engraver copied the other so that most of the ships in the Ortelius and Mercator collections can be recognized as stereotypes rather than original creations.[208] Münster's woodcut map of the world in the popular *Novus orbis* (Basel, 1532) includes among the other decorations in its bottom margin a figure named "Vartomanus" (Varthema) who was to become a symbol for "the traveler."[209] Laurent Fries' map of India in the Ptolemy of 1522 includes references in its vignettes and legends to medieval lore; it also shows the king of "Narsinga," a name not known in Europe before 1505, sitting on a throne.[210] The Italian cartographers provided little woodcut maps decorated with pictures of hitherto unknown plants, animals, and people for the various editions of the

[205] Based on Cortesão and Teixeira da Mota, *op. cit.* (n. 17), I, xxiii, 127.

[206] For the problems faced by the Spanish cosmographers in coming to terms with the scientific problems arising from the conflicts over the Moluccas see U. Lamb, "The Spanish Cosmographic Juntas of the Sixteenth Century," *Terrae incognitae*, VI (1974), 51–62.

[207] The maps of Lopo Homem regularly show Chinese junks too. See Cortesão and Teixeira da Mota, *op. cit.* (n. 17), I, 61.

[208] See J. Van Beylen, "Schepen op Kaarten ten tide van Gerard Mercator," *Duisburger Forschungen*, VI (1962), 131–33.

[209] For a reproduction see Bagrow-Skelton, *op. cit.* (n. 15), p. 85, fig. 19.

[210] For a reproduction see Skelton, *Decorative Printed Maps* (n. 10), pl. 4.

Jesuit letterbooks.[211] On the later Portuguese maps parrot-like birds, elephants, and rhinoceroses (related artistically not at all to Dürer's beast) cavort in the open spaces.[212]

The symbolism of the geographical globe, as an exact copy of the world that could be held in the hands, attracted the attention of artists, literati, and the public. Painted and engraved globes and armillary spheres graced the frontis-pieces and appeared on many maps and illustrations in the cosmographies and atlases.[213] The globes themselves were artistic creations, one of the finest being the golden globe (1561) manufactured for King Erik (reigned 1560–92) of Sweden.[214] For the information of his townsmen, Hondius sketched the Dutch voyages on the terrestrial sphere housed in the library of the University of Leyden.[215] To people everywhere the globe symbolized power, sovereignty, or supremacy. The extension of Christian supremacy in the East is probably repre-sented in the use that is made of a globe in the middle panel of the Rem altar triptych of about 1519. Lucas Rem, one of the first Germans to sail to India, visited Antwerp with his bride in 1519.[216] To celebrate the occasion the artist, Quentin Massys, painted the triptych now preserved in the Alte Pinakothek in Munich. The male figure in the middle panel is St. Luke, patron of Lucas Rem. He holds the crucifix atop a globe. The cross stands not on the middle of the globe, as might be expected, but to the right above India. In addition to its message on the spread of Christianity to the East, this portrait possibly suggests that Rem had utilized Behaim's globe while preparing for his expedition of 1505.[217] Holbein's "Ambassadors" painted in London in 1533 shows the French emissary with a celestial and terrestrial globe. The model used for the terrestrial globe is extant; it shows the northwest passage to Asia as Sebastian Cabot probably envisaged it.[218] Later in the century Marc Geerarts painted a portrait of the *annus mirabilis* of Queen Elizabeth which shows her with fingers lightly touching a celestial globe while outside her window the Spanish armada is being defeated.[219] Something of the mystery attached to the globe is well illustrated in John Donne's verse *A Valediction of Weeping* (1650–1711?):

[211] See Dainville, *La géographie des Humanistes* (n. 71), pp. 124–25.

[212] For example, see the reproduction of the map of the Orient from the Homem-Reinel atlas in W. B. George, *Animals and Maps* (Berkeley, 1969), pp. 28–29. Also see chap. vi for a general discussion, and *Asia*, II, Bk. 1, 131, 167, 170, 198.

[213] See F. de Dainville, "Les amateurs des globes," *Gazette des Beaux-Arts*, 6th ser. LXXI (1968), 52–53.

[214] It is preserved at Stockholm and shows clearly China, "Giapan," "Ins. Moluca," "Gilolo," and "Iava." See pl. 82.

[215] See E. Hulshoff Pol, "The Library," in Th. H. Lunsingh Scheurler and G. H. M. Posthumus Meyjes (eds.), *Leiden University in the Seventeenth Century* (Leyden, 1975), p. 416.

[216] On Rem's career in the spice trade see *Asia*, I, 108–9.

[217] Analysis based on H. Freiherr von Welser, "Der Globus des Lukas Rem," *Mitteilungen des Vereins für Geschichte der Stadt Nürnberg*, XLVIII (1958), pls. III and IX. See pl. 83.

[218] See H. Wallis, *loc. cit.* (n. 18), p. 204.

[219] For a reproduction see A. Fauser, *Die Welt in Händen, kurze Kulturgeschichte des Globus* (Stuttgart, 1967), p. 113.

On a round ball
A workeman that hath copies by, can lay
An Europe, Afrique and an Asia
And Quickly make that, which was nothing, *All*.[220]

The extension of discovery and the growth of geography were related and interdependent developments of the period from the thirteenth to the seventeenth centuries. The revelation of Asia that occurred from Marco Polo to Linschoten was decisive in bringing about a cartographic revolution. Sacred geography was overshadowed in this period by the development of a secular geography that gradually separated itself from all celestial and religious interests to become earthbound. The rediscovery of Ptolemy brought to Renaissance Europe a new respect for scientific exactitude and empirical methods in the making of maps. In navigation and cartography traditional trial and error techniques were replaced or modified by the more sophisticated calculations and ideas of space taught by academic cosmographers and mathematicians.

The involvement of the state, or of persons highly placed at court, in explorations and overseas trade brought to geographical study the stimulus of official patronage, particularly in Portugal, Spain, and the Low Countries. A growing sense of national identity and the feelings of national rivalry engendered by overseas competition produced incidents in which cartography and geography were subverted to the national interest. In Germany the religious hostilities attending the Reformation had the effect of stifling some very promising early developments in geographical science. Geography gradually became the business of craftsmen, printers, and other groups in related enterprises. As a result geography went into the service of business as well as the state. Engravings were put into convenient packages and marketed as atlases; pocket-sized atlases and geographical handbooks were spun off from the original creations; selling maps, globes, and cartographic instruments became an important trade in itself.

Asia was central to cartographic developments. Cathay and its placement on the map preoccupied cartographers from the fourteenth to the seventeenth centuries. Marco Polo's place names were introduced into the Ptolemaic atlas at an early date and many of them remained on maps to the end of the sixteenth century. Asia, unlike America, figured prominently in the Ptolemaic atlas. Its proper configuration, its extension eastward, and its relationship to America were among the most perplexing geographical problems of the century. When it gradually became obvious that Ptolemy's depiction of Asia was fanciful, eminent cartographers as well as makers of sea charts, began to produce separate maps of the East based on recent information. After Ptolemy's was reduced to the status of a historical atlas around 1570, the mapmakers also began to produce separates of the contemporary Asian nations. In certain cases the European cartographers employed maps of Asian provenance in their efforts to obtain a

[220] J. T. Shawcross (ed.), *The Complete Poetry of John Donne* (New York, 1967), pp. 125–26, 413.

[487]

truer depiction. But it was not until the Jesuit Matteo Ricci introduced European geography to China at the beginning of the seventeenth century that a two-way blending began to take place between the world's most advanced cartographic traditions.

As the map of the world unrolled, the general public learned of Asia through a host of sources. The world that could be held in the hands (the globe) provided all viewers with a new sense of the relationships between land and water and the approximate distances separating one continent from the other. The representations on the globes, like the configurations on the map, were regularly altered. For the common man the world was visibly becoming vaster and more complex. Debates about the northern routes to Cathay included a large public. The safe circumnavigation of the world by Magellan's men, Drake, and Cavendish excited responses which first brought Spain and Portugal into conflict and then Spain and England. By the last generation of the sixteenth century it was no longer possible for even the semiliterate to believe in a flat earth or in Ptolemy's picture of the world. That readers were stimulated to study these amazing geographical developments for themselves is amply attested by the constantly mounting sales of maps, cosmographies, and pocket-sized geographical handbooks. In England and Holland it was public pressure, motivated probably by desire for trade and treasure, which helped to keep alive the forlorn hope of finding a northern route to the riches of the East.

Geography as an academic discipline in its own right was gradually accepted in the universities. It still remained attached in many instances to cosmography, astronomy, navigation, and theology. But there were individual scholars who insisted in their writings and lectures in awarding to geography an integrity of its own. Most cosmographers were ready by mid-century to concede that study of the terrestrial sphere should be independent of the celestial sphere. The leading scholars of terrestrial subjects were inclined to give little more than lip service to biblical geography. They still believed, however, that nature is the mirror of God's plan and that he gave it form and unity. The Humanists, though they tried to preserve Ptolemy through retranslations of what they rightly thought were faulty texts, learned to accept his atlas as a historical document rather than as a true picture of the world. The new cosmographies and atlases explicitly compared regions in terms of latitudes, elevation, climate, and products. Some biological scientists, especially botanists, realized also that an understanding of geography had become essential to their studies.

What was most important, however, was a growing sense of cultural relativism about geography and its related branches of knowledge. The startling information was conveyed to Europe by the Jesuits that China and Japan possessed geographical and cartographical traditions of their own which were completely unrelated to the European and were sufficiently accurate and informed on Asia to be used in revising European maps and geographical beliefs. A kind of ethical relativism also developed as the Jesuits and others sought to explain moral and religious differences in terms of climate. Some, like Bodin, were forthrightly geographical determinists.[221] Juan Huarte, the Spanish physician, argued that natural aptitudes and characteristics were the products of the physical environment and climate.[222] The impact of environment on human affairs led finally to serious efforts to explain certain social phenomena, such as the city, exclusively in natural and empirical rather than in theological or humanistic terms.

[221] See above, pp. 306–9, as well as the discussion of Charron's ideas, pp. 297–300.
[222] His ideas analyzed in Dainville, *La géographie des Humanistes* (n. 71), pp. 143–44.

CHAPTER XI

Language and Linguistics

A flood of new and exotic words poured into Europe during the sixteenth century from the entire overseas world. The establishment of permanent political, commercial, and religious relations with Asia forced the adoption and incorporation of thousands of Eastern words into the vocabulary of every European language—probably more than in any other century before or since. New geographical, botanical, and zoological names; maritime terms; words for hundreds of varieties of textiles, spices, and jewels; and designations for places, natural features, and social practices swept like a tidal wave into the languages and letters of Europe. New words were coined in Europe to represent hitherto unknown customs, institutions, or ideas, and many words long established in the European languages were given extended or altered meanings as a result of the discoveries. The number of new words referring to the complicated geography, the established international commerce, and the high civilizations of Asia far exceeded those that originated in or referred to more primitive Africa and America.

Words, like techniques, products, and fables, had migrated to Europe from Asia long before the establishment of direct and permanent relations.[1] From the first century A.D. to 1500 the most significant import from Asia was silk. It is therefore not surprising that the Chinese *szŭ* should have become Latin *sericum*

---

[1] Some have postulated the unorthodox idea that the Dravidian languages of south India are survivors, comparable to Basque and Caucasian, of a "polysynthetic family of peri-Mediterranean and pre-Hamito-Semitic languages, . . . which stretched some five or six thousand years ago without a break over a vast zone of the Near East" (N. Lahovary, *Dravidian Origins and the West* [Bombay, 1963], pp. 1–2). While such a linguistic substratum may once have existed, we shall not speculate about what influence it, or its counterpart, the Indo-European family, might have had upon the languages of Mediterranean Europe as we know them.

and eventually English "silk."[2] The geographical term "China" was first adopted into Sanskrit (*Cīna*) from the name of the Ch'in dynasty (246–207 B.C.) and soon passed from India westward into the Roman empire.[3] A few other Indian words, mainly those associated with commerce, were similarly added to the vocabulary of medieval Europe. Even the word "India" itself, which ultimately derives from Sanskrit *Sindhu* (river), passed through Persian to Greek and Latin and was then incorporated in one recognizable form or another into the various European vernaculars as they developed into independent languages.[4]

Alexander the Great, his associates and successors, like most Greeks of Antiquity, took virtually no interest in "barbarian" languages. The Romans, as in so many other matters, retained the Greek attitude.[5] Medieval travelers to the Mongol court, for all their Christian bias, were the first Europeans to comment seriously on the languages of Asia. William of Rubruquis, in particular, noted the peculiarities of Chinese ideographic writing and commented on the printing of money and books. He delineated with surprising precision the differences which set off the Chinese, Tibetan, Tangut, and Uigur scripts from one another.[6] From the medieval accounts there also emerges a sense of the travelers' dismay about the multiplicity of languages in Asia and the feelings of relief experienced at being able to find interpreters at the court of the Grand Khan and at the commercial centers of inland and maritime Asia. On the basis of this quick survey it may be concluded that before the sixteenth century there was no substantial understanding in Europe for the nature of the Asian languages, for their differences and similarities to one another, or even for their contributions, meager as they were, to the European vocabulary.

[2] The Chinese word for silk traveled westward through Mongolia, where it acquired a suffix and became something like *sir-kek*. An analogue with respect to westward migration may be found in Chinese *p'i* (wild duck) which became Cantonese, *p'at*, Arabic *batt*, and Spanish *pato*. See August Conrady, "Alte westöstliche Kulturwörter," *Berichte über die Verhandlungen der sächsischen Akademie der Wissenschaften zu Leipzig, philologisch-historische Klasse*, (Leipzig 1925), III, 3–19; and E. C. Knowlton, "Words of Chinese, Japanese, and Korean Origin in the Romance Languages," (Ph.D. diss., Stanford University, 1959), pp. 10–14.

[3] This derivation has been the subject of learned and inconclusive controversy. For example, see B. Laufer, "The Name China," *T'oung pao*, 2d ser. XIII (1912), 710–26, and in the same volume the reply of P. Pelliot, "L'origine du nom de Chine," pp. 722–42. For further discussion see Margaret M. S. Yu, "Words and Things," *Studies in Linguistics*, XX (1968), 8–9. "China," as the name of the country, dates in English from *ca.* 1565. The words "Siam" and "Japan" were not used in Europe at all before the sixteenth century. See *Asia*, I, 524, 652. "Cochin-China" (from Chinese to Arabic to Portuguese), which means "to the east of China," was the name used in the European sources of the sixteenth century for the whole kingdom of Annam with its capital at Hanoi. This word first appeared in Europe on the Cantino map of 1502. See L. Aurousseau, "Sur le nom de Cochinchine," *Bulletin de l'École française d'Extrême-Orient* (Hanoi), XXIV (1924), 551–79.

[4] See G. S. Rao, *Indian Words in English* . . . (Oxford, 1954), pp. 67–69.

[5] The Greeks applied indifferently the word "barbarian" to all alien tongues because they were as unintelligible to them as the twittering of birds. See M. Leroy, *Main Trends in Modern Linguistics* (Berkeley and Los Angeles, 1967), p. 2.

[6] Cf. *Asia*, I, 30–48; also see B. Bischoff, "The Study of Foreign Languages in the Middle Ages," *Speculum*, XXXVI (1961), 214.

I

SOURCES

Sixteenth-century Europeans who often lived for many years in the port cities of Asia acquired a practical working vocabulary of the native words necessary for the conduct of government, business, war, evangelizing, and social relations. Many of the Portuguese in India learned the spoken tongues of their region of activity from their wives and mistresses. A patois also developed in the major Asian centers of trade that is best described as "pidgin Malay" and "pidgin Portuguese."[7] The accounts written by first-hand observers in the East naturally included references to many matters for which there were no equivalents in the European languages.[8] In most cases the informant in the field when writing to Europe felt compelled to add a word, phrase, or sentence explaining the terms which he assumed would be foreign to his readers. Indeed, modern language students have repeatedly argued for or against the alien provenance of a particular word or idea by reference to the explanation or lack of explanation in such writings. The reports of the observers in the field were published and given wide currency, particularly after 1550, in the travel collections, histories, and Jesuit letterbooks. By means of these publications and their translations a massive number of Asian words were first brought to the eyes and minds of European readers. In the port cities of Europe a certain number of words became current that had been transmitted orally by Asian visitors[9] and by European sailors, merchants, and missionaries.

Letters in the Malay language, sometimes accompanied by Portuguese translations, began to arrive in Lisbon soon after the conquest of Malacca in 1511.[10] Indians were retained at the Portuguese court to write letters to the rulers of their homelands in their native languages.[11] Certain of the first-hand

[7] For a discussion of the Portuguese language in the East see S. R. Dalgado and A. X. Soares, *Portuguese Vocables in Asiatic Languages* (Baroda, 1936), the authors' introduction.

[8] The Jesuit letters are particularly interesting in this regard. For example, the letters of Xavier in the hand of Balthazar Gago are sometimes written in a Portuguese spelled in the Castilian manner with Latin, Italian, and Tamil admixtures. For further comment see I. Elizalde, *San Francisco Xavier en la literatura española* (Madrid, 1961), p. 42.

[9] An example of an early Asian visitor is the chetty from Calicut who was known by the Christian name D. João da Cruz. A relative of the Zamorin of Calicut, the young Indian spent three years (1513–16) at the court of Lisbon. Since he learned to read and write Portuguese, he must have relayed to the Portuguese courtiers something about his native language, presumably "Malabaric." For further details on his career see G. Schurhammer, "Letters of D. João da Cruz...," in *Varia*, I, *Anhänge* (Rome and Lisbon, 1965), pp. 57–59.

[10] The Malay was written in Arabic letters. The originals today repose in the Torre do Tombo (Gavetas 15-4-1, 15-15-7, 15-15-27, 15-16-38). For details see C. O. Blagden (ed. and trans.), "Two Malay Letters from Ternate in the Moluccas, Written in 1521 and 1522," *Bulletin of the School of Oriental Studies* (London), VI (1930–32), 87–101.

[11] For example, King Manuel had the services of a *nāyar* of Cochin to indite correspondence in "Malabaric". See V. B. Nair, "A Nair Envoy to Portugal," *Indian Antiquary*, LVII (1928), 157–59.

reporters in the field meanwhile made conscious efforts to collect vocabularies necessary for the conduct of operations in Asia. Over the course of the sixteenth century lists were relayed to Europe of Malayālam, Malay, Bisayan, Tagalog, and Javan words. A list of 138 Malayālam words, or of "the language of Calicut," with their Portuguese equivalents was compiled by a participant in the first voyage of Vasco da Gama in 1497–99.[12] Antonio Pigafetta, a companion of Magellan, compiled and incorporated into his narrative a list of 426 Malay, Bisayan, and Tagalog words with their Italian equivalents.[13] Selections from Pigafetta's vocabulary were published in the French (1525) and Venetian (1536) epitomes of his account; these, in turn, were reissued in the travel collections of Ramusio (1550),[14] Eden (1555), and Purchas (1625). The companions of Sir Francis Drake on his voyage around the world in 1580 compiled a list of 32 Javan words with their English meanings and Hakluyt published the list in 1589.[15] In 1603 Frederick de Houtman returned to Holland after a sojourn in Sumatra and composed and published a Dutch-Malay vocabulary which included words from fifteen languages of the Malayo-Polynesian group.[16]

All the vocabularies of the sixteenth century focus on the native words of practical value or of personal interest to Europeans in the East: nautical and navigational terms, numbers, directions of the compass, names of weapons and precious metals, names of animals for eating, working, or collecting (i.e., parrots, etc.), parts of the human body, simple commands, and words and phrases of everyday usage. Even the most limited lists include the native word for "mirror," one of the few items of European manufacture that could be

---

[12] This vocabulary was not printed until 1838, but it certainly could have been used by later Portuguese voyagers to prepare themselves for their activities in south India. For the list see E. G. Ravenstein (ed.), *A Journal of the First Voyage of Vasco da Gama, 1497–1499*, Vol, XCIX, "Publications of the Hakluyt Society," O.S. No. 99 (London, 1898), pp. 105–8, and pl. 95.

[13] The scholarship on Pigafetta's work is voluminous. See *Asia*, I, 173–76. The best recent evaluation of his vocabularies and of the scholarship relating to them is Alessandro Bausani, "The First Italian-Malay Vocabulary by Antonio Pigafetta," *East and West* (Rome), XI (1960), 229–48.

[14] For a reproduction of the list in *Delle navigationi et viaggi* of Ramusio see *Asia*, I, facing p. 529.

[15] Reproduced in D. B. Quinn and R. A. Skelton (eds.), *The Principall Navigations Voiages and Discoveries of the English Nation* (Cambridge, 1965), p. 813. The compiler also gives a list of the "Kings or princes of Iava at the time of our English mens being there." For the language materials gathered by Cavendish see pl. 98.

[16] Entitled *Spraecke ende Woordboeck, inde Maleysche ende Madagaskarsche Talen* (Amsterdam, 1603). For commentary see K. J. Riemens, "Het spraekende woord-boeck van Fr. de Houtman en de vocabulaire van Noël de Barlaimont," *Het Boek*, VII (1918), 193–96. From Houtman's work Gotardus Arthusius (Gotthard Arthus) (1570–1630) derived his *Dialogues in the English and Malaiane Languages* (London, 1614), which was translated into English by Augustus Spalding. Also see J. C. Mollema (ed.), *De eerste Schipvaart der Hollanders naar Oost-Indië, 1595–97* (The Hague, 1935), pp. 46, 50. The oldest Malay vocabulary extant was compiled by Chinese traders who were active in Malacca before the arrival of the Europeans there. See E. D. Edwards and C. O. Blagden (eds. and trans.), "A Chinese Vocabulary of Malacca Malay Words and Phrases Collected between A.D. 1403 and 1511(?)," *Bulletin of the School of Oriental Studies* (London), VII (1930–32), 715–49. For later Malay vocabularies see A. C. Ruyl, *Spieghel van de maleysche taal* (Amsterdam, 1612), and David Haex, *Dictionarivm Malaico-Latinvm et Latino-Malaicvm cum aliis qvamplvrimus quae quarta pagina edocebit* (Rome, 1621).

readily traded in maritime Asia. Pigafetta's list is much more comprehensive and sophisticated than the others, for he also includes words relating to Islam and to family relationships, the names for a wide range of textiles, spices, and metals, household terms, personal raiment, and the winds. But then Pigafetta in all probability did not learn his Malay from chance encounters with local speakers. He had at his beck and call for the eighteen months of the voyage to the Philippines the personal slave of Magellan, a native of Sumatra called "Henrique," whom Magellan had earlier brought back to Europe while in the service of the Portuguese.[17] Pigafetta's list also reflects the common Malay current in the commercial centers of the East often called "the language of Malacca," an indication that Pigafetta probably did not learn his words locally, or in the Moluccas, as he seems to imply in the heading he gives his vocabulary.[18] Pigafetta, a man of curiosity and education, would almost certainly not have passed up the opportunity during a long, tedious voyage at sea to learn whatever he could about the language of the place that was the goal of the expedition.

The ideographic languages of East Asia were first introduced to sixteenth-century Europe by means of the Chinese books and maps that were acquired in Asia.[19] Specimen characters were also written by Chinese and Japanese individuals who appeared in Europe during the sixteenth century. These calligraphic samples, even though some were crudely written, were soon printed in European histories, geographies, and atlases.[20] The Jesuits, especially those based in Japan, sent sample characters to Europe that were well written in both their Chinese and hiragana forms. Many of these were printed in the Jesuit histories and letterbooks that were widely distributed throughout Europe.[21] Father Michele Ruggiero, the first Jesuit to study Chinese seriously, returned to Rome about 1590 to become the resident expert on Chinese language and printing.[22] The Japanese envoys who were in Europe from 1584 to 1586 brought gifts on which Japanese characters were written, and commentators on this mission provided lists of Japanese words and their European equivalents.[23] More importantly, the

[17] For further detail and interesting speculation about Pigafetta's sources see C. C. F. M. Le Roux, "Nogmaals Pigafetta's Maleische woorden," *Tijdschrift voor Indische taal-, land- en volkenkunde*, LXXIX (1939), 446–51.

[18] Bausani, *loc. cit.* (n. 13), p. 230.

[19] *Asia*, I, 738–39, 749–50, 754, 776–80; II, 13, 41, 74 n., 188.

[20] *Ibid.*, I, 743, 776. Also see O. Nachod, "Die ersten Kenntnisse chinesischer Schriftzeichen im Abendlande," in *Hirth Anniversary Volume* published by *Asia Major* (London), I (1923), 235–73. Sample characters appeared in the works on China of Escalante and Mendoza, and in A. Ortelius, *Theatrum orbis terrarum . . .* (Antwerp, 1584), p. 93. For a reproduction of the characters in Ortelius, see *Asia*, I, after p. 752.

[21] *Asia*, I, 679–80. Also see pl. 96.

[22] For his career in Macao and China, from 1579 to 1588, see P. M. D'Elia, *Storia dell' introduzione del Christianismo in Cina, scritta da Matteo Ricci, S.I.*, (3 vols.; Rome, 1942–49), I, xcvii–ix, 251; for his advent in Rome, see Angelo Rocca, *Bibliotheca apostolica vaticana a Sisto V in splendidiorem locum translata* (Rome, 1591), pp. 379, 410. Also see pl. 99.

[23] For example, see the list of eight Japanese words in Roman letters and their Italian meanings preceding the text in *Breve ragvaglio dell' isola Giappone* (Bologna, 1585).

young nobles and their masters sent letters of thanks in Japanese script to their European hosts.[24] Usually the letters in Japanese were accompanied by translations in Italian or Latin. It also appears that at least one Japanese book, a historical work, was sent to Italy.[25] Raw materials were certainly available in Italy and Portugal for serious study of both Chinese and Japanese before the end of the sixteenth century.[26]

The missionaries in Asia did their best in the latter half of the sixteenth century to command the language of the places in which they worked. Father Henrique Henriques began to learn and organize the Tamil language according to the principles of Latin grammar. He also contrived a system of romanization by which he and others could learn to speak Tamil.[27] In 1551 he sent to Lisbon a Portuguese translation of certain Malabar copper plates, a manuscript Tamil grammar, and translations in romanized Tamil of Christian prayers.[28] In 1554 a *Cartilha* was printed at Lisbon in Tamil, the first known publication in that language. An instructional manual for missionaries working in the Tamil country, the *Cartilha* includes prayers and the catechism in a romanized Tamil which is printed in large red letters. It also provides an interlinear translation in Portuguese and a syllabary (see pl. 91). The translations into Tamil were evidently made by three Indians known only by their Christian names: Vicente de Nazareth, Jorge Carvalho, and Thomé da Cruz. They possibly used the primitive system of transliteration devised by Henriques, for the *Prologo* in Portuguese outlining the principles followed in the transliteration was quite evidently prepared by a European who found Tamil "so barbaric" that the

---

[24] For a reproduction of the letter written by Itō Mancio to the duke of Mantua in 1585 see *Asia*, I, after p. 656. For Latin letters written for him to the pope from Goa (December 1, 1587) and from Macao (date not given) see Koda Shigetomo, "Itō Mancio's Two Epistles" [in Japanese; see Bibliography], *Shirin*, XVI, No. 2 (April, 1931), 81–91. Also see Tsuboi Kumazo, "A Letter of Appreciation Presented to the Government of Venice by the Envoy from the Ōtomo, Ōmura, and Arima Clans (daimyōs)" [in Japanese; see Bibliography], *Shigaku-Zasshi*, XII (1901), 616–20; and for a letter to Imola see Murakami Naojiro, "A Letter of Appreciation from the Envoys of the Three Clans of Ōtomo, Ōmura, and Arima" [in Japanese; see Bibliography], *ibid.*, pp. 496–98. And for a letter of the *daimyō* of Arima to Cardinal Antonio Caraffa (1538–91), see Hamada Kosaku, *Chronicle of a Mission to Europe in the Tensho Period* [in Japanese; see Bibliography] (Tokyo, 1931), pp. 73, 411–21.

[25] It was probably sent to Mantua. See Murakami Naojiro, "New Historical Materials concerning an Embassy to Spain and Italy" [in Japanese; see Bibliography], *Shigaku-Zasshi*, XIV (1903), 361.

[26] It should be observed that about ten Asian languages other than Chinese were being taught in China by 1549, and that the Chinese had compiled vocabularies of Malay and the language of Liu-ch'iu before the Europeans knew about these languages. See E. D. Ross, "New Light on the History of the Chinese Oriental College . . .," *T'oung pao*, 2d ser. IX (1908), 689–95.

[27] On Henriques' career see *Asia*, I, 436–39.

[28] For discussion of the copper plates see G. Schurhammer, "Some Remarks on Series 4 of the Kerala Society Papers," in *Varia*, I, *Anhänge* (Rome and Lisbon, 1965), pp. 51–52. The manuscript grammar of Henriques is available today in the National Library at Lisbon. See Xavier S. Thani Nayagam, "The First Books Printed in Tamil," *Tamil Culture*, VII (1958), 289. In a letter of January 27, 1552, Henriques wrote about compiling a Tamil-Portuguese dictionary. No trace of such a work, either in manuscript or in print, has yet been located. See X. S. Thani Nayagam, *Antão de Provença's Tamil-Portuguese Dictionary, A.D. 1679* (Kuala Lumpur, 1966), p. 7.

pronunciation of certain words could not be conveyed accurately by the Latin alphabet.[29]

After many pleas had been forwarded to Lisbon about the imperative need for printing Christian doctrine in the native languages, a printing press, originally intended for the mission in Abyssinia, was finally set up at Goa in 1556. The press was accompanied by Juan de Bustamente, a Spanish printer, and his helper Juan Gonsalves. They were aided by a man of Indian origin who had learned the printing trade in Portugal.[30] At Goa the first works issued were Christian writings in Portuguese and various secular works, such as Garcia da Orta's *Colóquios* (1563). Gonsalves, an expert blacksmith and type cutter, was the first to prepare types in Tamil characters. He then evidently taught João de Faria how to prepare such types. The characters prepared in Goa were taken to Quilon where Faria improved on them. These corrected types were then used in 1578 to print a Tamil translation by Henriques of Xavier's *Doctrina Christã* which had been published originally in 1557 in Portuguese at Goa. The first book in Indic print, the *Doctrina* of 1578, is sixteen pages long and was printed at Quilon on paper manufactured in China. On the last page it displays a shorter and a longer Tamil alphabet as well as a line of Tamil numbers. A copy of this book was probably sent to Rome in 1579.[31] Shortly thereafter the Jesuit press was evidently moved from Quilon to Cochin. Here in 1579 a *Doutrina Christão* was printed, a work unrelated to the Xavier book.[32] Written originally in Portuguese by Marcos Jorge, the Cochin *Doutrina* of 1579 was translated into Tamil by Henriques. A *Flos Sanctorum* in the Tamil of Henriques was printed in 1586, probably at Punicale on the Fishery Coast.[33]

The Jesuits at Macao appear not to have possessed a Western printing press until 1614.[34] But in 1585 Father Michele Ruggiero had a catechism printed at Macao from xylographic blocks prepared in the Chinese manner (see pl. 85).[35] This catechism was published in Chinese characters very likely written by a Chinese scholar. A Latin-Chinese vocabulary prepared by Ruggiero was also

[29] The only extant copy known of the *Cartilha* is in the Museu etnólogico de Belém. For a reproduction and a partial facsimile of the text see Jean Filliozat, *Un catéchisme Tamoul du XVIe siècle en lettres latines* (Pondichéry, 1967). For a reproduction of the title page see Américo Cortez-Pinto, *Da famosa arte da imprimissão* (Lisbon, 1948), pl. XVII.

[30] A. K. Priolkar, *The Printing Press in India, Its Beginnings and Early Development* (Bombay, 1958), pp. 8–9, 14–17. It is likely that the Indian was one of those who helped in the preparation of the *Cartilha* of 1554. Perhaps he was the Indian convert sent to Lisbon by Gaspar Barzaeus (in Barzée) in 1551. See *Asia*, I, 442.

[31] A copy of this earliest extant example of Indic printing was purchased in London in 1951 for the Harvard University Library. For further discussion of it see G. Schurhammer and G. W. Cottrell, "The First Printing in Indic Characters," *Harvard Library Bulletin*, VI (1952), 147–60. In 1963 this work, along with the *Doutrina* of 1579, were reissued at Tuticorin by R. P. Rajamanickam and the Tamil Literary Society.

[32] A copy is located today in the library of the Sorbonne.

[33] A copy is located today in the Vatican library.

[34] At that date their printing press from Japan was probably taken to Macao. See Kiichi Matsuda, *The Relations between Portugal and Japan* (Lisbon, 1965), p. 81.

[35] Entitled "True Account of God," its history is recounted in J. M. Braga, "The Beginnings of Printing at Macao," *Studia*, XII (1963), 33–34. See pl. 85.

printed at Macao in 1585. It may be surmised that Ruggiero brought back to Italy in 1590 the copies of these Chinese works as well as the unpublished translations of certain Chinese classical books which are today preserved in the Vatican and in the Roman archives of the Society of Jesus.[36] He certainly brought a Chinese slave to Rome, for Ruggiero appeared at a papal audience in December, 1590, with "his own Indian."[37]

The Japanese envoys to Rome had left Europe in 1586 with a printing press destined for their homeland. Their European companions of the Society took advantage of enforced halts at Goa and Macao to print Latin works on their new press for eventual distribution in Japan to the members of the mission. One of the two Latin works published at Macao was the *De missione legatorum Iaponensium* (1590), a dialogue on the experiences of the young Japanese envoys in Europe and Asia possibly composed by Alessandro Valignano, the Jesuit Visitor to the Asian missions.[38] It was this same press which returned to Macao in 1614 with Jesuit expellees from Japan and was eventually sold after 1620 to the Augustinians in Manila.

At the time of Valignano's first visit to Japan in 1579–82, he became convinced of the need to prepare and print Christian materials in Japan for the proper training of missionaries and converts and for the refutation of the Japanese sects. He himself prepared an apologetical "catechism" to provide answers raised by Japanese controversialists and sent it off to Lisbon with the Japanese envoys to be printed there. He also instructed Father Diego de Mesquita, the leader of the mission to Europe, to have a number of matrices cut in Flanders or Portugal of the *kana* script and of some Chinese characters. The young legates returned to Goa in 1587 with printed copies of the *Catechismus christianae fidei* (1586).[39] The new printing press that accompanied the returnees was the charge of two Japanese brothers who had learned in Portugal how to make matrices and types and how to operate the Western press.[40] It was probably these two Japanese printers who prepared the six characters in metal type for the names of Jesus and Mary which

[36] The Jesuit archives contain two copies of the complete Chinese *Doutrina* and one copy of the decalogue. See Schurhammer and Cottrell, *loc. cit.* (n. 31), p. 159. They also hold in manuscript the vocabulary as well as translations of the *Four Books* prepared by Ruggiero and Ricci. See Braga, *loc. cit.* (n. 35), p. 34. For a sample page from the unpublished vocabulary prepared between 1583 and 1588 see pl. 99.

[37] D'Elia, *op. cit.* (n. 22), I, 251, n. 2.

[38] See Johannes Laures, *Kirishitan Bunko: A Manual of Books and Documents on the Early Christian Missions in Japan* (Tokyo, 1940), pp. 4–5; also *Asia*, I, 809–10. The first work printed in Latin at Macao was a reprint of Ioão Bonifacio's treatise on Christian education entitled *Christiani pueri institutio* (Macao, 1588), a copy of which is located in the Biblioteca da Ajuda at Lisbon. For a reproduction of its title page see Cortez-Pinto, *op. cit.* (n. 29), p. 395.

[39] Two copies of this rare work are extant: one in the collection of the late ex-king Manuel II of Portugal and the other in the Liceu de Passos Manuel in Lisbon. A copy was sent to Archbishop Teotonio de Bragança of Évora, who was interested in the Jesuit mission of Japan. A Japanese screen recently found in Évora contains the Japanese text of a greater part of this work of 76 leaves. Its full Latin title is: *Catechismus Christianae Fidei, In Quo Veritas nostrae religionis ostenditur et sectae Iaponeses confutantur, editus a Patre Alexandro Valignano, societatis Iesu* (Lisbon, 1586).

[40] Known by their European names: Jorge de Loyola and Constantino Doyrado. See Matsuda, *op. cit.* (n. 34), p. 79.

appear on the title page of Valignano's catechism. It is likely also that they carried back to Japan with them these and other metal types of characters cast in Portugal.[41] When the printing press arrived in Japan in 1590, the government's repression of the Christians had already begun. So the new press had to be moved from place to place in western Japan as the Jesuits sought safety.

Despite turbulent political conditions the Christian press turned out at least twenty-nine books within the twenty-year period (1591–1611) of its productive existence in Japan.[42] The Japanese ideographs were ordinarily cut into wood, and the printing of them on Japanese paper was entrusted to the converts. Of six Christian works published in 1591–92 but two were issued in Japanese characters: *Dochirina Kirishitan* (Amakusa, 1592) and a book on baptism and penitence entitled in romanized transcription, *Bauchizumo no sazukeyō ...* (Amakusa, 1593?).[43] Copies of both these books were probably sent immediately to Évora to Archbishop Teotonio de Bragança, a great friend of the Jesuits and a supporter of their printing activities.[44] From 1593 to 1596 there were seven other books published at Amakusa, all in Roman type. An instructional manual for missionaries and converts was printed in colloquial Japanese which contained extracts from a classical Japanese history and Aesop's fables.[45] The idea behind translating the Western fables was to teach moral lessons through recounting pleasant stories. The third part of this collection contains 282 Chinese moralistic proverbs written in literary Japanese with terse explanations in the colloquial language.

The first publications of the mission press relating directly to language study were issued in 1594–95 at Amakusa. From Xavier's time onward the Jesuits had struggled valiantly to understand, speak, and write the Japanese language.[46]

---

[41] D. Schilling, "Christliche Druckereien in Japan (1590–1614)," *Gutenberg Jahrbuch*, XV (1940), 361–64.

[42] Copies of twenty-nine are extant; probably as many as fifty others were published. For a conveniently organized and scholarly listing of these works see *ibid.*, pp. 81–84; also Braga, *loc. cit.* (n. 35), pp. 116–26. Twenty-six works in Japanese characters were possibly published by the mission press. See Shigetomo Koda, "Notes sur la presse jésuite au Japon ... ," *Monumenta nipponica*, II, (1939), 42–53. For a full list of the books printed in Japan with up-to-date notes see J. Muller and E. Roth, *Aussereuropäische Druckereien im 16. Jahrhundert* (Baden-Baden, 1969), pp. 12–35.

[43] A copy of the *Dochirina* is in the Vatican library. The only extant copy of the *Bauchizumo* is in the Tenri library of Tokyo. On the date for the latter see A. Ebisawa (comp.), *Christianity in Japan. A Bibliography of Japanese and Chinese Sources* (Tokyo, 1960), pp. 6–7.

[44] Laures, *op. cit.* (n. 38), pp. 19, 20n.; on the archbishop's activities see *Asia*, I, 676, 692.

[45] *Heike Monogatari, Esopo no Fabulas, Kinkushū* (Amakusa, 1592–93). For discussion see Laures, *op. cit.* (n. 38), pp. 21–24. The only extant copy of the original work is in the British Museum. For a reproduction of its title page see Cortez-Pinto, *op. cit.* (n. 29).

[46] The literature on the language question is voluminous. For general discussion see J. Dahlmann, *Die Sprachkunde und die Missionen, ein Beitrag zur Charakteristik der älteren katholischen Missionsthätigkeit, 1500–1800* (Freiburg-im-Breisgau, 1891); for more specific analysis of the problem in Japan see J. A. de Freitas and A. R. Gonçálvez Viana, "Subsidios para a bibliographia portugueza, relativa ao estudo da lingua do Japão," *O Instituto*, LI (1904), 762–68; LII (1905), 115–28, 310–20, 437–38, 499–512; and the articles of Tadao Doi, "Researches in the Japanese Language Made by the Jesuit Missionaries in the XVIth and XVIIth Centuries," *Proceedings of the Imperial Academy of Japan* (Tokyo), XIII (1937), 232–36; "Das Sprachstudium der Gesellschaft Jesu in Japan im 16. und 17. Jahrhundert," *Monumenta*

Initially they had to be content with learning enough of the spoken language to hear confessions and to preach and debate. They had no dictionaries or grammars and were forced with the aid of their converts to provide their own technical aids. From the Jesuit letters it appears that Japanese-Portuguese dictionaries and grammars were already being compiled in 1563–64. These were constantly enlarged and corrected thereafter, particularly by Father Luis Fróis. In 1594 the Jesuits at Amakusa printed an abridgment of Manuel Alvarez' Latin grammar adapted to the needs of Japanese students.[47] In the following year they published an epitome of the Latin dictionary of Ambrosio Calepino with Portuguese and Japanese translations.[48]

In 1598–99 the Jesuits at Nagasaki printed a dictionary of the Chinese characters then in use in Japan which was called *Racuyoxu* (*Rakuyōshū*). What is particularly important about this dictionary is its presentation of the Chinese characters with *kana* and in the order of its syllabary.[49] The dictionary also includes an appendix of Japanese and Chinese official titles, and a list of the names of Japan's provinces. Father João Rodriguez, who probably had a part in preparing the *Racuyoxu*,[50] was possibly instrumental also in compiling the *Vocabulário da lingoa de Iapam* printed at Nagasaki in 1603–4. This work includes about thirty thousand Japanese characters and words written in Latin letters and arranged in alphabetical order. The meanings of the words are explained in Portuguese and the vocabulary is rich in terms relating to Buddhism, Japanese literature, provincial dialects, and slang. Several years later Rodriguez published at Nagasaki the *Arte de lingo do Iapam* (1604–8), a practical and sophisticated presentation of the nature of the Japanese language and its grammar that

---

nipponica, II (1939), 437–65; and "A Review of the Jesuit Missionaries' Linguistic Studies of the Japanese Language in the 16th and 17th Centuries," in *International Symposium on History of Eastern and Western Cultural Contacts, 1957* (Tokyo, 1959). Also consult C. R. Boxer, "Padre João Rodriguez Tçuzu, S.J., and His Japanese Grammars of 1604 and 1620," in *Miscelânea de filologia, literatura e história culturel a memória de Francisco Adolfo Coelho, 1874–1919* (Lisbon, 1950), II, 338–63.

[47] Entitled *De institutione grammatica*, the text is in Latin but the conjugations are given Portuguese and Japanese equivalents. A copy of this work was sent to Rome in 1605 (see Laures, *op. cit.* [n. 38], p. 24). Possibly it was addressed to Angelo Rocca, for it reposes today in the Biblioteca Angelica (Rome) which received its name and basic collection from Rocca.

[48] Entitled *Dictionarium Latino Lusitanicum ac Iaponicum* . . . (1595). For discussion see Laures, *op. cit.* (n. 38), p. 25. This was the first printed dictionary of the Japanese language. See Boxer, *loc. cit.* (n. 46), p. 349. In general, the Japanese were not inclined to print native works. Though printing was known in Japan from the tenth century, printed materials were limited to the reproduction of Buddhist charms. The printing of books by the Chinese method began in Japan only in 1592, two years after the Jesuit press arrived there. See Muller and Roth, *op. cit.* (n. 42), p. 7.

[49] The syllabary of the *kana* consists of fifty symbols which are used by the Japanese to express the sounds of the Sino-Japanese characters. The romanization of Japanese devised by the Jesuits was made possible by this practice. This dictionary, of course, was printed in Chinese characters with the *kana* alongside, a common practice in Japan to make easier the reading of the Chinese characters. For further analysis of the *Racuyoxu* see Tadao Doi, "Researches in the Japanese Language" (n. 46), pp. 233–34. Also cf. pl. 90.

[50] Rodriguez has commonly been thought to be the compiler. But Tadao Doi (*ibid.*) disagrees. The assumption of Rodriguez' leading role is based on the fact that he acted as Valignano's interpreter in his interview of 1591 with Hideyoshi and was thereafter more or less the official spokesman for the Jesuits in their dealings with Japanese officialdom.

remained the best available in Europe until after the reopening of Japan in the nineteenth century.[51]

The Spanish missionaries in the Philippines were also seriously engaged with language problems during the last generation of the sixteenth century.[52] The first Augustinians to work in Cebu were not outstanding as students of the local Bisayan language. Friar Martin de Rada was the exception among them for he quickly learned to speak both Bisayan and Chinese. Systematic study of the native tongues did not begin until the Franciscans decided to prepare a Tagalog catechism, grammar, and dictionary in 1580. Friar Juan de Plasencia, who was taught Tagalog by a Spanish boy born in the islands, was delegated to undertake this task. In the interest of preventing doctrinal disputes from arising between the orders, Philip II decreed that grammars or catechisms published in the islands required the approval of the bishop and the Audiencia. It was not until 1593 that a revised version of Plasencia's catechism was utilized in the publication of a *Doctrina Christiana* that appeared in Spanish and Tagalog; and another *Doctrina* in Chinese and Spanish were published by the wood-block method. Also in 1593 Brother Juan Cobo published a book in Chinese on the true God and the church which includes a fascinating woodcut of a realistic Chinese and a Dominican priest.[53] Two years later a printing press was brought to the Philippines by the Dominicans. Thereafter the other orders brought presses of their own to the islands, for the purpose of printing religious books in the native languages for the converts and of providing instructional materials to train the missionaries in the languages they needed for their work. By 1610 the Dominican friar Francisco de S. Joseph had published at Bataan the *Arte y reglas de la lengua tagala*, the first serious work ever to be published on this language.[54]

Publication of books in the languages of Asia was a joint enterprise involving missionaries in the field, native converts, the Portuguese crown, and the printing trade. Indians and Japanese were trained in Europe to operate the press, and many Asians of all nationalities were taught to work it at the mission stations in the East. Without cooperation from Asians, the Tamil *Cartilha* (1554) and the Japanese characters which grace the title page of Valignano's *Catechism* (1586) could probably never have been prepared in Lisbon. Copies of the books printed at the mission stations in Asia were often dispatched to Europe shortly after coming off the press. Because these books were frequently manuals prepared for the guidance of missionaries, they were generally Asian translations of Christian doctrinal texts familiar to most Europeans. They were sometimes provided also with parallel texts in Portuguese or Latin.

---

[51] For a detailed analysis of Rodriguez' *Arte* and for an appreciation of his command of Japanese see *ibid.*, pp. 235–36. Also see Boxer, *loc. cit.* (n. 46), pp. 358–61.

[52] See especially J. L. Phelan, "Philippine Linguistics and Spanish Missionaries, 1565–1700," *Mid-America* (Chicago), XXXVII (1955), 154–59.

[53] In Spanish this book is entitled *Tratado del verdadero Dios y de la Iglesia*. For a reproduction of the woodcut see L. C. Gutierrez, "Dos grandes bibliotecas del Extremo-Oriente para la Nacional de Madrid," *Gutenberg Jahrbuch*, XXXIV (1959), 123. See pls. 87, 88, 89, 92.

[54] For a discussion of this work and a reproduction of its title page see *ibid.*, pp. 123–25.

Some of the books prepared in Japan at the end of the sixteenth century were far more than mere translations of Christian teachings. They were fundamental efforts to analyze and organize the Japanese language, and its Chinese background, for the clear purpose of becoming better able to penetrate and understand the high civilizations of East Asia. To command the ideographic languages at the level of everyday usage is in itself a formidable task; the missionaries were determined to achieve a degree of competency in Japanese that would put them intellectually and socially on a level with learned natives. In the process they also provided the linguists of Europe with many of the materials necessary for analysis of the Asian languages and for their integration into the linguistic theory of the day. So the question naturally arises: What did the European scholarly world of the sixteenth century understand about the languages of the East and how did it fit them into prevailing ideas about the origin, development, and relationships of languages?

2

RENAISSANCE LINGUISTIC IDEAS

The reigning doctrines relative to the origin and history of language were biblical and humanistic in their assumptions.[55] From patristic writings and biblical exegesis a traditional view of language prevailed which permeated the thought and writings of Renaissance scholars. God in Paradise, it was generally believed, had concreated with Adam the first language. This original language, divinely given to mankind, was a perfect means of communication by which God and all men could speak one to the other without the aid of an interpreter. Its letters and words mirrored perfectly, or nearly so, the natures of the things they represented. Primitive Hebrew, not the Hebrew of the sixteenth century, was usually identified as the *lingua humana*. It had survived the universal flood, the first of God's punishments meted out to his erring children. Shortly after Noah's progeny had repeopled the earth, vainglorious tribes combined efforts to build at Babel a tower that would reach heaven itself. Angered by man's effrontery, God confounded the tongues of the builders and scattered the tribes over the face of the earth. To atone for their sins men were forced to live with a welter of vernaculars that made communication with God and one another a hardship and a constant reminder of the divine wrath.

From the linguistic muddle of Babel there emerged seventy-two profane

[55] For general discussions of Renaissance language study see Arno Borst, *Der Turmbau von Babel* (Stuttgart, 1960), III, Pt. I, 1048–50; H. Arens, *Sprachwissenschaft . . .* (2d ed.; Freiburg, 1969), pp. 62–65; R. H. Robins, *A Short History of Linguistics* (London, 1967), pp. 94–103; Louis H. Gray, *Foundations of Language* (New York, 1939), pp. 425–32; J. R. Firth, *The Tongues of Men* (2d ed.; London, 1964), chaps. iv and v; K. O. Apel, *Die Idee der Sprache in der Tradition des Humanismus von Dante bis Vico* (Bonn, 1963), chaps. ii and iii.

languages and a number of inferior variants and dialects.[56] The profane languages were not new creations but were produced quite simply from a reshuffling of the sounds, letters, and meanings of the primitive language. Since it was assumed that the *lingua humana* had not been permanently destroyed at Babel, its recovery became a goal of both religious and linguistic effort. Certain scholars tried to find the lost language by disentangling and rearranging primitive elements from the various profane languages. Others gradually came to believe, as the overseas discoveries revealed more of the world of language, that the primitive language and characters still existed intact somewhere. Most of the exotic languages therefore began to be examined by Renaissance scholars to discover those elements which related them to the original language of mankind.

During the Renaissance the Christian theory of linguistic origins and history competed with language ideas derived from the study of the classics. While the Greeks had ignored "barbarian" tongues, they studied their own language seriously. The ancient philosophers had debated vigorously whether language was created by nature or brought into being by convention as they sought, in working out their theories of knowledge, the relationship between the idea and the word denoting it. Aristotle took the view that the external world of nature impresses itself upon man through the senses. He declared that words are but symbols and not the precise image of the ideas or things they represent. After adopting the position that language is conventional rather than natural in its origins, Aristotle and his followers subjected language to logical analysis, or to an ordering that is generally called grammar. Aristotle's grammatical theories, which stressed the regularities in language structure, were elaborated upon by the Alexandrians and grouped into a coherent whole by Dionysius Thrax (second to first centuries B.C.). The cultural world of imperial Rome and early Christianity remained Greek and Latin until the sixth century. Throughout the Middle Ages the rules of grammar developed by the Greeks were held to be universal and completely independent of particular languages.

Most Roman and medieval students of language worked slavishly within the grammatical framework inherited from the Greeks. But some medieval thinkers, while debating niceties of grammar in the universities, had increasingly to concern themselves with the presentation of Christian teachings to the ordinary people in their own languages. To "go ye therefore and teach all nations" involved learning foreign languages. Pope Clement V by a decree issued at Vienne in 1311 had urged that Christianity, when necessary, be taught in infidel tongues, and he called upon the universities of Paris, Oxford, Bologna, and Salamanca to appoint two professors in Hebrew, Greek, Arabic, and Chaldean. Two experts in these languages were also to be employed by the papal curia to teach and to make translations. Because the hopes connected with this resolution far exceeded the results obtained from it, a renewal of the Vienne

---

[56] *Gen.* 11. The number seventy-two was arrived at by counting each of the descendants of the three sons of Noah as a representative of each language.

appeal was published at Basel in 1434.[57] In the meantime Dante was directing attention to the study of the vernacular languages of Italy and to a comparison of their dialects.[58] But for the rest of the languages of the world, Dante followed most of the conventional ideas related to the myth of Babel.[59]

Dante's absorption in the vulgar languages of Italy had the effect of encouraging others to cultivate and analyze other vernaculars. Serious study of Greek began at the end of the fourteenth century. Formal grammars, following the Latin model, were prepared in the fifteenth century for Italian, Spanish, and German. Study of Hebrew began at Charles University in Prague early in the fifteenth century, and before long a number of European universities actually began teaching Arabic and Chaldean.[60] While purists deplored these challenges to the supremacy of Latinity, the linguistic horizons of the fifteenth century were extended to include the languages of the Levant. Around 1427 a Bavarian named Johann Schiltberger, who had lived as a slave in Turkey for thirty-two years, gave to Europe a rendition of the Lord's Prayer in the Turkish, Armenian, and Tartar languages. He was thus the originator of the idea of using the Lord's Prayer as a *Sprachprobe*, a pioneering effort of syntactical comparison which developed into a venerable linguistic device.[61] Shortly thereafter Arnold von Harff, a noble of Cologne, included in the memoirs of his Eastern pilgrimages the alphabets as well as sample words and sentences from a number of Near Eastern languages.

While the Humanists busied themselves with the languages of Antiquity, the papacy directed its attention to a revival of relations with the contemporary Eastern Church. Priest Joseph of the Syro-Malabar church visited Rome in 1502 and was interviewed about south India by Pope Alexander VI.[62] While nothing startling resulted from this visit, Rome nonetheless continued its efforts to realign the Eastern Christians. Prelates from Syria, Ethiopia, and other parts of the East attended the Fifth General Council of the Lateran convened in 1512.[63] The Ottoman conquest of Syria and Egypt in 1516–17 further stimulated the papacy in its efforts to establish firm ties with the Eastern Christians in the hope of winning them as allies against the Turks. Study of the languages of the Christian East was also encouraged by these developments. The churchmen

[57] For discussion see G. Levi della Vida, *Ricerche sulla formazione del più antico fondo dei manoscritti orientali della Biblioteca Vaticana* (Vatican City, 1939), pp. 109–15.

[58] His most famous work on this subject is *De vulgari eloquentia* (ca. 1303).

[59] Dante was primarily dependent for his view of the confusion of tongues upon the synthesis of the patristic writers prepared by Thomas Aquinas. See A. Ewert, "Dante's Theory of Language," *Modern Language Review*, XXXV (1940), 358–59.

[60] See S. Segert and K. Beránek, *Orientalisk an der Prager Universität* (2 vols.; Prague, 1967), I, 9–10; on the spread of Arabic see J. Fueck, *Die arabischen Studien in Europa* ... (Leipzig, 1955), p. 50; and Moritz Steinschneider, *Die europäischen Übersetzungen aus dem Arabischen bis Mitte des 17. Jahrhunderts* (Graz, 1956).

[61] The last great collection of the Lord's Prayer in various languages and dialects was compiled by J. C. Adelung, *Mithridates oder allgemeine Sprachenkunde mit dem Vaterunser als Sprachprobe in beynahe fünf hundert Sprachen und Mundarten* (Berlin, 1806).

[62] See *Asia*, I, 157–58.

[63] W. Roscoe, *The Life and Pontificate of Leo X* (London, 1827), II, 280–81.

from the East, who were in attendance at the Lateran Council until 1517, were called upon to act as teachers of the Syriac, Arabic, and Ethiopic languages and asked to identify the Oriental books in the Vatican library and to compile a list of those whose titles they could read. The register issued in 1518 includes titles of twenty-two books; a note appended to the list indicates that other Oriental books, presumably in languages they could not read, were also part of the Vatican collection.[64] Possibly one of the unidentified titles was the Chinese book sent to Pope Leo X in 1514 by the king of Portugal.[65]

The Portuguese and the Spanish were more immediately affected by the revelation of new overseas languages than other Europeans. In 1492, the year of Columbus' departure in search of "the Indies," Antonio de Nebrija published his *Gramatica de la lengua castellana* (Salamanca), a book which inaugurated a new age in the study of the Iberian languages. In his prologue dedicated to Queen Isabella, the sponsor of Columbus, Nebrija stresses the relationship between political expansion and the flowering of the national language. To establish and maintain political unity the Castilian language should become the imperial language and should serve the cause of Spain as Latin had the cause of Rome. For Castilian to become an international language it had to be organized, and rules and standards had to be adopted to give it a solidity and authority comparable to Latin.[66] While Nebrija's fervor for Castilian was not shared by the Portuguese linguists, they were profoundly influenced by his ideas about the importance of language in the building and sustaining of empire.

The disparate colonies of the Portuguese, it was realized early in the sixteenth century, possessed little but a common language to bind them together. Religious books, about twenty-five hundred of them, were sent to Abyssinia in 1513; five years later the Franciscans sent a similar number to Cochin.[67] The indigenous converts, mainly the wives of the Portuguese, and the Christian children were initially taught the Portuguese language through these books. By 1570 as many as five hundred children were being taught in Goa the rudiments of Christian doctrine through Portuguese.

In Portugal itself a debate arose over the purity and independence of the national language. The importation into traditional Portuguese of Latin and Castilian words and syntax was assuming proportions far beyond anything previously known. Literati, like Gil Vicente, sometimes preferred to write their works in Castilian rather than Portuguese. Even while the Portuguese crown boasted of triumphs in distant places, tempers flared at home regarding the corruption of Portuguese, its relationship to Latin and Castilian, and its viability

---

[64] Levi della Vida, *op. cit.* (n. 57), pp. 109–15. The Lateran Council was seriously concerned with the religious problems raised by books. Finally it prescribed precensorship (that is, before publication) for all books without exception. See D. H. Wiest, *The Precensorship of Books* (Washington, D.C., 1953), p. 21.

[65] *Asia*, II, Bk. 1, 41.

[66] For further discussion of Nebrija's linguistic ideas see Werner Bahner, *La lingüistica española del Siglo de Oro* . . . (Madrid, 1966), pp. 41–47.

[67] For a list see S. da Silva Neto, *História da língua portuguêsa* (Rio de Janeiro, 1952), p. 543.

as an independent language. Damião de Góis, possibly because he shared so many of Erasmus' ideas, was a firm believer in the efficacy of popular languages and of their importance to the advancement of national culture. Others thought, as the Portuguese succeeded abroad, that it was imperative for the sake of empire and growing national pride to proclaim the independence of the language, to define its character, and to formulate the rules governing it.[68]

The first known Portuguese grammar was prepared by Fernão de Oliveira and published at Lisbon in 1536 under the title *Grammatica da lingoagem portuguesa*. Here the Portuguese language is organized according to the rules of Latin grammar. As in Nebrija's grammar, the independence and the worth of the vernacular is proclaimed, its superior clarity asserted, and the need for teaching it to the Brazilians, Asians, and Africans stressed. To posterity Oliveira is mainly remembered as a pioneer defender of the Portuguese language, and a herald of its future success.[69]

Oliveira's ideas about teaching the Portuguese languages systematically was implemented by João de Barros, the factor of the Casa da India and the historian of the Portuguese in Asia.[70] In 1539 he prepared for young Prince Philip of Portugal a brief catechism (*Cartinha*) preceded by a primer for learning to read the language. In the introductory letter addressed to Prince Philip, Barros asserts that the language a child learns at his mother's breast always remains the sweetest and most natural language to him. The Portuguese language, he points out, is carrying to Africa and Asia the message of the gospels. Four Malabar princes have expressed a desire to learn Portuguese for the purpose of reading the divine precepts of Christianity. No language can be so easily learned, he avers, as one which teaches salvation. To help the beginner Barros provides woodcut illustrations of common objects with their names, an alphabet, and a syllabary. Following these introductory language materials, he gives the beginner a short, simplified version of the precepts of the church.[71] It was this brief catechism from which Xavier first taught in Asia and which he had translated into Tamil (1542) and Japanese (1549).[72]

In their common aversion to Castilian, Oliveira and Barros stressed the

[68] Cf. especially J. Morais-Barbosa, *A língua portuguêsa no mundo* (2d rev. ed.; Lisbon, 1969), pp. 60–65.

[69] See J. P. Machado (ed.), *Duarte Nunes de Leão, Origem da língua portuguesa* (Lisbon, 1945), pp. 55–56. On the question of the chronological priority of Oliveira's grammar see H. Cidade, "João de Barros. O que pensa da lingua portuguesa—como a escreve," *Miscêlanea de filologia, literatura e história cultural a memória de Francisco Adolfo Coelho (1847–1919)* (Lisbon, 1950), II, 282–89.

[70] On his career see *Asia*, I, 190.

[71] Text in *Compilação de varias obras do insigne portuguez Joam de Barros . . .* (Lisbon, 1785), pp. 1–67.

[72] For the history of how Xavier and Barros used Barros' short catechism and instructional manual see G. Schurhammer and J. Wicki (eds.), *Epistolae S. Francisci Xavierii aliaque eius scripta* (2 vols.; Rome, 1945), I, 94–100. In Lisbon itself there were thirty-six reading teachers in the middle of the sixteenth century. João Soares, following Barros' lead, published in 1550 his *Cartinha para ensinar a ler e escrever* (Lisbon). See A. J. Saraiva, *História da cultura em Portugal* (2 vols.; Lisbon, 1955), II, 184–86.

undiluted purity of Portuguese and its linguistic proximity to classical Latin. Their grammars followed the organizational model of Latin, but Barros indicates that the subject matter of his grammar was derived from both common usage and the authority of the learned. He asserts that the learned in Portugal were not as Latinized in their speech and writing as the Humanists of Italy, France, and Spain, since most of them were involved directly or indirectly with expansion and exposed thereby to a variety of language influences.[73] The thousands of Portuguese with Asian experience who had returned to Lisbon by 1525 had brought back new words and expressions from the overseas world which at once left their imprint on the spoken language.[74] Asians and Africans were not uncommon sights on the streets of Lisbon, and the negro speaking Portuguese was caricatured in popular literature as a rude and comic figure.[75]

The grammars of Oliveira and Barros were especially designed to teach correct, metropolitan Portuguese to overseas peoples. As a consequence they employ exotic words from trade and seafaring to illustrate the orthographical and phonetical features of the Portuguese language. Barros in his dialogue in praise of the Portuguese language published in 1540 is already supremely conscious of its distinctive character and of its relative independence of Latin. He prophesied that Portuguese would one day conquer Latin, as its speakers had already conquered Asia and Africa. In his estimation the final victory of Portuguese as an international language was already being signaled by the vast number of Moorish words adopted: "all those which begin with *al* and *xa*, and terminate with *z*." But this is not all. Barros has the father of the dialogue tell his son:

And now from the conquest in Asia we receive *chatinar* for "to trade," *beniaga* for "merchandise," *lascarim* for "soldier," *çumbaya* for "a reverence" and "a bow," and other words which are now just as natural to the tongues of the men who go to those places as their own Portuguese.[76]

[73] See also H. Cidade, *A literatura portuguesa e a expansão ultramarina* (2d ed.; 2 vols.; Coimbra, 1968), I, 284–85.

[74] By this date around 70,000 Portuguese had embarked for the Orient; about one-tenth of that number had returned. See Morais-Barbosa, *op. cit.* (n. 68), pp. 75–79.

[75] Three of the *autos* of Gil Vicente include characters who speak the argot of negro slaves, a version of colonial Portuguese in which phonetic elements were introduced from the Sudanese languages and Bantu. See W. Giese, "Notas sôbre a fala dos negros em Lisboa no principio do século XVI," *Revista lusitania*, XXX (1932), 251–57. Generally the teachers of reading were mulattoes and other simple folk who also read and wrote for the illiterate. See Saraiva, *op. cit.* (n. 72), II, 184–86. For further discussion of the negro dialect in Iberian literature see Edmundo de Chasca, "The Phonology of the Speech of the Negroes in Early Spanish Drama," *Hispanic Review*, XIV (1946), 322–39.

[76] L. Stegagno Picchio (ed.), *João de Barros Dialogo em louvor da nossa linguagem . . .* (Modena, 1959), p. 81. On *chatinar* see Appendix to this chapter. *Beniaga* (*Veniaga*) was current in Portuguese for a long time, but is now listed in ordinary dictionaries of Portuguese as an Indian word meaning "merchandise." The other word is Arabic in origin. For Barros' efforts in the *Decadas* to give etymologies of certain Asian geographical names see *Asia*, I, 342–43. Also cf. Duarte Nunes de Leão, *Origem da língua portuguesa* (1601), who gives as examples of words imported from India: "catle, cabaia, lascarim, chatim, de que fizemos chatinar, vaniaga, corja . . .." See Machado (ed.), *op. cit.* (n. 69), p. 239, and for the editor's commentary see pp. 112–13.

While Barros and his fellow Iberians coped with practical problems of the national language, more conventional Humanists elsewhere continued to uphold the ideal of the *homo trilinguis*. From the ninth century the Greek, Hebrew, and Latin languages were held to be sacred tongues in that they had the distinction of appearing on the *titulus* of Christ's cross. They were also the languages of the learned world; trilingual colleges were established in the first third of the sixteenth century at Oxford (1517), Louvain (1517), Alcalá (1528), and Paris (1529). In these colleges it was recognized that Greek and Hebrew were as valuable as Latin for the study of philosophy and religion. But to strict Latinists both Greek and Hebrew were Oriental languages which had infiltrated the learned world only gradually and under highly dubious auspices.

Roger Bacon reported in 1267 that only four individuals in Latin Europe knew anything of the language of Homer. Beginning in the late fourteenth century the contacts between Italy and Byzantium inaugurated serious study of Greek in Latin Europe. The first Greek grammar prepared in Europe was published at Venice in 1495, but it was only in the sixteenth century that study of Greek became part of the regular language curriculum. Hebrew was studied by Jewish scholars in the Middle Ages, but Roger Bacon was the first Christian churchman to work with it seriously. While courses in Hebrew were offered at a number of major universities in the thirteenth, fourteenth, and fifteenth centuries, the returns in research and in preparation of students were minimal. Students of both Greek and Hebrew were accused of heresy and of trying to corrupt the purity of Latin Christianity. To these attacks the trilingual colleges and the Humanists interested in Oriental languages responded by asserting the vital need for studying the Old Testament and the philosophers of Greece in the original languages. Nicolas Clenard argued that the purpose of learning the languages of the Hebrews and Arabs was to enable Christians to refute their false teachings and to convert them to the true faith.[77]

The courtly society of Castiglione had no deep interest in the *homo trilinguis*, for the courtier had to command the modern languages to relate to his own society and to that of his neighbors.[78] This trend toward adoption of the vernacular languages prompted discussion and debate about their worthiness for philosophical discourse. Sperone Speroni, the Humanist, in his *Dialogue on Languages* (*ca.* 1540) raises the question: Why study foreign languages? The response to this question he places in the mouth of Peretto Pomponazzi, the eminent Aristotelian philosopher. Languages were created, as Aristotle asserted, by an act of the human will and were therefore all products of the human spirit. Thought is consequently not limited by linguistic form; all languages are of equal value, even the Arabic and Indian languages. That Speroni had in mind the languages of India (and not of Ethiopia) is supported by his subsequent reference

---

[77] For further discussion of the problems of Greek and Hebrew in the Latin world see L. Kukenheim, *Contributions à l'histoire de la grammaire grecque, latine et hebraïque à l'époque de la Renaissance* (Leyden, 1951), pp. 1, 7–10, 88–95. Also see Arens, *op. cit.* (n. 55), p. 64.

[78] Borst, *op. cit.* (n. 55), III, 1108–10.

to the merchants who send the spices and other Oriental commodities to Italy.[79]

The transition from the supremacy of Latin to the increased use of the vernaculars was accepted in the later sixteenth century without much debate. Latin grammar was used as a model for the organization of the European vernaculars, Greek, and Hebrew. Every new language encountered was likewise organized in terms of Latin. It was only among those who sought to ascertain the nature and causes of linguistic change that debate became heated. The general theory of change advanced by Theodor Bibliander (1504-64) was the one most widely accepted. In his commentaries published in 1548, Bibliander argued that the profane languages continued to develop after Babel as a result of external factors rather than because of the gradual evolution of their own inner forms. Changes occurred because of migrations and wars, of shifts in dominant political groups, and of the demands of new occupations, social classes, and popular modes. He recognized that the conquests in Asia and America might produce similar linguistic changes in the future.[80]

The biblical and Humanistic doctrines regarding the nature, origin, and history of language remained supreme until the middle years of the cinquecento. Challenge to the dominance of Latin steadily mounted from the vernacular languages and from the exaltation of Greek and Hebrew as the languages of philosophy and the Scriptures. While Greek and Hebrew became the equals of Latin in the trilingual colleges, the vernacular languages rapidly acquired respectability and received systematic organization. The equality of all languages was recognized by Speroni; the Florentine Academy was founded in 1540 for the express purpose of translating the sciences into the Tuscan vernacular. The Iberian grammarians proclaimed the importance of the vernacular languages to the conquest and maintenance of empire. The languages of the Levant and Africa began to be studied and organized by churchmen interested in evangelizing and in welding closer ties between Rome and the Christians of the Eastern rite. In the work of Bibliander the changes in the profane languages were attributed unhesitatingly to the cultural and social milieu rather than to the inner nature of the language. The most vexing of the theoretical problems that remained unresolved was the puzzling question of the extent of linguistic diversity,[81] a problem that was daily being widened and complicated by the discovery of a multitude of new languages in the overseas world about whose nature students of language possessed little or no knowledge.

---

[79] *Dialogo delle lingue e dialogo rettorica. Con introduzione di Giuseppe de Robertis* (Lanciano, 1912), pp. 72-73. For further comment see P. O. Kristeller, *Studies in Renaissance Thought and Letters* (Rome, 1956), pp. 489-90.

[80] Theodor Bibliander, *De ratione communi omnium linguarum et literarū commentarius . . .* (Zurich, 1548), pp. 5, 58-61. For commentary on the general theory see Robert A. Hall, Jr., "Linguistic Theory in the Italian Renaissance," *Language*, XII (1936), 103-4. Also see Arens, *op. cit.* (n. 55), pp. 71-72.

[81] Later Protestant writers used the diversity of languages to attack the claim of the Latin church to universality. For example, see Edward Brerewood, *Enquiries Touching the Diversity of Languages and Religions throughout the Chief Parts of the World* (London, 1614).

84. Printed in Quilon, probably on the printing press carried back to Asia by the Japanese emissaries. The woodcut is identical with that on *Christiani pueri institutio . . .* (Macao, 1588). Reproduced from J. Muller and E. Roth, *Aussereuropäische Druckereien im 16. Jahrhundert* (Baden-Baden, 1969), pl. XXXIV.

85. Title page of the first book printed at Macao by Europeans (1585). Prepared under the direction of Father Michele Ruggiero for xylographic reproduction. From J. Braga, "The Beginning of Printing at Macao," *Studia*, XII (1963), facing p. 3.

CHRISTIANI
PVERI INSTITVTIO,
ADOLESCENTIÆQVE
perfugium: autore Ioanne Bonifacio
SOCIETATIS IESV.
cum libri unius, & rerũ accefsione plurimarũ.

Cum facultate Superiorum
apud Sinas, in Portu Macaenſi
in Domo Societatis IESV.
Anno   1588.

86. First book printed in China on a European press, 1588. Copy in the Biblioteca da Ajuda of Lisbon. Reproduced from A. Cortez-Pinto, *Da famosa arte da impressão* (Lisbon, 1948), p. 395.

Doctrina Christiana, en
lengua española y tagala, cor
regida por los Religiosos de las
ordenes. Impressa con licencia, en
S. Gabriel, de la orden de S. Domingo
En Manila. 1593.

87, 88. Title page and final page of a *Doctrina Christiana* (Manila, 1593). Printed in Spanish and Tagalog. Reproduced from J. Muller and E. Roth, *Aussereuropäische Druckereien im 16. Jahrhundert* (Baden,–Baden, 1969), pls. XXII and XXIII.

89. Title page of a *Doctrina Christiana* printed at Manila in 1593 in Chinese characters for use of the Dominican fathers. Reproduced from J. Muller and E. Roth, *Aussereuropäische Druckerein im 16. Jahrhundert* (Baden-Baden, 1969), pl. XXI.

90. Title page of a *Doctrina Christam* printed in Japanese characters at Nagasaki by a Japanese lay brother in 1600. Reproduced from J. Muller and E. Roth, *Aussereuropäische Druckereien im 16. Jahrhundert* (Baden-Baden, 1969), pl. XIX.

r ,bento be ——— hofruito do teu — ventre — Jhu — Sancta —
viçsapattá palam vnare vaetile ihu. Xuddama⸱
Ebento be — bo fruito do teu vétre Jhu : Sancta ma⸱

— maria — de deos — madre — nos — peccadores
na mariá tambiránaré madáue : éngale pauigale
ria — madre de — deos — : — roga — por —

por — roga. ————— Amen. _
vénddi iránducolauénú. Amen.
nos — peccadores. ——Amen:

¶ Seguesse ho Credo.

O Credo in deum patré omnipotentem crea⸱ torem celi et terre . Et in Jesum xpum filium eius vnicum dominum nostrú. Qui conceptus est de spú sancto : natus ex maria vir⸱ gine . Passus sub pontio pilato/crucifixus/mortuus/ et sepultus : Descendit ad inferos : tertia die resur rexit a mortuis. Ascendit ad celos : sedet ad dex⸱ teram dei patris omnipotentis . Inde venturus est iudicare viuos et mortuos. Credo in spúz san⸱ ctú : sanctá ecclesiam catholicaú . Sanctorum có

91. A page from the *Cartilha* (1554) in Tamil and Portuguese showing the end of the "Ave Maria." The top line in Portuguese, written in red, is a word-for-word translation of the Tamil version—a device for language instruction. Reproduced from A. Cortez-Pinto, *Da famosa arte da impressão* (Lisbon, 1948), pl. XVIII.

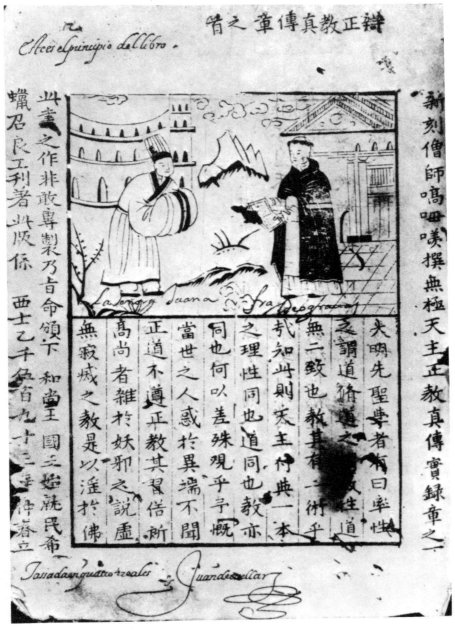

92. First page of a "Treatise on the True God and the Church," printed in Chinese characters at Manila with woodcut of a Chinese and a friar (1593). Reproduced from L. Gutierrez, "Dos grandes bibliotecas del Extremo-Oriente para la Nacional de Madrid," *Gutenberg Jahrbuch*, XXXIV (1959), 123.

93. Guillaume Postel, French linguist, geographer, and Japanophile. From A. Thevet, *Les vrais pourtraits* . . . (Paris, 1584), p. 588ʳ. Courtesy of the Newberry Library.

94. Portrait (1595) of Blaise de Vigenère (1523–96) by Thomas de Leu. Original in Cabinet des Estampes, Bibliothèque Nationale (Paris). Reproduced from D. Métral, *Blaise de Vigenère* . . . (Paris, 1939), pl. I.

THIS IS THE LANGUAGE OF CALECUT.

See, look ! . .	nocane [nōkka].
Hearest thou? . .	que que ne [kēlka].
Take him away .	criane.
To draw . .	balichene [walikkān].
Rope . .	coraoo [kayara].
Largely . .	lacany.
Give me . .	cornda.
To drink . .	carichany [kutippān].
Eat . . .	tinane [tinmān].
Take . . .	y na.
I do not wish to .	totenda.
To go . .	mareçane.
Go away ! . .	poo [pō].
Come here ! . .	baa [bā or wā]
Be silent ! . .	pote.
Rise ! . .	legany.
To throw . .	carecane [karikkān].
To speak . .	para ne [parane, speak thou].
Mad, silly . .	moto.
Serious . .	monday decany.
Lame . . .	mura call [murakāl].
To fall . .	biamçe.
Many, much . .	balidu [walare].
Bad . . .	betall [chītta].
Wind . . .	clarle [kātta].
Little . . .	chiredu [chiratu?].

95. Part of the first Malayālam vocabulary sent to Europe. From E. G. Ravenstein (ed.), *A Journal of the First Voyage of Vasco da Gama*, Publications of the Hakluyt Society, Old Series, Vol. XCIX (London, 1898), p. 105.

¶ Alem da renda, e campos de que faláo as cartas acima, que deu el Rey de Bungo aos padres, para no Facata, e Bungo fazerem Igreijas lhes deu outro na cidade de Amanguche cincoenta legoas de Bungo. A doaçáo se pos aqui para verem a maneyra de suas escrituras, aluaras, e letra. E cada figura destas sinifica o que vay sobrella.

O Duque   do Reyno de Çuo,   do Reyno Nangato,

do Reyno Bugen,   do Reyno Chicugen caqui,   do Reyno Iuami.

X

96. Japanese characters taken from the letter of Gaspar Vilela written in 1557, and reproduced from the preface by Artur Viegas to the second edition of *Relação Anual* of Fernão Guerreiro. Reproduced from A. Cortez-Pinto, *Da famosa arte da impressão* (Lisbon, 1948), facing p. 408.

Alphabetum Idiomatis
DE CINA
Ex bibliotheca Vaticana Romæ. In tertia aula
conclusa. Ex schedula manu Marcelli
Papæ scripta, ut aiunt. Sunt &
illic libri hoc idiomate perscri-
pti et manuscripti plures.

上 xam   几 pa
大 ta   扎 guin
人 im   子 zu
互 heu   隹 cua
乙 y   作 ze
已 qui   亻二 ju
屮 fa   凵丁 co
三 Sam   口 Chi
干 Zem   弘 li
七 Zi   巴 ey
十 xi
土 Su
丁 ye
刂 Sin
主 Cam

In eadem Bibliotheca videntur
Liber manuscriptus manu Henrici 8.
Anglorum Regis contra Lutherum ad
Leonem X. missus ab eodem. cum
disticho antecedente manu eius Regis
perscripto. Titulus libri hic est.
Assertio septem sacramentorū contra Lutherū
Anglorum Rex Henricus Leo decimæ mittit.
distichon: Hoc opus et fidei testem, et amicitiæ.

97. A Chinese alphabet from a document preserved in the Vatican Library reportedly
written by Pope Marcellus II (d. 1555). Reproduced with permission from British Museum
PS6/6126, Lansdowne, 720, p. 275.

Iulp.   The fourth of Iuly 1588. we paſſed the equinoctiall line, which was the fourth time that
Augnſt.   we had trauerſed the ſame in this our iourney. The 24.day of Auguſt wee had ſight of two I-
         lands of ẏ Aſores the one called Flores,the other Coruo,and directed our way from them for the
September. Liſard vntill the third of September, at which time we eſpied a Flemiſh Hulke that came from
         Portingale,which tolde vs the iopful newes of our Fleets good ſucceſſe againſt the huge armie
         of the Spaniards. And on the fift day we met with a ſhip of Southhampton, which had taken
         a Braſilian prife,whoſe Captaine informed vs at large of the trueth of that which had paſſed:
         We tooke ſome refreſhing of them, which was recompenſed with treble curteſie, and ſo entred
         into the narrow Seas where we had as terrible a night as euer men endured : for all our ſayles
         were blowen quite away: but making as good ſhift as we could with certaine olde ſayles wee
Their arriuall had within borde, on the next morning being the ninth of September 1588,like wearied men
at Plimu- through the fauour of the Almightie, we gate vnto Plymmouth : where the Townes men re-
mouth the 9. ceiued vs with all humanitie. In this voyage we burnt twentie ſayles of Spaniſh ſhippes,be-
of September ſides diuers of their Townes and Uillages.

                                           Written by N. H.

The names of the Kings or Princes of Iaua at the time of our *Englifh mens being there.*

Raia	Donaw.	Raia	Tymbanton.
Raia	Rabacapala.	Raia	Mawgbange.
Raia	Bacabatra.	Raia	Patimara.

Certaine wordes of the naturall language of Iaua, learned *and obferued by our men there.*

Sabuck, ſilke.		Gula, blacke ſugar.	
Sagu, bread of the Countrey.		Tadon,a woman.	
Larnike, drinke.		Bebeck, a ducke.	
Paree, ryce in the huſke.		Aniange, a beere.	
Braas, ſodden ryce.		Popran, oyntment.	
Calapa, coquos.		Coar, the head.	
Cricke, a dagger.		Endam, raine.	
Catcha, a looking glaſſe.		Ionge, a ſhippe.	
Arbo, an oxe.		Chay, the ſea.	
Vados, a goate.		Sapelo, ten in number.	
Cabo, golde.		Dopolo, twentie.	
Gardange, a plantine.		Treda, no.	
Hiam, a henne.		Lau, vnderſtand you.	
Seuit, linnen cloth.		Bayer, goe.	
Doduck, blewe cloth.		Adadizano, I will fetch it.	
Totopps, one of their caps.		Suda, ynough.	

Certaine notes or references taken out of the large Mappe of *China, brought home by Maſter Thomas* Candiſh. 1588.

THe great kingdome of the Mogores, is vpon the Northweſt and fals vpon Ta-
naſſacin beyond Mallaca, and ioynes vpon Bengala: they are men of warre,and
vſe no fight but on horſebacke, they goe in their apparel like Portingales.
  2 A City wherein is Captaine a Chinian,a man very deformed,hauing vnder
him many men of warre: he maketh warre both againſt the Tartarians, and the
Mogores lying betweene them,and lyeth without the circuite of the wall.
  3 Certaine hils beyond which the Tartarians do inhabite,who heretofore were great friends
with the Chinians,and now mainteine continual warres againſt them,ſo great that ſometimes
                                                       there

98. Historical, geographical, and language materials collected by Thomas Cavendish (1588). From Hakluyt, *Principall Navigations* (London, 1589), p. 813.

99. A page from the first European-Chinese dictionary. Composed by Ricci and Ruggiero in China between 1583 and 1588. Preserved in the Jesuit Archives (Rome), Jap.-Sin., I, 198, f. 33ᵛ. Reproduced from P. D. d'Elia, *Fonti Ricciane* . . . (3 vols.; Rome, 1942–49), Vol. II, pl. V.

1.vduelelſen.
.v.isvolenie.
on. wibranie.
ie.woleni.
m. iz biranie.
nga válaſztás.

Elector.

br.bochér.
ec. ixλoγeis.
in.electior.
l.elettore.
ſpan elegidor.
ll.electeur.
r. ein Erwehler.
g.een wthieſer.
igl. a chooſer.
l. wiborca.
ing. váliſzto.

Electrum.

ec ἤλεωτϱον.
t. electrum, ſucci-
num.
l. ambra di coro-
na, ambra gialla.
ſp.el ambar, escla-
rimiente.
ill. ambre.
rman. Agſtein/
Bornſte n.
lg. emmerē, amer,
amber.
ngl.amber.
oat. ambar.
olon.burſztin.
oh. cziſtec.agſtein.
ung.gyanta.

Eleemoſyna.

cbr.tſedhakah.
ræc.ἐλεηϱοσύνη.
Græc.

Græc. Vulg. ψυ-
χης.
Latin. e'eemoſyna.
Ital. elemoſina, limo-
ſina.
Hiſp.limoſina.
Gall.aumoſne.
German. Almuſen/
daß man dē Ar-
men gibt.
Belg. almoes.
Ang.almeſſe.
Dan.almiſſe.
Sclavon. vbvoſhie.
Carniol. almoſhen.
Bohem. almuz na,
peniz ktery z ſe
chudym pro buh
dlawa.
Polon. jal'muz na.
Turc. tſchadaka.
Hung. alamiſna.

Elegans.

Hebr. tob,iapheh.
Græc.Φιλόκαλ@,ἐλ-
λόγιμος.
Græc. Vulg. λόγ@.
Lat. elegans.
Ital.elegante.
Hiſpa.lindo.
Gall.de chois.
Germa. wolgeziert/
ſchön.
Belg. vercierdt.
Angl. elegant,polite,
fine.
Dan.deyligt.
Sclavon. leip, z.he-
den.
Dalm. naredan.

Carniol. leipu ziran.
Turc. chas.
Hung.ekens.
Bohem. poſtawy á
craſy.

Elegantia.

Hebr. tiphebeth.
Græc. Φιλοκαλία.
Lat.elegantia.
Ital.eleganza.
Hiſpan.lindeza.
Gall. bonne grace.
Germa.ſchöne/ Zier-
lichkeit.
Belg. fraeiheyt, cier-
licheyt.
Angl. preatineſſe.
Dan.deyligt.
Sclav. leipota,zhed-
noſt.
Dalm.vreha.
Polon. czudnoſcz.
Hung.ekeſſegh.
Bohe.peknoſt.

Eleganter.

Græc.κϱμψῶς.
Latin.eleganter.
Ital. elegantemente,
convenevelmēte.
Hiſpan linda.
Gall. elegamment.
German. zierlich/
fein.
Belg.fraeiheyt, cier-
licken.
Angl.neatly.
Sclav. leipu.
Pol. czudnie.
Dalm.doztoyne.
Hung. ekeſen.
Gg

Boh. oz dobne,

Elephas.

Hebr.behemah,phil.
Chald.beira.
Arab. behiz., fil,elſil,
elphil,alſil.
Græc. Ελίφας,πι-
είοςας.
Græc. Vulg. λίφας.
Latin. elephas, ele-
phantus.
Antiq. Lat.bos luca.
Sabinor.barrus.
Punic.Caſar.
Ital. lionfante.
Gall. elephant.
Hiſp. elephante.
Germ. ein Helfant.
Belg.elephant.
Angl. olyphant.
Sclav.ſion, ellefans.
Polo.elefánt.
Hung. elfánt.
Boh.ſloun.
Carniol. ellefans.
Turc ful,fül,phil.
Perſic.bebad.
Æthiop.ytembo.
Indic.barre.
Benomotap. Sofa-
lenſ. almana-
char.
Malac.cargba.
Cefalenſ. almana-
char.
Gedroſior,Decanēſ
ati.
Malavar.ane.
Canarin.azete.
Calecut.ane.

Elephan.

100. Sample page from H. Megiser, *Thesaurus polyglottus* (Frankfurt, 1603), p. 465. Notice under entry "Elephas" (Elephant) the equivalents in Asian languages. Courtesy of the Newberry Library.

101. A Japanese *kana* syllabary and *kanji* numerals from C. Duret, *Thresor des langues* (Cologne, 1613), pp. 913–15.

Mainte nant comme c'est que ces simples lettres se ordónent & a-gencent en vn contexte d'e-scriture, enuoi cy vn essay presenté à mó-sieur le Com-te d'Auuer-gne lors qu'il estoit grand Prieur de Frá-ce dont nous auons esté se-courus pour la satisfaction du public par monsieur de Roüé son tres docte & digne precepteur.

Ce qui suit, est vne copie de lettres patétes du Roy de Bŏgo dedás l'isle du Iappō; par lesquelles il permet aux Peres de la S. societé de Iesus estás ar riuez sur ses terres pour y pláter l'Euágile, de bastir en la ville d'Amágu-tie, vne Eglise appelée Day Dogie, c'est à dire la grande aduenue & entree du ciel. Les caractéres au demeurant sont tissus de plusieurs lettres accou-plées enseble par des entrelas, à la façon des notes Cicerŏniénes, & des ab-breuiatiŏs ou chiffres; signifiants ce qui est escrit au dessus, partie en lágue Iappŏnoise, & le reste accŏmodé à nostre parler pour plus facile intelligé ce. Par là on peut assez cŏprendre ce qui a esté dit cy deuát de la difficulté de lire & peindre ceste escriture ainsi abbregee & embarrassee; dŏt il y a in-finies sortes de liaisŏs & desguisemés. A propos dequoy Osorius vers la fin du 3. liu. de son hist. de Portugal, met qu'à Malipur, ville du Royaume de Naringue, l'an 561. furent trouuees au dessus d'vn autel, certaines lettres gra-

(marginalia): Ce morua à l'imita-tiŏ de ce qui est dis en Gene-se 18. c'est icila maison de Dieu, & la porte du ciel.

grauees fort ancienes, d'ŏt chaque caractére en exprimoit 10. 15. ou 20. au rapport d'vn Brachmane qui les leut & interpreta; cŏtenants en substáce que S. Thomas artiué en ces quartiers là du téps du Roy Sagan, pour prescher l'Euangile és Indes, y auoit basty vne Eglise; là où cŏme il faisoit vn iour ses prieres à genoulx au pied d'vne croix, vn Brachmane le massacra d'vn coup d'espieu. Voyez ce qu'escrit de ceste hist. amplement Pierre du Iarric. liu. 2. ch. 17. 18. & 19. de son histoire des Indes Orientales.

Le Roy & gouuerneur   du Royaume de Zuo,   du Royaume de N angati,

du Royaume de Bugen,   du Royaume de Chicu gen Caqui,   du Royaume de Iuami,

du Royaume de Bongo   du Royaume de Bichyi,   A ob'r. yé Day (le grád)

Dogie, acces du ciel,   aux Peres

102. Sample *kanji* script from C. Duret, *Thresor des langues* (1613), p. 916.

103. Sample *kanji* script taken from a patent of the King of Bungo (Japan) giving the Jesuits the right to build a church in his land. From C. Duret, *Thresor des langues* (1613), p. 917.

104. Sample of Timothy Bright's shorthand. Reproduced from G. L. Keynes, *Dr. Timothie Bright* (London, 1962), pl. I.

3

CLASSIFICATION AND COMPARISON

So long as Hebrew, Greek, and Latin were the only languages to which serious study was devoted, the simple divisions of language into sacred and profane, classical and Oriental, and living and dead remained adequate as working categories. But the extension of scholarly interest to the vernacular languages of Europe, the Levant, and eventually the overseas world quickly made apparent the inadequacy of these earlier divisions and made essential the invention of new and more exact classifications. Students of the Near Eastern languages recognized that Hebrew, Arabic, Chaldean, and Syriac possessed common characteristics which set them apart from the family of the Greek and Latin languages. Still the belief prevailed that Hebrew was the mother of all languages whatsoever and in the sixteenth and seventeenth centuries an astounding amount of scholarly effort continued to be directed to the laborious and fruitless task of trying to discover and explain the process by which Hebrew was split into a variety of languages and dialects. While the description and classification of new languages was delayed by the search for the affinities of all languages to Hebrew, the linguists and theologians of the sixteenth century began slowly and timidly to group the languages of the world according to their characteristic features. In the process they developed techniques of linguistic comparison that were to remain the standard equipment of the philologist until the nineteenth century.

Guillaume Postel (1510–81), the French linguist and cabalist, has been hailed many times as the father of comparative philology.[82] While at the College of Sainte-Barbe in Paris, Postel displayed a rare talent in learning foreign languages. Here he also became acquainted with the young men from Spain and Portugal who were sent to Paris at the expense of their rulers. The Iberian students were full of tales about the discoveries, and the Jesuits vibrant with enthusiasm for the religious conquests that awaited them in the overseas world. Initially, however, Postel followed secular linguistic studies and in 1536 was chosen to accompany the French mission to Constantinople. Under the tutelage of a Turkish Christian, Postel studied Arabic in the city on the Bosphorus. In 1537 he appeared at Venice and associated himself with the circle of Daniel Bomberg, the printer of books in Hebrew and other Oriental languages. It was probably with the aid of Teseo Ambrogio (1469–1540) that Postel collected the

---

[82] For evaluations of his language studies see Paul Colomiès, *Gallia orientalis* (Hamburg, 1655), pp. 59–66; G. Dugat, *Histoire des orientalistes de l'Europe du XIIᵉ au XIXᵉ siècle* (Paris, 1868), pp. xvi–xviii; Theodor Benfey, *Geschichte der Sprachwissenschaft und orientalischen Philologie in Deutschland* . . . (Munich, 1869), pp. 225–26. For the relation of his language studies to Postel's total thought see William J. Bouwsma, *Concordia Mundi: The Career and Thought of Guillaume Postel* (Cambridge, Mass., 1957), pp. 7, 104–6. For his portrait see pl. 93.

alphabets and grammars which he published the following year in his first book.

The collecting of foreign and contrived alphabets had begun as early as the eighth century. Sacred names and invocations to God or the Devil were written or engraved in letters from a secret or magical alphabet. The medieval talismanists had manuals that showed in tabular form which sacred letters to use in relation to particular astrological signs for the best magical results.[83] In the Middle Ages Greek letters and runes were often the basis for the ciphers invented to protect the secrecy of messages.[84] Even students of language did not escape the general feeling that exotic alphabets possessed a mysterious meaning or a semisacred character. Such beliefs were given substance by the clear affinities which existed among the letters of all known alphabets and of their obvious relationship to Hebrew.

Postel's *Linguarum duodecim characteribus differentium alphabetum introductio* (Paris, 1538) describes and gives illustrations of the alphabets and grammars of eleven Balkan and Near Eastern languages, and one called "Indian" (pp. 33–38). Like most of his contemporaries, Postel sought the affinities between Hebrew and the profane languages he assumed were descended from it. The characters of primitive Hebrew, like the divine words themselves, had been confused at Babel. Consequently the collection and comparison of alphabets might lead, it was thought, to the recovery of the primitive characters which were alleged to be in almost perfect conformity with the nature of the things they represented. More of the primitive characters were thought to be better preserved in the Semitic than in other languages. But it was recognized that the characters of every language, including Hebrew, had changed with the passage of time. Comparison of the modern Hebrew with other alphabets might therefore lead to the isolation of the universal characters of the *lingua humana*, a first step in bringing an end to the "confusion of tongues."

The "Indian alphabets" of Postel and his contemporaries actually are examples from what we now call Geez, the leading Semitic language of Ethiopia. That such alphabets were named "Indian" is not surprising when it is recalled that Ethiopia was often included in the sixteenth-century definition of India.[85] Bernard von Breydenbach's *Journey*, published in 1486, included the first samples of the Ethiopic alphabet to appear in a printed European book. Johannes Potken, a German priest who was present at the Lateran Council, published at Cologne a *Psalterium aethiopice* (1513) in Geez with a Latin translation. His contemporaries began to refer to the language of the *Psalterium* as "Chaldean" and to its alphabet as "Indian." Following Potken, Sebastian Münster in 1527

---

[83] J. Marquès-Rivière, *Amulettes, talismans et pantacles dans les traditions orientales et occidentales* (Paris, 1950), pp. 306–7.

[84] See Bischoff, *loc. cit.* (n. 6), p. 213.

[85] Even before the sixteenth century, the Ethiopians were called "Indians." The hostel founded for the Ethiopian pilgrims to Rome was named "S. Stefano degli Indiani." For its history see Renato Lefevre, "Appunti sull'ospizio di S. Stefano degli Indiani nel Cinquecento," *Studi romani*, XV (1967), 16–33.

and Teseo Ambrogio in 1539 included the Ethiopic letters in their books of the "Chaldean" language and in both cases they caption them "Indian."[86] Postel follows Ambrogio in these identifications, and later linguists perpetuated their misleading designations.[87] In 1552 Mariano Vittorio published at Rome his grammar entitled *Chaldeae seu Aethiopicae linguae institutiones* dedicated to Cardinal Marcello Cervini.[88] It was not until the latter half of the seventeenth century that Europeans clearly distinguished between the languages of Ethiopia and India. Even in the nineteenth century, scholars continued to be titillated by the relationships they saw between the Ethiopic and Indian letters.[89]

The authors of writing books were also fascinated by exotic scripts. Giovanbattista Palatino, one of the foremost exponents of writing according to geometrical principles, published a book in 1540 in which he professed to teach by precept and example "every sort of ancient and modern letters of all nations."[90] He includes among his examples an "Indian alphabet" that appears opposite an "Egyptian alphabet," both framed in decorative cartouches. No elucidatory text is provided but the implication is clear that Palatino is trying to show that his method of italic writing is applicable to even the most remote alphabetical symbols. While some of his "Indian" characters resemble their counterparts in the Brahmi and south Indian scripts, the similarities are probably attributable to the fact that these scripts had common Semitic progenitors rather than to any direct knowledge of the Indian scripts themselves.[91]

The appearance in Europe of Chinese books and sample Chinese and Japanese characters, along with assertions about the great antiquity and the universality of the Chinese language in East Asia, could only have added more confusion to the search for primitive characters. Particularly illuminating to the problem is a

---

[86] *Chaldaica grammatica antehac a nemine attentata sed iam primum per Seb. Munsterum conscripta et edita . . .* (Basel, 1527), pp. 14–18; for the history of Münster's books see K. H. Burmeister, *Sebastian Münster: Versuch eines biographischen Gesamtbilder* (Basel, 1963), pp. 48–49; T. Ambrogio, *Introductio in chaldaicam linguam . . .* (Pavia, 1539), pp. 203ᵛ–204ʳ. Ambrogio learned that "Indian" was not Chaldean from the Syrian priests who attended the Lateran Council. In his later controversy with Potken, Ambrogio proclaimed the independence of the "Indian" (Ethiopian) language. He used "Chaldean" thereafter as a synonym for Syriac. See E. Nestle, "Aus einem sprachwissenschaftlichen Werk von 1539," *Zeitschrift der deutschen morgenländischen Gesellschaft*, LVIII (1904), 602–3. Also see the article on Teseo Ambrogio degli Albonesi (under Albonesi) in the *Dizionario biografica degli italiani.*

[87] For example, see Claude Duret, *Thresor de l'histoire des langues de cest universe . . .* (Yverdon, 1619), pp. 580–86.

[88] See below, p. 512, on Cervini.

[89] For example, see W. Deecke, "Ueber das indische Alphabet in seinem Zusammenhang mit den übrigen südsemitischen Alphabeten," *Zeitschrift der deutschen morgenländischen Gesellschaft*, XXXI (1877), 598–612.

[90] *Libro . . . nel quale s'insegna a'scrivere ogni sorti lettera, antica, et moderna, di qualunque natione, con le sue regole, et misure, et essempi: et con un breve, et util discorso de la cifre* (Rome, 1540). This was a popular and influential work and was republished with additions in 1543, 1545, and 1547. For comment see James Wardrop, "*Civis Romanus sum*, Giovanbattista Palatino and His Circle," *Signature*, N.S., XIV (1952), pp. 15–16.

[91] For sample scripts see David Diringer, *The Alphabet . . .* (New York, 1948), and his book *Writing* (The Hague, 1962). Also see I. J. Gelb, *A Study of Writing: The Foundations of Grammatology* (Chicago, 1952), chap. v.

manuscript book preserved in the British Museum (Lansdowne 720) which includes a facsimile of a Chinese "alphabet" (see pl. 97).[92] The caption at its head, probably written by a copyist or a curator, records that the original of this document was housed in the third court of the Vatican library and was written, "as they say," in a document by the hand of Pope Marcellus II. The caption also states that there are Chinese books in the Vatican as well as many manuscripts. The copyist notes at the bottom of the "alphabet" that the Vatican library possesses the manuscript written against Luther by King Henry VIII which was sent to Pope Leo X. The "Chinese alphabet" is preserved in this manuscript book along with a page on which are written just two characters of an "Armenian alphabet," a page on which an "Etruscan alphabet" appears, another page on which additional "Etruscan letters" are set down, and a page which gives "a scale and a system of music composed of numerals."

Marcellus II (reigned April 9–May 1, 1555), the presumed writer of this strange document, was widely known in political, religious, and intellectual circles before being elected pope as the Cardinal Marcello Cervini. Early in his career Cervini had won the patronage of Cardinal Alessandro Farnese who became Pope Paul III (reigned 1534–49). Under the Farnese pope the influence of Cervini mounted at the papal court, particularly in diplomatic and intellectual affairs. Cervini was sent on diplomatic missions in 1539 to the court of Charles V at Madrid and shortly thereafter to Paris and Ghent.[93] On his return to Rome around 1540, Cervini again took up humanistic studies, particularly the pursuit of ancient languages. He and his associates advanced the idea at this time of establishing at Rome a press for printing the Greek manuscript works in the Vatican collections.[94] And in 1548, upon becoming the librarian, he set into motion the vast project of cataloging the holdings of the Vatican library.

The catalog of the Latin manuscripts sponsored by Cervini was prepared in three volumes between 1550 and 1555 and remained the standard inventory of the Vatican library until 1620.[95] The compiler and transcriber of the catalog was Ferdinando Ruano, the Latin scrivener of the Vatican library from 1541 to his death in 1560. Ruano was a native of Badajoz, a city on the Spanish-Portuguese frontier which had been host to the conference of 1524 between Castile and Portugal over the question of the Moluccas.[96] That he was also a student of ancient scripts and interested in comparative alphabets is attested by

---

[92] On pp. 275–76 of this manuscript, "Voyage d'Italie," which was written by "some very learned and intelligent Frenchmen, between the years 1574 and 1578" (*A Catalogue of the Lansdowne Manuscripts in the British Museum with Indexes of Persons, Places, and Matters* [London, 1819], p. 163).

[93] P. Paschini, "Un cardinale editore: Marcello Cervini," in *Miscellanea . . . in memoria di Luigi Ferrari* (Florence, 1952), pp. 384–85.

[94] G. Tiraboschi, *Storia della letteratura italiana* (9 vols. in 20; Florence, 1805–13), VII, Pt. I, 205.

[95] Eugène Müntz, *La bibliothèque du Vatican au XVIe siècle: Notes et documents* (Paris, 1886), pp. 81, 86. The first volume (No. 3967) was completed in 1550; the other two volumes (Nos. 3968 and 3969) bear the arms of Julius III who was pope from 1550 to 1555.

[96] Cf. *Asia*, I, 116–17.

his only published book, *Setti alphabeti di varie lettere* (Rome, 1554), which he dedicated to Cervini.[97] On January 5, 1554, the Jesuit Superior, Peter Canisius, wrote from Vienna to Polanco in Rome saying that the imperial chancellor (Johann Albrecht von Widmanstetter [1506–57],[98] a student of Syriac and Arabic) would like if possible to have a copy of the alphabet of the Japanese language and as much pertinent information as was available on the Indian language.[99] From this suggestive evidence we may surmise that the Chinese (or Japanese) "alphabet," since it was said to be in the hand of Marcellus, was in existence by 1555 and known to Ruano.

The Chinese characters which comprise the "alphabet" in the Vatican document are arranged in two vertical lines of uneven length. They are written awkwardly, possibly by a Western hand; the French copyist of the facsimile document in the British Museum may also have added touches of his own. Nonetheless a few of the individual characters are readily identifiable. Most of the others seem at best to be but parts of characters. The twenty-five characters in the "alphabet" make no sense as a literary passage, and so they were not copied from some readily available Chinese book. The romanizations of the characters follow the conventional method employed and diffused by the Portuguese. For example, the Chinese character for "three" is usually romanized today as "san," but the Portuguese of the sixteenth century regularly wrote "sam," as in *sampão*.[100]

Probably Cervini or Ruano obtained the Chinese characters of the "alphabet" through intermediaries. A number of possibilities present themselves. Between 1548 and 1555 Cervini received at Rome several Eastern prelates, mostly Syrian and Ethiopian bishops, who might have brought the Chinese materials to him.[101] Both Cervini and Ruano had close friends in Iberia and in the Iberian colony in Rome who might have forwarded the characters.[102] Or they might have come through Paolo Giovio, to whom Barros sent "a book of the writing of the '*chis*'" (possibly Shiites or Chinese) while Giovio was working at the Vatican.[103] It is conceivable that Ruano, working from such materials and from the Chinese books already in the library, extracted from the Chinese writing what he thought were the root characters, copied them down, and added the romanizations, perhaps with the help of a Portuguese. It is most likely, however, that the characters were originally written by Bernard of Kagoshima, the young Japanese convert who visited Rome from early January to late

[97] On Ruano see James Wardrop, "The Vatican Scriptors: Documents for Ruano and Cresci," *Signature*, N.S., V (1948), pp. 4–11. For discussion of his book see R. Bertieri, "Un disegnatore di caratteri italiano del XVI secolo, poco noto," *Gutenberg Jahrbuch*, XV (1940), 63–70.

[98] See Max Müller, *Johann Albrecht von Widmanstetter, 1506–1557: Sein Leben und Werken* (Bamberg, 1908), pp. 66–80. Possibly he heard about such a "Japanese alphabet" from Postel, who visited Vienna during 1554.

[99] O. Braunsberger (ed.), *Beati Petri Canisii . . . epistulae et acta* (5 vols.; Freiburg, 1923), I, 450.

[100] See Appendix to this chapter under *champão*.

[101] See Levi della Vida, *op. cit.* (n. 57), pp. 140–45.

[102] Cervini corresponded regularly with Angelo Colocci, the Spanish Humanist.

[103] See *Asia*, I, 410, n. 532.

October, 1555, and was there during the election and brief pontificate of Marcellus II.[104]

However the "alphabet" was obtained, it is clearly a collection of genuine Chinese characters, and parts of them. Explicit in this document is the determination on the part of some language student to find an alphabetical key to Chinese, a vain enterprise that was commonly followed by linguists of the seventeenth century.[105] No reason is indicated for the inclusion in this documentary material of the musical scale composed of numbers. Perhaps the copyist had in mind a method for understanding or analyzing the tones of Chinese, or saw the nonphonetic similarity in Western musical notation and the characters of the Chinese. Certainly similar efforts were made in the seventeenth century by students of language who were intent upon deciphering the tonal system of Chinese.

That writers, printers, and scholars were fascinated by the Chinese characters and puzzled by the language is similarly brought out in the correspondence of Filippo Sassetti. Around 1582 Baccio Valori, governor of Pisa and a Humanist, sent a Chinese "alphabet" from Florence to Sassetti in Lisbon with a request to learn there what he could about it.[106] Possibly this was a copy of the "Cervini alphabet," for by this date Cardinal Fernando de' Medici was collecting documents and other materials essential to his enterprise of printing books at Rome in the languages of the Orient.[107] Sassetti, perhaps following Valori's usage, refers to the characters as "hieroglyphs." He reports that the Jesuits told him, as he had reported before, "that this writing by notes [*per note*] is employed throughout China and Japan, and in all the neighboring lands where the script is common and where the spoken languages [*le lingue*] differ more [from one another] than Tuscan does from German." Sassetti concludes that there is no question about the languages of East Asia being written in characters. The problem is to decide how this is done.

Sassetti evidently took the "alphabet" of Valori in his baggage to India. From Cochin he wrote to Valori on January 17, 1588, that "the Chinese appear to possess no alphabet or basic characters and that such characters as they have represent an idea [*un concetto*] and are consequently infinite in number."[108] But even though this feature of the Chinese script makes it most difficult to learn, its

---

[104] Bernard knew Portuguese and a smattering of Latin and Italian. See *ibid.*, p. 673.

[105] See "A Discourse on the Diversity of Letters . . .," in *Hakluyt Posthumus, or Purchas His Pilgrimes* . . . (Glasgow, 1905), Vol. I, chap. xvii; Paul Cornelius, *Languages in Seventeenth- and Early Eighteenth-Century Imaginary Voyages* (Geneva, 1965), chaps. i and ii; and Madeleine V. David, *Le débat sur les écritures et l'hiéroglyphe aux XVIIᵉ et XVIIIᵉ siècles* . . . (Paris, 1965), chap. ii.

[106] E. Marcucci (ed.), *Lettere edite e inedite di Filippo Sassetti* (Florence, 1855), p. 239. Also see *Asia*, I, 475–77.

[107] G. E. Saltini, "Della stamperia orientale medicea . . .," *Giornale storico degli archivi toscani*, IV (1860), 239. The documents of Cervini passed on his death into the hands of his family. In the eighteenth century they were acquired by the Archivio do Stato in Florence. Today they are bound in sixty volumes entitled "Mss. Cerviniani." See L. Dorez, "Recherches et documents sur la bibliothèque du Cardinal Sirleto," *Mélanges d'archéologie et d'histoire*, XI (1891), 460–61.

[108] Marcucci (ed.), *op. cit.* (n. 106), p. 408.

ideographic nature enables people of utterly different tongues to write down their languages in the same characters. Of the reaction in Florence to Sassetti's essentially correct description of Chinese we have no record. It was not long, however, before Father Michele Ruggiero arrived at Rome in 1590 and was able to apprise the scholars of Europe of the accuracy of Sassetti's general conclusions.[109]

Words as well as letters and characters were analyzed and compared as the search went on for common elements, resemblances, and incontrovertible differences in vocabulary and syntax. Translations of the Lord's Prayer were systematically collected and examined for clues to the pedigrees and the ethnic descent of the various languages. Postel, Ambrogio, and Bibliander provided the learned world with renditions of the Lord's Prayer in most of the Near Eastern languages. Konrad Gesner in his *Mithridates* (1555) gives it in twenty-two different languages. Twenty years later, André Thevet in his *Cosmographie* added a version in the Carib language of America.[110] And in 1591, Angelo Rocca (1524–1620), a Roman collector of books and director of the Vatican printing press, published the Lord's Prayer in a romanized Chinese version obtained from Father Ruggiero.[111]

A classification of the recognized seventy-two languages of the world was first undertaken systematically by Bibliander in his *De ratione communi* (1548) and by Gesner in his *Mithridates* (1555). While both of these Swiss authors still believed in the primacy of the "three sacred languages," they sought to order the known languages of the world according to their linguistic characteristics. The only Asian language noticed by Bibliander is the tongue of Tartary. Gesner, who is more encyclopedic in his survey, includes all the information available on as many languages as he can possibly learn about.[112] He also seeks to group the languages in terms of their cognate or related elements. To determine relatedness, Gesner centers his attention upon similarities in place names and proper names and seeks to discover the "true meanings" of these words. As a consequence, he is forced when dealing with geographically distant names to wrestle with the contradictions and the disorientations in his sources.

For Gesner the Chaldean, Ethiopic, and Arabic languages, the lineal descendants of Hebrew, reign over almost two-thirds of the earth. He includes sample Ethiopian and Chaldean words from Breydenbach, and refers to Postel and

---

[109] Cf. above, p. 497. Father Pietro Paolo Rossi, rector of the Jesuit seminary in Rome, wrote a letter on July 14, 1590, to the rector of the Jesuit college in Florence announcing the arrival of Ruggiero and noting that he brought Chinese vestments and more than twenty-four Chinese books with him. See D'Elia, *op. cit.* (n. 22), I, 250.

[110] For a general review of the polyglot Lord's Prayer to this point see Adelung, *op. cit.* (n. 61), pp. 646–48.

[111] Rocca, *op. cit.* (n. 22), pp. 365–76. Also cf., above, p. 234.

[112] For a general analysis see George J. Metcalf, "The Views of Konrad Gesner on Language," *Studies in Germanic Language and Literatures in Memory of Fred O. Nolte* (St. Louis, 1963), pp. 15–26. Also see Henry M. Hoenigswald, "Linguistics in the Sixteenth Century," *Library Chronicle*, XX (1954), 1–4.

Pierre Belon in his comments on Arabic.[113] For his references to the languages of India he relies on the general, terse comments of Herodotus, Pliny, and Aelian.[114] "On the various languages of the remotest lands of the Tartar empire and the New World," he limits himself to the collection of place names garnered from Marco Polo, Maximilian of Transylvania, Peter Martyr, and the Venetian voyagers to Tana. For his discussion of the Tartar languages Gesner relies on Marco Polo and Matthias à Michou, a Polish canon of Krakow whose major work is entitled *Descriptio Sarmatiarum Asianae et Europianae* (1517).[115] In the revised edition of Gesner's *Mithridates* prepared by Caspar Waser and published in 1610 at Zurich, commentaries were added on the languages of Bengal, Malabar, China, and Japan.[116]

As scholars became increasingly aware of the existence of a group of living languages whose phonological, grammatical, and lexical organizations differed markedly from any previously known, the compilers and translators of polyglot religious writings and Bibles more frequently included versions of the Scriptures in the languages of the Near East.[117] The lexicographers at first limited their polyglot dictionaries to the languages of Europe. Ambrogio Calepino's (1435?–1510) polyglot dictionary, first published in 1502, was enlarged in 1579 to include words from seven languages and in 1598 to include words from eleven languages.[118] In the following year J. J. Scaliger divided the languages of Europe into four major and seven minor classes.[119] It was left to Hieronymus Megiser (1553–1618), the German historian, philologist, and editor and translator of travel books,[120] to undertake the compilation and publication of the earliest dictionary of the known languages of the world.

Megiser's *Thesaurus polyglottus* (1603) endeavors to identify, group, and list words from over four hundred different languages and dialects.[121] Like Gesner

---

[113] *Mithridates. De differentiis linguarum tum veterum tum quae hodie apud diversas nationes in toto orbe terrarum in usu sunt, Conradi Gesneri Tigurini observationes. Anno MDLV. Tiburi excudebat Froschouerus.*, pp. 6–9.

[114] *Ibid.*, p. 56.

[115] *Ibid.*, pp. 68–71. On Michou and his influence see Bohdan Baranowski, *Znajomość wschodu w dawnej Polsce do XVIII wieku* (*Knowledge of the Orient in Poland before the Eighteenth Century*) (Lodz, 1950), pp. 25–27.

[116] *Mithridates Gesneri, exprimens differentias linguarum, tum veterum, tum quae hodie, per totum terrarum orbem, in usu sunt*, pp. 88, 92, 97.

[117] *Complutensian polyglot*, 1514–17, in Greek, Hebrew, Latin, and Chaldean; *Psalterium*, 1516, in Arabic, Chaldean, Greek, Hebrew, and Latin; the *Antwerp polyglot*, 1569–72, in Chaldean, Greek, Hebrew, Latin, and Syriac.

[118] Arens, *op. cit.* (n. 55), p. 64.

[119] H. Pedersen, *Linguistic Science in the Nineteenth Century: Methods and Results* (Cambridge, Mass., 1931), p. 6; also Leroy, *op. cit.* (n. 5), pp. 7–8.

[120] He translated both Varthema and Marco Polo into German. See his *Hodeporicon Indiae Orientalis* (Leipzig, 1608), and his *Chorographia Tartariae* (Leipzig, 1610).

[121] Full title is: *Thesaurus polyglottus: vel, dictionarium multilingue: ex quadringentis circitur tam veteris, quam novi (vel potius antiquis incogniti) orbis nationum linguis, dialectis, idiomatibus, et idiotismis, constans* (Frankfurt, 1603). For discussion see R. C. Alston *et al.*, "The Earliest Dictionary of the Known Languages of the World," *Newberry Library Bulletin*, VI (1966), 211–15. Also see pl. 100 for a sample page.

he sought to assemble all the information available on ancient and contemporary languages according to their cognate and derivative affinities. In addition to six principal European groupings based on linguistic interrelationships, he postulates Asiatic, African, and American classifications, The languages of insular Southeast Asia and Japan he places under his third American division devoted to insular languages. He, like the cosmographers, includes as part of the "New World" those parts of Asia unknown to classical Antiquity. He also gives equivalents, whenever he has them and in as many languages as possible, for the common and technical words of the Latin vocabulary.

In his geographical table of language groups Megiser names the following languages for the region from India eastward. For India proper he designates Malabar, Gujarati, Deccanese or Konkani, Bengali, the languages of Cambay, Vijayanagar (Telugu) and Coromandel (Tamil), Kanarese or the language of Goa, and "Brachmanum" (Sanskrit).[122] East of India he lists the languages of Pegu, Martaban, Malay, China, and Champa (Cham). The islands of the "New World" in Asia include the languages of Japan ("which has sixty-six kingdoms"), Diu, Anjediva, the Maldives, Ceylon ("Chingallae"), Sumatra ("which has twenty-nine kingdoms"), Borneo, Java Major, Java Minor, Banda, the Moluccas (including Ternate, Tidor [or "Timor?"], and Gilolo [Halmahera]), and the Philippines.

A study of Megiser's equivalents from the Asian languages shows that they come mainly from the Malayan and Javanese words of commerce. There is clear evidence from spelling peculiarities that he used Pigafetta's list, probably the one published in Ramusio. Whenever he gives equivalents in Chinese or Japanese, they are romanized and appear to be extracted from the Jesuit letterbooks. For example, he places under *Deus* (God) the following equivalents: from the language of Calicut, "Tamerani," (Malayālam, *Tamburān*)[123] and "Natigai" (Tartar for earth god); from Japanese, "Deniche" (*Dainichi* or "Great Sun"), and "cogi" (*Go-chi*, name for "five Buddhas"); from Tidorese, "Ala" (*Allah*); from Malay, "Dios"; from Javanese, "Ala" (*Allah*). His renditions of the Asian names for various spices he obviously obtained from Orta or one of the works based on the *Colóquios*.[124] A perusal of Megiser's dictionary quickly shows that he collected his Asian words from the best available European sources and collated them for comparative purposes with their equivalents in the languages of Europe and America.

Comparisons of alphabets, words, and syntax of the ancient and modern

[122] The Europeans meant by "Malabar" both Malayālam and Tamil; "Kanarese" was usually a misnomer for Konkani; "Badaga" was Telugu, and "Hindustani" was applied even to Marathi; "Bracmana" or "Bracmanum" did not necessarily mean Sanskrit, for it was applied sometimes to the languages of Goa, the Konkani and Marathi languages. For further discussion of these early language labels see L. Cardon and H. Hosten, "Early Jesuit Printing in India . . .," *Journal of the Asiatic Society of Bengal*, IX (1913), 150.

[123] Varthema, his probable source, writes "Tamarani."

[124] See *Asia*, I, 194–95, and above, pp. 434–35, for a discussion of the translations and adaptations of Orta's work.

languages over the course of the sixteenth century revealed that similarities exist among all known languages. The vernacular and exotic languages continued to be studied, analyzed, and organized in terms of Latin and in relation to the search for the primitive language. The ideographic languages presented a peculiar challenge, but they too were subjected to analysis by the same limited linguistic techniques. Perhaps new techniques were not developed because of the preoccupation of the best linguistic scholars of the age with the problems of Latin and the vernacular languages of Europe. Or this deficiency might also be attributed to the limited amount of solid information that was available on the nature of the new languages regularly being discovered. Still, scholars like Postel, Bibliander, Gesner, and Megiser began gradually to move away from their initial concern with the common nature of all languages to a concern for elements of difference. As difference began to assume greater importance, the linguists gradually tried to group the languages into families in terms of geography and common characteristics. Megiser separated the languages of the overseas world from the languages of Europe, a necessary first step to the study of these languages in their own terms. And, at the same time, he accumulated from the available sources an impressive number of words from the overseas languages to produce a dictionary that was in itself a compendium of the state of Europe's knowledge about the languages of Asia at the end of the sixteenth century.

4

HARMONY AND UNIVERSALITY

The quest for the *lingua humana* had proved to be long, frustrating, and unproductive. Belief in the existence of the original language remained nonetheless an article of faith. The search for it intensified in the sixteenth century because of the problems posed by the multitude of new languages and dialects being discovered. Comparisons of alphabets, words, and syntax seemed to reveal the existence of a harmony among the languages which lay beneath the apparent discord. The universal language, some thought, might even be found intact in one of the known natural languages or in one yet to be discovered. While the search continued for the original language, a few impatient linguists optimistically tried to contrive artificial languages that could be universally understood. Such endeavors failed then, as they have ever since, to bring an end to diversity through the recovery or the manufacture of a universal tongue.

Some of the intellectual trends, religious aspirations, and mystical movements popular in the sixteenth century helped to inspire, sustain, and broaden the quest for a common means of communication. In the period of the later Crusades, Ramon Lull (*ca.* 1236–1315), a writer in the Augustinian-Franciscan tradition whose works were widely quoted in the sixteenth century, had advocated the peaceful conversion of the world through mastery of language. In the sixteenth century the Neo-Platonists continued to believe that the religious unity of the world could be achieved and the perfect language of mankind recovered only by those enlightened enough to penetrate the mysteries of Revelation and nature through contemplation and occult techniques. The cabalists, Jewish and Christian, believed that the Scriptures contain divine mysteries and that every word, letter, number, and accent in the sacred writings is endowed with occult meaning.[125] The publication in 1505 of the *Hieroglyphica* (Venice) of Horapollo led to the growth of a popular cult which viewed the enigmatic hieroglyphs as ideographical devices for conveying philosophical insights and moral maxims which could be interpreted by the enlightened everywhere without reference to literary or verbal explanations. The etymologists of the Renaissance, who traced their ancestry to the *Etymologiae* of Isidore of Seville, held that the name reveals the nature of its subject and that the etymology reveals the force of the name. The common element in all these movements was a preoccupation with finding the best means of overcoming the barrier of language diversity which stood in the way of universal understanding.

Most students of Oriental languages were devotees or tolerant observers of one or more of the occultist movements. The eclectic Postel was a conscious follower of the missionary ideals of Lull and an ardent student of cabalistic literature. For Postel language is more than merely a means of communication among men; it is God's greatest gift and the means through which men communicate with God and one another. Through language the benefits of reason are communicated and the happiness and order of society secured. Hebrew, the mother of all languages, is the language of ultimate truth and the vehicle necessary for restoring the unity of man with God and for bringing about the reunion of the human race.[126]

In *Des merveilles du monde* (Paris, 1552) Postel celebrates the continuing miracle of the revelation of the Orient that God had vouchsafed to his age. To show that God speaks to all men in the same way, and that a universal harmony exists, Postel equates Buddhism with Christianity, Buddha with Christ, and the Tartars with the lost tribes of Israel. As harbingers of the imminent concord of the world he points out that a single missionary baptized 100,000 men in a month, and that the Jesuits have converted as many pagans in a decade in the East as were brought to Christianity over the entire world in the previous eight hundred years. With religious unity being speedily realized, the Christian world had quickly to find a universal ruler and a common means of communication.[127]

Neither Postel nor the other Orientalists of his persuasion were able, as they

---

[125] For some examples of cabalistic techniques and interpretations see J. L. Blau, *The Christian Interpretation of the Cabala in the Renaissance* (New York, 1944), pp. 56–60.

[126] See Bouwsma, *op. cit.* (n. 82), pp. 104–6.

[127] *Des merveilles du monde*, I, 4ʳ, 50ʳ, 82ᵛ, 84ʳ, 92ᵛ.

so ardently hoped, to find by linguistic analysis the lost language of mankind. But others, less well informed on the languages of the East, made a new attack on the problem by seeking a natural language of universal dimensions. In his *Mithridates* Gesner directed attention to "Rotwelsch," the secret language of beggars, magicians, sorcerers, thieves, and lovers which never gets into the books but exists in all vernaculars. He, like Bonaventura Vulcanius in his book on the language of the Goths, saw in the gypsy language a form of "Rotwelsch" which was spoken by wandering tribes all over the world. Gesner also observed that, though tinctured by local languages, the gypsy language was ancient, persistent, and widespread. Students of language in the sixteenth century thought the gypsies originated in Egypt, the ancient land of the hieroglyphs. It was not until the eighteenth century, when fuller documentation became available, that the gypsy language was recognized to be Indian in origin.[128]

Most striking as an example of the prevailing beliefs in the harmony of languages are the observations of Filippo Sassetti. He was not only impressed by the universality of the Chinese script in East Asia; he was also convinced of its antiquity and its possible relationship to the hieroglyphic writing of Egypt.[129] In India, where he was stationed from 1583 to 1588 and where he had direct, personal experience with the native languages, Sassetti was quick to recognize that the learned employed an ancient, uncorrupted language called "Sanscruta," which means "well articulated."[130] The Brahmans, who possessed a monopoly on Sanskrit, he considered to be the caste to whom Herodotus had attributed great wisdom. Traces of this ancient language can readily be found, Sassetti observes, in the vernacular languages of India even though Sanskrit itself is no longer spoken. He reports that Sanskrit has an alphabet of fifty-three letters and a well-organized grammar. He also notices that in both Sanskrit and the vernacular languages there exist words which resemble the Italian words for the numbers six, seven, eight, and nine.[131] The Italian words *Dio* (God) and *serpe* (serpent) are also similar to the Sanskrit *devo* (*deva*) and *sarpant* (*sarpa*). European languages, he believes, could easily be translated into Sanskrit. The reverse would not be true because the Europeans, owing to the "tonal differences" (*differente temperatura*) of their languages, could not imitate the numerous and crisp vowels of Sanskrit.[132]

Sassetti implies that ancient India was the motherland of all languages. But while his few remarks may seem to anticipate the discovery of the Indo-European family, Sassetti's observations must be carefully appraised in terms of

---

[128] See Arens, *op. cit.* (n. 55), pp. 71–72; Pedersen, *op. cit.* (n. 55), pp. 16–17; Gray, *op. cit.* (n. 55), p. 38. The gypsy tongue probably originated with a tribal group of northwest India.

[129] Cf., above, p. 216; and below, p. 536.

[130] Actually it means "refined" or "polished."

[131] Ital. sei = Skt. ṣaṣ; sette = sapta; otto = aṣṭa; nove = nava.

[132] For his observations on Sanskrit see Marcucci (ed.), *op. cit.* (n. 106), pp. 45, 251, 283, 408, 415–16. These remarks were addressed to Bernardo Davanzati (1529–1606) and Pier Vettori (1499–1585). For discussion see Benfey, *op. cit.* (n. 82), pp. 222–23; Borst, *op. cit.* (n. 55), III, Pt. I, 1180–81; Arens, *op. cit.* (n. 55), p. 73; and G. Bonfante, "Ideas on the Kinship of the European Languages from 1200 to 1800," *Journal of World History*, I (1953), 686–87.

his own time. None of his correspondents in Europe reacted excitedly about these acute observations. They, like Sassetti himself, probably judged his observations to be but additional confirmation for their belief in language harmony and in the common descent of all languages from primitive Hebrew. But it should also be recognized that implicit in Sassetti's remarks is a new inquiring spirit: he wishes that he had gone to India at the age of eighteen so that he might have had the time necessary to learn the ancient and beautiful Sanskrit language.

The failures of scholars to find a truly universal and practicable idiom within the natural languages of the world stimulated speculation about the possibility of constructing a universal language by artificial means. A created, universal language would be composed of ideal words or characters derived from forms which occur commonly in the various natural languages. These contrived words could in some measure be understood by the speakers of every natural language. Other artificial languages could be contrived which would be different enough from all natural languages to perform as a cryptography for use in secret diplomatic, commercial, and military communications. Scholars of various language backgrounds might compensate themselves for the loss of Latin by contriving an artificial language especially designed to meet their needs.

It is not surprising that professional translators should have become active in collecting materials on universal idioms, secret languages, and ciphers. Especially interesting in this regard is Blaise de Vigenère (1523–96), a student of Greek, Hebrew, and the cabalistic writings who became secretary and translator to King Henry III of France. For over seventeen years he collected materials on secret languages and occult lore which he published in a lengthy *Traicté des chiffres* (Paris, 1586).[133] Designed as a free gift to the public, this book is a collection of ancient, modern, and exotic epigraphy, a manual of diplomatic cryptography, a repository of occult lore from alchemy, magic, and the Cabala, a prodigious compilation of diverse texts from ancient, modern, rabbinical, cabalistic, and Arab authors, and a pot-pourri of symbolic explanations of letters, numbers and signs. It also includes a method of enciphering and deciphering which today still bears his name and which has been used in a number of cipher machines.[134]

Vigenère is perhaps most interesting in this context for the understanding he displays of the Chinese language. He clearly bases his analysis upon the materials in the Jesuit letters from Japan, particularly those of Fróis.[135] He inserted this

---

[133] For commentary on the relation of this book to his other activities see D. Métral, *Blaise de Vigenère, archéologue et critique d'art (1523–1596)* (Paris, 1939), pp. 57–59. For his position among the Christian Cabalists see F. Secret, *Les kabbalistes chrétiens de la Renaissance* (Paris, 1965), chap. vii. For his portrait see pl. 94.

[134] On this aspect of Vigenère's contribution see David Kahn, *The Codebreakers: The Story of Secret Writing* (New York, 1967), pp. 145–47.

[135] He was probably alerted to the Jesuit letters and to the Japanese mission of 1584 to 1586 (*Traicté*, p. 323ʳ) by Edmond Auger (1530–91), the Jesuit confessor of King Henry III and rector of Tournon, Toulouse, and Lyons. Auger was the translator of Maffei's first book. See *Asia*, I, 324.

Asian material into his own scheme for organizing the languages of the world according to their dual roles of secret languages and ordinary tongues. In ancient times, he asserts, the mysteries of philosophy and theology were kept secret in the sacred written languages of the Hebrews, Chaldeans, Egyptians, Ethiopians, and Indians.[136] Clearly he has in mind here primitive Hebrew, the south Semitic scripts, hieroglyphs, and Sanskrit. These languages were displaced by vernaculars, and all that remains today of secret languages are the ciphers used in business and diplomacy.[137]

After asserting unequivocally that the art of printing spread from China to Europe, Vigenère concludes that the Chinese like the ancient Egyptians have two forms of writing, "hieroglyphs" and ordinary letters for forming words.[138] The Chinese "hieroglyphs" are commonly in use throughout East Asia but are reserved entirely for religious purposes. To learn to read and write the "hieroglyphs" is a difficult undertaking because they consist of pictures of objects in the natural world which are sometimes combined or modified to represent more than a single word or idea. They seem indeed, like the Sphinx,[139] to be "monstrosities composed of diverse natures." A Japanese bonze called "Cicatara" is reported by Fróis to be the best calligrapher in Japan; indeed he appears to be something of a magician for he writes his Christian name "Simon" in Japanese characters which mean "that which is taught by the master."[140] From this observation Vigenère concludes that the Chinese "hieroglyphs" are contrived and are therefore comparable to Ciceronian notes (shorthand), devices, and ciphers.[141]

To Vigenère Chinese is a sacred language that has preserved its secret character throughout history. And so it is no wonder that even the most enlightened must spend their entire lives mastering it. Study of this language, he implies, might lead to great achievements and even to the recovery or the production of a universal cipher. While one of his pages is entitled "the alphabet of China and Japan," it is left blank.[142] He is able, however, to present specimens of a number of other Asian alphabets. In 1613 Claude Duret, a follower of Vigenère, was

[136] *Traicté des chiffres*, p. 3^v, 10^v, 11^r.

[137] On code and cipher in sixteenth-century diplomacy see Charles Carter, *The Western European Powers, 1500–1700* (Ithaca, N.Y., 1971), chap. vi.

[138] The Greek word *hieroglyphika* literally means "sacred carved letters" and reveals the Greek belief that hieroglyphic writing was designed primarily for religious purposes, especially for monumental inscriptions on temples and tombs. Hence, if Chinese were "hieroglyphic" it was also thought to be a religious language known only to its devotees. See *Traicté des chiffres*, pp. 323^r–323^v.

[139] Cf. A. Chastel, "Notes sur le sphinx à la Renaissance," in *Archivio di filosofia, umanesimo e simbolismo* (Padua, 1958), pp. 179–82.

[140] *Traicté des chiffres*, p. 325^v.

[141] Cf. the remark of John Dee, the English geographer, in his *Monas hieroglyphica* (Antwerp, 1564): "And if the twenty-first speculation of our Hieroglyphic Monad gave satisfaction to a *Voarchadumicus* [a person concerned with the mystical discipline of names] and provided him with . . . a subject of speculation, he will confess that, for the sake of philosophizing, he need not travel to the inhabitants of India or America." See C. H. Josten, "A Translation of John Dee's 'Monas Hieroglyphica' (Antwerp, 1564)," *Ambix*, XII (1964), 137.

[142] *Traicté des chiffres*, p. 327^r.

finally able to publish the Chinese and Japanese "alphabets" that Edmond Auger had promised to supply for Vigenère.[143] He also gives the "numbers" in Chinese characters, numbers being especially fascinating since that were not dependent even in Western languages upon the alphabet and hence were supposed to possess extraordinary occult power. He provides an example of how European names are written in Japanese and includes the *Kanji* script (pl. 102). Duret also includes a copy in Japanese, with French interlinear translation, of the patent by the "king" of Bungo granting to the Jesuits the right to build a church in the city of Yamaguchi.[144] The characters of the patent are intended to show Europeans how difficult this cipher is to read and write.

While Vigenère compiled and analyzed his materials on the ciphers of the world, Dr. Timothie Bright (*ca.* 1550–1615) in England was inventing a form of writing which has earned for him the title of "father of modern shorthand." In 1588 Bright published an instructional manual entitled *Characterie: An Arte of Shorte, Swifte and Secrete Writing by Character* (London).[145] In his dedication to Queen Elizabeth, Bright observes that "nothing remaineth extant" of Ciceronian tachygraphy (shorthand) and claims that he has now "invented the like." He asserts that his *Characterie* is easy to learn, secret, and superior to "the writing by letters and alphabets, in that nations of strange languages may hereby communicate their meaning together in writing, though of sundrie tongues." And he goes on to observe:

It is reported of the people of China that they have no othere kinde (but a language of characters), and so trafficke together many Provinces of that kingdom, ignorant one of an others speach. Their Characters are very long, and harde to make, that a dousen of mine, may be written as soone as one of theirs: Besides, they wanting an Alphabet fal into an infinite number, which is a thing that greatlie chargeth memory, and may discourage the learner.[146]

Modern students of Bright's work, including specialists in literature, linguistics, writing, and stenography, have vainly tried to explain the mystery that surrounds the birth of modern shorthand in the Elizabethan age. They have sought antecedents in Greek and Roman tachygraphy, in the notes of John of Tilbury in his *Ars notaria* (1174), in the recovery of the Ciceronian notes in

---

[143] *Thresor de l'histoire des langues de cest univers* (Cologne, 1613), pp. 913–15. Included are 47 hiragana and the numbers in Chinese characters are 1 to 10, 1,000, 100,000, and 1,000,000. See pl. 101. These characters were probably written originally by a Japanese and cut for publication by a European printer. The simpler characters, such as the numbers and the hiragana, are reproduced quite accurately; the more complex and elegant characters of the patent are less accurately reproduced. For this opinion, I am indebted to my colleague Edwin McClellan.

[144] *Ibid.*, pp. 917–20. Also see *Asia*, I, 680; also see pl. 103.

[145] A duodecim book of great rarity, only six copies are known to be extant. According to the title page, Queen Elizabeth granted Bright the exclusive privilege for fifteen years to teach or print "in or by characters." For commentary see G. C. Keynes, *Dr. Timothie Bright, 1550–1615: A Survey of His Life, with a Bibliography of His Writings* (London, 1962), p. 15. For a sample page see pl. 104.

[146] Bright's system was also criticized for requiring "such understanding and memory, as that few of the ordinary sort of men could attaine to the knowledge thereof." See "preface to the reader" in Edmond Willis, *An Abbreviation of Writing by Character* (London, 1618).

1496 and in the subsequent efforts to decipher them, and in the shorthand of
Bishop John Jewell of Salisbury.[147] Bright himself insists on the originality of
his invention of writing by symbol and sign. And he has been credited by others
with inventing the idea and the word *Characterie*, a collective singular noun
which means a written language not translatable into speech.[148]

Bright's script, though based partially on the Latin alphabet, is fundamentally
a form of writing by sign and word. It starts with an alphabet of eighteen signs;
to these he adds a variety of ticks, hooks, and circles by which he writes the 537
basic words of the English language, or the *Characterie*. The "charactericall"
symbol for the basic words must be memorized by the learner. Additional
words are formed by writing a synonym in *Characterie* and by placing the initial
letter of the desired word to the left of the symbol: dove = d + symbol for bird.
Since a synonym does not exist for every word, it is sometimes necessary to use
an antonym and to indicate this by writing the initial letter on the right side
of the symbol. The words are written "one directly under the other," or in
vertical columns, which, unlike Chinese, proceed from left to right.[149] Certain
grammatical forms such as number ("two man" not "two men") are to be
understood as in Chinese by context. Tenses are likewise "declared by the
language." Various forms of a word are indicated by the same sign: the sign
for ship is placed beneath the character for "neighbor" to write "neighborhood."
"For no man," Bright asserts, "will read either neighbourship, or friendhood."

Bright, according to his own preface, knew something of the nature of the
Chinese language. He might also have gathered from reading Vigenère that it
was thought to be similar to the Ciceronian notes, that is, a contrived cipher not
translatable into speech. His emphasis upon obtaining plurality and tense from
context is a feature of Chinese that he could easily have read about in the Jesuit
letterbooks.[150] His device for writing "neighborhood" with the "ship" sign is
reminiscent of the techniques by which the Japanese adapted their language
to the Chinese script.[151] Whatever the case may or may not be for the influence of Chinese and Japanese upon Bright's *Characterie*, it should not be
overlooked that language theorists of the seventeenth century were repeatedly
inspired by Chinese in their search for a "real character" as the basis for a
universal language.[152]

The failure to recover the universal, primitive language did not eradicate the
belief in the harmony of languages. To orientalists and occultists the discovery
of new languages merely reinforced their belief in the biblical tradition. They

[147] See especially Francesco Giuletti, *Storia delle scritture veloci (dall'antichità ad oggi)* (Florence,
1968), pp. 59, 311–13.

[148] E. H. Butler, *The Story of British Shorthand* (London, 1951), pp. 11–12.

[149] In 1911 W. J. Bayliss wrote his *Perpendicular Shorthand* in this manner. See *ibid.*

[150] Gago's letter on language was first published in 1570. See *Asia*, I, 680, 806–7.

[151] Suggestion of Robins, *op. cit.* (n. 55), p. 117, who apparently did not realize that Bright had
mentioned his interest in the Chinese and Japanese languages.

[152] Gaspar Schott of Würzburg and Anathasius Kircher, the great Jesuit polyglot, sought to
contrive universal languages through the use of Chinese characters. Also see John Wilkins, *Essay
toward a Real Character* (London, 1668).

were not able, however, to progress beyond the mere assertion that the known languages of the world possessed common elements testifying to their common origin. They could only express vague hopes that God, while revealing to the age the great range and extent of linguistic diversity, would also show the way to recovery of the common language by leading the rest of the world to Christianity. Tentative efforts to find the universal language in the vestigial tribal languages of the gypsies likewise produced nothing but speculation and debate. The identification of Chinese characters with Egyptian hieroglyphs, and observations about the universality of Chinese and Sanskrit in their geographical regions, helped to confirm the belief in harmony while raising new questions about universality. Faced by such a multitude of possibilities, it is little wonder that men of a more practical turn of mind became impatient with the search for a universal cipher derived from the natural languages. And so speculation began, and experiments were made in the contriving of artificial languages. But the artificial language, it soon became apparent, was limited in usefulness, as in the case of shorthand, to special interest groups. Since the artificial languages appealed only to special groups with particular needs, they could never become truly universal and could do nothing whatsoever to halt the seemingly endless multiplication of languages and dialects.

5

REBABELIZATION

Shortly after Speroni in 1540 proclaimed the suitability of the vernacular languages for philosophical discourse, the strict Latinists, secular and ecclesiastical alike, were shocked by another attack from an unexpected quarter. At the Council of Trent, Cardinal Cristoforo Madruzzo (1512–78) proclaimed that all languages, even the lowliest folk languages, are a gift of God and fitting mediums in which to praise him. Heresy does not originate with translations of the Bible and other sacred texts, for the Protestant reformers, who had led the revolt against the universal church, were men learned in Hebrew, Greek, and Latin. The simple people of every land are pious and they must praise God in the language familiar to them.[153] Like Madruzzo, the leading Jesuits were likewise opposed to strict Latinity and were, as we have seen, avid students of overseas languages. While the church preserved its official Latinity, strong internal forces were at work after Trent urging the cultivation of the European vernaculars and the overseas languages as mediums of evangelization.

Both ecclesiastical and lay authors increasingly wrote in the vernacular languages. This was especially true of the books that dealt with the overseas world. The letterbooks and histories of the Jesuits, even when they were first

[153] Borst, *op. cit.* (n. 55), III, Pt. 1, 1119.

issued in Latin, were quickly translated into a variety of local languages. The great travel collections were published only in vernacular languages for they sought to appeal to a broad reading public. Varthema wrote in Italian, Barros and Castanheda in Portuguese, Cristobal de Acosta in Spanish, and Linschoten in Dutch. While some of the secular writers may not have been able to write a book in Latin, there were others like Ramusio and Barros who chose quite deliberately for commercial or patriotic reasons to issue their great works in their native languages. Even the Jesuit history of Maffei, written originally in Latin, reached a wide public before the end of the sixteenth century because it was soon translated into vernacular versions.[154]

It was primarily through the books in the vernacular languages that the literary public of Europe began to be exposed to a new vocabulary. Strange places, persons, and products carried new names and terms with them. The place names of the countries just discovered were repeated in Portuguese writings as a proud litany of national achievement: Goa, Narsinga, Cambaya, Caúl, Cananor, Cochin, Cilan, Pegu, Malaca, Sião, Macao, Japão. And it was these place names in Portuguese orthography which rapidly found their way into general literature and the new atlases being prepared. Names and terms for the persons, products, and customs of Asia followed a similar route, though many of them were known earlier through Venetian sources. Asian words for which there were no European equivalents were incorporated in one form or another into all the major languages. These loan words were rarely completely at home in their new linguistic environment, but they, like the products and arts of the East, titillated a growing taste for the exotic. And they also revealed by their very existence and persistence that Europe was being exposed physically, culturally, and psychologically to new experiences for which there was no existing vocabulary in Latin or the vernacular languages.[155]

Among those who contributed heavily to the rebabelization of Europe were the publishers and printers. As merchants and members of the literati, the printers were usually abreast of the latest developments in both spheres. The printers of Venice, Rome, Antwerp, Amsterdam, and Lisbon were particularly well informed about the European economy. The publishers were often the confidantes and patrons of leading Humanists. The interest of the Vatican in sponsoring printing activities established closer working relationships between clerical scholars and a few printers. Because they were businessmen interested in profits, the printers encouraged the writing and publication of salable books in the vernacular languages. Certain of them sponsored financially the collecting of travel literature to promote the publication of books that would appeal to a broad public. By these efforts the printers contributed significantly to the formation and crystallization of the European vernaculars.[156]

But there was also a class of printers who concentrated on producing books

154 See *Asia*, I, chap. iv, and pp. 314–31 for further discussion of these authors and their works.
155 Cf. Leo Spitzer, *Linguistics and Literary History: Essays in Stylistics* (Princeton, 1948), p. 8.
156 L. Febvre and H. J. Martin, *L'apparition du livre* (Paris, 1958), p. 477.

for limited markets. At Venice some of the leading houses specialized in publishing books in Greek and Hebrew characters, and the publication in 1505 by the Aldine press of Horapollo's *Hieroglyphica* made Venice the Italian center of Egyptian studies.[157] Religious writings were printed there in Serbian characters beginning in 1519.[158] The Koran in Arabic letters was published there in 1530; it was probably from these type fonts that Postel obtained the Arabic letters for his *Linguarum duodecim* (1538).[159] Books in Ethiopic characters were usually printed at Genoa. Printers from other Italian cities and other European countries journeyed to Venice and Genoa to learn how to cut Oriental typefaces.[160] And Cervini, as we have seen,[161] inaugurated before mid-century an interest in printing books at Rome in Oriental characters.

But it was in Portugal that European printers first had direct experience with the languages of the more distant East. Around 1554 Indians were being trained in the use of the Western press, and through their efforts a catechism in romanized Tamil was published.[162] The earliest book printed in India in Tamil letters was probably sent to Rome by the Jesuits in 1579, to be followed shortly by others. At Coimbra in 1570 Chinese characters were first printed on a European press.[163] Fifteen years later two Japanese were in Lisbon learning how to operate the European press and evidently showing their tutors how to cut characters more correctly.[164] By 1598 the printers of the *Cartas* (Évora) were able to improve on the characters included in earlier Jesuit letterbooks and to eliminate some of the omissions and distortions which had marked the earliest European efforts to print ideographs. In the case of the Chinese characters, in contrast to their printing of Egyptian hieroglyphs, the printers of Europe had the benefit of learning from natives and of having their work criticized by missionaries well versed in Japanese.

At Rome in the pontificate (1572–85) of Gregory XIII, Cardinal Fernando de' Medici (1551–1609) sought to establish a press especially dedicated to the publication of Christian works in Oriental languages. As second son of Cosimo I, grand duke of Tuscany, the cardinal was able to count on the financial support of his family for this enterprise. His interest in the Eastern church was acknowledged by the pope when he appointed the cardinal to be the Protector of the Patriarchate of Antioch and Alexandria and superintendent of religious affairs in the kingdom of Ethiopia. Papal emissaries were sent to Ethiopia, Egypt, Syria, and Persia at Medici expense to acquire manuscripts that could be published in Rome for distribution to the missions in those Eastern countries.

[157] Guy de Tervarent, "Un humaniste: Piero Valeriano," *Journal des Savants*, 1967, pp. 164–68.

[158] D. S. Radojičič, "Die ersten Serbischen Druckereien," *Gutenberg Jahrbuch*, XV (1940), 248–54.

[159] C. Frede, *La prima traduzione italiana del Corano* ... (Naples, 1967), pp. 32–33.

[160] For example, Guillaume Le Bé, one of Garamond's pupils in Paris, worked in 1545 as a type-cutter of Hebrew fonts in Venice. See A. F. Johnson, *Periods of Typography: The Italian Sixteenth Century* (London, 1926), pp. 24–25.

[161] H. Brown, *The Venetian Printing Press* ... (London, 1896), pp. 104–7.

[162] See above, p. 495, and pl. 91.

[163] See *Asia*, I, 680.

[164] See above, p. 497.

In 1584, the year when the Japanese emissaries arrived in Europe, a papal bull proclaimed that the Medici press was to have a monopoly of printing books in "foreign languages." Direction of the press was assigned to Giovan Battista Raimondo of Cremona, a learned man who had long been collecting manuscripts in Oriental languages and descriptions of Eastern lands. Robert Granjon of Paris was employed to cut Oriental typefaces by both the Typographia Vaticana and the Typographia Medicea.[165] The first work published by the Medici press was an Arabic version of the Four Gospels that appeared in 1590. The death of Gregory XIII in 1585 had evidently brought a halt to official enthusiasm for the Medici press, and so no other works were issued by it. The manuscripts collected by Raimondo, now conserved in the Biblioteca Magliabechiana of Florence, include some which list "Indian" words (Codex XI, No. 3) and a memoir relating to the island of Borneo (Codex XVII, No. 11), perhaps an indication that the Medici group intended also to print in the languages of South Asia.[166]

The Augustinian Angelo Rocca was put in charge of the Typographia Vaticana in 1585 by Pope Sixtus V. Rocca was a great collector of books who also had responsibilities in the administration of the Vatican library. He was present at Rome when the Japanese mission visited there and in his book on the Vatican library published in 1591 he reproduces the Latin inscription in the library of Sixtus V commemorating this mission.[167] Rocca was also in touch with the Jesuit Michele Ruggiero, who arrived at Rome in 1590 shortly after his return from China. Rocca was fascinated by Ruggiero's Chinese books printed on double pages of thin paper and by the Christian writings which had been translated into Chinese and printed in characters by the xylographic method. He notes that the Chinese do not print with lead type, but that they incise their monosyllabic characters in wood. This information, like his Chinese version of the Lord's Prayer, came through Ruggiero.[168] The Jesuit also supplied Antonio Possevino (1534–1611) with a highly favorable "moral portrait" of the Chinese which was incorporated into the *Bibliotheca* (1593) prepared for the *ratio studiorum* of the Jesuits.[169]

But, despite their initial enthusiasm for Ruggiero, his Roman friends were soon to learn from Valignano that Ruggiero "knows very little about Chinese literature and language." Valignano wrote this judgment to the General in 1596 in a letter declaring his opposition to a project which envisaged the publication of Ruggiero's translations of the *Four Books*, the Mencius, and a miscellany of extracts from various Chinese authors.[170] The opinion of Valignano apparently carried enough weight in Rome to prevent the publication of Ruggiero's

---

[165] See Johnson, *op. cit.* (n. 160), p. 12.

[166] See Saltini, *loc. cit.* (n. 107), especially pp. 235–39, 260–62, 267, 301, and 304.

[167] Rocca, *op. cit.* (n. 22), p. 8. For the reception of the Japanese by Sixtus V, see *Asia*, I, 698.

[168] Rocca, *op. cit.* (n. 22), pp. 341, 362–63, 376, 379, 410. Also see above, p. 515.

[169] See Book IX of A. Possevino, *Biblioteca selecta qua agitur de ratione studiorum* (Rome, 1593).

[170] D'Elia, *op. cit.* (n. 22), I, 43 n. 1.

translations. As a consequence the sixteenth century drew to a close before any of the classical Chinese, Japanese, or Indian works were printed in European translations. Nor, of course, were the printers of Europe able to publish anything in the scripts of the East but sample characters. They had, however, learned in Rome and elsewhere that printing was older in eastern Asia than in Europe, that the printing process of Asia was different from theirs, that the Western press could be used to produce books in Oriental languages, and that the incising of ideographs in lead type was best left to people who commanded this form of writing.[171]

But it was the printers of works in Western languages, rather than those who sought to specialize in Oriental typefaces, who brought general information on the languages of Asia to the public of Europe. Mambrino Roseo (*fl.* 1544–71), Venetian chronicler and continuator of the world history of Giovanni Tarchagnota, notes that Malay is the universal language of the East Indies.[172] G. L. d'Anania in *L'universale fabrica del mondo* . . . (Venice, 1576) observes that "the Indians use diverse languages, possess a script of their own, and write from left to right as we do."[173] Their alphabet "(as I have seen) is truly of a barbaric type, and similar to that of the Arabs."[174] Thomas Stevens, the English Jesuit at Goa, was an ardent student of the Marathi language, but his translations and writings in and about Marathi were not known in Europe until the seventeenth century. Still, in October, 1583, Stevens wrote from Goa to his brother in England: "Very many are the languages of these places [in India]. Their pronunciation is not disagreeable and the structure is allied to Greek and Latin. The phrases and constructions are of a wonderful kind."[175] Aside from the remarks of Stevens and the later observations of Filippo Sassetti already recounted,[176] the Europeans of the sixteenth century evince but slight interest in the languages of India. Their indifference can possibly be accounted for by the great diversity of the Indian languages, by their similarities, real and imagined, to the south Semitic languages of the Levant, by the greater enthusiasm which the Jesuit commentators had for the civilizations of East Asia, and by the spectacular differences which quickly became apparent between the alphabetical and ideographical realms of language.

[171] In 1595 Pope Clement VIII ordained that the Jesuit press in Japan might print books without submitting them for prepublication censorship to the Inquisition of Goa. See Muller and Roth, *op. cit.* (n. 42), p. 9.

[172] He writes on the period from 1513 to 1559 in his *Delle historie del mondo* . . . (Venice, 1573). His comments on Malay may be found on pp. 125^r–125^v.

[173] P. 204.

[174] It should be recalled that the "Indian" alphabets published in Europe were Ethiopic letters. See above, p. 510.

[175] Stevens also observes that they have their own letters. For the Latin original of this quotation see Georg Schurhammer, "Der Marathidichter Thomas Stephens, S.I. Neue Dokumente," in L. Szilas (ed.), *Orientalia* (Lisbon, 1963), pp. 385–86. Stevens later wrote appreciatively of the beauty of Marathi: "Like a jewel among pebbles, like a sapphire among jewels, is the excellence of the Marathi tongue." As quoted in H. G. Rawlinson, "India in European Literature and Thought," in G. T. Garratt (ed.), *The Legacy of India* (Oxford, 1962), p. 27.

[176] Above, p. 514.

In 1569, before the Jesuits had penetrated China, the Portuguese Dominican Gaspar da Cruz announced that the Chinese, Japanese, and Annamites could communicate with one another in writing, that their spoken tongues were quite different, and that the dialects of China were infinite in number.[177] D'Anania, who saw the ideographs in the Jesuit letterbooks, asserts that their characters resemble no other letters whatsoever.[178] The Jesuit historian G. P. Maffei, who looked at the Chinese books in the Vatican library and at the Escorial, observes that their characters are like the hieroglyphs in that each represents a word or an idea. From his sources Maffei learned that many dialects exist in each province of China even though the script is everywhere the same. But there is a language, he reports, "like Latin that is commonly spoken by the educated—courtiers, secretaries, lawyers, judges, and magistrates—which they learn with great care and which we commonly called 'Mandarin.'"[179] Agosto Lapini in his discussion of the Japanese emissaries notes in his *Diary* that "the first names [of the emissaries] are the names of their lineage, because in their country they place their lineage names before their proper names."[180] Renward Cysat, a Swiss who learned about Japan from the Jesuit letters, included in his book published in 1576 a short lexicon of Japanese words and placenames arranged alphabetically according to their romanizations.[181] Luis de Guzman in his *Historia de las missiones* . . . (Alcalá de Henares, 1601) esteems Japanese more than Greek and Latin for its numerous synonyms and its courtesy forms.[182] From the New World the Jesuit Father José de Acosta pointed out in 1590 that Japanese has a phonetic system not employed in Chinese and that there are striking resemblances between the ideographs of Asia and the pictographs of the American Indians.[183]

More important than the presence in Europe of Asian books and the general descriptions of languages is the story of how quickly the Asian letters and words infiltrated the popular literature of the cinquecento. Writers of imaginary travels were particularly inclined to provide their narratives with exotic alphabets and words to lend their stories an air of authenticity. Sir John Mandeville, for example, included in his *Travels* the alphabets for a number of Asian languages. Not all these alphabets are contrived; the Syrian and Greek letters are perfectly authentic but were probably thought of in the fourteenth century as being exotic or fanciful.[184] The alphabet which Sir Thomas More provides in the sixteenth century for his Utopians is usually described as imaginary or compounded of elements from various alphabets. The words of the Utopians

---

[177] See *Asia*, I, 776.

[178] G. L. d'Anania, *L'universale fabrica del mondo* (Venice, 1576), p. 235.

[179] G. P. Maffei, *Historiarum Indicarum libri XVI* (Venice, 1589), p. 95ʳ. Note that "mandarin" here has a different meaning from the functionary "mandarin," an indication of the way Asian words developed secondary meanings for Europeans.

[180] G. A. Corazzini (ed.), *Diario fiorentino di Agostino Lapini* (Florence, 1900), under 1585.

[181] See *Asia*, I, 704.

[182] *Ibid.*, p. 714.

[183] *Ibid.*, pp. 806–7.

[184] See J. W. Bennett, *The Rediscovery of Sir John Mandeville* (New York, 1954), pp. 65–66.

are usually related to Greek prototypes.[185] Recent scholars have asserted that Raphael Hythlodaeus, More's informant, was a pseudonym for a Portuguese from whom More possibly obtained a description of the Malayālam script.[186] This conclusion is based on the argument that certain of the Utopian letters recall Malayālam script in their shape and general appearance. It is also alleged that the characteristic features of Malayālam script "must have been known to many Europeans at the time."[187] Since resemblance plays such a strong role in this circumstantial case, it should be pointed out, as mentioned earlier,[188] that confusion reigned in sixteenth-century Europe about "Indian" alphabets. Also it should be recalled that the Jesuits in India published the Tamil alphabet (very similar to Malayālam) only in 1578.[189] On the other hand, the case for preferring Malayālam gains substance by the fact that the Portuguese began collecting Malayālam words with the first voyage of Vasco da Gama in 1497–98,[190] or eighteen years before the publication in Latin of More's *Utopia*.

While the search for the origins of the Utopian alphabet is inconclusive, study of the introduction of exotic words into popular literature proves more productive. The sixteenth-century authors of imaginary voyages, whether in poetry or prose, evidently had no hesitation in employing new names and terms to heighten the exotic appeal of their offerings.[191] Nor did they hesitate to revise their works in deference to the latest geographical information. Study of the words they introduce, particularly the spellings, helps to determine the sources and establish dates for versions, sections, or passages over which there has been scholarly debate. Examination of the words they decide to include in their presentations also occasionally reveals something about the predispositions of the authors and their public and how they both viewed the discoveries.

Ariosto and Rabelais, whose works were among the most popular creations of the sixteenth century, brought the names of Asia to a wide public.[192] That contemporaries were aware of how they were using strange names for exotic

---

[185] See Émile Pons, "Les langues imaginaires dans le voyage utopique, un précurseur: Thomas More," *Revue de littérature comparée*, X (1930), 589–607.

[186] For the general argument that Hythlodaeus was a Portuguese voyager and an informant of More about India see G. B. Parks, "More's Utopia and Geography," *Journal of English and Germanic Philology*, XXXVIII (1938), 224; and J. D. M. Derrett, "Thomas More and Joseph the Indian," *Journal of the Royal Asiatic Society*, April, 1962, pp. 18–19.

[187] The conclusion of J. D. M. Derrett in "The Utopian Alphabet," *Moreana*, XII (1966), p. 62.

[188] Above, p. 510.

[189] Above, p. 496.

[190] See above, p. 493, and pl. 98.

[191] For a list of the place names mentioned in European literature produced before 1500 see Ivar Hallberg, *L'Extrême Orient dans la littérature et la cartographie de l'Occident des XIIIᵉ, XIVᵉ et XVᵉ siècles* (Göteborg, 1906).

[192] On Ariosto see above, pp. 205–7. Rabelais, who castigated as "barbarous" the prevailing fad for hieroglyphical emblems and allegories, was nonetheless a rabid amateur collector of exotic names and terms. Indeed, he may have been the first writer to employ the word "exotic" to describe Asian merchandise ("marchandises exotiques" [see above, p. 264]). For commentary see G. Bandmann, "Das Exotische in der europäischen Kunst," in *Der Mensch und die Künste: Festschrift Heinrich Lützeler* (Düsseldorf, 1962), p. 337 n. 2.

effects is borne out by the commentaries of the time. Nor is it too far-fetched to speculate that they helped to produce a taste for the travel literature that became so popular in the latter half of the century. Poets, writers of romances, dramatists, and essayists also continued after mid-century to write popular works in the vernacular in which a constantly greater number of foreign names appeared. The *Lusiads* of Camoëns is the most obvious example of a literary masterpiece that could not have been written without the discoveries.[193] A relatively obscure romance in prose even took the name of a Chinese folk hero as its title. *Il magno Vitei* (Verona, 1597) of Ludovico Arrivabene celebrates the chivalrous exploits of the founder of China's government. Arrivabene derived his primitive transliteration (i.e., "Vitei") from the popular book on China by Mendoza.[194] Similar examples, too numerous to list, could be provided to show how the names of Asia were employed in various types of popular literature in prose and poetry.

Popular literature was but one of the routes through which Asian words entered the European languages. Specialists in almost all fields had to add many new names to their professional vocabularies. Geographers, cosmographers, and cartographers were forced to learn hundreds of new geographical names for natural features (rivers, bays, lakes, mountains, plateaus, valleys), countries, provinces, cities, and towns.[195] Naturalists had to add to their vocabularies and schemes of classification the names of new plants and animals, in many cases by adopting the native names. Even animals known to Antiquity, and for which names already existed in Greek or Latin, were often referred to in the sixteenth century by their Asian names.[196] Navigators added to their vocabularies the local Asian words for matters essential to sailing: points of the compass, winds, and currents. Words for the multitude of new textiles, spices, and jewels were borrowed and many of these loan words became standard in European vocabularies. Historians annexed to their working vocabularies the names and titles of Asian dynasties, monarchs, and officials.

Practices that were foreign to Europe, such as running "amuck," were known only by their native names. For the caste names of India no European equivalents existed and so the native names ("Pariah," "Nāyar," "Chetty") were simply adopted.[197] Words for conveyances that were unknown in Europe,

---

[193] For the geographical names mentioned in the *Lusiads* see A. C. Borges de Figueiredo, *A geographia dos Lusíadas de Luis de Camoës* (Lisbon, 1883), pp. 55–61; for the flora of Asia see Conde de Ficalho, *Flora dos Lusíadas* (Lisbon, 1880), and R. Machado, *A flora da India nos Lusíadas* (Lisbon, 1947).

[194] For further discussion see above, pp. 219–23. Mendoza writes: "Vitey, who was the first that did reduce the kingdoms to one government . . ." See G. T. Staunton (ed.), *The Historie of the great and mightie Kingdome of China* . . ., "Hakluyt Society Publications," O.S. Nos. 14–15 (2 vols.; London, 1853–54), I, 69–70.

[195] On the changed meaning of many technical terms of geography see François de Dainville, *La géographie des Humanistes* (Paris, 1940), pp. 161–63.

[196] For example, the "rhinoceros" was commonly called in Portuguese, *Ganda* (Skt. gaṇḍa) or *Abada* (Malay); in Spanish, *Abada*. See Appendix to this chapter.

[197] The word "caste" was invented by the Portuguese as a generic description for the social classes of India. It is derived from the Latin adjective *casta* meaning "pure" which became a feminine noun

or different in certain ways from their European analogues, were often known by their Asian names: "andor" (litter), "sampan," "jangada" (raft), "junk," "Lantea" (Chinese rowing vessel), "palanquin," "pangara" (small boat of India), "parão" (pinnace), and "dhoney." Names for secular administrators ("mandarin," "nabob," "naique," "rajah," "shabandar," "zamorin") as well as religious personages ("bonze" [Buddhist priest], "brahmin," "yogi") were adopted in many European languages. The names of Asian deities ("Shaka" [Buddha], Ganesha, Confucius) and religious buildings ("pagoda" and "varela" [Buddhist temple]) were all used after a time in European writings without explanation. Uniquely Asian products were commonly referred to by their original names: "achar" (pickles), "areca" (palm seed), "baju" (short jacket), "bamboo," "bhang" (Indian hemp), "coir," "calambec" (aloes-wood), "calico," "cha" (tea), "curry," "charao" (lacquerware), "saia" (root for red dye), "copra," "datura" (thorn-apple), "gingham," "hing" (asafetida), "jaggery" (palm-sugar), "lac" (varnish), "litchi" (dried fruit), "mango," "ola" (palm leaf), "patola" (silk cloth), "kimono," "rota" (rattan), "sago" (palm starch), "zerumbit" (aromatic root). Commercial terms which became permanent additions to the European vocabulary were words such as "banian" (trader of Gujarat), "caixo" (cash), "chop" (seal), "chatinar" (to trade), "chit," "coolie," "fanani" (small coin of south India), "godown" (warehouse), "mangelim" (weight equal to a carat), "tanga" (a small coin of south India). Words which reflect the daily life and the intellectual and artistic advancement of the East are notable for their scarcity. But still there are a few that crept into the European languages at this period: "biombo" (Japanese folding screen), "boy" (servant), "catana" (large Japanese broadsword), "catel" (cot), "lacai" (lacquerware), "pundit," "tank" (place of ceremonial bathing in India).

Many words already established in the European languages acquired extended or different meanings in the sixteenth century. The word "typhoon," for example, probably originated in the learned world of Greece and passed into the medieval vocabulary through Aristotle's *Meteorologica* and the Vulgate. Humanist writers of the sixteenth century use it in their works to mean "violent winds" and refer to it as a Greek term. By the seventh century this Greek word was adopted into Arabic as a specific designation for the intense tropical storms of the East. Arabic traders were possibly responsible subsequently for introducing it into Persian, the Indian languages, and commercial Malay. By the middle of the sixteenth century the Portuguese mariners and missionaries had adopted the Arabic term as their name for the violent Eastern storms. From Portuguese it quickly passed into the vernaculars of the rest of Europe where it was gradually blended during the sixteenth century with the Greco-Latin "typhon" of the Humanists. In popular etymology it has been common to

---

in Portuguese meaning "pure people." See D. Enrico Zaccaria, *Contributo allo studio degl'iberismi in Italia*... (Turin, 1905), pp. 28–30. It was first used in English in 1555, and was frequently spelled "cast" in the sixteenth century.

assume that "typhoon" was derived from the Chinese *tai-fung*, meaning "great storm." It is more likely that the Arabic term was so generally associated with the storms of the China Sea that even sensitive students of language felt impelled to find its origin in Chinese.[198] But what is historically most significant about this word is its migration westward and eastward from Greece, and its ultimate blending into a term that still preserves the popular maritime meaning of a hurricane in the seas of India and the Far East.[199]

Other established European words also underwent a change of meaning even though they did not migrate eastward and return to Europe with the Portuguese. The name "bird of paradise" was applied from the thirteenth to the sixteenth century to all birds of exquisite beauty.[200] After Magellan's men returned with plumages of what the natives and some Europeans after the fifteenth century called the "manucodiata" (from Malay, *mameq deviata*), the term "bird of paradise" was transferred to the Moluccan bird and has since been used exclusively with reference to it.[201] "Porcelain," the ultimate etymology of which is unknown, was applied more and more regularly to the hard-paste ceramics of China. Standard geographical terms had to be extended in their meanings to include the physical features of the overseas world within their definition. The word "archipelago," for example, which had previously referred only to the Greek islands was now applied to the island chains of the Indian Ocean.[202] The word "climate" which had originally been the name for one of the sectors in the terrestrial sphere came to be applied in common parlance to the complex of meteorological phenomena that we include now in our definition of climate. And in the hands of literary artists "climate" quickly acquired a host of figurative meanings as well.[203] Even the word "barbarian," which had been a term of contempt, underwent modification in the sixteenth

---

[198] Based on H. and R. Kahane, "Two Nautical Terms of Greek Origin: *Typhoon* and *Galley*," in *Etymologica: Walther von Wartburg zum siebzigsten Geburtstag* ... (Tübingen, 1958), pp. 417–28.

[199] A similar etymological study should be worked out for the word "Brahman." Clearly of Sanskrit origin, it was used by the Greeks as early as the fourth century B.C. It was preserved through the Middle Ages in the spelling "Brachman" or "Bragman." The Portuguese writers of the sixteenth century write it regularly without the "c." In the sixteenth century it acquired the figurative meaning of "high caste" persons of any country, as in the contemporary "Boston Brahmans." In fact, there are many words of this sort known to Europe in Antiquity, retained through the Middle Ages, and then given new attention, or a change in meaning, during the sixteenth century. A few of the most important are: "sugar," "candy," "rice," "camphor," "musk," "opal," and "sandal." A good model for works of this kind is Alan S. C. Ross, *Ginger: A Loan-Word Study* (Oxford, 1952). He derives "ginger" from the Middle Indian forms—Prakrit, *Singabera*, and Pali, *singivera*—through Greek and Latin to the European vernaculars. Also see, for figurative usage of these words, Rao, *op. cit.* (n. 4), pp. 67–68.

[200] See P. A. Robin, *Animal Lore in English Literature* (London, 1936), p. 155.

[201] Linschoten, probably prompted by Paludanus, wrote in 1596, "the bird which the Portingales call passaros de Sol, that is Fowle of the Sunne, the Italians call it Manucodiatas, and the Latinists, Paradiseas, and by us [Dutch] called Paradice birds." A. C. Burnell and P. A. Tiele (eds.), *The Voyage of John Huyghen van Linschoten to the East Indies*, "Hakluyt Society Publications," O.S. Nos. 70–71 (2 vols.; London, 1885), I, 307.

[202] Dainville, *op. cit.* (n. 195), p. 162.

[203] *Ibid.*, pp. 162–63.

century as Europeans began to realize that the "barbarians" of Asia were capable of producing admirable works.[204]

Most of the Asian words and concepts which entered Europe at this period were relayed through the Portuguese language. The Asian words imported into Portuguese were borrowed from the Indo-Aryan (Konkani, Marathi, Gujarati, Hindustani, Bengali, and Sinhalese), the Dravidian (Malayālam, Tamil, Kanarese [Kannada], and Telugu), the Japanese, the Sino-Tibetan (Burmese, Chinese, Thai, and Cambodian), and the Malay-Polynesian (Malay, Javanese, and Teto [of Timor]) languages. Most of the loan words were nouns: the names of places, flora, fauna, titles, ceremonies, natural phenomena, and inanimate objects. Once adopted these nouns often acquired figurative and pejorative meanings, as in "chatim" (originally a "great merchant," now also "a cunning or conniving person") and "veniaga" (originally an "Indian temple or coin," now also "debauchery"). From many of the borrowed words new forms were derived: "chatim" > "chatinar" (to deal in things of small value), "mandarim" > "mandarinado" (the office of mandarin), "bonzo" > "bonzaria" (a community of Buddhist priests), and "bonzeiro" (a friend of the Buddhists).

While the influence on Portuguese of a given Asian language was ordinarily directly proportional to the influence of Portuguese on it, the case of Chinese is somewhat different. The Chinese language borrowed next to nothing from Portuguese.[205] But the Portuguese writers of the sixteenth century, who vastly admired China, were forced to introduce into their writings a host of Chinese terms of government, commerce, and industry for which they had no equivalents in their own language. Finally, from examination of contemporary dictionaries and grammars it may be asserted that the Portuguese of the sixteenth and seventeenth centuries normally employed a more orientalized vocabulary than have their descendants. The decline of the Asian empire was accompanied by a tendency for Asian words and their derivatives to fall into disuse and in many cases to drop out of the Portuguese vocabulary.[206]

Asian words entered the other European vernaculars of the sixteenth century by divers routes. The Spanish, who had little trouble reading Portuguese authors in the original, were quick to adopt a number of Oriental words. But it was mainly after the union of the crowns in 1580, after the publication (1585) in Spanish of Mendoza's popular account of China, and after the visit of the Japanese emissaries to Spain in 1585 that Asian place names and terms became more prominent in Castilian literature. Throughout most of the sixteenth century, the Spanish language absorbed a multitude of Americanisms. Spain's preoccupation with America certainly delayed the impact on its languages of the new words from Asia.[207] Still, by the last generation of the sixteenth

[204] See *Asia*, II, Bk. I, 199.

[205] On the resistance of particular languages to the borrowing of words see E. Sapir, *Language* (New York, 1921), pp. 108–10.

[206] For further discussion see the introduction to the monumental work of lexicography by S. R. Dalgado, *Glossário luso-asiático* (2 vols.; Coimbra, 1919, 1921).

[207] See R. Lapesa, *Historia de la lengua española* (6th ed.; Madrid, 1965), p. 199.

century, Castilian writers such as Lope de Vega had become sufficiently aware of Japan to write dramas about it. But, as in the case of Portuguese, the influence of Oriental words on Castilian declined with the waning of empire. Only about twenty nouns in today's common vocabulary are recognized as borrowings of the sixteenth century from the Indian and Malay languages, and only two each from Chinese and Japanese.[208]

The Italian language received its influx of Oriental words through a number of channels. The Venetian merchants and political agents of the fifteenth and sixteenth centuries were responsible for introducing many of the terms and names of commerce which they learned in the marts of the Levant and at Lisbon. The newsletters of Florentines in the service of the Portuguese also brought Asian words before the eyes of Italian readers. More extensive accounts were written by those who traveled with the Iberians to the East (for example, Varthema and Pigafetta) and these reports were widely circularized. Jesuit letterbooks in Italian began to be issued at Rome in 1546. The Italian accounts and the translations from other languages which appeared in Ramusio's collection of travel literature constituted perhaps the single richest source of exotic words.[209] Alfonso Ulloa translated the first two *Décadas* of Barros in 1562, and the first seven books of Castanheda in 1577–78. But it was Sassetti, with his profound interest in foreign languages and words, who strove with utmost care to record and explain for his Florentine correspondents the new vocabulary which he encountered during his stay in Portugal and India.[210] In Italian, even more so than in the Iberian languages, the Asian words did not find a secure home. Perhaps they fell out of Italian so quickly because the Italian cities had no direct, political interest in Asia, and only a declining involvement in Eastern trade in comparison to the interests of the Atlantic powers.

The French language received its infusion of Asian words mainly through translations of Portuguese and Italian writings. But it should also be recalled that the epitome of Pigafetta was published in French in 1525, long before it appeared in print in any other language. The translation in 1553 by Nicholas de Grouchy of Castanheda's first book (1551) brought a large number of Asian words into French for the first time. Since Grouchy prided himself on the literal quality of his translation, about fifty Asian words passed intact into French. A number of others retained their Lusitanian forms and a few were Gallicized.[211] In 1552 Postel brought many Japanese names from the Jesuit letters into French in the pages of his *Des merveilles du monde*. Varthema was

[208] M. Alvar *et al.*, *Enciclopedia lingüística hispánica* (2 vols.; Madrid, 1967), II, 250. Also see A. A. Fokker, "Quelques mots espagnols et portugais d'origine orientale, dont l'étymologie ne se trouve pas ou est insuffisamment expliquée dans les dictionnaires," *Zeitschrift für romanische Philologie*, XXXIV (1910), 560–68; XXXVIII (1914), 481–85.

[209] See E. Zaccaria, *op. cit.* (n. 197), especially pp. 28–30, 71, 141; also see by the same author, *L'elemento iberico nella lingua italiana* (Bologna, 1927). For a general statement on the importation of new words into Italian see Bruno Migliorini, *The Italian Language* (New York, 1966), pp. 253, 256.

[210] Marcucci (ed.), *op. cit.* (n. 106), pp. 147, 231, 229, 304–5.

[211] See J. G. C. Herculano de Carvalho, "O vocabulário exótico na *Histoire des Indes* (1553)," *Biblos*, XXVII (1951), 397–98. On Castanheda see *Asia*, I, 187–90.

translated into French in 1556, thus bringing Asian words into French through the Italian route. Thevet and Belleforest relied heavily for their Asian terms upon the Italian accounts in Ramusio. A French translation of Mendoza's book on China was published in 1588 and reissued twice by 1600. In the course of the sixteenth century about sixty Asian words entered the French language and became permanent additions to its common vocabulary.[212] And this, despite the fact that France had no empire or direct trading connections with Asia—only hopes!

The words of Asia first migrated into the Germanic languages through the Iberian and Italian languages. The Germans and the Dutch, like the Italians, were involved early in the sixteenth century in the spice trade. In their commercial newsletters the Germans and the Dutch did bring Asian names into their languages,[213] but after 1520 direct commercial reports became fewer and the northern countries had to rely almost exclusively upon translations. Varthema was translated into German as early as 1515, but it was not until after mid-century and the breakdown of the Portuguese monopoly on news that the Germanic languages received new infusions of Asian words. The English travel collections of Richard Eden (1555) and Richard Willes (1577) were the first translations to introduce a substantial number of Asian names into English.[214] From 1577 to 1582 Thomas Nicholas and John Frampton translated from Castilian into English the authoritative works of Escalante and Castanheda and other incidental matter on the East.[215] The Asian materials were slight in Hakluyt's first edition (1589), but the great collector did encourage the translation and publication of Mendoza's book on China which appeared in 1588 in the English of R. Parke. The last decade of the sixteenth century saw the appearance of the first volumes in the great collections of De Bry and Hulsius as well as Hakluyt's expanded second edition. And in 1596 the *Itinerario* of Linschoten appeared in Dutch, followed two years later by versions in German and English. Through these numerous works the Germanic languages received a heavy supplement of Asian words. The English language, for example, retained permanently in its common vocabulary about fifty of the words of Asian origin current before 1600.[216]

Asian place names, proper names, and general terms were also engrafted upon

---

[212] Number derived from analysis of R. Arveiller, *Contribution à l'étude des termes de voyage en français (1505–1722)* (Paris, 1963); F. V. Peixoto da Fonseca, "Vocábulos franceses de origem portuguesa exótica," *Revista de Portugal*, XXXI (1966), 105–8; XXXIII (1968), 115–17; E. C. Knowlton, *op. cit.* (n. 2); and Urban T. Holmes, "French Words of Chinese Origin," *Language*, X (1934), 280–85.

[213] See *Asia*, I, 161–64.

[214] *Ibid.*, pp. 209–12.

[215] *Ibid.*, p. 212.

[216] Number determined by study of Rao, *op. cit.* (n. 4), especially pp. 107–34; also see John Florio, *A Worlde of Wordes* ... (London, 1598), pp. 60, 75, 176, 195, 216. For German words see Enno Littmann, *Morgenländische Wörter im Deutschen* ... (2d ed.; Tübingen, 1924), pp. 117–36; and Karl Lokotsch, *Etymologisches Wörterbuch der europäischen* ... *Wörter orientalischen Ursprungs* (Heidelberg, 1927). On Dutch borrowings see H. H. Post, "A terminologia portuguesa ou aportuguesada do *Itinerario* ... de ... Linschoten," *Revista de Portugal*, XXV (1960), 349–61, 454–72.

the Latin language of the learned world. Latin translations of the early news-letters and of Varthema were the first important publications on the discoveries in that language. Jakob Stoppell in his *Repertorium* . . . (Memmingen, 1519) uses place names garnered from the writings of the medieval travelers to Asia. Willibald Pirckheimer appended to his *Germaniae* . . . (1530) a list of place names which includes a number from the contemporary reports on Asia. The report (1523) of Maximilian of Transylvania on the voyage of Magellan was followed by the *Novus orbis* (1532) of Simon Grynaeus and the *Cosmographia* (1550) of Sebastian Münster. Little else was published in Latin on the Asian discoveries until the last generation of the sixteenth century. In 1570 Ortelius issued the first edition of his *Theatrum orbis terrarum*, which contained a separate map of Asia as well as regional maps of Tartary and the East Indies. In this and subse-quent editions Ortelius relied heavily for his place names upon the Portuguese cartographers. His captions and legends are in Latin; only the Ptolemaic features on the maps retain Latin names. For example, the map of China added to his edition of 1584 has virtually nothing on it but Lusitanized place names. In the meantime Charles de L'écluse published at Antwerp in 1576 his epitomized Latin version of Orta's *Colóquios* (1563).[217] This Latin abbreviation of Orta's work became the leading authority on Asian botany in Europe and was revised and republished four times before the end of the century. The problem of providing a correct scientific nomenclature for the new Asian plants was one of the major reasons for the repeated revisions. In 1581 the annual letterbooks of the Jesuits began to be issued in Latin on a regular basis. They, along with G. B. Maffei's *Historiarum Indicarum libri XVI* (Florence, 1588) and the Latin translation (1589) of Mendoza probably constituted the best Latin materials on Asia available in sixteenth-century Europe.

The Latin language, like the vernaculars, usually adopted the Asian words intact or in their Lusitanized forms. The spelling of the Asian words varied greatly even within the Portuguese sources, for the reporters noted down as well as they could what they *heard* individually. The problem was further com-plicated by the unsettled condition of European orthography. Inconsistencies in spelling often led to confusion in the identification of places and peoples When Asian words in their Lusitanized forms were subjected to Gallicization, Italian-ization, and Germanization, the problem was exacerbated. Proper and consistent spellings were particularly important for cartographers who had to distinguish between Cambay, Cambala (of Marco Polo), and Cambodia. It was even more difficult for them when they sought to reconcile the new place names with the designations of Ptolemy. For botanists the problem was similar for they were forced by their discipline to seek out the corresponding name, if it existed, in the nomenclature of Dioscorides. And for the cosmographer, who dealt in all subjects, it was next to impossible to be accurate on the differences between

---

[217] See the list of scientific terms used by Orta as compiled in J. P. Machado, "Lexicologia científica de origem oriental nos *Colóquios dos Simples e Drogas*," in special commemorative number of the periodical *Garcia de Orta*, XI (1963), 755–88.

Mon (language of Burma), "Mugs" (people of Arakan), and "Mara" (Makian island) when they appeared in a variety of spellings. It is no wonder that later authors who used Varthema's *Itinerario* (1510), the earliest of the comprehensive accounts, in the original Italian or in the Latin, German, or Spanish translations, should have questioned the credibility of his account because of his vague and inaccurate names for the regions, peoples, and places east of India.[218]

Vocabulary is the part of language which is most subject to quick and capricious innovation. And the borrowing of words rather than the translation of them, is most likely to occur when the languages concerned are of altogether different types.[219] Adoption of foreign words on a wholesale basis is especially likely to occur when the civilizations have had no direct contacts previously and when the civilizations encountered are complex and culturally alien. Borrowing becomes a virtual necessity when a confrontation occurs between the phonetic and the ideographic languages. For example, the Portuguese writers on China simply transliterated the local administrative titles without making serious efforts to translate them. As distant as the Indian tongues were from Europe's languages, they were still multisyllabic and phonetic. The great difficulty in India was the multiplicity of languages and the existence of two different families. This undoubtedly produced the confusion in the minds of Europeans between Konkani (Indo-Aryan) and Kanarese (Dravidian). Nonetheless, the languages of Malabar could allegedly be mastered in six months. The ideographic languages, it was recognized, involved a lifetime of study for correct usage. What more could be done than to romanize the ideographs and try to explain them?

Thousands of Asian place names and proper names invaded all the languages of western Europe over the course of the sixteenth century. They became increasingly common as the number of writings on Asia mounted. From the literary descriptions in the Iberian languages and Italian they invaded the cosmographies, natural histories, geographies, atlases, and popular literature. With the passage of time some words dropped out of both the popular and the specialized vocabularies. Those which were retained acquired the spelling of the receiving language and were adapted to its grammar through derivative forms: mandarin > mandarinate; curry > curried. About one hundred words of Asian origin were added to the permanent, common vocabulary of Europe during the sixteenth century (see Appendix to this chapter).[220] Hundreds of new words of Asian provenance became part of the specialized vocabularies of geographers, cartographers, botanists, and linguists. Those Asian words of the specialized vocabularies which became permanent were worked into the

---

[218] Cf. *Asia*, I, 165.

[219] See A. Meillet and M. Cohen, *Les langues du monde* (Paris, 1924), pp. 6–7.

[220] Knowlton, *op. cit.* (n. 2), p. 53, calculates that 65 Chinese and 128 Japanese loan words were introduced into the Romance languages, mostly into Portuguese. His list includes a few common place names (Kuang-tung > Cantão) and numerous political administrative terms. He does not consider whether or not the word has become fixed in the language—a mere mention is recorded in some instances.

standard nomenclature of the discipline where usually they received a stricter definition and delineation. The "China root" of the sixteenth century became the *Smilax china* of Linnaeus in the eighteenth century. The words "Serica" and "Cathay" gave way to "China" and were dropped from the scientific vocabulary of the geographer; Siam, previously unknown to cartographers, became a permanent feature of their repertory. Examples of this kind are countless—as countless as the number of new Asian words that entered the vocabulary of Europe in the sixteenth century.

At the opening of the sixteenth century, there was in Europe no substantial information about the languages of Asia. No understanding existed of their similarities to one another or to the languages of Europe and the Levant. Vague references in the writings of medieval and Renaissance travelers to the ideographic nature of Chinese went unnoticed or unappreciated by students of language. The place names mentioned by the travelers were sometimes inserted on maps or incorporated into chronicles and works of popular literature. But in no sense can it be argued that the intrusion of new place names into geographical conceptions produced any interest in the languages of Asia. Asian names were merely added to the repertory of Ptolemaic place names. It was mainly in the absorption of popular writers with exotic alphabets that there can be discerned in Europe a primitive awakening to the existence of the numerous languages of Asia.

Europeans became acquainted with the many tongues of Asia only after the establishment of direct and permanent relations. From the outset sailors, merchants, and administrators were forced to acquire a working knowledge of the languages of Eastern commerce. The missionaries, particularly in the latter half of the century, were required to have a practical command of the languages prevailing in the places where they evangelized. In every instance the Europeans in Asia had to acquire their language skills through native informants and teachers. They then had to prepare rudimentary vocabularies, dictionaries, and grammars for their own use and for their successors. At no time during the sixteenth century was it possible to find in Europe the materials necessary for teaching a merchant or a missionary any of the languages of Asia. Since most of the missionaries adept in the languages of Asia never returned to Europe, there were likewise no teachers of Asian languages available. The only language student who returned to Europe, Father Michele Ruggiero, was described by his superiors in the field as a man who was old, weary, and inept at Chinese.

The information on Asian languages acquired by hard, direct experience was relayed to Europe through vocabularies compiled in Asia and through literary descriptions. The dispatch of books to Europe also provided the literati in Portugal and Italy with printed and manuscript examples of Asian languages. Asian persons visiting in Europe also left samples of their writing. About the most that the general public of Europe was prepared to understand and accept were the literary descriptions of the Asian languages incorporated into the travel accounts and the Jesuit letterbooks. Fortunately, the literary descriptions were full enough to make it clear that a welter of new languages had been discovered and that they were sophisticated and quite different from the known languages.

Malay was early recognized to be the main language of commerce in southern Asia. The languages of Malabar, Malayālam and Tamil, were reported to be easy to learn and quite different from other Indian languages. Sanskrit, while generally recognized as the sacred language of the Hindus, was studied by no one but Sassetti. The Europeans gave serious attention only to the languages of Goa and Malabar, although they clearly understood that India possessed a host of other languages. While it was possible, even in Europe, to name many of the languages of Southeast Asia, there existed no understanding in depth of any of them except Malay and Tagalog. The Sinic form of writing (Chinese, Japanese, and Annamese) because of its ideographic nature received far more attention from students of language than the other Asian tongues. By the end of the century it was clearly understood that the Chinese ideographs had been adapted to Japanese and Annamese even though these were different spoken languages. And it was likewise recognized that in China itself there existed a vast number of dialects and a language of the educated called "Mandarin."

The Europeans in Asia, especially the learned missionaries, were quite naturally dominated by Latin in their linguistic thought and activity. As a practical measure, they romanized the Tamil alphabet and contrived romanizations for many of the Chinese and Japanese characters. The romanizations were recognized as but poor approximations of the original sounds—even as they are yet for Chinese. The failure of the Latin letters to convey the sounds of the Asian languages was usually ascribed to the "barbarity" of these languages. Most of the romanizations passed into the other languages of Europe through Portuguese, and so they often retained Lusitanized features. Nonetheless, the romanizations apparently served their purpose, for many of the most important Jesuit publications were issued in romanized form for the use of practicing missionaries. The dictionaries and the grammars of the Asian languages that they published also followed Latin models, a technique that was being employed contemporaneously in the organization of the vernaculars of Europe.

Printing by movable type was another European invention that the missionaries turned to advantage in the East. They printed religious works first in romanizations, and then gradually in the native scripts. Several Christian books were printed by the Chinese xylographic method, but this technique was never adopted permanently in the mission stations. Rather Indians, Japanese, and Chinese were taught to work the European press. A few Asians were even sent to Lisbon to learn how to cut typefaces, presumably so that they could return to their homelands to cut characters in their own scripts. The printers were also involved in developing the techniques of romanization. As in Europe, they were essential in Asia to compiling and preparing for the press the dictionaries and grammars of the vernaculars.

Biblical and classical ideas about the origin, history, and development of language remained unchallenged in Europe until the middle of the sixteenth century. But, even in this early period, the vernacular languages were becoming more independent of Latin though organized in terms of Latin models. The Humanists' interest in Greek and the theologians' concern with Greek and Hebrew had the effect of elevating these two Eastern languages to the level of Latin. The papacy meanwhile encouraged study of the modern languages of the Levant and Africa as it sought to realign the Eastern church and to evangelize there. Around 1540 the national languages were proclaimed, both in Italy and Portugal, to be perfectly appropriate and respectable vehicles of philosophical discourse. In the Iberian states they were hailed as the languages of empire. While the church preserved its official Latinity, ecclesiastical proponents of the vernaculars advanced the idea openly that God could be worshipped equally well in all languages. The Jesuits extended this point of view to the mission field of Asia and quickly tried to master the languages of their converts. As a consequence of all this, the vernaculars of both Europe and Asia were increasingly recognized as worthy of study in their own right.

The rapid growth in the number and variety of recognized languages posed a gigantic problem for European students of linguistics. The nature and causes of linguistic change, while continuing to be hotly debated, were attributed with increasing frequency, following Bibliander, to external social and cultural factors rather than to internal evolution of the language. But such a conclusion helped very little to explain the origin of language or to account for its unending diversity. The idea of primitive Hebrew as the *lingua humana* continued to be accepted on faith; but the relationships of the profane languages to Hebrew and to one another still defied understanding. Given the accepted antiquity of Chinese, it was theologically important to prove that it was related to Hebrew. The general assumption that the pictographs were primitive and that the alphabetical languages were derived from them was shaken by the revelation of Chinese as a living language of great vitality and influence.

That harmony existed among the languages of the world was a conclusion supported by both doctrine and comparative study. Alphabets, words, and syntax were compared in the hope of discovering the elements common to all languages, a necessary first step to the unscrambling of the confused tongues. The languages of Asia, including Chinese and Japanese, were brought into the systems of comparison devised for the generically related languages of Europe and the Levant. For example, efforts were made to find a Chinese alphabet and to compare its words in romanized form to the words of other languages. But these efforts uncovered no significant similarities between Chinese and the phonetic languages of Europe. About all that could be done was to incorporate Chinese words into polyglot dictionaries, to reclassify the languages of the world into families, and to treat the overseas languages as independent problems.

Not all students of language were so easily satisfied. Those who stressed linguistic harmony persisted in their efforts to recover the universal idiom.

Occultists hoped with the aid of divine wisdom to recover the perfect language from the Scriptures or the "hieroglyphs," Egyptian and Chinese. Other scholars sought to locate a universal idiom in the natural languages, as in Gesner's studies of "Rotwelsch." The failure of these efforts led others of a more immediate and practical turn of mind to contrive artificial languages for universal use which, like the numerical system, musical notes, or shorthand, had no phonetic equivalents. Even though these efforts failed either to uncover or to produce universal language, many serious students of language of the seventeenth century followed the lead of sixteenth-century students in a fruitless search for the *lingua humana* and the primitive characters.[221]

The widest and most permanent influence of Asia on the languages of sixteenth-century Europe was the introduction of new words into the common vocabulary. Most of the new Asian words entered Europe through the medium of the Portuguese language. They then filtered, through translations primarily, into the other languages of Europe. Once adopted they were often phonetically and orthographically modified to fit the usages of the borrowing language. The languages that were most permanently affected were those of the Atlantic states involved in the overseas spice trade. The Italian language was less influenced than the other vernaculars by the influx of Asia words, even though most of the travel accounts and many special works on Asia appeared in that language. This was perhaps a function of Latin's predominance in Italy and of the less intimate involvement of the Italians with the Atlantic spice trade. Although the vernaculars of Europe were unequal in their readiness to accept new words from Asia, the reception of Asian terms into the professional vocabularies of navigators, geographers, scientists, and cosmographers was practically universal.

The languages of Asia, as they were slowly and irregularly revealed to Europe, produced bewilderment and perplexity among scholars and linguists. Speculation throve on partial or mistaken information or interpretation. The discovery of languages written in ideographs was particularly disconcerting, especially as it began to be understood that they could not be satisfactorily integrated into prevailing linguistic conceptions. The introduction of exotic words on a large scale had the effect of upsetting traditional schemes of nomenclature and classification in geography, cartography, and the natural sciences. "Name," wrote Francis Bacon in the next century, "though it seem but a superficial and outward matter, yet it carrieth much impression and enchantment." It was this "impression and enchantment" of exotic names from Asia, as well as the peculiar nature of the ideographic languages, that helped to confound the languages as well as the linguists of Europe. The study of language in Europe was to be handicapped by the effects of the "rebabelization" of the sixteenth century until new linguistic theories and techniques had evolved in the following centuries.

---

[221] The best general discussion for the seventeenth century is to be found in Cornelius, *op. cit.* (n. 105), chaps. i, ii, and iv.

Words of Asiatic Origin Introduced into the European Vocabulary (Sixteenth Century)

All the words in this table were derived during the sixteenth century from one Asian language or another, excluding Arabic, Persian, and other Near Eastern languages. They then became permanent words in one European language or another. All can be found in modern dictionaries. Not all of the words listed became permanent or common words in all European languages, but each did become part of at least one modern European language. The list includes mainly the words of the common vocabulary and omits most titles, place names, and other specialized terms. Most of the words entered the European vocabulary through the Portuguese language. Only representative examples of secondary borrowings are given.

Source Word (Eur. lang, and date of first use)	Meaning	Derivation	In other European languages	Remarks
abada or bada (P., 1541)	rhinoceros	Malay, badak(?)	bada (Ital, 1579) abada (Sp., 1585) abath (Eng., 1592)	"a" is possibly an Arabic prefix. Cobarruvias (1611) calls it the common name for rhinoceros. On derivation see Yule and Burnell, p. 1.
achár (P., 1563)	pickles	Malay, àchár	achar (Dutch, 1596) machar (Eng., 1598) Later, achar in English	"achar" is still used as a commercial name.
amouco (P., 1516)	people who run wild	Malay, amuk	amouco (Fr., 1553) amocchi (It., 1566) amuck (Eng., 1663)	
andor (P., 1500)	a litter	Malayàlam, andōla; Konkani, ãndôr	andor (Fr. 1553) andore (Ital., ca. 1555)	Etymology is much disputed; perhaps related to Skt., hindola.
anil (P., 1516)	indigo	Skt., nīla	anyll (Ital, 1525) neel (Eng., 1583)	
areca (P., 1510; Ital, 1510)	seed of the palm, used in making a quid of betel	Malayàlam, adekka or adakka	arecca (Fr., 1521) arecca (Eng., 1599)	
baju (P., 1515)	a short jacket	Malay, baju	bàju (Fr., 1553) baiu (Dutch, 1596)	Modern Dutch dictionary gives "baadje" and "baaitje."
bambu; see "mambu"				
baneanes, banianes (P., 1516)	traders from Gujarat	Skt., vānija Gujarati, vāṇiyo	banian (Fr., 1575) banian (Eng., 1599)	

(continued)

Source word (Eur. lang, and date of first use)	Meaning	Derivation	In other European languages	Remarks
bangue (P., 1554)	Indian hemp	Skt., bhaṅga Hindi, bhāṅg	bhang (Eng., 1563) bangue (Sp., 1578) bangue (Dutch, 1596) bengi (Fr., 1638)	
bate (P., 1531)	rice in the husk	Kannada, batta Konkani, bhāta Malay, pādi	batte (Dutch, 1596) paddy (Eng., 1598)	
bétele, betre (P., 1500)	betel leaf	Malayālam, veṭṭila	betel (Ital., 1510) betel (Fr., 1515) betele (Eng., 1553)	cf. note of Schmidt, in ZDMG, LXVII, 653–59, for further detail.
biombo (P., 1569)	folding screen	Japanese, byōbu	biombo (Sp., ca. 1585) biomba (Ital., ca. 1585)	Examples brought by Japanese emissaries to Europe.
bói, boia (P., 1511)	a servant	Telugu and Malayālam, bōyi	boye (Fr., 1610) boye (Eng., 1673)	Usage extended to East Asia. For details see Vermeer.
bonzo (P., 1500)	Buddhist priest	Japanese, bōzu	bonzii (Lat., 1552) bonsos (Eng., 1585)	
cairo (P., 1502)	coir, or palm rope	Tamil, kayiru Malayālam, kāyar	cayro (Fr., 1552) cayro (Eng., 1582)	
caixa (P., 1510; Ital., 1510)	small monies, cash	Skt., karṣa Tamil, kāsu	caixa (Dutch, 1596) caixa (Eng., 1598) cas (Fr., 1609)	English word "cash" appears in 1621.
calaim (P., 1510)	fine Indian tin	Malay, kālang Arabic, kalaʻi	calaia (Ital., 1582) calin (Fr., 1610)	
calampat (Ital., 1510)	finest aloes-wood	Japanese(?), kalambak	calamba (P., 1516) calambour (Fr., ca. 1525) calambac (Eng., 1594)	

calico (Eng., *ca.* 1540)	calico cloth	cloth of Calicut	calicoe (Lat., 1627)	Loss of final "e" in Eng. may have occurred because the word came from Fr. "calicot" where the "t" is not pronounced.
cambolim (P., 1514)	blanket or cloak	Skt., kambala Konkani, kamblim	cambolim (Fr., 1610) cumbly (Eng., 1673)	
canfora (P., 1516)	camphor	Hindi, kapūr	comfora (Ital., 1506) canfore (Fr., 1553)	Word also mentioned by Marco Polo.
carambola (P., 1563)	acid fruit of *Averrhoa carambola*	Skt., karmara Konkani-Marathi, karambal	carambola (Cast., 1578) carambolar (Dutch, 1596) carambola (Eng., 1598) carambole (Fr., 1602)	
caril (P., 1563)	curry	Kanarese (Kannada), karil Tamil, kari	carriel (Dutch, 1596) cariel (Eng., 1598) caril (Fr., 1610)	
catamaran (Ital., 1583)	raft formed of three of four logs lashed together	Tamil, kaṭṭremaram	gatameroni (Ital., 1583)	
catana (P., 1582)	large broadsword	Japanese, katana		
cate, cato, cacho, catechu (P., 1516)	astringent extract of acacia	Skt., kvath cate = Konkani, kāt; cacho = Malay, kachu; catechu from both	cato (Cast., 1578) catu (Ital., 1585)	
catele, cátel (P., 1510)	a light bedstead	Tamil and Malayālam, kaṭṭil Hindi, khāt	catele (Cast., 1578) catu (Ital., 1585)	English cot (1634).
cha (Ital., 1559)	tea	Chinese, ch'a	chá (P., 1565) chaa (Eng., 1598)	Cha also in Greek and Russian.
champana, champão (P., 1516)	small boat or skiff	Chinese, san-pan	chiampana (Ital., 1510) sampang (Fr., 1540) sampan (Eng., 1620)	Chinese means "three boards,"

(continued)

Source word (Eur. lang, and date of first use)	Meaning	Derivation	In other European languages	Remarks
chapa (P., 1518)	seal or stamp	Hindi and Gujarati, chāp	chapa (Fr., 1553), chop (Eng., 1614)	Usage extended to East Asia. Many different spellings in English.
charão, acharão, xarão (P., 1569)	Japan ware, or japanning	Chinese, ch'i yáu(?)	charol (Sp., 1572), achiran (Ital., 1582)	Etymology not certain.
chatim (P., 1552)	chetty, a trading caste	Malayālam, chetti	chatins (Fr., 1553), chitini (Ital., 1566), chettijns (Dutch, 1596)	
chatinar (P., 1552)	to trade, derived from chatim			In modern Portuguese it means to sell small things of little price and value.
chay, choy, chaya (Ital., ca. 1566)	root of Indian plant which yields red dye	Tamil, says	saia (Eng., 1598), zage (Dutch, 1672)	
chito (P., 1563)	letter or note	Konkani, citthi		Eng. "chit" for bill is commonly used in East.
coles (P., 1563)	hired servant or coolie	Gujarati and Marathi, koli	colles (Dutch, 1596), colles (Eng., 1598)	
copra (P., 1563)	dried kernel of the coconut used for its oil	Malayālam, koppara; Hindi, khopā; Gujarati, khoprū	copra (Sp., 1578), chopra (Eng., 1584), copra (Dutch, 1596)	
corja (P., 1514)	a score; fig, multitude or rabble	Malayālam, kórchchu; Telugu, khorjam	corge (Eng., 1605)	
datura (P., 1563)	thorn apple	Skt., dhattūra	datyro (Sp., 1578), datura (Lat., ca. 1580), deutroa (Dutch, 1596), deutroa (Eng., 1598)	

Portuguese form	Meaning	Source language	Variant forms	Notes
durian (Lat., 1444)	aromatic fruit of Southeast Asia	Malay, duriyan	duriões (P., 1552) durion (Sp., 1585) durian (Eng., and Fr., 1588)	
eme (Dutch, ca. 1598)	emeu, cassowary, bird of Southeast Asia	Javanese, eme	emeu (Fr., 1598) eme (Ger., ca. 1598)	cf. Asia, II, Bk. I, 95.
fanão (P., 1498)	small coin long in use in south India	Skt, paṇa Malayālam and Tamil, paṇam	fanone (Ital., 1505) fanam (Eng., 1555) panan (Fr., 1610)	First mentioned in Travels of Ibn Batuta.
fotoqués (P., 1562)	Buddhist deities of Japan: generic name	Japanese, hotoke (Buddha)		
gong (P., 1513)	bell	Malay, gŏng	ghong (Eng., 1673)	In modern dicts: Fr., gong; Sp., gongo; Dutch, gong; Ger., gong
gudão (P., 1552)	warehouse	Malay, gadong	gudoes (Fr., 1553) godown (Eng., 1583) gottoni (Ital., 1585)	Borrowed through Anglo-Indian into Hindi and Bengali.
guingão (P., 1552)	gingham cloth	Malay, guingong Javanese, ging-gang	guingoes (Fr., 1553) gingani (Ital., 1567) gingham (Eng., 1615)	
ingo (P., 1554)	the drug, asafetida	Skt, hingu Konkani-Marathi, hing	ingn (Sp., 1578) hing (Eng., 1583) hin (Lat., 1631)	
jaca (P., 1535)	jack fruit and tree	Malayālam, chakka	jaque (Fr., 1553) iaca (Dutch, 1596) jack (Eng., 1613)	Mentioned by overland travelers in fourteenth century.
jagra, jágara (P., 1510)	palm sugar	Malayālam, chakkara Skt, śarkarā	jagra (Fr., 1553) jaggery (Eng., 1583) iagra (Dutch, 1596)	Originally same word as "sugar,"
jambo (P., 1563)	rose apple	Sanskrit, jambu	iambos (Dutch, 1596) iambos (Eng., 1598)	Often confused with guava.

(continued)

Source word (Eur. lang. and date of first use)	Meaning	Derivation	In other European languages	Remarks
jangada (P., 1504)	a raft (usually)	Tamil-Malayālam, shangadam	iangada (Dutch, 1596), jangada (Eng., 1598)	Dalgado, Glossário, gives seven different meanings in Portuguese.
jogue (P., 1498)	name of Hindu ascetic, yogi	Skt., yogī Hindi, jogī	ioghe (Ital., 1510), yoghi (Fr., 1553), yogi (Eng., 1619)	Name also mentioned by Marco Polo and Ibn Batuta.
junco, jungo (P., 1510)	large Eastern ship, usually Chinese	Malay, djong	iuncum (Lat., 1549), guinco (Ital., 1550), junk (Eng., 1616)	
kris, cris (P., 1552)	a dagger with a wavy blade	Malay, kris	kris (Eng., 1577)	Modern Eng, kris, creese.
laca, lácar (P., 1498)	Asian varnish; lacquer-varnish	Hindi, lākh	lacca (Ital., 1510), lac (Eng., 1533), lacre (Fr., 1553)	English words lake (red color) and shellac also derived from Hindi, lākh.
lantea, lanteia (P., 1569)	a rowing vessel	Chinese, ling-t'ing (slipper boat) Cantonese, lang-t'eng	lantea (Cast., 1585), lantec (Ital., 1588)	Etymology from E. C. Knowlton, Words, p. 51.
lechia, lichia (P., 1513)	fruit of the Nephelium litchi; litchi nuts	Chinese, li-chi; Malay, lichi, from Cantonese, lai-chi	litchi (Eng., 1588), lechya (Dutch, 1596), laices (Lat., 1631)	
mambu (P., 1563)	bamboo	Kanarese, bambou Malay, bambu	mambu (Sp., 1578), bambos (Eng., 1586), bambus (Dutch, 1596), bambou (Fr., 1598), mambu (Lat., 1608)	
mandarim (P., 1514)	generic term for Asian officials	Hindi and Malay, mantri	mandarin (Fr., 1553), mandarin (Eng., 1588), mandarijns (Dutch, 1596)	Often associated incorrectly with mandar, "to command," and with China exclusively.

manga (Ital., 1510)	fruit of the *Mangifera indica*: mango	Malayalam, manga	manga (P., 1525) mango (Eng., 1582)	
mangelim (P., 1516)	small weight of south India for weighing precious stones	Telugu, manjali	mangelim (Fr., 1553) mangelim (Eng., 1555)	Modern Portuguese dictionary gives meaning "carat."
mão (P., 1515)	name of a weight long current in western Asia and India	Marathi and Hindi, mān	maund (Eng., 1584) mao (Dutch, 1596)	Variations of this name occur in several ancient languages.
manucodiata (Fr., *ca.* 1525)	bird of paradise	Malay, māmeq dēivāta Javanese, manuk-devata	manucodiata (Ital., 1552) manucodiata (Eng., 1555)	Buffon gave bird of paradise the name "manucode."
nababo (P., 1600)	deputy or viceroy	Hindi, navāb	nabob (Eng., 1612)	
naique (P., 1511)	native headman	Skt, nāyaka Hindi, nāyak	naic (Ital., 1565) naik (Eng., 1588)	
naire (P., 1503)	ruling caste in Malabar	Malayālam, nāyar	naeri (Ital., 1510) naire (Fr., 1515) naire (Lat., 1571) naire (Cast., 1578) nayre (Eng., 1582)	Originally same as *naique.*
negundo (P., 1563)	shrub of India, *Vitex negundo*	Konkani, ningūd Marathi, nigūd	negundo (Sp., 1578) negundo (Fr., 1602)	
noira (P., 1516)	bird of the Moluccas; lory in Eng.	Malay, nūri	noyra (Dutch, 1598)	
ola (P., 1511)	palm leaf	Malayālam, ōla	ola (Dutch, 1598) olla (Eng., 1622)	
pagode (P., 1516)	used in three senses: idol; temple for idols; name of Indian coin	obscure; possibly from Skt, bhagavat; Malayālam, pakōti	pagode (Fr., 1553) pagod (Eng., 1582) pagode (Dutch, 1596)	Extended (cf. *varela*) to Far East in English word "pagoda."
palanquim (P., 1535)	a box litter	Telugu, pallaki Malay, palañgki	palanquin (Fr., 1553) palanchino (Ital., 1567) palanquin (Eng., 1588)	

(*continued*)

Source word (Eur. lang. and date of first use)	Meaning	Derivation	In other European languages	Remarks
pandito (P., 1574)	learned man	Skt., paṇḍita	pandit (Fr., 1625) pundit (Eng., 1661)	
pangaio (P., 1555)	a small boat	Konkani, pangáy	pangara (Eng., 1591) pangaio (Dutch, 1596)	
paran, paró, parão (P., 1504)	small war or trading vessel comparable to a pinnace	Malay, parahu or parau	parao (Ital., 1510) praõ (Fr., 1525) parones (Lat., 1571)	
parea (P., 1516)	low caste of south India, pariah	Tamil, paraiyan	paria (Ital., ca. 1550) paria (Fr., 1575) paria (Eng., 1613)	
parseo, parse, parsi (P., 1552)	Persian emigrants in India, the Parsees	Hindi, parsi	parcees (Eng., 1616)	Perhaps Hindi took this name from European languages.
patola (P., 1509)	a silk cloth	Kanarese and Malayālam, paṭṭuḍa	patole (Fr., 1525) patole (Ital., ca. 1550)	
pucho (P., 1516)	a fragrant root, the costus of the ancients	Malay, pūchuq	pucho (Fr., 1553) puchio (Ital., ca. 1563) putchuh (Eng., 1588)	Debated derivation.
quimão, queimão (P., 1559)	a flowing garment	Japanese, kimono	kimono (Lat., 1585) kimone (Fr., 1588)	Found in Jesuit letters and Maffei.
raja (P., 1553)	ruler in India	Skt., rājā	raja (Eng., 1555) raja (Ital., 1578)	Mentioned by Ibn Batuta.
rota (P., 1552)	palm stems of which canes are made, rattan	Malay, rótan	rota (Cast., 1578) rota (Dutch, 1596) rotan (Fr., ca. 1610)	English "rattan" does not appear until 1660.

sagu (P., 1552)	palm starch	Malay, sagū	çagu (Fr., 1553) sago (Eng., 1555) sagu (Ital., 1550)	
samorin (P., 1498)	ruler of Calicut	Malayālam, sāmūri	samory (Ital., 1510) çamorim (Fr., 1553) zamorin (Eng., 1583)	Mentioned by Ibn Batuta.
sapão (P., 1570)	sappan-wood, or brazilwood	Malay, sapang	sapon (Dutch, 1596) sapon (Eng., 1598)	
sura (P., 1537)	toddy, or fermented sap of several kinds of palm	Skt., surā	sura (Sp., 1578) sura (Dutch, 1596) sura (Eng., 1598)	
tabaxer (P., 1563)	sugar of bamboo, or salty bamboo	Pers., tabāshīr, from Skt., tvakkṣīrā	tabaxir (Sp., 1578) tabixir (Lat., 1580) tabaxiir (Eng., 1598)	
tanga (P., 1513)	a coin of India	Marathi, ṭāṅk Hindi, ṭaṅgā	tanga (Fr., 1553) tanga (Ital., 1578) tanga (Eng., 1598)	
tanque (P., 1498)	reservoir	Gujarati-Marathi, ṭāṅki	tanga (Ital., 1510) tanque (Fr., 1553) tank (Eng., 1616)	
the (Fr., 1565)	tea	Chinese (Amoy dialect), ti	Latin (1631) Eng. (1653)	See Holmes, p. 285.
tona, tone (P., 1504)	small riverine sailing vessel of south India	Tamil, tōṇi	doni (Eng., 1582) tone (Dutch, 1598)	"Dhoney" in modern English.
tufão (P., ca. 1560)	typhoon			For discussion see p. 533.
varela (P., 1552)	Buddhist idols or temples	Malay, barhālā	varelle (Ital., 1569) varelle (Eng., 1588)	cf. pagode.
veniaga (P., 1552)	merchant	Malay, běrnyága		

Alvar, M., *et al. Enciclopedia lingüística hispánica*. 2 vols. Madrid, 1967.

Arveiller, Raymond. *Contribution á l'étude des termes de voyage en français (1505–1722)*. Paris, 1963.

Barbosa, Jorge Morais. *A língua portuguesa no mundo*. 2d ed., rev. Lisbon, 1969.

Cobarruvais, Don Sebastian de. *Tesoro de la lengua Castellana o Espanola*. Madrid, 1611.

Corominas, J. *Diccionario crítico etimológico de la lengua castellana*. 4 vols. Berne, 1954.

Dalgado, Sebastião Rodolfo. *Glossário Luso-Asiático*. 2 vols. Coimbra, 1919, 1921.

———. *Portuguese Vocables in Asiatic Languages*. Translated into English with notes, additions, and comments by Anthony Xavier Soares (Baroda, 1936). Gaekwad's *Oriental Studies*, edited by B. Bhattacharyya, Vol. LXXIV.

Dauzat, Albert. *Dictionnaire étymologique de la langue française*. Paris, 1949.

Florio, John. *A Worlde of Wordes*. London, 1598.

Fokker, A. A. "Quelques mots espagnols et portugais d'origine orientale, dont l'étymologie ne se trouve pas ou est insuffisamment expliqué dans les dictionnaires." *Zeitschrift für romanische Philologie*, XXXVIII (1914), 481–85.

Herculano de Carvalho, J. G. C. "O vocabulário exótico no *Histoire des Indes* (1553)." *Estudos linguísticos*, I (Lisbon, 1964), 9–38.

Hirth, Friedrich. "Fremdwörter aus dem Chinesischen." *Archiv für das Studium der neueren Sprachen und Litteraturen*, LXVII (1882), 197–212.

Holmes, Urban T. "French Words of Chinese Origin." *Language*, X (1935), 280–85.

Knowlton, Edgar C. Jr. "Antão de Proença's *Vocabulario Tamulico*: Lustitano-Indo-Portuguese Elements." *Tamil Culture*, XI (1964), 135–64.

———. *Words of Chinese, Japanese, and Korean Origin in the Romance Languages*. Ann Arbor, Mich.: University Microfilms, 1959.

König, K. "Ueberseeische Wörter im Französischen vom 16–18 Jahrhundert." *Beihefte zur Zeitschrift für romanische Philologie*, No. 91 (Halle, 1939).

Little, William, *et al. The Oxford Universal Dictionary on Historical Principles*. Revised and edited by C. T. Onions. 3d ed. Oxford, 1955.

Littmann, Enno. *Morgenländische Wörter im Deutschen*. 2d ed. Tübingen, 1924.

Loewe, R. "Über einige europäische Wörter exotischer Herkunft." *Zeitschrift für vergleichende Sprachforschung*, LX (1933), 145–84; LXI (1933), 37–136.

Lokotsch, K. *Etymologisches Wörterbuch der europäischen Wörter orientalischen Ursprungs*. Heidelberg, 1927.

Machado, José Pedro. "Lexicologia científica de origem oriental nos *Colóquios dos Simples e Drogas*." *Garcia de Orta*, XI (1963), 755–88.

Michaelis, H. *A New Dictionary of the Portuguese and English Languages*. New York, 1945.

Nicot, Jean. *Thresor de la langue française*. Paris, 1606.

Peixoto da Fonseca, Fernando V. "Vocábulos franceses de origim portuguesa exótica." *Revista de Portugal*, XXXI (1966), 105–8; XXXIII (1968), 115–17.

Post, H. Houwens. "A terminologia portuguesa ou aportuguesada do *Itinerário viagem ou navegacão à India Oriental ou portuguesa* de João Huyghen van Linschoten." *Revista de Portugal*, XXV (1960), 349–61, 454–72.

Rao, G. Subba. *Indian Words in English; A Study in Indo-Birtish Cultural and Linguistic Relations*. Oxford, 1954.

São Luiz, D. Francisco de [Cardinal Saraiva]. *Glossário de vocábulos portuguezes derivados das línguas orientaes e africanas, excepto a Arabe*. Lisbon, 1837.

Scott, Charles P. G. "The Malayan Words in English." *Journal of the American Oriental Society*, XVII (1896), 93–144; XVIII (1897), 49–124.

Serjeantsen, Mary S. *A History of Foreign Words in English*. 2d ed. London, 1961.

Vermeer, Hans J. "'Indisch' boy." In *Donum Indogermanicum: Festgabe für Anton Scherer*, pp. 70–81. Edited by Robert Schmitt-Brandt. Heidelberg, 1971.

Yu, Margaret M. S. "Words and Things." *Studies in Linguistics*, XX (1968), 7–36.

Yule, Henry, and Burnell, A. C. *Hobson-Jobson*. First published in 1886. Rev. ed. by William Crooke (London, 1903). Reprinted at Delhi in 1968.

Zaccaria, Enrico. *L'elemento iberico nella lingua italiana*. Bologna, 1927.

———. *Contributo allo studio degl'iberismi in Itali e della Wechselbeziehung fra le lingue romanze ossia voci e frasi spagnuole e portoghesi nel Sassetti aggiantievi quelle del Carletti e del Magalotti*. Turin, 1905.

Epilogue

The European world, so long undisturbed in its familiar patterns, underwent a transformation in the sixteenth century which produced in observers a sense of mild shock, wary fascination, or deep wonderment. Some men of the Renaissance, preoccupied as they were with the classical revival, the Christian schism, and the organization of new national institutions, seemingly remained oblivious to the new rents in the curtain obscuring the East. But in all walks of life and in all nations perceptive individuals and groups understood that the limits of their world were being widened and that fundamental changes were consequently portended for the future of Europe. As in all historical periods, there were those who insisted that the resources and energies of society should be directed to the solution of immediate, pressing problems and not wasted on distant ventures of unpredictable value and consequence. Such unreceptivity and passivity toward the overseas discoveries provoked and irritated the curious and adventurous. For example, the Italian physician and student of "subtleties," Girolamo Cardano, stormed in his autobiography: "O, what arrogant poverty of intellectual humility not to be moved to wonder!"[1]

Among those who were "moved to wonder" the responses to the revelation of the East were not uniform. The Iberians, whether practical men of affairs or literati, were inclined to be more concerned about the costs of expansion than about its broader artistic or intellectual implications. The Italians and French, possibly because they were not directly involved in the explorations and conquests in the East, responded more slowly and abstractly to the challenge implicit in the discovery of high civilizations in Asia. This non-involvement as well as the integrated and sophisticated Renaissance of Italy and France assured in those two countries a calmer and more unruffled appraisal of the news about the East.

[1] *The Book of My Life* (New York, 1930), p. 54.

And the preoccupation of their artists, intellectuals, and statesmen with more immediate European issues helped to delay reactions for a time. But once the facts had been tested, evaluated, and put into perspective, the Italians and the French reacted more sensitively than others to the meaning of the discoveries for European civilization. The Germans and the Netherlanders, although initially eager to participate directly in the overseas voyages, were forced after 1530 to direct their attention to domestic problems arising from the Protestant Reformation. They and their English co-religionists did not become seriously involved in eastward expansion until the last quarter of the century. Nor did the Protestants produce evaluations of the significance of the discoveries comparable to those issued in Catholic lands.

All sixteenth-century Europeans inherited from the pre-discovery era a picture of the East as a shadowy place obscured by the mists of time and space. The broad public, informed by the medieval tradition as preserved in the romance of Alexander, the encyclopedias, cosmographies, sermon books, and bestiaries, continued to visualize Asia as a rich region inhabited by strange peoples who practiced mysterious and magical arts, excelled in a number of unknown and exotic crafts, and lived exemplary lives. Isolated examples of Asian art, technology, and ideas had migrated to Europe before 1500, but their provenance was not usually recognized; in the sixteenth century also, artistic motifs, tools, devices, and mathematical ideas were borrowed, sometimes only semiconsciously, from Asian originals. Most Europeans were unable to distinguish between the Islamic Orient and the rest of Asia. Consequently, the growing fear of an Ottoman attack upon central Europe was accompanied by anxiety and uneasiness about invasions of strange and unfathomable ideas from the distant East; many writers connected the Portuguese wars against the Muslims in India with the unrelenting struggle against the hostile Turks. Thus for the public in all parts of Europe the East was the homeland of the Islamic enemy as well as of fabulous peoples, magical arts, superior craftsmanship, moral kings, and mass armies.

Foretastes of the Asia of *reality* were first given to Europe by the direct imports of spices, metals, and other portable products. Collections of the "wonders" brought back from the overseas world were assembled by many of the leading rulers, prelates, merchants, and scholars of Europe. Contemplation of these "silent sources" provoked discussion and inspired reflection about the civilizations which had produced them. Artists and craftsmen, in particular, were fascinated by the "subtle *ingenia*" of the Asian oddities, and they soon prepared naturalistic depictions of many of them. Asian animals, jewels, and woods that Europeans had long known acquired new symbolic attributes as they became more familiar. In engraving and painting, Asia itself was represented emblematically in depictions wherein the products, plants, and animals of the East figure as exotic symbols. Decorative motifs, devices, and patterns based on Asian products or artistic models were periodically added to the vocabulary of European ornament and to the decorative features in many art forms.

Epilogue

The Portuguese, as they explored, traded, warred, and evangelized in Asia, also began more peaceably to penetrate the intellectual community of Europe for the first time in history. This movement was carried out less systematically but quite as effectively as the overseas expansion. Through its official missions to the papacy, its king's letters to his fellow monarchs, and its emissaries of government and trade, Portugal brought news of its Asian conquests to Spain, Italy, France, and the Netherlands. The commercial enterprises at Lisbon and Antwerp provided further tangible evidence of Portuguese successes in the marts of Asia. Individual heralds of empire, especially Damião de Góis, related the news orally and in print to Europe's intellectuals. The close association of Portugal with the Society of Jesus also helped to bring Jesuit missionary achievements to the eyes and ears of Christian peoples everywhere. Visitors and emissaries to Lisbon from other countries served in their own ways as "living letters." When Portugal came under the rule of Philip II in 1580, its official relationships with the other states of Europe generally passed into Spanish hands. Nonetheless the Japanese embassy to Europe of 1584 to 1586 dramatized the joint successes of the Portuguese and the Jesuits in Japan, the most remote yet thriving of Europe's religious enterprises.

Visual materials produced in Portugal, especially maps of the overseas world, conveyed to the other European countries a more permanent record of the Portuguese achievements in the East. Literary accounts of the Portuguese expansion began to appear in substantial numbers after the breakdown at mid-century of the spice monopoly. The Portuguese texts were translated in whole or in part into Italian and other vernaculars, and these, as well as adaptations of them, began to be sold widely at book stalls and fairs. The extant catalogs of royal, papal, and private libraries indicate that substantial numbers of books on the recent discoveries were collected in every European country from Spain to England and from England to Germany. In Catholic Europe the tightening of censorship led to the publication of a greater amount of noncontroversial literature, including materials on the recent overseas discoveries and conquests. In Protestant Europe, however, the books of Sir John Mandeville and Marco Polo retained their popularity as folkbooks and as the reigning descriptions of Asia.

In addition to the books of Polo and Mandeville, the "old Asia" of the pre-discovery era was kept alive by the collectors of moralistic Indian fables. Writers of romances from Boiardo to Lope de Vega also preserved a traditional Orient as the backdrop for the imaginary chivalric deeds of their heroes. By close study of the individualistic spellings of the Asian place names and exotic references they employed, it emerges clearly that the writers of romances—especially Rabelais and Barahona de Sota—did not hesitate to modernize their peregrinations from the latest cartographic and literary materials available. As a result the Orient of the romances and of the French sentimental novels of the last years of the century became increasingly less fantastic and its peoples less monstrous and more human. Indeed the ordinary reader to whom the romances appealed was often unable to distinguish between the fictional and the authentic travelogues.

The "New World" of the cartographers, cosmographers, poets, and linguists initially included all parts of the overseas world not known to Ptolemy and his followers. The recently discovered parts of Asia—especially insular Southeast Asia, Japan, and the islands of the Pacific—were comprehended, along with the Americas, within Münster's authoritative definition. It was only in the latter half of the century that certain observers began to identify the New World exclusively with the Americas—possibly because some cartographers and cosmographers had come to realize from the Jesuit letters and other sources that the insular reaches of Asia were more distant from America, and their geographical and historical connections to continental Asia much closer, than had been originally supposed. The French poets nonetheless continued to think of the "New World" as an ideal totality, one in which the unspoiled natives lived sublime and noble lives in a setting reminiscent of the "Age of Gold," quite removed from the ravages of life in Europe. The linguists, too, as they began to reorganize the languages of the world into geographical groupings, helped to keep alive the idea that the "new Asia" was part of the "New World."

For intellectuals the discovery of Japan and its high civilization was a momentous event. That Ptolemy and the other Ancients had not known America was hardly surprising, but their ignorance of Japan was deemed truly inexcusable. From the European viewpoint, civilized Japan—even though it was quickly identified with the "Zipangu" of Marco Polo—appeared above the horizon after primitive America. Following its physical discovery in 1543, the Europeans were informed gradually through the Jesuits of the character of Japan's religion and its sophisticated culture. Guillaume Postel was the first to attempt to bring Japan within the pale of Eurasiatic civilization by identifying Buddhism as a form of primitive Christianity and by praising the Japanese as moral exemplars and the best of the Asian peoples. Once the realization dawned in Europe that Japan was a part of the Sinic world, China began to share its glory. The penetration of Chinese civilization after 1583, and the subsequent persecution of the Christians in Japan, was watched closely by European intellectuals. Partially as a result of developments in Asia, the adulation originally given to Japan was transferred to China over the last two decades of the century.

From the intellectual's viewpoint the discoveries had proceeded chronologically over the course of the century from the most primitive to the most civilized parts of the world. This, coupled with the existence in Europe of a traditional view of Asia, slowed the reaction of the national literatures and scholarly disciplines to the challenge posed by the revelation of a non-Western civilization that rivaled Europe's own. The responses that occurred in the first half of the century were consequently minor in all forms of endeavor, with perhaps the exceptions of cartography and navigation. In cosmography note was taken of the latest discoveries, but generally without questioning the authority of the Ancients. While the Asian scene was gradually transformed in the romances, litanies of exotic place names and words were introduced into popular poetry and prose in all countries. But such literary symbols of Asia, like the artistic symbols which appeared in ornament and design, evoked primarily the successes, adventure, and glory gained by Europeans through overseas conquests. In effect, these literary and artistic symbols were emblems which quietly praised the conquerors and their exploits in remote places but showed only a slight interest in Asia for its own sake. Also because a fear persisted that treasure and lives were being wasted merely for trade and glory, a long time passed before Europeans recognized that they had anything fundamental to learn from Asia.

Only in the latter half of the century did new literary subjects, forms, and devices develop that reflected a considerable debt to the unfolding of the world map. The Portuguese maritime tragedies and siege triumphs grew directly out of the problems faced by the empire-builders in India and the Indian Ocean. Secular dramas, prose pieces, and speculative literature debated the morality of the treatment given by Christians to the heathen peoples of America and Asia. In England the pattern poems of Puttenham and the shorthand experiments of Bright were possibly inspired by Asian models, at least according to the testimony of their authors. Certainly the epic *Lusiads* of Camoëns could not have been written without the author's historical interest in the discoveries and his personal experience with the route to India.

The discovery of Asia had a remarkable effect upon the definition, theory, and organization of history. Portugal's history, as written by Góis and Osório and popularized by Goulart, was conceived almost entirely in terms of the Asian conquest, possibly the only national history ever constructed with overseas expansion as its dominant theme. Juan de Mariana, who wrote his basic Spanish history after Philip assumed the Portuguese throne, felt compelled to bring the Asian conquest into the history of Spain, and José d'Acosta appended it to the history of the Spanish conquest of America. The compilers of chronicles—Franck, Giovio, and De Thou—gradually included references to events from Asia in contemporary world history. Other chroniclers—especially Barros and Castanheda—expanded chronicle entries relating to the discoveries into narrative chapters to produce a chronicle-narrative form of historical discourse. The Spanish and Portuguese—Oviedo, Cruz, and Mendoza—created ethnohistories in which the geography, history, resources, and the prevailing conditions of an overseas region or country were described. Maffei and Guzman, in their accounts of Jesuit activities in Asia, were responsible for originating the genre of mission history. Following Bodin, some historians sought self-consciously to examine the implications of the discoveries for historical thought and the history of civilization. In the process they quickly came to realize the inadequacy of Europe's traditional historical theories. History, they came to think, should henceforward be conceived in world terms, designed to study problems of universal impact, and directed to understanding the motives and workings of the history of civilization.

In history, as well as in other forms of literature, Asia was regularly elevated to the level of a moral exemplar. More's *Utopia* possibly had India as its locale. The moralistic tales of the Middle Ages exalted the rulers of India almost to the level of sainthood; writers of the later sixteenth century, possibly to escape the charge of heresy, Christianized and Europeanized many of the Indian tales— Barlaam (Buddha) was canonized! Out of deference to prevailing opinions, the secular romances were similarly Christianized and moralized. The failures of the Portuguese and the missionaries in India contributed to a growing feeling in Europe that the Indians were stubborn, wrong-headed, and immoral. After its discovery, Japan replaced India as the model state of Asia in the writings of Postel, Jean Macer, and many of the Jesuits. At the end of the century, especially after the publication in 1585 of Mendoza's adulatory and popular ethnohistory, the "great and mighty kingdom of China" became a chief model of secular morality. Arrivabene lauded its early rulers as exemplary princes in *Il magno Vitei*, his prose romance based on Mendoza and Maffei. To Botero the prosperity and peace of China could best be accounted for by reference to the prudence of its rulers and the industry of its people. Montaigne and Charron saw in the Eastern societies support for their beliefs about the universality of ethical precepts.

The products of Asia, the writings about its countries and peoples, and the new maps helped to introduce a new realism to European art, romance, and epic. The elephant of Raphael and the rhinoceros of Dürer, both representations based ultimately on living examples brought to Europe, were delineated naturalistically for the first time since Antiquity, were incorporated into ornament and design, and were sometimes Mannerized. The flora and fauna of Asia appeared in graphic and faithful depiction in the poetic descriptions of Camoëns and Du Bartas as well as in the naturalistic drawings shown in herbals and animal books. The new maps and discussions of maritime routes lent realism to the poetic compositions of Ariosto, Barahona, Du Bartas, and Marlowe. In the creations of the English writers—Mandeville, More, Rastell, and Marlowe— there is a fascination with the circumnavigation of the earth as a genuine possibility or accomplishment which distinguishes their works from those of the Continental literati. On maps also, vivid portraits show Asian animals and contrivances such as junks and "land ships"; in costume books the peoples of Asia dress in native garb. In their literary and artistic depictions of individual items known either through concrete examples or through literary descriptions the Europeans tend throughout the century to become more naturalistic, objective, and factual.

Comparisons and contrasts between the products of Europe and Asia existed implicitly in the early collections of curiosities, travel compendia, cosmographies, and herbals. With the passage of time they became more self-conscious and explicit. In the earlier encyclopedic cosmographies and atlases all pertinent information on Asia was included without making distinctions between the traditional and the new knowledge: before the end of the century the new sources assumed primary importance as the maps of Ptolemy, for example, became the basis for the historical rather than the contemporary atlas. The Jesuit missionaries in Asia, especially Valignano and Fróis, began self-consciously to draw comparisons, even to the point of making lists of them, between the social and cultural practices of Asia and Europe. It was not long before artists and writers in Europe followed suit. The superiority of Chinese porcelain and lacquerware as well as Indian and Chinese textiles forced invidious comparisons that were followed by efforts at imitation. The infinite variety and diversity existing in their expanding world impelled Louis Le Roy, Bodin, and Montaigne to draw explicit distinctions between their own traditions, institutions, and values and those of Asia. At a more specific level Torelli compared European to Indian knighthood and Arrivabene contrasted the ideal prince of China to the contemporary rulers of Europe. In literary techniques, the strange practices and customs of the Asians gave the English Euphuists the materials for the literary contrasts and antitheses they vied with one another in concocting. In many of the comparisons set forth both in Asia and Europe the social and cultural practices of Europe came off second best.

The tolerance and objectivity implied by explicit comparison reflected a growing uneasiness about the completeness and adequacy of Europe's own understanding. Even in popular literature—as in the cosmography of Anania or *Les Serées* of Bouchet—the writers exhibited a tolerance for diversity and a willingness to suspend judgment until all the evidence could be weighed. In the various fields of learning, except for theology, no implacable hostility existed to the new knowledge brought from overseas. Artists, geographers, botanists, and literati, while often suspiciously cautious, experienced no serious difficulty in bringing the new information into their creations and in dealing with it objectively and realistically. In some cases tolerance was possible because the older traditions, art forms, or literary genres could readily be adjusted to accommodate the new knowledge without fundamental changes. In such instances the revelation of Asia enriched without threatening the traditional understanding.

Basic modifications in Europe's established viewpoints and disciplines came but slowly. Artists, collectors, and literati recognized at an early date that the works of nature and art from Asia were remarkable and worthy of close attention, contemplation, and imitation. Navigators and merchants reported that the Asians produced admirable sailing craft, maps, charts, and books which owed no debt to Europe. While the religions of Asia were initially dismissed as superstitious rites or works of the devil, the Europeans were forced gradually to admit that the temples of India, the monasteries of Burma and Japan, and the devotion of their masses demonstrated the sophistication and vigor of the native cults. Postel and others sought the origins of Buddhism and other organized Asian religions in a primitive Christianity that was thought to be universal before the dispersal of Babel. Asian religious edifices, rites, and beliefs were ordinarily remarked upon for the purpose of showing their relations to

Christian analogues. A few of the earliest commentators also sought the origins of Indian civilization in the exploits of Alexander the Great. Some Humanists, in their efforts to fit the ancient civilizations of the East into their historical schema, merely enlarged their definitions of Antiquity to include Asia.

Such stratagems failed to satisfy the intellectually curious who were convinced of the reality and independence of Asia and felt obliged to respond forthrightly to the challenges it posed to Europe's traditional learning. A growing uneasiness about the infallibility of Antiquity as well as an omnipresent fear that a religiously divided Europe would not be able to withstand a Turkish invasion helped to produce a sentiment for self-reassessment. From all reports it was clear that the Japanese and Chinese enjoyed a civilization that in some respects was superior to Europe's own. Printing and the manufacture of books in type, one of Europe's proudest achievements, had been developed centuries earlier in China. All the Asian peoples, it was understood, possessed mathematics and astronomical traditions of their own which they used in devising sophisticated calendars. The Indians, despite their backwardness and stubborn ignorance, had long employed metals in the preparation of drugs, an idea that was new to Europe. Javans, Indians, Chinese, and Japanese held their own views of the outlines of the world and its regions and placed geographical sketches of them on globes, charts, and maps. The ideographic languages of Asia had retained an ancient script and were also modern vehicles of everyday oral communication and literary production. Without benefit of the Greek sages, the Ten Commandments of the Hebrews, or the Sermon on the Mount, the societies of Asia enjoyed an orderly civil life, lived under law, and exhibited a flourishing material prosperity. All that was lacking in Asia was the divine gift of the Christian religion.

Not all European intellectuals reacted positively to this conclusion. And to those who did, Asia meant many different things. To some it proved that a high civilization was possible in non-Christian societies. For others the history of Asia's various parts lent support to their ideas of geographical determinism or theories of progress. To Botero the Chinese city was a model of the urban agglomerate. Taken as a group, the late sixteenth-century admirers of Japan and China seem to anticipate the Sinophile *philosophes* of the eighteenth century. Their sometimes uncritical praise of the Japanese and Chinese, as well as their denigration of the Indians, were of course derived from the Portuguese histories, the great travel collections, the encyclopedic cosmographies, and the Jesuit newsletters. The "China enthusiasm" of the eighteenth century, it should also be noted, was based on similar and often equally biased sources. Whatever else might be concluded about the European's view of Asia, it becomes patently clear that a representative group of artists, scientists, scholars, and literati were willing to admit, sometimes begrudgingly, that Europe had much to learn from its experiences in Asia and from many of the societies found there.

In conjunction with these admissions, changes began to occur. Artists, craftsmen, mechanics, and shipbuilders experimented with and imitated a number of Asian techniques: porcelain manufacture, textile design, lacquer, land ships, mapping conventions, fireworks, and drug preparation. In response to the Asian experience, new genres of popular literature were created: the maritime tragedy, the siege drama, the travel collection, and the geographical atlas. Elements of realism were added to the romance, the sentimental novel, and the epic. The literary form most radically altered was history. Most of its theoretical presuppositions with respect to mankind's origins and to periodization were questioned and sometimes modified. New historical genres—ethnohistory, chronicle-narrative, and history of civilization—were attempted and the older forms of historical discourse were expanded to make possible the inclusion of the overseas world.

The introduction into the European languages of a host of new words relating to the discoveries and to Asia shook the foundations of language study in Europe, broadened the base of comparative philology, and led to the reform of language groupings. A growing understanding of the nature of the ideographic script raised a multitude of questions in linguistic theory and possibly accelerated the development of modern shorthand and romanization techniques. Asian plants, like Asian words, had to be accommodated. The European botanists, like the linguists, were required by the new imports to begin restructuring their discipline. Dioscorides' authoritative manual was tested against the new knowledge and was found to be wanting. Herbals prepared by Orta and Acosta on the basis of their observations in India quickly became the fundamental texts on exotic plants and drugs. Before the end of the century the botanists of Europe had brought a new world of plant descriptions and engraved depictions into their compilations and had begun to classify the flora according to natural affinities.

The scholarly discipline most affected was of course geography, and its allied subjects of cosmography, navigation, and cartography. Europe's changing perceptions of both the heavens and the earth helped to divide cosmography into the increasingly independent disciplines of astronomy, geography, and history. The navigators discovered new stars as well as new islands and strange peoples. An influx of new data, as well as other developments both related and unrelated to these intellectual subjects, forced the various disciplines to define more sharply their specializations and to reexamine their inherited conventions and methods. In the process astronomy concerned itself more and more exclusively with charting the heavens, and geography with mapping the earth. The geographers had also to readjust completely their perception of water and land relationships while trying to reconcile a new and changing picture of the earth with the traditional Ptolemaic representations. The business of geography turned away from cosmography toward cartography, a science which seeks accurately and precisely to determine geographical location, extent, and direction and to depict it on a globe or plane surface. It was the revelation of Asia from Polo to Linschoten which more than any other discovery undermined the authority of Ptolemy and contributed to the cartographic revolution of the sixteenth century. The new discipline of geography, patronized by government, church, and business, brought a new world picture to all elements of society. Related to the new map was a revised view of Europe in its spatial relationship to Asia and the rest of the world. A better knowledge of physical features helped to produce the preoccupation with geographical determinism and cultural relativism that characterized the writings of Bodin, Botero, and Charron as well as many lesser lights.

The most fundamental and universal of the changes effected in Europe's view of itself and the world was to be found in the growth of a new form of cultural relativism. Throughout the Renaissance the Europeans had compared and contrasted their achievements to those of Antiquity. This vertical or temporal relativism usually ended, at least until 1540, with a paean of praise, sometimes purely rhetorical, for the superior attainments of the Ancients. The opening of Asia to the European mind helped to create a new relativism that was both vertical and horizontal, or both temporal and spatial. The civilizations of Asia were recognized by the end of the sixteenth century as being the equal of contemporary Europe and as having a continuous history that went back to Antiquity. The Chinese, in particular, were acknowledged to possess superior attainments in the arts and crafts, in social and cultural organization, and in historical continuity. The realization that China was both an ancient and a modern civilization of high attainments contributed to a growing belief, based on a host of other sources as well, that the assumed superiority of Western Antiquity was simplistic and no longer completely acceptable. China, like Greece and Rome, was a fount of ancient wisdom; furthermore, unlike the empires of the West, China had maintained its language and civilization intact throughout recorded history.

This new relativism possibly had its origins among the Europeans who actually worked in Asia. For the first time in history significant numbers of Europeans resided in Asia and provided first-hand and relatively regular reports on activities and events there. In India the Portuguese inaugurated a social compromise by subsidizing marriages between Portuguese and native women of low caste. The offspring of these unions, though often held in slight esteem by both Indians and Europeans, were living testimonies to the possibilities inherent in assimilation. The subsequent refusal of the higher castes, and even the Christians of St. Thomas, to accept Latin Christianity led to a denigration of Hindu culture among the European traders and administrators as well as the missionaries. The Jesuits, before the late sixteenth-century visits to Akbar, were vitriolic in their denunciation of the caste system, the morals, and the religions of the Indians. The failures in south India, when coupled with the meager successes in Africa, led Valignano and others to denounce the dark-skinned natives as intellectual inferiors who were unready to appreciate and accept Christian truth when it was offered to them.

The policy of cultural hostility was reversed in East Asia. Christian successes in Japan led the Jesuits, following Xavier's early remark that the Japanese are "the best people who have yet been discovered," to laud the lighter-skinned Asians and their civilization. The leaders of the Society in Japan, especially Valignano and Fróis, discouraged inflexibility among the missionaries and gradually began to propound a policy of cultural and social accommodation in all matters except the Christian faith. Compromise with native customs, traditions, institutions, and secular thought was advocated to make conversion easier for the missionaries and more palatable to the natives. In his penetration of China, Matteo Ricci likewise followed a policy of accommodation and went perhaps one step further in his open admiration for Chinese culture as he understood it. In Europe the missionaries' praise of China and Japan was accepted and repeated by many artists, literati, and scholars. While only a few disciplines underwent structural change in deference to the new knowledge from overseas, no branch of European intellectual activity except Christian theology went unshaken. The century that had begun with a robust confidence in European secular ideals, ideas, institutions and arts ended in a wondering doubt about their superiority and permanence.

General Bibliography

This catalog of works consulted attempts to be comprehensive but makes no pretense at being exhaustive. The listings are of two types: (1) general, which includes books and articles useful for background or for the analysis of problems and ideas common to more than a single chapter; (2) separate bibliographies of books and articles for each chapter. The only exception to the "Chapter Bibliography" scheme is the division of the Germanic Literatures (Chap. VIII) into two separate listings entitled "German and Netherlandish Literature" and "English Literature."

No effort has been undertaken to separate primary from secondary materials. A few entries appear under "General Bibliography" which were inadvertently omitted from the earlier books of this series and which should have been included, and a number which are generally relevant to the series but were published after the appearance of my earlier books. Certain titles appear in more than one of the chapter bibliographies. Chinese and Japanese titles are given in characters, transliteration, and translation.

BOOKS

Ainslie, Whitelaw. *Materia Indica; or, some Account of those Articles which are Employed by the Hindoos and other Eastern Nations in their Medicine, Arts and Agriculture; Comprising also Formulae, with Practical Observations, Names of Diseases in Various Eastern Languages, and a Copious List of Oriental Books immediately connected with General Science, etc.* 2 vols. London, 1826.

Albuquerque, Luis G. M. de. *Introdução a história dos descobrimentos.* Coimbra, 1962.

Alexandrowicz, C. H. *An Introduction to the History of the Law of Nations in the East Indies.* Oxford, 1967.

Allemagne, Henri d'. *Les cartes à jouer du 14me au 20me siècle.* 2 vols. Paris, 1906.

Allen, Don Cameron. *The Legend of Noah: Renaissance Rationalism in Art, Science and Letters.* Urbana, 1949.

——. *Doubt's Boundless Sea: Skepticism and Faith in the Renaissance.* Baltimore, 1964.

——. *Image and Meaning: Metaphoric Traditions in Renaissance Poetry*. New enlarged ed. Baltimore, 1968.

——. *Mysteriously Meant: The Rediscovery of Pagan Symbolism and Allegorical Interpretation in the Renaissance*. London and Baltimore, 1976.

Allen, J. W. *A History of Political Thought in the Sixteenth Century*. 2d ed. London, 1941.

Allison, C. Fitzsimmons. *The Rise of Moralism*. New York, 1966.

Amaral Abranches, Pinto J.; Okamoto, Yoshitomo; and Bernard, Henri. *La première ambassade du Japon en Europe, 1582–1592*. Tokyo, 1942.

Anselmo, Antonio Joaquim. *Bibliografia das obras impressas em Portugal no século XVI*. Lisbon, 1926.

Arciniegas, German. *Amerigo and the New World*. New York, 1955.

Avenir, Tchemerzine. *Bibliographie d'ouvrages sur les sciences et les arts édités aux XVᵉ et XVIᵉ siècles*. Courbevoie, 1933.

Baglione, G. B. *Le vite de' pittori, scultori, architetti dal pontificato di Gregorio XIII*. Rome, 1640.

Bagrow, Leo, and Skeleton, R. *A History of Cartography*. Cambridge, 1964.

Baião, A., et al. *História da expansão portugueza no mundo*. 3 vols. Lisbon, 1937–40.

Baldensperger, Fernand. . . . *Études d'histoire littéraire, quatrième série*. . . . Paris, 1939.

Baldensperger, Fernand, and Friedrich, Werner. *Bibliography of Comparative Literature*. Chapel Hill, N.C., 1950.

Balen, W. J. van. *Naar de Indische Wonderwereld met Jan Huyghen van Linschoten*. Amsterdam, 1946.

Baltrušaitis, Jurgis. *Le moyen-âge fantastique*. Paris, 1955.

Banha de Andrade, António Alberto. *Mundos novos do mundo. Panorama da difusão, pela Europa, de notícias dos descobrimentos geográficos portugueses*. 2 vols. Lisbon, 1972.

Baranowski, Bohdan. *Znajmość wschodu w dawnej Polsce do XVIII wieku* (Knowledge of the Orient in Poland before the Eighteenth Century). Lodz, 1950.

Barthold, V. V. *La découverte de l'Asie: Histoire de l'Orientalisme en Europe et en Russie*. Translated from Russian and annotated by B. Nikitine. Paris, 1947.

Basalla, George, ed. *Rise of Modern Science: External or Internal Factors?* Lexington, Mass., 1968.

Bataillon, Marcel. *Études sur le Portugal au temps de l'humanisme*. Coimbra, 1952.

Batiffol, Pierre. *Le Vatican de Paul III à Paul V*. Paris, 1890.

Baudet, Henri. *Paradise on Earth: Some Thoughts on European Images of Non-European Man*. New Haven, 1965.

Bausum, Henry. "Primitivism in English Books of Travel, 1511–1626." Ph.D. diss., University of Chicago, Department of History, 1963.

Beard, Miriam. *A History of the Business Man*. New York, 1938.

Beckmann, Johann. *Litteratur der älteren Reisebeschreibungen*. 2 vols. Göttingen, 1808, 1810.

Belon, Pierre. *Les observations de plusieurs singularitez et choses memorables, trouvées en Grèce, Asie, Judée, Egypte, Arabie, e autres pays estranges*. Paris, 1553.

Bennett, Josephine Waters. *The Rediscovery of Sir John Mandeville*. New York, 1954.

Berges, Wilhelm. *Die Fürstenspiegel des hohen und späten Mittelalters*. Stuttgart, 1952.

General Bibliography

Bergier, J. F. *Genèse de l'économie européenne de la Renaissance.* Paris, 1963.

Berlin. Japan-Institut. *Bibliographischer Alt-Japan-Katalog, 1542–1853.* Kyoto, 1940.

Berlin. Verwaltung der staatlichen Schlösser und Gärten. *China und Europa. Chinaverständnis und Chinamode im 17. und 18. Jahrhundert.* Ausstellung vom 16. September bis 11. November 1973 im Schloss Charlottenburg. Berlin, 1973.

Bernal, John D. *Science in History.* 4th ed. 4 vols. London, 1969.

Bernard, Henri. *Les premiers rapports de la culture Européene avec la civilisation japonaise.* Tokyo, 1938.

Biker, Julio ed. *Collẽão de tratados e concertos de pazes que o estado da India portugueza fez com os reis e senhores com que teve relações nas partes da Asia e Africa oriental.* 14 vols. Lisbon, 1881–87.

Blau, Joseph L. *The Christian Interpretation of the Cabala in the Renaissance.* New York, 1944.

Boas, George. *Essays on Primitivism and Related Ideas in the Middle Ages.* Baltimore, 1948.

Bodde, Derk. *China's Gifts to the West.* Washington, D.C., 1942.

———. *Chinese Ideas in the West.* Washington, D.C., 1948.

Bolgar, Robert R. *The Classical Heritage and Its Beneficiaries.* London, 1954.

Bolte, Johannes, and Mackensen, Lutz. *Handwörterbuch des deutschen Märchens.* 2 vols. Berlin and Leipzig, 1930–33, 1934–40.

Boncompagni, Francesco L. *Le prime due ambasciate dei Giapponesi a Roma (1585–1615). Con nuovi documenti.* Rome, 1903.

Borst, Arno. *Der Turmbau von Babel: Geschichte der Meinungen über Ursprung und Vielfalt der Sprachen und Völker.* 4 vols. Stuttgart, 1957–63.

Boscaro, Adriana. *Sixteenth-Century European Printed Works on the First Japanese Mission to Europe: A Descriptive Bibliography.* Leyden, 1973.

Boulnois, Luce. *The Silk Road.* Translated from the French. London, 1966.

Bouwsma, William J. *Concordia Mundi: The Career and Thought of Guillaume Postel.* Cambridge, Mass., 1957.

Bowie, Theodore, *et al. East-West in Art: Patterns of Cultural and Aesthetic Relationships.* Bloomington, Ind., 1966.

Boxer, Charles R. *Race Relations in the Portuguese Colonial Empire, 1415–1825.* Oxford, 1963.

———. *The Portuguese Seaborne Empire, 1415–1825.* London, 1969.

Branca, Vittore. *Venezia e l'oriente fra tardo medioevo e rinascimento.* Florence, 1966.

Braudel, Fernand. *La civilisation matérielle.* Paris, 1967.

Breuer, Hans. *Kolumbus war Chineser: Erfindungen und Entdeckungen des Fernen Ostens.* Frankfurt, 1970.

Brown, Horatio F. *The Venetian Printing Press: An Historical Study Based upon Documents for the Most Part Hitherto Unpublished.* London, 1896.

Burke Peter. *The Renaissance Sense of the Past.* New York, 1970.

Bush, Douglas. *Classical Influences in Renaissance Literature.* Cambridge, Mass., 1952.

Bush, Michael L. *Renaissance, Reformation, and the Outer World.* London, 1967.

Caillois, Roger. *Au coeur du fantastique.* Paris, 1965.

Callot, Emile. *La renaissance des sciences de la vie au XVIe siècle*. Paris, 1951.

Camus, A. G. *Mémoire sur la collection des grands et petits voyages.* . . . Paris, 1802.

Carter, Charles H. *The Western European Powers, 1500–1700*. Ithaca, N.Y., 1971.

————, ed. *From the Renaissance to the Counter-Reformation: Essays in Honor of Garrett Mattingly*. London, 1966.

Carter, Thomas F., and Goodrich, L. C. *The Invention of Printing in China and Its Spread Westward*. New York, 1955.

Carvalho, Joaquim de. *Estudos sobre a cultura portuguesa do século XVI*. Vol. I. Coimbra, 1947.

Cassirer, Ernst. *Sprache und Mythos: Ein Beitrag zum Problem der Götternamen*. Darmstadt, 1959.

Chabod, Federico. *Storia dell' idea d'Europa*. Bari, 1971.

Charbonnel, J. Roger. *La pensée italienne au XVIe siècle et le courant libertin*. Paris, 1919.

Charmot, François. *La pédagogie des jésuites*. Paris, 1925.

Chartrou, Josephe. *Les entrées solennelles et triomphales à la Renaissance (1484–1551)*. Paris, 1928.

Chastel, André, and Klein, Robert. *Die Welt des Humanismus: Europa 1480–1530*. Brussels, 1954.

Chaunu, Pierre. *Les Philippines et le Pacifique des Ibériques (XVIe–XVIIe siècle)*. 2 vols. Paris, 1960–66.

————. *Conquête et exploitation des nouveaux mondes (XVIe siècle)*. Paris, 1969.

Chauvin, Victor C. *Bibliographie des ouvrages arabes publiés dans l'Europe chrétienne de 1810 à 1885*. 12 vols. Liège, 1892–1905.

Chu Ch'ien-chih [朱謙之]. Chung-kuo ssu-hsiang tui-yü ou-chou wen-hua chih yin-hsiang [中國思想對於歐洲文化之影響]. ("The Influence of Chinese Thought on European Culture"). Shanghai, 1940.

Chudoba, B. *Spain and the Empire, 1519–1643*. Chicago, 1952.

Cipolla, Carlo M. *Literacy and Development in the West*. Baltimore, 1969.

Cirlot, Juan E. *A Dictionary of Symbols*. New York, 1962.

Clements, R. J. *"Picta Poesis": Literary and Humanistic Theory in Renaissance Emblem Books*. Rome, 1960.

Clouston, William A. *Popular Tales and Fictions: Their Migrations and Transformations*. 2 vols. London, 1887.

Cochrane, Eric, ed. *The Late Italian Renaissance, 1525–1630*. London, 1970.

Cornelius, Paul. *Languages in Seventeenth and Early Eighteenth-Century Imaginary Voyages*. Geneva, 1965.

Cortelazzo, Manilo, ed. *Méditerranée et Océan Indien*. Venice, 1970.

Cortesão, Armando. *History of Portuguese Cartography*. Vol. I. Coimbra, 1969.

Cortesão, Armando, and Teixeira da Mota, Avelino. *Portugaliae monumenta cartographica*. 5 vols. Lisbon, 1960–62.

Cortesão, Jaime. *Os descobrimentos portugueses*. 2 vols. Lisbon, 1960.

Costantini, Celso, ed. *Le missioni catholiche e la cultura dell' Oriente*. Rome, 1943.

Couchoud, Paul-Louis. *Asiatic Mythology*. London, 1932.

Coutinho, C. V. G. *A naútica dos descobrimentos: Os descobrimentos vistos por um navegador.* 2 vols. Lisbon, 1951–52.

Crombie, Alistair C., ed. *Scientific Change: Historical Studies in the Intellectual, Social and Technical Conditions for Scientific Discovery and Technical Invention, from Antiquity to the Present.* London, 1963.

Curcio, Carlo. *Dal Rinascimento alla Controriforma.* Rome, 1934.

———. *Europa, storia di un'idea.* Florence, 1958.

Curtius, Ernst Robert. *European Literature and the Latin Middle Ages.* New York, 1953.

Dalgado, Sebastião Rodolfo. *Glossário Luso-asiático.* 2 vols. Coimbra, 1919, 1921.

Daniel, Norman. *Islam and the West: The Making of an Image.* Edinburgh, 1960.

———. *Islam, Europe and Empire.* Edinburgh, 1966.

Dannenfeldt, Karl H. "Late Renaissance Interest in the Ancient Orient." Ph.D. diss., University of Chicago, Department of History, 1948.

Daumas, Maurice. *Histoire générale des techniques.* Vol. I. Paris, 1962.

Dawson, Raymond. *The Chinese Chameleon: An Analysis of European Conceptions of Chinese Civilization.* London, 1967.

———, ed. *The Legacy of China.* Oxford, 1964.

De Bry, Theodor. *Indiae Orientalis. . . . .* Frankfurt, 1599.

D'Elia, Pasquale M. *Storia dell'introduzione del Cristianismo in Cina scritta da Matteo Ricci S. I.* 3 vols. Rome, 1942–49.

Denis, Ferdinand. *Scènes de la nature sous les tropiques, et leur influence sur la poésie; suivies de Camoens et Jozé Indio.* Paris, 1824.

———. *Le monde enchanté: Cosmographie et histoire naturelle fantastique du moyen âge.* Paris, 1843.

De Solla Price, Derek John. *Science Since Babylon.* New Haven and London, 1961.

Dickson, Sarah Augusta. *Panacea or Precious Bane: Tobacco in Sixteenth Century Literature.* New York, 1954.

Diffie, Bailey W. *Prelude to Empire: Portugal Overseas before Henry the Navigator.* Lincoln, Neb., 1965.

Dionsotti-Casalone, Carlo. *Geografia e storia della litteratura.* Turin, 1967.

Doucet, Roger. *Les institutions de la France au XVIe siècle.* 2 vols. Paris, 1948.

Droulers, Eugène. *Dictionnaire de attributs, allégories, emblèmes et symboles.* Turnhout, Belgium, 1948.

Duyvendak, J. J. L. *Holland's Contribution to Chinese Studies.* London, 1950.

Ebersolt, Jean. *Orient et occident: Recherches sur les influences byzantines et orientales en France avant et pendant les croisades.* 2d ed. Paris, 1954.

Edwardes, Michael. *East-West Passage: The Travel of Ideas, Arts, and Inventions between Asia and the Western World.* New York, 1971.

Ehrman, Albert, and Pollard, G. *The Distribution of Books by Catalogue from the Invention of Printing to A.D. 1800.* Cambridge, 1965.

Elliot, John H. *Imperial Spain.* New York, 1964.

———. *The Old World and the New, 1492–1650.* Cambridge, 1970.

Errera, Carlo. *L'epoca delle grandi scoperte geografiche.* Milan, 1926.

General Bibliography

Evans, Joan. *Magical Jewels of the Middle Ages and the Renaissance, Particularly in England.* Oxford, 1922.

——. *Nature in Design: A Study of Naturalism in Decorative Art from the Bronze Age to the Present.* London, 1933.

Fairchild, Hoxie Neale. *The Noble Savage: A Study in Romantic Naturalism.* New York, 1928.

Febvre, Lucien. *Le problème de l'incroyance au XVIe siècle.* Paris, 1943.

——. *Au coeur religieux du XVIe siècle.* Paris, 1957.

Febvre, Lucien, and Martin, H. J. *L'apparition du livre.* Paris, 1958.

Fechner, M. V. *Torgovlia russkogo gosudarstva so stranami vostoka v XVI vieke* (The Trade of the Russian State with the Countries of the East in the Sixteenth Century). Moscow, 1952.

Fernández Alvarez, Manuel. *La España del Emperador Carlos V.* Madrid, 1966.

Ferrand, Gabriel. *Relations de voyages et textes géographiques arabes, persanes et turcs relatifs à l'Extrême-Orient, du VIIIe au XVIIIe siècle.* Paris, 1913.

Ferrara, Orestes. *Le XVIe siècle, vu par les ambassadeurs vénitiens.* Paris, 1954.

Fiore, L. B. *La scoperta dell' America e gli umanisti del cinquecento.* Arpino, 1920.

Forbes, Robert J. *Bibliographia Antiqua: Philosophia Naturalis.* 11 vols. Leyden, 1940–52.

——, and Dijksterhuis, Eduard Jan. *History of Science and Technology.* 2 vols. Baltimore, 1963.

Foulché-Delbosc, Raymond. *Bibliographie des voyages en Espagne et en Portugal.* Paris, 1896.

Frankl, Paul. *The Gothic: Literary Sources and Interpretations through Eight Centuries.* Princeton, N.J., 1960.

Frenz, Horst, and Anderson, G. L., eds. *Indiana University Conference on Oriental-Western Literary Relations.* Chapel Hill, N.C., 1955.

Friedrich, Werner P., and Malone, David H. *Outline of Comparative Literature from Dante Alighieri to Eugene O'Neill.* Chapel Hill, N.C., 1954.

Garin, Eugenio. *La cultura del Rinascimento: Profilo storico.* Bari, 1967.

Garratt, Geoffrey T., ed. *The Legacy of India.* Oxford, 1937.

Gerard, P. *Anvers à travers les âges.* 2 vols. Brussels, 1888.

Giamatti, A. Bartlett. *The Earthly Paradise and the Renaissance Epic.* Princeton, 1966.

Gifford, Henry. *Comparative Literature.* London, 1969.

Gillispie, Charles, C. *Edge of Objectivity: an Essay in the History of Scientific Ideas.* Princeton, 1960.

Goldschmidt, Ernst P. *The Printed Book of the Renaissance.* Cambridge, 1950.

González de Mendoza, Juan. *The History of the Great and Mighty Kingdom of China. . . .* Reprinted from the translation of R. Parke. Edited by Sir George T. Staunton. "Hakluyt Society Publications," O.S., Nos. 14–15. 2 vols. London, 1853–54.

Goris, Jan A. *Étude sur les colonies marchandes méridionales (Portugais, Espagnols, Italiens) à Anvers de 1448 à 1587.* Louvain, 1925.

Gottschalk, Paul. *The Earliest Diplomatic Documents on America.* Berlin, 1927.

Gray, Louis H., and Moore, George F., eds. *Mythology of All Races.* 13 vols. New York, 1964.

Green, Otis H. *Spain and the Western Tradition: The Castilian Mind in Literature from El Cid to Calderon.* 4 vols. Madison, Wis., 1964–66.

Greene, Thomas M. *The Descent from Heaven: A Study in Epic Continuity.* New Haven and London, 1963.

Grün, K. *Kulturgeschichte des 16. Jahrhunderts.* Heidelberg, 1872.

Hall, Marie Boas. *The Scientific Renaissance, 1450–1630.* New York, 1962.

Hallam, Henry. *Introduction to the Literature of Europe in the Fifteenth, Sixteenth and Seventeenth Centuries.* 3d ed. 3 vols. London, 1847.

Hamann, Günther. *Der Eintritt der südlichen Hemisphäre in die europäische Geschichte.* Vienna, 1968.

Hampe, Theodor. *Die fahrende Leute in der deutschen Vergangenheit.* Leipzig, 1902.

Hart, Henry H. *Sea Road to the Indies.* New York, 1950.

Haskell, Francis. *Patrons and Painters: A Study in the Relations between Italian Art and Society in the Age of the Baroque.* New York, 1963.

Hay, Denis, ed. *The Age of the Renaissance.* London, 1967.

Hayden, Hiram. *The Counter-Renaissance.* New York, 1950.

Henkel, Arthur, and Schöne, Albrecht. *Emblemata: Handbuch zur Sinnbildkunst des XVI. und XVII. Jahrhunderts.* Stuttgart, 1967.

Herculano, Alexandre, ed. and trans. *Opusculos.* 10 vols. Lisbon, 1873–1908.

Herman, Jean Baptiste. *La pédagogie des Jésuites au XVIe siècle.* Louvain, 1914.

Hilton, Ronald. *Handbook of Hispanic Source Materials and Research Organizations in the United States.* 2d ed. Stanford, Calif., 1959.

Hirsh, Rudolf. *Printing, Reading, and Selling: 1450–1550.* Wiesbaden, 1967.

Hirst, Desirée. *Hidden Riches: Traditional Symbolism from the Renaissance to William Blake.* London, 1963.

Hirth, Georg. *Kulturgeschichtliche Bilder aus drei Jahrhunderten.* 6 vols. Leipzig, 1881–90.

Hocke, René. *Manierismus in der Literatur.* Hamburg, 1959.

Hodgen, Margaret T. *Early Anthropology in the Sixteenth and Seventeenth Centuries.* Philadelphia, 1964.

Hopper, Vincent F. *Medieval Number Symbolism: Its Sources, Meaning and Influence on Thought and Expression.* New York, 1938.

Hughes, Charles, ed. *Shakespeare's Europe.* London, 1903.

Humboldt, Alexander von. *Examen critique de l'histoire de la géographie du Nouveau Continent et des progrès de l'astronomie aux XVe et XVIe siècles.* 4 vols. Paris, 1835–39.

Inalcik, Halil. *The Ottoman Empire: The Classical Age, 1300–1600.* Translated by N. Itzkowitz and C. Imber. London, 1973.

Iversen, Erik. *The Myth of Egypt and Its Hieroglyphs in European Tradition.* Copenhagen, 1961.

Jacob, Ernst Gerhard. *Deutschland und Portugal: Ihre kulturellen Beziehungen, Rückschau und Ausblick. Eine Bibliographie.* Leyden, 1961.

Jacob, Georg. *Der Einfluss des Morgenlands auf dem Abendland vornehmlich während des Mittelalters.* Hanover, 1924.

Jacobs, Hubert, trans. and ed. *A Treatise on the Moluccas (ca. 1544)*. Rome and St. Louis, 1970.

Jacobs, Norman. *The Origin of Modern Capitalism and Eastern Asia*. Hong Kong, 1958.

Jacquot, Jean, ed. *Fêtes et cérémonies au temps de Charles Quint*. Paris, 1960.

Jeannin, Pierre. *Les marchands au XVIme siècle*. Paris, 1957.

Johnson, Jerah. *Africa and the West*. Hinsdale, Ill., 1974.

Jones, Eldred D. *The Elizabethan Image of Africa*. Folger Booklets on Tudor and Stuart Civilization. Washington, D.C., 1971.

Julien, C. A. *Les voyages de découverte et les premiers établissements (XVᵉ–XVIᵉ siècle)*. Paris, 1948.

Kaser, Kurt. *Das Zeitalter der Reformation und Gegenreformation von 1517–1660*. Gotha-Stuttgart, 1922.

Kayser, Wolfgang. *The Grotesque in Art and Literature*. Translated by U. Weinstein. Bloomington, Ind., 1963.

Keith, A. Berriedale. *A History of Sanskrit Literatrue*. London, 1961.

Kelly, Donald R. *Foundations of Modern Historical Scholarship*. New York, 1970.

Kern, Hendrik. *Manuel of Indian Buddhism*. Delhi, 1968.

Kernodle, George R. *From Art to Theatre: Form and Convention in the Renaissance*. Chicago, 1944.

Kiewe, Heinz Edgar, et al. *Civilisation on Loan*. Oxford, 1973.

Klempt, Adalbert. *Die Säkularisierung der universal-historischen Auffassung: Zum Wandel des Geschichtsdenkens im 16. und 17. Jahrhundert*. Göttingen, 1960.

Konetzke, R. *Das spanische Weltreich: Grundlagen und Entstehung*. Munich, 1943.

Koyré, Alexandre. *Mystiques, spirituels, alchemistes du XVIᵉ siècle allemand*. Paris, 1955.

Kristeller, Paul O. *Studies in Renaissance Thought and Letters*. Rome, 1956.

Lach, Donald F., and Flaumenhaft, Carol, eds. *Asia on the Eve of Europe's Expansion*. Englewood Cliffs, N.J., 1965.

Lacroix, P. *Science and Literature in the Middle Ages and Renaissance*. New York, 1964.

Lagoa, Visconde J. de. *Glossário toponímico da antiga historiografia portuguesa ultramarina, Asia e Oceania*. 2 vols. Lisbon, 1953–54.

Lansberg, Heinrich. *Handbuch der literarischen Rhetorik: Eine Grundlegung der Literaturwissenschaft*. 2 vols. Zurich, 1960.

Lavedan, Pierre. *Dictionnaire illustré de la mythologie et des antiquités grecques et romaines*. Paris, 1931.

———. *Histoire de l'urbanisme, Renaissance et temps modernes*. Paris, 1941.

Le Gentil, Georges. *Découverte du monde*. Paris, 1954.

Lecler, Joseph. *Toleration and the Reformation*. 2 vols. New York, 1960.

Leonard, Irving A. *Books of the Brave*. Cambridge, Mass., 1949.

Lepszy, Hans-Joachim. *Die Reiseberichte des Mittelalters und der Reformationszeit*. Hamburg, 1953.

Lestrange, Robert. *Les animaux dans la littérature et dans l'histoire*. Paris, 1937.

Levin, Harry. *The Myth of the Golden Age in the Renaissance*. Bloomington, Ind., 1969.

Lowie, Robert. *The History of Ethnological Theory.* New York, 1937.

Lubac, Henri de. *La rencontre du bouddhisme et de l'Occident.* Paris, 1952.

Lundberg, Mabel. *Jesuitische Anthropologie und Erziehungslehre in der Frühzeit des Ordens.* (*1540–1650*). Uppsala and Stockholm, 1966.

Macdonell, Arthur A. *History of Sanskrit Literature.* Delhi, 1962.

Mackail, John W. *Studies in Humanism.* London, 1938.

Magalhães-Godinho, Vitorino. *História dos descobrimentos: Colectânea de esparsos.* 2 vols. Lisbon, 1959–62.

————. *L'économie de l'Empire portugais aux XVe et XVIe siècles. L'or et le poivre. Route de Guinée et route du Cap.* Paris, 1969.

————. *Os descobrimentos e a economia mundial.* 2 vols. Lisbon, 1963, 1971.

Magnino, Leo. *Pontificia Nipponica: Le relazioni tra la Santa Sede e il Giappone attraverso i documenti pontifici.* Rome, 1947.

Majumdar, R. C., ed. *The Classical Accounts of India.* Calcutta, 1960.

Mâle, Émile. *L'Art religieux après le Concile de Trente.* Paris, 1932.

Martineau, Alfred, and May, L. P., comps. *Tableau de l'expansion européenne à travers le monde de la fin du XIIe au début du XIXe siècle.* Paris, 1935.

Mazzeo, John Anthony. *Renaissance and Seventeenth Century Studies.* London, 1964.

Merriman, R. B. *The Rise of the Spanish Empire in the Old World and in the New.* 4 vols. 2d ed. New York, 1962.

Mesnard, Pierre. *L'Essor de la philosophie politique au XVIe siècle.* Paris, 1936.

Meyer-Bayer, Kathi. *Music of the Spheres and the Dance of Death.* Princeton, 1970.

Mezhow, Vladimir. *Bibliographia Asiatica: Bibliographie des livres et articles des journaux russes concernant l'Asie, la Sibérie exceptée.* St. Petersburg, 1891.

Miller, William. *The Latins in the Levant: A History of Frankish Greece (1204–1566).* New York, 1908.

Miranda da Costa Lobo, Francisco. *A acção diplomática dos portugueses nos séculos XV e XVI, destinada a realização de descobertas e conquistas.* Lisbon, 1937.

Mollat, Michel, and Adam, Paul, eds. *Les aspects internationaux de la découverte océanique aux XVe et XVIe siècles.* Paris, 1966.

Mols, Roger. *Introduction à la démographie historique des villes d'Europe du XIVe au XVIIIe siècle.* 3 vols. Louvain, 1954–56.

Monroe, James T. *Islam and the Arabs in Spanish Scholarship (Sixteenth Century to the Present).* Leyden, 1970.

More, St. Thomas. *The Complete Works.* Edited by E. Surtz, and J. H. Hexter. 4 vols. New Haven, 1963–65.

Moreau, Edouard, et al., eds. *La crise religieuse du XVIe siècle.* Paris, 1950.

Moule, A. C., and Pelliot, Paul. *Marco Polo: The Description of the World.* London, 1938.

Mousnier, Roland. *Les européens hors d'Europe de 1492 jusqu'à la fin du XVIIe siècle.* Paris, 1957.

Needham, Joseph. *Science and Civilization in China.* 5 vols. Cambridge, 1965–76.

Nicholl, Robert, ed. *European Sources for the History of the Sultanate of Brunei in the Sixteenth Century.* Brunei, [1975].

Noël, François. *Dictionnaire de la fable ou mythologie grecque, latine, égyptienne, celtique, persanne, indienne, chinoise.* . . . 2 vols. Paris, 1810.

Nowell, Charles E., ed. *Magellan's Voyage around the World: Three Contemporary Accounts.* Evanston, Ill., 1962.

Nys, Ernest. *Les publicistes espagnoles du XVIᵉ siècle et les droits des Indiens.* Brussels, 1890.

O'Gorman, Edmundo. *The Invention of America: An Inquiry into the Historical Nature of the New World and the Meaning of Its History.* Bloomington, Ind., [1961].

Okamoto Yoshitomo [岡本良知]. *Jūrokuseiki Nichi-Ō kōtsūshi no kenkyū* [十六世紀日欧交通史の研究]. ("The Study of the Intercourse between Japan and Europe during the Sixteenth Century"). Tokyo, 1944.

O'Kelly, Bernard. *The Renaissance Image of Man and the World.* Columbus, Ohio, 1966.

Oliveira-Marques, A. M. de. *A sociedade medieval portuguesa.* Lisbon, 1964.

Olschki, Leonardo. *Storia letteraria delle scoperte geographiche.* Florence, 1937.

———. *Marco Polo's Asia.* Berkeley, Calif., 1960.

Onians, Richard B. *The Origins of European Thought about the Body, the Mind, the World, Time, and Fate.* 2d ed. Cambridge, 1954.

Ortelius, Abraham. *Theatrum orbis terrarum.* . . . Antwerp, 1584.

Parker, John. *Books to Build an Empire: A Bibliographical History of English Overseas Interests to 1620.* Amsterdam, 1965.

Parks, George B., comp. *The Contents and Sources of Ramusio's "Navigationi."* New York, 1955.

Parry, John H. *The Spanish Theory of Empire in the Sixteenth Century.* Cambridge, 1940.

———. *The Establishment of the European Hegemony, 1415–1715: Trade and Exploration in the Age of the Renaissance.* New York, 1961.

———. *The Age of Reconnaissance.* New York, 1964.

———. *The Spanish Seaborne Empire.* New York, 1966.

Paulitschke, Philipp Viktor. *Die Afrika-Literatur in der Zeit von 1500 bis 1750 nach Christ: Ein Beitrag zur geographischen Quellenkunde.* Vienna, 1882.

Pecchiai, Pio. *Roma nel Cinquecento.* Bologna, 1949.

Pedro, V. de. *América en las letras españolas del siglo de oro.* Buenos Aires, 1954.

Peery, William, ed. *Studies in the Renaissance.* 3 vols. Geneva, 1954–56.

Pelsener, Jean. *La réforme du XVIᵉ siècle à l'origine de la science moderne.* Paris, 1960.

Penrose, Boies. *Travel and Discovery in the Renaissance, 1420–1620.* Cambridge, Mass., 1952. Reprinted 1965.

Pertusi, Agostino, ed. *Venezia e l'Oriente fra tardo Medioevo e Rinascimento.* Florence, 1966.

Poliakov, Léon. *Le mythe aryen: Essai sur les sources du racisme et des nationalismes.* Paris, 1971.

Poujade, J. *La route des Indes et ses navires.* Paris, 1941.

Ramusio, G. B., comp. *Delle navigationi et viaggi.* . . . 3 vols. Venice, 1550–59.

Rego, Antonio da Silva. *Portuguese Colonization in the Sixteenth Century.* Johannesburg, 1959.

Ribeiro, Orlando. *Portugal, o mediterrâneo e o Atlântico: Esboço de relações geográficas.* Rev. ed. Lisbon, 1963.

Rice, Eugene F. *The Renaissance Idea of Wisdom.* Cambridge, Mass., 1958.

Richards, Gertrude R. B., ed. *Florentine Merchants in the Age of the Medicis.* Cambridge, 1932.

Robb, Nesca. *Neoplatonism of the Italian Renaissance.* London, 1935.

Robinson, Margaret V. *Fictitious Beasts: A Bibliography.* London, 1961.

Rogers, Francis, ed. *Europe Informed: An Exhibition of Early Books Which Acquainted Europe with the East.* Cambridge, Mass., 1966.

Romeo, Rosario. *Le scoperte americane nella coscienza italiana de Cinquecento.* Milan, 1954.

Roscoe, William. *The Life and Pontificate of Leo X.* 4 vols. London, 1827.

Roux, Jean Paul. *Les explorateurs au moyen âge.* Paris, 1961.

Salis, Arnold von. *Antike und Renaissance.* Zurich, 1947.

Sanz, Carlos. *Primitivas relaciones de España con Asia y Oceanía: Los dos primeros libros impresos en Filipinas, mas un tercero en discordia.* Madrid, 1958.

Schierlitz, E. *Die bildlichen Darstellungen der indischen Gottestrinität in der älteren ethnographischen Literatur.* Munich, 1927.

Schurhammer, Georg. *Varia.* Edited by László Szilas. 2 vols. Lisbon, 1965.

Scrivano, Riccardo. *Il Manierismo nella letteratura del Cinquecento.* Padua, 1959.

Sedlar, Jean. "India and the Greek World: An Essay in the Transmission of Ideas." Forthcoming.

Sella, Domenico. *European Industries, 1500–1700.* London, 1970.

Shaabar, Matthias A. *Check List of Sixteenth-Century Editions of Works of Sixteenth-Century Latin Authors.* New York, 1963.

Simon, Jean. *La Polynésie dans l'art et la littérature de l'Occident.* Paris, 1939.

Singleton, C. S., ed. *Art, Science, and History in the Renaissance.* Baltimore, 1968.

Sinor, Denis. *Orientalism and History.* Cambridge, 1955.

Skachkov, Petr Emel'îanovich. *Bibliografîìa Kitaîa Akademia nauk USSR.* Moscow, 1960.

Slicher van Bath, B. H. *The Agrarian History of Western Europe, A.D. 500–1850.* London, 1963.

Smith, Alan G. R. *Science and Society in the Sixteenth Century.* London, 1972.

Smith, Ronald Bishop, ed. *The First Age of the Portuguese Embassies, Navigations, and Peregrinations to the Ancient Kingdoms of Cambay and Bengal, 1500–1521.* Potomac, Md., 1969.

Steensgaard, Niels. *Carracks, Caravans, and Companies: The Structural Crisis in the European Asian Trade in the Early Seventeenth Century.* Copenhagen, 1973.

Stillwell, Margaret Bingham. *The Awakening Interest in Science during the First Century of Printing, 1450–1550: An Annotated Checklist of First Editions Viewed from the Angle of Their Subject Content, Astronomy, Mathematics, Medicine, Natural Science, Physics, Technology.* New York, 1970.

Stone, Donald. *France in the Sixteenth Century: A Medieval Society Transformed.* Englewood Cliffs, N.J., 1969.

Streit, Robert, *et al.*, comps. *Bibliotheca missionum.* 21 vols. Aachen, 1916–55.

Surtz, E. and Hexter, J. H. S. See More, St. Thomas.

Tayler, E. W. *Nature and Art in Renaissance Literature.* New York, 1964.

Teixeira, Manuel. *Early Portuguese and Spanish Contacts with Borneo.* Lisbon, 1964.

———. *The Portuguese Missions in Malacca and Singapore, 1511–1958.* 3 vols. Lisbon, 1961–63.

Theal, George McCall. *Records of South-Eastern Africa.* 9 vols. London, 1898–1903.

Thomas, Keith. *Religion and the Decline of Magic.* London, 1971.

Thorndike, Lynn. *A History of Magic and Experimental Science up to the Seventeenth Century.* 8 vols. New York, 1929–58.

Toffanin, Giuseppe. *History of Humanism.* New York, 1954.

Toulmin, Stephen, and Goodfield, June. *The Discovery of Time.* New York, 1965.

Toussaint, A. *Histoire de l'Océan Indien.* Paris, 1961.

Tuveson, Ernest Lee. *Millennium and Utopia: A Study in the Background of the Idea of Progress.* Berkeley and Los Angeles, 1949.

Van Tieghem, Paul. *La littérature latine de la Renaissance.* Paris, 1944.

———. *La littérature comparée.* 4th rev. ed. Paris, 1951.

Verlinden, Charles. *L'Esclavage dans l'Europe médiévale.* Bruges, 1955.

Villey-Desmeserets, Pierre. *Les sources d'idées au XVIe siècle.* Paris, 1912.

Vindel, Pedro, *Biblioteca oriental comprende 2.747 obras relativas à Filipinas, Japón, China y otras partes de Asia y Oceaniá. . . .* 2 vols. in one. Madrid, 1911–12.

Wagner, Fritz. *Der Historiker und die Weltgeschichte.* Munich, 1965.

Walker, Daniel P. *Spiritual and Demonic Magic from Ficino to Campanella.* London, 1958.

Weber, Henry. *Tales of the East.* 3 vols. Edinburgh, 1812.

White, Lynn, Jr. *Machina ex Deo: Essays in the Dynamism of Western Culture.* Cambridge, Mass., 1968.

Williams, Ralph C. *The Merveilleux in the Epic.* Paris, 1925.

Wilpert, Gero von. *Sachwörterbuch der Literatur.* 5th rev. ed. Stuttgart, 1969.

Winternitz, Moriz. *History of Sanskrit Literature.* Calcutta, 1927.

Yates, Francis A. *Theatre of the World.* London and Chicago, 1969.

Yule, Henry, and Burnell, A. C. *Hobson-Jobson: A Glossary of Colloquial Anglo-Indian Words and Phrases, and of Kindred Terms, Etymological, Historical, Geographical, and Discursive.* New edition by William Crooke. 2d ed. Delhi, 1968.

Yule, Henry, and Cordier, Henri, eds. *The Book of Ser Marco Polo.* 2 vols. London, 1938.

Zoli, Sergio. *La Cina e la cultura italiana da '500 al '700.* Bologna, 1973.

Zoltowski, Adam. *East and West in European History: Three Lectures.* London, 1954.

ARTICLES

Allen, D. C. "The Degeneration of Man and Renaissance Pessimism." *Studies in Philology,* XXV (1938), 202–27.

Babelon, Jean. "Découverte du monde et littérature." *Comparative Literature,* II (1950), 157–66.

Baron, Hans. "The *Querelle* of the Ancients and Moderns as a Problem for Renaissance Scholarship." *Journal of the History of Ideas,* XX (1959), 3–22.

Bezzola, Reto R. "L'Oriente nel poema cavalleresco del primo Rinascimento." *Lettere italiane*, XV (1963), 385–98.

Boxer, Charles R. "Portuguese and Spanish Projects for the Conquest of Southeast Asia." *Journal of Asian History*, III (1969), 118–36.

Cessi, Roberto. "L'India in una descrizione sconosciuta del principio del secolo XVI." *Studi colombiani* (Genoa), III (1952), 213–16.

Cipolla, Carlo M. "The Diffusion of Innovations in Early Modern Europe." *Comparative Studies in Society and History*, XIV (1972), 46–52.

Cordier, Henri. "Deux voyageurs dans l'Extrême-Orient . . . Essai bibliographique. Nicolo De'Conti—Lodovico de Varthema." *T'oung pao*, X (1899), 390–404.

Dales, J. H. "The Discoveries and Mercantilism: An Essay in History and Theory." *Canadian Journal of Economics and Political Science*, XXI (1955), 141–53.

Diffie, Bailey W. "Portugal's Preparation for Exploration: A Functional-Cultural Interpretation." *Colóquio (III) internacional de estudos Luso-Brasileiros, Lisbon, 1957, Actas* (Lisbon), II (1960), 251–65.

Du Pront, A. "Espace et humanisme." *Bibliothèque d'humanisme et renaissance*, VIII (1946), 7–104.

Formichi, Carlo. "Cultural Relations between Italy and India during the Middle Ages and Renaissance." *East and West (Rome)*, I (1950), 82–85.

Frankel, Hans H. "Poetry and Painting: Chinese and Western Views of Their Convertibility." *Comparative Literature*, IX (1957), 289–307.

Goto, Souéo. "Les premiers échanges de civilisation entre l'Extrême-Orient et l'Occident dans les temps modernes." *Revue de littérature comparée*, VIII (1928), 401–19, 601–18.

Hodgen, Margaret T. "Ethnology in 1500." *Isis*, LVII (1966), 315–24.

Koebner, R. "Despot and Despotism: Vicissitudes of a Political Term." *Journal of the Warburg and Courtauld Institutes*, XIV (1951), 275–302.

Lach, Donald F. "China in European Thought and Culture." *Dictionary of the History of Ideas*.

———. "The Far East." In D. B. Quinn, ed. *The Hakluyt Handbook*, I, 214–22. 2 vols. London, 1974.

Lach, Robert. "Der Orient in der ältesten abendlandischen Musikgeschichte." *Bericht des Forschungsinstituts für Osten und Orient*, III (1923), 162–74.

Momigliano, Arnoldo. "The Place of Herodotus in the History of Historiography." *History*, XLIII (1958), 1–13.

Putscher, Marielene. "Ordnung der Welt und Ordnung der Sammlung, Joachim Camerarius und die Kunst- und Wunderkammern des 16. und frühen 17. Jahrhunderts." In *Circa Tiliam: Studia historiae medicinae Gerrit Arie Lindeboom septuagenario oblata*, pp. 256–77. Leyden, 1974.

Rawlinson, Hugh G. "India in European Literature and Thought." In G. T. Garratt, ed., *The Legacy of India*, pp. 1–37. Oxford, 1962.

———. "Indian Influence on the West." In L. S. S. O'Malley, ed., *Modern India and the West: A Study of the Interaction of Their Civilizations*, pp. 535–75. London, 1941.

Rein, Adolf. "Ueber die Bedeutung der überseeischen Ausdehnung für das europäische Staatensystem." *Historische Zeitschrift*, CXXXVII (1927), 28–90.

Reynolds, Beatrice R. "Latin Historiography: A Survey 1400–1600." *Studies in the Renaissance*, II (1955), 7–66.

Rowe, John Howland. "Ethnography and Ethnology in the Sixteenth Century." *Kroeber Anthropological Society Papers*, XXX (1964), 1–19.

Scammell, G. V. "The New Worlds and Europe in the Sixteenth Century." *Historical Journal*, XII (1969), 389–412.

Silva Dias, J. S. da. "Portugal e a cultura europeia (séculos XVI a XVIII)." *Biblos*, XXVIII (1952), 203–498.

Singer, Charles. "East and West in Retrospect." In Charles Singer *et al.*, eds., *A History of Western Technology*, II, pp. 753–76. 5 vols. Oxford, 1956.

Tenenti, Alberto. "L'utopia nel Rinascimento (1450–1550)," *Studi storici*, VII (1966), 689–707.

Van Kley, Edwin J. "Europe's 'Discovery' of China and the Writing of World History." *American Historical Review*, CXXVI (1971), 358–85.

Van Tiegham, Paul. "La littérature latine de la Renaissance." *Bibliothèque d'humanisme et renaissance*, IV (1944), 177–418.

Venturi, Franco. "Oriental Despotism." *Journal of the History of Ideas*, XXIV (1963), 133–42.

White, Lynn, Jr. "Medieval Borrowings from Further Asia." In O. B. Hardison, ed., *Medieval and Renaissance Studies*, No. 5 (1974), pp. 3–26.

Wicki, Josef. "Zum Humanismus in Portugiesisch-Indien des 16. Jahrhunderts." *Analecta Gregoriana*, cura Pontificiae Universitatis Gregorianae edita, v. LXX, ser. Facultatis historiae ecclesiasticae sectio A (n. 3); *Studi sulla chiesa antica e sull'umanesimo* . . ., pp. 193–246. Rome, 1954.

Wittkower, Rudolf. "Marvels of the East: A Study in the History of Monsters." *Journal of the Warburg and Courtauld Institutes*, V (1942), 159–97.

Yüan, Tung-li. "Russian Works on China, 1918–1958." *Monumenta serica*, XVIII (1959), 388–430.

Chapter Bibliographies

I. HERALDS OF EMPIRE

BOOKS

Aitken, James M., trans. *The Trial of George Buchanan before the Lisbon Inquisition*. Edinburgh, 1939.

Allen, P. S. *et al.*, eds. *Opus epistolarum Des. Erasmi Roterdami*. 12 vols. Oxford, 1906–58.

Almeida, Fortunato de. *História das instituições em Portugal*. Porto, 1903.

Babeau, Albert A. *Les voyageurs en France depuis la Renaissance jusqu'à la Révolution*. Paris, 1938.

Bataillon, Marcel. *Études sur le Portugal au temps de l'humanisme*. Coimbra, 1952.

Battelli, Guido, comp. and ed. *Documentos para o estudo das relações culturais entre Portugal e Italia: D. Miguel de Sylva, dos Condes de Portalegre, Bispo de Vizeu, Cardeal de Santa Maria Transtiberina*. 4 vols. Florence, 1934–35.

Battelli, Guido, and Coelho, Henrique Trindade. *Filippo Terzi, architette e ingenere militaire in Portogallo (1577–97)*. Florence and Lisbon, 1960.

Beau, Albin Eduard. *As relações germânicas do humanismo de Damião de Góis*. Coimbra, 1941.

Bell, Aubrey Fitzgerald. *Un humanista Portugûes: Damião de Góis*. Lisbon, 1942.

Bernardes Branco, Manuel. *Portugal e os estrangeiros*. 5 vols. Lisbon, 1879–95.

Braga, Theophile. *História da litteratura portugeza*. 2 vols. Porto, 1914.

——. *História da universidade de Coimbra*. 2 vols. Lisbon, 1892, 1895.

Brandão, Mário. *A Inquisição e os professores do Colégio das Artes [Coimbra]*. Coimbra, 1948.

Brásio, António. *Uma carta inédita de Valentim Fernandes*. Coimbra, 1959.

Burmeister, Karl. *Sebastian Münster, Versuch eines biographischen Gesamtbildes*. Basel and Stuttgart, 1963.

——, ed. See Münster, Sebastian.

Chapter Bibliographies

Cabié, Edmond. *Ambassade en Espagne de Jean Ebrard, Seigneur de St. Sulpice, de 1562 à 1565 et mission de ce diplomate dans le même pays en 1566.* Albi, 1903.

Carter, Charles. *The Western European Powers, 1500–1700.* Ithaca, N.Y., 1971.

Castro, José de. *Portugal em Roma.* 2 vols. Lisbon, 1939.

———. *Portugal no Concilio de Trento.* 6 vols. Lisbon, 1944–62.

Cerejeira, M. Gonçalves. *Clenardo e a sociedade portuguesa do seu tempo.* Coimbra, 1949.

Chauvin, E. and Roersch, A. *Étude . . . sur Clénard.* Brussels, 1900.

Clenard, Nicolas. *Correspondance.* Edited by Alphonse Roersch. 3 vols. Brussels, 1940–41.

Douais, Marie Jean Celestin, ed. *Dépèches de M. de Fourquevaux, ambassadeur du roi Charles IX en Espagne, 1565–72.* 3 vols. Paris, 1896–1904.

Duhr, Bernhard. *Die Jesuiten an den deutschen Fürstenhöfen des 16. Jahrhunderts.* Freiburg-im-Breisgau, 1901.

Estaço, Aquilas. *Statii lusitani Oratio.* . . . Rome, 1574.

Evans, R. J. W. *Rudolf II and His World: A Study in Intellectual History, 1576–1612.* Oxford, 1973.

Fabié y Escudero, Antonio María, ed. and trans. *Viajes por España.* . . . Madrid, 1879.

Falgairolle, E., ed. see Nicot, Jean.

Farinelli, Arturo. *Viajes por España y Portugal desde la edad media hasta el siglo XX; divagaciónes bibliograficas.* Madrid, 1920.

Fischer, Béat de. *Dialogue luso-suisse: Essai d'une histoire des relations entre la Suisse et le Portugal du XVe siècle à la Convention de Stockholm de 1960.* Lisbon, 1960.

Ford, J. D. M., and Moffat, L. G., eds. *Letters of the Court of John III, King of Portugal.* Cambridge, 1965.

Forjaz de Sampaio, Albino. *História da literatura portuguesa.* 3 vols. Paris and Lisbon, n.d.

Foulché-Delbrosc, R. *Bibliographie des voyages en Espagne et en Portugal.* Paris, 1896.

Gamelo, Benito. *Relaciones entre España e Italia durante la edad media.* . . . El Escorial, 1927.

Gamo, José Maria Alonso, trans. See Navagero, Andrea.

Garcia Mercadal, José. *Viajes de extranjeros por España y Portugal.* 2 vols. Madrid, 1959.

Godet, Marcelo. *La Congrégation de Montaigu (1490–1580).* Paris, 1912.

Góis, Damião de. *Aliquot opuscula.* Louvain, 1544.

———. *Lisboa de quinhentos.* Translated by Raúl Machado. Lisbon, 1937.

Gomes, João Pereira. *Os professores de filosofia da universidade de Évora.* Évora, 1960.

Gomes de Carvalho, M. E. *D. João III e os Francezes.* Lisbon, 1909.

Gomes dos Santos, Domingos M. *Jorge Buchanan e o ambiente coimbrão do século XVI.* Coimbra, 1962.

Gonçalves Guimarães, A. J., ed. See Resende, Garcia de.

Goris, Jan Albert. *Études sur les colonies marchandes méridionales (Portugais, Espagnols, Italiens) à Anvers de 1488 à 1567.* Louvain, 1925.

Gouveia, Antonio de. *The Latin Letters of Antonio de Gouveia.* Translated by Martha Katherine Zeeb. Philadelphia, 1932.

Grande, Stephano. *Le relazioni geografiche G. Gastaldi.* Rome, 1906.

Hanke, Lewis. *Aristotle and the American Indians.* Chicago, 1959.

Chapter I

Harrisse, Henry. *Fernand Colomb, sa vie, ses oeuvres, essai critique.* Paris, 1872.

Henry, W. J. C., ed. *Inéditos Goesianos.* 2 vols. Lisbon, 1896–99.

Hirsch, Elizabeth F. *Damião de Gois: The Life and Thought of a Portuguese Humanist, 1502–1574.* The Hague, 1967.

Jedin, Hubert. *Papal Legate at the Council of Trent, Cardinal Seripando.* St. Louis, 1947.

Klatt, David. *David Chytraeus als Geschichtslehrer und Geschichtschreiber.* Rostock, 1908.

Kubler, George, and Soria, Martin. *Art and Architecture in Spain and Portugal.* Baltimore, 1959.

Laire, Francis Xavier. *Index Librorum ab inventa typographia ad annum 1500 chronologica dispositus.* Sains, 1791.

Le Gentil, Georges. *Les français en Portugal.* Coimbra, 1928.

Lestocquoy, Jean, ed. *Correspondance des nonces en France, Carpi et Ferrerio, 1535–1540.* . . . Rome, 1961.

Lopes de Mendonça, Antonio Pedro. *Damião de Góes e a Inquisição de Portugal, estudo biographico.* Lisbon, 1859.

Machado, Augusto Reis, ed. See Souza, Luiz de.

Matthews, George T., ed. *News and Rumor in Renaissance Europe.* New York, 1959.

Matos, Luis de. *Les Portugais à l'université de Paris entre 1500 et 1550.* Coimbra, 1950.

——. *Les Portugais en France au XVIe siècle.* Coimbra, 1952.

Miranda da Costa Lobo, F. *A accção diplomática dos portugueses . . . destinada à realização de descobertas e conquistas.* Lisbon, 1937.

Münster, Sebastian. *Briefe.* Edited by K. H. Burmeister. Frankfurt-am-Main, 1964.

Navagero, Andrea. *Viaje a Espagna del . . . señor Andres Navagero (1524–26).* Translated by José Maria Alonso Gamo. Valencia, 1951.

Navarro, Alberto. *"Orações obediencias" . . . ; algumas achegas para o estudo das relações entre Portugal e a Santa Sé.* Lisbon, 1965.

Nicot, Jean. *Jean Nicot, ambassadeur de France en Portugal au XVIe siècle, sa correspondance diplomatique inédite.* Edited by E. Falgairolle. Paris, 1897.

Nouvel, E. *Le Collège de Sainte-Barbe, la vie d'un collège parisien de Charles VII à nos jours.* Paris, 1948.

Peragallo, Prospero, ed. *Carta de El-Rei D. Manuel ao Rei Catholico narrando as viagens portuguezas à India desde 1500 até 1505.* Lisbon, 1892.

Pike, Ruth. *Enterprise and Adventure: The Genoese in Seville and the Opening of the New World.* Ithaca, N.Y., 1966.

——. *Aristocrats and Traders: Sevillian Society in the Sixteenth-Century.* Ithaca, N.Y., 1972.

Quicherat, Jules E. J. *Histoire de Sainte-Barbe.* 3 vols. Paris, 1860–64.

Rau, Virgínia, and Borges Nunes, Eduardo, eds. *Carta de D. Manuel I ao rei de Aragão, D. Fernando, . . . sobre a tomada de Goa.* Lisbon, 1968.

Resende, Garcia de. *Cancioneiro Geral de Garcia de Resende.* Edited by A. J. Gonçalves Guimarães. 5 vols. Coimbra, 1910–17.

Reusch, Fr. Heinrich, ed. *Die Indices librorum prohibitorum des sechzehnten Jahrhunderts.* Tübingen, 1886.

Révah. I. S. *La censure inquisitoriale portugaise au XVIe siècle.* Lisbon, 1960.

Rodrigues, Francisco. *História da Companhia de Jesus . . . de Portugal.* 5 vols. Porto, 1931.

Roersch, Alphonse. *L'Humanisme belge à l'époque de la Renaissance: Études et portraits.* Louvain, 1933.

———, ed. See Clenard, Nicolas.

Sampaio Ribeiro, Maria de. *O retrato de Damião de Góis por Alberto Dürer; processo e história de uma atoarda.* Coimbra, 1943.

Saraiva, António José, *et al. História da cultura em Portugal.* 2 vols. Lisbon, 1955.

Schott, Andreas. *Hispania illustrata.* . . . 4 vols. Frankfurt-am-Main, 1603–8.

Silva Dias, J. S. da. *A política cultural da época de D. João III.* 2 vols. Coimbra, 1969.

Sobieski, Jacques. *Dwie Podróże Jakóba Sobieskiego ojca króla Jana III. Odbyte po krajach europejskich w latach 1607–13 i. 1638 waydane z rekopismu przez Edwarda Raczijnskiego.* Poznan, 1833. Spanish portions of his travels (pp. 96–126) translated into Spanish and published in the collection by Javier Liske, comp., *Viajes de extranjeros por España y Portugal en los siglos XV, XVI, y XVII,* pp. 233–67. Madrid, 1880.

Souza, Luiz de. *Vida de Dom Frei Bartolomeu dos Martires.* Edited by Augusto Reis Machado. 2 vols. Lisbon, 1946.

———. *Anais de D. João III.* Edited by M. R. Lapa. 2d ed. 2 vols. Lisbon, 1951, 1954.

Spitz, Lewis William. *Conrad Celtis, the German Arch-Humanist.* Cambridge, Mass., 1957.

Strasen, E. A., and Gandara, A. *Oito séculos de história Luso-Alemã.* Lisbon, 1944.

Trindade Coelho, H., and Mattelli, G., eds. *Documentos para o estudo das relações culturaes entre Portugal e Italia.* 4 vols. Florence, 1934–35.

Vasconcellos, Joaquim António da Fonseca. *Damião de Goes, sua descendéncia em Flandres, Allemanha e Austria.* Porto, 1897.

Vasconcelos, Carolina Michaëlis de. *A Infanta D. Maria de Portugal (1521–1577).* Porto, 1902.

Veríssimo Serrão, Joaquim. *A Infanta Dona Maria (1521–1577) e a sua fortuna no sul da França.* Lisbon, 1954.

———. *Antonio de Gouveia e o seu tempo (1510–66).* Coimbra, 1966.

———. *A embaixada em França de Brás de Alvide (1548–1554).* Paris, 1969.

———. *Les portugais à l'université de Toulouse (XIIIᵉ–XVIIᵉ siècles).* Paris, 1970.

Vocht, Henry de. *History of the Foundation and Rise of the Collegium Trilingue Lovaniense, 1517–1550.* 4 vols. Louvain, 1951–55.

ARTICLES

Almagià, R. "Un fiorentino in Spagna al principio del seculo XVI." In *Studi in onore de Gino Luzzato,* II, 138–50. 2 vols. Milan, 1950.

Aquarone, J. B. "Brantôme à la cour de Portugal et la visite à Lisbonne du Grand Prieur de Lorraine." *Bulletin des études portugaises et de l'Institut français au Portugal,* XI (1947), 66–102.

Bauer, C. "Conrad Peutingers Gutachten zur Monopolfrage," *Archiv für Reformationsgeschichte,* XLV (1954), 1–43, 145–96.

Beckmann, J. "Die Universitäten von 16. bis 18. Jahrhundert im Dienste der Glaubenverbreitung." *Neue Zeitschrift für Missionswissenschaft,* XVII (1961), 23–46.

Bell, Aubrey F. G. "The Humanist Jeronymo de Osorio." *Revue hispanique*, LXXIII (1928), 525–66.

Bertoni, Giulio. "Umanisti portoghesi a Ferrara (Hermico e Didaco)." *Giornale storico della letteratura italiana*, CXIV (1939), 46–50.

Bourdon, Léon. "Le voyage de Jeronimo Osorio . . . en Italie (1576–77)." *Annales publiées par la faculté des lettres de Toulouse*, I (1951), 71–83.

———. "Deux adventuriers portugais, Gaspar Caldeira et Antão Luis (1564–1568)." *Bulletin des études portugaises et de l'Institut français au Portugal*, XVIII (1954), 5–33.

Cermenati, M. "Un diplomatico naturalista del Rinascimento, Andrea Navagero." *Nuovo archivio veneto*, XXIV (1912), 164–205.

Claverie, Charles, ed. "Relation d'un voyage en Espagne (1612)." *Revue hispanique*, LIX (1923), 359–555.

Gomes Branco, J. "Un umanista portoghese in Italia, Achiles Estaço." In Reale Accademia d'Italia, *Relazione storiche fra l'Italia e il Portogallo: Memorie e documenti*, pp. 135–43. Rome, 1940.

Hamy, E. T. "Nouveaux documents sur les frères d'Albaigne et sur le projet de voyage de découvertes présenté en 1566 à la Cour de France." *Bulletin de géographie historique et descriptive*, 1899, pp. 101–10.

———. "Francisque et André d'Albaigne, cosmographes lucquois au service de la France." *Bulletin de géographie historique et descriptive*, 1894, pp. 405–23.

Henriques, G. J. C. "Buchanan in Portugal." In D. A. Millar, ed. and comp. *George Buchanan: A Memorial, 1506–1906*, pp. 60–78. St. Andrews and London, 1907.

Jubinal, Achille. "Études critiques; voyages en Espagne et en Portugal au XVIᵉ siècle." *Revue espagnole, portugaise, brasilienne et hispano-américaine*, IV (1857), 253–63, 374–97.

Kästner, Alfred. "Die Geschichte des spanischen Zeitungswesens von 1500–1800." *Zeitungswissenschaft*, XVII (1942), 370–383.

La Ville de Mumont, H. de. "George Buchanan à Bordeaux." *Revue philomatique de Bourdeaux et du Sud-ouest*, IX (1906), Nos. 7, 8, 9 (July, August, and September), 289–312, 337–59, 410–20.

Lebèque, Raymond. "George Buchanan: Sa Vie, son oeuvre, son influence en France et au Portugal." *Boletim do instituto francês em Portugal*, III (Coimbra, 1931), 190–210.

Le Gentil, Georges. "Nicolas de Grouchy, traducteur de Castanheda." *Bulletin des études portugaises et de l'Institut français au Portugal*, IV (1937), 31–47.

Leite de Faria, Francisco. "Un impresso de 1531 sobre as impressas dos Portugueses no Oriente." *Boletim internacional da bibliografia Luso-Brasileira*, VII (1966), 90–109.

Lemos, M. "Damião de Goes." *Revista de história*, IX (1920), 5–19, 208–26; X (1921), 41–66; XI (1922), 34–66.

Maranzoni, G. "Lazzaro Buonamico e lo studio Padovano nella prima metà del cinquecento." *Nuovo archivio veneto*, 3d. ser. I (1901), 118–51, 301–13; II (1902), 131–96.

Mathorez, J. "Notes sur les espagnoles en France depuis le XVIᵉ siècle jusqu'au règne de Louis XIII." *Bulletin hispanique*, XVI (1914), 337–71.

———. "Notes sur l'histoire de la colonie portugaise de Nantes." *Bulletin hispanique*, XV (1913), 317–20.

Matos, Luis de. "Un umanista portoghese en Italia, Damião de Goes." *Estudos italianos em Portugal*, No. 19 (1960), pp. 41–61.

———. "L'Humanisme portugaise et ses relations avec l'Europe." *Bulletin des études portugaises et de l'Institut français au Portugal*, XXVI (1965), 45–65.

Mollat, Michel. "Quelques aspects de la vie économique et sociale de la France dans la première moitié du XVIᵉ siècle vus à travers la correspondance des diplomates portugais." *Bulletin des études portugaises et de l'Institut français au Portugal*, XII (1948), 224–53.

———. "Passages français dans l'Océan Indien au temps de Francois Iᵉʳ." *Studia*, XI (1963), 239–50.

Nair, V. B. "A Nair Envoy to Portugal." *Indian Antiquary*, LVII (1928), 157–59.

Oliveira Marques, A. H. D. "Damião de Góis e os mercadores de Danzig." *Arquivo de bibliografia portuguesa*, IV (1958), 133–63.

Özbaran, Salih. "The Ottoman Turks and the Portuguese in the Persian Gulf, 1534–1581." *Journal of Asian History*, VI (1972), 45–87.

Peixoto, Jorge. "A informação em França, Espanha e Portugal nos séculos XVI, XVII e XVIII." *Arquivo de bibliografia portuguesa*, VII (1961), 131–36.

Piccinini, Prassitele. "Rapporti fra Italia e Portogallo nel campo delle scienze mediche." In Reale Accademia d'Italia, *Relazioni storiche fra l'Italia e il Portogallo*, pp. 387–401. Rome, 1940.

Pinto, Elena. "La biblioteca Vallicelliana in Roma." In *Miscellanea della R. Società Romana di Storia Patria*, No. 8. Rome, 1932.

Rivadeneira, Pedro de. "Vida del Padre Ignacio de Loyola," In *Obras escogidas . . .*, pp. 8–118. Madrid, 1868.

Silva Dias, J. S. da. "Portugal e a cultura europeia (sécs. XVI à XVIII)." *Biblos*, XXVIII (1952), 203–498.

Šimeček, Zdeněk. "Rožmberské zpravodajstír o nových zemích Asii a Africe v 16. století" (Rosemberk Reports about the New Lands of Asia and Africa in the Sixteenth Century). *Československý časopis historický*, XIII (1965), 428–43.

———. "L'Amérique au 16ᵉ siècle à la lumière des nouvelles du service de renseignements de la famille des Rožmberk." *Historica* (Prague), XI (1966), 53–93.

Sousa Costa, António Domingues de. "Estudantes portugueses na reitoria de Colégio de S. Clemente de Bolonha na primeira metade do século XV." *Arquivos de história da cultura portuguesa*, Vol. III, No. 1. Lisbon, 1969.

Tacchi Venturi, Pietro. "I portoghesi e Paolo III per la diffusione della civiltà cristiana nelle Indie e nell'Estremo Oriente." In Reale Accademia d'Italia, *Relazione storiche fra l'Italia e il Portogallo*, pp. 361–74. Rome, 1940.

Venturino, João Baptista. "Viagem do Cardeal Alexandrino, 1571." In A. Herculano, *Opusculos*, VI, 49–90. 10 vols. Lisbon, 1873–1908.

Veríssimo Serrão, Joaquim. "O humanista Diogo de Teive. Novos dados para a sua biografia." *Revista portuguesa de história*, IV, Pt. I (1949), 329–41.

———. "Manuel Álvares (1545–1612): Um desconhecido português professor de Medicina na Universidade de Toulouse." *Boletim da biblioteca geral da Universidade de Coimbra*, XXII (1953), 241–50.

Verlinden, Charles. "Lanzarotto Malocello et la découverte portugaise des Canaries." *Revue belge de philologie et d'histoire*, XXXVI (1958), 1173–1209.

Witte, Charles-Martial de. "Saint Charles Borromée et la couronne de Portugal." *Boletim internacional de bibliografia Luso-Brasileira*, VII (1966), 114–56.

II. BOOKS, LIBRARIES AND READING

BOOKS

Adams, Herbert M. *Catalogue of Books Printed on the Continent of Europe, 1501–1600, in Cambridge Libraries.* London, 1967.

Almagià, Roberto. *Monumenta cartographica Vaticana.* 4 vols. Vatican City, 1944–55.

Alvisi, Eduardo, ed. *Index bibliothecae Mediceae.* Florence, 1882.

Anselmo, António Joaquim. *Bibliografia das obras impressas em Portugal no século XVI.* Lisbon, 1926.

Arlolí y Farando, Servando, *et al.*, comps. *Biblioteca Colombina: Catálogo de sus libros impresos.* . . . 7 vols. Seville, 1888–1948.

Augustinus, Antonius. *Bibliothecae.* Tarragona, 1587.

Austin, Gabriel. *The Library of Jean Grolier, a Preliminary Catalogue.* New York, 1971.

Babelon, Jean. *La bibliothèque française de Fernand Colomb.* Paris, 1913.

Baridon, Silvo F. *Inventaire de la bibliothèque de Pontus de Tyard.* Geneva, 1950.

Barros, João de. *Grammatica da língua portuguesa.* Lisbon, 1540.

Bassaeus, Nicolaus, publ. *Collectio in unum corpus, omnium librorum hebraeorum, graecorum, latinorum necnon germanice italice, gallicè, et hispanicè scriptorum, qui in nundinis Franco-furtenibus ab anno 1564, usque ad nundinas autumnales anni 1592. partim novi, partim nova forma, et diversis in locis editi, venales extiterunt: desumpta ex omnibus Catalogis Willerianis singularum nundinarum . . . melioríque ratione quam hactenus disposita. . . .* Frankfurt, 1592.

Bates, William. *Vitae selectorum aliquot virorum.* . . . London, 1681.

Baudrier, Henri Louis, and Baudrier, Julien. *Bibliographie Lyonnaise: Recherches sur les imprimeurs, libraires, relieurs, et fondeurs de lettres de Lyon au XVIᵉ siècle.* 12 vols. Lyons, 1895–1921.

Bell, Robert (Belus). *Rerum hispanicarum scriptores aliquot.* . . . 2 vols. in 3. Frankfurt, 1579–81.

Bertoni, G. *La biblioteca estense e la coltura ferrarese ai tempi del Duca Ercole I (1471–1505).* Turin, 1903.

Bogeng, G. A. E. *Die grossen Bibliophilen: Geschichte der Büchersammler und ihrer Samlungen.* 3 vols. Leipzig, 1922.

Bonaffé, Edmond. *Inventaire des meubles de C. de Médicis en 1589.* Paris, 1874.

Boscaro, A. *Sixteenth-Century European Printed Works of the First Japanese Mission to Europe.* Leyden, 1973.

Braga, Theophile. *História da universidade de Coimbra.* . . . 2 vols. Lisbon, 1892, 1895.

Brandão, Mario, *Alguns documentos respeitantes à Universidade de Coimbra na época de D. João III.* Coimbra, 1937.

British Museum. Dept. of Printed Books. *The Lumley Library, the Catalogue of 1609.* Edited by Sears Jayne and Francis R. Johnson. London, 1956.

——. *Short-title Catalogue of Portuguese Books Printed before 1601 now in the British Museum.* Edited by Henry Thomas. London, 1940.

——. *Short-title Catalogue of Books Printed in the Netherlands and Belgium and of Dutch and Flemish Books Printed in Other Countries from 1470 to 1600.* London, 1965.

——. *Short-title Catalogue of Books Printed in Spain and of Spanish Books Printed Elsewhere in Europe before 1601 now in the British Museum.* By Henry Thomas. London, 1921.

——. *Short-title Catalogue of Books Printed in France and of French Books Printed in Other Countries from 1470–1600 now in the British Museum.* London, 1924.

——. *Short-title Catalogue of Books Printed in Italy and of Italian Books Printed in Other Countries from 1465–1600.* London, 1958.

Brito Aranha, Pedre Wenceslau de. *A imprensa em Portugal nos séculos XV e XVI. As ordenaçoes d'elrei D. Manuel.* Lisbon, 1898.

Brown, Horatio F. *The Venetian Printing Press: An Historical Study Based upon Documents for the Most Part Hitherto Unpublished.* London, 1896.

Burckhard, Jacob. *Historiae bibliotheca augustae quae Wolffenbutteli.* . . . 3 vols. Leipzig, [1744].

Burger, Konrad. *Die Drucker und Verleger in Spanien und Portugal von 1501 bis 1536.* Leipzig, 1913.

Burke, Redmond A. *What Is the Index?* Milwaukee, Wis., 1952.

Burmeister, K. H. *Sebastian Münster.* Basel, 1963.

Camerarius, Joachim. *De rebus turcicis commentarii.* Frankfurt, 1598.

Castellani, Carlo, comp. *Catalogo ragionato delle più rare o più importanti opere geografiche a stampa che si conservano nella Bibliotheca del Collegio Romano.* Rome, 1876.

——. *Pietro Bembo, bibliotecario della libreria di S. Marco in Venezia (1530–1543).* Venice, 1896.

Chantilly. Musée Condé. Bibliothèque. *Cabinet des livres imprimés antérieurs au milieu du XVIᵉ siècle, par Chantilly.* Paris, 1905.

Christ, Karl. *Die Bibliothek des Klosters Fulda im 16. Jahrhundert.* Leipzig, 1933.

Cicogna, Emmanuele A, comp. *Delle inscrizioni veneziana.* 6 vols. Venice, 1824–53.

Cidade, Hernani, and Múrias, M., eds. *Asia de João de Barros.* 4 vols. Lisbon, 1945.

Clair, Colin. *Christopher Plantin.* London, 1960.

Claudin, Anatole. *Les enlumineurs, les relieurs, les libraires et les imprimeurs de Toulouse aux XVᵉ et XVIᵉ siècles (1480–1530).* Paris, 1893.

Coimbra. University Library. *Catálogo de manuscritos da biblioteca da universidade de Coimbra.* Published in *Boletim da biblioteca da universidade de Coimbra,* 1935–67.

Collinson, J. *The Life of Thuanus with Some Account of His Writings.* . . . London, 1807.

Como, Ugo da. *Girolamo Muziano, 1528–92: Noti e documenti.* Bergamo, 1930.

Corella, A. Sierra. *La censura de libros y papelos en España y los indices y catálogos españoles de los prohibidos y expurgados.* Madrid, 1947.

Costa Coutinho, Bernardo Xavier da. *Bibliographie Franco-Portugaise, essai d'une bibliographie chronologique de livres français sur le Portugal.* Porto, 1939.

[588]

Chapter II

Cushing, Harvey. *A Bio-Biography of Andreas Vesalius.* 2d ed. New York, 1962.

Deacon, Richard. *John Dee: Scientist, Geographer, Astrologer, and Secret Agent to Elizabeth I.* London, 1968.

Delumeau, Jean. *Vie économique et sociale de Rome dans la seconde moitié du XVIᵉ siècle.* Paris, 1957.

Denis, Michael. *Wiens Buchdruckergeschichte bis MDLX.* Vienna, 1782.

Denucé, Jean. *Inventaire des archives plantiniennes.* Antwerp, 1926.

Doni, Anton Francisco. *La libraria del Doni Fiorentino: Nella quale sono scritti tutti gl' autori vulgari con 100 discorsi sopra quelli.* Venice, 1550.

Doucet, Roger. *Les bibliothèques parisiennes au XVIᵉ siècle.* Paris, 1956.

Droz, Eugénie. *Barthélemy Berton, 1563-1573.* Geneva, 1960.

Duncker, Albert. *Landgraf Wilhelm IV von Hessen, genannt der Weise, und die Begründung der Bibliothek zu Kassel im Jahre 1580.* Kassel, 1881.

Durme, Maurice van. *El cardinal Granvela.* Barcelona, 1957.

Ehrman, A., and Pollard, B. *The Distribution of Books by Catalogue from the Invention of Printing to A.D. 1800.* Cambridge, 1965.

El Escorial. 1563-1963. *IV Centenario de la fundación del Monasterio de San Lorenzo el Real.* 2 vols. Madrid, 1963.

Escudero y Perosso, Francisco. *Tipografía Hispalense: anales bibliográficos de la ciudad de Seville desde el establecimiento de la imprenta hasta fines del siglo XVIII.* Madrid, 1894.

Fava, Domenico. *La biblioteca Estense nel suo sviluppo storico.* Modena, 1925.

Febvre, Lucien. *Philippe II et la Franche-Comté.* Paris, 1912.

Febvre, Lucien, and Martin, H. J. *L'apparition du livre.* Paris, 1958.

Fischer, H., *et al. Conrad Gessner, 1516-65, Universalgelehrter, Naturforscher, Arzt.* Zurich, 1967.

Franck, Adolphe. *Reformateurs et publicistes de l'Europe.* 3 vols. Paris, 1864-93.

Franklin, Alfred L. *Les anciennes bibliothèques de Paris.* Paris, 1867-70.

French, P. J. *John Dee: The World of an Elizabethan Magus.* London, 1972.

Fulton, John Farquhar. *The Great Medical Bibliographers: A Study in Humanism.* London, 1951.

Gabrieli, Giuseppe. *Manoscritti e carte orientali nelle biblioteche e negli archivi d'Italia.* Florence, 1930.

Gachard, Louis P., ed. *Lettres de Philippe II à ses filles les infantes Isabella et Catherine écrites pendant son voyage en Portugal (1581-83).* Paris, 1884.

Gallardo, Bartolomé José. *Ensayo de una biblioteca española de libros raros curiosos.* 4 vols. Madrid, 1863-89.

García Lopez, Juan Catalina. *Ensayo de una tipografía complutense.* Madrid, 1899.

Garcia-Villoslada, Riccardo. *Storia del Collegio Romano dal suo inizo (1551) alla sopressione della Compagnia di Gesù (1773).* Rome, 1954.

Gaselee, Stephen. *The Early Printed Books in the Library of Corpus Christi College.* Cambridge, 1921.

Geanakoplos, Deno J. *Greek Scholars in Venice.* Cambridge, 1962.

Gesner, Konrad. *Bibliotheca universalis, sive Catalogus omnia scriptorum locupletissimus, in tribus lingis Latina, Graeca, et Hebraica extantium et non extantiū, veterum et recentiorem.* . . . 2 vols. Zurich, 1545.

————. *Bibliotheca instituta et collecta primum a Conrado Gesnero . . . locupletata . . . per Iosiam Simlerum Tigurinum.* Zurich, 1574.

Goldschmidt, Ernst P. *Hieronymus Münzer und seine Bibliothek.* London, 1938.

Gollob, Eduard. *Die Bibliothek des Jesuitenkollegiums in Wien und ihre Handschriften.* Vienna, 1909.

Gottlieb, Theodor. *Über mittelalterliche Bibliotheken.* Leipzig, 1890.

————. *Büchersammlung Kaiser Maximilians I: mit einer Einleitung über älteren Bücherbesitz im Hause Habsburg.* Leipzig, 1900.

Gualtieri, Guido. *Relationi della venuta de gli ambasciatori giaponesi à Roma, sino alla partita di Lisbona. Con una descrittione del lor paese, e costumi.* . . . Venice, 1586.

Haebler, Konrad. *The Early Printers of Spain and Portugal.* London, 1897.

————. *Deutsche Bibliophilen des 16. Jahrhunderts: Die Fürsten von Anhalt, ihre Bücher und Bucheinbände.* Leipzig, 1923.

Händler, G. *Fürstliche Mäzene und Sammler in Deutschland von 1500 bis 1620.* Strassburg, 1933.

Harrisse, Henri. *Fernand Colomb, sa vie, ses oeuvres: Essai critique.* Paris, 1872.

————. *La Colombine et Clément Marot.* 2d ed. Paris, 1886.

————. *Excerpta Colombieniana: Bibliographie de quatre cents pièces gothiques françaises, italiennes et latines du commencement du XVIe siècle non décrites jusqu'ici. Précédée d'une histoire de la bibliothèque Colombine et de son fondateur.* Paris, 1887.

————. *Le Prèsident de Thou et ses descendants, leur célèbre bibliothèque, leurs armoires, les traductions françaises de J.-A. Thuani Historiarum sui temporis.* Paris, 1905.

Hartig, Otto. *Die Gründung der Münchener Hofbibliothek durch Albrecht V und Johann Jakob Fugger.* . . . Munich, 1917.

Herculano, Alexandre. *History of the Origins and Establishment of the Inquisition in Portugal.* Stanford, Calif., 1926.

Hessel, Alfred. *A History of Libraries.* Washington, D.C., 1950.

Hessels, J. H., ed. See Ortelius, Abraham.

Hirn, Josef. *Erzherzog Ferdinand II von Tyrol.* 2 vols. Innsbruck, 1885–88.

Hirsch, Rudolf. *Printing, Selling, and Reading, 1450–1550.* Wiesbaden, 1966.

Ilic, Ursula D. "Book Ownership in Sixteenth-Century France: A Study of Selected Notarial Inventories." M. A. thesis, Graduate Library School, University of Chicago, 1967.

Innsbruck Exposition (Ausstellung). *Katalog Österreich-Tirol, 1363–1963.* Innsbruck, 1963.

Irwin, Raymond. *The Origins of the English Library.* London, 1958.

Jayne, Sears. *Library Catalogues of the English Renaissance.* Berkeley and Los Angeles, 1956.

Jayne, Sears, and Johnson, F. R. *The Lumley Library: The Catalogue of 1609.* London, 1956.

Kibre, Pearl. *The Library of Pico.* New York, 1936.

Chapter II

Klemm, G. *Zur Geschichte der Sammlungen für Wissenschaft und Kunst in Deutschland.* Zerbst, 1837.

Kloosterboer, W. *Bibliografie van nederlandse publikaties over Portugal en zijn overzeese gebiedsdelen.* The Hague, 1957.

Koemans, C. *Collections of Maps and Atlases in the Netherlands: Their History and Present State.* Leyden, 1961.

Kramm, Heinrich. *Deutsche Bibliotheken unter dem Einfluss von Humanismus und Reformation.* Leipzig, 1938.

Krauss, Werner. *Altspanische Drucke im Besitz der ausserspanische Bibliotheken.* Berlin, 1951.

Lambeck (Lambecius), Peter. *Commentarii de aug. bibliotheca Caesarea Vindobonensi libri II.* 8 vols. Vienna, 1665–69.

Lamma, Ernesto. *Saggio di una bibliografia intorno Andrea Navagero.* Venice, 1927.

Lehmann, Paul. *Eine Geschichte der alten Fuggerbibliotheken.* Tübingen, 1956.

Leite, Duarte. *História dos descobrimentos. Colectânea de esparsos. Organização, notas e estudo final de V. Magalhães Godinho.* 2 vols. Lisbon, 1960.

Lenhart, John Mary, O. M. Cap. *Pre-Reformation Printed Books and Applied Bibliography.* New York, 1935.

Leon Pinelo, Antonio de. *Epítome de la Biblioteca oriental i occidental, náutica y geografica.* Madrid, 1629.

Le Roux de Lincy, Adrien Jean Victor. *Notice sur la bibliothèque de Catherina de Medicis avec des extraits de l'inventaire de cette bibliothèque.* Paris, 1859.

————. *Recherches sur Jean Grolier, sur sa vie et sa bibliothèque: Suivies d'un catalogue des livres que lui ont appartenu.* Paris, 1866.

Levi della Vida, Giorgio. *Ricerche sulla formazione del più antico fondo dei manoscritti orientali della Biblioteca vaticana.* Vatican City, 1939.

Lhotsky, Alphons. Die Geschichte der Sammlungen. Vol. II of *Festschrift zur Feier des fünfzigjährigen Bestandes.* 2 vols. Vienna, 1941–45.

Lisbon, Camâra Municipal. *Documentos do arquivo histórico da Câmara Municipal de Lisboa, Livros de Reis.* Vols. 1–8. Lisbon, 1957–65.

Lisbon. Museu nacional de arte antiga. *Influences do Oriente na arte portuguesa continental, a arte nas provincias portuguesas do ultramar.* Lisbon, 1957.

Luchner, Laurin. *Denkmal eines Renaissancefürsten: Versuch einer Rekonstruktion des Ambraser Museums von 1586.* Vienna, 1958.

Lunsingh Scheurleer, Th. H., and Posthumus Meyjes, G. H. M., eds. *Leiden University in the Seventeenth Century: An Exchange of Learning.* Leyden, 1975.

Luxoro, Maria. *La biblioteca di San Marco nella sua storia.* Florence, 1954.

Luzio, Alessandro, and Renier, Rodolfo. *Mantova e Urbino: Isabella d'Este ed Elisabetta Gonzaga nelle relazioni famigliari e nelle vicende politiche.* Turin and Rome, 1893.

Madurell Marimon, José Maria, and Rubio y Balaguer, Jorge, comps, and eds. *Documentos para la historia de la imprenta y librería en Barcelona (1474–1553).* Barcelona, 1955.

Manuel II of Portugal. *Livros antigos Portugueses, 1489–1600, da biblioteca da Sua Magestade Fidelissima.* 3 vols. London, 1929–32.

Matos, Luis de. *Les portugaises en France au XVIe siècle.* Coimbra, 1952.

Chapter Bibliographies

McCurdy, Edward, trans. *The Notebooks of Leonardo*. 2 vols. in 1. New York, 1958.

Menhardt, Hermann. *Das älteste Handschriftenverzeichnis der Wiener Hofbibliothek von Hugo Blotius, 1576*. Vienna, 1957.

Mistretta di Paolo, Vincenzo. *Biblioteche private e scuole pubbliche e private in Alcamo nel '500*. Alcamo, 1967.

McDonald, Robert H., ed. *The Library of Drummond of Hawthornden*. Edinburgh, 1971.

Müntz, Eugene. *La bibliothèque du Vatican au XVIᵉ siècle*. Paris, 1886.

Nolhac, Pierre de. *La bibliothèque de Fulvio Orsini: Contribution à l'histoire des collections d'Italie et à l'étude de la Renaissance*. Paris, 1887.

Norton, Frederick J. *Printing in Spain, 1501-1520*. Cambridge, 1966.

Omont, Henri Auguste. *Anciens inventaires et catalogues de la Bibliothèque nationale*. 5 vols. Paris, 1908-21.

Ortelius, Abraham. Abraham Ortelii, geographi antwerpiensis, et virorum eruditorum . . . Epistulae . . . 1524- . . . Edited by J. H. Hessels. Cambridge, 1887.

Pansa, Muzio. *Della libraria Vaticana*. Rome, 1590.

Parr, George M. *Jan van Linschoten: The Dutch Marco Polo*. New York, 1964.

Picatoste y Rodriguez, Felipe. *Apuntes par una bibliografia científica española del siglo XVI*. Madrid, 1891.

Pittoni, Laura. *La libreria di S. Marco*. Pistoia, 1903.

Pottinger, David D. *The French Book Trade in the Ancien Régime, 1500-1791*. Cambridge, Mass., 1958.

Primisser, Alois. *Die kaiserlich-königliche Ambraser Sammlung*. Vienna, 1819.

Quentin-Bauchart, Ernest. *La bibliothèque de Fontainebleau et les livres des derniers Valois à la Bibliothèque nationale (1515-1598)*. Paris, 1891.

Renouard, Antoine Augustin. *Les annales de l'imprimerie des Aldes, ou histoire des trois Manuce et de leurs éditions*. 3d ed. Paris, 1834.

Retana, W. E. *Tablas cronológica y alfábetica. . . .* Madrid, 1908.

Reusch, Franz Heinrich. *Die Indices Librorum Prohibitorum des sechzehnten Jahrhunderts*. Stuttgart, 1886.

Révah, I. S. *La censure inquisitoriale portugaise au XVIᵉ siècle*. Lisbon, 1960.

Rodríguez-Marín, Francisco. *Luis Barahona de Soto: estudio biográfico, bibliográfico y crítico*. 2 vols. Madrid, 1903.

Rodríguez-Moñino, Antonio R. *La biblioteca de Benito Arias Montano, noticias y documentos para su reconstitución, 1548-1598*. Badajoz, 1929.

Rogers, Francis, ed. *Europe Informed: An Exhibition of Early Books Which Acquainted Europe with the East*. Cambridge, Mass., 1966.

Saba, Agostino. *La biblioteca di S. Carlo Borromeo*. Florence, 1936.

Sacken, Freiherr von. *Die K. K. Ambraser Sammlung*. 2 vols. Vienna, 1855.

Sánchez Cantón, Francisco. *La librería de Vélasquez*. Madrid, 1905.

Saraiva, António José. *História da cultura em Portugal*. 3 vols. Lisbon, 1950-62.

Schutz, Alexander Herman. *Vernacular Books in Parisian Private Libraries of the Sixteenth Century According to the Notarial Inventories*. Chapel Hill, N.C., 1955.

Seguin, Jean Pierre. *L'information en France de Louis XII à Henri II*. Geneva, 1961.

———. *L'information en France avant le périodique: 517 canards imprimés entre 1529 et 1631*. Paris, 1964.

Selig, Karl Ludwig. *The Library of Vincencio Juan de Lastanosa, patron of Gracián*. Geneva 1960.

Silva Bastos, José Timóteo. *História da censura intelectual em Portugal*. Coimbra, 1926.

Skallerup, Harry R. *Books Afloat and Ashore: A History of Books, Libraries, and Reading among Seamen during the Age of Sail*. Hamden, Conn., 1974.

Smital, Ottokar. *Die beiden Hofmuseen und die Hofbibliothek*. Vienna and Leipzig, 1920.

Sousa Viterbo, Francisco M. de. *A Livraria Real, especialmente no reinado de D. Manuel*. Lisbon, 1901.

Stauber, Richard. *Die Schedelsche Bibliothek*. Freiburg, 1908.

Steinmann, M. *Johannes Oporinus*. Basel and Stuttgart, 1967.

Stummvoll, Josef L. *Geschichte der österreichischen Nationalbibliothek*. Vienna, 1968.

Tacchi-Venturi, Pietro, ed. *Opere storiche del P. Matteo Ricci, S. J.* 2 vols. Macerata, 1913.

Taylor, Archer. *Book Catalogues: Their Varieties and Uses*. Chicago, 1957.

———. *Renaissance Guides to Books: An Inventory and Some Conclusions*. Berkeley, 1945.

Thompson, James W. *The Medieval Library*. Chicago, 1939.

Thou, Jacques Auguste de. *Catalogus bibliothecae Thuanae a clariss. viv. Petro et Iacobo Puteanis, ordine alphabetico primum distributus. Tum secundum scientias et artes à clariss. viro Ismaela Bullialdo digestus nunc vero editus à Josepho Quesnel Parisino et bibliothecario. Cum indici alphabetico authorum*. Paris, 1679.

———. *Les éloges des hommes savans, tirez de l'Histoire de M. de Thou . . . par Antoine Teissier*. 4 vols. Leyden, 1715.

Tomasino, Jacopo Filippo. *V. C. Laurentii Pignorii . . . bibliotheca et museum. . . .* Venice, 1632.

Valdenbro y Cisneros, José Maria de. *La imprenta en Cordoba, ensayo bibliográfico*. Madrid, 1900.

Vienna, National Library. *Ambraser Kunst- und Wunderkammer. Die Bibliothek. Katalog der Ausstellung im Prunksaal 28. Mai bis 30. September 1965*. Vienna, 1965.

Villey-Desmeserets, Pierre. *Les livres d'histoire moderne utilisés par Montaigne . . . suivi d'un appendice sur les traductions françaises d'histoires anciennes utilisées par Montaigne*. Paris, 1908.

Vocht, Henry de. *History of the Foundation and Rise of the Collegium Trilingue Lovaniense, 1517–1550*. 4 vols. Louvain, 1951–55.

Voet, Leon. *The Golden Compasses: A History and Evaluation of the Printing and Publishing Activities of the Officina Plantiniana at Antwerp*. 2 vols. Amsterdam, 1969.

Waters, D. W. *The Art of Navigation*. London, 1958.

Watt, Joachim de (Vadianus). *Epitome trium terrae partium Asiae, Africae et Europae*. Zurich, 1534.

Wiest, Donald H. *The Precensorship of Books*. Washington, D.C., 1953.

Chapter Bibliographies

ARTICLES

Anon. "Old Inventories of Maps." *Imago mundi*, V (1948), 18–20.

————. "Viagem a Portugal dos Cavaleiros Tron e Lippomani, 1580." In Alexandre Herculano, ed. and trans., *Opusculos*, VI, pp. 113–26. 10 vols. Lisbon, 1873–1908.

Almagià, R. "La diffusion des produits cartographiques flamands en Italie au XVIe siècle." *Archives internationales d'histoire des sciences*, XXXIII (1954), 40–50.

Bagrow, Leo. "A Page from the History of the Distribution of Maps." *Imago mundi*, V (1948), 53–62.

Barbieri, Torquato, comp. "Indice delle cinquecentine conservate nella Biblioteca Carducci, I (1501–1550)." *Archiginnasio*, LVII (1962), 184–256.

Bay, J. E. "Conrad Gesner, the Father of Bibliography." *Papers of the Bibliographical Society of America*, X, Pt. 2 (1916), 60–65.

Bec, Christian. "Une librairie florentine de la fin du XVe siècle." *Bibliothèque d'humanisme et renaissance*, II (1969), 321–32.

Beer, Rudolf, ed. "Niederländische Büchererwerbungen des Benitos Arias Montano für den Eskorial im Auftrage König Philip II von Spanien." *Jahrbuch der kunsthistorischen Sammlungen des allerhöchsten Kaiserhauses*, XXV (1905), Pt. 2, i–xi.

Boeheim, Wendelin, ed. "Urkunden und Regesten aus der K.K. Hofbibliothek." *Jahrbuch der kunsthistorischen Sammlungen des allerhöchsten Kaiserhauses*, VII (1888), Pt. 2, xci–cccxiii.

Boinet, Amédée. "Un bibliophile français du XVIe siècle, Claude Gauffier." *Gutenberg Jahrbuch*, 1953, pp. 176–79.

Bonnefon, P. "La bibliothèque de Montaigne." *Revue d'histoire littéraire de la France*, II (1895), 310–69.

Boxer, Charles R. "Some Portuguese Sources for Indonesian Historiography." In Soedjatmoko *et al.*, eds., *An Introduction to Indonesian Historiography*, pp. 217–33. Ithaca, N.Y., 1965.

Brandão, Mario. "Contribuições para a história da universidade de Coimbra: a livraria do Padre Francisco Suarez." *Biblos*, III (1927), 325–49.

Brockhaus, H. "Ein altflorentiner Kunstverlag." *Mitteilungen des kunsthistorischen Instituts in Florenz*, I (1910), 97–110.

C. R. "Inventaire des meubles et effets du chateau de Vianen en 1567." *Le bibliophile belge*, 3d ser. IX (1874), 106–14, 274–79.

Carvalho, Joaquim de. "A livraria dum letrado do século XVI. Frei Diogo de Murça." *Boletim bibliografico da universidade de Coimbra*, Nos. I–VII (1927), 1–27.

Clough, C. H. "Pietro Bembo's Library Represented in the British Museum." *British Museum Quarterly*, XXX (1966), 3–17.

Connat, M., and Megret, J. "Inventaire de la bibliothèque des Du Prat." *Bibliothèque d'humanisme et renaissance*, III (1943), 72–128.

Corraze, Abbé R. "Notes pour servir à l'histoire de la librairie à Toulouse (1500–1540)." *Bulletin philologique et historique*, 1934–35, pp. 59–81.

Coyecque, E. "Quatre catalogues de livres (1519–1520)." *Revue des bibliothèques*, V (1895), 2–12.

Cristofari, Maria. "La tipografia vicentina nel secolo XVI." In *Miscellanea di scritti di bibliografia ed erudizione in memoria di Luigi Ferrari*, pp. 191–214. Florence, 1952.

Deherain, H. "Fernand Colomb et sa bibliothèque." *Journal des Savants* (Paris), VIII (1914), 342–51.

Des Coudres, Hans P. "Das verbotene Schrifttum und die wissenschaftlichen Bibliotheken." *Zentralblatt für Bibliothekswesen*, LII (1935), 459–71.

Dorez, Léon. "La bibliothèque privée du pape Jules II." *Revue des bibliothèques* (Paris), VI (1896), 97–124.

————. "Recherches sur la bibliothèque du Cardinal Girolamo Aleandro." *Revue des bibliothèques* (Paris), VII (1897), 49–68.

————. "Recherches sur la bibliothèque de Pier Leoni, médecin de Laurent de Medicis." *Revue des bibliothèques* (Paris), IV (1894), 73–83; VII (1897), 81–103.

————. "Le registre des dépenses de la Bibliothèque Vaticane de 1548 à 1555." In *Fasciculus Ioanni Willis Clark dicatum*, pp. 142–85. Cambridge, 1909.

Droz, Eugénie. "Le libraire Jean de Campenon (d. 1580)." *Bulletin de la société des bibliophiles de Guyenne*, XXXVI (1967), 131–45.

Fletcher, John. "Athanasius Kircher and the Distribution of His Books." *Library*, XXIII (1968), 108–17.

Galizia, Giovanna. "Inventari quattro e cinquecenteschi di libri appartenenti alla sacrestia della cattedrale di Macerata." *Aevum*, XLI (1967), 160–65.

Gérard, Charles. "Quelques livres curieux de la bibliothèque nationale St. Marc, de Venise." *La bibliofilia*, X (1908–9), 413–34.

Goris, J. A. "De intellectueele bagage van een Spanjaard in de XVIe eeuw." *Het Boek*, XI (1922), 337–41.

————. "Twee kleine zestiende-eeuwsche bibliotheken te Antwerpen (1584)." *Het Boek*, XIII (1924), 255–57.

Gutierrez, Luis Cuesta. "Dos grandes bibliotecas del Extremo Oriente para la Nacional de Madrid." *Gutenberg Jahrbuch*, XXXIV (1959), 120–26.

Hervouet, Yves. "Les bibliothèques chinoises d'Europe occidentale." *Mélanges publiée par l'Institut des hautes études chinoises* (University of Paris), I (1957), 451–511.

Hildebrandt, Ernst. "Die kurfürstliche Schloss- und Universitätsbibliothek zu Wittenberg 1512–1547: Beiträge zu ihrer Geschichte." *Zeitschrift für Buchkunde*, II (1925), 34–42, 109–29, 157–88.

Hoff, van't B. "De catalogus van de bibliothek van Gerard Mercator." *Het Boek*, XXV (1961–62), 25–27.

Hughes, Barnabas B., O.F.M. "The Private Library of Johann Scheubel, Sixteenth-Century Mathematician." *Viator*, III (1972), 417–32.

Hülle, Hermann. "Die Erschliessung der chinesischen Bücherschätze der deutschen Bibliotheken." *Ostasiatische Zeitschrift*, 1919–20, pp. 199–219.

Husner, Fritz. "Die Bibliothek des Erasmus." In *Gedenkschrift zum 400. Todestage des Erasmus von Rotterdam*, pp. 228–59. Basel, 1936.

Joachimsohn, Paul. "Aus der Bibliothek Sigismund Gossembrots." *Zentralblatt für Bibliothekswesen*, XI (1894), 249–68, 297–307.

Chapter Bibliographies

Jonghees, J. H. "Stephanus Ninandies Pighius Compensis." *Mededelingen van het Nederlands Historisch Instituut te Rome*, 3d ser. VIII (1954), 120–85.

Kirchhoff, Albrecht. "Die Leipziger Büchermesse von 1550 bis 1650." *Archiv für Geschichte des deutschen Buchhandels*, XI (1888), 183–203.

——. "Leipziger Sortimentshändler im 16. Jahrhundert und ihre Lagervorräthe." *Archiv für Geschichte des deutschen Buchhandels*, XI (1888), 204–82.

——. "Lorenz Finckelthaus in Leipzig Nachlassinventar vom Jahre 1581." *Archiv für Geschichte des deutschen Buchhandels*, XIV (1891), 99–113.

Klaiber, L. "Die altspanischen und altportugiesischen Drucke und Handschriften der Universitätsbibliothek Freiburg i.B." *Revue hispanique*, Part I (1933), 498–525.

Kronenberg, M. E. "Pastor Johannes Phoconius (Zwolle 1527–Deventer 1560) en zijn bibliothek." *Het Boek*, III (1914), 345–51, 374–83, 454–69.

Lattès, S. "Recherches sur la bibliothèque d'Angelo Colocci." *Mélanges d'archéologie et d'histoire*, XLVIII (1931), 308–44.

Le Gentil, Georges. "Les français en Portugal." *Bulletin des études portugaises*, I (1931), 1–25.

Liu, James J. Y. "The Feng-yüeh Chin-nang [風月錦囊]; A Ming Collection of Yüan and Ming Plays and Lyrics Preserved in the Royal Library of San Lorenzo, Escorial Spain." *Journal of Oriental Studies* (Hong Kong), IV, Nos. 1–2 (1957–58), 79–107.

Luzio, A., and Renier, R., eds. "La coltura e le relazioni letterarie di Isabella d'Este Gonzaga, appendice prima." *Giornale storico della letteratura italiana*, XLII (1903), 75–89.

Martín-González, J. J. "El palacio de Carlo V en Yuste." *Archivo español de arte*, XXIII (1950), 246–47.

Matos, Luis de. "Obras raras do século XVI." *Boletim internacional de bibliografia Luso-Brasileira*, III (1962), 74–83.

Matsuda Kiichi. "Catálgo de los documentos japoneses existentes en Europe Meridional." *Boletim da filmoteca ultramarina portuguesa*, XX (1962), 7–29.

Mercati, Giovanni. "Un indice di libri offerti a Leone X." *Il libro e la stampa*, N.S. II (1908), 41–47.

Offenbacher, Emile. "La bibliothèque de Wilibald Pirckheimer." *La bibliofilia*, XL (1939), 241–63.

Omont, Henri. "Inventaire de la bibliothèque de Guillaume Pelicier, évêque de Montpelier (1529–1568)." *Revue des bibliothèques*, I (1891), 161–72.

Pelliot, Paul. "Une liasse d'anciens imprimés chinois des Jésuites retrouvée à Upsal." *T'oung pao*, XXIX (1932), 114–18.

Petitot, C. B., ed. "Mémoires de Jacques-August de Thou." In *Collection complète des mémoires relatifs à l'histoire de France*, Ser. I, Vol. XXXVII, pp. 189–530. 130 vols. in 131. Paris, 1820–29.

Piquard, Maurice. "La bibliothèque d'un homme d'état [Cardinal de Granvelle] au XVIe siècle." In *Mélanges d'histoire du livre . . . offerts à M. Frantz Calot*, pp. 227–35. Paris, 1960.

Pogson, K. M. "List of Books Presented by the Earl of Essex in 1600, Still in the Bodleian." *Bodleian Quarterly Record*, III (1920–22), 241–44.

Prandtl, Wilhelm. "Die Bibliothek des Tycho Brahe." *Philobiblon*, V (1932), 291–99, 321–29.

Preisendanz, Karl. "Die Bibliothek Johannes Reuchlins." In *Johannes Reuchlin, 1455–1522, Festgabe*, pp. 35–82. Pforzheim, 1955.

Prideaux, W. R. B. "Books from John Dee's Library." *Notes and Queries*, 9th ser. VIII (1901), 137–38; 10th ser. I (1904), 241–42.

Quelle, Otto. "Die ibero-amerikanischen Länder in Manuscriptatlanten des 16. und 17. Jahrhunderts der Wiener Nationalbibliothek." *Ibero-Amerikanisches Archiv*, XIII (1939), 130–49.

Reiffenberg, Baron de. "Bibliothèque de Joseph Scaliger." *Le bibliophile belge*, IV (1847), 228–31.

Ridolfi, Roberto. "La biblioteca del Cardinale Niccolo Ridolfi (1501–50)." *Bibliofilia*, XXXI (1929), 173–93.

Robathan, Dorothy M. "The Catalogues of the Princely and Papal Libraries of the Italian Renaissance." *Transactions and Proceedings of the American Philological Association*, LXIV (1933), 138–49.

Schelven, A. A. van. "Een catalogus van den Amsterdamschen boekverkooper Cornelis Claesz." *Het Boek*, XI (1922), 329–34.

Schütte, Joseph Franz, S.J. "Christliche japanische Literatur, Bilder und Druckblaetter in einem unbekannten Vatikanischen Codex aus dem Jahre 1591." *Archivum historicum Societatis Iesu*, IX (1940), 226–80.

Schutz, A. H. "Gleanings from Parisian Private Libraries of the Renaissance (1494–1558)." *Romance Philology*, V (1951), 25–34.

Selig, K. L. "A German Collection of Spanish Books." *Bibliothèque d'humanisme et renaissance*, XIX (1957), 71–80.

Sondheim, M. "Die Bibliothek des Hans Sachs." In *Sondheims gesammelte Schriften*, pp. 259–60. Frankfurt, 1927.

Stahleder, Erich. "Die verschollene Bibliothek des Benediktinklosters Eschenbrunn." *Jahrbuch des historischen Vereins Dillingen*, LXIX (1967), 25–41.

Steiger, C. F. de. "Die Bibliothek des Berner Schultheissen Johannes Steiger (1518–81)." *Stultifera navis*, X (1890), 44–54.

Stern, Virginia F. "The Bibliotheca of Gabriel Harvey." *Renaissance Quarterly*, XXV (1972), 1–62.

Strauss, Felix F. "The 'Liberey' of Duke Ernest of Bavaria (1500–1560)." *Studies in the Renaissance*, VIII (1961), 128–43.

Thani Nayagam, Xavier S. "Tamil Manuscripts in European Libraries." *Tamil Culture*, III (1954), 219–28.

Vajda, Georges. "Un inventaire de bibliothèque juive d'Italie." *Revue des études juives*, CXXVI (1967–68), 473–83.

Van der Feen, G. B. C. "Noord-nederlandsche boekerijen in der 16ᵉ eeuw." *Het Boek*, VII (1918), 81–92, 318–34; VIII (1919), 219–24.

Veríssimo Serrão, Joaquim. "António de Gouveia e Miguel de Montaigne: seu provável contacto." *Revista filosófica* (Coimbra), II (1952), 84–89.

Voet, Leon. "Les relations commerciales entre Gerard Mercat et la maison Plantinienne." *Duisburger Forschungen*, VI (1962), 221–24.

Walde, O. "Neue bücher- und bibliotheksgeschichtliche Forschungen in deutschen Bibliotheken." *Nordisk tidskrift för bok- och biblioteksväsen* (Stockholm), XXIX (1942), 165–262.

Warner, George F., ed. "The Library of James VI, 1573–83." *Miscellany of the Scottish Historical Society* (Edinburgh), I (1893), i–lxxv.

Wicki, Joseph. "Der älteste deutsche Druck eines Xaveriusbriefes aus dem Jahre 1545, ehemals im Besitz des Basler Humanisten Lepusculus." *Neue Zeitschrift für Missionswissenschaft*, IV (1948), 105–9.

III. THE INHERITED THEMES

BOOKS

Alexander the Great. Curtius Rufus, Quintus. *La historia d'Alexandro Magno*. Florence, 1478.

———. Curtius Rufus, Q. . . . *De Rebus gestis Alexandri Magni, regis Macedonum*. . . . Argentière, 1518.

———. *Alexandri Macedonis ad Aristotelem. De mirabilibus Indie in Secreta secretorum Aristotelis*. Lyons, 1528.

———. *Q. Curtii De rebus gestis Alexandri Magni rêgis Macedonum, libri*. . . . Cologne, 1542.

———. *Q. Curtii . . . De rebus gestis Alexandri Magni*. . . . Basel, 1545.

———. *De fatti d'Alessandro Magno . . . tradotto per Tomaso Porcacchi*. . . . Venice, 1559.

———. Curtius Rufus, Quintus. *The History of Quintus Curtius, Conteyning the Actes of the Greate Alexander, translated out of Latin into Englishe by Iohn Brende*. London, 1570.

Altheim, Franz. *Alexander und Asien: Geschichte eines geistigen Erbes*. Tübingen, 1953.

Amalfi, Gaetano. *Il Panciatantra in Italia*. Trani, 1893.

Baethgen, Friedrich, trans. *Sindban, oder die Sieben Weisen Meister: Syrisch und Deutsch*. Leipzig, 1879.

Baltrušaitis, Jurgis. *Le moyen âge fantastique*. Paris, 1955.

Barlaam and Joasaph. S. *Ioannis Damasceni Historia de vitis et rebus gestis SS Barlaam eremitae et Iosaphat, Indiae regis, Iacobo Billio . . . interprete*. Antwerp, 1593.

Benfey, Theodor, ed. and trans. *Pantschatantra: Fünf Bücher indischer Fabeln, Märchen, und Erzählungen*. 2 vols. Leipzig, 1859.

Berges, W. *Die Fürstenspiegel des hohen und späten Mittelalters*. Stuttgart, 1952.

Bernheimer, Richard. *Wild Men in the Middle Ages*. Cambridge, Mass., 1952.

Blochet, Edgar. *Les sources orientales de la Divine Comédie*. Paris, 1901.

Bodnar, Edward W. *Cyriacus of Ancona and Athens*. Brussels, 1960.

Bolte, Johannes, and Mackensen, Lutz. *Handwörterbuch des deutschen Märchens*. 2 vols. Berlin and Leipzig, 1930–33, 1934–40.

Braunholtz, Eugen. *Die erste nichtchristliche Parabel des Barlaam und Josaphat ihre Herkunft und Verbreitung*. Halle, 1884.

Breloer, B., and Bömer, F. *Fontes historiae religionum Indicarum*. Bonn, 1939.

Chapter III

Brummach, Jürgen. *Die Darstellung des Orients in den deutschen Alexandergeschichten des Mittelalters.* "Philologische Studien und Quellen," Vol. 29. Berlin, 1966.

Budge, E. A. Wallis. *Barlaam and Yewâsef.* Cambridge, 1923.

Burlingame, Eugene Watson, trans. and ed. *Buddhist Parables Translated from the Original Pali.* New Haven, 1922.

Burmeister, Karl Heinz. *Sebastian Münster, eine Bibliographie.* Wiesbaden, 1964.

Buron, E. *Ymagi Mundi de Pierre d'Ailly.* Paris, 1930.

Bysshe, Sir Edward. *Palladius de gentibus Indiae.* London, 1665.

Camerarius, Joachim. *Libellus gnomologicus.* . . . Leipzig, 1569.

Campbell, Killis. *The Seven Sages of Rome.* Boston, 1907.

Cary, George A. *The Medieval Alexander.* 2d ed. Cambridge, 1967.

Cassel, D. Paulus, ed. *Mischle Sindbad, Secundus Syntipas.* 3d ed. Berlin, 1891.

Comparetti, Domenico. *Ricerche intorno al Libro di Sindibad.* Milan, 1869.

Corrêa de Lacerda, Margarida. *Vida do honrado infante Josaphate, filho del Rey Avenir. Versão de frei Hilário da Lourinhã e o identificação por Diogo do Couto (1542–1616) de Josaphate com o Buda.* Lisbon, 1963.

Cosquin, Emmanuel Georges. *Etudes folkloriques: recherches sur les migrations des contes populaires et leur point de départ.* Paris, 1922.

————. *Les contes indiens et l'occident.* Paris, 1922.

Crane, Thomas F., ed. *The Exempla . . . of Jacques de Vitry.* London, 1890.

Dahlquist, Allan. *Megasthenes and Indian Religion: A Study in Motives and Types.* Stockholm, 1962.

der Nersessian, Sirarpie. *L'illustration du roman de Barlaam et Joasaph.* Paris, 1937.

Di Francia, Letterio. *La leggenda di Turandot nella novellistica e nel teatro.* Trieste, 1932.

Dresbach, L. *Der Orient in der altfranzösischen Kreuzzugsliteratur.* Breslau, 1901.

Edgerton, Franklin, trans. and ed. *The Panchatantra Reconstructed.* 2 vols. New Haven, 1924.

Falugio, Domenico. *Triomphe Magno.* Rome, 1521.

Funk, Philipp. *Jakob von Vitry, Leben und Werke.* "Beiträge zur Kulturgeschichte des Mittelalters," Vol. III. Leipzig and Berlin, 1909.

Gabrieli, Giuseppe. *Dante e l'Oriente.* Bologna, 1921.

Gaedertz, K. T. *Gabriel Rollenhagen, sein Leben und seine Werke.* Leipzig, 1881.

Graf, Arturo. *Miti, leggende, e superstizioni del Medio Evo.* Turin, 1892–93.

Guerri, Domenico. *La corrente popolare nel Rinascimento.* Florence, 1931.

Günter, Heinrich. *Buddha in der abendländischen Legende.* Leipzig, 1922.

Haight, Elizabeth H. *Life of Alexander of Macedon.* New York, 1955.

————. *Essays on the Greek Romances.* New York, 1943.

————. *More Essays on Greek Romances.* New York, 1945.

Herodotus. See Selincourt, Aubrey de, trans.

Hertel, Johannes. *Das Pañcatantra, seine Geschichte und seine Verbreitung.* Leipzig and Berlin, 1914.

Hervieux, Léopold. *Les fabulistes latins depuis le siècle d'Auguste jusqu'à la fin du moyen âge.* 2 vols. Paris, 1884–99.

Hirsch, Siegmund. *Das Alexanderbuch Johann Hartliebs.* Berlin, 1909.

Hoffman, Agnes. *Untersuchungen zu den altdeutschen Marco Polo-Texten.* Ohlau, 1936.

Holmes, Urban Tigner. *A History of Old French Literature from the Origins to 1300.* Rev. ed. New York, 1962.

Hölscher, Tonio. *Ideal und Wirklichkeit in den Bildnissen Alexanders des Grossen.* Heidelberg, 1971.

Husselman, Elinor. *Kalilah and Dimnah.* London, 1938.

Jacobs, Joseph. *Indian Fairy Tales.* London, 1892.

Jacobs, Joseph ed. *Barlaam and Josaphat. English Lives of Buddha.* London, 1896.

Janson, Horst W. *Apes and Ape Lore.* London, 1952.

Keith, A. Berriedale. *A History of Sanskrit Literature.* Reprint of 1920 edition. London, 1961.

Keith-Falconer, Ian G. N. *Kalilah and Dimnah or the Fables of Bidpai: Being an Account of Their Literary History.* . . . Cambridge, 1885.

Klijn, Albertus F. J. *The Acts of Thomas.* Leyden, 1962.

Landau, Marcus. *Die Quellen des Dekameron.* Stuttgart, 1884.

Lang, David Marshall. *The Balavariani (Barlaam and Josaphat): A Tale from the Christian East Translated from the Old Georgian.* Berkeley, 1966.

———. *The Wisdom of Balahvar, a Christian Legend of the Buddha.* London, 1957.

Lavro, Pietro, trans. *Arriano di Nicomedia, chiamato nuovo Xenofonte de i fatti del Magno Alessandro re di Macedonia Novamente di greco tradotto in italiano per Pietro Lavro modonese.* . . . Venice, 1544.

Lee, A. C. *The Decameron: Its Sources and Analogues.* London, 1909.

Lepszy, Hans-Joachim. *Die Reiseberichte des Mittelalters und der Reformationszeit.* Hamburg, 1953.

Lévêque, Eugène. *Les mythes et les légendes de l'Inde et de la Perse dans Aristophane, Platon, Aristote, Virgile, Ovide, Tite-Live, Dante, Boccace, Arioste, Rabelais, Perrault, La Fontaine.* Paris, 1880.

Loiseleur-Deslongchamps, Auguste Louis Armand. *Essai sur les fables indiennes.* Paris, 1838.

Macdonell, Arthur A. *History of Sanskrit Literature.* London, 1928.

———. *India's Past: A Survey of Her Literatures, Religions, Languages and Antiquities.* Oxford, 1927.

Magoun, F. P. *The Gestes of Alexander of Macedon.* Cambridge, Mass., 1929.

Majumdar, Ramesh, ed. *The Classical Accounts of India: Being a Compilation of the English Translations of the Accounts left by Herodotus, Megasthenes, Arrian, Strabo, Quintus, Diodorus Siculus, Justin, Plutarch, Frontinus, Nearchus, Apollonius, Pliny, Ptolemy, Aelian and Others, with Maps, Editorial Notes, Comments, Analysis, and Introduction.* Calcutta, 1960.

Manni, Eugenio. *Introduzione allo studio della storia greca e romana.* Palermo, 1952.

McCrindle, John W. *Ancient India as Described in Classical Literature.* Westminster, 1901.

Merkelbach, Reinhold. *Die Quellen des griechischen Alexanderromans.* Munich, 1954.

Meyer, Paul. *Alexandre le Grand dans la littérature française du moyen âge.* Vol. I. Paris, 1886.

Mierow, Charles C., trans. *The Two Cities: A Chronicle of Universal History to the Year 1146 A.D. by Otto, Bishop of Freising.* New York, 1966.

Moldenhauer, Gerhard. *Die Legende von Barlaam und Josaphat auf der iberischen Halbinsel.* Halle, 1929.

Monneret de Villard, Ugo. *Le leggende orientali sui Magi evangelici.* Rome, 1952.

Monti, Gennaro M. *Le Crociate e i rapporti fra Oriente mediterraneo e Occidente europeo.* Rodi, 1936.

Müller, Max. *Chips from a German Workshop.* Vol. IV. New York, 1890.

Münster, Sebastian. *Briefe . . ., Lateinisch und Deutsch.* Edited by K. H. Burmeister. Frankfurt-am-Main, 1964.

———. *Cosmographei.* . . . Basel, 1550.

Oesterley, H., ed. *Gesta Romanorum.* Berlin, 1872. English translation by C. Swan. London, 1888.

Olschki, Leonardo. *Marco Polo's Asia.* Berkeley, 1960.

Paris, Gaston. *Les contes orientaux dans la littérature française du moyen âge.* Paris, 1875.

Patch, Howard R. *The Otherworld According to Descriptions in Medieval Literature.* Cambridge, Mass., 1950.

Peri (Pflaum), Hiram. *Der Religionsdienst der Barlaam-Legende, ein Motiv abendländischer Dichtung.* Salamanca, 1959.

Perry, Ben Edwin. *Studies in the Text History of the Life and Fables of Aesop.* Haverford, Pa., 1936.

———. *Babrius and Phaedrus.* London, 1965.

Pfister, Friedrich. *Kleine Texte zum Alexanderroman. Commonitorium Paladii Briefwechsel zwischen Alexander und Dindimus, Brief Alexanders über die Wunder Indiens nach die Bamberger Handschrift herausgegeben.* Heidelberg, 1910.

Pforr, Anton von. *Das Buch der Beispiele der alten Weisens (1483).* Berlin, 1964.

Pupo-Walker, Constantino Enrique. "A Critical Edition of the Old Portuguese Version of Barlaam and Josaphat." Ph.D. diss., University of North Carolina, Chapel Hill, 1966.

Rapson, Edward James, ed. *The Cambridge History of India.* Delhi reprint, 1962.

Rawlinson, Hugh G. *Intercourse between India and the Western World from the Earliest Times to the Fall of Rome.* 2d ed. Cambridge, 1926.

Raymond, Irving W., ed. *Seven Books of History against the Pagans.* New York, 1936.

Reicke, Emil, ed. *Willibald Pirckheimers Briefwechsel.* 2 vols. Jena, 1930.

Ringbom, Lars-Ivar. *Graltempel und Paradies: Beziehungen zwischen Iran und Europe im Mittelalter.* Stockholm, 1951.

Robinson, Charles A. *The History of Alexander the Great.* 2d ed. Providence, R.I., 1953.

Rogers, Francis M. *The Quest for Eastern Christians. Travels and Rumor in the Age of Discovery.* Minneapolis, 1962.

Ross, David John Athold. *Alexander Historiatus: A Guide to Medieval Illustrated Alexander Literature.* London, 1963.

Chapter Bibliographies

Rüdiger, Wilhelm. *Petrus Victorius aus Florenz: Studien zu einem Lebensbilde.* Halle, 1896.

Rypins, Stanley, ed. *Three Old English Prose Texts.* London, 1924.

Sander, M. *Le livre à figures italien depuis 1467 jusqu'à 1530.* Milan, 1942.

Schofield, Margaret, ed. *The Dicts and Sayings of the Philosophers: A Middle English Version by Stephen Scrope.* Philadelphia, 1936.

Sedlar, Jean. *India and the Greek World: An Essay in the Transmission of Ideas.* Forthcoming.

Selincourt, Aubrey de, trans. *Herodotus. The Histories.* Edinburgh, 1960.

Sjöberg, Lars-Olaf. *Stephanites und Ichnelates: Überlieferungsgeschichte und Text.* Stockholm, 1962.

Slepčevič, Pero. *Buddhismus in der deutschen Literatur.* Vienna, 1920.

Sonet, Jean. *Le roman de Barlaam et Josaphat. Recherches sur la tradition manuscrite latine e française.* 2 vols. Louvain, 1949–52.

Stählin, Friedrich. *Humanismus und Reformation im bürgerlichen Raum, eine Untersuchung der biographischen Schriften des Joachim Camerarius.* Leipzig, 1936.

Stein, Otto. *Megasthenes und Kautilya.* Vienna, 1922.

Storost, Joachim. *Studien zur Alexandersage in der älteren italienischen Literatur.* Halle, 1935.

Tawney, C. H., and Penzer, N. M., eds. and trans. *The Ocean of Story: Somadeva's Kathā Sarit Sōgara.* Reprint of the 2d revised and enlarged edition of 1923. 10 vols. Delhi, 1968.

Thomas, Edward, J. *The Life of Buddha as Legend and History.* London, 1931.

Thompson, Stith. *Motif-Index of Folk-Literature.* 6 vols. Helsinki, 1932.

———. *The Folk Tale.* New York, 1946.

Thompson, Stith and Balys, J. *The Oral Tales of India.* Folklore Series No. 10. Bloomington, Ind., 1958.

Thompson, Stith, and Roberts, Warren E. *Types of Indic Oral Tales: India, Pakistan, and Ceylon.* F. F. Communications No. 10. Helsinki, 1960.

Timmer, Barbara C. J. *Megasthenes en de indische Maatschappij.* Amsterdam, 1930.

Urwick, Edward J. *The Message of Plato: A Re-Interpretation of the "Republic."* London, 1920.

Vernero, M. *Studi critici sopra la geografia nell' Orlando Furioso.* Turin, 1913.

Waters, W. G., trans. *The Nights of Straparola.* 2 vols. London, 1894.

Winternitz, Moriz. *History of Sanskrit Literature.* Calcutta, 1927.

Woodward, G. R., and Mattingly, H. *St. John Damascene: Barlaam and Joasaph.* London, 1914.

Yankowski, S. V. *The Brahman Episode.* Ansbach, 1962.

Zacher, Gustav. *Die "Historia Orientalis" des Jacob von Vitry.* Königsberg, 1885.

ARTICLES

Andrée, J. "Vergile et les Indiens." *Revue des études latines,* XXVII (1949), 158–63.

Avery, M. "The Miniatures of the Fables of Bidpai." *Art Bulletin,* XXIII (1941), 103–16.

Becker, H. "Die Brahmanen in der Alexandersage." *Zeitschrift für deutsche Philologie,* XXIII (1891), 424–25.

Benfey, Theodor. "Einige Bermerkungen über das indische Original der zum Kreise der Sieben Weisen Meister gehörigen Schriften." *Mélanges asiatiques* (St. Petersburg Academy of Sciences), VIII (1858), 188–90.

Bertolini, Virginio. "Le carte geografiche nel' 'Filocolo.'" *Studi sul Boccaccio*, V (1969), 211–25.

Bolton, W. F. "Parable, Allegory, and Romance in the Legend of Barlaam and Josaphat." *Traditio*, XIV (1958), 359–66.

Bossuot, R. "Vasque de Lucene, traducteur de Quinte Curce (1468)." *Bibliothèque d'humanisme et renaissance*, VIII (1946), 215–17.

Brincken, Anna-Dorothea v. den. "Die universalhistorischen Vorstellungen der Johann von Marignola OFM, der einzige mittelalterliche Weltchronist mit Fernostkenntnis." *Archiv für Kulturgeschichte*, XLIX (1967), 297–339.

Chalmers, Robert. "The Parables of Barlaam and Josaphat." *Journal of the Royal Asiatic Society*, N.S. XXIII (1891), 423–49.

Conybeare, F. C. "The Barlaam and Josaphat Legend . . .." *Folk-Lore*, VII (1896), 101–42.

Cosquin, Emmanuel Georges. "Les mongols et leur prétendu rôle dans la transmission des contes indiens vers l'Occident européen." *Revue des traditions populaires*, XXVII (1912), 337–73, 393–430, 497–526, 545–66.

———. "La légende des saints Barlaam et Josaphat, sa origine." *Revue des questions historiques*, XXVIII (1880), 579–600.

Crane, Thomas F. "Medieval Sermon-Books and Stories." *Proceedings of the American Philosophical Society*, XXI (1883), 49–78.

D'Ancona, Alessandro. "Le fonti del 'Novellino.'" *Romania*, III (1874), 167–68.

Dawkins, R. M. "The Story of Griselda." *Folk-Lore*, LX (1949), 363–74.

Derrett, J. Duncan M. "The History of Palladius on 'the Races of India and the Brachmans.'" *Classica et mediaevalia*, XXI (1960), 64–135.

———. "Greece and India: The Milindapanha, the Alexanderromance and the Gospels." *Zeitschrift für Religions- und Geistesgeschichte*, XIX (1967), 33–63.

Devos, Paul. "Les origines du 'Barlaam et Joasaph' grec." *Analecta Bollandiana*, LXXV (1957), 83–104.

Dihle, Albrecht. "Indische Philosophen bei Clemens Alexandrinus." In *Mullus. Festschrift Theodor Klauser*, pp. 60–71. Münster, 1964.

Filliozat, Jean. "Les premières étapes de l'indianisme." *Bulletin de l'Association Guillaume Budé*, 3d ser., No. 3 (1953), pp. 80–96.

———. "La doctrine des brâhmanes d'après saint Hippolyte." *Revue de l'histoire des religions*, CXXX (1945), 59–91.

———. "La naissance et l'essor de l'indianisme." *Bulletin de la société des études indochinoises*, N.S. XXIX (1954), 265–96.

Giles, Lionel. "Two Parallel Anecdotes from Greek and Chinese Sources." *Bulletin of the London School of Oriental and African Studies*, II (1922), 609–11.

Goetz, Hermann. "Der Orient der Kreuzzüge in Wolframs Parzival." *Archiv für Kulturgeschichte*, XLIX (1967), 1–42.

Gubernatis, Angelo de. "Le type indien de Lucifer chez le Dante." *Giornale dantesco*, III (1896), 49–58.

Halliday, W. R. "Notes upon Indo-European Folk-Tales and the Problem of Their Diffusion." *Folk-Lore*, XXXIV (1923), 117–40.

Harris, J. Rendell. "The Sources of Barlaam and Joasaph." *John Rylands Library Bulletin* (Manchester), IX (1925), 119–29.

Hartmann, R. "Alexander und der Rätselstein aus dem Paradies." In *Oriental Studies Presented to E. G. Browne*, pp. 179–85. Cambridge, 1922.

Hatto, A. T. "The Elephants in the Strassburg Alexander." *London Medieval Studies*, I (1937–39), 399–429.

Hawickhorst, Horst. Über die Geographie bei Andrea de' Magnabotti." *Romanische Forschungen*, XIII (1902), 689–784.

Hennig, Richard. "Indienfahrten abendländischer Christen im frühen Mittelalter." *Archiv für Kulturgeschichte*, XXV (1935), 277–80.

Hertz, W. "Die Sage von Giftmädchen." *Abhandlungen der philosophisch-philologischen Classe der königlichen bayerischen Akademie der Wissenschaften*, XX (1897), 89–166.

Hilke, A. "Eine lateinische Übersetzung der griechischen Version des Kalila Buchs." *Abhandlungen der Gesellschaft der Wissenschaften zu Göttingen, Phil.-hist. Kl.*, N.S. XXI, No. 3 (1928), 59–166.

Keith, A. B. "Pythagoras and the Doctrine of Transmigration." *Journal of the Royal Asiatic Society*, 1909, pp. 569–79.

Krappe, Alexander H. "The Seven Sages." *Archivum Romanicum*, VIII (1924), 386–407; IX (1925), 345–65; XI (1927), 163–76; XVI (1932), 271–82; XIX (1935), 213–26.

———. "The Indian Provenance of a Medieval Exemplum." *Traditio*, II (1944), 499–502.

Kuhn, Ernest. "Barlaam and Joaseph: Eine bibliographisch-literargeschichtliche Studie." In *Abhandlungen der philosophisch-philologischen Classe der königlichen bayerischen Akademie der Wissenschaften*, XX (1897), 1–88.

Lane, Richard. "Saikaku and Boccaccio: the Novella in Japan and Italy." *Monumenta nipponica*, XV (1959–60), 87–118.

Lang, David Marshall. "The Life of the Blessed Joasaph: A New Oriental Christian Version of the Barlaam and Joasaph Romance." *Bulletin of the School of Oriental and African Studies* (London), XX (1957), 389–407.

Liebrecht, Felix. "Die Quellen des Barlaam und Josaphat." *Jahrbuch für romanische und englische Literatur*, II (1860), 314–34.

Manselli, Raoul. "The Legend of Barlaam and Joasaph in Byzantium and in the [*sic*] Romance Europe." *East and West* (Rome), VII, No. 4 (1957), 331–40.

Martin, W. A. P. "Plato and Confucius: A Curious Coincidence." *Proceedings of the American Oriental Society* in *Journal of the American Oriental Society*, XIV (1890), xxxi–xxxiv.

Meier, F. "Turandot in Persien." *Zeitschrift der deutschen morgenländischen Gesellschaft*, XCV (1941), 1–27.

Meyer, R. W. "Pico della Mirandola und der Orient." *Asiatische Studien*, XVIII–XIX (1965), 308–36.

Müller, Max "On the Migration of Fables." In *Chips from a German Workshop*, IV, pp. 139–80. New York, 1890.

Olschki, Leonardo. "Dante e l'Oriente." *Giornale Dantesco*, XXXIX (1936), 65–90.

————. "I 'Cantari dell'India' di Giuliano Dati," *La bibliofilia*, XL (1938), 289–316.

Padoan, Giorgio. "Petrarca, Boccaccio e la scoperta delle Canarie." *Italia medioevale e umanistica*, VII (1964), 263–77.

Peters, Rudolf. "Über die Geographie im *Guerino Meschino* des Andrea de' Magnabotti." *Romanische Forschungen*, XXII (1906–8), 426–505.

Pfister, Friedrich. "Die Brahmanen in der Alexandersage." *Berliner philologische Wochenschrift*, Vol. XLI (1921), cols. 569–75.

————. "Das Nachleben der Überlieferung von Alexander und den Brahmanen." *Hermes*, LXXVI (1941), 143–69.

Průšek, Jaroslav. "Boccaccio and His Chinese Contemporaries." In *Chinese History and Literature: Collection of Studies*, pp. 449–66. Prague, 1970.

Radcliff-Umstead, D. "Boccaccio's Adaptation of Some Latin Sources for the *Decameron*" *Italica*, XLV (1968), 171–94.

Rawlinson, Hugh G. "India in European Literature and Thought." In G. T. Garratt, ed., *The Legacy of India*, pp. 1–37. Oxford, 1962.

Rintelen, Wolfgang von. "Kult und Legendenwanderung von Ost nach West im frühen Mittelalter." *Saeculum*, I (1971), 71–100.

Robinson, Charles H. "The Extraordinary Ideas of Alexander the Great." *American Historical Review*, LXII (1957), 326–44.

Ruffini, M. "Les sources de Don Juan Manuel." *Les lettres romanes* (Louvain), VII (1953), 37–41.

Schoff, W. H. "Navigation to the Far East under the Roman Empire." *Journal of the American Oriental Society*, XXXVII (1917), 240–49.

Schwarzbaum, H. "International Folklore Motifs in Petrus Alfonsi's *Disciplina clericalis*." *Sefarad*, XXI (1961), 267–99; XXII (1962), 17–59, 321–44; XXIII (1963), 54–73.

Searles, Colbert. "Some Notes on Boiardo's Version of the Alexandersagas." *Modern Language Notes*, XV (1900), 45–48.

Stankiewicz, E. "The Legend of Opulent India, Marin Držić, and South Slavic Folk Poetry." In *Languages and Areas: Studies Presented to George V. Bobrinskoy . . .*, pp. 161–67. Chicago, 1967.

Thorley, J. "The Silk Trade between China and the Roman Empire at Its Height, *circa* A.D. 90–130." *Greece and Rome*. N.S., 1971, pp. 71–80.

Viksit S. K. "Was the Bhagavad-Gītā Known to Megasthenes?" *Annals of the Bhandarkar Oriental Research Institute* (Poona), XXX (1949), 296–99.

White, Lynn, Jr. "Medieval Borrowings from Further Asia." *Medieval and Renaissance Studies*, No. 5 (1974), pp. 3–26.

Wilcken, Ulrich. "Alexander der Grosse und die indischen Gymnosophisten." *Sitzungsberichte der preussischen Akademie der Wissenschaft, Phil.-Hist. Kl.* (Berlin), 1923–24, pp. 150–83.

Wittkower, Rudolf. "Marvels of the East." *Journal of the Warburg Institute*, V (1942), 157–97.

Wolf, Werner. "Der Vogel Phönix und der Gral." In *Studien zur deutschen Philologie des Mittelalters, Friedrich Panzer zum 80. Geburtstag dargebracht*, pp. 730–95. Heidelberg, 1950.

Abraham, Richard D. "A Portuguese Version of the Life of Barlaam and Josephat." Ph.D. diss., University of Pennsylvania, 1938.

Adamson, John, ed. *Memoirs of the Life and Writings of Luis de Camoens.* 2 vols. London, 1820.

Agostinho, Nicolau. *Relação summária da vida do Illustríssimo e Reverendíssimo Senhor D. Teotónio de Bragança, quarto Arcebispo de Évora.* Évora, 1614.

Albrecht, Johannes. *Beiträge zur Geschichte der portugiesischen Historiographie des sechszehnten Jahrhunderts.* Halle a.S., 1915.

Amezúa, Agustín G. de, ed. See Torquemada, Antonio de.

Andrade, Francisco de. *O primeiro cêrco de Diu: poema épico.* Coimbra, 1589. Reprinted in *Biblioteca portuguêsa.* Lisbon, 1852.

Andrade Caminha, Pêro de. *Poesias inéditas de P. de Andrade Caminha publicadas pelo Dr. J. Priebisch.* Halle, 1898.

Anselmo, António Joaquim. *Bibliografia das obras impressas em Portugal no século XVI.* Lisbon, 1926.

Aquarone, J. B. D. *João de Castro, gouverneur et viceroi des Indes orientales (1500–1548).* 2 vols. Paris, 1968.

Asensio, Eugenio, ed. *Jorge Ferreira de Vasconcelos: Comedia* Eufrosina. Madrid, 1951.

Atkinson, William C., trans. See Camões, Luis de.

Baião, António. *História quinhentista (inédita) do segundo cêrco de Diu.* Coimbra, 1925.

Barata, Antonio Francisco. *Subsidios para a biographia do poeta Jeronymo Côrte Real.* Évora, 1899.

Barros, João de. *Dialogo em louvor de nossa linguagem letture critica dell'edizione del 1540 con una introduzione su la question delle lingua in Portogallo.* Edited by Luciana Stegagno Picchio. Modena, 1959.

———. *Asia de João de Barros dos feitos que os portugueses fizeram no descobrimento e conquista dos mares e terras do Oriente. Actualizada no ortografia e anotada por Hernani Cidade; Notas históricas finais por Manuel Murias.* 6th ed. 4 vols. Lisbon, 1945–46.

———. *Panegíricos.* Edited by Manuel Rodrigues Lapa. Lisbon, 1943.

———. *Compilação de varias obras do insigne Portuguez João de Barros. Contem a Ropica Pnefma, e o Dialogo com dous filhos seus sobre preceitos moraes. Serve de segunda parte á Compilação que de outros opusculos do mesmo auctor fizeram imprimir em Lisboa no anno de 1785 os monges de Evora. Feita esta reimpressão por diligências e cuidado do Viconde de Azevedo.* Porto, 1869.

———. *Crónica do Imperador Clarimundo com prefácio et notas do Prof. Marques Braga.* 3 vols. Lisbon, 1953.

Bataillon, Marcel. *Études sur le Portugal au temps de l'humanisme.* Coimbra, 1952.

Batllori, Miguel, and Garcia-Villoslada, R. *Il pensiero della rinascenza in Spagna e Portogallo.* Milan, 1964.

Beau, Albin Eduard. *Die Entwicklung des portugiesischen Nationalbewusstseins.* Hamburg, 1945.

Chapter IV

Bell, Aubrey F. G. *Studies in Portuguese Literature*. Oxford, 1914.

————. *Gaspar Correa*. Oxford, 1924.

————. *Luis de Camoens*. Oxford, 1923.

————. *Gil Vicente*. London, 1921.

————. *Un humanista Português: Damião de Góis*. Translated from English by A. A. Doria. Lisbon, 1942.

————. *Four Plays of Gil Vicente*. Edited from the *editio princeps* (1562), with translation and notes. Cambridge, 1920.

————. *Diogo do Couto*. London, 1924.

————. *Portuguese Literature*. Rev. ed. Oxford, 1970.

————. *Lyrics of Gil Vicente*. 2d ed. Oxford, 1921.

Bernardes, Diogo. *Obras completas com prefácio e notas do Prof. Marques Braga*. 3 vols. Lisbon, 1945–46.

Betencourt, J. Barbosa de. *História comparativa da literatura Portuguêsa*. Paris, 1923.

Bourdon, Leon. *Jeronimo Osorio et Stanislas Hosius d'après leur correspondance (1565–78)*. Coimbra, 1956.

————. *Autour de la controverse Jeronimo Osorio–Walter Haddon*. Coimbra, 1957.

Bowra, Cecil M. *From Virgil to Milton*. London, 1963.

Boxer, Charles R., trans. and ed. *The Tragic History of the Sea, 1589–1622*. "Hakluyt Society Publications," 2d ser. No. 112. Cambridge, 1959.

————, trans. and ed. *Further Selections from the Tragic History of the Sea, 1559–1565*. "Hakluyt Society Publications," 2d ser. No. 132. Cambridge, 1968.

Braga, Marques, ed. See Barros, João de; Bernardes, Diogo; Ferreira, Antonio; Vicente, Gil.

Braga, Téofilo. *História das novelas portuguêsas de cavalaria*. Porto, 1873.

————. *Bibliografia Camoniana*. Lisbon, 1880.

————. *História de Camões*. 2 vols. Porto, 1873.

————. *História da litteratura portugueza*. Vol. II. Porto, 1914.

————. *Sá de Miranda e a eschola italiana*. Porto, 1896.

————. *História dos quinhentistas. Vida de Sá de Miranda e sua eschola*. Porto, 1871.

————. *Gil Vicente e as origens do teatro naçional*. Porto, 1898.

————, ed. *Romanceiro geral português*. 3 vols. Lisbon, 1906–9.

Camões, Luis de. *Obras completas de Camões*. Edited by Hernani Cidade. 5 vols. Lisbon, 1946–47.

————. *The Lusiads*. Translated by William C. Atkinson. Harmondsworth, Middlesex, 1952.

Carvalho, Joaquim de. *Estudos sobre a cultura Portuguesa do século XVI*. 2 vols. Coimbra, 1947–48.

Carvalho, Joaquim Barradas de. *As fontes de Duarte Pacheco Pereira no "Esmeraldo de situ orbis."* São Paulo, 1967.

Casimiro, Augusto, ed. and trans. *D. Teodósio II, Segunda o codice 51–111–30 da Biblioteca da Ajuda*. Porto, 1944.

Chapter Bibliographies

Castilho, A. Feliciano de. *Notícia da vida e obras de Garcia de Resende.* Lisbon, 1845.

Castilho, António. *Commentario do cêrco de Goa e Chaul no anno MDLXX.* Lisbon, 1573.

Castilho, Julio, Visconde de. *Antonio Ferreira, poeta quinhentista.* 3 vols. Rio de Janeiro, 1875.

————. *Indices do Cancioneiro de Resende e das obras de Gil Vicente.* Lisbon, 1900.

Castro Azevedo, Luisa M. de. *Bibliografia Vicentina.* Lisbon, 1942.

Castro Osório ,João de. *O além-mar na literatura portuguêsa (Época dos descobrimentos).* Lisbon, 1948.

———— (comp.). *Cancioneiro de Lisboa, séculos XII–XX.* 2 vols. in 1. Lisbon, 1956.

Cidade, Hernani, ed. *Luís de Camões, Obras completas.* 3d ed. 5 vols. Lisbon, 1962.

————. *A literatura portuguêsa e a expansão ultramarina. As ideias, os factos, as formas de arte.* 2 vols. 2d ed. Coimbra, 1963–64.

————. *História da expansão portuguesa no mundo.* Lisbon, 1937.

Cidade, H., and Murias, M., eds. See Barros, João de.

Coelho, Adolfo. *Bibliografia critica de história e literatura comparanda.* 2 vols. Porto, 1873–75.

Correia, Maximino. *Sobre a medicina dos Lusíadas.* Lisbon, 1920.

Côrte Real, Jerónimo. *Sucessos do segundo cêrco de Dio.* Lisbon, 1574.

Corte Real, João Alfonso. *Estelas indianas em Sintra.* Lisbon, 1942.

Cortesão, Jaime. *Camões e o descobrimento do mundo.* Lisbon, 1944.

————. *L'expansion des Portugais dans l'histoire de la civilisation.* Lisbon-Brussels, 1930.

Cortez Pinto, Américo. *Da famosa arte da imprimissão.* Lisbon, 1948.

Costa, Joaquim. *Antonio Galvão, a "Apóstulo das Molucas."* Lisbon, 1943.

Coutinho, Carlos V. Gago. *O roteiro da viagem de Vasco da Gama e a sua versão nos Lusíadas.* Lisbon, 1930.

Crabbe Rocha, André de. *Aspectos do Cancioneiro Geral.* Coimbra, 1950.

Crespo, Firnino. *André de Resende, humanista e poeta latino e sue participação no movimento cultural português do século XVI.* Lisbon, 1934.

Dalgado, Sebastião Rodolpho. *Florilegio da provérbios Concanis . . .* Coimbra, 1922.

Denis, Ferdinand. *Résumé d'histoire littéraire du Portugal.* Paris, 1826.

————. *Scènes de la nature sous les tropiques et de leurs influences sur la poesie; suivies de Camoens Jozé Indio.* Paris, 1824.

Dias, José Sebastião da Silva. *A politica cultural da época de D. João III.* 2 vols. Coimbra, 1969.

Duffy, James. *Shipwreck and Empire.* Cambridge, Mass., 1955.

Fernandez Almazara, Eugenio. *Relaçiones de la épica de Lope de Vega y la de Camões.* Coimbra, 1936.

Ferreira, Antonio. *Poemas lusitanas.* Edited by Marques Braga. 2 vols. Lisbon, 1939–40.

Ferreira, Joaquim, ed. *Da vida e feitos de El-Rei D. Manuel [Osório].* 2 vols. Porto, 1944.

Ficalho, Conde de. *Flora dos Lusíadas.* Lisbon, 1880.

Figueiredo, A. C. Borges de. *A geografia dos Lusíadas.* Lisbon, 1883.

Figueiredo, Fidelino de. *A épica portuguesa no século XVI.* Madrid, 1931.

————. *História literaria de Portugal.* Coimbra, 1944.

Chapter IV

Ford, J. D. M., ed. *Os Lusíadas*. Cambridge, Mass., 1946.

Forjaz de Sampaio, Albino. *História da literatura portuguesa*. 4 vols. Paris, n.d.

Frèches, Claude-Henri. *Introdução ao teatro de Simão Machado*. Lisbon, 1971.

Freire, Anselmo Braamcamp. *Crítica e história*. Lisbon, 1910.

———. *Vida e obras de Gil Vicente*. 2d ed. Lisbon, 1944.

Freire de Andrada, Jacinto. *Vida de Dom João de Castro Quarto Vice-Rei da India*. Lisbon, 1940.

Freitas, Jordão de. *Subsidios para a bibliographia portugueza relativa ao estudo da Lingua Japoneza e para a biographia de Fernão Mendes Pinto*. Coimbra, 1905.

Freitas, William. *Camoëns and His Epic: A Historic, Geographic, and Cultural Survey*. Stanford, 1963.

Gaspar Simoẽs, João. *Itinerário histórico da poesia portuguesa de 1189–1964*. Lisbon, 1964.

———. *História do romance português*. Lisbon, 1967.

Gibb, James, trans. *The History of the Portuguese People*. 2 vols. London, 1752. See Osório.

Góis, Damião de. *Commentarii rerum gestarum in India citra Gangem a Lusitanis anno 1538. . . .* Louvain, 1539.

———. *De bello Cambaico ultimo comment*. Louvain, 1548.

———. *De rebus aethiopicis, indicis, lusitanicis, et hispanicio, opuscula etc. . . .* Cologne, 1574.

———. *Chronica do felicissimo rei Dom Emanuel*. Lisbon, 1566. Modern edition by David Lopes. 4 vols. Coimbra, 1943–55.

———. *Opúsculos históricos*. Translated from the original Latin by Dias de Carvalho. Porto, 1945.

Gomes de Brito, Bernardo, comp. *História Tragico-Maritima em que se escrevem cronolōgicamente os naufrágios que tiveram as naus de Portugal. . . .* 2 vols. Lisbon, 1735–36.

Gonçalves, António Manuel. *A custódia de Belém*. Lisbon, 1958.

Govea, Antoine. *Histoire orientale, de grans progres de l'eglise Catholique, Apostolique, & Roman en la reduction des anciens Chrestiens, dits de S. Thomas, de plusiers autres Schismatiques & Heretiques a l'vnion de la vraye Eglise. Conuersion encor les Mahometains, Mores & Payens. Par les bons deuoirs du Rᵐᵉ. Sr. Dom Alexis de Meneses, de l'Ordre des Eremites de S. Augustin, Archevesque de Goa, & Primat en tout l'Orient. Composée en langue portugaise par R. P. F. Antoine Gouea, & puis mise en espagnol par venerable P. F. Francois Munoz, & tournée en françois par F. Jean Baptiste de Glen. Docteur en Théologie, tous Religieux de mesme Ordre*. Antwerp, 1609.

Guimarães, A. J. Gonçalves, ed. See Resende, Garcia de.

Hart, Henry H. *Luis de Camoëns and the Epic of the Lusiads*. Norman, Okla., 1962.

Henry, William J. C., ed. *Inéditos Goesianos*. 2 vols. Lisbon, 1896–99.

Herculano de Moura, João. *Inscripções indianas em Sintra*. Lisbon, 1891.

Hirsch, Elizabeth F. *Damião de Góis: The Life and Thought of a Portuguese Humanist. 1502–1574*. The Hague, 1967.

Keates, Laurence. *The Court Theatre of Gil Vicente*. Lisbon, 1962.

Lapa, Manuel Rodrigues. *Historiadores quinhentistas*. Lisbon, 1943.

———, ed. See Barros, João de.

Le Gentil, Georges. *La littérature portugaise*. Paris, 1935.

————. *Camoëns, l'oeuvre épique et lyrique.* Paris, 1954.

————. *Fernao Mendes Pinto, un precurseur de l'éxotisme au XVIe siècle.* Paris, 1947.

————. *Tragiques histoires du mer au XVIe siècle, récits portugais.* Paris, 1939.

Leitão Ferreira, F. *Notícias de André de Resende.* Lisbon, 1916.

Lemos, Jorge de. *Hystória dos cêrcos qve em tempo de Antonio Monis Barreto governador que foi dos estados da India, os Achens, & Iaos puserão â fortaleza de Malaca, sendo Tristão Vaz de Veiga capitão della. Breuemente composta por Iorge de Lemos.* Lisbon, 1585.

Lopes de Castanheda, Fernão. *História do descobrimento e conquista da India pelos portugueses.* 3d ed. Edited by Pedro de Azevedo. 4 vols. Coimbra, 1924.

Machado, Roque. *Vasco da Gama nos Lusíadas.* Lisbon, 1936.

————. *A flora da India nos Lusíadas.* Lisbon, 1947.

Machado, Simão. *Comedias portuguesas.* . . . Lisbon, 1601.

Manuel II. *Livros antiquos portugueses.* 3 vols. London, 1921.

Martin, Mário. *Vide e obra de Frei João Claro (c. 1520) Doctor Parisiensis e Professor Universitário.* Coimbra, 1956.

Martins, Cristiano. *Camões: temas e motivos da obra lirica.* Rio de Janiero, 1944.

Matos, Luís de. *A corte literária dos duques de Bragança no Renascimento.* Lisbon, 1956.

Menendez Pelayo, M. *Historia de las ideas estéticas en España.* Santander, 1940.

Moisés, Massaud. *A novela da cavalaria no quinhentismo Português.* "Boletim da faculdade. de filosofia, çiencias e letras (Literatura portuguesa series)," No. 13. São Paulo, 1957.

————, et al. *Bibliografia da literatura portuguêsa.* São Paulo, 1968.

Moldenhauer Gerardo. *Die Legende von Barlaam und Josaphat auf der iberischen Halbinsel.* Halle, 1929.

Monçon, Francisco de. *Libro primero del espejo del principe Christiano.* Lisbon, 1571.

Mustard, Wilfred P., ed. *The Eclogues of Henrique Caiado.* Baltimore, 1931.

Noronha, Tito de. *Autos de Antonio Prestes.* Porto, 1871.

————. *O Cancioneiro geral de Garcia de Rezende.* Porto, 1871.

Nykl, Alois R. *Algumas observações sôbre as linguas citadas na "Peregrinacam" de Fernam Mendes Pinto.* Lisbon, 1941.

Oliveira, Fernão. *Arte da guerra no mar.* Coimbra, 1555.

Oliveira Marques, A. H. de. *Daily Life in Portugal in the Late Middle Ages.* Madison, Wis., 1971.

Osório da Fonseca, Jerónimo. *Histoire de Portugal, contenant les entreprises, navigations et gestes memorables des portugallois, tout en la côqueste des Indes Orientales par eux descouvertes qu' és guerres d'Afrique et autres exploits depuis l'an [1496] jusques [1578].* Paris, 1581.

————. *The History of the Portuguese during the Reign of Emmanuel.* Translated into English by James Gibb. 2 vols. London, 1752.

————. *Da vida e feitos de el-rei D. Manuel. XII livros.* Translated by Francisco Manuel do Nascimento. 2 vols. Porto, 1944.

Parker, Jack H. *Gil Vicente,* New York, 1967.

Peixoto, Afránio. *Dicionário dos Lusíadas.* Rio de Janeiro, 1924.

Pereira, Gabriel. *Estudos eborenses, história e arquelogia.* 3 vols. Évora, 1947–50.

———. *Documentos históricos da cidade de Évora.* Évora, 1885.

Peres, Damião, ed. *História Trágico-Maritima.* 6 vols. Porto, 1942–43.

Pereyra, Carlos. *Monardes y el exotismo medico en el siglo XVI.* Madrid, 1936.

Pimenta, A. *Dom João III.* Porto, 1936.

Pimpão, Alvaro Julio da Costa. *Poetas do Cancioneiro Geral.* Lisbon, 1942.

Portugal. Junta de investigações do ultramar. *Colóquio sobre a influencia do ultramar na arte.* "Estudo de çiências politicas e sociais," No. 76. Lisbon, 1965.

Prescott, William H. *History of the Reign of Philip II King of Spain.* 2 vols. Boston, 1855–59.

Prestage, Edgar, ed. *Crítica contemporanea à chronica de D. Manuel de Damião de Goes. MS. do Museu Britanico.* Lisbon, 1914.

———. *Minor Works of Camões—Not Hitherto Made English.* London, 1924.

Priebisch, J. ed. See Andrade Caminha, Pêro de.

Ramos, Feliciano Ferreira. *História da literatura portuguesa desde o século XII aos meados do século XX.* 4th ed. Braga, 1960.

Ramos, Vitor, ed. *Os Lusíadas.* São Paulo, 1966.

Rau, Virgínia. *Estudos de história.* Lisbon, 1968.

Rêgo, Paul, ed. *O processo de Damião de Goes na Inquisição.* [Lisbon], [1971].

Remedios, Mendes dos, ed. See Resende, Garcia de.

Resende, Andre de. *Obras portuguesas.* Edited by José Pereira Tavares. Lisbon, 1963.

Resende, Garcia de. *Cancioneiro geral.* Edited by A. J. Gonçalvez Guimarães. 5 vols. Coimbra, 1910–17.

———. *Miscellanea e variedade de histórias, costumes, casos, e cousas que em seu tempo aconteceram.* Edited by Mendes dos Remedios. Coimbra, 1917.

Révah, I. S. *La censure inquisitoriale portugaise au XVIe siècle.* Lisbon, 1960.

———, ed. *Rópica Pnefma.* 2 vols. Lisbon, 1952.

Reyes, Antonio dos, ed. *Corpus illustrium poetarum lusitanorum.* 7 vols. Lisbon, 1745–48.

Rodrigues, Francisco. *História da Companhia de Jesus na Assistência de Portugal.* 4 vols. in 7 parts. Porto, 1931–50.

Rodríguez-Moñino, Antonio R. *Viaje a Oriente de Fray Antonio de Lisboa (1507).* Badajoz, 1949.

———. *Fray Diego de Mérida, jerónimo de Guadalupe, "Viaje a Oriente" (1512).* Barcelona, 1946.

Rossi, Giuseppe C. *A poesia épica italiana do século XVI na literatura portuguesa.* Lisbon, 1945.

———. *La letteratura italiana e le letterature di lingua portoghese.* Turin, 1967.

———. *Storia della lettaratura portoghese.* Florence, 1953.

Rüegg, August. *Luis de Camões und Portugals Glanzzeit im Spiegel seines Nationalepos.* Basel, 1925.

Sá de Miranda, Francisco de. *Poesias.* Edited by C. Michaëlis de Vasconcellos. Halle, 1885.

———. *Obras completas.* Edited by Rodrigues Lapa. 2 vols. Lisbon, 1942–43.

Salgado, Antonio, Jr. *Os Lusíadas e a viagem de Gama. O tratemento mitológico de uma realidade histórica*. Porto, 1939.

Saraiva, António Jose. *Luis de Camões*. Lisbon, 1960.

——. *Gil Vicente e o fim do teatro medieval*. 3d ed. Lisbon, 1907.

Schneider, Reinhold. *Das Leiden des Camoes oder Untergang und Vollendung der portugiesischen Macht*. 2d ed. Cologne, 1957.

Scudieri-Ruggieri, Jole. *Il Canzoniere di Resende*. Geneva, 1931.

Sérgio, António, ed. *História Trágico-Marítima*. 3 vols. Lisbon, 1955–56.

Serrão, Joel. *Dicionário de história de Portugal*. 4 vols. Lisbon, 1960–69.

Silva, Pereira da. *A astronomia dos Lusíadas*. Lisbon, 1918.

Silva Dias, J. S. da. *A política cultural da época de D. João III*. 2 vols. Coimbra, 1969.

Simões, João Gaspar. *História do romance portugûes*. Lisbon, 1967.

——. *História da poesia portuguesa das origens aos nossos dias*. 3 vols. Lisbon, 1955–59.

Soares Amora, A., *et al.*, eds. *Os Lusíadas*. Edition monumental. São Paulo, 1956.

Sousa Coutinho, Lopo de. *Livro primeyro do cerco de Diu, que os Turcos poseram a fortaleza de Diu*. Lisbon, 1556.

——. *História do cerco de Dio*. Coimbra, 1556.

Sousa de Macedo, Antonio de. *Flores de España, excelencias de Portugal*. . . . Lisbon, 1631.

Sousa Viterbo, Francisco Marques de. *Trabalhos náuticos dos portugueses nos séculos XVI e XVII*. 2 vols. Lisbon, 1898–1900.

——. *Curiosidades históricas e artisticas*. Coimbra, 1919.

Stegagno Picchio, Luciana, ed. See Barros, João de.

——. *Storia del teatro portoghese*. Rome, 1964.

Stegmüller, Friedrich. *Filosofia e teologia nas universidades de Coimbra e Évora no século XVI*. Coimbra, 1959.

Storck, Friedrich Wilhelm Paul. *Vida e obras de Luis de Camões*. Translated and annotated by C. M. de Vasconcelos. Lisbon, 1897.

Tavares, José Pereira, ed. See Resende, André de.

Teive (Tevius), Diogo de. *Commentarius de rebus in India apud Dium gestis anno salutis nostri MDXLI*. Coimbra, 1548. Reprinted in *Jacobi Tevii, Bracarensis, Opuscula, quibus accessit commentarius de rebus ad Dium gestis, denuò in lucem edi curavit Joseph Caietanus Mesquita, Lusitanus, Parisiis, ecudebat Franc. Ambr. Didot, 1762*. Paris, 1762.

Teyssier, Paul. *Simão Machado. Comédia de Dio. Édition critique, introduction et commentaire*. Rome, 1969.

——. *La langue de Gil Vicente*. Paris, 1959.

Theal, George McCall. *Records of South-Eastern Africa*. 9 vols. London, 1898–1903.

Tom, Henry Y. K. "The Wonderful Voyage: Chivalric and Moral Asia in the Imaginations of Sixteenth-Century Italy, Spain, and Portugal." Ph.D. diss., Department of History, University of Chicago, 1975.

Torquemada, Antonio de. *Jardín de flores curiosas (Lérida, 1573)*. Edited by Agustin G. de Amezúa. Madrid, 1955.

Valbuena Prat, Angel. *El teatro español en su siglo de Oro*. Barcelona, 1969.

Chapter IV

Vasconcellos-Abreu, Guilherme de. *Os contos apologos e fábulas da India: influência indirecta no Auto da Mofina Méndez, de Gil Vicente.* Lisbon, 1902.

Vasconcelos, C. Michaëlis de, ed. *Sá de Miranda. Poesias.* Halle, 1885.

————. *Vida e obras de Luís de Camões. Primiera Parte,* Lisbon, 1898.

Vasconcelos, José Augusto do Amaral Frazão de. *Naufrágio da nao 'S. Paulo' em um ilheu próximo de Sumatra no ano de 1561. Narração inédita, escrita em Goa em 1562 pelo Padre Manuel Alvares, S.J.* Lisbon, 1948.

Veríssimo Serrão, Joaquim. *História breva da históriografia portuguesa.* Lisbon, 1962.

Vicente, Gil. *Obras completas.* Edited by Marques Braga. 4th ed. 6 vols. Lisbon, 1968.

————. *Farsa de Ines Pereira.* Porto, 1941.

Vindel, Pedro. *Biblioteca oriental. Comprende 2,747 obras relativas à Filipinas, Japón, China y otras partes de Asia y Océano.* . . . 2 vols. in 1. Madrid, 1911–12.

————. *Biblioteca ultramarina . . . referentes a América, China, Japón.* . . . Madrid, 1917.

ARTICLES

Almeida, F. Vieira de. "Le théâtre de Camões dans l'histoire du théâtre portugais." *Bulletin d'histoire du théâtre portugais,* I, Pt. 2 (1950), 250–66.

Alves, Paulo Durão. "Significado histórico-cultural da Universidade de Évora." *A Cidade de Évora,* XVI, Nos. 41–42 (January–December, 1959), 17–27.

Asensio, Eugenio. "El teatro de Antônio Prestes." *Bulletin d'histoire du théâtre portugais,* V (1954), Pt. I, 89–145.

Atkinson, William C. "Comedias, tragicomedias and farças in Gil Vicente." In *Miscelânea de filologia, literatura e história cultural a memória de Francisco Adolfo Coelho (1847–1919),* II, 268–80. Lisbon, 1950.

Ayres, Christovam. "Fernão Mendes Pinto e o Japão." *História e memórias da Academia Real das Sciências de Lisboa, Classe de Sciências Moraes.* N.S. X, Pt. II. Lisbon, 1906.

Azevedo, N. de. "O Chi-King [of Confucius] e os Cancioneiros medievais." In *A arte literária na idade média,* pp. 115–44. Porto, 1947.

Bataillon, Marcel. "Erasme et la cour de Portugal." *Arquivo de história e bibliografia,* II (1927), 258–91.

Bell, Aubrey F. G. "The Humanist Jeronymo de Osorio." *Revue hispanique,* LXXIII (1928), 525–56.

Blanc, José. "Influência do ultramar na dança." In *Colóquio sobre a influência do ultramar na arte,* pp. 105–20. "Junta de investigacões do ultramar," No. 76. Lisbon, 1965.

Bossuat, R. "Vasque de Lucène, traducteur de Quinte-Curce (1468)." *Bibliothèque d'humanisme et renaissance,* VIII (1946), 197–245.

Bourdon, Léon. "Le voyage de Jerónimo Osório, éveque de Silves, en Italie (1576–77)." *Annales publiées par la faculté des lettres de Toulouse,* I (1951), 71–85.

————. "Rites et jeux sacrés de la mission japonaise des Jésuites vers 1560–1565." In *Miscelânea . . . Francisco Adolfo Coelho,* II (1950), 320–27.

Boxer, Charles R. "Three Historians of Portuguese Asia." In *Istituto português de Hongkong, Secção de História,* pp. 1–30. Macao, 1948.

————. "Was Camoëns Ever in Macau?" *T'ien Hsia Monthly,* X (1940), 324–33.

[613]

————. "Portuguese and Spanish Projects for the Conquest of Southeast Asia, 1580–1600." *Journal of Asian History*, III (1969), 118–36.

————. "An Introduction to the *História Trágico-Máritima*." In *Miscelânea de estudos em honra do Professór Hernâni Cidade*, pp. 48–99. Lisbon, 1957.

Calado, Adelino de Almeida. "Livro que trata das cousas da India e do Japão." *Boletim da biblioteca da universidade de Coimbra*, XXIV (1960), 1–138.

Camara Ficalho, Madalena da. "João de Barros-históriador do império." *Congresso do mundo portugues, Publicações* (Lisbon, 1940), V, 383–96.

Cardozo, Manoel. "The Idea of History in the Portuguese Chroniclers of the Age of Discovery." *Catholic Historical Review*, XLIX (1963), 1–19.

Castelo-Branco, Maria. "Significado do cómico do 'Auto da India.'" *Ocidente*, LXX (1966), 129–36.

Castro Osório, João de. "Estudos sobre o Renascimento Portugues, o testemunho de Garcia de Resende." *Ocidente*, LXV (1963), 33–48, 49–63.

Chaves, Luis. "As tradições e lendas portuguesas de S. Francisco Xavier." *Archivum historicum Societatis Jesu*, III (1953), 94–106.

Cidade, Hernani. "Camões e a India." *Ocidente*, XLII (1952), 225–28.

————. "Devidas de Camões a poesia espanhola." In *Homentage a Antoni Rubio*, III, 387–408. Barcelona, 1936.

————. "Os portugueses no Renascimento. Sua contribuição para a mundividência quinhentista." *Proceedings of the International Colloquium on Luso-Brazilian Studies* (Nashville, Tenn., 1953), pp. 133–48.

————. "João de Barros. O que pensa da língua portuguesa-Como a escreve." In *Miscelânea de filologia, literatura e história cultural a memória de Francisco Adolfo Coelho (1847–1919)*, II, 281–303. Lisbon, 1950.

Costa, António Domingues de Sousa. "A expansão portuguesa a luz do direito." *Revista da universidade de Coimbra*, XX (1962), 1–243.

Ducarme, P. "Les Autos de Gil Vicente." *Le Muséon*, V (1885), 369–74, 649–56; VI (1886), 120–30, 155–62.

Entwhistle, William J. "The 'Lusiads', da Gama and Modern Criticism." In *Lusitania*, Vol. IV, fasc. 10. Lisbon, 1927.

Esteves Pereira, Francisco Maria. "A História de Barlaam e Josaphat en Portugal." *Boletim de segunda classe da Academia das Sciênçias de Lisboa*, X (1916), 350–68.

Faria, J. de. "O teatro escolar dos séculos XVI, XVII, e XVIII." In *A evolução e o espirito de teatro em Portugal*, I, 255–78. Lisbon, 1948.

Faria, Manuel Severim de. "Vida de João de Barros." In *Discursos varios politicos*, pp. 22–59. Évora, 1924.

Figueiredo, Fidelino de "Camões as an Epic Poet." *Romanic Review*, XIII (1926), 217–29.

————. "Camões as Lyric Poet." *Romanic Review*, XVI (1925), 287–305.

————. "O teatro primitivo e os descobrimentos." In *A épica portuguesa no Séc. XVI*, pp. 117–44. "Bol. da Faculdade de filosofia, ciências e letras," No. 101, Letras, No. 6. São Paulo, 1950.

————. "The Geographical Discoveries and Conquests of the Portuguese." *Hispanic American Historical Review*, VI (1926), 47–70.

Chapter IV

——. "De re japonica:Evolução do japonismo literário português desde Fernão Mendes Pinto a Wenceslau de Morais." *Vasco da Gama*, I (1925–26), 202–19.

——. "Garcia de Resende." In *Crítica do exílio*, pp. 77–154. Lisbon, 1930.

——. "Camoẽs e Lope." *Revue de littérature comparée*, XVIII (1938), 160–70.

Fitzler, Hedwig M. A. Kömmerling. "Fünf Jahrhunderte portugiesischen Kolonial-geschichtsschreibung." *Die Welt als Geschichte*, VII (1941), 101–23; VIII (1942) 97–121, 331–58.

Frèches, Claude-Henri. "Les 'Comédias' de Simão Machado: I. Comédia do Cêrco de Dio. II. Comédias da Pastora Alfea." *Bulletin d'histoire du théâtre portugais* (Lisbon), II (1951), Pt. II, 151–80; III (1952), Pt. I, 1–42.

——. "Gil Vicente. Les Indes. Avant-propos." *Bulletin des études portugaises de l'Institut français au Portugal* (Coimbra), XIX (1955–56), 141–57.

Freire, Natércia. "Influência do ultramar na poesia." In *Colóquio sobre a influência do ultramar na arte*, pp. 123–69. Lisbon, 1965.

Guy, Alain. "L' 'homo novus' du Portugal au XVIᵉ siècle," *Congresso internacional de história dos descobrimentos. Actas*, IV (1960), 225–39.

Hooykaas, R. "The Impact of the Voyages of Discovery on Portuguese Humanist Literature." *Revista da universidade de Coimbra*, XXIV (1971), 551–66.

Janeiro, Armando Martins. "O teatro de Gil Vicente e o teatro clássico japonês." *Boletim da sociedade de geografia de Lisboa*, LXXXIV (1966), 323–58.

Macgregor, I. A. "Some Aspects of Portuguese Historical Writings of the Sixteenth and Seventeenth Centuries on South East Asia." In D. G. A. Hall, ed., *Historians of South East Asia*, pp. 172–199. London, 1961.

Machado, José Pedro. "Versão desconhecida de uma carta de João de Barros (1531)." *Revista de Portugal*, XXIX (1964), 175–83.

Matos, Luís de. "Das relações entre Erasmo e os Portugueses." *Boletim internacional de bibliografia luso-brasileira*, IV (1963), 241–51.

——. "O humanista Diogo de Teive." *Revista da universidade de Coimbra*, XIII (1937), 215–70.

Maurício, Domingos. "Os Jesuitas e a filosofia portuguêsa do séc. XVI–XVIII." *Brotéria*, XXI (1935), 257–66, 310–29; XXII (1936), 395–410.

Moser, Gerald M. "A 16th Century Portuguese Finds Korea Fascinating." *Korean Report*, II (1962), 13–16.

——. "A volta do marido [on the theme of the 'Auto da India' of Gil Vicente]." *Vértice*, XXV (1965), 795–98.

Peixoto da Fonseca, F. V. V. "Les chroniques portugaises des *Portugaliae Monumenta Historica*." *Revue des langues romanes*, LXXVII (1967), 55–84.

Post, H. H. "Une source peu connue des 'Lusiades,'" *Boletim de filologia*, XIX (1960), 77–93.

Quilinan, E. "The Autos of Gil Vicente." *Quarterly Review*, LXXIX (1845), 168–202.

Randles, W. G. L. "Quelques modifications apportées par les grandes découvertes à la conception médiévale du monde." *Revista da Faculdade de Letras* (de Lisboa), 3d ser., No. 3 (1959), pp. 66–88.

——. "Le nouveau monde, l'autre monde, et la pluralité des mondes." In International

Chapter Bibliographies

Congress for the History of the Discoveries, *Resumo dos comunicações*, pp. 162–63. Lisbon, 1960.

Reali, Erilde M. "Note sull'esotismo linguistico nella 'Peregrinacão' di Fernão Mendes Pinto." *Annali della sezione romanza dell'istituto universitario orientale* (Naples), XI (1969), 225–33.

Révah, I. S. "'Antiquité et christianisme,' 'Anciens et Modernes,' dans l'oeuvre de João de Barros." *Revue philosophique de la France et de l'étranger*, CLVII (1967), 165–85.

Ribeiro, Luciano. "Em torno do primeiro cerco de Diu." *Studia* (Lisbon), XIII–XIV (1964), 41–104.

Rodrigues, José Maria. "Fontes dos Lusíadas." *O Istituto*, LI (1904), 754–61; LII (1905), 56–62, 183–92, 357–66, 426–36, 627–40, 757–64; LIII (1906), 54–61, 171–80, 228–36, LIV (1907), 298–312, 355–63, 436–48, 498–512, 552–66, 621–34, 709–21; LV (1908), 60–86, 142–60; LVI (1909), 530–45, 657–70, 751–58; LVII (1910), 20–32, 85–94, 154–64, 282–92, 354–65, 481–96, 544–57, 611–23, 748–57; LVIII (1911), 55–64, 277–85, 415–26, 460–72, 527–36, 662–72, 732–39; LIX (1912), 85–97, 134–42, 235–42, 280–83, 358–64, 410–18, 660–66; LX (1913), 1–7, 65–72, 116–23.

Rogers, Francis M. "Portugal's Literary Relations with the Outside World." *Yearbook of Comparative and General Literature*, IV (1956), 26–30.

——. "The Manuscript Latin Translation of Mendes Pinto's *Peregrinacam*," in *Homenaje a Rodriguez-Moñino*, II, 143–52. Madrid, 1966.

Ross, E. Denison. "Camoens and His Adventures in the East." *Nineteenth Century*, XIX–XX (July–December, 1938), 64–75.

Rossi, Giuseppe Carlo. "Il commercio nella letteratura portoghese del Cinquecento." *Economia e storia*, XIV (1967), No. 3, 330–48.

Sanceau, Elaine. "Portuguese Women during the First Two Centuries of Expansion Overseas." *Congresso internacional de história dos descobrimentos*, V (1960), Pt. I, 237–62.

Saviotti, Gino. "Gil Vicente poeta cómico." *Bulletin historique du théâtre portugais* (Lisbon), II (1951), Pt. II, 181–211.

Sequeira, Eduardo. "Fauna dos Lusíadas." *Boletim do sociedade de geografia de Lisboa*, VII (1887), 7–68.

Silva, Luciano Pereira da. "A concepção cosmológica nos 'Lusíadas,'" *Lusitania*, II, 263–89.

Sousa Viterbo, Francisco Marques de. "O orientalismo português no século XVI." *Boletim da sociedade de geografia de Lisboa*, XII (1892–93), 317–30.

——. "Henrique Garcez, traductor dos 'Lusíadas' em hespanhol." *Circulo Camoniano* (Porto), I (1889), 316–23.

——. "O theatro na corte de D. Filippe II." *Archivo histórico portuguez*, I (1903), 1–17.

Stegmüller, Friedrich. "Zur Literaturgeschichte der Philosophie und Theologie an den Universitäten Evora und Coimbra im XVI. Jahrhundert." In *Gesammelte Aufsätze zur Kulturgeschichte Spaniens*, III, 385–438. Münster, 1931.

Tejada, F. Elias de. "Los doctrinas politicas de Jeronimo Osorio." *Anuario de Historia del derecho español*, XVI (1945), 341–88.

Thomas, Henry. "English Translations of Portuguese Books before 1640." *Library*, 4th ser. VII (1927), 1–30.

Vasconcelos, Carolina Michaëlis de. "Lucius Andreas Resendius Lusitanus." *Archivo histórico portuguez*, III (1905), 161–78.

Ventura, Augusta F. S. "Subsidios para o estudo da Flora Camoniana." *Biblos*, IX (1933), 128–39; XI (1935), 72–84; XII (1936), 212–22.

Zachariae, T. "Aufführungen von Jesuitendramen in Indien." *Archiv für das Studium der neueren Sprachen und Literaturen*, CXXX (1913), 32–39.

V. SPANISH LITERATURE

BOOKS

Acosta, José de. *Obras*. Edited by Francisco Mateos, S. J. Madrid, 1954.

Achútequi, Pedro S. *La universalidad del concimiento de Dios en los paganos, según los primeros téologos de la Compañía de Jésus, 1534–1648*. Pamplona, 1951.

Aguado Beye, Pedro. *Manual de historia de España*. 3 vols. 8th ed. Madrid, 1958–59.

Alenda y Mira, Jenaro. *Relaciónes de solemnidades publicas de España*. Madrid, 1903.

Andrews, James R. *Juan del Encina: Prometheus in Search of Prestige*. Berkeley, Calif., 1959.

Anghiera, Pietro Martire d'. *Lettres ... relatives aux découvertes maritimes des espagnols et des portugais*. Edited and translated by P. Gaffarel and F. Louvot. Paris, 1885.

———. *De orbe Nove ... of Peter Martyr*. Edited and translated by F. A. MacNutt. 2 vols. New York and London, 1912.

Arco y Garay, Ricardo del. *La idea de imperio en la politica y la literatura españolas*. Madrid, 1944.

Artigas, Miguel. *Don Luis de Gongora y Argote: Biografia y estudio critico. . . .* Madrid, 1925.

Ausejo, Luz U. "The Philippines in the Sixteenth Century." Ph.D. diss., Dept. of History, University of Chicago, 1972.

Azevedo, Pedro de, ed. See Lopes de Castanheda, Fernão.

Ballesteros y Beretta, Antonio. *La genesis del descubrimentos*. Barcelona, 1947.

Barahona, Luis de Soto. *Las lagrimas de Angelica*. Granada, 1586.

———. *Primera parte de la Angelica (1586)*. New York, 1904.

Barlow, Roger. *A Brief Summe of Geographie*. Edited by E. G. R. Taylor. "Hakluyt Society Publications," 2d ser., No. 69. London, 1932.

Bataillon, Marcel. *Erasme et l'Espagne: Recherches sur l'histoire spirituelle du XVIe siècle*. Paris, 1937.

———. *Études sur le Portugal au temps de l'humanisme*. Coimbra, 1952.

Baumel, Jean. *Les problèmes de la colonisation et de la guerre dans l'oeuvre de Francisco de Vitoria*. Paris, 1936.

Bell, Aubrey. *Benito Arias Montano*. London, 1922.

———. *Castillian Literature*. Oxford, 1938.

Bernays, Jakob. *Peter Martyr Angherius und sein "Opus epistolarum."* Strassburg, 1891.

Bertaux, Émile. *La Renaissance en Espagne et en Portugal*. Paris, 1916.

Blecua, José Manual, ed. See Manuel, Don Juan.

Chapter Bibliographies

Boaistuau, Pierre. *El theatro del mūdo.* Alcalá, 1569.

———. *Historias prodigiosas y maravillosas de diversos sucessos acaescidos en el mundo.* Medina del Campo, 1586.

Boria, Juan de. *Empresas morales a la S.C.R.M. del Rey Don Philipe nuestro Señor.* Madrid, 1581.

———. *Emblemata moralia, scripta quodam hispanice a Johanne de Boria.* Berlin, 1697.

Bouwsma, William J. *Concordia Mundi: The Career and Thought of Guillaume Postel (1510–1581).* Cambridge, Mass., 1957.

Brenan, Gerald. *The Literature of the Spanish People.* Cambridge, 1951.

Calbrick, Gladys. "A Critical Text of *La gran conquista de Ultramar.*" Ph.D. diss., Department of Romance Languages, University of Chicago, 1939.

Carreras y Artau, Joaquín. *Louis Vives, philosophe de l'humanisme. Apports hispaniques à la philosophie chrétienne de l'Occident.* Louvain, 1962.

Carreras y Candí, Francisco. *Folklore y costumbres de España.* 3 vols. Barcelona, 1931.

Castellanos, Juan de. *Elegías de varónes ilustres de Indias.* Madrid, 1589.

Castillo, Hernando del. *Cancionero general . . . según la edición de 1511, con un apéndice de lo añadido en las de 1527, 1540 y 1557.* "La sociedad de bibliofilos españoles." 2 vols. Madrid, 1882.

Centeno, Amaro. *Historia de cosas del Oriente primera y segunda parte. Contiene una descripción general de los Reynos de Assia con las cosas mas notables dellos.* Cordova, 1595.

Cervantes, Miguel de. *Don Quixote.* Translated by Thomas Skeleton. New York, 1909.

Chandler, Frank W. *Romances of Roguery: The Picaresque Novel in Spain.* New York, 1899.

Chevalier, Maxime. *L'Arioste en Espagne (1530–1650): Recherches sur l'influence du "Roland furieux."* Bordeaux, 1966.

Churton, Edward. *Gongora: An Historical and Critical Essay on the Times of Philip III and IV of Spain with Translations.* 2 vols. London, 1862.

Cicogna, Emmanuelle A. *Delle vita e delle opere di Andrea Navagero.* Venice, 1855.

Cirot, Georges. *Mariana historien.* Paris, 1904.

Coster, Adolphe. *Fernando de Herrera "el Divinio."* Paris, 1908.

Cotarelo y Mori, Emilio. *Colección de entremeses, loas, bailes . . . desdes fines del siglo XVI a mediádos del XVIII.* Madrid, 1911.

Crawford, J. P. Wickersham. *Spanish Drama before Lope de Vega.* Rev. ed. Philadelphia, 1937.

Croce, Benedetto. *La Spagna nella vita italiane durante la Rinascenza.* 4th ed. Bari, 1949.

Cummins, J. S., trans and ed. See Morga, Antonio de.

———. ed. *Triunfo de la fee en los reynos del Japón of Lope de Vega.* London, 1967.

Deferrari, Harry A. *The Sentimental Moor in Spanish Literature before 1600.* Philadelphia, 1927.

Defourneaux, Marcelin. *La vie quotidienne en Espagne au Siècle d'Or.* Paris, 1965.

Doetsch, C. *Benito Arias Montano.* Madrid, 1928.

Donato, Leonardo. *La corrispondenza da Madrid (1570–1573).* Edited by Mario Brunetti and Eligio Vitale. Venice, 1963.

Dusmet de Arizcun, Xavier. *Una expedición española a Cambodja en el siglo XVI.* Madrid 1932.

Eguiagaray Bohigas, Francisco. *Los intellectuales españoles de Carlos V.* Madrid, 1965.

Elizalde, Ignacio. *San Francisco Xavier en la literatura española.* Madrid, 1961.

Elliott, John H. *The Old World and the New.* Cambridge, 1970.

Encina, Juan del. *Cancioneiro.* Madrid, 1928.

Entrambasaquas, Joaquín de. *Estudios sobre Lope de Vega.* 2 vols. Madrid, 1946–47.

Escalante, Bernardino de. *B. Escalante: Primera historia de China.* Edited by Carlos Sanz. Madrid, 1958.

Fernandez Alvares, Manuel. *Política mundial de Carlos V y Felipe II.* Madrid, 1966.

Fernandez de Retana, Luiz. *Cisneros y su siglo.* 2 vols. Madrid, 1929–30.

Figueiredo, F. de, ed. See Torres Naharro, Bartolomé de.

Fígueroa, Alonso Gomez de. *Alcaçar imperial.* . . . Valencia, 1513.

Figueroa, Martín Fernández de. *Conquista de las indias de Persia & Arabie que fizo la armada del rey don Manuel de Portugal.* . . . Salamanca, 1512.

Fortescue, Thomas, trans. See Mexía, Pedro.

Foulché-Delbosc, Raymond. *Bibliographie des voyages en Espagne et en Portugal.* Paris, 1896.

Fucilla, Joseph G. *Relaciónes hispanoitalianas.* Madrid, 1953.

Gaffarel, P., and Louvot, F., trans. and eds. See Anghiera, Pietro Martire d'.

Gandía, Enrique de. *Historia crítica de los mitos de la conquista americana.* Madrid, 1929.

Garcia López, José. *Historia de la literatura española.* 8th ed. Barcelona, 1964.

Garcia Villoslada, Ricardo. *La universidad de Paris durante los estudios de Francisco Vitoria (1507–1522).* Rome, 1938.

Gillet, Joseph E., ed. See Torres Naharro, B. de.

Gomara, Francisco López de. *Historia general de las Indias.* Zaragoza, 1552.

Góngora y Argote, Luis de. *Obras completas.* Edited by Juan Mille y Gimenez and Isabel Mille y Gimenez. Madrid, 1956.

Gonzalez de Clavijo, Ruy. *Vida del Gran Tamerlane.* Madrid, 1582.

———. *Narrative of the Embassy of Ruy Gonzalez de Clavijo to the Court of Timour at Samarcand, A.D. 1403–06.* London, 1859.

———. *Embassy to Tamerlane, 1403–06.* Translated from the Spanish by Guy Le Strange. London, [1928].

González Palencia, Angel. *Del Lazarillo a Queveda.* Madrid, 1946.

———, ed. *Pedro de Medina. Libro de grandezas y cosas memorabiles de España.* Madrid 1944.

———, and Mele, Eugenio. *Vida y obras de Don Diego Hurtado de Mendoza.* Madrid, 1941–43.

Gossart, Ernest. *Espagnols et flamands au XVIe siècle.* Brussels, 1910.

Green, Otis H. *Spain and the Western Tradition: The Castilian Mind in Literature from El Cid to Calderon.* 4 vols. Madison, Wis., 1964–66.

Guevara, Antonio de. *Relox de principes.* Seville, 1543.

Hamilton, Bernice. *Political Thought in Sixteenth-Century Spain.* Oxford, 1963.

Hanke, Lewis. *Colonisation et conscience chrétienne au XVIe siècle*. Paris, 1957.

———. *The Spanish Struggle for Justice in the Conquest of America*. Boston, 1965.

———. *Bartolomé de las Casas, Historian*. Gainesville, Fla., 1952.

———. *Aristotle and the American Indians: A Study of Race Prejudice in the Modern World*. Chicago, 1959.

Harrisse, Henry. *Bibliotheca Americana vetustissima*. Reprint. Madrid, 1958.

Hazañas y la Rua, Joaquín. *La imprenta en Seville (1475–1800)*. Seville, 1892.

Heidenheimer, Heinrich. *Petrus Martyr Angherius und sein Opus epistolarum*. Berlin, 1881.

Hernandez, Francisco. *Opera cum edita tum inedita.* . . . 5 vols. in 3. Madrid, 1790.

Herrera y Tordesillas, Antonio de. *Historia general del mundo del tiempo del señor rey don Felipe el segundo, desde el año 1559 hasta su muerte*. 3 vols. Madrid, 1599–1612.

Höffner, Joseph. *Christentum und Menschenwürde: Das Anliegen der spanischen Kolonialethik im goldenen Zeitalter*. Trier, 1947.

Jones, Royston O. *The Golden Age: Prose and Poetry*. London, 1971.

———, ed. *Poems of Gongora*. Cambridge, 1966.

Kendall, John Dickinson. "Juan Gonzales de Mendoza and His *Historia de la China:* An Essay in Historical Bibliography." M.A. thesis, Department of Spanish, University of Minnesota, 1965.

Keniston, Hayward. *Francisco de los Cobos, Secretary of the Emperor Charles V*. Pittsburgh, 1960.

Klempt, Adalbert. *Die Säkularisierung der universalhistorischen Auffassung: Zum Wandel des Geschichtsdenkens im 16. und 17. Jahrhundert*. Göttingen, 1960.

Lamb, Ursula, ed and trans. See Medina, Pedro de.

Ledda, Giuseppina. *Contributo allo studio della letteratura emblematica in Spagna (1549–1613)*. Pisa, 1970.

Le Gentil, Pierre. *La poésie lyrique espagnole et portugaise à la fin de moyen âge*. 2 vols. Rennes, 1949–54.

Le Strange, Guy, trans. See Gonzalez de Clavijo, Ruy.

Leonard, Irving A. *Books of the Brave*. Cambridge, Mass., 1949.

Lipsius, Justus. *Epistolario de Justo Lipsio y los españoles (1577–1606)*. Edited by A. Ramirez. Madrid, 1966.

Lodge, Louise F. *Angelica in El Bernardo and Las lágrimas de Angelica*. Urbana, Ill., 1937.

Lopes de Castanheda, Fernão. *História do descobrimento e conquista da India pelos portugueses*. Edited by Pedro de Azevedo. 4 vols. Coimbra, 1924–33.

Lyte, Herbert. *A Tentative Bibliography of Spanish-German Literary and Cultural Relations*. Minneapolis, 1936.

MacNutt, F. A., ed. and trans. See Anghiera, Pietro Martire d'.

McKenna, James B., ed. and trans. *A Spaniard in the Portuguese Empire: The Narrative of Martín Fernández de Figueroa*. Cambridge, Mass., 1967.

Madrid, Dirección general de archivos y bibliotecas, Biblioteca nacional. *Guía de la exposicion Oriente-Occidente*. 1958.

Manuel, Don Juan. *El Conde Lucanor*. Edited by José Manuel Blecua. Madrid, 1969.

Mar, Juan del. *La lucha contra il pirata en nuestra poesía*. Madrid, 1942.

Mariana, Juan de. *Historia general de España.* "Biblioteca de autores españolas," Vol. XXXI. Madrid, 1872.

Mariéjol, Jean H. *Un lettré italien à la cour d'Espagne (1488–1526): Pierre Martyr d'Anghera, sa vie et ses oeuvres.* Paris, 1887.

Marsh, J. O., Jr. "The Spanish Version of Sir John Mandeville's *Travels:* A Critical Edition." Ph.D. diss., University of Wisconsin, 1950.

Martyr, Peter. See Anghiera, Pietro Martire d'.

Mas, Albert. *Les turcs dans la littérature espagnole du siècle d'or.* 2 vols. Paris, 1967.

Mateos, Francisco, ed. See Acosta, José de.

Mazur, Oleh. "The Wild Man in the Spanish Renaissance and Golden Age Theatre: A Comparative Study." Ph.D. diss., University of Pennsylvania, 1966.

Medina, José Toribio. *Bibliografía española de la Islas Filipinas (1523–1810).* Santiago, Chile, 1897.

Medina, Pedro de. *A Navigator's Universe: The "Libro de Cosmographia" of 1538 by Pedro de Medina.* Edited and translated by Ursula Lamb. Chicago, 1972.

Menéndez y Pelayo, Marcellino. *Historia de las ideas estéticas en España.* 8 vols. Madrid, 1883–91.

Merriman, Roger B. *The Rise of the Spanish Empire in the Old World and the New.* 4 vols. New York, 1918–34. Reprinted 1962.

Mexía, Pedro. *Dialogos.* . . . Seville, 1547.

———. *The Forest.* . . . Translated by Thomas Fortescue. London, 1576.

———. *Silva de varia lección.* Edited by J. Garcia Soriano. 2 vols. Madrid, 1933–34.

Mille y Gimenez, Juan, and Mille y Gimenez, Isabel, eds. See Góngora y Argote, Luis de.

Mir, Miguel, ed. *Conquista de las islas Malucas . . . escrita por el liceniado Bartolome Leonardo de Argensola.* "Bibliotheca de escritores aragoneses, Sección literaria," Vol. VI. Zaragoza, 1891.

Montesinas, José, ed. See Vega, Lope de.

Morga, Antonio de. *Antonio de Morga: Sucesos de las islas Filipinas.* Translated and edited by J. S. Cummins. "Hakluyt Society Publications," 2d ser. Vol. CXL. Cambridge, 1971.

Morel-Fatio, Alfred. *L'Espagne au XVIe et au XVIIe siècle.* Paris, 1878.

Morínigo, Marcos A. *América en el teatro de Lope de Vega.* Buenos Aires, 1946.

Morton, F. Rand. *Notes on the History of a Literary Genre: The Renaissance Epic in Spain and America.* Mexico, 1962.

Nougué, André. *L'oeuvre en prose de Tirso de Molina.* Toulouse, [1962].

Nys, Ernst. *Les origines du droit international.* Brussels, 1894.

Ortiz de Urbina, Ignacio. *San Ignacio de Loyola y los orientales.* Madrid, 1950.

Olmedo, Felix G. *Juan Bonifacio (1538–1606) y la cultura literaria del Siglo de Oro.* Santander, 1938.

Parker, A. A. *Valor actual del humanismo español.* Madrid, 1952.

Pavia, Mario N. *Drama of the Siglo de Oro: A Study of Magic, Witchcraft, and Other Occult Beliefs.* New York, 1959.

Chapter Bibliographies

Peeters-Fontaines, Jean. *Bibliographie des impressions espagnols des Pays-Bas.* 2 vols. Louvain and Antwerp, 1933.

Pellicer y Pilares, Juan Antonio. *Ensayo de una bibliotheca de traductores españoles.* . . . Madrid, 1778.

Penzer, Norman M., ed. *The Most Notable and Famous Travels of Marco Polo.* London, 1929.

Pérez Pastor, Cristóbal. *La imprenta en Medina del Campo.* Madrid, 1895.

Pierce, Frank, comp. and ed. *The Heroic Poem of the Spanish Golden Age: Selections.* New York, 1947.

Pike, Ruth. *Aristocrats and Traders: Sevillian Society in the Sixteenth Century.* Ithaca, N.Y., 1972.

Pinta Llorente, M. de la. *Actividades diplomáticas de P. José de Acosta.* Madrid, 1952.

Portnoy, Antonio. *Ariosto y su influencia en la literatura española.* Buenos Aires, 1932.

Predmore, Richard L. *The World of Don Quixote.* Cambridge, Mass., 1967.

Ramirez, A., ed. See Lipsius, Justus.

Randall, Dale B. *The Golden Tapestry: A Critical Survey of Non-chivalric Spanish Fiction in English Translation, 1543-1657.* Durham, N.C., [1963].

Rekers, Bernard. *Benito Arias Montano, 1527-98.* Amsterdam, 1961.

Rennert, Hugo A. *The Life of Lope de Vega (1562-1635).* New York, 1968.

Ribadeniera, Marcelo de. *Historia de las islas del archipielago Filipino y reinos de la Gran China, Tartaria, Cochin-China, Malaca, Siam, Cambodge y Japon.* Barcelona, 1601.

Rodríguez Marín, Francisco. *Luis Barahona de Soto: Estudio biográfico, bibliográfico, y crítico.* 2 vols. Madrid, 1903.

Rogers, Francis M. *The Quest for Eastern Christians: Travel and Rumor in the Age of Discovery.* Minneapolis, 1962.

Rohlfs, Gerard. *Manual de filogia hispanica: Guía bibliográfica, crítica y metódica.* Bogotá, 1957.

Román y Zamora, Friar Jerónimo. *Relación del descubrimiento de las Philippinas y del ataque a Manila par el pirate Limahon con noticias de Fr. Martin de Rada.* Salamanca, 1595.

―――. *Repúblicas del mundo: Divididas en tres partes.* . . . Salamanca, 1595.

―――. *Repúblicas de Indias; idolatrias y gobierno en México y Perú antes de la conquista.* . . . *Fielmente reimpresas, según la édición de 1575, con una addenda de las noticias que hay en la Crónica, del mismo autor, impresa en 1569.* . . . 2 vols. Madrid, 1897.

Rumea de Armas, Antonio. *Historia de la censura literaria gubernativa en España.* Madrid, 1940.

Saavedra, Guzmán. *El peregrino indiano.* Madrid, 1599.

Sánchez, Juan Manuel. *Bibliografía aragonesa del siglo XVI.* . . . 2 vols. Madrid, 1913-14.

Sánchez Alonso, Benito. *Fuentes del la historia española e hispanoamericana.* 3d ed. 3 vols. Madrid, 1952.

―――. *Historia de la historiografía española. Ensayo de un examen de conjunto.* 2 vols. Madrid, 1941-44.

Santaella, Rodrigo de. *Cosmographia breve introductoria enel libro de Marco Paulo. El libro del famoso Marco Paulo veneciano.* . . . *Con otro tratado de Micer Pogio florentino.* Seville, 1503.

Sanz, Carlos, ed. See Escalante, Bernardino de.

————. *Primitivas relaciones de España con Asia y Oceania: Los dos primeros libros impresos en Filipinas, mas un tercero en discordia.* Madrid, 1955.

Schafer, Ernesto. *El Consejo Real y Supremo de las Indias: Su historia, organizacion y labor administrativa hasta la terminación de la Casa de Austria.* 2 vols. Seville, 1935, 1947.

Schumacher, Hermann. *Petrus Martyr, der Geschichtsschreiber des Weltmeers.* New York and Leipzig, 1879.

Schütte, F. J. *El "Archivo del Japon," vicisitudines de Archivo Jesuitico del Extremo Oriente y descripción del fondo existente en la Real Academia de la Historia de Madrid.* Madrid, 1964.

Scott, James B. *The Spanish Origins of International Law.* London, 1934.

Serís, Homero. *Manual de bibliografía de la literatura española.* Syracuse, N.Y., 1948.

Sierra Corella, Antonio. *La censura de libros y papeles en España, y los indices y catalogos españoles de los prohibidos y expurgados.* Madrid, 1947.

Simón Díaz, José. *Bibliografía de la literatura hispanica.* 10 vols. Barcelona, 1966–72.

Southern, Richard W. *Western Views of Islam in the Middle Ages.* Cambridge, Mass., 1962.

Strelka, Josef. *Der burgundische Renaissancehof: Margarethes von Österreich und seine literarhistorische Bedeutung.* Vienna, 1957.

Swecker, Zoe. "The Early Iberian Accounts of the Far East, 1550–1600." Ph.D. diss., Department of History, University of Chicago, 1960.

Tafur, Pedro. *Andancas e viajes por diversas partes del mundo avidos (1435–1439).* 2 vols. "Colleccion de libros españoles, raros e curiosos, Vol. VIII. Madrid, 1874.

Taylor, E. G. R., ed. See Barlow, Roger.

Terry, Arthur. *Anthology of Spanish Poetry, 1500–1700.* Oxford, 1965.

Thomas, Henry. *Spanish and Portuguese Romances of Chivalry.* Cambridge, 1920.

Ticknor, George. *History of Spanish Literature.* 3 vols. Boston, 1882.

Tirso de Molina (pseudonym for Telléz, Gabriel, 1570–1648). *Obras.* Madrid, 1910.

Tom, Henry Y. K. "The Wonderful Voyage: Chivalric and Moral Asia in the Imagination of Sixteenth-Century Italy, Spain, and Portugal." Ph.D. diss., Department of History, University of Chicago, 1975.

Torquemada, Antonio de. *Jardín de flores curiosas (Lérida, 1573).* Facsimile reproduction. Edited by A. G. de Amezúa. Madrid, 1955.

Torres Naharro, Bartolomé de. *Propalladia and Other Works of Bartolomé de Torres Naharro.* Edited by Joseph E. Gillet. 4 vols. Bryn Mawr, Pa., 1943–61.

————. *Comedia trofeo.* Edited by F. de Figueiredo. São Paulo, 1942.

Valbuena Prat, Angel. *Historia de la literatura española.* 6th ed. 3 vols. Barcelona, 1960.

————. *La vida española en el Siglo de Oro según sus fuentes literarias.* Barcelona, 1943.

Valera, Juan. *Morsamor. Obras,* Vol. XI. Madrid, 1907.

Vargas Machuca, Bernardo de. *Milicia y descripción de las Indias.* Madrid, 1599.

Vega, Lope de. *Lope de Vega. Barlaán y Josafat.* "Teatro antiguo español, textos y estudios," Vol. III. Edited by José Montesinas. Madrid, 1935.

————. *La hermosura de Angélica.* "Colleccion de las obras sueltas," Vol. III. Madrid, 1776.

Vilanova, Antonio. *Las fuentes y los temas del Polifemo de Góngora.* 2 vols. Madrid, 1957.

Villarroel, Fidelis, O. P. "The Life and Works of Fray Jerónimo Román with Special Reference to the Unpublished MS. in the British Museum 'Predicación y conversión de las gentes.'" M. A. thesis, University of London, 1957.

Wagner, Henry R., and Parish, Helen R. *The Life and Writings of Bartolomé de las Casas.* Albuquerque, N.M., 1967.

Wilson, Edward M., and Moir, Duncan. *A Literary History of Spain: The Golden Age: Drama.* London, 1971.

Wosler, Karl. *Lope de Vega y su tiempo.* Madrid, 1933.

Zaccaria, Enrico. *Bibliografia italo-iberica: Ossia, edizioni e versioni di opere spagnuole e portoghesi fattesi in Italia.* 2d rev. ed. Capri, 1908.

ARTICLES

Asensio, Eugenio. "España en la épica filipina." *Revista de filologia espagñol,* XXXIII (1949), 66–109.

Bataillon, Marcel. "L'idée de la découverte de l'Amérique chez les Espagnols du XVI⁰ siècle (d'apres un livre récent)." *Bulletin hispanique,* LV (1953), 23–55.

————. "Philippe Galle et Arias Montano." *Bibliothèque d'humanisme et renaissance,* II (1942), 132–60.

Benfey, Theodor. "Die alte spanische Übersetzung des Kalîlah und Dimnah." *Orient und Occident,* I (1862), 497–507.

Bernard, Henri. "Lope de Vega et l'Extrême-Orient." *Monumenta nipponica,* IV (1941), 278–83.

————. "La théorie du protectorat civil des missions en pays infidèles; ses antécédents historiques et sa justification théologique par Suarez." *Nouvelle revue de théologie,* LXIV (1937), 261–83.

Bonneville, Henry. "Sur la poésie à Seville au Siècle d'Or." *Bulletin hispanique,* LXVI (1964), 311–48.

Boxer, Charles R. "Some Aspects of Spanish Historical Writings on the Philippines." In D. G. E. Hall, ed., *Historians of South East Asia,* pp. 195–208. London, 1961.

————. "Portuguese and Spanish Projects for the Conquest of Southeast Asia." *Journal of Asian History,* III (1969), 118–36.

————, and Cummins, J. S. "The Dominican Mission in Japan (1602–22) and Lope de Vega." *Archivum fratrum praedicatorum,* XXXIII (1963), 1–88.

Capote, Higinio. "Las Indias en la poesía del Siglo de Oro." *Estudios americanos,* VI (1953), 5–36.

Caravaggi, Giovanni. "Un capitolo della fortuna spagnuola del Boiardo: La tradizione dell'Innamorato iniziata da Hernando de Acuña." In G. Anceschi, ed., *Il Boiardo e la critica contemporanea,* pp. 117–55. Florence, 1970.

Cidade, Hernani. "La literatura portuguesa y la expansión ultramarina." *Estudios americanos,* XX (1960), 219–40.

Elliott, John H. "The Mental World of Hernán Cortés." *Transactions of the Royal Historical Society,* XVII (1967), 41–58.

Chapter IV

Entwistle, William J. "The Search for the Heroic Poem." *Studies in Civilization* (Philadelphia, 1941), 89–105.

Ferrando, R. "F. de Oviedo y el concimiento del Mar del Sur." *Revista de Indias*, XVIII (1958), 469–82.

Gay, Jesús López, S. J. "Un documento inédito del P. G. Vázquez (1549–1604) sobre los problemas morales del Japón." *Monumenta nipponica*, XVI (1960), 118–60.

Green, Otis H. "A Critical Survey of Scholarship in the Field of Spanish Renaissance Literature." *Studies in Philology*, XLIV (1947), 228–64.

Huerga, A. "Fray Luis de Granada y S. Carlos Borromeo." *Hispania sacra*, XI (1958), 299–347.

Jameson, A. K. "The Sources of Lope de Vega's Erudition." *Hispanic Review*, V (1937), 124–39.

Kilger, L. "Die Peru-Relation des José de Acosta 1576 und seine Missionstheorie." *Neue Zeitschrift für Missionswissenschaft*, I (1945), 24–38.

Lopetegui, Leon. "Contactos entre España y China en el siglo XVI." *Missionalia hispanica*, I (1944), 341–52.

Lopez de Meneses, Amada. "Andrea Navagero, traductor de Gonzalo Férnandez de Oviedo." *Revista de Indias*, XVIII (1958), 63–72.

Marsden, C. A. "Entrées et fêtes espagnoles au XVIᵉ siècle." In J. Jacquot, ed., *Fêtes et cérémonies au temps de Charles Quint*, II, 389–411. Paris, 1960.

Meregalli, Franco. "Las relaciones literarias entre Italia y España en el Renacimiento." *Thesaurus*, XVII (1962), 606–24.

Molinaro, J. A. "Barahona de Sota and Aretino." *Italica*, XXXII (1955), 22–26.

Retana, W. E. "La literatura historica de Filipinas de los siglos XVI y XVII." *Revue hispanique*, LX (1924), 293–325.

Rogers, F. M. "Valentim Fernandes, Rodrigo de Santaella and the Recognition of the Antilles as 'Opposite-India.'" *Boletim da sociedade de geografia de Lisboa*, LXXV (1957), 281–96.

Ruffini, Mario. "Les sources de Don Juan Manuel." *Les lettres romanes* (Louvain), VII (1953), 27–49.

Sanz, Carlos. "Primitivas relaciones de España con el Japón." *Boletín de la Real Sociedad geográfica*, CII (1966), 257–78.

Schütte, Josef Franz. "Documentos sobre el Japón conservados en la Coleccion 'Cortes,'" *Conclusión: Boletín de la Real Academia de la Historia*, CXLVII (1960), 149–259.

Thomas, Henry. "The Output of Spanish Books in the Sixteenth Century." *Library*, 4th ser. I (1921), 69–94.

Urtiaga, Alfonso. "El indiano en la dramática de Tirso de Molina." *Estudios*, XXI (1965), 529–774.

Vilanova, Antonio. "Preceptistas de los siglos XVI y XVII." In D. Guillermo Diaz-Plaja et al., *Historia general de las literaturas hispánicas*, III, 565–692. Barcelona, 1953.

Wagner, Henry R. "Peter Martyr and His Works." *Proceedings of the American Antiquarian Society*, LVI, Pt. 2 (October, 1946), 239–88.

Weber de Kurlat, Frida. "El tipo cómico del negro en el teatro prelopesco. Fonética." *Filología*, VIII (1962), 139–68.

Whinnom, K. "El origen de las comparaciónes religiosas del Siglo de Oro: Mendoza, Montesino y Román." *Revista de filología española*, XLVI (1963), 263–85.

Williams, G. S. "The 'Amadis Question.'" *Revue hispanique*, XXI (1909), 1–167.

VI. ITALIAN LITERATURE

BOOKS

Anon. *La victoria de lo serenissimo ed invictissimo Emanuele Re de Portugallo.* . . . Rome, 1515.

Albertazzi, Adolfo. *Romanzieri e romanzi del cinquecento e del seicento.* Bologna, 1891.

———. *Storia dei generi letterari italiani: Il romanzo.* Milan, 1902.

Aleandro, Girolamo. *Vitae et res gestae pontificum romanorum.* 2 vols. Rome, 1630.

Allulli, Ranieri. *Marco Polo e il libro della meraviglie.* Milan, 1954.

Almagià, Roberto. *Monumenta cartographica Vaticana.* 4 vols. Rome, 1944–55.

Anania, Lorenzo d'. *L'universale fabrica del mondo.* Naples, 1573.

Anceschi, Giuseppe, ed. *Il Boiardo e la critica contemporanea.* Florence, 1970.

Araujo, J. de. *Centenario da India. O soneto de T. Tasso a Camoëns e Vasco da Gama. Carta a Antonio de Portugal de Faria.* Genoa, 1898.

Arcari, Paolo Maria. *Il pensiero politico di Francesco Patrizi da Cherso.* Rome, 1935.

Arciniegas, German. *Amerigo and the New World.* New York, 1955.

Aretino, Pietro. *Pietro Aretino. Il secondo libro delle lettere.* Edited by F. Nicolini. 1 vol. in 2 parts, Bari, 1916.

Ariosto, Ludovico. *Ludovico Ariosto. Orlando Furioso. An English Translation with Introduction, Notes, and Index.* Edited by Allan Gilbert. 2 vols. New York, 1954.

———. *Ludovico Ariosto. Orlando Furioso.* Translated by William Stewart Rose. Edited by S. A. Baker and A. B. Giamatti. Indianapolis, 1968.

Arrivabene, Lodovico. *Dialogo delle cose più illustri di Terra Santa.* . . . Verona, 1592.

———. *Il Magno Vitei.* . . . *In questo libro, oltre al piacere, che porge la narratione delle alte cavallerie del glorioso Vitei primo Rè della China, e del valoroso Iolao, si hà nella persona di Ezonlom, uno ritratto di ottimo Prencipe, & di Capitano perfetto. Apresso si acquista notitia di molti paesi, di varij costumi di popoli, di animali, sì da terra, & sì da acqua, di alberi, di frutti, & di simiglianti cose moltissime.* . . . Verona, 1597.

———. *Istoria della China di Lodovico Arrivabene . . . nella quale si tratta di molte cose marovigliose di quell'amplissimo regno.* . . . Verona, 1599.

Bacci, P. *Giovanni da Verazzano, navigatore fiorentino.* Bologna, 1965.

Baker, S. A., and Giamatti, A. B., eds. See Ariosto, Ludovico.

Baldi da Urbino, Bernardino. *La nautica e le egloghe.* Reprint of Venice, 1590 edition. Edited by G. Romeo. Lanciano, 1913.

———. *Vita e fatti di Federigo di Montefeltro, duca di Urbino.* . . . 3 vols. in 2. Rome, 1824.

Banchieri, Adriano. *La Nobilità dell' Asino di Attahalippa dal Perú Provincia del Mondo novo.* Venice, 1592.

Bandello, Matteo. *Matteo Bandello. Le novelle.* Edited by Gioachino Brognoligo. 5 vols. Bari, 1910–12.

Barbagli, Danilo Agnuzzi, ed. See Patrizi, Francesco.

Barera, A. *L'Opera scientifico letteraria del card. Federico Borromeo*. Milan, 1931.

Barros, João de. *L'Asia del S. Giovanni di Barros*. . . . Translated by Alfonso Ulloa, Venice, 1562.

Bartoli, Cosimo. *Discorsi historici universali*. Venice, 1569.

Bassano, Luigi. *Costumi et i modi particolari della vita de' Turchi*. Rome, 1545.

Battistini, Mario, ed. See Guicciardini, Giovanbattista.

Becutti, Francisco. *Rime*. Venice, 1580.

Belloni, Antonio. *Il poema epico e mitologico*. Milan, 1912.

Bembo, Pietro. *Historiae venetae libri XII*. . . . Venice, 1551.

———. *Della historia viniziana de Monsignor M. Pietro Bembo, volgarmente scritta*. Venice, 1552.

———. *Della historia vinitiana*. . . . *volgarmente scritta libri XII*. Venice, 1570.

Benci, Francesco. *Ergastus Francisci Bencii, Societatis Jesu . . . Drama, arte, distributionem praemiorum in gymnasio eiusdem societatis*. . . . Rome, 1587.

———. . . . *Orationes et carmina*. . . . Ingolstadt, 1599.

———. *Quinque martyres e Societate Jesu in India libri sex*. Venice, 1591.

Benfey, Theodore, trans. and ed. *Die Reise der drei Söhne des Königs von Serendippo*. Helsinki, 1932.

Bennett, Joan W. *The Rediscovery of Sir John Mandeville*. New York, 1954.

Berengo, Marino. *Nobili e mercanti nella Lucca del Cinquecento*. Turin, 1965.

Bernardo, Aldo S. *Petrarch, Scipio, and the "Africa": The Birth of Humanism's Dream*. Baltimore, 1962.

Beroaldo, Filippo. *Carminum*. Rome, 1530.

Berti, Luciano. *Il principe dello studiolo: Francesco I dei Medici e la fine del Rinascimento fiorentino*. Florence, 1967.

Bertoni, Giulio. *La biblioteca Estense e la coltura ferrarese ai temps del duca Ercole I (1471–1505)*. Turin, 1903.

———. *L' "Orlando furioso," e la rinascenza a Ferrara*. Modena, 1919.

Betussi, Giuseppe. *La Leonora. Ragionamento sopra la vera bellezza*. Lucca, 1557.

———. *Il Raverta, dialogo d'amore*. "Biblioteca rara pubblicata da G. Daelli," Vol. XXX, Milan, 1864.

———. *Le imagini del tempio della signora donna Giovanni Aragona, dialogo*. Venice, 1557.

———. *Ragionamento . . . sopra il Cathaio*. . . . Padua, 1573.

Bittner, Max, and Tomaschek, W. *Die topographischen Capitel des indischen Seespiegels Mohît*. Vienna, 1897.

Boiardo, Matteo Maria. *Orlando innamorato*. Edited by F. Foffani. "Collezione di classici italiani." Turin, 1944–48.

Bonardi, Giovan Maria. *La minera del mondo*. Venice, 1589.

Boncompagni, Francesco L. *Le prime due ambasciate dei Giapponesi a Roma (1585–1615). Con nuovi documenti*. Rome, 1903.

Chapter Bibliographies

Bordone, Benedetto, *Libro di Benedetto Bordone nel qual si ragiona de tutte l'Isole de mondo.* . . . Venice, 1528.

Botero, Giovanni. *Relations of the Most Famous Kingdoms and Common-wealths thorowout the World: Discoursing of their Situations, Religions, Languages, Manners, Customes, Strengths, Greatnesse and Policies.* Translated by R. Johnson. London, 1630.

――――. *Thesoro politici.* Venice, 1612.

――――. *Ioann. Boteri . . . Epistolarum . . . D. Caroli Cardinalis Borromaei nomine scriptarum. Libri II.* Paris, 1586.

――――. *Giovanni Botero. The Reason of State and the Greatness of Cities.* Edited by P. J. Waley and D. P. Waley. Translated by R. Peterson (1606). New Haven, 1956.

Boxer, Charles R., ed. and trans. *South China in the Sixteenth Century.* "Hakluyt Society Publications," 2d ser., Vol. CVI. London, 1953.

Bozza, Tommaso. *Scrittori politici italiani dal 1550 al 1650.* Rome, 1949.

Bracciolini, Poggio, and Varthema, Ludovico de. *Travelers in Disguise: Narratives of Eastern Travel by Poggio Bracciolini and Ludovico de Varthema.* Edited by Lincoln D. Hammond. Cambridge, Mass., 1963.

Brand, Charles P. *Torquato Tasso: A Study of the Poet and of His Contribution to English Literature.* Cambridge, 1965.

Brasavola, Antonio. *Examen simplicium medicamentorum in publicis disciplinis et officinis usus est.* Rome, 1536.

Bresciano, Giovanni. *Neapolitana: Contributi alla storia della tipografia in Napoli nel secolo XVI.* . . . Halle, 1965.

Brickman, Benjamin. *An Introduction to Francesco Patrizi's " Nova de universis philosophia."* New York, 1941.

Brognoligo, Gioachino, ed., See Bandello, Matteo.

Brown, Horatio F. *The Venetian Printing Press: An Historical Study Based upon Documents for the Most Part Hitherto Unpublished.* London, 1896.

Brugi, Biagio. *Gli scolari dello Studio di Padova nel Cinquecento.* Padua, 1905.

Brusoni, Girolamo. *Varie osservazioni sopra le Relazioni Universali di G. Botero.* Venice, 1659.

Buonamici, Lazaro. *Carmina.* Venice, 1553.

Calcagnini, Celio. *Opera aliquot.* Basel, 1544.

Calderini, Apollinare. *Discorsi sopra la ragione di stato del Signor Giovanni Botero.* Milan, 1609.

Cammarosano, Francesco. *La vita e le opere di Sperone Speroni.* Empoli, 1920.

Campana, Cesare. *Delle historie del mondo, descritte dal Sig. C. C., gentil huomo Aquilano, libri sedici; ne' quali diffusamente si narrano le cose avvenute dall'Anno 1580 fino al 1596.* . . . Turin, 1598.

――――. *Delle istorie del Mondo . . . libri 4.* Venice, 1591.

Capparoni, Pietro. *Profili bio-bibliografici dei medici e naturalisti celebri italiani.* 2 vols. Rome, 1925.

Caraci, Giuseppe. *Introduzione al Sassetti epistolografo: Indagini sulla cultura geografica del secondo Cinquecento.* Rome, 1960.

Cardano, Girolamo. *The Book of My Life.* New York, 1930.

Carletti, Francesco. *Ragionamenti di Francesco Carletti Fiorentino sopra le cose da lui vedute ne' suoi viaggi si dell' Indie Occidentali, e Orientali come d'altri paesi.* . . . Florence, 1701.

————. *My Voyage around the World.* Translated by Herbert Weinstock. London, 1965.

Carradori, G. *Sulla vita e sugli studi d' G. B. Ramusio.* Rimini, 1883.

Carrara, Enrico. *I due Orlandi.* Turin, 1935.

————. *Tra il Furiose e la Gerusalemme Liberata, Lezioni.* Turin, 1936.

Casella, M. T., and Pozzi, G. *Francesco Colonna—Bibliografia e opere.* 2 vols. Padua, 1959.

Catalano, Michele. *Vita di Ludovico Ariosto.* 2 vols. Geneva, 1930–31.

Cavalli, Ferdinando. *La scienza politica in Italia.* New York, 1968.

Caviceo, Jacobo. *Libro de peregino.* Parma, 1508.

Cermenati, Mario. *U. Aldrovandi e l'America.* Rome, 1906.

Chabod, Federico. *Storia dell' idea d'Europa.* Bari, 1971.

————. *Giovanni Botero.* Rome, 1934.

————. *Lo stato di Milano nella prima metà del secolo XVI.* Rome, 1954.

————. *Machiavelli and the Renaissance.* New York, 1965.

————. *Scritti sul Rinascimento.* Turin, 1967.

Charbonnel, J. Roger. *La pensée italienne au XVIᵉ siècle.* Paris, 1919.

Cian, Vittorio. *Un decennio della vita di M. Pietro Bembo (1521–31).* Turin, 1885.

————, ed. *"Motti" inediti e sconosciuti di M. Pietro Bembo pubblicati e illustrati.* Venice, 1888.

Ciappi, Marc' Antonio. *Compendio delle heroiche et gloriose attioni, et santa vita di Papa Greg. XIII.* Rome, 1591.

Cicogna, Emanuele Antonio. *Delle vita e delle opere di Andrea Navagero, oratore, istorico, poeta veneziano del secolo decimosesto.* Venice, 1855.

Clubb, Louise G. *Giambattista Della Porta, Dramatist.* Princeton, 1965.

Cocchiara, G. *Il mito del buon selvaggio.* Messina, 1948.

Cochrane, Eric. *Florence in the Forgotten Centuries, 1527–1800.* Chicago, 1973.

Conestaggio, Girolamo Franchi. *Storia dell' unione del regno di Portagallo alla Corona di Castiglia.* Genoa, 1585.

Corazzini, G. A., ed. See Lapini, Agostino.

Cortesão, Armando, and Teixeira da Mota, Avelino. *Portugaliae monumenta cartographica.* 5 vols. Lisbon, 1960–62.

Costa, Emilio. *Pel settimo centenario della università di Padova.* Bologna, 1922.

————. *Ulisse Aldrovandi e la studio bolognese.* . . . Bologna, 1907.

Crane, Thomas F. *Italian Social Customs of the Sixteenth Century.* New Haven, 1920.

Croce, Benedetto. *La Spagna nella vita italiana durante la Rinascenza.* Bari, 1917.

————. *Storie e leggende napoletane.* Bari, 1919.

De Angelis, Vincenzo di. *Introduzione a* . . . *Orlando Furioso. Canti scelti commentati e organicamente collegati.* Florence, 1938.

Dionigi da Fano, Bartolomeo. *Delle historie del mundo di M. Giovanni Tarcagnota . . . con l'aggiunta di M. Mambrino Roseo, e dal Reverendo M. Bartolomeo Dionigi da Fano, sino all' anno 1582.* Venice, 1585.

————, ed. See Federici, Cesare.

Doglioni, Giovanni Nicolò. *Compendio historico universale di tutte le cose notabili gia successe nel mondo. . . .* Venice, 1605.

Dolci, Pietro. *Compendio di geografia storica comparata e storia della geografia.* Naples, 1889.

Donato, Giannatti. *Lettere a Pieri Vettori, pubblicate sopra gli originali del British Museum da R. Ridolfi e C. Roth.* Florence, 1932.

Doni, Anton Francesco. *Mondi celesti, terrestri, et infernali.* Venice, 1567.

Dragonetti, Alfonso. *Le vite degli illustri aquilani.* Aquila, 1847.

Edwards, Ernest Wood. *The "Orlando Furioso" and its Predecessors.* Cambridge, 1924.

Elwert, W. T. *Studi di letteratura veneziana.* Venice, 1958.

Erizzo, Sebastiano. *Le sei giornate.* Venice, 1567.

Estaço, Aquiles. *Statii Lusitani Oratio oboedientialis ad. Gregorium. XIII. Pont. Max. Sebastiani. I., regis, Lusitaniae nomine, habita, eiusdem monomachia. navis. Lusitaniae versib. descripta.* Rome, 1574.

————. *Monomachia navis Lusitanae cum ingenti regis Dachenor classe.* Rome, 1574.

Fabié y Escudero, Antonio Maria, ed. and trans. *Viajes por España de Jorge de Einghen, del baron Leon de Rosmithal de Blatna, de Francisco Giucciardini y de Andres Navagero.* Madrid, 1879.

Fairfax, Edward, trans. *Godfrey of Boulogne, or the Recoverie of Jerusalem.* London, 1600.

Fantuzzi, Giovanni. *Memorie della vita di Ulisse Aldrovandi, medico e filosofo bolognese.* Bologna, 1774.

Faria, Antonio de Portugal. *Portugal e Italia: Ensaio de Diccionario Bibliographia.* 3 vols. Leorne, 1898–1901.

————. *Centenarii da India. T. Tasso a Luiz de Camoëns' soneto: "Vasco da Gama."* Leorne, 1898.

Fatini, Giuseppe. *Agnola Firenzuola (1493–1543).* Turin, 1932.

————. *Bibliographia della critica Ariostea (1510–1956).* Florence, 1958.

Federici, Cesare. *Viaggio . . . nell' India orientale.* Edited and enlarged by Bartolomeo Dionigi da Fano. Venice, 1587.

Ferrara, Stefano. *Un mercante del sec. XVI, storico difensore della Commedia di Dante e poeta. . . .* Novara, 1906.

Ferrero, G. G., and Visconti, D., eds. See Giovio, Paolo.

Fiore, L. B. *La scoperta dell' America e gli umanisti del cinquecento.* Arpino, 1920.

Flamini, Francesco. *Il cinquecento.* Milan, 1898–1902.

Flora, Francesco. *Storia della letteratura italiana. Il Cinquecento,* Vol. II, Pt. 1. Verona, 1947.

Foffani, F., ed. See Boiardo, Matteo Maria.

Fornari, Simone. *La spositione sopra l'Orlando Furioso di M. Lodovico Ariosto.* 2 vols. Florence, 1549.

Fornaris, Fabrizio de. *Angelica Comedia.* Paris, 1585.

Foscarini, Marro. *Della letteratura veneziana.* Venice, 1854.

Fracastoro, Girolamo. *Opera omnia.* Venice, 1555.

———. *Homocentricorum.* Venice, 1538.

———. *Syphilis, sive de morbo Gallico.* Verona, 1530.

Frachetta, Girolamo. *Il seminario de' governi di stato, et di gverra.* Venice, 1624.

Fulin, Rinaldo, ed. *Diarii e diaristi veneziani.* Venice, 1881.

Furno, Albertina. *Il sentimento del mare nella poesia italiana.* Turin, 1905.

Gambara, Lorenzo. *Laurentii Gambarae Brixiani De navigatione Christophori Columbi libri quattuor, Ad Antonium Perennotum Cardinalem Granvellanum.* Rome, 1581.

———. *Poemata omnia.* Rome, 1586.

Garin, Eugenio. *Italian Humanism: Philosophy and Civic Life in the Renaissance.* New York, 1965.

Garzoni, Tomaso. *La piazza universale di tutte le professioni del mondo.* Venice, 1587.

Gentile, Giovanni. *Il pensiero italiano del Rinascimento.* 3d ed. Florence, 1940.

Getto, Giovanni. *Nel mondo della "Gerusalemme."* Florence, 1968.

———. *La composizione della Gerusalemme liberata.* Turin, 1959.

Giacomini Tebalducci Malespini, Lorenzo. *Oratione de le lodi di Francesco Medici, gran duca di Toscana, fatta per ordine de l'Academia fiorentina. . . .* Florence, 1587.

Giannoti, Donato. *Lettere a Pier Vettori.* Edited by Roberto Ridolfi and Cecil Roth. Florence, 1932.

Gigli, G., and Nicolini, Fausto. *Novellieri minore del cinquecento. G. Barabosco—S. Eriggo.* Bari, 1912.

Gilbert, Allan, trans. 2nd ed. See Ariosto, Ludovico; Machiavelli, Niccolò.

Giles, H. A. *A Chinese Biographical Dictionary.* Taipei, 1964.

Gioda, Carlo. *La vita e le opere di Giovanni Botero.* 3 vols. Milan, 1895.

Giovio, Paulo. *Opera. . . .* Edited by G. G. Ferrero and D. Visconti. 4 vols. Rome, 1956–64.

———. *Turcicarum rerum commentarius.* Paris, 1538.

———. *Historiarum sui temporis.* 2 vols. in 1. Paris, 1558–60.

———. *Elogia virorum . . . illustrium.* Basel, 1575.

———. *Dialogo dell'imprese militari et amorose.* Rome, 1555.

———. *Illustrium virorum vitae.* Florence, 1551.

———. *De legatione Moscovitarum. . . .* Antwerp, 1557.

———. *Elogios o vidas breves de los cavalleros antiguos y modernos, q estan al bivo pintados en el museo de Paulo Iovico.* Translated from Latin into Spanish by Gaspar de Baeca. Granada, 1568.

———. *Le vite del Gran Capitano e del Marchese di Pescara.* Edited by C. Panigada. Translated from Latin into Italian by Ludovico Domenichi. Bari, 1931.

Giraldi, Lilio Gregorio. *De re nautica libellus.* Basel, 1540.

Giudici, Paolo, ed. See Varthema, Ludovico di.

Gobbi, Ulisse. *L'economia politica negli scrittori italiani del seculo XVI–XVII.* Milan, 1889.

González de Mendoza, Juan. *The History of the Great and Mighty Kingdom of China. . . .*

Reprinted from the translation of R. Parke. Edited by Sir George T. Staunton. "Hakluyt Society Publications," O.S. Nos. 14–15. 2 vols. London, 1853–54.

Grande, S. *Le relazioni geografiche fra P. Bembo, G. Fracastoro, G. B. Ramusio, G. Gastaldi.* Rome, 1906.

Green, Otis Howard. *Spain and the Western Tradition.* 4 vols. Madison, Wis., 1966.

Grendler, Paul F. *Critics of the Italian World, 1530–1560: Anton Francesco Doni, Nicolò Franco, and Ortensio Lando.* Madison, Wis., 1969.

Griffith, T. Gwynfor. *Bandello's Fiction: An Examination of the Novelle.* Oxford, 1955.

Grillo, Giacomo. *Poets of the Court of Ferrara: Ariosto, Tasso, and Guarini.* Boston, 1943.

Groto, Luigi. *La Dalida.* Venice, 1572.

Gualdo, Paolo. *Vita di Gian Vicenzo Pinelli.* Augsburg, 1607.

Guazzo, M. *Historie di tutti i fatti degni di memoria nel mondo successi dal MDXXIIII sino all'anno MDXLIX.* Venice, 1549.

Guazzo, Steffano. *Lettere del Signor Steffano Guazzo. . . .* Turin, 1591.

———. *La civile conversation. . . .* Lyons, 1582.

Gubernatis, Angelo de. *Torquato Tasso.* Rome, 1908.

———. *Letteratura indiana.* Milan, 1883.

———. *Matériaux pour servir à l'histoire des études orientales en Italie.* Paris, 1876.

Guicciardini, Francesco. *The History of Italy.* 4 vols. London, 1753.

Guicciardini, Giovanbattista. *Lettere di Giovan Battista Guicciardini a Cosimo e Francesco de' Medici (1559–77).* Edited by Mario Battistini. Brussels and Rome, 1949.

Güntert, Georges. *Un poeta scienziato del seicento, Lorenzo Magalotti.* Florence, 1966.

Hammond, Lincoln D., ed. See Bracciolini, Poggio, and Varthema, Ludovico de.

Hauvette, Henri. *L'Arioste et la poésie chevalresque à Ferrara au début XVIe siècle.* Paris, 1927.

Hazlitt, W. Carew. *The Venetian Republic: Its Rise, Its Growth, and Its Fall, A.D. 409–1797.* London, 1915.

Herrick, Marvin T. *Italian Comedy in the Renaissance.* Urbana, Ill., 1960.

Imperato, Ferrante. *Dell' historia naturale libri XXVIII.* Naples, 1599.

Jesuits. Letters from Missions (the East). *Diversi avisi particolari dall' Indie di Portogallo ricevuti, dall' anno 1551 sino al 1558.* Venice, 1559.

———. *Avvisi del Giapone de gli anni M.D.LXXXII. LXXXIII. et LXXXIV . . . Riceuute il mese di Dicembre M.D.LXXXV.* Rome, 1586.

———. *Avvisi della Cina, et Giappone del fine dell' anno 1587 . . . Cavati dalle lettere della Compagnia di Giesù, ricevute il mese d' Ottobre 1588.* Venice, 1588.

———. *Raguaglio d'un notabilissimo naufragio, cavato da una lettera del P. Pietro Martinez, scritta da Goa, al Molto Rever. P. Generale . . . alli 9. di Dicembre M.D.LXXXVI.* Venice, 1588.

Johnson, Alfred F. *Periods of Typography: The Italian Sixteenth Century.* London, 1926.

Koelliker, Oscar. *Die erste Umsegelung der Erde.* Munich and Leipzig, 1908.

Lagomaggiore, Carlo. *L'Istoria viniziana di M. Pietro Bembo: Saggio critico con appendice di documenti inediti.* Venice, 1905.

Lane, Frederic C. *Venice and History.* Baltimore, 1966.

Lapini, Agostino. *Diario Fiorentino di Agostino Lapini.* Edited by G. A. Corazzini. Florence, 1900.

Laste, Natale della, and Forcellini, Marco, eds. See Sperone degli Alvarotti, Speroni.

Leo, Emilio di. *Scienza e umanesimo in Girolamo Fracastoro.* Salerno, 1937.

Leo, Ulrich. *Torquato Tasso: Studien zur Vorgeschichte des Secentismo.* Berne, 1951.

Lévèque, Eugène. *Les mythes et les legendes de l'Inde et de la Perse dans Aristophane, Platon . . . Arioste, Rabelais, etc.* Paris, 1880.

Lievsay, John L. *Stefano Guazzo and the English Renaissance, 1575–1675.* Chapel Hill, N.C., 1961.

Litta, Pompeo. *Le famiglie celebri italiane.* 10 vols. in 4. Milan, 1819–74.

Logan, Oliver. *Culture and Society in Venice, 1470–1790.* London, 1972.

Longhena, Mario, ed. *Viaggi in Persia.* . . . Milan, 1929.

Lucas-Dubreton, Jean. *Le monde enchanté de la Renaissance: Jerôme Cardan l'halluciné.* Paris, 1954.

Luzio, Alessandro. *Isabella d'Este, nei primordi del papato di Leone X e il suo viaggio a Roma nel 1514–15.* Milan, 1906.

———, and Renier, Ridolfo. *Mantova ed Urbino: Isabella d'Este ed Elisabetta Gonzaga.* . . . Turin and Rome, 1893.

Machiavelli, Niccolò. *Niccolò Machiavelli: The Chief Works and Others.* Translated by Allan Gilbert. 3 vols. Durham, N.C., 1965.

Maffei, G. C. *Scala naturala.* Venice, 1564.

Maffi, Pietro. *La cosmografia nelle opere di Torquato Tasso.* Milan, 1898.

Magnaghi, Alberto. *D'Anania e Botero, a proposito di una "Fantastica" storico-geografica sul Cinquecento.* Ciriè, 1914.

Maier, Bruno, ed. See Tasso, Torquato.

Mâle, Emile. *L'Art religieux après le Concile de Trente.* Paris, 1932.

Manfroni, Camillo. *Relazione del primo viaggio intorno al mondo di Antonio Pigafetta.* Milan, 1928.

Manuzio, Antonio, comp. *Viaggi fatti da Vinetia, alla Tana, in Persia, in India, et in Constantinopoli.* . . . Venice, 1545.

Manzi, Pietro. *La tipografia napoletana dell' 500.* 2 vols. Rome, 1971–72.

Marcucci, Ettore, ed. See Sassetti, Filippo.

Marsili-Libelli, Cecilia R. *Anton Francesco Doni, scrittore e stampatore: Bibliografia delle opere e delle critica e annali tipografici.* Florence, 1960.

Masson, Georgia. *Italian Gardens.* New York, 1961.

Mazzotti, Giuseppe. *Ville venete.* Rome, 1963.

Medina, Pedro de. *Obras.* Edited by A. González Palencia. 2 vols. Madrid, 1944.

Meneghetti, Gildo. *La vita avventurosa di Pietro Bembo: umanista, poeta, cortigano.* Venice, 1961.

Mengaldo, Pier Vicenzo. *La lingua del Boiardo lirico.* Florence, 1963.

Montalboddo, Francanzano da. *Itinerarium Portugalensium.* . . . Milan, 1508.

———. *Paesi novamente retrovati.* Venice, 1507.

Moretti, Alfredo, ed. *Corrispondènza di Niccolò Machiavelli con Francesco Vettori dal 1513 al 1515.* Florence, 1948.

Mori, Ascanio Pipino de. *Delle novelle.* London, 1794.

Multineddu, Salvatore. *Le fonti della Gerusalemme Liberata.* Turin, 1895.

Nagler, Alois M. *Theatre Festivals of the Medici.* New Haven, Conn., 1964.

Navagero, Andrea. *Opera omnia.* Venice, 1754.

Navarro, Alberto. *Orações obedienciais: Algumas achegas para o estudo das relações entre Portugal e a Santa Sé.* Lisbon, 1965.

Nelson, John Charles, ed. See Patrizi, Francesco.

Niccolai, Francesco. *Pier Vettori.* Florence, 1912.

Nicolini, Fausto. *Novèllièri minore del Cinquecento, G. Parabosco-S. Erizzo.* Bari, 1912.

————, ed. See Aretino, Pietro.

Noberasco, Filippo. *Un compagno di Magellano: Leon Pancaldo savonese.* Savona, 1929.

Olschki, Leonardo. *Storia letteraria delle scoperte geografiche.* Florence, 1937.

Ore, Oystein. *Cardano: The Gambling Scholar.* Princeton, 1953.

Palagi, Giuseppe, ed. *Quattro lettere inediti di Ulisse Aldrovandi a Francesco I de' Medici, granduca di Toscana.* Bologna, 1873.

Panciroli, Guido. *The History of Many Memorable Things Lost, Which Were in Use among the Ancients.* London, 1715.

Papi, Fulvio. *Antropologia e civiltà nel pensiero di Giordano Bruno.* Florence, 1968.

Pardi, Giuseppe. *Lo studio di Ferrara nei secoli XV e XVI.* Ferrara, 1903.

Parks, George B., comp. *The Contents and Sources of Ramusio's "Navigationi."* New York, 1955.

Paruta, Paolo. *Delle perfettione della vita politica.* Venice, 1579.

Pasio, Francesco. *Copia d'una breve relatione della Cristianita di Giappone de mese del Marzo del 1598, in sino ad Ottob. del medesimo: e della morte di Taicosama sign. di detto Regno.* Venice, 1601.

Pasqualigo, Luigi, Conte. *Lettere amorose.* Venice, 1569.

Passano, Giambattista. *I novellieri italiani in prosa.* 2d ed. Part 1. Turin, 1878.

Passi, Carlo. *Tavola della provincie, città, castella, popoli, monti, mari, fiume, et laghi de quali il Giovio ha fatto nelle sue istorie mentione. . . .* Venice, 1570.

Pastorello, Ester. *Tipografi, editori, librai a Venezia nel secolo XVI.* Florence, 1924.

Patrizi, Francesco. *Della historia diece dialoghi . . . ne qveli si ragiona di tvtte le cosse apparten-enti all' historia, & allo scriverla, & all' osservarle.* Venice, 1560.

Pedot, Lino, O.S.M. *La S. C. De Propaganda Fide e le missioni del Giappone (1622–1838).* Vicenza, 1946.

Pellegrini, Francesco. *Fracastoro.* Trieste, 1948.

————, ed. *Scritti inediti di Girolamo Fracastoro.* Verona, 1955.

Pellizzari, Achille. *Portogallo e Italia nel secolo XVI: Studi e ricerche storiche e letterarie.* Naples, 1914.

Peregallo, Prospero. *Cenni intorna alla colonia italiana in Portogallo nei secoli XIV, XV, e XVI.* Genoa, 1907.

Pertusi, Agostino, ed. *Venezia e l'oriente fra tardo medioevo e rinascimento.* Florence, 1966.

———. *La storiografia veneziana fino al seculo XVI.* Venice, 1970.

Pinto, Olga, ed. *Viaggi di C. Federici e G. Balbi, alle Indie Orientali.* Rome, 1962.

Piromalli, Antonio. *La cultura a Ferrara al tempo dell' Ariosto.* Florence, 1953.

Porcacchi, Thommaso. *L'isole piu famose del mondo.* Venice, 1576.

Possevino, Antonio. *Apparato all' historia di tutte le nationi. Et il modo di studiare la geografia.* Venice, 1598.

———. *Bibliotheca selecta qua agitur de ratione stvdiorvm. . . .* Rome, 1593.

———. *Judicium de quator scriptoribus (la Nove, Bodin, Philip de Morney et Machiavelli).* Rome, 1592.

Raimondi, Giovan Battista. *Viaggio per terra de Lindia [sic] Orientale a Venetia.* Venice, 1575.

Rajna, Pio. *Le fonti dell' Orlando Furioso.* 2d rev. ed. Florence, 1900.

Ramusio, G. B., comp. *Delle navigationi et viaggi. . . .* 3 vols. Venice, 1550–59.

Raya, Gino. *Il romanzo.* Milan, 1950.

Reichenbach, Giulio. *L'Orlando innamorato di M. M. Boiardo.* Florence, 1936.

Remer, Theodore G., ed. *Serendipity and the Three Princes: From the "Peregrinaggio" of 1557.* Norman, Okla., 1965.

Resta, Gianuito. *Studi sulle lettere del Tasso.* Florence, 1957.

Reumont, Alfred von. *The Carafas of Maddaloni.* London, 1884.

Revelli, Paolo. *Terre d'America e archivi d'Italia.* Milan, 1926.

Ridolfi, Roberto. *Vita di Francesco Guicciardini.* Rome, 1960.

Ridolfi, Roberto, and Roth, Cecil, eds. See Giannoti, Donato.

Rocca, Angelus. *Bibliotheca Apostolica Vaticana a Sixto V in splendidiorem locum translata.* Rome, 1591.

Röhricht, R., ed. *Bibliotheca geographica Palaestinae. . . .* Berlin, 1890.

Romei, Annibale. *Ferrara e la corte Estense nella seconda metà del secolo XVI. I Discorsi di Annibale Romei, gentiluomo ferrarese.* Edited by A. Solerti. Castello, 1891.

Romeo, Girolamo, ed. See Baldi da Urbino, Bernardino.

Romeo, Rosario. *Le scoperte americane nella coscienza italiana del cinquecento.* Milan and Naples, 1954.

Roncinotto, Alvise. *El viazo de Colocut.* Venice, 1539.

Roscoe, William. *The Life and Pontificate of Leo X.* 4 vols. London, 1805–27.

Roseo, Mambrino. *Vita di Alessandro Magno.* Venice, 1570.

———. *Historia de' successori di Alessandro Magno. Raccolta da diversi auttori, et in gran parte da Diodoro Siculo. . . .* Venice, 1570.

———. *Delle historie del mondo . . . parte terza. Aggiunta alla . . . Historia di M. Giovanni Tarchagnota.* Venice, 1573.

———. *La prima parte del terzodecimo libro di Amadis di Gaula. . . .* Venice, 1584.

———. *Aggiunta al secondo volume di don Rogello di Grecia. . . .* Venice, 1594.

———. *L'historia de Amadis de Grecia. Il secondo libro delle prodezze di Splandiano.* Venice, 1600.

————. *Della historia del principe Sferamundi.* . . . Venice, 1610.

————. *Aggiunta di Amadis di Grecia.* Venice, 1629.

————. *Lisuarte di Grecia, figliuola dello imperatore Splandiano.* . . . Venice, 1630.

Rossi, Giuseppe. *Girolamo Fracastoro in relazione all' Aristotelismo e alle scienza nel Rinascimento.* Pisa, 1893.

Rossi, M. *Un letterato e mercante fiorentino del secolo XVI, Filippo Sassetti.* Città di Castello, 1899.

Rovelli, Luigi. *L'opera storica ed artistica di Paolo Giovio.* Como, 1928.

Rüdiger, Wilhelm. *Petrus Victorius aus Florenz.* Halle, 1896.

Ruggieri, Ruggero M. *L'umanesimo cavalleresco italiano da Dante al Pulci.* Rome, 1962.

Sá, Artur Moreira de. *Manuscritos e obras impressas de Aquiles Estaço, separata do Arquivo de Bibliografia portuguesa.* Coimbra, 1958.

Sansovino, Francesco. *Del governo et amministratione di diversi Regni et Republiche così antiche come moderne.* Venice, 1578.

————. *Trofeo della victoria sagra ottenuta della cristianissima lega contro i Turchi.* Venice, 1571.

————. *Sopplimento delle croniche universali del mondo di Fra Jacopo Filippo da Bergamo tradotto nouvamente da M. Francesco Sansovino.* . . . Venice, 1575.

————. *Cronologia del mondo.* . . . Venice, 1580.

————. *Venezia città nobilissima et singolare.* Venice, 1581.

Sassetti, Filippo. *Lettere di Filippo Sassetti sopra i suoi viaggi nelle Indie Orientali dal 1578 al 1588.* Edited by Prospero Viani. Reggio, 1844.

————. *Lettere indiane, a cura di Arrigo Benedetti.* 2d ed. Turin, 1961.

————. *Lettere edite e inedite di Filippo Sassetti, raccolte e annotate da Ettore Marcucci.* Florence, 1855.

————. *Lettere scelte, con introd. e note di Gino Raya.* Milan, 1932.

Scaduto, Mario. *Storia della Compagnia di Gesù in Italia.* Rome, 1964.

Schefer, Charles, ed. *Les voyages de Ludovico de Varthema ou Le Viateur en la plus grande partie d'Oriente.* . . . Paris, 1888.

Schück, Julius. *Aldus Manutius und seine Zeitgenossen in Italien und Deutschland.* Berlin, 1862.

Schulte, Aloys. *Die Fugger in Rom.* Leipzig, 1904.

Segre, Cesare, ed. *Ludovico Ariosto: Opere minori.* Milan, 1954.

Sereno, Aurelio. *Theatrum capitolum.* . . . Rome, 1514.

Sgrilli, Gemma. *Francesco Carletti, mercatore e viaggiatore fiorentino, 1573 (?)–1636.* Rocca, 1905.

Solerti, A., ed. See Romei, Annibale.

Sorivano, R. *Il Manierismo nella letteratura del Cinquecento.* Padua, 1959.

Sperone degli Alvarotti, Speroni. *Opere.* . . . Edited by Natale della Laste and Marco Forcellini. 5 vols. Venice, 1740.

Spontone, Ciro. *Dodici libri del governo di stato.* Verona, 1600.

Staunton, Sir George T., ed. See González de Mendoza, Juan.

Straparola, Francesco. *Piacevoli notti.* 2 parts. Venice, 1550, 1553.

――――. *The Nights of Straparola.* Translated by William G. Waters. London, 1894.

Strauch, Alfons. *Die Kosmographie in Ariosts Orlando Furioso.* Bonn, 1921.

Tappert, Wilhelm. *Bilder und Vergleiche aus dem Orlando innamorato Bojardo's und dem Orlando furioso Ariosto's.* Marburg, 1886.

Tarcagnota, Giovanni. *Delle historie del mondo.* 3 vols. in 5. Venice, 1598.

Tassin, Charles. *Giannotti, sa vie, son temps, et ses doctrines. Étude sur un publiciste florentin du XVIᵉ siècle.* Paris, 1869.

Tasso, Torquato. *Torquato Tasso. Jerusalem Delivered.* Edited by R. Weiss. London, 1962.

――――. *Opere.* Edited by Bruno Maier. 5 vols. Milan, 1963.

Thérault, Suzanne. *Un cénacle humaniste de la Renaissance autour de Vittoria Colonna [1492–1547], châtelaine d'Ischia.* Florence, 1968.

Thomas, Henry. *Spanish and Portuguese Romances of Chivalry in the Spanish Peninsula and Its Extension and Influence Abroad.* Cambridge, 1920.

Tinto, Alberto. *Annali tipografici dei Tramezzino.* Venice, 1966.

Tiraboschi, Girolamo. *Storia della letteratura italiana.* Vol. VII, Pt. 1. Florence, 1809.

Tom, Henry Y. K. "The Wonderful Voyage: Chivalric and Moral Asia in the Imagination of Sixteenth-Century Italy, Spain, and Portugal." Ph.D. diss., Department of History, University of Chicago, 1975.

Torelli, Pomponio. *Trattato del debito del cavalliero, di Pomponi Torelli Conte di Montechiarugolo, nell' Academia de' Signori Innominati di Parma, Il Perduto.* Parma, 1596.

――――. *Tancredi.* Parma, 1597.

Tramezzino, Michele. *Peregrinaggio di tre giovani del re di Serendippo.* Venice, 1557.

Trindade Coelho, H., and Mattelli, G., eds. *Documentos para o estudo das relações culturaes entre Portugal e Italia.* 4 vols. Florence, 1934–35.

Turner, Richard A. *The Vision of Landscape in Renaissance Italy.* Princeton, 1966.

Ulivi, Ferruccio. *Il manierismo del Tasso, e altri studi.* Florence, 1966.

Ulloa, Alfonso, trans. See Barros, João de.

Varthema, Ludovico di. *Itinerario di Ludovico di Varthema.* Edited by Paolo Giudici. Milan, 1928.

――――. *Les voyages de Ludovico di Varthema ou le Viateur en la plus grande partie d'Orient.* Translated from Italian into French by J. Balarin de Raconio. "Recueil de voyages et de documents pour servir à l'histoire de la geographie depuis le XIIIᵉ jusqu' à la fin du XVIᵉ siècle," Vol. IX. Paris, 1888.

Vasques, Alberto, and Rose, R. Selden, eds. *Algunas cartas de Don Diego Hurtado de Mendoza escritas 1538–1552.* New Haven, 1935.

Vecchietti, F., and Maro, T. *Biblioteca picena.* 5 vols. Osimo, 1790–96.

Vernero, Michele. *Studi critici sopra la geografia nell' Orlando Furioso.* Turin, 1913.

Viperani, Giovanni Antonio. *De rege, et regno liber.* Antwerp, 1569.

Viviani, Ugo, ed. *Vita e opere di Andrea Cesalpino.* Arizzo, 1922.

Waley, P. J., and Waley D. P., eds. See Botero, Giovanni.

Waters, W. G., trans. See Straparola, Francesco.

Weiss, R., ed. See Tasso, Torquato.

Chapter Bibliographies

Williams, Ralph C. *The Merveilleux in the Epic.* Paris, 1925.

Yriarte, Charles. *La vie d'un patricien de Venise.* Paris, 1874.

Zoli, Sergio. *La Cina e la cultura italiana dal '500 al '700.* Bologna, 1973.

ARTICLES

Azevedo, João Lucio d'. "Francesco Sassetti." In *Novas epanáforas: Estudos de história e literatura*, pp. 97–135. Lisbon, 1932.

Barberi, Francesco. "Le edizioni romane di Francesco Minizio Calvo." In *Miscellanea di scritti di bibliografia ed erudizione in memoria di Luigi Ferrari*, pp. 57–98. Florence, 1952.

Barilli, Renato. "Il Boiardo e l'Ariosto nel giudizzio del Rajna." In G. Anceschi, ed., *Il Boiardo e la critica contemporanea.* pp. 61–72. Florence, 1970.

Beltrami, G. "La chiesa Caldea nel secolo dell'unione." *Orientalia Christiana* (Rome), XXIX (1933), 35–39, 86–137.

Berchet, Guglielmo, ed. "Fonti italiani per la storia della scoperta del Nuovo Mondo." In *Raccolta . . . Colombiana*, Pt. III, Vol. I, pp. 170–80. Rome, 1892.

Bertolotti, A. "Le tipografie orientali e gli orientalisti a Roma nei secoli XVI e XVII." *Rivista Europea*, IX (1878), 217–68.

Bertoni, Giulio. "Umanisti portoghesi a Ferrara (Hermico e Didaco)." *Giornale storico della letteratura italiana*, CXIV (1939), 46–51.

Bezzola, Reto R. "L'Oriente nel poema cavalleresco del primo Rinascimento." *Lettere italiane*, XV (1963), 385–98.

Bradner, Leicester. "Columbus in Sixteenth-Century Poetry." In *Essays Honoring Lawrence C. Wroth*, pp. 15–30. Portland, Me., 1951.

Bramanti, Vanni. "Lettere inedite di Filippo Sassetti." *Giornale storico della letteratura italiana*, CXLIII (1966), 390–406.

Briggs, Helen M. "Tasso's Theory of Epic Poetry." *Modern Language Review*, XXX (1930), 457–73.

Caramella, S. "L'Asia nell' 'Orlando Innamorato,'" *Bollettino della società geografica italiana*, 5th ser. XII (1923), 44–59, 127–50.

Carletti, Francesco. "The Carletti Discourse: A Contemporary Italian Account of a Visit to Japan in 1597–98." Translated by M. N. Trollope. In *Transactions of the Asiatic Society of Japan*, 2d ser. IX (1932), 1–35.

Casamassima, E. "Ludovico degli Arrighi detto Vicentino copista dell' 'Itinerario' del Varthema." *La bibliofilia*, LXIV (1962), 117–62.

Cavicchi, Filippo. "Un poemetto di Girolamo Casio e l'ingresso in Bologna (1525) del card. Legato Innocenzo Cibo." *Atti e memorie della R. Deputazione di Storia Patria per la provincie di Romagna* (Bologna), 4th ser. III (1913), 111–12.

Cermanati, Mario. "Un diplomatico naturalista del Rinascimento Andrea Navagero." *Nuovo archivio veneto*, N.S. XXIV (1912), 164–205.

Cessi, Roberto. "L'India in una descrizione sconosciuta del principio del secolo XVI." *Studi Colombiani*, III (1952), 213–16.

Chabod, Federico. "Paulo Giovio." In *Scritti sul Rinascimento*, pp. 243–67. Turin, 1967.

Cian, Vittorio. "P. Bembo e Isabella d'Este." *Giornale storico della letteratura italiana*, IX (1887), 81–136.

Comfort, W. William. "The Saracenos in Italian Epic Poetry." *PMLA*, LIX (1941), 882–919.

Cristofari, Maria. "La tipografia vicentina nel secolo XVI." In *Miscellanea di scritti di bibliografia ed erudizione in memoria di Luigi Ferrari*, pp. 191–214. Florence, 1952.

D'Elia, Pasquale. "L'Italia alle origini degli studi sulla Cina." *Nuovo antologia*, CDXXII (1942), 148–60.

Del Piero, Antonio. "Delle vita e delle opere di G. B. Ramusio." *Nuovo archivio veneto*, N.S. IV (1902), 5–109.

Diener, Hermann. "Die 'Camera Papagalli' im Palast des Papstes." *Archiv für Kulturgeschichte*, XLIX (1967), 43–97.

Dionisotti, Carlo. "La guerra d'Oriente nella letteratura veneziana del Cinquecento." In A. Pertusi, ed., *Venezia e l'Oriente fra tardo Medioevo e Rinascimento*, pp. 471–93. Venice, 1966.

Divrengues, A. "La société milanese d'après Bandello au temps de la Renaissance." *Revue du seizième siècle*, XVIII (1931), 223–30.

Elwert, W. T. "Pietro Bembo e la vita letteraria del suo tempo." In *La civiltà veneziana del Rinascimento*, pp. 125–76. Florence, 1958.

———. "Venedigs literarische Bedeutung." *Archiv für Kulturgeschichte*, XXXVI (1954), 261–300.

Fanelli, Vittorio. "Apetti della Roma cinquecentesca. Note sulla diffusione della cultura iberica a Roma." *Studi Romani*, XV (1967), 277–88.

Fantini, Bianca Saraceni. "Prime indagini sulla stampa padovana del cinquecento." In *Miscellanea di scritti di bibliografia ed erudizione in memoria di Luigi Ferrari*, pp. 415–85. Florence, 1952.

Ferri, Luigi. "Pietro Pomponazzi e la Rinascenza." *Archivio storico italiano*, 3d ser. XV (1872), 65–96.

Fiorentino, F. "Vita ed opere di A. Cesalpino." *Nuovo antologia*, XLVI (1879), 657–83.

Fucilla, J. G. "European Translations and Imitations of Ariosto." *Romanic Review*, XXV (1934), Pt. 1, 45–51.

Gabrieli, G. "L'Ariosto e l'Oriente." *Atti Arcadia*, XI–XII (1933), 29–50.

Gallina, A. M. "Un intermediario fra la cultura italiana e spagnola nel secolo XVI; Alfonso de Ulloa." *Quaderni ibero-americani*, XVII (1955), 4–12; XVII (1956), 194–209.

Gilbert, Felix. "The Renaissance Interest in History." In C. S. Singleton, ed., *Art, Science, and History in the Renaissance*, pp. 373–86. Baltimore, 1968.

Gioffré, Domenico. "Documenti sulle relazioni fra Genova ed il Portogallo dal 1493 al 1539." *Bulletin de l'institut historique belge de Rome*, XXXIII (1961), 179–316.

Goldstein, Thomas. "Florentine Humanism and the Vision of the New World." In International Congress for the History of the Discoveries, *Resumo das comunicações*, pp. 132–35. Lisbon, 1960.

Gomes Branco, J. "Un umanista portoghese in Italia: Achilles Estaço." In Reale Accademia d'Italia, *Relazioni storiche fra l'Italia e il Portogallo: Memorie e documenti*, pp. 135–43. Rome, 1940.

Chapter Bibliographies

Goodman, Leo A. "Notes on the Etymology of Serendipity and Some Related Philological Observations." *Modern Language Notes*, LXXVI (1961), 454–81.

Grendler, Paul F. "Francesco Sansovino and Italian Popular History." *Studies in the Renaissance*, XVI (1969), 139–80.

Heikamp, Detlef. "Les Médicis et le Nouveau Monde." *Oeil*, CXLIV (1966), 16–23, 50.

Lagomaggiore, C. "L'Istoria viniziana di M. Pietro Bembo." *Nuovo archivio veneto*, 3d ser., VIII (1905), 162–80; IX (1905), 33–113.

Lefèvre, Renato. "Due cinquecentine di Andrea Corsali viaggiatore nelle Indie." In *Almanacco dei bibliotecari italiani*, pp. 42–52. Rome, 1967.

———. "Una corrispondenza dal Mar Rosso di Andrea Corsali nel 1516." *Il libro italiano*, IV, Pt. 2 (1940), 433–48.

———. "Appunti sull'ospizio di S. Stefano degli 'indiani" nel Cinquecento." *Studi Romani*, XV (1967), 16–33.

Le Goff, J. "L'Occident médiéval et l'Océan Indien: Un horizon onirique." In Manilo Cortelazzo, ed., *Méditerranée et Océan Indien*, pp. 243–65. Venice, 1970.

Leite de Faria, Francisco. "Un impresso de 1531 sobre as empressas dos Portugueses no Oriente." *Boletim internacional da bibliografia Luso-Brasileira*, VII (1966), 90–109.

Lubac, H. de, and Bernard-Maitre, H. "La découverte du buddhisme." *Bulletin de l'association Guillaume Budé*, 3d ser. III (October, 1953), 97–115.

Luzio, Alessandro, and Renier, Rodolfo. "La cultura e le relazioni letterarie di Isabella d'Este Gonzaga." *Giornale storico della letteratura italiana*, XXXIII (1899), 1–62.

———. "La cultura e le relazioni letterarie di Isabella d'Este Gonzaga. 4 Gruppo veneto." *Giornale storico della letteratura italiana*, XXXVIII (1901), 41–70.

Luzio, L. "La fortuna dell' Itinerario di Ludovico de Varthema bolognese nella letteratura e nella cartografia contemporanea." In *Atti del XIV Congresso geografico tenuto a Bologna dall' 8 al 12 aprile 1947*, pp. 511–14. Bologna, 1949.

Magnino, Leo. "António de Noli e a colaboração entre Portugueses e Genoveses nos descobrimentos." *Studia*, X (1962), 99–115.

Marangoni, Giuseppe. "Lazzaro Buonamico e lo studio Padovano nella prima metà del cinquecento." *Nuovo archivio veneto*, 3d ser. I (1901), 118–51, 301–18; II (1902), 131–96.

Matos, L. "Natura, intelletto, e costumi dell' elefanta." *Boletim internacional da bibliografia Luso-Brasileira*, I (1960), 44–55.

Mazzoni, G. "Ludovico Ariosto e Magellano." *L'Ape* (Ferrara), Nos. 3–4 (March–April, 1939), pp. 2–3.

Mercati, G. "Un indici di libri offerti a Leone X." *Il libro e la stampa*, N.S. II (1908), 40–45.

Moreira de Sá, Artus. "Manuscritos e obras impressos de Aquilos Estaço," *Arquivo de bibliografia portuguesa*, III (1957), 167–78.

Morison, Stanley. "The Earliest Known Work of Arrighi." *Fleuron*, VII (1930), 167–68.

Müntz, C. "Le musée de portraits de Paul Jove." *Mémoires de l'institut national de France, Académie des inscriptions et belles lettres*, XXXVI (1901), 249–343.

Pavolini, P. E. "Di alcuni altri paralleli orientali alla novella del Canto XXVIII del Furioso." *Giornale della società asiatica italiana* (Florence), XI (1897–98), 165–73.

Pettinelli, R. A. "Di alcuni fonti del Boiardo." In G. Anceschi, ed., *Il Boiardo e la critica contemporanea*, pp. 1–11. Florence, 1970.

Pinto, Olga. "Viaggiatori veneti in Oriente (secoli XIII–XVI)." In A. Pertusi, ed., *Venezia e l'Oriente fra tardo medioevo e rinascimento*, pp. 389–401. Venice, 1966.

————. "Ancora il viaggiatore veneziano Gasparo Balbi a proposito della ristampa italiana di una carta dell' Asia di W. J. Blaev." *Atti dell' Academia nazionale dei Lincei*, 8th ser. III (1948), 465–71.

Po, Guido. "La collaborazione italo-portoghese alle grandi esplorazioni geografiche ed alla cartographia nautica." In Reale Accademia d'Italia, *Relazioni storiche fra l'Italia e Portogallo: Memorie e documenti*, pp. 261–322. Rome, 1940.

Polein, Stanislas. "Une tentative d'Union au XVIᵉ siècle: la mission religieuse du Père Antoine Possevin, S. J. en Moscovie (1581–82)." *Orientalia Christiana analecta*, CL (1957), 1–135.

Pullé, Francesco L. "Originali indiani della novella Ariostea nel XXVIII canto del Furioso." *Giornale della società asiatica italiana*, IV (1890), 129–64.

Rees, D. G. "John Florio and Anton Francesco Doni." *Comparative Literature*, XV (1963), 33–38.

Rizzi, Fortunato. "Un maestro d'umanità: F. Beroaldo." *L'Archiginnasio*, XLVIII (1953), 75–111.

Rossi, Ettore. "La leggenda di Turandot." In *Studi orientalistici in onore di Giorgio Levi della Vida*, II, 457–76. Rome, 1956.

Saltini, Guglielmo Enrico. "Della stamperia orientale Medicea e di Giovan Battista Raimondi." *Giornale storico degli archivi toscani*, IV (1860), 237–308.

Sanesi, Giuseppe. "Alcuni osservazioni e notizie intorno a tre storici minori del cinquecento." *Archivio storico italiano*, 5th ser. XXIII (1899), 261–88.

————. "Ragionamento sopra il commercio dal Granduca Cosimo I tra i sudditi." In *Archivio storico italiano*, 1st ser. IX, appendix (1853), 165–88.

Searles, Colbert. "The Leodilla Episode in Bojardo's *Orlando Innamorata*." *Modern Language Notes*, XVII (1902), 328–42, 406–11.

————. "Some Notes on Boiardo's Version of the Alexandersagas." *Modern Language Notes*, XV (1900), 89–95.

Sforza, Giovanni. "Francesco Sansovino e le sue opere storiche." *Memorie delle R. Accademia delle scienze di Torino*, ser. 2ª, XLVII (1897), 27–66.

Sparrow, John. "Latin Verse of the High Renaissance." In E. F. Jacob, ed., *Italian Renaissance Studies*, pp. 354–409. London, 1960.

Spini, Giorgio. "Historiography: The Art of History in the Italian Counter-Reformation." In E. Cochrane, ed., *The Late Italian Renaissance, 1525–1630*, pp. 91–133. London, 1970.

Vaganay, Hugues. "Les Romans de chevalerie italiens d'inspiration espagnole." *La bibliofilia*, XI (1909–10), 171–82; XII (1910–11), 112–25, 205–11, 280–300, 390–99.

Verci, Giambattista. "Vita di Giuseppe Betussi." In *Biblioteca rara pubblicata da G. Daelli*, XXX, pp. xvii–xlviii. Milan, 1864.

Vernero, Michele. "I concetti cosmografici e le cognizioni geografiche dell' Ariosto in rapporto a quelle del suo tempo." *Geografia*, IV (1916), 62–73.

Volpati, Carlo. "Paolo Giovio e Venezia." *Archivio veneto*, 5th ser. XV (1934), 132–56.

Waterhouse, E. K. "Tasso and the Visual Arts." *Italian Studies*, III (1946–49), 146–62.

Weinberg, Bernard. "The Accademia degli Alterati and Literary Taste from 1570 to 1600." *Italica*, XXXI (1954), 207–14.

———. "Argomenti di discussioni letterarie nell' Accademia degli Alterati." *Giornale storico della letteratura italiana*, CXXXI (1954), 175–94.

Zaccagnini, Guido. "Le fonti della 'Nautica' di B. Baldi." *Giornale storico della letteratura italiana*, XL (1902), 366–96.

VII. FRENCH LITERATURE

BOOKS

Anon. *La salade nouvellement imprimée à Paris, laquelle fait mention de tous les pays du monde.* . . . Paris, 1527.

Anon. *La institution . . . du royaume de la Chine.* Paris, 1556.

Anon. *Le desespere contentement d'amour.* Paris, 1599.

Anon. *L'Ile des hermaphrodites.* Paris, ca. 1600.

Anon. *Les pudiques amours de Celestine avec ses disgraces et celles d'Angelie.* Paris, 1605.

Adams, M. A., ed. *The Earliest French Play about America.* . . . New York, 1931.

Adhémar, Jean. *Frère André Thevet, grand voyageur et cosmographe des rois de France au XVIᵉ siècle.* Paris, 1947.

Albert-Buisson, François. *Le Chancelier Antoine Duprat.* Paris, 1935.

Alexandrowicz, C. H. *An Introduction to the History of the Law of Nations in the East Indies.* Oxford, 1967.

Alfonse, Jean. *Voyages aventureux.* Poitiers, 1559.

———. *La cosmographie . . . par Jean Fonteneau dit Alfonse de Saintonge.* Edited by Georges Musset. Paris, 1914.

Apomazar, Ibn Sirìn. *Des significations et événements des songes selon la doctrine des Indiens, Perses, et Egyptiens, tourné du Grec en Latin, et mis en François.* Paris, 1586.

Armstrong, Robert. *Ronsard and the Age of Gold.* New York, 1968.

A[shley], R[obert], trans. See Le Roy, Louis.

Atkinson, Geoffroy. *Les nouveaux horizons de la Renaissance française.* Paris, 1935.

———. *La littérature géographique française de la renaissance: Répertoire bibliographique.* Paris, 1927.

Auger, Edmond, trans. See Maffei, Giovanni Pietro.

Baif, Jean Antoine de. *Le premier des meteores.* Paris, 1567.

Baridon, Silvio. *Pontus de Tyard (1521–1605).* Milan, 1950.

———. *Inventaire de la bibliothèque de Pontus de Tyard.* Geneva, 1950.

Bates, Blanchard W. *Literary Portraiture in the Historical Narrative of the French Renaissance.* New York, 1945.

Battista, Anna Maria. *Alle origini del pensiero politico libertino: Montaigne e Charron.* Milan, 1966.

Baudrier, Le Président. *Bibliographie lyonnaise . . . quatrième série.* Lyons, 1899.

Bauer, Albert. *Maurice Scève et la Renaissance lyonnaise.* Paris, 1906.

Belevitch-Stankevitch, H. *Le goût chinois en France au temps de Louis XIV.* Paris, 1910.

Belleau, Remy. *Les amours et nouveaux eschanges des pierres precieuses.* Paris, 1576.

Belleforest, François de. *L'histoire universelle du monde, contenant l'entière description et situatiõ des quatres parties de la terre.* Paris, 1570.

————, et al. *Histoire prodigieuses extraicts de plusiers fameux auteurs.* Antwerp, 1594.

Belon, Pierre. *Les observations de plusieurs singularitez et choses memorables . . . en Grèce, Asie . . . et autres pays estranges.* Paris, 1553.

Bembo, Pierre. *L'histoire du nouveau monde decouvert par les Portugalois, escrite par le seigneur Pierre Bembo.* Paris, 1556.

Bernard-Maitre, Henri. *Sagesse chinoise et philosophie chrétienne.* Paris, 1935.

————. *Le Japon et la France à l'époque de la Renaissance (1545–1619).* Tientsin, 1942.

Béroalde de Verville, François. *Les aventures de Floride, l'Infante determinee et le Cabinet de Minerve. . . .* 5 vols. Tours and Rouen, 1593–1601.

————. *L'histoire des vers qui filent la soye, en cette Serodokimasie ou recherche de ces vers est discourse de leur nature, gouvernement, utilité, plaisir et profit qu'ils rapportent.* Tours, 1600.

————. *Le moyen de parvenir.* Reprint of Paris edition of 1596. Edited by C. Royer. 2 vols in 1. Geneva, 1970.

————. *L'histoire véritable, ou le voyage des princes fortunéz.* Paris, 1610.

————. *Le palais des curieux.* Paris, 1612.

Bigard, Louis. *Le trafic maritime avec les Indes sous François 1er.* Paris, 1939.

Blachiere, Loïs de la. *Histoire veritable de certains voiages perilleux et hazardeux sur la mer.* Niort, 1599.

Blignières, Auguste de. *Essai sur Amyot et les traducteurs françaises du XVIe siècle.* Paris, 1851.

Boaistuau, Pierre. *Histoires prodigieuses extraictes de plusiers fameux autheurs, Grecz et Latins, sacrez et prophans: mises en nostre langue par P. Boaistuau, surnommé Launay, natif de Bretaigne avec les pourtraicts et figures.* Paris, 1561.

Bodin, Jean. *Reponses aux paradoxes de M. de Malestroict.* Edition of 1588. Edited by H. Hauser. Paris, 1932.

————. *Colloque de Jean Bodin des secrets cachez des choses sublimes entre sept scavans qui sont de differens sentimens.* Translated by Roger Chauviré. Paris, 1914.

————. *The Six Books of a Commonweale.* Facsimile reprint of the English translation of 1600. Edited by Kenneth Douglas McRae. Cambridge, Mass., 1962.

————. *Universae naturae theatrum. . . .* Lyons, 1596.

————. *Jean Bodin. Method for the Easy Comprehension of History.* First published at Paris in 1566 in Latin. Translated by Beatrice Reynolds. New York, 1945.

Boemus, Johann. *Recueil de diverses Histoires touchant les situations de toutes regiõs & pays côtenuz es trois parties du monde. . . .* Paris, 1539.

Boissard, Jean Jacques. *Habitus variarum orbis gentium. Habitz de nations estranges.* Cologne, 1581.

Bouchet, Guillaume, sieur de Brocourt. *Les sérées de Guillaume Bouchet, sieur de Brocourt.* Edited by C. E. Roybet. 6 vols. Paris, 1873–82.

Boulenger, Jacques. *Rabelais.* Paris, 1942.

Bouwsma, William J. *Concordia Mundi: The Career and Thought of Guillaume Postel (1510–81).* Cambridge, Mass., 1957.

Brand, Friedrich J. *P. Emundus Augerius, S.J.* Cleves, 1903.

Brown, John L. *The Methodus ad Facilem Historiarum Cognitionem of Jean Bodin.* Washington, D.C., 1939.

Brunet, G., *et al.* eds. See L'Estoile, Pierre de.

Buchanan, George. See Naiden, James R., ed.

Buffereau, François. *Le mirouer du monde.* Geneva, 1517.

Busson, Henri. *Les sources et développement du rationalisme dans la littérature française de la Renaissance (1533–1601).* Paris, 1922.

Cabeen, David C., ed. *A Critical Bibliography of French Literature: The Sixteenth Century.* Syracuse, 1956.

Cabié, Edmond. *Ambassade en Espagne de Jean Ebrard, Seigneur de Saint-Sulpice, de 1562 à 1565 et mission de ce diplomate dans le même pays en 1566. Documents.* . . . Albi, 1903.

Camerarius, Phillip. *The Living Librarie, or Meditations and Observations Historical.* . . . London, 1621.

Cameron, Alice. *The Influence of Ariosto's Epic and Lyric Poetry on Ronsard and His Group.* Baltimore, 1930.

Castanheda, Fernão Lopes de. *Le premier livre de l'histoire de l'Inde . . . faict par Fernand Lopes de Castanheda.* . . . Translated by N. de Grouchy. Paris, 1553.

Cayet, Palma. *Chronologie septenaire.* Paris, 1605.

Centellas, Joachim. *Les voyages et conquestes des Roys de Portugal es Indes d'Orient. Recueilly de fideles tesmoignages et memoires du seigneur Ioachim de Centellas.* Paris, 1578.

Chamard, Henri. *Histoire de la Pléiade.* 3 vols. Paris, 1939–40.

———, ed. See Du Bellay, Joachim.

Champion, Pierre. *Paris au temps de la Renaissance.* Paris, 1936.

Charron, Jean Daniel. *The "Wisdom" of Pierre Charron.* Chapel Hill, N.C., 1961.

Charron, Pierre. *Les trois veritez, contres les athées, idolatres, Ivifs, Mahumetans, heretiques, & schismatiques. Le tout traicté en trois livres.* 1st ed. 1593. Brussels, 1595.

———. *Traicté de sagesse.* Bordeaux, 1606.

———. *De la sagesse livres trois.* Bordeaux, 1601.

———. *Of Wisdom.* Translated by Samson Lennard. London, 1651.

Chartrou, Josephe. *Les entrées solennelles et triomphales à la Renaissance (1484–1551).* Paris, 1928.

Chinard, Gilbert. *L'éxotisme américain dans la littérature française au XVIᵉ siècle.* Paris, 1911.

Chrétien des Croix, Nicolas. *Les Portugaiz infortunés.* Rouen, 1608.

Cioranescu, Alexandre. *L'Arioste en France, des origines à la fin du XVIIIᵉ siècle.* Vol. I. Paris, 1939.

———. *Bibliographie de la littérature française du XVIᵉ siècle.* Paris, 1959.

Cohen, Gustave. *Ecrivains français en Hollande, dans la première moitié du XVIIe siècle*. Paris, 1920.

Cohen, J. M., trans. See Rabelais, François.

Cohen, R. S. "The Use of Rhetoric in Béroalde de Verville's *Le moyen de parvenir*." Ph.D. diss., Department of Romance Languages, University of Chicago, 1973.

Conestaggio, Jeronimo de Franchi. *Dell' unione del regno di Portugallo alla corono di Castiglia, istoria del Ieronimo de Franchi Conestaggio, gentilhuomo genovese*. Genoa, 1585.

Coornaert, Émile. *Les français et le commerce international à Anvers (fin XVme et XVIme siècles)*. 2 vols. Paris, 1961.

Corrozet, Giles. *Blasons domestiques*. Paris, 1865.

Dejob, V. Charles. *Marc-Antoine Muret, un professeur français en Italie dans la seconde moitié du XVIe siècle*. Paris, 1881.

Delisle, Leopold. *Fabri de Peiresc*. Toulouse, 1889.

Deserpz, François. *Recueil de la diversité des habits qui sont de present en usage, tant es pays d'Europe, Asie, Affrique et Isles sauvages*. Paris, 1567.

Dorigny, Jean. *La vie du P. Emond Auger, de la Compagnie de Jésus*. Lyons, 1716.

Douais, M., ed. *Dépèches de M. de Fourquevaux, ambassadeur du roi Charles IX en Espagne, 1565–72*. 3 vols. Paris, 1896, 1900, 1904.

Du Bartas, Guillaume de Salluste. *The Works of Guillaume de Salluste, Sieur du Bartas*. Edited by U. T. Holmes, Jr., *et al*. 3 vols. Chapel Hill, N.C., 1935.

———. *Bartas, His Divine Weekes and Works*. Translated by Joshua Sylvester. London, 1605. Edited by Francis C. Haber. Gainesville, Fla., 1965.

———. *Les oeuvres.* . . . 2 vols. in 1. Paris, 1611.

Du Bellay, Joachim. *Oeuvres poétiques*. Edited by Henri Chamard. Paris, 1908.

———. *The Defense and Illustration of the French Language by Joachim Du Bellay*. Translated by Gladys M. Turquet. London, 1939.

Du Hamel, Jacques. *Acoubar ou la loyauté trahie*. Rouen, 1603.

Du Perier, Anthoine. *Les amours de Pistion*. Paris, 1602.

Du Pinet, Antoine. *Plans . . . villes . . . Europe, Asie, Afrique*. Lyons, 1564.

Du Plessis-Mornay, Philippe de. *De la verité de la religion Chrestienne contre les athées, Epicuriens, payens, Juifs, Mahmudistes, et autres infideles*. Antwerp, 1581.

Estancelin, Louis. *Recherches sur les voyages et découvertes des navigateurs normands en Afrique, dans les Indes Orientales et en Amérique*. Paris, 1832.

F. G. L., trans. See Polo, Marco.

Falgairolle, Edmond, ed. *Jean Nicot, ambassadeur de France en Portugal au XVIe siècle, sa correspondance diplomatique inédite*. Paris, 1897.

Febvre, Lucien. *Au coeur religieux du XVIe siècle*. Paris, 1957.

———. *Le problème de l'incroyance au XVIe siècle*. Paris, 1943.

Feist, Elisabeth. *Weltbild und Staatsidee bei J. Bodin*. Halle, 1930.

Feugère, L., ed. *Oeuvres complétes d'Etienne de la Boëtie*. Paris, 1846.

Fouqueray, Henri. *Histoire de la Compagnie de Jésus en France des origines à la suppression*. 4 vols. Paris, 1910.

Frame, Donald M. *Montaigne: A Biography*. New York, 1965.

————, ed. and trans. See Montaigne, Michel.

Franklin, Julian H. *Jean Bodin and the Sixteenth Century Revolution in the Methodology of Law and History*. New York, 1963.

————. *Jean Bodin and the Rise of Absolutist Theory*. Cambridge, 1973.

Gabriel-Robinet, Louis. *La censure*. Paris, 1965.

Gaffarel, P. L. J. *Les decouvreurs français du XIVᵉ au XVIᵉ siècle*. Paris, 1888.

————, ed. *André Thevet: Les singularitez de la France Antarctique*. Paris, 1878.

Gambier, Henri. *Italie et renaissance poétique en France: La renaissance poétique en France au XVIᵉ siècle et l'influence de l'Italie*. Padua, 1936.

Gascon, Richard. *Grand commerce et vie urbaine au seizième siècle: Lyon et ses marchands (environs de 1520–environs de 1580)*. 2 vols. Paris, 1971.

Gerig, John L. *Antoine Arlier and the Renaissance at Nîmes*. New York, 1929.

Gonnard, René. *La légende du bon sauvage: Contribution à la étude des origines du socialisme*. Paris, 1946.

González de Mendoza, Juan. *Histoire du grand royaume de la Chine, situé aux Indes orientales. Par R. P. Juan Gonsales de Mendoce, traduite par Luc de la Porte*. N.p., 1588.

Gordon, Amy. "The Impact of the Discoveries on Sixteenth-Century French Cosmographical and Historical Thought." Ph.D. diss., Department of History, University of Chicago, 1974.

Goulart, Simon. *Histoire de Portual contenant les enterprises, navigations, et gestes memorables des Portugallois, tant en la conqueste des Indes orientales par eux descouvertes, qu'ès guerres d'Afrique et autres exploits, depuis l'an mil cinq cens novante six, jusques a l'an mil cinq cens septante huit, sous Emmanuel premier. . . . Comprinse en vingt livres, dont les douze premiers sont traduits du latin de Jerosme Osorius, Evesque de Sylves en Algarve, les huit suivans prins de Lopes de Castanhede et d'autres historiens, nouvellement mise en François par S. G. S. Avec un discours du fruit qu'on peut recueiller de la lecture de ceste histoire et ample Indice des matieres principales y contenues*. Geneva, 1581.

————. *A Learned Summary upon the Famous Poeme of William of Saluste Lord of Bartas . . . translated out of French by T. L. D. M. P*. London, 1621.

————. *Histoires admirables*. Paris, 1600.

————. *Thrésor d'histoires. . . . First published at Paris in 1600*. 4 vols. in 2. Geneva, 1610–28.

Grouchy, Nicolas de, trans. See Castanheda, Fernão Lopes de.

Grouchy, Le Vicomte de, and Travers, Emile. *Étude sur Nicolas de Grouchy et son fils Timothée de Grouchy*. Paris, 1878.

Gruget, Claude. *Les diverses leçons*. Paris, 1552.

Gundersheimer, Werner. *The Life and Works of Louis Le Roy*. Geneva, 1966.

Guy, Henri. *Histoire de la poésie française au XVIᵉ siècle*. Paris, 1910.

Guyon, Loys. *Les diverses leçons*. Lyons, 1625.

Haber, Francis C., ed. See Du Bartas, Guillaume de Salluste.

Hall, Kathleen M. *Pontus de Tyard and his "Discours philosophiques."* Oxford, 1963.

Harrisse, Henry. *Le Président de Thou et ses descendants, leur célèbre bibliothèque, leurs armoires, et la traduction française de J. A. Thuani Historiarum sui Temporis*. Paris, 1905.

Hennebert, Frederic. *Histoire des traductions françaises d'auteurs grecs et latins pendant le XVIe* et le XVIIe siècles. Brussels, 1861.

Herval, René. *Giovanni da Verazzano et les Dieppois à la recherche du Cathay (1524–1528). Étude historique accompagnée d'une traduction integrale de la celebre Lettre de Verazzano à François Ier (Relation du Voyage de la "Dauphin")*. Rouen and Caen, n.d.

Hessels, J. H., ed. See Ortelius, Abraham.

Hodgen, Margaret T. *Early Anthropology in the Sixteenth and Seventeenth Centuries*. Philadelphia, 1964.

Holmes, U. T., Jr., et al., eds. See Du Bartas, Guillaume de Salluste.

Honour, H. *Chinoiserie*. London, 1961.

Huppert, George. "The 'New History' of the French Renaissance." Ph.D. diss., Department of History, University of California at Berkeley, 1962.

————. *The Idea of Perfect History*. Urbana, Ill., 1970.

Jarric, Pierre du. *Histoire des choses plus memorables advenues tant ez Indes Orientales que autres pays de la decouverte des Portugais.* . . . 3 vols. Bordeaux, 1608–14.

Jesuits. Letters from Missions (the East). *L'Institution des loix, covstumes et avtres choses merveilleuses & memorables tant du Royaume de la Chine que des Indes contenues en plusiers lettres missives envoyées aux religieux de la Compagnie du Nom de Jesus. Traduictes d'Italien en Françoys.* . . . Paris, 1556.

————. *Lettres novvelles du Iappon. Touchant l'aduancement de la chrestienté en ces pays là, de l'an 1579. iusques à l'an 1581*. Paris, 1584.

————. *Novveaux advis des Indes Orientales et Iappon.* . . . Paris, 1581.

————. *Novveaux advis de l'estat du Christianisme es pays et royaulmes des Indes Orientales & Iappon.* . . . Paris, 1582.

————. *Advis du Jappon des années 1582, 83 et 84, avec quelques autres de la Chine des années 1583–84*. Paris, 1586.

————. *Advertissement de la Chine et Iapon de l'an 1585, 86, et 87 . . . tirez des lettres de la Compagnie de Jesus . . . et traduitz d'Italien en François*. Paris, 1589.

Jones, Leonard Chester. *Simon Goulart, 1543–1628, étude biographique et bibliographique*. Geneva, 1917.

Jugé, Abbé Clement. *Jacques Peletiers du Mans (1517–82): Essai sur sa vie, son oeuvre, son influence*. Paris, 1946.

Julien, Charles A. *Les voyages de découverte et les premiers établissements (XVe–XVIe siècles)*. Paris, 1948.

Kelley, Donald R. *Foundations of Modern Historical Scholarship*. New York, 1970.

Kinser, Samuel. *The Works of Jacques-Auguste de Thou*. The Hague, 1966.

La Boderie, Guy Le Fèvre de. *L'Encyclie*. Antwerp, 1571.

————. *La Galliade*. Paris, 1578.

Lalanne, Ludovic. *Brantôme, sa vie et ses écrits*. Paris, 1896.

La Perrière, Guillaume de. *The Mirrour of Policie. A Work nolesse Profitable than Necessarie for all Magistrates, and Governours of Estates and Commonweales*. London, 1599.

————. *Le miroir politique.* . . . Paris, 1567.

La Popelinière, Henri Lancelot, sieur de Voisin. *Histoire des troubles et guerres civiles en France pour le fait de la religion depuis 1555 jusqu'en 1581.* 2 vols. La Rochelle, 1581

————. *Les trois mondes par le Seigneur de la Popelliniere.* Paris, 1582.

————. *L'histoire des histoires.* Paris, 1599.

————. *L'idée d'histoire accomplie.* Paris, 1599.

La Porte, Luc de, trans. See González de Mendoza, Juan.

Lapp, John C. *The Universe of Pontus de Tyard: A Critical Edition of "L'Univers."* Ithaca, N.Y., 1950.

Laumonier, Paul. *Ronsard, poéte lyrique: Étude historique et littéraire.* 3d ed. Paris, 1932.

La Ville, Léonard de. *Lettres envoyées des Indes orientales, contenans la conversion de cinquante mille personnes à la religion chrestienne és isles de Solor et de Ende. Traduites de latin en françois par L. de L. V.* Lyons, 1571.

Lefranc, Abel. *Les navigations de Pantagruel: Étude sur la géographie rabelaisienne.* Paris, 1905.

————, ed. See Margaret of Navarre.

————, and Marichal, Robert, eds. See Rabelais, François.

Le Goffic, Charles. *Les poétes de la mer.* Paris, 1928.

Lennard, Samson, trans. See Charron, Pierre.

Lenormant, Charles. *Rabelais et l'architecture de la Renaissance.* Paris, 1840.

Léon, J. *Historiale description de l'Afrique.* 2 vols. Lyons, 1556.

Le Roy, Louis. *Considerations par l'histoire française et l'universelle de ce temps....* Paris, 1567.

————. *De l'origine, antiquité, progres, excellence, et utilité de l'art politique.* Paris, 1567.

————. *Des troubles et differens advenans entre les hommes par la diversité des religions.* Lyons, 1568.

————. *De la vicissitude ou varieté des choses en l'univers.* Paris, 1575.

————. *Of the Interchangeable Course, or Variety of Things in the Whole World.* Translated by R[obert] A[shley]. London, 1594.

Léry, Jean de. *Histoire d'un voyage fait en la terre du Brésel.* Geneva, 1578.

L'Estoile, Pierre de. *Mémoires-journaux de Pierre de L'Estoile.* Edited by G. Brunet *et al.* 12 vols. Paris, 1875–96.

Le Vayer, Paul. *Les entrées solonnelles à Paris des rois et reines de France....* Paris, 1896.

Levêque, Eugène. *Les mythes et légendes de l'Inde et de la Perse....* Paris, 1880.

Liotard, Charles. *Étude philologique sur "Les Serées" de G. Bouchet.* Nîmes, 1875.

Lote, G. *La vie et l'oeuvre de François Rabelais.* Aix-en-Provence, 1938.

Lucinge, René de. *De la naissance, durée et cheute des estats.* Paris, 1587.

Macer, Johannes. *Indicarum historiarum ex oculatis et fidelissimis testibus perceptarum libri tres.* Paris, 1555.

————. *Les trois livres de l'histoire des Indes ... composez en latin, et depuis nagueres faictz en françoys.* Paris, 1555.

McRae, Kenneth Douglas, ed. See Bodin, Jean.

Maffei, Giovanni Pietro. *Histoire des choses memorables sur le faict de la religion chrestienne, dictes et executées és pays et royaumes des Indes orientales. Par ceux de la Compagnie du nom de Jesus, depuis l'an 1552 jusques à present. Traduit du latin de Jean Pierre Maffeo en françois par M. Edmond Auger.* Lyons, 1571.

Margaret of Navarre. *Heptameron [of Margaret of Navarre].* Edited by George Saintsbury. 5 vols. London, 1894.

———. *Les dernières poésies de Marguerite de Navarre.* Edited by Abel Lefranc. Paris, 1896.

Margry, Pierre. *Les navigations françaises et la révolution maritime du XIVᵉ au XVIᵉ siècle.* Paris, 1867.

Martin, François. *Description du premier voyage fait aux Indes Orientales par un François en l'an 1603.* . . . . Paris, 1604.

Martínez, Pedro. *Recueil d'un fort notable naufrage tiré des lettres du Pere Pierre Martinez.* . . . Paris, 1588.

Matos, Luís de. *Les portugais à l'université de Paris entre 1500 et 1550.* Coimbra, 1950.

———. *Les portugais en France au XVIᵉ siècle.* Coimbra, 1952.

Meuton, Anton. *Bodins Theorie von der Beeinflüssung des politischen Lebens der Staaten durch ihre geographische Lage.* Bonn, 1904.

Montaigne, Michel Eyquem de. *The Complete Works of Montaigne: Essays, Travel Journals, Letters.* Edited and translated by Donald M. Frame. Stanford, 1948.

———. *The Diary of Montaigne's Journey to Italy in 1580 and 1581.* Edited and translated by E. J. Trechmann. London, 1929.

Moreau-Reibel, Jean. *Jean Bodin et le droit comparé dans ses rapports avec la philosophie de l'histoire.* Paris, 1933.

Mourgues, Odette de. *Metaphysical, Baroque, and Précieux Poetry.* Oxford, 1953.

Musset, Georges, ed. See Alfonse, Jean.

Myres, John Linton. *The Influence of Anthropology on the Course of Political Science.* Berkeley, Calif., 1916.

Naiden, James R., trans. and ed. *The "Sphera" of George Buchanan (1506–82), a Literary Opponent of Copernicus and Tycho Brahe.* Seattle, 1952.

Nicot, Jean. *Dictionaire Francois-Latin, augmenté outre les precedentes impressions d'infinies dictions françoises, specialement des mots de Marine, Venerie et Faulconnerie. Recueilli des observations de plusieurs hommes doctes, entre autres de M. Nicot.* Paris, 1573.

———. *Thrésor de la langue française.* Paris, 1606.

Norton, G. *Studies in Montaigne.* New York, 1904.

Ortelius, Abraham. *Abraham Ortelii . . . epistulae.* Edited by J. H. Hessels. Cambridge, 1887.

Oviedo y Valdes, Gonzalo Fernández de. *Histoire naturelle et generale des Indes, ysles, et terre ferme de la grande Mer Oceane, traducte par luy [Jean Poleur] de Castillan.* Paris, 1555.

Pallister, Janis Louise. *The World View of Béroalde de Verville Expressed through Satirical Baroque Style in "Le moyen de parvenir."* Geneva, 1971.

Papi, F. *Antropologià e civiltà nel pensiero di Giordano Bruno.* Florence, 1968.

Paquot, Marcel. *Les étrangers dans les divertissements de la cour de Beaujoyeulz à Molière (1581–1673).* Brussels, 1933.

Parfaict, François. *Histoire du théâtre françois, depuis son origine jusqu'à présent.* 15 vols. Paris, 1735–49.

Parmentier, Jean. *Description novvelle des merveilles de ce mõde, & de la dignite de lhomme, composee en rithme francoyse en maniere de exhortation, par Ian parmentier, faisant sa derniere nauigation, auec Raoul son frere, en lisle Taprobane, altrement dicte Samatra. Item vu champ royal specialement cõpose par maniere de paraphrase sur loraison dominicale. Item plusieurs chãps royaule faictz par ledit Jan Parmentier soubz termes astronomiques, geo-graphiques, maritimes (a lhonneur de la tresheureuse voerge Marie mere di Dieu, Item Moralite treselegante) composee par le susdit Jan parmentier (a dix personnaiges a lhonneur de lassumption de la vierge Marie. Deploration sur la mort desditz Parmentiers composee par Pierre crignon compaignon desditz Paramentiers en ladicte nauigation.* Facsimile of Paris edition of 1531. Boston, 1920.

———. *Moralité très excellente à l'homme de la glorieuse Assumption Nostre Dame . . . composé par Jan Parmentier, bourgeois de la ville de Dieppe, et jouée audit lieu, le jour du Puy de ladicte Assomption, l'an de grâce mil cinq cens vingt et sept. . . .* Paris, 1839.

———. *. . . Le discours de la navigation de Jean et Raoul Parmentier de Dieppe. Voyage à Sumatra en 1529. Description de l'isle de Sainct-Domingo.* Edited by Charles Schefer. Paris, 1883.

Peletier, Jacques. *Art poétique.* Paris, 1555.

Piaget, Edouard. *Histoire de l'établissement des Jésuites en France (1540–1640).* Leyden, 1893.

Pillehotte, Jean, comp. *Histoires prodigieuses. . . .* Lyons, 1598.

Plattard, Jean. *Les textes françaises.* 5 vols. Paris, 1919.

———. *Rabelais: L'homme et l'oeuvre.* Paris, 1939.

———. *The Life of François Rabelais.* Translated by Louis P. Roche. New York, 1931.

———. *Montaigne et son temps.* Paris, n.d.

Poleur, Jean, trans. See Oviedo y Valdes, Gonzalvo Fĕrnández de.

Polo, Marco. *La description géographique des provinces et villes plus fameuses de l'Inde Orien-tale . . . par Marc Paule gentilhomme Venetien, et nouvellement reduit en vulgaire François.* Translated by F. G. L. Paris, 1556.

———. *The Book of Ser Marco Polo.* Edited by Sir Henry Yule and Henri Cordier. 2 vols. London, 1938.

Posadowsky-Wehner, Kurt Graf von. *Jean Parmentier (1494–1529): Leben und Werk.* Munich, 1937.

Postel, Guillaume. *De orbis terrae concordia.* Basel, 1544.

———. *Des merveilles du monde, Et principalemẽt desadmirables choses des Indes, & du nouveau monde, Histoire extraicte des escriptz tresdignes de foy. . . .* Paris, 1553(?).

———. *Des histoires orientales et principalement des Turkes ou Turchikes et schitiques ou Tartaresques et aultres que en sont descendues. . . .* Paris, 1575.

Rabelais, François. *Oeuvres de Rabelais.* Edited by Abel Lefranc and Robert Marichal. 7 vols. Paris and Geneva, 1912–65.

———. *The Histories of Gargantua and Pantagruel by François Rabelais.* Translated by J. M. Cohen. London, 1957.

Rabinowitz, Sally. *Guillaume Bouchet: Ein Beitrag zur Geschichte der französischen Novelle.* Weida, 1910.

Raymond, Marcel. *L'influence de Ronsard sur la poésie française (1550–1585).* New ed. Geneva, 1965.

Reichenberger, Kurt. *Die Schöpfungswoche des Du Bartas. Themen und Quellen der Sepmaine.* 2 vols. Tübingen, 1963.

Reynier, Gustave. *Le roman sentimental avant l'Astrée.* Paris, 1908.

Reynolds, Beatrice, trans. See Bodin, Jean.

Rice, Eugene F., Jr. *The Renaissance Idea of Wisdom.* Cambridge, Mass., 1958.

Rouillard, Clarence Dana. *The Turk in French History, Thought, and Literature, 1520–1660.* Paris, 1938.

Roybet, C. E., ed. See Bouchet, Guillaume, sieur de Brocourt.

Royer, Charles, ed. See Béroalde de Verville, François.

Sabrié, Jean Baptiste. *De l'humanisme au rationalisme. Pierre Charron (1541–1603), l'homme, l'oeuvre, l'influence.* . . . Paris, 1913.

Sainéan, Lazare. *L'histoire naturelle et les branches connexes dans l'oeuvre de Rabelais.* Paris, 1921.

————. *La langue de Rabelais.* 2 vols. Paris, 1922–23.

Sainte Marie, Fernand de. *Lettres Envoyees Des Indes Orientales Contenans la conversion de cinquante mille personnes à la Religion Chrestienne, es Isles de Solor & de Ende. Traduites de Latin en Francois par Leonard de la Villes Charolais . . . sur la copie envoyee à Rome.* Lyons, 1571.

Saintsbury, George, ed. See Margaret of Navarre.

Saulnier, Verdun L. *Maurice Scève (ca. 1500–1560).* 2 vols. Paris, 1948–49.

————. *La littérature française de la Renaissance (1500–1610).* 8th rev. ed. Paris, 1967.

Schefer, Charles, ed. See Parmentier, Jean.

————, and Cordier, Henri, eds. *Recueil de voyages et de documents pour servir à l'histoire de la géographie depuis le XIIIe jusqu'à la fin du XVIe siècle,* Vol. IV, *Le discours de la navigation de Jean et Raoul Parmentier de Dieppe.* Paris, 1882–97.

————. *Recueil de voyages et de documents pour servir à l'histoire de la géographie.* . . . Vol. XX, *La cosmographie.* Paris, 1904.

Schenda, Rudolf. *Die französische Prodigienliteratur in der zweiten Hälfte des 16. Jahrhunderts.* Munich, 1961.

Schmidt, Albert-Marie. *La poésie scientifique en France au seizième siècle.* Paris, 1938.

Schurhammer, G., and Wicki, J., eds. See Xavier, Francis.

Secret, François. *L'ésotérisme de Guy Le Fèvre de La Boderie.* Geneva, 1969.

Séguin, Jean-Pierre. *L'information en France de Louis XII à Henri II.* Geneva, 1961.

Signot, Jacques. *La division du monde, contenant la déclaration des provinces et regions d'Asie, Europe, et Affrique.* . . . Lyons, 1555.

Silver, Isidore. *The Intellectual Evolution of Ronsard.* St. Louis, 1969.

Steinmann, Martin. *Johannes Oporinus, ein Basler Buchdrucker um die Mitte des 16. Jahrhunderts.* Basel and Stuttgart, 1967.

Sylvester, Joshua, trans. See Du Bartas, Guillaume de Salluste.

Tannenbaum, Samuel A. *Michel Eyquem de Montaigne: A Concise Bibliography.* New York, 1942.

Tchemerzine, Avenir. *Bibliographie d'éditions originales et rares d'auters français des XVe, XVIe, XVIIe, et XVIIIe siècles contenant environ 6,000 facsimiles de titres et de graveurs.* 10 vols. Paris, 1927–33.

Thevet, André. *Cosmographie du Levant*. Lyons, 1554.

———. *Singularites de la France Antarctique*. Paris, 1557.

———. *La cosmographie universel.* . . . Paris, 1575.

———. *Les vrais portraits et vies des hommes illustres, grecz, Latins, et payens*. 2 vols. in 1. Paris, 1584.

———. *Histoire des plus illustres et sçavans hommes de leurs siècles*. 2 vols. Paris, 1584.

Thibaudet, Albert. *Montaigne*. Paris, 1963.

Thou, J. A. de. *Histoire universelle depuis 1543 [sic] jusqu'en 1607*. 16 vols. London, 1734.

Thourin, George. *Choses diverses des ambassadeurs de trois roys de Japon naguîeres venuz à Rome. Traduit du latin par G. T.* Liège, 1585.

Tilley, Arthur. *Studies in the French Renaissance*. Cambridge, 1922.

———. *François Rabelais*. Philadelphia and London, 1907.

———. *The Literature of the French Renaissance*. 2 vols. Cambridge, 1904.

Trechmann, E. J., ed. and trans. See Montaigne, Michel Eyquem de.

Turquet, G. M. trans. See Du Bellay, Joachim.

Tyard, Pontus de. *L'Universe, ou discours des parties et de la nature du monde*. Lyons, 1557.

———. *Le premier curieux ou premier discours de la nature du monde et de ses parties*. Edited by John L. Lapp. Ithaca, N.Y., 1950.

———. *Discours philosophiques*. Paris, 1587.

Van Tieghem, Philippe. *Les influences étrangères sur la littérature française (1550–1880)*. Paris, 1961.

Vaschalde, Henri. *Olivier de Serres, seigneur du Pradel, sa vie et ses travaux*. Paris, 1886.

Vigenère, Blaise de. *Traicté des chiffres, ou secretes manieres d'escrire*. Paris, 1586.

Vignier, Nicolas. *Bibliothèque historiale*. 3 vols. Paris, 1588.

Villey-Desmeserets, Pierre. *Les sources d'idées au XVIᵉ siècle*. Paris, 1912.

———. *Les sources et l'évolution des Essais de Montaigne*. Paris, 1908.

Vivier, P. *Montaigne, auteur scientifique*. Paris, 1920.

Vordermann, Elisabeth. *Quellenstudien zu dem Roman "Le Voyage des Princes Fortunez" von Béroalde de Verville*. Göttingen, 1933.

Weber, Henri. *La création poétique au XVIᵉ siècle en France, de Maurice Scève à Agrippa d'Aubigne*. Paris, 1956.

Williams, Ralph C. *The Merveilleux in the Epic*. Paris, 1925.

Wilson, D. B. *Ronsard, Poet of Nature*. Manchester, 1961.

Wroth, Lawrence C. *The Voyages of Giovanni da Verrazzano, 1524–28*. New Haven and London, 1970.

Xavier, Francis. *Epistolae S. Francisci Xaverii.* . . . Edited by G. Schurhammer and J. Wicki. Rome, 1944.

———. *Copie dunne lettre missive envoiée des Indes, par monsieur maistre Francois Xavier . . . Item deux aultres epistres faictes et envoiées par ledit seigneur maistre Francois Xavier*. Paris, 1545.

Yates, Frances A. *The French Academies of the Sixteenth Century*. London, 1947.

————. *Giordano Bruno and the Hermetic Tradition*. Chicago, 1964.

Yule, Henry, and Cordier, Henri, eds. See Polo, Marco.

ARTICLES

Aquarone, J. B. "Brantôme à la cour de Portugal et la visite à Lisbonne du Grand Prieur de Lorraine." *Bulletin des études portugaises et de l'Institut français au Portugal*, XI (1947), 66–102.

Auerbach, Eric. "The World in Pantagruel's Mouth." In *Mimesis; The Representation of Reality in Western Literature*, pp. 229–49. Princeton, 1953.

Babelon, Jean. "Découverte du monde et littérature." *Comparative Literature*, II (1950), 157–66.

Baron, Hans. "The *Querelle* as a Problem for Renaissance Scholarship." *Journal of the History of Ideas*, XX (1959), 3–22.

Barrère, J. "A propos d'un épisode du voyage de Montaigne." *Revue historique de Bordeaux*, XXVIII (1930), 145–52.

Bernard-Maitre, Henri. "L'orientaliste Guillaume Postel et la découverte spirituelle du Japon en 1552." *Monumenta nipponica*, IX (1953), 83–108.

————. "Humanisme Jésuite et Humanisme de l'Orient." *Analecta Gregoriana, cura Pontificiae Universitatis Gregorianae edita, v. LXX, ser. Facultatis historiae ecclesiasticae sectio A (n. 3): Studi sulla chiesa antica e sull'umanesimo; studi presentati nella Sezione di storia ecclesiastica del Congresso Internazionale per il IV Centenario della Pontificia Università Gregoriana, 1953* (Rome, 1954), pp. 187–92.

————. "Le passage de Guillaume Postel chez les premiers Jésuites de Rome (mars 1544– decembre 1545)." In *Mélanges . . . offerts à Henri Chamard*, pp. 227–43. Paris, 1951.

————. "Aux origines françaises de la Compagnie de Jésus. L'Apologie de Guillaume Postel." *Recherches de science religieuse*, XXXVIII (1952), 209–33.

Bezold, F. von. "Jean Bodins Colloquium *Heptaplomeres* und der Atheismus des 16. Jahrhunderts." *Historische Zeitschrift*, CXIII (1914), 260–315.

Biermez, Jean. "Sur Montaigne et la sagesse taoiste." *Revue de Paris*, LXXVI (1969), 18–28.

Bonnefon, Paul. "La bibliothèque de Montaigne." *Revue d'histoire littéraire de la France*, II (1895), 313–71.

Bouillane de Lacoste, Henry de. "La première navigation de Pantagruel." *Mercure de France*, CCCXX (1954), 604–29.

Boulenger, Jacques. "Notes sur la vie de Rabelais." *Bibliothèque d'humanisme et renaissance*, I (1941), 30–42.

Chartrou, Joseph M. "Les entrées solonnelles à Bordeaux au XVIe siècle." *Revue historique de Bordeaux*, XXIII (1930), 49–59, 97–104.

Chaunu, Pierre. "Les romans de chevalerie et la conquête du Nouveau Monde." *Annales: économies, sociétés, civilisations*, X (1955), 216–28.

Clouzot, H. "La sériculture dans Béroalde de Verville." *Revue du XVIe siècle*, III (1915), 281–86.

Craeybeckx, Jan. "Les français et Anvers au XVIe siècle." *Annales: économies, sociétés, civilisations*, XVII (1962), 542–54.

Dawkins, Jasmine. "The Sea in Sixteenth-Century French Poetry." *Nottingham French Studies*, IX (1970), 3–15.

Delaunay, Paul. "L'aventureuse existence de Pierre Belon du Mans." *Revue du seizième siècle*, IX (1922), 251–68; X (1923), 1–34, 125–47; XI (1924), 30–48, 222–32; XII (1925), 78–97, 256–82.

Denizet, Jean. "Le livre imprimé en France aux XVᵉ et XVIᵉ siècles." In M. Mollat and P. Adam, eds., *Les aspects internationaux de la découverte océanique aux XVᵉ et XVIᵉ siècles*, pp. 31–37. Paris, 1966.

Denoix, L. "Les connaissances nautiques de Rabelais." In *François Rabelais, ouvrage publié pour le quatrième centenaire de sa mort (1553–1953)*, *Travaux d'humanisme et renaissance*, VII (1953), 171–80.

Du Pront, A. "Espace et humanisme." *Bibliothèque d'humanisme et renaissance*, VIII (1946), 7–104.

Durkan, John. "George Buchanan: Some French Connections." *Bibliotheck*, IV (1963), 66–72.

Febvre, L. "L'universalisme de Jean Bodin." *Revue de synthèse*, XXXVII (1934), 165–68.

Françon, Marcel. "Pantagruel et le Prestre Jehan." *Studi francesi*, IX (1965), 86–88.

Geneste, Pierre. "Gabriel Chappuys, traducteur de Jerónimo de Urrea." In *Mélanges offerts à Marcel Bataillon*, pp. 448–66. Bordeaux, 1962.

Guignard, Jacques. "Imprimeurs et libraires parisiens, 1525–36." *Bulletin de l'association Guillaume Budé*, 3d ser., No. 2 (1953), pp. 43–73.

Huppert, George. "The Idea of Civilization in the Sixteenth Century." In A. Molho and J. A. Tedeschi, eds., *Renaissance Studies in Honor of Hans Baron*, pp. 759–69. Florence, 1971.

———. "The Renaissance Background of Historicism." *History and Theory*, V (1966), 48–60.

———. "Naissance de l'histoire en France: Les 'Recherches' d'Estienne Pasquier." *Annales: économies, sociétés, civilisations*, XXX (1968), 69–105.

Ivanoff, Nicholas. "Fêtes à la cour des derniers Valois." *Revue du XVIᵉ siècle*, XIX (1932), 96–122.

Kinser, Samuel. "Ideas of Temporal Change and Cultural Progress in France, 1470–1535." In A. Molho and J. A. Tedeschi, eds., *Renaissance Studies in Honor of Hans Baron*, pp. 705–55. Florence, 1971.

Koebner, R. "Despot and Despotism: Vicissitudes of a Political Term." *Journal of the Warburg and Courtauld Institutes*, XIV (1951), 275–302.

Lapp, John C. "Defeat of the Armada in French Poetry of the Sixteenth Century." *Journal of English and Germanic Philology*, XLII (1944), 98–100.

———. "An Explorer-Poet: Jean Parmentier." *Modern Language Quarterly*, VI (1945), 83–92.

———. "The New World in French Poetry of the Sixteenth Century." *Studies in Philology*, XLV (1948), 151–64.

———. "Pontus de Tyard and the Science of His Age." *Romanic Review*, XXXVIII (1947), 16–22.

Le Gentil, Goerges. "Nicholas de Grouchy, traducteur de Castanheda." *Bulletin des études portugaises et de l'Institut français au Portugal,* N.S. IV (1937), 31–46.

McFarlane, I. D. "George Buchanan's Latin Poems from Script to Print: A Preliminary Survey," *Library,* 5th ser. XXIV (1969), 275–85.

———. "George Buchanan and French Humanism." In A. H. T. Levi, ed., *Humanism in France at the End of the Middle Ages and in the Early Renaissance,* pp. 295–319. New York, 1970.

Mathorez, J. "Notes sur l'histoire de la colonie portugaise de Nantes." *Bulletin hispanique,* XV (1913), 316–39.

Michaud, G. L. "The Spanish Sources of Certain Sixteenth Century French Writers." *Modern Language Notes,* XLIII (1928), 157–63.

Michel, Pierre. "Cannibales et cosmographes." *Bulletin de la société des amis de Montaigne,* 4th ser., No. 11 (1967), pp. 23–37.

Mollat, Michel. "Passages français dans l'Océan Indien au temps de François Ier." *Studia,* No. 11 (1963), pp. 239–50.

Morf, H. "Die französische Literatur in der 2. Hälfte des 16. Jahrhunderts." *Zeitschrift für französische Sprache und Literatur,* XVIII (1896), 157–201; XIX (1897), 1–61.

Paschal, Mary. "The New World in *Les Sepmaines* of Du Bartas." *Romance Notes,* XI (1969–70), 619–22.

Perrochon, H. "Simon Goulart, commentateur de la première semaine de Du Bartas." *Revue d'histoire littéraire de la France,* XXXII (1925), 397–401.

Richter, B. L. O. "The Thought of Louis Le Roy According to His Early Pamphlets." *Studies in the Renaissance,* VIII (1961), 173–96.

Romier, Lucien. "Lyon et le cosmopolitisme au début de la Renaissance française." *Bibliothèque d'humanisme et renaissance,* XI (1949), 28–42.

Rowe, John Howland. "Ethnography and Ethnology in the Sixteenth Century." *Kroeber Anthropological Society Papers,* No. 30 (1964), pp. 1–19.

Sainéan, Lazare. "Rabelaisiana —*Le Monteville* de Rabelais." *Revue des études rabelaisiennes,* IX (1911), 265–75.

———. "Les sources modernes du roman de Rabelais." *Revue des études rabelaisiennes,* X (1912), 375–420.

———. "La cosmographie de Jean-Alfonse Saintongeais." *Revue des études rabelaisiennes,* X (1912), 19–67.

———. "L'histoire naturelle dans l'oeuvre de Rabelais." *Revue du seizième siècle,* III (1915), 186–277.

Salomon, Richard. "A Trace of Dürer in Rabelais." *Modern Language Notes,* LVIII (1943), 498–500.

Saulnier, Verdun L. "Dix années d'études sur Rabelais." *Bibliothèque d'humanisme et renaissance,* XI (1949), 105–28.

———. "Position actuelle des problèmes rabelaisiens." *Actes du congrès de Tours et Poitiers,* 1954, pp. 83–104.

———. "Etude sur Béroalde de Verville." *Bibliothèque d'humanisme et renaissance,* V (1944), 209–326.

Schenda, Rudolf. "Bibliographie und kurze Beschreibung einiger Prodigienschriften." *Zeitschrift für französische Sprache und Literatur*, LXIX (1959), 150–67.

Scott, C. P. G. "The Malayan Words in English." *Journal of the American Oriental Society*, XVIII (1897), 74–80.

Schrader, Ludwig. "Die Rabelais-Forschung der Jahre 1950–1960: Tendenzen und Ergebnisse." *Romanistisches Jahrbuch*, XI (1960), 161–201.

Secret, François. "Jean Macer, François Xavier, et Guillaume Postel, ou un épisode de l'histoire comparée des religions au XVIᵉ siècle." *Revue de l'histoire des religions*, CLXX (1966), 47–69.

See, Henri. "La philosophie de l'histoire de Jean Bodin." *Revue historique*, CLXXV (1939), 497–505.

Telle, Emile von. "La situation géographique(?) de la Dive Bouteille." *Bibliothèque d'humanisme et renaissance*, XIV (1952), 329–30.

Tilley, M. A. "Rabelais and Geographical Discovery." *Modern Language Review*, II (1906), 316–26.

Tooley, Marian J. "Bodin and the Medieval Theory of Climate." *Speculum*, XXVIII (1953), 64–83.

Venturi, Franco. "Oriental Despotism." *Journal of the History of Ideas*, XXIV (1963), 133–42.

Veríssimo, Serrão J. "António de Gouveia e Miguel de Montaigne: Seu provável contacto." *Revista filosófica (Coimbra)*, II (1952), 84–88.

Vivanti, Corrado. "Alla origini dell'idea di civiltà: le scoperte geografiche e gli scritti di Henri de la Popelinière." *Revista storica italiana*, LXXIV (1962), 225–49.

Vogel, E. G. "Ueber W. Postels Reisen in den Orient." *Serapeum*, XIV (1853), 49–58.

Weinberg, Bernard. "Montaigne's Readings for *Des Cannibales*." In George B. Daniel, Jr., ed., *Renaissance and Other Studies in Honor of William Leon Wiley*, pp. 261–79. Chapel Hill, N.C., 1968.

VIII. THE GERMANIC LITERATURES

GERMAN AND NETHERLANDISH LITERATURE

BOOKS

Anon. *General Chronica, das ist, wahrhafftige Beschreibung vieler bisher unbekandter Landschafften, erstlich die Königreich und Herrschafften Priester Johannis in Morgenland. 2. gemeine Beschreibung dess gantzen Erdbodens. 3. eine summarischer Auszug der newen erfunden Insulen, Americae und Magelonae, so man die newe Welt pfleget zu nennen, in 3 unterschiedliche Bücher getheilet.* Frankfurt, 1581.

Adam, Melchior. *Vitae germanorum philosophorum.* Heidelberg, 1615.

Adel, Kurt. *Das Wiener Jesuitentheater und die europäische Barockdramatik.* Vienna, 1960.

———. *Das Jesuitendrama in Österreich.* Vienna, 1957.

———, ed. *Conradi Celtis . . . opuscula.* Leipzig, 1966.

Albertinus, Aegidius, trans. *Historii und eigentliche Bechreibung was gestalt das Evangelium*

Christi in China eingeführt, gepflanzt und gepredigt wird. Verteutscht durch Aegidium Albertinum. Munich, 1608.

————. *Historische Relation, was sich inn etlichen Jaren hero im Königreich Iapon, so wol im geist—als auch weltlichem Wesen, namhafftes begeben und zugetragen* (pp. 1–253). *Zum andern, von der Stadt und Gelegenheit der gantzen Ostindien* (pp. 254–317). *Drittens, kurtze Beschreibung dess Landts Guinea und Serra Lioa in Africa ligendt.* . . . *Durch Aegidium Albertinum übersetzt.* Munich, 1609.

Allen, Percy S.; Allen, M. H.; and Garrod, H. W., eds. *Opus epistolarum Des. Erasmi Roterdami.* 12 vols. Oxford, 1906–58.

Alsdorf, Ludwig. *Deutsch-indische Geistesbeziehungen.* Berlin, 1942.

Alsleben, A., ed. *Johann Fischarts Geschichtklitterung (Gargantua).* Halle, 1891.

Amiel, Émile. *Un publiciste du XVIᵉ siècle: Juste Lipse.* Paris, 1884.

Appelbaum, Stanley, ed. and trans. *The Triumph of Maximilian I.* New York, 1964.

Arthus, Gotthard. *Historia Indiae Orientalis, ex variis auctoribus collecta, et iuxta seriem topographicam regnorum, provinciarum et insularum . . . ad extremos usque Iaponios deducta.* . . . Cologne, 1608.

Bagdat, Elise C. *La "Querela Pacis" d'Érasme (1517).* Paris, 1924.

Bahder, K. von, ed. *Das Lalebuch (1597) mit den Abweichungen und Erweiterungen der Schiltbürger (1598) und des Grillenvertreibers.* Halle, 1914.

Balen, Wilhelm J. van. *De Ontdekking van de Wereld.* 2 vols. Amsterdam, 1932.

————. *Naar de indische Wonderwereld met Jan Huyghen van Linschoten.* 2 vols. Amsterdam, 1946.

Barzée, Gaspar. *Epistolae indicae in quibus luculenta extat descriptio rerum nuper in India orientali praeclaré gestarum a Theologis societatis Jesu.* Dillingen, 1563.

Baudet, Henri. *Paradise on Earth.* Translated by Elisabeth Wentholt. New Haven, 1965.

Baur, Frank. *Geschiedenis van de letterkunde der Nederlanden.* . . . 4 vols. Brussels, 1939.

Bennett, Josephine Waters. *The Rediscovery of Sir John Mandeville.* New York, 1954.

Benzing, Josef. *Der Buchdruck des 16. Jahrhunderts im deutschen Sprachgebiet: Eine Literatur-übersicht.* Leipzig, 1936.

Bergh, Laurent P. C. van den, ed. *Correspondance de Marguerite d'Autriche, gouvernante des Pays-Bas, avec ses amis, sur les affaires des Pays-Bas de 1506–1528.* 2 vols. Leyden, 1845–47.

Berlin. Austellung . . . im Schloss Charlottenburg. *China und Europa.* Berlin, 1973.

Bernays, Jakob. *Joseph Justus Scaliger.* Berlin, 1855.

Bertau, Karl. *Deutsche Literatur im europäischen Mittelalter.* 2 vols. Munich, 1972.

Beyrleins, Jacob. *Reyssbuch. Wegweiser etlicher Reysen durch gantz Teutschlandt, Polen, Sibenburg, Dennenmarck, Engelandt, Hispanien, Franckreich, Italien, Sicilien, Egypten, Indien, Ethiopien und Türckey.* Strassburg, 1606.

Bibliotheca exotica. See Draud, Georg.

Bischof, Hermann. *Sebastian Franck und deutsche Geschichtschreibung.* Tübingen, 1857.

Bock, Eugeen de. *John Baptist Houwaert.* Antwerp, 1960.

Boemus, Johann. *Omnium gentium mores, leges, et ritus ex multis clarissimus rerum scriptoribus.* Landshut, 1520.

Chapter Bibliographies

Bogeng, G. A. E. *Die grossen Bibliophilen: Geschichte der Büchersammler und ihrer Sammlungen.* 3 vols. Leipzig, 1922.

Bolte, Johannes, ed. *Georg Rollenhagens Spiel von Tobias 1576.* Halle, 1930.

Bonger, Hendrik. *Dirck Volckertszoon Coornhert: Studie over een nuchter en vroom Nederlander.* Lochem, 1942.

Boogerd, L. van den. *Het Jezuietendrama in de Nederlanden.* Groningen, 1961.

Boulting, William. *Aeneas Silvius, Orator, Man of Letters, Statesman and Pope.* London, 1918.

Boyd, James. *Ulrich Füetrer's "Parzival": Material and Sources.* Oxford, 1936.

Brandt, Geeraert. *Historie der vermaerde zee- en koopstadt Enkhuisen.* . . . Rev. ed. 2 vols. in 1. Nieuwendijk, 1971.

Braunsberger, Otto. *Petrus Canisius, ein Lebensbild.* Freiburg-im-Breisgau, 1917.

Breloer, B., and Bömer, F., eds. *Fontes historiae religionum Indicarum.* Bonn, 1939.

Brodrick, James. *Saint Peter Canisius, S.J.* Chicago, 1962.

British Museum. *Short-title Catalogue of Books Printed in the German-speaking Countries and German Books Printed in Other Countries from 1455 to 1600.* London, 1962.

Bucher, Otto. *Bibliographie der deutschen Drucke des XVI. Jahrhunderts.* Vol. 1: *Dillingen.* Vienna, 1960.

Buchner, E. *Das Neueste von Gestern. Kulturgeschichtlich-interessante Dokumente aus alten deutschen Zeitungen.* Vol. 1: *Das 16. und 17. Jahrhundert.* Frankfurt, 1911.

Burmeister, Karl Heinz. *Sebastian Münster: Versuch eines biographischen Gesamtbildes.* Basel and Stuttgart, 1963.

———. *Georg Joachim Rhetikus, 1514–1574: Eine Bio-Bibliographie.* Wiesbaden, 1967.

Bussche, Emile van den. *Flandre et Portugal.* Bruges, 1874.

Canisius, Petrus. *Epistula et acta.* 8 vols. Freiburg-im-Breisgau, 1896–1923.

Caverel, Philippe de. *Ambassade en Espagne et en Portugal (en 1582) de R. P. en Dieu, Dom Jean Sarrazim, abbé de St. Vaast, du Conseil d'estat de Sa Magesté Catholique, son premier conseiller en Arthois etc.* Arras, 1860.

Celius, Caspar. *Caspari Celii Zeitung auss Jappon was in derselben nechst verschienen 1582. von den Jesuitern, so wohin bekehrung der Heyden, als in erzehlung der neuwen Christenheit gehandelt worden.* Dillingen, 1586.

Celtis, Konrad. See Pindter, F., ed.

Chauvin, Victor, and Roersch, Alphonse. *Étude sur la vie et les travaux de Nicolas Clénard.* Brussels, 1900.

Chemnitz, Martin. *Navigatio Lusitanorum in Indiam Orientalem, heroico carmine descripta per Martinum Chemnitium secundum.* Leipzig, 1580.

Chytraeus, David. *Was zu dieser Zeit in Griechenland, Asien, Africa, unter der Türcken und Priester Johans Herrschafften. Item, in Ungern und Behemen etc. der Christlichen Kirchen zustand sey. Sampt etlichen Schreiben so von Constantinopel, vom Berge Sinai, und andern Örten aus Orient, newlicher Zeit abgangen.* . . . *Henrico Arnoldo aus Churland in Liffland verdeutschet.* Leipzig, 1581.

Chytraeus, Nathan. *Hodoeporica; sive, Itineraria, a diversis clariss. doctissimisq́; viris, tum veteribus, tum recentioribus . . . carmine conscripta.* . . . Frankfurt, 1575.

[658]

Clair, Colin. *Christopher Plantin.* London, 1960.

Clark, James M. *The Abbey of St. Gall as a Center of Literature and Art.* Cambridge, 1926.

Clenard, Nicolas. See Roersch, Alphonse, ed.

Cockx-Indestige, Elly, and Glorieux, Geneviève. *Belgica typographica, 1541–1600.* Nieuwkoop, 1968.

Coignet, Michel. *Abraham Ortelius. His Epitome. Supplement Added by Michel Coignet.* Antwerp, 1603.

Conestaggio, Girolamo Franchi di. *Historien der Königreich Portugal und Aphrica, darauss zusehen in welcher Zeit sonderlich Portugal seinen Anfang genommen von wem dasselbige Land zum Königreich erhaben, was dieselbigen für Kreige und Gewerbe zu Wasser und Land geführet, auch wie das Königreich wiederumb zur Kron Spanien gebracht worden.* Munich, 1598.

Conrady, Karl Otto. *Lateinische Dichtungstradition und deutsche Lyrik des 17. Jahrhunderts.* Bonn, 1962.

Coornhert, Dirk V. *Dirck Volckertsen Coornhert en zijne Wellevenskunst.* Amsterdam, 1860.

Corsali, Andreas. *Ein schreiben Andree Corsali von Florentz an den durchleuchtigen fürsten Herrn Julianum den Andern aussgangen zu Cochin welchs ein statt in Indien den 6. januarij in 1515. jhar. — Das ander schreiben Andree Corsali von Florentz an den durchleuchtigen fürsten vnd herren Hertzogen Lorentzen de Medici von dem Rotenmeer vnd Sinu Persico biss gen Cochin ein statt in Indien dess datum stehet den achtzehenden septembris tausend fünff hundert siebent zehen.* Frankfurt, 1576.

Crone, Ernst, ed. *The Principal Works of Simon Stevin.* Amsterdam, 1953.

Dannenfeldt, Karl H. *Leonhard Rauwolf, Sixteenth-Century Physician, Botanist, and Traveler.* Cambridge, Mass., 1968.

Daris, J. *Histoire du diocèse et de la principauté de Liège pendant le XVIe siècle.* Liège, 1884.

Davids, William. *Verslag van een anderzoek betreffende de betrekkingen tusschen de Nederlansche en de Spaansche letterkunde in de 16–18e eeuw.* 's-Gravenhage, 1918.

Davies, David William. *Dutch Influences on English Culture, 1555–1625.* Ithaca, N. Y., 1964.

Daxhelet, E. *Adrien Barlandus, humaniste belge, 1486–1538: Sa vie, ses oeuvres, sa personalité·* Louvain, 1938.

Delen, Adrien Jean Joseph. *Christophe Plantin, imprimeur de l'humanisme.* . . . Brussels, 1944.

Del Rio, Martin Antoine. *Syntagma tragoediae Latinae in tres partes distinctum.* 3 vols. in 2. Antwerp, 1593–94.

De Witt, André. "Het humanisme in Brugge (1515–1579)." Lic. hist. diss., University of Louvain, 1955–56.

Dhassels, Hieronymi. *Itinerarium, oder Reissbüchlein, darinnen summarische Beschreibung auff 100 vornemer Stätte in Europa, und andern Ländern in der Welt, welche sich in andere 4257 grosse und kleine Handels und andere Stätt ausstheilen zubefinden, wie viel gemeiner teutscher Meiln solche von gedachten 100 Stätten gelegen, un alles nach dem Alphabet verzeichnet.* Leipzig, 1589.

Dietz, Alexander. *Zur Geschichte der Frankfurter Büchermesse, 1462–1792.* Frankfurt, 1921.

Doesborch, Jan van, comp. *Pape Ian landen.* Facsimile of 1506 edition. Amsterdam, 1873.

Dorey, T. A., ed. *Latin Historians.* London, 1966.

Dorsten, J. A. van. *Poets, Patrons, and Professors.* Leyden, 1962.

———. *The Radical Arts: First Decade of an Elizabethan Renaissance.* Leyden, 1970.

Draud, Georg. *Bibliotheca exotica sive Catalogus officinalis librorum peregrinis linguis usualibus scriptorum.* . . . Frankfurt, 1610.

Dréano, Maturin. *Humanisme chrétien: La tragédie latine commentée pour les chrétiens du XVIe siècle par Martin Antoine del Rio.* Paris, 1936.

Dresser, Matthias. *Historien und bericht von dem newlicher zeit erfundenden Königreich China wie es nach umbstenden, so zu einer rechtmessigen beschreibung gehören darumb beschafften. Item, von dem auch new erfundenen lande Virginia. Jetzund auffs newe übersehen und mitt einem zusatz vermehret, nemlich: wie es umb die religion in Perser und Mohren land, unter Priester Johan bewand sey.* Leipzig, 1598.

———. *Isagoge historica, Historische Erzehlung der denkwürdigsten Geschichten von Anfang der Welt, biss auff unsere Zeit, nach den 6000 Jahren verfasst, wurd in 4. Bücher getheilt. Durch Mattaeum Dresserum Professoren zu Leipzig in fol. bey Bart. Voigt,* 1601.

———. *Memorabilia mundi.* Halle, 1589.

Duhr, Bernhard. *Geschichte der Jesuiten in den Ländern deutscher Zunge.* 2 vols. Freiburg-im-Breisgau, 1907, 1913.

———. *Die Jesuiten an den deutschen Fürstenhöfen des 16. Jahrhunderts.* Freiburg-im-Breisgau, 1901.

Duncan, Martin, trans. *Die vruchten der ecclesie Christi. Van wõderlicke Wonderheyden dwelcken geüonden eñ gedaen wordẽ met Godts gratie in veel eñ grottelanden van Indien dwelcken nu in onse tijden eersten geüõden sijn eñ totten Christelicken geloof nu dagelijer bekeert worden: tot Gods glorie, tot salicheyt der Heydenen, eñ tot troost der Christenen, een corte verclaeringhe ut veel bueuen van daergesonden, ende alsulckr certifiterende metter waerheyt. Ende nu eerst ut den Latijne in onser duijtssche spraeckẽ overgeset door Martinum Duncanum Quempensim, Pastor* . . . *te Delf.* Leyden, 1567.

Durme, Maurice van. *Supplément à la correspondance de Christophe Plantin.* . . . Antwerp, 1955.

Duyse, Florimond van. *Het oude Nederlandische lied.* 4 parts. 's-Gravenhage, 1903–8.

Egenolff, Christian. *Chronica, Beschreibung und gemeyne Anzeyge, vonn aller Welt herkommen, Fürnamen, Landen, Stande, Eygenschafften, Historien, Wesen, Manier, Sitten, An-und Abgang. Auss den glaubwirdigsten Historie* . . . *nach historischer Warheit beschriben.* Frankfurt-am-Main, 1535.

———. *Chronica von an uñ abgang aller Welt wesenn. Ausz den glaubwirdigsten Historien beschriben.* . . . Frankfurt, 1533.

Ehrenberg, Richard. *Das Zeitalter der Fugger.* 2 vols. Jena, 1896.

Ellerbroek-Fortuin, Else. *Amsterdamse Rederijkersspelen in den XVIe eeuw.* . . . Groningen, 1937.

Ellinger, Georg. *Geschichte der neulateinischen Literatur Deutschlands im 16. Jahrhundert.* 3 vols. Berlin, 1929–33.

Engel, Karl. *Bibliotheca Faustiana.* Oldenburg, 1885.

Esserhens, D. Henrici. *Dreyzehn Christliche Predigten auss dem acht und dreyssigsten und neun und dreyssigsten Cap. Ezechielis von Gog und Magog oder den Türcken.* Strassburg, 1571.

Everart, Martin, trans. *Cort Onderwijs van de Conste de Seevaert bechreven deur den Licentiaet "Rodrigo Zamorano."* . . . Amsterdam, 1598.

Favolius, Hugo. *Theatri orbis terrarum enchiridion, minoribus tabulis per Philippum Gallaeum exaratum: et carmine heroico, ex variis Geographis et Poëtis collecto, per Hugonem Favolium illustratum.* Antwerp, 1585.

Feyerabend, Sigmund. *General chronicen, das ist: Warhaffte eigentliche vnd kurtze beschreibung, vieler namhaffter, vnd zum theil biss daher vnbekannter landtschafften* . . . *Darinnen alle völcker vnd nationen, die in der gantzen welt* . . . *wohnen, sampt jhrer ankunfft vnd herkommen, auch art vnd natur, item ceremonien vnd gebräuchen in geistlichen vnd weltlichen sachen, treuwlich beschrieben* . . . *werden. Jetzt auffs neuw mit sonderni grossen fleiss, besser als zuvor, beschreiben vnd verteutscht, auch mehrer richtigkeit halben in drey vnderschliedliche bücher getheilt.* . . . Frankfurt, 1576.

———. *Cosmographia. Das ist: Warhaffte eigentliche und kurtze Beschreibung des gantzen Erdbodens, und die nach Petolemeo neuw erfundenen Inseln Americe und Magellane* . . . *in Verlegung Sigmund Feyerabents.* Frankfurt, 1576.

———. *Historia rerum in Oriente gestarum. Apud P. Fabricium imprensis S. Feyerabendij.* Frankfurt, 1587.

Fischart, Johann. *Geschichtklitterung* (Gargantua). Edited by A. Alsleben. Halle, 1891.

———. *Sämmtliche Dichtungen.* Edited by H. Kurz. 3 vols. Leipzig, 1861–67.

Fischer, Hans, *et al. Conrad Gessner, 1516–1565: Universalgelehrter, Naturforscher, Arzt.* Zurich, 1967.

Fischer, Hermann, and Bolte, Johannes, eds. *Peregrinnagio—Die Reise der Söhne Giaffers.* . . . "Bibliothek des litterarischen Vereins in Stuttgart," Vol. 208. Stuttgart, 1896.

Flemming, Willi. *Geschichte des Jesuitentheaters in den Landen deutscher Zunge.* Berlin, 1923.

———. *Das Ordensdrama: Deutsche Literatur in Entwicklungsreihen.* 2d ed. Darmstadt, 1965.

Floerke, Hanns. *Studien zur niederländischen Kunst- und Kulturgeschichte.* Munich, 1905.

Forster, Edward Seymour, trans. *The Turkish Letters of Ogier Ghiselin de Busbecq.* Oxford, 1927.

Franck, Sebastian. *Weltbuch: spiegel vñ bildtnisz des gantzen erdbodens von Sebastiano Franco Wördensi in vier bücher, nemlich in Asiam, Aphricam, Europam, vnd Americam gestelt vnd abteilt.* . . . Tübingen, 1534.

———. *Chronica zeÿtbuch vnd geschÿchtbibel von anbegyn biss inn diss gegenwertig M.D. XXXJ jar. Dariñ beide Gottes vnd der welt lauff, hendel, art, wort, werck, thun, lassen, kriegen, wesen, vnd leben ersehen vñ begriffen wirt.* . . . Strassburg, 1531.

———. *Erst Theil dieses Weltbuchs, von newen erfundnen Landtschafften* . . . *Durch S. F. zum ersten am Tag geben, jetzt aber mit sondern Fleiss auf ein neuwes ubersehen, vnd in ein wolgeformtes Handtbuch verfasset.* . . . Frankfurt, 1567.

Fricius, Valentine, trans. *Indianischer Religionstandt der gantzen newen Welt, beider Indien gegen Auff und Niedergang der Sonnen: Schleinigster Form auss gründtlichen Historien sonderlich des Hochwürdigen Vatters Francisci Gonzagen Barfüsserische Ordenscroniken, und Didaci Vallades, geistlicher Rhetorie zusammen gezogen und aussm Latein in hochteutsch verwendent durch F. Valentinum Fricium.* Ingolstadt, 1588.

Gaedertz, Karl Theodor. *Gabriel Rollenhagen, sein Leben und seine Werke.* Leipzig, 1881.

Gassar, Achilles P. *Historiarum et chronicorum mundi epitome usque ad annum 1533.* Antwerp, 1533.

Geiger, Ludwig. *Johann Reuchlin: Sein Leben und seine Werke.* Leipzig, 1871.

———, ed. *Johann Reuchlins Briefwechsel.* Tübingen, 1876.

———. *Conrad Celtis in seinen Beziehungen zur Geographie.* Munich, 1896.

Genée, Rudolf. *Hans Sachs und seine Zeit.* Leipzig, 1902.

Gerard, P. *Anvers à travers les ages.* 2 vols. Brussels, 1888.

Gerlo, Aloïs, comp. *Bibliographie de l'humanisme belge.* Brussels, 1965.

Goedeke, Karl. *Grundriss zur Geschichte der deutschen Dichtung aus den Quellen.* 2d ed. Vol. II: *Das Reformationszeitalter.* Dresden, 1886.

———, ed. *Froschmeuseler von Georg Rollenhagen.* In K. Goedecke and J. Tittmann, eds., *Deutsche Geschichte des sechszehnten Jahrhunderts,* Vols. VIII–IX. Leipzig, 1876.

Goetz, Walter, ed. *Beiträge zur Geschichte Herzog Albrechts V und des Landsberger Bundes, 1556–1598.* 5 vols. Munich, 1898.

Götze, Alfred August Woldemar. *Die hochdeutschen Drucker der Reformationszeit.* Strassburg, 1905.

Goris, Jan A. *Étude sur les colonies marchandes méridionales (Portugais, Espagnols, Italiens) à Anvers de 1488 à 1587.* Louvain, 1925.

Graf, Wilhelm. *Doktor Christoph Scheurl von Nürnberg.* In W. Goetz, ed., *Beiträge zur Kulturgeschichte des Mittelalters und der Renaissance,* Vol. XLIII. Leipzig and Berlin, 1930.

Grafton, Anthony T. "Joseph Scaliger (1540–1609) and the Humanism of the Later Renaissance." Ph.D. diss., Department of History, University of Chicago, 1975.

Gramaye, Jan Baptiste. *Asia, sive historia universalis asiaticorum gentium.* Antwerp, 1604.

Graubard, Mark, trans., and Parker, John, ed. *Tidings Out of Brazil.* Minneapolis, 1957.

Greiff, R., ed. *Briefe und Berichte über die frühesten Reisen nach Amerika und Ostindien aus den Jahren 1497 bis 1506 aus Dr. Conrad Peutingers Nachlass. XXVI Jahresbericht des Hist. Kreis Vereins im Reg. Bez. von Schwaben und Neuburg, für das Jahr, 1860.* Augsburg, 1861.

———. *Tagebuch des Lucas Rem aus den Jahren 1494–1541.* Augsburg, 1861.

Grote, L. *Die Tucher.* Munich, 1961.

Grouchy, Vicomte de, and Travers, E. *Étude sur Nicolas de Grouchy.* Paris, 1878.

Grün, K. *Kulturgeschichte des 16. Jahrhunderts.* Heidelberg, 1872.

Guicciardini, Lodovico. *Description de touts les Pays-Bas.* Arnhem, 1593.

———. *Lettere di Giovan Battista Guicciardini a Cosimo e Francesco de' Medici scritte dal Belgio 1559 al 1577.* Brussels, 1950.

Gundolf, Friedrich. *Anfänge deutscher Geschichtsschreibung.* Amsterdam, 1938.

Günther, H., ed. *Fortunatus: Nach dem Augsburger Druck von 1509.* "Neudrucke deutscher Litteraturwerke des XVI. und XVII. Jahrhunderts," Nos. 240–41. Halle, 1914.

Haas, C. M. *Das Theater der Jesuiten in Ingolstadt: Ein Beitrag zur Geschichte des geistlichen Theaters in Süddeutschland.* Emsdetten, 1958.

Haebler, Konrad. *Deutsche Bibliophilen des 16. Jahrhunderts: Die Fürsten von Anhalt, ihre Bücher und Bucheinbände.* Leipzig, 1923.

Hagen, K. *Deutschlands literarische und religiöse Verhältinisse im Reformationszeitalter.* 3 vols. Erlangen, 1844.

Haitz, Michael. *Hartmann Schedel's Weltchronik.* . . . Munich, 1899.

Halkin, Léon Ernest. *Réforme protestante et réforme catholique au diocèse de Liège. Le cardinal de la Marck, prince évêque de Liège (1505–1538).* Liège, 1930.

Handwerker, Otto. *Geschichte der Würzburger Universitätsbibliothek.* Würzburg, 1904.

Hantsch, Viktor. *Deutsche Reisende des sechzehnten Jahrhunderts.* Leipzig, 1895.

———. *Sebastian Münster.* Leipzig, 1898.

Hartfelder, Karl, ed. *Fünf Bücher Epigramme von Konrad Celtes.* Berlin, 1881.

Hartmann, A., ed. *Die Amerbach-Korrespondenz.* Basel, 1953.

Haszler, K. D., ed. *Reisen und Gefangenschaft Hans Ulrich Kraffts aus der Originalhandschrift.* "Bibliothek des literarischen Vereins in Stuttgart," Vol. LXI. Stuttgart, 1861.

Hauffen, Adolf. *Johann Fischart: Ein Literaturbild aus der Zeit der Gegenreformation.* 2 vols. Berlin, 1921–22.

Hay, John. *De rebus Iaponicis, et Peruanis epistolae recentiores.* . . . Antwerp, 1605.

Hedio, Kaspar. *Ein auserlesene Chronik von Anfang der Welt biss auf das Jahr . . . 1543.* . . . Strassburg, 1549.

Heekelingen, H. de Vries de, ed. *Correspondance de B. Vulcanius pendant son séjour à Cologne, Genève et Bâle (1573–1577).* The Hague, 1923.

Henne, Alexandre. *Histoire du regne de Charles-Quint en Belgique.* 10 vols. Brussels and Leipzig, 1858–60.

Herbermann, C. G., ed. *The Cosmographiae introductio of Martin Waldseemüller in Facsimile.* . . . New York, 1907.

Herberstein, Siegmund von. *Rerum Moscoviticarum commentarii.* Basel, 1551.

Herman, Jean Baptiste. *La pédagogie des Jésuites au XVIᵉ siècle.* . . . Louvain, 1914.

Hertz, W. *Gesammelte Abhandlungen.* Stuttgart and Berlin, 1905.

Heussen, A. H. *Het leven van Ogier Ghislain de Busbecq (1522–91).* Brussels, 1955.

Hirten, William James, ed. *The Complaint of Peace by Erasmus.* New York, 1946.

Hodgen, Margaret T. *Early Anthropology in the Sixteenth and Seventeenth Centuries.* Philadelphia, 1964.

Hoffman, Agnes. *Untersuchungen zu den altdeutschen Marco Polo-Texten.* Ohlau, 1936.

Hoffman von Fallersleben, August H., ed. *Antwerpener Liederbuch vom Jahre 1544.* Hanover, 1855.

Holzmann, M. and Bohatta, H. *Deutsches Anonymen-Lexikon.* 7 vols. Weimar, 1902–28.

Homberg, Johann. *Historia moralis, Beschreibung aller fürnembsten Geistlichen und Weltlichen Regenten mancherlei Sitten und Gewohneiten, aller und jeder Völcker in Africa, Asia, Europa und America.* Frankfurt, n.d.

Hooykaas, J. C. *Repertorium op de koloniale Litteratuur.* . . . Vol. I. Amsterdam, 1877.

Horowitz, A. *Zur Bibliothek und Correspondenz Reuchlins.* Vienna, 1872.

Houwaert, Ian Baptista. *Sommare beschrijvinghe van de triumphantelycke Incompst vanden . . . Aertshertoge Matthias.* . . . Antwerp, 1579.

Jacob, Ernst Gerhard. *Deutschland und Portugal, ihre kulturellen Beziehungen.* Leyden, 1961.

Ijzerman, Jan Willem. *Dirck Gerritsz Pomp, 1544–1604.* The Hague, 1915.

Jesuits. Letters from Missions (The East). *Iohan Georgii Götzen verzeichniss und Beschreibung deren Dingen, so von den Jesuitern in Orient von Anno 1552 biss auff 68. gehandelt worden.* Ingolstadt, 1576.

————. *Historischer Bericht, wz sich Jahr 1577, 79, 80, und 81 in bekehrung der gewaltigen Landschafft und Insel Jappon, in politischen und auch in Geistlichen Sachen zugetragen, in etlichen underschiedlichen Missiven der Jesuiten auss gemelter Insel Jappon an ihren Generaln und andere Jesuiten in Europam gethan.* Dillingen, 1585.

————. *Zeitung auss Jappon dess 1582. 83. und 84 Jahrs sampt der frölichen Botchafft auss China dess 83. und 84. Jahrs von dem daselbst angehenden Christenthumb. Gezogen auss den Briefen der Jesuiter die zu Rom ankommen im December, 1585.* Dillingen, 1586.

————. *Bechreibung der jüngst abgesandten Japponischen Legaten gentzen Reiss auss Jappon biss gen Rom und widerumb von dannẽ in Portugal, biss zu ihrem abschied auss Lisbona, auch von grossen Ehren, so ihnen allenthalben von Fürsten und Herrn erzeigt, und was sich sonst mit ihnen verlauffen mit vorgehender Beschreibung der Japponischen Landtsart, Gebrauch, Sitten, und Natur.* Dillingen, 1587.

————. *Schreiben auss China und India an der Jesuiten General den 9. Decembr. 1586 gethan, sampt erzelhung eines mercklichen Schiffbruchs.* Dillingen, 1589.

————. *Avisi della Cina e Giapone del fine dell' anno 1586, con larrivo delli Signori Giaponesi nell' India.* Antwerp, 1589.

————. *Annales Indiques, contenantes la vraye narration et advis de ce qu'est advenue et succede en Iapon, et aultres lieux voisins des Indes, envoyez par les Peres de la Societé de Iesus au R. P. Claude Aquauiua General de la dicte Compagnie, en l'an 1588. Nouuellement traduictes en Francois.* Antwerp, 1590.

————. *Lodoici Froys 3 Jahrschreiben auss Japonia, was darin im Anno 75. aussgericht und vom schrecklichen Ableiben, Quabercuden und seines Anhangs.* Mainz, 1598.

————. *Newe Historische Relation und sehr gute fröliche Bottschaft, was sich in viel gewaltigen Königreichen der Orientalischen Indien zugetragen.* Dillingen, 1601.

————. *Newe historische Relatio der Orientalischen Indien und Königreich China, im Jahr 98. und 99 durch die Patres soc. Iesu gestellet.* Dillingen, 1602.

————. *Zwey Japonische Sendschreiben, wz sich nemlich nach Taicosamae dess gantzen Jappons Oberherrn absterben, wunderbarlich daselbst zugetragen.* Mainz, 1603.

Joachimsen, Paul. *Geschichtsauffassung und Geschichtschreibung in Deutschland unter dem Einfluss des Humanismus.* "Beyträge zur Kulturgeschichte des Mittelalters und der Renaissance," Vol. VI. Edited by Walter Goetz. Part I. Leipzig, 1910.

Jonge, Johan K. L. de, ed. *De Opkomst van het Nederlandisch Gezag in Oost-Indië.* 3 vols. The Hague, 1862–65.

Kalff, Gerrit. *Geschiedenis der nederlandsche Letterkunde in de 16de eeuw.* 2 vols. Leyden, 1889.

Kallen, Gerhard. *Aeneas Silvius Piccolomini als Publizist.* Cologne, 1939.

Kapp, F. *Geschichte des deutschen Buchhandels.* Leipzig, 1886.

Keller, Adelbert von, and Goetze, E., eds. *Hans Sachs. Gesamtausgabe.* 26 vols. Stuttgart, 1870–1908.

Kiechel, Samuel. *Die reisen des Samuel Kiechel. Aus drei Handschriften Hrsg. von K. D. Harszler.* "Bibliothek des litterarischen Vereins in Stuttgart," Vol. LXXXVI. Stuttgart, 1866.

Klatt, Detloff. *David Chytraeus als Geschichtslehrer und Geschichtschreiber.* Rostock, 1908.

Klemm, Gustav. *Zur Geschichte der Sammlungen für Wissenschaft und Kunst in Deutschland.* Zerbst, 1837.

Kloosterboer, W. *Bibliografie van Nederlandse publikatis over Portugal en zijn overzeese gebiedsdeelen.* Utrecht, 1957.

Knuvelder, Gerard. *Handboek tot de Geschiedenis der Nederlandse Letterkunde van de aanvang tot heden.* 4 vols. Malenberg, 1953.

Koepp, Johannes. *Untersuchungen über das Antwerpener Liederbuch vom Jahre 1544.* Antwerp, 1927.

Kollarz, Christian. "Die beiden Indien im deutschen Schrifttum des 16. und 17. Jahrhunderts." Ph.D. diss., University of Vienna, 1966.

König, Erich. *Peutingerstudien.* Freiburg-im-Breisgau, 1914.

——, ed. *Konrad Peutingers Briefwechsel.* Munich, 1923.

Körner, Josef. *Bibliographisches Handbuch des deutschen Schrifttums.* Bern and Munich, 1966.

Kreps, J. *Le Mecenat de la Cour de Bruxelles, 1430–1559.* Paris, 1956.

Kriegk, G. L. *Geschichte von Frankfurt.* Frankfurt, 1871.

Kronenberg, M. E., ed. and trans. *De novo mondo. Antwerp. Jan van Doesborch* [*about 1520*]. The Hague, 1927.

Kühne, August, ed. *Das älteste Faustbuch. Wortgetreuer Abdruck der editio princeps des Spies'schen Faustbuches vom Jahre 1587.* Zerbst, 1868. Reprint of 1970.

Kury, Hans. *Simon Grynaeus von Basel.* Zurich and Leipzig, 1935.

Kurz, Heinrich, ed. *Johann Fischart's sämmtliche Dichtungen.* 3 vols. Leipzig, 1866–67.

Lagerway, Walter. *Guide to Netherlandic Studies: Bibliography.* Grand Rapids, Mich., 1964.

Lanz, Karl, ed. *Correspondenz des Kaisers Karl V.* 3 vols. Leipzig, 1844–46.

Lepszy, Hans-Joachim. "Die Reiseberichte des Mittelalters und der Reformationszeit." Ph.D. diss., University of Hamburg, 1952.

Leüblfing, Johann von. *Ein schön lustig Reissbuch.* . . . Ulm, 1612.

Liebrecht, Henri. *Les chambres de rhétorique.* Brussels, 1948.

Lipsius, Justus. *Sixe bookes of politickes or civil doctrine.* . . . London, 1594.

——. *Opera.* 5 vols. Antwerp, 1603.

——. *Admiranda, sive de magnitudine Romana.* Antwerp, 1605.

——. *Dissertationum ludicrarum et amoenitatum, Scriptores varij.* Leyden, 1638.

——. *Epistolarum selectarum centuria prima* [*tertia*] *ad Belgas.* 3 vols. in 1. Antwerp, 1602–5.

Lodewijcksz, Willem. *Prima pars descriptionis itineris navalis in Indiam Orientalem, earvmqve rervm qvae navibvs battavis occvrrervnt; vna cvm particvlari enarratione conditionum, morum, oeconomiae popularum, quos adnavigarunt. Praeterea de numismatis, aromatibus, speciebus & mercibus ibidem venalibus, eorumque pretio. Insuper de insularem apparentijs, tractibus, orisque regionum maritimis, vna cum incolarum ad vivum delineatione; cuncta diversis tabulis illustrata: omnibus mare navigantibus & rerum exterarum studiosis, lectu periucunda.* Amsterdam, 1598.

——. *Premier Livre de la navigasion aux Indes Orientales par les Hollandais et des choses a aux advenues.* . . . Amsterdam, 1595.

———. *Le second Livre, journal ou comtoire contenant le vrai discours et narration historique du voyage fait par les huit navires a Amsterdam au mois de mars de l'an, 1598, sous la conduite de l'amiral Jacques Corneille Necq, et du Vice-Amiral Wibrant de Warwicq.* Calais, 1601.

Lossen, M. *Briefe von Andreas Masius und seinen Freunden 1538 bis 1573.* "Publikationen der Gesellschaft für rheinische Geschichtskunde," Vol. II. Leipzig, 1886.

Lycosthenes, Conradus. *Prodigiorum ac ostentorum chronicon.* . . . Basel, 1557.

Mackensen, L., and Bolte, J. *Handwörterbuch des deutschen Märchens.* Berlin and Leipzig, 1930–33.

Markwart, Otto. *Willibald Pirckheimer als Geschichtsschreiber.* Zurich, 1886.

Mayer, Johannes. *Compendium cronologicum seculi à Christo nato decimi sexti. Das ist: Summarischer Inhalt aller gedruck und glaubwirdigen Sachen so sich auff gantzem Erdenkreisz in den nechsten hundert Jaren zu Wasser und Landt hier und wider zugetragen mit kurtzer Beschreibung etlicher Völcker und Länder mancherley sittin und gebräuchen ausz ansehelichen authoribus zusamb getragen und in dise formb verfasset.* Munich, 1598.

Megiser, Hieronymus. *Thesaurus polyglottus: vel, dictionarium multilingue: ex quadringentis circiter tam veteris, quam novi (vel potius antiquis incogniti) orbis nationum linguis, dialectis, idiomatibus, & idiotismis, constans.* Frankfurt, 1603.

———. *Hodoeporicon Indiae Orientalis.* Leipzig, 1608.

———. *Chorographia Tartariae.* Leipzig, 1610.

———. *Septentrio novantiquus, oder Die newe nort welt. Das ist: Gründliche vnd warhaffte beschreibung aller der mitternächtigen vnd nortwerts gelegenen landen vnd insulen, so . . . von etlichen berühmten . . . adelspersonen, schiffern, befelschshabern . . . seynd erfunden worden. . . . Zuvor in teutscher sprach nie aussgangen, sondern an jetzo erst alles aus vielen vnterschiedenen schrifften vnd büchern . . . verdeutschet, mit artigen darzu gehörigen figuren vnd land tafeln gezieret, vnd in druck verfertiget, durch Hieronymum Megiserum. Sampt angehengter relation, welcher gestalt in dem . . . 1612. jahr, beydes, eine newe kurtze schiffart nach der China gegen nortwerts, vnd dann auch ein vnsegliche grosse vnd reiche landschafft sudwerts im fünften theil der welt Magellanica erfunden worden.* . . . Leipzig, 1613.

Meijer, Reinder P. *Literature of the Low Countries: A Short History of Dutch Literature in the Netherlands and Belgium.* Assen, 1971.

Melanchthon, Philipp. *Omnium operum.* . . . 4 vols. Wittenberg, 1562–77.

———. *Epistolarum.* . . . Basel, 1565.

Mermnan, Arnold *Theatrum conversionis gentium totius orbis.* . . . Antwerp, 1572.

Meyer, Christian. *Geschichte der Stadt Augsburg.* Tübingen, 1907.

Moorrees, F. D. J. *Dirk Volckertszoon Coornhert.* . . . Schoonhoven, 1887.

Müller, Günther. *Deutsche Dichtung von der Renaissance bis zum Ausgang des Barocks.* Potsdam, 1929.

Müller, J. *Das Jesuitentheater in den Ländern deutscher Zunge vom Anfang bis zum Hochbarock.* 2 vols. Augsburg, 1930.

Müller, Max. *Johann Albrecht Widmanstetter, 1506–1557: Seine Leben und Werken.* Munich, 1907.

Münster, Sebastian. *Cosmographei oder Beschreibung aller Länder-Herrschafften etc.* . . . Basel, 1550.

————. *La cosmographie universelle de tout le monde ... auteur en partie Mvenster, mais beaucoup augmentée, ornée & enrichée, par François de Belleforest. ...* Paris, 1575.

————. *A Briefe Collection and Compendious Extract of Straūge and Memorable Thinges, Gathered Oute of the Cosmographye of Sebastian Munster. ...* London, 1572.

————. *A Treatyse of the Newe India, with Other New Founde Landes and Ilands, as well Eastwarde as Westwarde, as They are Knowen and Found in these Oure Days, after the Descripcion of Sebastian Munster in His Boke of vniuersall Cosmographie: Wherin the Diligent Reader May See the Good Successe and Rewarde of Noble and Honest Enterpryses, by the Which Not Only Worldly Ryches are Obtayned, but also God Is Glorified, and the Christian Fayth Enlarged. Tr. Out of Latin into Englishe. By Rycharde Eden. ...* London, 1553.

Murray, John Joseph. *Antwerp in the Age of Plantin and Brueghel.* Norman, Okla., 1970.

Mylius, Arnold. *De rebus Hispanicis Aragonicis, Indicis et Aethiopicis.* Cologne, 1602.

Näf, Werner. *Vadian und seine Stadt St. Gallen.* St. Gall, 1944.

Nauert, Charles G. *Agrippa and the Crisis of Renaissance Thought.* Urbana, Ill., 1965.

Nauwelaerts, René. *Bibliografie over de Vlaamse letterkundigen. ...* [Duffel], [1969].

Newald, Richard. *Die deutsche Literatur vom Späthumanismus zur Empfindsamkeit, 1570– 1750.* In H. de Boor and R. Newald. *Geschichte der deutschen Literatur von den Anfangen bis zur Gegenwart,* Vol. V. Munich, 1963.

Nijhoff, Wouter, and Kronenberg, Maria E. *Nederlandsche bibliographie van 1500 tot 1540.* 3 vols. The Hague, 1919–61.

Nordman, V. A. *Justus Lipsius als Geschichtsforscher und Geschichtslehrer.* Helsinki, 1932.

Nürnberg Stadtarchiv. *Beiträge zur Wirtschaftsgeschichte Nürnbergs.* 2 vols. Nuremberg, 1967.

O'Malley, Charles D. *Andreas Vesalius of Brussels, 1514–1564.* Berkeley, 1964.

Ortelius, Abraham. *Theatri orbis terrarum enchiridion, minoribus tabulis per Philippum Gallaeum exaratum: et carmine Heroico, ex variis Geographis et Poëtis collecto, per Hugonem Favolium illustratum.* Antwerp, 1585.

————. *The Theatre of the Whole World.* London, 1606.

Ortroy, Fernand Gratien van. *Bibliographie de l'oeuvre de Pierre Apian.* Amsterdam, 1963.

Overdiep, Gerrit S., *et al.,* eds. *De letterkunde van de Renaissance. ...* Antwerp, 1947.

Pallmann, H. *Sigmund Feyerabend, sein Leben und seine geschäftlichen Verbindungen.* "Archiv für Frankfurts Geschichte und Kunst." N.S., Vol. VII. Frankfurt, 1881.

Pannwitz, Max, ed. *Deutsche Pfadfinder des 16. Jahrhundert in Afrika, Asien u. Südamerika. ... Springer ... Staden ... Schmidel ... Rauwolf.* Stuttgart, 1911.

Paquier, Jules. *Jerome Aleandre et la principauté de Liège, 1514–1540.* Paris, 1896.

Parr, C. M. *Jan van Linschoten: The Dutch Marco Polo.* New York, 1964.

Peeters-Fontainas, Jean. *Bibliographie des impressions espagnoles des pays-bas méridionaux.* 2 vols. Nieuwkoop, 1965.

Peixoto, Jorge. *Relações de Plantin com Portugal: Notas para o estudo da tipografia no século XVI.* Coimbra, 1962.

Perquin, W., *et al.,* comps. *Bibliotheca catholica neerlandica impressa, 1500–1727.* The Hague, 1954.

Petry, Karl. *Handbuch zur deutschen Literaturgeschichte*. 2 vols. Cologne, 1949.

Peuckert, Will-Erich. *Sebastian Franck, ein deutscher Sucher*. Munich, 1943.

Peutinger, Konrad. *Sermones convivales . . . : de mirandis Germaniae antiquitatibus*. Strassburg, 1506.

Pindter, Felicitas, ed. *Der Briefwechsel des Konrad Celtis*. Munich, 1934.

———. *Conradus Celtis Protucius, Quattuor Libri Amorum secundum quattuor latera Germaniae etc.* Leipzig, 1934.

———. *Conradus Celtis Protucius, Libri odarum quattuor*. Leipzig, 1937.

Pölnitz, G. F. von. *Jacob Fugger: Kaiser, Kirche, und Kapital in der oberdeutschen Renaissance*. 2 vols. Tübingen, 1949–51.

Polet, Amédée. *Une gloire de l'humanisme belge, Petrus Nannius 1500–1559*. Louvain, 1936.

Poncelet, Alfred. *Histoire de la Compagnie de Jésus dans les anciens Pays Bas: Établissement de la Compagnie de Jésus en Belgique et ses developpements jusqu' à la fin du règne d'Albert et d'Isabelle*. Brussels, 1927–28.

Praag, Jonas A. van. *La comedia espagnole aux Pays-Bas*. Amsterdam, 1922.

Pressel, Theodor. *David Chytraeus*. Elberfeld, 1862.

Prims, Florin. *Geschiedenis van Antwerpen*. 13 vols. Antwerp, 1941–43.

Proctor, Robert. *Jan van Doesborgh, Printer at Antwerp: An Essay in Bibliography*. London, 1894.

Prost, A. *Les sciences et les arts occultes au XVIe siècle: Corneille Agrippa*. Paris, 1881–82.

Prÿs, Joseph. *Der Staats-roman des 16. und 17. Jahrhundert und sein Erziehungsideal*. Würzburg, 1913.

Quaden [Quad], Matthias. *Matthaei Quaden Enchiridion Cosmographicum, Handtbüchlein der gantzen Welt gelegenheit begreiffende*. Cologne, 1598.

Ramirez, Alejandro, ed. *Epistolario de Justo Lipsio y los Españoles*. St. Louis, Mo., 1966.

Reicke, E. *Willibald Pirckheimer*. Jena, 1930.

———, ed. *Willibald Pirckheimers Briefwechsel*. "Veröffentlichungen der Kommission zur Erforschung der Geschichte der Reformation," Vol. I. Munich, 1940.

Rem, Lucas. *Tagebuch . . . 1494– . . . 1541 mit Briefen und Berichten über die Entdeckung des neuen Seeweges nach Amerika und Ostindien*. In B. Greiff, ed., *Jahresbericht des Vereins für Geschichte von Schwaben und Neuburg*, Vol. XXVI. Augsburg, 1861.

Remy, A. F. J. *The Influence of India and Persia on the Poetry of Germany*. New York, 1901.

Robertson, J. G., et al. *A History of German Literature*. 6th ed. Edinburgh and London, 1970.

Robson-Scott, W. D. *German Travellers in England, 1400–1800*. Oxford, 1953.

Roersch, Alphonse. *L'Humanisme belge à l'époque de la Renaissance: Études et portraits*. Louvain, 1933.

———, ed. *Correspondance de Nicolas Clenard*. 3 vols. Brussels, 1940–41.

Rollenhagen, Gabriel. *Wahrhaffte Lügen vom geist- und natürlichen Dingen, oder deutliche Beschreibung etlicher Wahrhafftigen, aber bey vielen alten und neuen Scribenten und Gelehrten, Geistlichen und Weltlichen eingerissenen, ausgebreiteten glaubwürdigen Lügen*. Leipzig, 1603. As reproduced in Gabriel Rollenhagen, ed., *Vier Bücher . . . indianischer reisen. . . .* Frankfurt and Leipzig, 1717.

Rollenhagen, Georg. *Froschmeuseler.* Edited by Karl Goedeke. In K. Goedeke and J. Tittmann, eds., *Deutsche Dichter des sechszehnten Jahrhunderts,* Vols. VIII–XI. Leipzig, 1876.

———[?]. *Alte newe Zeitung: A Sixteenth-Century Collection of Fables.* Edited by Eli Sobel. Berkeley, Calif., 1958.

———. *Georg Rollenhagens Spiel von Tobias, 1576.* Edited by Johannes Bolte. Halle, 1930.

Roloff, Hans-Gert, ed. See Wickram, Georg.

Rooses, Max, and Denucé, J., eds. *Correspondance de Christophe Plantin.* 9 vols. in 6. Antwerp and Ghent, 1883–1918.

Roth, Paul. *Die neuen Zeitungen in Deutschland im 15. und 16. Jahrhundert.* Leipzig, 1914.

Rupprich, Hans. *Die deutsche Literatur vom späten Mittelalter bis zum Barock.* In H. de Boor and R. Newald, eds., *Geschichte der deutschen Literatur von den Anfangen bis zum Gegenwart,* Vol. IV, Pts. 1 and 2. Munich, 1970, 1973.

———. *Willibald Pirckheimer und die erste Reise Dürers nach Italien.* Vienna, 1930.

Sabbe, Maurits. *La vie des livres à Anvers aux XVIᵉ, XVIIᵉ, et XVIIIᵉ siècles.* Brussels, 1926.

Sachs, Hans. See Keller, Adalbert von.

Saunders, Jason Louis. *Justus Lipsius: The Philosophy of Renaissance Stoicism.* New York, 1955.

Scaliger, J. J. *Autobiography.* Translated by G. W. Robinson. Cambridge, Mass., 1927.

Schedel, Hartmann. *Liber chronicarum.* Nuremberg, 1493.

Scheurleer, Theodor H. Lunsingh, and Meyjez, G. H. M. Posthumus, eds. *Leiden University in the Seventeenth Century: An Exchange of Learning.* Leyden, 1975.

Schick, Léon. *Un grand homme d'affaires au début du XVIᵉ siècle: Jacob Fugger.* Paris, 1957.

Schmidt, Charles Guillaume Adolph. *Histoire littéraire de l'Alsace à la fin du XVᵉ et au commencement du XVIᵉ siècle.* 2 vols. Paris, 1879.

Schneegans, H. *Geschichte der grotesken Satire.* Strassburg, 1892.

Schneider, J. Adam. *Spaniens Anteil auf der deutschen Literatur des 16. und 17. Jahrhunderts.* Strassburg, 1898.

Schorbach, K. *Studien über das deutsche Volksbuch Lucidarius.* Strassburg, 1894.

Schott, Andreas. *Hispania illustrata: Hispania illustratae seu rerum urbiumque Hispaniae Lusitaniae, Aethiopiae, et Indiae scriptores varii. Partim editi nunc primum, partim aucti et emendati.* 4 vols. Frankfurt, 1603–8.

———. *Hispaniae bibliotheca seu de academiis ac bibliothecis.* 3 vols. in 1. Frankfurt, 1608.

———, trans. *Rodriguez Giram literae japonica ex italicis lat. factae.* Antwerp, 1615.

Schulze, Franz. *Die wissenschaftliche Bedeutung der Reiseberichte Balthasar Springers, das ersten bekannten Indienfahrer aus Deutschland.* Strassburg, 1902.

Seelmann, Wilhelm. *Georg Rollenhagen.* Magdeburg, 1889.

Seidenfaden, I. *Das Jesuitentheater in Konstanz. Grundlagen und Entwicklung. Ein Beitrag zur Geschichte des Jesuitentheaters in Deutschland.* Stuttgart, 1963.

Shaaber, Matthias A. *Check List of Sixteenth-Century Editions of Works of Sixteenth-Century Latin Authors.* New York, 1963.

Soden, Franz von, and Knaacke, J. K. F., eds. *Christoph Scheurl's Briefbuch.* 2 vols. in 1. Potsdam, 1867, 1872.

Chapter Bibliographies

Sommerhalder, H. *Johann Fischarts Werke: Eine Einführung*. Berlin, 1960.

Specht, Thomas. *Geschichte der ehemaligen Universität Dillingen (1549–1804)*. Freiburg-im-Breisgau, 1902.

Spitz, Lewis W. *Conrad Celtis, the German Arch-Humanist*. Cambridge, Mass., 1957.

Springer, Balthasar. *Die Merfart uñ Erfarung nüwer Schiffung und Wege zu viln overkaufen Inseln und Künigreichen*. . . . Reproduced in Franz Schulze, *Balthasar Springers Indienfahrt 1505–6*. Strassburg, 1902.

Stammler, Johannes. *Dialogos de diversarum gentium sectis*. Ulm, 1508.

Stammler, W. *Von der Mystik zum Barock (1400–1600)*. Stuttgart, 1950.

Steinruck, Josef. *Johann Baptist Fickler*. Münster, 1965.

Stevin, Simon. . . . *de thiende 1585*. Facsimile with an Introduction by A. J. E. M. Smeur. Nieuwkoop, 1965.

Stiefel, A. L., ed. *Hans Sachs Forschungen*. Nuremberg, 1894.

Stier, H. P. *Vlämischer Bericht über Vasco da Gamas 2. Reise, 1502–03*. Braunschweig, 1887.

Strasen, E. A., and Gandara, Alfredo. *Oito séculos de história Luso-Alemã*. Lisbon, 1914.

Strauss, Gerald. *Sixteenth-Century Germany: Its Topography and Topographers*. Madison, Wis., 1959.

——. *Nuremberg in the Sixteenth Century*. Bloomington, Ind., 1967.

Strelka, Josef. *Der Burgundische Renaissancehof Margarethes von Österreich und seine literarhistorische Bedeutung*. Vienna, 1957.

Tamara, Francisco. *De las costumbres de todas las gentes*. Antwerp, 1556.

Taylor, Archer. *Problems in German Literary History of the Fifteenth and Sixteenth Centuries*. New York, 1939.

Tello, Francisco. *Relation. Ausz befelch Herrn Francisco Taglej Gubernators, und general Obristens der Philippinischen Inseln in welcher kürtzlich angezeigt wirdt welcher Gestallt sechs geistliche Brüder ausz Hispania desz Orden S. Francisci von der Observantz sambt andern 20 newlich von jnen bekehrten Japonesern im Königreich. Japon den 14. Martij desz verschinen Jars umb desz Christlichen Glaubens willen seyn gecreutziget worden und durch die Gnaden Gottes die seligste Marte Cron erlangt haben*. Munich, 1599.

Tesser, J. H. M. *Petrus Canisius als humanistisch geleerde*. . . . Amsterdam, 1932.

Theunisz, Johannes. *Carolus Clusius, het merkwaardige leven van een pionier der wetenschap*. Amsterdam, 1939.

Tiele, Pieter A. *Bibliothek van Nederlandsche pamfletten . . . Eerste deel: 1500–1648*. Amsterdam, 1858.

Tiemann, Hermann. *Das spanische Schrifttum in Deutschland von der Renaissance bis zur Romantik*. Hamburg, 1936.

Trigault, Nicolas. *Vita Gasparis Barzaei Belgae e Societa Jesu B. Xavieri in India Socii*. Antwerp, 1610.

Tscharner, Eduard H. von. *China in der deutschen Dichtung bis zur Klassik*. Munich, 1939.

Ulrich, Christoph. *Wahrhafftige und Ewiger Gedechtnusz würdige, Geschichts Erzelung. Welcher massen die new erfundene Insulen Königreich und Fürsternthumb im Japonien genandt zur Christlichem Glauben bekert und dann von Bäpstlicher Heyligkeit deren sie sich beneben der Heyligen Kirchen undterwürffig gemacht. Derselben abgesandte und Königliche*

Legaten auffgenommen worden alles an öffentlichem Consistorio vorgenommen und gehalten inn Rom den 23. Martij anno M. D. LXXXV. Ausz sonderm Eyffer und dem gemainen Mann zu gütem ausz Lateinischer inn Teutsche Sprach Vertiert Durch Christophen Vlrich den Eltern von Nürnberg. Augsburg, n.d.

Vadian (Vadianus), Joachim. *Pomponii Melae Hispani. Libri de situ orbis tres.* . . . Vienna, 1518.

Vocht, Henry de. *Monumenta humanistica lovaniensia: Texts and Studies about Louvain Humanists in the First Half of the Sixteenth Century: Erasmus—Vives—Sorpius—Clenardus—Goes—Moringus.* Louvain, 1934.

————. *History of the Foundation and the Rise of the Collegium Trilingue Louaniense 1517–1554.* 4 vols. Louvain, 1951–55.

Vries, Tiemens de. *Holland's Influence on English Language and Literature.* Chicago, 1916.

Waller, G. F. *Catalogus van Nederlandsch en vlaamsch populaire boeken.* 's-Gravenhage, 1936.

Weevers, Theodor. *Coornhert's Dolinghe van Ulysee, de eerste Nederlandsche Odyssee.* . . . Groningen, 1934.

Wegg, Jervis. *The Decline of Antwerp under Philip of Spain.* London, 1924.

Weller, Emil Ottokar. *Die ersten deutschen Zeitungen. Mit einer Bibliographie, 1505–1599.* Tübingen, 1872.

Wetzel, Johann. *Die Reise der Söhne Giaffers, aus dem italienischen des Christoforo Armeno übersetzt durch Johann Wetzel 1583, hrg. von H. Fischer u. J. Bolte.* Tübingen, 1895.

Weyrauther, M. *Konrad Peutinger und Wilibald Pirckheimer in ihren Beziehungen zur Geographie: Eine geschichtliche Parallele.* Munich, 1907.

Wichmann, Arthur. *Dirck Gerritsz.* Groningen, 1899.

Wickram, Jörg. *Von Goten und Bösen Nachbaurn. Strassburg, 1556.* Edited by Hans-Gert Roloff. In *Georg Wickrams sämtliche Werke,* Vol. IV. Berlin, 1969.

Wijnaendts Francken, C. J. *Vier Moralisten: Confucius, Plutarchus, Montaigne, Coornhert.* Amsterdam, 1946.

Willehad, P. E. *Willibald Pirckheimer, Dürers Freund im Spiegel seines Lebens, seine Werke, und seine Umwelt.* Cologne, 1971.

Wolf, Gustav. *Aus Kurköln im 16. Jahrhundert.* Berlin, 1905.

Zeidler, J. *Studien und Beiträge zur Geschichte der Jesuitenkomödie und des Klosterdramas.* Leipzig, 1891.

Zeydel, Edwin H. *Sebastian Brant.* New York, 1967.

————, trans. *The Ship of Fools by Sebastian Brant. Translated into Rhyming Couplets with Introduction and Commentary.* New York, 1944.

ARTICLES

Barassin, J. "Jean Huges Linschoten." *Studia* (Lisbon), No. 11 (1963), pp. 251–55.

Bartlett, D. M. M. "Münsters *Cosmographia universalis.*" *Journal of the Gypsy Lore Society,* XXXI (1952), 83–90.

Bataillon, Marcel. "La cour découvre le nouveau monde." In Jean Jacquot, ed., *Fêtes et cérémonies au temps de Charles Quint,* pp. 13–27. Paris, 1960.

Bauer, C. "Conrad Peutingers Gutachten zur Monopolfrage." *Archiv für Reformationsgeschichte*, XLV (1954), 1–43, 145–96.

Bay, J. C. "Conrad Gessner (1516–65), the Father of Bibliography." *Papers of the Bibliographical Society of America*, X, Pt. 2 (1916), 53–86.

Beckmann, Johannes. "Die Universitäten vom 16. bis 18. Jahrhundert im Dienste der Glaubensverbreitung." *Neue Zeitschrift für Missionswissenschaft*, XVII (1961), 24–47.

Berger, Samuel. "Melanchthons Vorlesungen über Weltgeschichte." *Theologische Studien und Kritiken*, LXX (1897), 781–90.

Boisacq, Émile. "Les philologues classiques et orientales en Belgique." In *L'Encyclopedie belge*, pp. 515–21. Brussels, 1933.

Bolte, Johannes. "Quellenstudien zu Georg Rollenhagen." *Sitzungsberichte der preussischen Akademie der Wissenschaften (Berlin) philosophisch-historische Klasse*, 1929, pp. 668–89.

Bonaparte, Roland (Prince). "Les premiers voyages des Néerlandais dans l'Insulinde, 1595–1602." *Revue de géografie*, XIV (1884), Pt. 1, 446–55; Pt. 2, 46–55.

Boxer, C. R. "Uma raridade bibliográfica sobre Fernão Cron." *Boletim internacional de bibliografia Luso-Brasileira*, XII (1971), 5–46.

Brásio, António. "Uma carta inédita de Valentim Fernandes." *Boletim da biblioteca da universidade de Coimbra*, XXIV (1960), 338–58.

Brulez, W. "Venetiaanse handelsbetrekkingen met Perzië en Indië omstreeks 1600." *Orientalia Gandensia*, I (1964), 1–27.

Carreras Artau, J. "Louis Vives, philosophe de l'humanisme." In *Apports hispaniques à la philosophie chrétienne de l'Occident*, pp. 55–71. Louvain, 1962.

Christ, Karl. "Die Bibliothek Reuchlins in Pforzheim." *Zentralblatt für Bibliothekswesen*, LIII (1924), 1–96.

Debaene, Luc. "Rederijkers en Prozaromans." *De Gulden Passer*, XXVII (1949), 1–23.

Delcourt, Marie. "L'humanisme aux Pays-Bas au temps de Plantin." *De Gulden Passer*, XXXIII (1955), 208–18.

Doehaerd, Renée. "Commerce et morale à Anvers au XVIᵉ siècle; a propos d'un manuscrit de la Bibliothèque de Leyde." *Revue historique*, CCIV (1950), 226–33.

Drewes, G. W. J. "Oriental Studies in the Netherlands: A Historical Survey." In *Higher Education and Research in the Netherlands: Bulletin of the Netherlands Universities Foundation for International Co-operation*, I, No. 4 (1957), 3–13.

Edighoffer, Roland. "La correspondance de Sebastian Münster." *Études germaniques*, XXI (1966), 249–51.

Ellinger, Georg. "Zu den Quellen des Faustbuchs von 1587." *Zeitschrift für vergleichende Literaturgeschichte*, I (1888), 156–81.

Fabri, J. "Un ami de Juste Lipse: L'humaniste André Schott 1552–1629." *Les études classiques*, XXI (1953), 188–208.

Gerlo, Aloïs. "L'apport de l'humanisme belge au développement de la pensée scientifique." *Revue de l'université de Bruxelles*, VIII (1956), 328–61.

———; Vertersen, Irène; and Vervliet, H. D. L., eds. "La correspondance inédite de Juste Lipse conservée au musée Plantin-Moretus." *De Gulden Passer*, XLII (1964), 5–232.

Gernez, D. "Lucas Janszoon Wagenaer: A Chapter in the History of Guide-Books for Seamen." *Mariner's Mirror*, XXII (1937), 190–97.

Hantzsch, Viktor. "Sebastian Münster." In *Abhandlungen der historische-philosophische Klasse der Gesellschaft der Wissenschaften* (Leipzig), XVIII (1898), 1–187.

Hartig, Otto. "Die Gründung der Münchener Hofbibliothek durch Albrecht V. und Johann Jakob Fugger." *Abhandlungen der königlich bayerischen Akademie der Wissenschaften, Philosophisch-philologische und historische Klasse*, Vol. XXVIII (1917).

Hecker, V. "Ein Gutachten Conrad Peutingers in Sachen der Handelsgesellschaften." *Zeitschrift des historischen Vereins für Schwaben*, II (1879), 188–217.

Heyd, Wilhelm von. ". . . Valentin Fernandez Aleman." *Akademie der Wissenschaften (Munich), Philosophisch-philologische und historische Klasse, Sitzungsberichte*, II (1872), 479–83.

Hidber, B. "Renward Cysat, der Stadtschreiber zu Luzern; Lebensbild eines katholisch-schweizerischen Staatsmannes aus dem sechzehnten Jahrhundert." *Archiv für schweizerische Geschichte*, XIII (1862), 160–224; XX (1875), 3–88.

Horák, Bohuslav. "Ohlas zámořských objevů v české literatuře" ("Responses to Overseas Discoveries in Czech Literature"). In his translation of Jean de Lery, *Histoire o plavení se do Ameriky kteráž i Brasilia slave*, pp. 27–31. Prague, 1957.

Kellenbenz, Hermann. "Le front hispano-portugais contre l'Inde et le rôle d'une agence de renseignements au service de marchands allemands et flamands." *Studia* (Lisbon), No. 11 (1963), pp. 263–90.

———. "Die Beziehungen Nürnbergs zur iberischen Halbinsel besonders im 15. und in der ersten Hälfte des 16. Jahrhunderts." *Beiträge zur Wirtschaftsgeschichte Nürnbergs*, I (1967), 456–93.

———. "Os mercadores alemães de Lisboa por volta de 1530." *Revista portuguesa de história*, IX (1960), 125–39.

Kömmerling-Fitzler, Hedwig. "Der Nürnberger Georg Pock (d. 1528–29) in Portugiesisch-Indien und im Edelsteinland Vijayanagara." *Mitteilungen des Vereins für Geschichte der Stadt Nürnberg*, LV (1967–68), 137–84.

———. "Der Anteil der Deutschen an der Kolonialpolitik Philipps II. von Spanien in Asien." *Vierteljahrschrift für Sozial- und Wirtschaftsgeschichte*, XXVIII (1935), 243–81.

Kronenberg, Maria Elizabeth. "Bijdragen over Jan van Doesborgh drukker te Antwerpen," *Het Boek*, 3d ser. XXXV (1961), 221–28.

Lapeyre, Henri. "Anvers au XVIᵉ siècle d'après des travaux récents." *Revue d'histoire moderne et contemporaine*, XI (1964), 191–202.

Lucke, Wilhelm. "Deutsche Geschichtsblätter aus den ersten Jahren der Reformation." *Deutsche Geschichtsblätter*, IX (1908), 183–205.

Lütge, Friedrich. "Der Handel Nürnbergs nach dem Osten im 15./16. Jahrhundert." In *Beiträge zur Wirtschaftsgeschichte Nürnbergs*, I (1967), 318–76.

Maes, Léon. "Lettres inédites d'André Schott." *Le Muséon*, VII (1906), 67–102, 325–61; IX (1908), 368–411; XI (1910), 239–70.

———. "Une lettre d'A. Schott à Abr. Ortelius." *Musée belge*, IX (1905), 315–18.

Murray, John J. "The Cultural Impact of the Flemish Low Countries on 16th and 17th Century England." *American Historical Review*, LXII (1957), 837–54.

Offenbacher, Emile. "La bibliothèque de Wilibald Pirckheimer." *La bibliofilia*, XL (1939), 241–63.

Chapter Bibliographies

Oliveira Marques, A. H. de. "Relações entre Portugal e a Alemanha no século XVI." *Revista da Faculdade de Letras* [*de Lisboa*], 3d ser., No. 4 (1960), 36–55.

Oncken, Hermann. "Sebastian Franck als Geschichtsschreiber." *Historisch-politische Aufsätze und Reden* (Munich), I (1914), 273–319.

Reiffenberg, Baron de. "Bibliothèque de Joseph Scaliger." *La bibliophile belge*, IV (1847), 229–33.

Roobaert, E., and Moerman, A. "Librairies et imprimeurs à Anvers de XVIe siècle. I. Jean de Loet, imprimeur de la ville d'Anvers, 1549–1566." *De Gulden Passer*, XXXIX (1961), 188–210.

Sarazin, Anny. "Joannes Bochius, secretaris van Antwerpen 1555–1609." *Bijdragen tot de Geschiedenis*, XXVIII (1937), 241–67.

Schmeller, J. "Ueber Valentin Fernandez Alemã und seine Sammlung von Nachrichten über die Entdeckungen und Besitzungen der Portugiesen in Afrika und Asien bis zum Jahre 1508. . . ." *Abhandlungen der philosophisch-philologische Classe der Königlichen Bayerischen Akademie der Wissenschaften*, Pt. III (1847), Vol. IV, 1–73.

Sobel, Eli. "Georg Rollenhagen, Sixteenth-Century Playwright, Pedagogue, and Publicist." *PMLA*, LXX (1955), 762–80.

Sondheim, Moriz. "Die Bibliothek des Hans Sachs." In Sondheim, *Gesammelte Schriften*, p. 260. Frankfurt-am-Main, 1927.

Strauss, Gerald. "A Sixteenth-Century Encyclopedia: Sebastian Münster's Cosmography and Its Editions." In C. H. Carter, ed., *From the Renaissance to the Counter-Reformation: Essays in Honor of Garrett Mattingly*, pp. 130–50. London, 1966.

Thompson, L. S. "German Translations of the Classics between 1450 and 1550." *Journal of Germanic Philology*, XLII (1943), 343–63.

Unger, Willem S. "Nieuwe literatur over Antwerpen als internationale handelsstad in de 15e en 16e eeuw." *Tijdschrift voor Geschiedenis*, LXXVI (1963), 430–36.

Valentin, J. M. "Études récentes sur le théâtre des Jesuites." *Études germaniques*, XXII (1967), 247–53.

Van Houtte, J. A. "Anvers aux XVe et XVIe siècles. Expansion et apogée." *Annales: économies, sociétés, civilisations*, XVI (1961), 248–78.

Voet, L., and Dodoens, R. "Geleerden en Kunstenaars rond Plantin en de Moretussen: Plantiana, 1943–1958." *De Gulden Passer*, XXXVII (1959), 36–38.

Werner, Theodor Gustav. "Die Beteiligung der Nürnberger Welser und Augsburger Fugger in der Eroberung des Rio de La Plata und der Gründung von Buenos Aires." *Beiträge zur Wirtschaftsgeschichte Nürnbergs*, I (1967), 494–592.

Zeydel, E. H. "Sebastian Brant and the Discovery of America." *Journal of English and Germanic Philology*, XLII (1943), 410–11.

ENGLISH LITERATURE

BOOKS

Abbot, George. *A Briefe Description of the Whole Worlde*. London, 1599.

Allott, Robert, comp. *England's Parnassus, or the Choicest Flowers of Our Modern Poets* (*1600*). Edited by C. Crawford. Oxford, 1913.

Alston, R. C. *A Bibliography of the English Language from the Invention of Printing to the Year 1800.* Vols. II and VII. Leeds, 1965–69.

Alter, Robert. *Rogue's Progress: Studies in the Picaresque Novel.* Cambridge, Mass., 1964.

Anders, Heinrich. *Shakespeare's Books: A Dissertation on Shakespeare's Reading and the Immediate Sources of His Works.* Berlin, 1904.

Andrews, Kenneth R. *Elizabethan Privateering: English Privateering during the Spanish War, 1585–1603.* Cambridge, 1964.

Ansell, Robin P. *Animal Lore in English Literature.* London, 1932.

Arnold, Paul. *Ésotérisme de Shakespeare.* Paris, 1955.

Arthusius, Gotardus. *Dialogues in the English and Malaians Languages . . . faithfully translated into the English Tongue by Augustus Spalding.* London, 1614.

Atkins, John W. H. *English Literary Criticism: the Renascence.* London, 1951.

Baildon, H. Bellyse, ed. See Dunbar, William.

Bakeless, John Edwin. *The Tragicall History of Christopher Marlowe.* 2 vols. Cambridge, Mass., 1942.

Baldwin, William. *A Treatise of morall philosophy Contaynynge the sayings of the wyse.* London, 1579.

Barlow, Roger. *A brief summe of geographie.* Edited by E. G. R. Taylor. London, 1932.

Battenhouse, Roy W. *Marlowe's Tamburlaine: A Study in Renaissance Moral Philosophy.* Nashville, Tenn., 1941.

Baxter, J. W. *William Dunbar: A Biographical Study.* Edinburgh, 1952.

Bennett, Henry Stanley. *English Books and Readers, 1475 to 1557.* 2d ed. Cambridge, 1969.

———. *English Books and Readers, 1558 to 1603. . . .* Cambridge, 1965.

Bergeron, David M. *English Civic Pageantry (1558–1642).* Columbia, S.C., 1971.

Boaistuau, Pierre. *Certaine Secrete Wonders of Nature . . . Gathered out of Divers Authors.* Translated by C. Fenton. London, 1569.

Boemus, Johann. *The Fardle of Facions.* London, 1555.

———. *The Manners, Lawes and Custumes of all Nations.* Translated by Edward Aston. London, 1611.

Bond, R. W., ed. See Lyly, John.

Botero, Giovanni. *Relations of the Most Famous Kingdoms.* London, 1603.

———. *Observations upon the Lives of Alexander, Caesar, Scipio.* Newly Englished. London, 1602.

Bowers, Fredson, ed. See Dekker, Thomas; Marlowe, Christopher.

Boxer, Charles R., ed. *South China in the Sixteenth Cnetury.* "Hakluyt Society Publications," 2d series, Vol. CVI. London, 1953.

Boyd, Evelyn Mae. "A Study of the Character Tamburlaine and Evidences of Its Influence on Drama from 1587–1605." M.A. thesis, Department of English, University of Chicago, 1920.

Bradbrook, Muriel C. *The School of Night: A Study in the Literary Relationships of Sir Walter Raleigh.* Cambridge, 1936.

Brerewood, Edward. *Enquiries Touching the Diversity of Languages and Religions throughout the Chief Parts of the World.* London, 1614.

Bright, Timothy. *Characterie: An Art of Shorte, Swifte, and Secrete Writing by Character.* London, 1588.

Brown, Huntington. *Rabelais in English Literature.* Cambridge, Mass., 1933.

——, ed. See Hall, Joseph.

Brown, Peter Hume. *George Buchanan, Humanist and Reformer.* Edinburgh, 1890.

——, ed. See Buchanan, George.

Buchanan, George. *Vernacular Writings of George Buchanan.* Edited by Peter Hume Brown. Edinburgh and London, 1892.

Camman, Schuyler. *China's Dragon Robes.* New York, 1952.

Carroll, William M. *Animal Conventions in English Renaissance Nonreligious Prose (1500–1600).* New York, 1954.

Cawley, Robert R. *The Voyagers and Elizabethan Drama.* Boston, 1938.

——. *Unpathed Waters: Studies in the Influence of the Voyagers on Elizabethan Literature.* Princeton, 1940.

Chalmers, Alexander, ed. *The Works of the English Poets.* London, 1910.

Chambers, Raymond Wilson. *Thomas More.* New York, 1935.

Chan (Chen), Shou-yi. "Influence of China on English Culture in the Eighteenth Century." Ph.D. diss., Department of English, University of Chicago, 1928.

Chew, Samuel C. *The Crescent and the Rose: Islam and England during the Renaissance.* New York, 1969.

Clair, Colin. *A History of Printing in Britain.* London, 1965.

Clark, Cumberland. *Shakespeare and National Character.* New York, 1932.

Clark, Eleanor G. *Raleigh and Marlowe: A Study in Elizabethan Fustian.* New York, 1941.

Conestaggio, Girolamo Franchi. *The Historie of the Uniting of the Kingdom of Portugall to the Crowne of Castill. . . .* London, 1600.

Connell-Smith, Gordon. *Forerunners of Drake: A Study of English Trade with Spain in the Early Tudor Period.* London and New York, 1954.

Cornelius, Paul. *Languages in Seventeenth- and Early Eighteenth-Century Imaginary Voyages.* Geneva, 1965.

Couldridge, F. T. "Voyages and Travels in the Works of Some Prominent Men of Letters of the Shakespearian Age (1558–1625)." M.A. thesis, University of South Africa, 1940.

Craig, Hardin. *The Enchanted Glass: The Elizabethan Mind in Literature.* Rev. ed. Oxford, 1950.

——. *New Lamps for Old: A Sequel to the Enchanted Glass.* Oxford, 1960.

Cunliffe, John W., ed. See Gascoigne, George.

Davenport, A., ed. See Hall, Joseph.

Davies, David W. *Dutch Influences on English Culture 1558–1625.* Ithaca, N.Y., 1964.

Davys, John. *The Voyages and Works of John Davis, the Navigator.* Edited by Albert Hasting Markham. "Hakluyt Society Publications," O. S. Vol. LIX, 2 vols. London, 1880.

Dekker, Thomas. *The Dramatic Works.* Edited by Fredson Bowers. Cambridge, 1953.

——. *Non-Dramatic Works.* Edited by Alexander Grosart. 5 vols. Cambridge, 1884–86.

Delony, Thomas. *The Works of Thomas Deloney.* Edited by Francis Oscar Mann. Oxford, 1912.

Doni, Antonio Francesco. *The Moral Philosophie of Doni—the Earliest Version of the Fables of Bidpai.* Translated by Sir Thomas North. Edited by Joseph Jacobs. London, 1888.

Dunbar, William. *The Poems.* Edited by H. Bellyse Baildon. Cambridge, 1907.

———. *The Poems.* Edited by W. Mackay MacKenzie. Edinburgh, 1932.

Dunlop, John Colin. *A History of Prose Fiction.* London, 1906.

Eden, Richard, ed. and trans. *The History of Travayle in the West and East Indies . . . newly set in order, augmented, and finished by Richard Willes.* London, 1579.

Edwards, H. L. R. *Skelton: The Life and Times of an Early Tudor Poet.* London, 1949.

Ellis-Fermor, U. M. *Tamburlane the Great in Two Parts.* London, 1930.

Escalante, Bernardino. *A Discourse of the Navigation which the Portugales doe make to the Realmes and Provinces of the East Partes of the Worlde. . . .* Translated by John Frampton. London, 1579.

Falconer, Alexander Frederick. *Shakespeare and the Sea.* London, 1964.

Farmer, J. S., ed. See Rastell, John.

Ferguson, Arthur B. *The Articulate Citizen and the English Renaissance.* Durham, N.C., 1965.

Feuillart, Albert, ed. See Sidney, Philip.

Fortescue, Thomas, trans. *The Forest, or Collection of Historyes No Lesse Profitable, Then Pleasant and Necessary. Done out of the French into English by Thomas Fortescue.* London, 1576.

Foster, William. *England's Quest of Eastern Trade.* London, 1933.

———. *Early Travels in India, 1583–1619.* London, 1921.

———, ed. *Letters Received by the East India Company from Its Servants in the East, 1602–1617.* 6 vols. London, 1896–1902.

Fowler, Alastair D. S., ed. and trans. See Willes, Richard.

Freeman, Rosemary. *English Emblem Books.* London, 1948.

Furness, Horace Howard, et al. eds. *A New Variorum Edition of Shakespeare.* 25 vols. Philadelphia, 1871–1919.

Fussner, Frank Smith. *The Historical Revolution: English Historical Writing and Thought, 1580–1640.* New York, 1962.

Gascoigne, George. *The Complete Works of George Gascoigne.* Edited by John W. Cunliffe. 2 vols. Cambridge, 1907, 1910.

Gillespie, James Edward. *The Influence of Overseas Expansion on England to 1700.* New York, 1920.

Giovio, Paolo. *The Worthy Tract of Paulus Iovius, contayning a discourse of rare inventions, both militaire and amorous called Impresse.* Translated by Samuel Daniel. London, 1585.

Gordon, Ian Alastair. *John Skelton, Poet Laureate.* Melbourne, 1943.

Greene, Robert. *Life and Complete Works.* Edited by Alexander B. Grosart. 15 vols. London, 1881–86.

Greenlaw, Edwin, et al., eds. See Spenser, Edmund.

Guttman, Selma. *The Foreign Sources of Shakespeare's Works.* New York, 1947.

Hakluyt, Richard, comp. *Principall Navigations, Voyages, and Discoveries of the English Nation . . . within the Compasse of these 1500 Yeeres. . . .* 3 vols. London, 1598–1600.

Hale, John R. *England and the Italian Renaissance.* London, 1963.

Hall, Joseph. *The Collected Poems of Joseph Hall, Bishop of Exeter and Norwich.* Edited by A. Davenport. Liverpool, 1949.

———. *The Discovery of a New World.* Edited by Huntington Brown. Cambridge, Mass., 1937.

Harting, James Edmund. *The Ornithology of Shakespeare.* London, 1871.

Heiserman, Arthur R. *Skelton and Satire.* Chicago, 1961.

Henderson, Philip, ed. See Skelton, John.

Hirst, Desirée. *Hidden Riches: Traditional Symbolism from the Renaissance to Blake.* London, 1964.

Hortop, Job. *The rare travailes of Iob Hortop, an Englishman, who was not heard of in three and twentie yeeres space. Wheren is declared the dangers he escaped in his voiage to Gynnie also of sundri monstrous beasts. . . .* London, 1591.

Hughes, Charles, ed. *Shakespeare's Europe.* London, 1903.

Hume, Martin. *Spanish Influence in English Literature.* London, 1905.

Hunter, G. K. *John Lyly: The Humanist as Courtier.* Cambridge, Mass., 1962.

Irwin, Raymond. *The English Library: Sources and History.* London, 1966.

Jacobs, Joseph, ed. *The Morall Philosophie of Doni: Drawne out of the Ancient Writers. Englished out of Italian by T. North. With Introductory Essay upon the Buddhistic Origin and Literary History of the "Fables of Bidpai." . . .* London, 1888.

James, David G. *The Dream of Prospero.* Oxford, 1967.

Jayne, Sears. *Library Catalogues of the English Renaissance.* Berkeley and Los Angeles, 1956.

Johnson, Robert, trans. *The Travellers Breviat, or an historicall description of the most famous Kingdomes in the World.* London, 1601.

Johnson, Ronald C. *George Gascoigne.* New York, 1972.

Jones, Eldred D. *Othello's Countrymen: The African in English Renaissance Drama.* London, 1965.

Jorgensen, Paul A. *Shakespeare's Military World.* Berkeley and Los Angeles, 1956.

Judge, C. B. *Elizabethan Book Pirates.* Cambridge, Mass., 1934.

Kerr, Robert, ed. *A General History and Collection of Voyages and Travels.* 18 vols. Edinburgh and London, 1824.

Keynes, Sir Geoffrey Langdon. *Dr Timothie Bright, 1550–1615: A Survey of His Life with a Bibliography of His Writings.* London, 1962.

Kinghorn, A. M. *The Chorus of History: Literary Historical Relations in Renaissance Britain 1485–1558.* London, 1971.

Kinsman, Robert S., ed. See Skelton, John.

Kraus, Hans Peter. *Sir Francis Drake: A Pictorial Biography.* Amsterdam, 1970.

Lesher, Clara R. *The South Sea Islanders in English Literature, 1519–1798.* Chicago, 1940.

Lewis, C. S. *English Literature in the Sixteenth Century, Excluding Drama.* Oxford, 1954.

Lievsky, John L. *The Sixteenth Century: Skelton through Hooker.* New York, 1968.

Linschoten, Jan Huyghen Van. *The Voyage to the East Indies from the English Translation of 1598.* Edited by A. C. Burnell and P. A. Tiele. "Hakluyt Society Publications," O.S., Nos. 70–71. 2 vols. London, 1885.

Lodge, Thomas. *Complete Works.* 4 vols. The Hunterian Club edition. Glasgow, 1883.

Lyly, John. *The Complete Works of John Lyly.* Edited by Robert W. Bond. 3 vols. Oxford, 1902. Reissued 1967.

Lynam, Edward, ed. *Richard Hakluyt and his Successors; a volume issued to commemorate the centenary of the Hakluyt Society.* "Hakluyt Society Publications," 2d ser., No. 93. London, 1967.

McKerrow, Ronald B., and Wilson, F. P., eds. See Nashe, Thomas.

Mann, Francis Oscar, ed. See Deloney, Thomas.

Mansinha, Mayadhai. *Kalidasa and Shakespeare.* Delhi, 1969.

Marlowe, Christopher. *Tamburlaine the Great.* Parts I and II. Edited by John D. Jump. Lincoln, Neb., 1967.

———. *The Complete Works of Christopher Marlowe.* Edited by Fredson Bowers. 2 vols. Cambridge, 1973.

Martyr, Peter. *The Decades of the newe worlde or west India contayning the navigations and conquests of the Spanyardes . . . Written in the Latine tounge by Peter Martyr of Angheria and translated into Englysshe by Richard Eden.* London, 1555.

Matthiessen, Francis O. *Translation: An Elizabethan Art.* New York, 1965.

Mendoza, Juan Gonzalez de. *The Historie of the great and mightie kingdome of China, and the situation thereof: togither with the great riches, huge cities, politike gouernement, and rare inventions in the same.* Translated by R. Parke. London, 1588.

Mexía, Pedro. See Fortescue, Thomas.

Millar, David A., comp. and ed. *George Buchanan: A Memorial, 1506–1906.* St. Andrews and London, 1906.

Miller, Edwin H. *The Professional Writer in Elizabethan England.* Cambridge., 1959.

Monardes, Nicholas. *Joyfull Newes, Out of the Newe Founde World.* 2 vols. New York, 1925.

More, Thomas. *The Complete Works.* Edited by E. Surtz and J. H. Hexter. 5 vols. New Haven, 1963–65.

Moryson, Fynes. *Shakespeare's Europe: Unpub. Chapters of Fynes Moryson's Itinerary being a Survey of the Condition of Europe at the End of the Sixteenth Century.* Edited by Huntington Brown. London, 1903.

Münster, Sebastian. *A Briefe Collection and Compendious Extract of Strange and Memorable Thinges, Gathered Oute of the Cosmographye of S.M.* London, 1572.

Nashe, Thomas. *The Works of Thomas Nashe.* Edited by Ronald B. McKerrow and F. P. Wilson. 5 vols. Reprint and revision of the edition of 1904–10. Oxford, 1958.

Nelson, William. *John Skelton, Laureate.* New York, 1939.

Newdigate, Bernard H. *Michael Drayton and His Circle.* Oxford, 1941.

Nichols, John, ed. *Progresses of Queen Elizabeth.* 3 vols. London, 1788–1805.

North, Thomas, trans. *The Morall Philosophie of Doni: Drawne out of the Ancient Writers. . . .* London, 1888.

Orr, David. *Italian Renaissance Drama in England before 1625.* Chapel Hill, 1970.

Oxford, Earl of. *A Collection of Voyages and Travels Compiled from the Curious and Valuable Library of the late Earl of Oxford.* 2 vols. London, 1745.

Paige, P. S., trans. See Pigafetta, Antonio.

Paradise, N. Burton. *Thomas Lodge: The History of an Elizabethan.* New Haven, 1931.

Parke, R., trans. See Mendoza, Juan Gonzalez de.

Parker, John. *Books to Build and Empire: A Bibliographical History of English Overseas Interests to 1620.* Amsterdam, 1965.

Parre, R. U. *English Translations from the Spanish, 1484–1943.* New Brunswick, N. J., 1944.

Penrose, Boies. *Travel and Discovery in the Renaissance, 1420–1620.* Cambridge, Mass. 1955.

———. *Tudor and Early Stuart Geography.* Washington, D. C., 1962.

Phipson, Emma. *The Animal Lore of Shakespeare's Time.* London, 1883.

Pigafetta, Antonio. *The Voyage of Magellan: The Journal of Antonio Pigafetta.* Translated by P. S. Paige. Englewood Cliffs, N.J., 1969.

Plant, Marjorie. *An Economic History of the English Book Trade.* London, 1965.

Platt, Hugh. *The Jewell House of Art and Nature. Conteining divers rare and profitable inventions, together with sundry new experiments in the Art of Husbandry, Distillation, and Moulding. . . .* London, 1594.

Platter, Thomas. *Thomas Platter's Travels in England.* Edited and translated by C. Williams. London, 1937.

Pollard, Alfred W., and Redgrave, G. R. *A Short-Title Catalogue of Books Printed in England, Scotland, and Ireland and of English Books Printed Abroad, 1475–1640.* London, 1926.

Pollet, Maurice. *John Skelton: Poet of Tudor England.* London, 1971.

Pompen, Aurelius, O.F.M. *The English Versions of the Ship of Fools: A Contribution to the History of the Early French Renaissance in England.* London, 1925.

Prasad, Ram Chandra. *Early English Travellers in India: Study in Travel Literature of the Elizabethan and Jacobean Periods, with Particular Reference to India.* Delhi, 1965.

Prouty, Charles C. T. *George Gascoigne, Elizabethan Courtier, Soldier and Poet.* New York, 1942.

Puttenham, George. *The Arte of English Poesie.* Edited by G. D. Willcock and A. Walker. Cambridge, 1936.

Quinn, David Beers. *Raleigh and the British Empire.* London, 1970.

———. *England and the Discovery of America, 1481–1620.* New York, 1974.

———, ed. *The Hakluyt Handbook.* "Hakluyt Society Publications," 2d ser., Nos. 144 and 145. Cambridge, 1974.

———, ed. *The Last Voyage of Thomas Cavendish, 1591–92.* Chicago, 1975.

Raleigh, Walter. *The English Voyages of the Sixteenth Century.* Glasgow, 1906.

Raleigh, Sir Walter. *Works.* 8 vols. Oxford, 1829.

Ramasaran, J. A. "The West Indies in English Literature Mainly during the Sixteenth and Seventeenth Centuries." M.A. thesis, University of London, 1951.

Randall, Dale B. J. *The Golden Tapestry: A Critical Survey of Non-Chivalric Spanish Fiction in English Translation, 1543–1657.* Durham, N. C., 1963.

Rao, G. Subba. *Indian Words in English: A Study in Indo-British Cultural and Linguistic Relations.* Oxford, 1954.

Rastell, John. *The Nature of the Four Elements.* Edited by J. S. Farmer in "The Tudor Facsimile Texts." London, 1908.

———. *A New Boke of Purgatory Which Is a Dyalogue & Dysputation between One Comyngo an Almayne a Christian Man and One Gynaemyn a Turke of Mahomett Law....* [London, 1530?].

Recorde, Robert. *The Castle of Knowledge.* London, 1556.

———. *Whetstone of Witte.* London, 1557.

Reed, Arthur W. *Early Tudor Drama.* London, 1926.

Ringler, William A., Jr., ed. See Sidney, Sir Philip.

Robinson, Margaret V. *Fictitious Beasts: A Bibliography.* London, 1961.

Routh, E. M. G. *Sir Thomas More and His Friends, 1477–1535.* London, 1934.

Rowlands, Samuel. *The Complete Works of Samuel Rowlands.* 2 vols. Hunterian Club edition. Glasgow, 1880.

Rowse, Alfred Leslie. *The Elizabethans and America.* London, 1959.

Rye, William Benchley. *England as Seen by Foreigners.* London, 1865.

Ryley, J. Horton. *Ralph Fitch, England's Pioneer to India and Burma: His Companions and Contemporaries.* London, 1899.

Schelling, Felix E. *Foreign Influences in Elizabethan Plays.* New York and London, 1923.

———. *English Literature during the Lifetime of Shakespeare.* New York, 1910.

———. *Elizabethan Drama, 1558–1642.* 2 vols. London, 1911.

Scott, Edmund. *An Exact Discourse of the Subtilities, Fashions, Pollicies, Religion, and Ceremonies of the East Indians, as well as Chynese and Iauans there abyding and dwelling. Where unto is added a briefe Description of Iaua Maior.* London, 1606.

Sellman, Roger R. *The Elizabethan Seaman.* London, 1957.

Sells, Arthur L. *Animal Poetry in French and English Literature and the Greek Tradition.* Bloomington, Ind., 1955.

Serjeantson, Mary S. *History of Foreign Words in English.* London, 1935.

Shaaber, Matthias A. *Some Forerunners of the Newspaper in England, 1476–1622.* Philadelphia, 1929.

Shillington, Violet, and Chapman, A. B. W. *The Commercial Relations of England and Portugal.* London, 1907.

Sidney, Sir Philip. *The Poems of Sir Philip Sidney.* Edited by William A. Ringler, Jr. Oxford, 1962.

———. *Defense of Poesie.* London, 1595.

———. *The Prose Works of Sir Philip Sidney.* Edited by Albert Feuillerat. 4 vols. Cambridge, 1912. Reprinted 1963.

Sisson, C. J. *Thomas Lodge and Other Elizabethans.* Cambridge, Mass., 1933.

Skelton, John. *The Complete Poems of John Skelton, Laureate.* Edited by Philip Henderson. London, 1959.

――――. *John Skelton. Poems*. Edited by Robert S. Kinsman. Oxford, 1969.

Smith, John, ed. *Asia's Influence on English Literature*. Rev. ed. London, 1961.

Spencer, Dorothy Mary. *Indian Fiction in English: An Annotated Bibliography*. Philadelphia, 1960.

Spenser, Edmund. *The Works of Edmund Spenser: A Variorum Edition*. Edited by Edwin Greenlaw, *et al*. 8 vols. Baltimore, 1932–47.

Sprague, Allan B. *Tides in English Tastes*. 2 vols. Cambridge, Mass., 1937.

Sprague, A. C. ed. *Poems and a Defense of Rhyme*. Cambridge, Mass., 1930.

Srinivasa Iyengar, K. R. *The Indian Contribution to English Literature*. Bombay, 1945.

Staunton, George T., ed. See Mendoza, Juan Gonzalez de.

Strathmann, Ernest A. *Sir Walter Raleigh: A Study in Elizabethan Skepticism*. New York, 1951.

Stubbings, Hilda U., comp. *Renaissance Spain in Its Literary Relations with England and France: A Critical Bibliography*. Nashville, Tenn., 1969.

Surtz, E., and Hexter, J. H., eds. See More, Thomas.

Taylor, Eva Germaine Rimington. *Late Tudor and Early Stuart Geography (1583–1650)*. London, 1934.

――――. *Tudor Geography; 1485–1583*. London, 1930.

――――, ed. See Barlow, Roger.

Taylor, Hilda. "Topographical Poetry in England during the Renaissance." Ph.D. diss., Department of English, University of Chicago, 1926.

Thomas, Henry. *Spanish and Portuguese Romances of Chivalry: The Revival of the Romance of Chivalry in the Spanish Peninsula, and Its Extension and Influence Abroad*. Cambridge, 1920.

Topsell, Edward. *The Historie of Foure-Footed Beastes: Describing the True and Lively Figure of Every Beast . . . Collected out of all the Volumes of Conradus Gesner; and all other Writers of This Present Day*. London, 1607.

Torquemada, Antonio de. *The Spanish Mandevile of Miracles. Or the Garden of Curious Flowers, wherein are Handled Sundry Points of Humanity, Philosophy, Divinitie, and Geography. Beautified with Many Strange and Pleasant Histories*. London, 1600.

Tragen, Cecil. *Elizabethan Venture*. London, 1953.

Tuve, Rosemond. *Elizabethan and Metaphysical Imagery*. Chicago, 1957.

Ungerer, Gustav. *Anglo-Spanish Relations in Tudor Literature*. Berne, 1956.

Van Dorsten, J. A. *Poets, Patrons and Professors: An Outline of Some Literary Connections between England and the University of Leiden, 1575–1586*. Leyden, 1962.

――――. *The Radical Arts: First Decade of an Elizabethan Renaissance*. Leyden, 1970.

Warner, William. *Albion's England*. London, 1602.

Waterman, William. *The fardle of facions, conteining the annciente maners, customes, and lawes of the peoples enhabiting the two partes of the earth, called Affriche and Asie*. "Hakluyt Society Publications," Supplement. London, 1812.

Watson, George, ed. *The New Cambridge Bibliography of English Literature*. Vol. I, *600–1660*. Cambridge, 1974.

Webbe, Edward. *The Rare and Most Wonderful Things Which Edward Webbe and Englishman Borne Hath Seene and Passed in His Troublesome Travailes.* 2d ed. London, 1590.

Welsby, Paul Anthony. *George Abbot, the Unwanted Archbishop.* London, 1962.

Whitney, Geoffrey. *A Choice of Emblems and other Devises.* Leyden, 1586. Edited in facsimile by H. Green. London, 1866.

Willcock, G. D., and Walker, A., eds. See Puttenham, George.

Willes, Richard. *The History of Travayle in the West and East Indies . . . newly set in order, augmented and finished by Richard Willes.* London, 1577.

————. *De Re poetica by Richard Wills [Willes].* Edited and translated by A. D. S. Fowler. Oxford, 1958.

————. *Poematum liber.* London, ca. 1573.

Williams, C., ed. and trans. See Platter, Thomas.

Williams, S. Wells. *The Middle Kingdom.* 2 vols. London, 1883.

Williamson, James A. *The Cabot Voyages and Bristol Discovery under Henry VII.* Cambridge, 1962.

————. *Maritime Enterprise (1485–1558).* Oxford, 1913.

Wilson, Frank P., ed. *The English Drama, 1485–1585.* Oxford, 1969.

Wright, Louis B. *Middle-Class Culture in Elizabethan England.* Chapel Hill, N.C., 1935.

Yates, Frances. *John Florio.* Cambridge, 1934.

Yoder, Audrey E. *Animal Analogy in Shakespeare's Character Portrayal.* New York, 1947.

ARTICLES

Atkinson, A. D. "Marlowe and the Voyagers." *Notes and Queries,* CXCIV (1949), 247–50, 273–75.

Baer, Elizabeth. "Richard Eden's Copy of the 1533 *Decades* of Peter Martyr." In *Essays Honoring Lawrence C. Wroth,* pp. 3–14. Portland, Me., 1965.

Basherville, Charles Read. "John Rastell's Dramatic Activities." *Modern Philology,* XIII, No. 9 (January, 1960), 557–60.

Borish, M. E. "Sources and Intentions of the *Four Elements.*" *Studies in Philology,* XXXV (1938), 149–63.

Braddy, Haldeen. "The Oriental Origin of Chaucer's Canacee-Falcon Episode." *Modern Language Review,* XXXI (1936), 11–19.

Bradner, Leicester. "Columbus in Sixteenth-Century Poetry." In *Essays Honoring Lawrence C. Wroth,* pp. 15–30. Portland, Me., 1965.

Brooke, C. F. Tucker. "Marlowe's Tamburlaine." *Modern Language Notes,* XXV (1910), 93–94.

Brownlow, F. W. "The Boke Compiled by Maister Skelton Poet Laureate, Called *Speake Parrot.*" *English Literary Renaissance,* I (1971), 3–26.

Cawley, Robert R. "Shakespeare's Use of the Voyages in *The Tempest.*" *PMLA,* XLI (1926), 688–726.

Ch'ien Chung-shu. "China in the English Literature of the Seventeenth Century." *Quarterly Bulletin of Chinese Bibliography* (Kunming), N.S. I, No. 4 (December, 1940), 351–84.

Church, Margaret. "The First English Pattern Poems." *PMLA*, LXI (1946), 636–50.

Cunliffe, John W. "The Queenes Majesties Entertainment at Woodstocke." *PMLA*, N.S. XIX (1911), 92–141.

Derrett, J. Duncan M. "Thomas More and Joseph the Indian." *Journal of the Royal Asiatic Society*, April, 1962, pp. 18–34.

———. "The Utopian Alphabet." *Moreana*, No. 12 (1966), pp. 61–65.

Dick, Hugh G. "Tamburlaine Sources Once More." *Studies in Philology*, XLVI (1949), 154–66.

Dindinger, Johann, O.M.I. "Thomas Stephens und sein Purâna." *Die katholischen Missionen*, LVII (1929), 100–103, 133–36, 162–67.

Draper, John W. "Shakespeare and India." In *Littératures: Études de littérature moderne* (*Annales publiées par la Faculté des Lettres de Toulouse*), II (November, 1953), 1–12.

———. "Indian and Indies in Shakespeare." *Neuphilologische Mitteilungen*, LVI (1955), 103–12.

Duyvendak, J. J. L. "An Old Chinese Fragment in the Bodleian." *Bodleian Library Record*, February, 1949, pp. 245–47.

Ebel, Julia G. "A Numerical Survey of Elizabethan Translations." *Library*, 5th ser. XXII (1967), 104–27.

Esler, Anthony. "Robert Greene and the Spanish Armada." *Journal of English Literary History*, XXXII (1965), 314–32.

Evans, John. "Extracts from the Private Account Book of Sir W. More." *Archaelogia*, XXXVI (1855), 284–92.

Feinstein, Blossom. "The *Faerie Queene* and Cosmogonies of the Near East." *Journal of the History of Ideas*, XXIX (1968), 531–50.

Fisher, A. S. T. "Birds of Paradise." *Notes and Queries*, CLXXXVIII (1945), 95–98.

Gatenby, E. V. "The Influence of Japanese on English Literature." *Studies in English Literature* (Tokyo), XIV (1934), 508–20, 595–609.

Gilbert, Allan. "Tamburlaine's 'Pampered Jades.'" *Rivista di letterature moderne*, IV (1953), 208–10.

Heiserman, Arthur R. "Satire in the *Utopia*." *PMLA*, LXXVIII (1963), 163–74.

Henriques, G. J. C. "Buchanan in Portugal." In D. A. Millar, ed. and comp., *George Buchanan: A Memorial*, pp. 60–79. London, 1907.

Hodgen, Margaret T. "Montaigne and Shakespeare Again." *Huntington Library Quarterly*, XVI (1952), 23–42.

Holzhausen, Wilhelm. "Übersee in den Darstellungsformen des Elisabethanischen Dramas." In W. Horn, ed., *Beiträge zur Erforschung der Sprache und Kultur Englands und Nordamerikas*, pp. 156–65. Breslau, 1928.

Izard, Thomas C. "The Principal Source for Marlowe's Tamburlaine." *Modern Language Notes*, LVIII (1943), 411–18.

Jorgensen, Paul A. "Foreign Sources for the Elizabethan Notion of the Spaniard." *Viator*, I (1970), 337–44.

Kilger, Laurenz. "Die Peru-Relation des José de Acosta 1576 und seine Missionstheorie." *Neue Zeitschrift für Missionswissenschaft*, I (1945), 24–38.

Korn, A. L. "Puttenham and the Oriental Pattern-Poem." *Comparative Literature*, VI (1954), 289–303.

Markino, Yoshio. "Chaucer and Chinese Odes." *English Review*, XXVII (1918), 29–38.

Martin, G. Currie. "China in English Literature." *Asiatic Quarterly Review*, N.S. XI (1917), 407–33.

Mathews, Ernest G. "English Translations from Spanish." *Journal of English and Germanic Philology*, XLIV (1945), 387–424.

Matthews, W. "Peter Bales, Timothy Bright, and Shakespeare." *Journal of English and Germanic Philology*, XXXIV (1935), 483–510.

McLachlan, R. "A Sixteenth-Century Account of China . . . by Thomas Nicholas." *Papers on Far Eastern History* (Canberra), No. 12 (1975), pp. 71–86.

Morley, Morris. "John Willis: Elizabethan Stenographer." *Notes and Queries*, CLXXXIX (1945), 222–27.

Nugent, Elizabeth M. "Sources of John Rastell's *The Nature of the Four Elements*." *PMLA*, LVII (1962), 74–88.

Parks, George B. "The Geography of the 'Interlude of the Four Elements.'" *Philological Quarterly*, XVII (1938), 251–62.

———. More's *Utopia* and Geography." *Journal of English and Germanic Philology*, XXXVII (1938), 224–36.

Parr, Johnstone. "More Sources of Rastell's *Interlude of the Four Elements*." *PMLA*, XL (1945), 48–58.

———. John Rastell's Geographical Knowledge of America." *Philological Quarterly*, XXVII (1948), 229–40.

Pearce, Roy Harvey. "Primitivistic Ideas in the *Faerie Queene*." *Journal of English and Germanic Philology*, XLIV (1945), 139–51.

Plomer, Henry Robert. "John Rastell and His Contemporaries." *Bibliographica* (London), II (1896), 437–51.

Pratt, S. M. "Antwerp and the Elizabethan Mind." *Modern Language Quarterly*, XXIV (1963), 53–60.

Schurhammer, Georg. "Der Marathidichter Thomas Stephens S.I., neue Dokumente." *Archivum historicum Societatis Iesu*, XXVI (1957), 67–82.

Scott, Charles P. G. "The Malayan Words in English." *Journal of the American Oriental Society*, XVII (1896), 93–144; XVIII (1897), 49–124.

Seaton, Ethel. "Marlowe's Map." *Essays and Studies by Members of the English Association*, X (Oxford, 1924), 13–25.

Southwood, James. "Thomas Stephens, 1549–1619." *Month*, CXCIX (1956), 197–210.

Stern, Virginia F. "The Bibliotheca of Gabriel Harvey." *Renaissance Quarterly*, XXV, No. 1 (1972), 1–62.

Stroup, Thomas B. "Shakespeare's Use of a Travel-Book Commonplace." *Philological Quarterly*, XVII (1938), 351–58.

Swallow, Alan. "John Skelton: The Structure of the Poem." *Philological Quarterly*, XXXII (1953), 29–42.

Taylor, Eva Germaine Rimington. "Richard Hakluyt." *Geographical Journal*, CIX (1947), 165–74.

Thomas, David H. "John Eliot's Borrowings from Du Bartas in His Minor Works." *Revue de littérature comparée*, XLIII (1969), 263–76.

Thomas, Henry. "English Translations of Portugese Books before 1640." *Library*, 4th ser. VII (1926), 1–30.

Trattner, Walter J. "God and Expansion in Elizabethan England: John Dee, 1527–1583." *Journal of the History of Ideas*, XXV (1964), 17–34.

Trimble, William R. "Early English Historiography, 1485–1548." *Journal of the History of Ideas*, X (1950), 30–41.

Waith, Eugene M. "Marlowe and the Jades of Asia." *Studies in English Literature, 1500–1900*, V (1965), 229–45.

Wann, Louis. "The Oriental in Elizabethan Drama." *Modern Philology*, XII (1914), 423–47.

Whitney, Lois. "Spencer's Use of the Literature of Travel in *Faerie Queene*." *Modern Philology*, XIX (1921), 143–62.

Winstedt, Richard. "The East in English Literature." *Indian Art and Letters*, N.S. XXI (1947), 1–12.

IX. TECHNOLOGY AND THE NATURAL SCIENCES

BOOKS

Acosta, Christoval [Cristóbal]. *Tractado delas drogas, y medicinas de las Indias Orientales, con sus plantas debuxadas al bivo por Christoval Acosta medico y cirujano que las vio ocularmente.* Burgos, 1578.

———. *Trattato di Christoforo Acosta Africano della historia, natura, et virtu delle droghe medicinali, et altri semplici rarissimi, che vengono partati dalle Indie Orientali in Europa.* Venice, 1585.

Agricola, Georgius. *Georgius Agricola. De re metallica. Translated from the First Latin Edition of 1556.* Translated and edited by Herbert C. Hoover and Lou Henry Hoover. New York, 1950.

Agrippa, Henry Cornelis. *The Vanity of Arts and Sciences.* London, 1684.

Albertinus, Aegidius. *Der welt tummel und schau-platz, sampt der hetter suessen warheit. Darinn . . . nicht allein die naturliche, sondern auch moralische unnd sitliche eygenschafften unnd geheimnussen der fuernembsten creaturen unnd geschoepff Gottes. . . .* Munich, 1614.

Aléchamps, Jacques d'. *Historia generalis plantarum.* Lyons, 1586–87.

Allen, Richard H. *Star Names: Their Lore and Meaning.* New York, 1963. Reprint of the work first issued in 1899 as *Star-Names and Their Meanings.*

Alpini, Prosper. *Prosperi Alpini. De plantis Aegypti liber.* Padua, 1640.

———. *De medicina aegyptiorum, libri quatuor.* Paris, 1645. 1st ed. Venice, 1591.

Amato Lusitano. *Curationum medicinalium Amati Lusitani medici physici praestantissimi centuriae quatuor.* Venice, 1557.

———. *In Dioscoridis anazarbei de medica materia libros quinque.* Lyons, 1558.

Arber, Agnes. *Herbals: Their Origins and Evolution.* 2d rev. ed. Cambridge, 1938.

Archer, Peter. *The Christian Calendar and the Gregorian Reform.* New York, 1941.

Chapter IX

Audemard, Louis. *Les jonques chinoises*. Rotterdam, 1957.

Avenir, Tchemerzine. *Bibliographie d'ouvrages sur les sciences et les arts édités aux XVe et XVIe siècles*. Courbevoie, 1933.

Bacon, Francis. *Of the advancement and proficience of learning or the partitions of sciences IX books*. Oxford, 1640.

Baillon, Henri E. *Dictionnaire de botanique*. 5 vols. Paris, 1876–92.

Baldacci, Antonio. *Intorno alla vita e alle opere di U. Aldrovandi*. Bologna, 1907.

Barbensi, Gustavo. *Il pensiero scientifico in Toscana disegno storico dalle origini al 1859*. Florence, 1969.

Barsaud, Georges. *L'humanisme et la médicine au XVIe siècle*. Paris, 1942.

Bassaeus, Nicolaus. *Catalogus oder Register, aller apoteckischen Simplicien und Compositen, so in den beyden Messen zu Frankfurt am Meyn . . . verkauft werden*. Frankfurt, 1582.

Bauhin, Jean. *Historia plantarum universalis*. Embrun (France), 1550–51.

Bauhin, Kaspar. *Histoire des plantes de l'Europe, et des plus usitees qui viennent d'Asie, d'Afrique et d'Amerique. Où l'on voit leurs figures, leurs noms, en quel temps elles fleurissent, et le lieu où elles croissent*. Lyons, 1689.

———. *De lapidis Bezoar Orient et Occident. Cervini item et Germanici ortu, natura, differentijs, veróque usu ex veterum et recentiorum placitis liber hactenus non editus*. Basel, 1613.

Beaujouan, Guy. *La science en Espagne aux XVe et XVIe siècles*. Paris, 1967.

Bechtel, Guy. *Paracelse, ou la naissance de la médicine alchemique*. Paris, 1970.

Beckmann, Johann. *Beyträge zur Geschichte der Erfindungen*. 5 vols. Leipzig, 1780–1805.

Bellini, Angelo. *Gerolamo Cardano e il suo tempo*. Milan, 1947.

Benedict, Susan Rose. *A Comparative Study of the Early Treatises Introducing into Europe the Hindu Art of Reckoning*. Concord, N.H., 1916.

Bensaude, Joachim, ed. *Histoire de la science nautique portugaise*. Geneva, 1917.

Bernal, J. D. *Science in History*. 4th ed. 4 vols. London, 1969.

Bernard, Henri. *Matteo Ricci's Scientific Contribution to China*. Translated by E. C. Werner. Peking, 1935.

Biringuccio, Vanucio. *Pirotechnica (Venice, 1540)*. Translated by C. Smith and M. T. Gnudi. New York, 1943.

Blundeville, Thomas. *His Exercises*. 2d rev. ed. London, 1597.

Blunt, Wilfred. *The Art of Botanical Illustration*. London, 1950.

Bobroff, Sara. "Exotic Plants in Linnaeus' *Species Plantarum* (1753)." Ph.D. diss., Department of History, University of Chicago, 1973.

Bock, Hieronymus. *Kreüter buch. Darinn underscheidt namen unnd würkung der kreütter standen hecken und beümen sampt iren früchten so inn teütschen landen wachsen*. Strassburg, 1539.

Bodenheimer, Friedrich S. *The History of Biology: An Introduction*. London, 1958.

Bodin, Jean. *Universae naturae theatrum*. Lyons, 1596.

Boetius de Boodt, Anselm. *Gemmarum et lapidum historia*. Hanau, 1609.

Bondt, Jakob de. *Tropische geneeskunde—Bontius on Tropical Medicine*. Facsimile of Amsterdam 1658 edition. Amsterdam, 1951.

Bonnin, Alfred. *Tutenag and Paktong: With Notes on Other Alloys in Domestic Use during the Eighteenth Century.* London, 1924.

Bose, D. M., et al. *A Concise History of Science in India.* New Delhi, 1971.

Bowers, John Z. *Western Medical Pioneers in Feudal Japan.* Baltimore, 1970.

Boxer, Charles R. *Two Pioneers of Tropical Medicine: Garcia d'Orta and Nicolas Monardes.* London, 1963.

Brasavola, Antonio (called Musa). *Examen omnium simpl. medicament. quorum usus in publius est officinis.* Venice, 1545.

———. *De medicamentis tam simplicibus, quam compositis catharticis, quae unicuq; humori sunt propria. . . .* Venice, 1552.

Bretschneider, Emilei Vasel'evich. *History of European Botanical Discoveries in China.* Leipzig, 1962.

———. *Botanicum sinicum: Notes on Chinese Botany from Native and Western Sources.* Nendeln, 1967.

———. *Medieval Researches from Eastern Asiatic Sources.* 2 vols. London, 1888. New ed. London, 1937. Reprint, 1967.

Brunfels, Otto. *Herbarum vivae eicones: Appendix isagogica novi herbarii. Tomus Herbarii.* 3 vols. Strassburg, 1530–36.

Bucher, Bruno. *Geschichte der technischen Künste.* 3 vols. Stuttgart, 1875.

Calcagnini, Celio. *Opera aliquot. . . .* Basel, 1544.

Callery, Bernadette Gabrielle. "The Printable Plant: The Impact of Popular Vernacular Printing on the English Herbals Produced in the Sixteenth and Seventeenth Centuries." M.A. thesis, Graduate Library School, University of Chicago, 1971.

Cap, Paul Antoine. *La science et les savants au XVIᵉ siècle.* Tours, 1867.

Capivaccio, Girolamo. *Opera omnia, quinque section comprehensa.* Frankfurt, 1603.

Cardano, Girolamo. *De subtilitate libri XXI.* Lyons, 1580.

———. *Opera omnia. Faksimile-Neudruck der Ausgabe, Lyon, 1663.* Stuttgart, 1966.

———. *De rerum varietate.* Avignon, 1558.

———. *Offenbarung der Natur unnd natürlicher Dingen auch mancherly subtiler Würkungen.* Basel, 1559.

———. *The Book of My Life.* Translated from the Latin by Jean Stoner. New York, 1962.

Carus, Julius Victor. *Histoire de la zoologie depuis l'antiquité jusqu'au XIXᵉ siècle.* Paris, 1880.

Cermenati, Mario. *Ulisse Aldrovandi e l'America.* Paris, 1906.

Cervantes Saavedra, M. de, and Marin, F. R., eds. *El ingenioso hidalgo, Don Quijote de la Mancha.* 10 vols. Madrid, 1947–49.

Cesalpino, Andrea. *De plantis libri XVI.* Florence, 1583.

Chatterton, Edward K. *Sailing Ships: The Story of Their Development from the Earliest Times to the Present Day.* Philadelphia, 1909.

Chŏn, Sangŭn. *Science and Technology in Korea; Traditional Instruments and Techniques.* Cambridge, Mass., 1974.

Chopra, Ram Nath. *Glossary of Indian Medicinal Plants.* New Delhi, 1956.

Choulant, Johann Ludwig. *Graphische Incunabeln für Naturgeschichte und Medicin.*

Geschichte und Bibliographie der ersten naturhistorischen und medicinischen Drucke des XV. und XVI. Jahrhunderts, welche mit illustrirenden Abbildlungen versehen sind. Leipzig, 1858.

Cian, Vittorio. *Un decennio della vita di M. Pietro Bembo, 1521–31.* Turin, 1885.

Cipolla, Carlo. *Guns, Sails, and Empire.* New York, 1965.

———. *Clocks and Culture (1300–1700).* London, 1967.

———. *Literacy and Development in the West.* Baltimore, 1969.

Clusius. See L'écluse, Charles de.

Coats, Alice M. *The Plant Hunters: Being a History of the Horticultural Pioneers, Their Quests, and Their Discoveries from the Renaissance to the Twentieth Century.* New York, 1970.

Colmeiro, D. Miguel. *Ensayo historico sobre los progresos de la botánica desde su origen hasta el dia, considerados mas especialmente con relacion a España.* Barcelona, 1842.

———. *La botánica y los botánicos en la peninsula hispanolusitania.* Madrid, 1858.

Copernicus, Nikolas. *De revolutionibus orbium coelestium.* Nuremberg, 1543.

Cordus, Valerius. *Pharmacorum omnium, quae in usu poliss. sunt componendorum ratio.* Nuremberg, 1592.

———. *Dispensatorium, hoc est. Pharmacorum conficiendorum ratio.* Venice, 1556.

Cortes, Martin. *Breve compendio de la sphera y de la arte de navegar.* Seville, 1551.

Costa, Emilio. *Ulisse Aldrovandi e lo studio bolognese nella seconda metà del secolo XVI.* Bologna, 1907.

Cox, Evan Hellhouse Methven. *Planthunting in China: A History of Botanical Exploration in China and the Tibetan Marches.* London, 1945.

Crescentio, Pietro de. *De omnibus agriculturae partibus et de plantarum animalium natural et utilitate lib. XII.* Basel, 1548.

Crosby, Alfred W., Jr. *The Columbian Exchange: Biological and Cultural Consequences of 1492.* Westport, Conn., 1972.

Dannenfeldt, Karl H. *L. Rauwolf, Sixteenth-Century Physician, Botanist, and Traveler.* Cambridge, Mass., 1968.

Datta, B., and Singh, A. N. *History of Hindu Mathematics: A Source Book.* Parts I and II. Bombay, 1962.

Davy de Verville, Adrien. *Histoire de la botanique en France.* Paris, 1954.

Day, K. L. *Indigenous Drugs of India.* Calcutta, 1896.

Debus, Allen G. *Alchemy and Chemistry in the Seventeenth Century.* Los Angeles, 1966.

———, ed. *Science, Medicine, and Society in the Renaissance: Essays to Honour Walter Pagel.* New York, 1973.

De Jode, Gerard. *Speculum orbis terrarum.* Antwerp, 1593.

D'Elia, Pasquale. *Galileo in China.* Cambridge, Mass., 1960.

Diccionario universal das moedas assim metallicas, como ficticios imaginarias, ou de conclus, etc. que se conhecem na Europa, Asia, Africa, e America. Lisbon, 1793.

Diergart, Paul. *Beiträge aus der Geschichte der Chemie dem Gedächtniss von Georg W. A. Kahlbaum.* Leipzig and Vienna, 1909.

Dijksterhuis, Eduard Jan. *Simon Stevin.* The Hague, 1970.

———. *The Mechanization of the World Picture.* Oxford, 1961.

———, ed. *The Principal Works of Simon Stevin.* 6 vols. Amsterdam, 1955–66.

Dodoens, Rembert. *Histoire des Plantes en laquelle est contenue la description entiere des herbes etc. traduicte de Bas-Aleman par Charles de l'Escluse en Anvers.* Antwerp, 1557.

———. *Cruydeboeck.* Facsimile reprint of the 1554 edition. Leyden, 1968.

———. *A nieuve herball, or Historie of plantes . . . and that not onely of those . . . in . . . Englande, but of all others also of forayne realms, commonly used in Physicke.* Translated by Henry Lyte. London, 1578.

Donnelly, Ivon A. *Chinese Junks and Other Native Craft.* Shanghai, 1939.

Drury, Heber. *The Useful Plants of India: With Notice of Their Chief Value in Commerce, Medicine and the Arts.* Madras, 1873.

Dubler, César E. *La 'Materia Medica' de Dioscorides; Transmisión medieval y renacentista.* 5 vols. Barcelona, 1953–55.

Duchesne, Joseph. *Opera medica, scilicet, ad Jacobi Auberti de ortu & causis metallorum . . . explicationem brevis responsio.* Lyons, 1600.

Dupleix, Scipio N. *La curiosité naturelle redigée en questions selon l'ordre alphabétique.* Paris, 1606.

Durante, Castore. *Herbario nuovo di Castore Durante medico e cittadino Romano. Con figure, che rappresentano le vive piante che nascono en tutta Europa, e nell' Indie orientali e occidentali. . . .* Rome, 1585. 1st ed. Venice, 1584.

Duveen, Denis I. *Bibliotheca Alchemica et Chemica: Annotated Catalogue of Printed Books on Alchemy, Chemistry and Cognate Subjects in the Library of D. I. Duveen.* London, 1965.

Dymock, William. *Pharmacographia Indica: A History of the Principal Drugs of Vegetable Origin, Met with in British India.* London, 1890–93.

Ercher, Lazarus. *Treatise on Ores and Assaying.* Translated by A. G. Sisco and C. S. Smith. Chicago, 1951.

Farber, Edward. *The Evolution of Chemistry: a History of Its Ideas, Methods, and Materials.* New York, 1952.

Ferguson, Eugene Shallcross. *Bibliography of the History of Technology.* Cambridge, Mass., 1968.

Ferguson, John. *Bibliographical Notes on Histories of Inventions and Books of Secrets.* 2 vols. Glasgow, 1898. Reprinted London, 1959.

Ficalho, Conde de. *Flora dos Lusíadas.* Lisbon, 1880.

Figard, Leon. *Un medecin philosphe au XVIᵉ siècle: Étude sur la psychologie de Jean Fernel.* Geneva, 1970.

Filliozat, Jean. *La doctrine classique de la médicine indienne: Ses origines et ses parallèles grecs.* Paris, 1949.

Flückiger, Friedrich A., and Hanbury, Daniel. *Pharmacographia: A History of the Principal Drugs of Vegetable Origin Met with in Great Britain and British India.* London, 1874.

Fontura da Costa, Abel. *A marinharia dos descobrimentos.* Lisbon, 1934.

Fournier, Paul. *Voyages et découvertes scientifiques des missionnaires naturalistes français à travers le monde . . . (XVᵉ à XXᵉ siècles).* Paris, 1932.

Fragoso, Juan. *Discursos de las cosas aromaticas, arboles y frutales, y de otras muchas medicinas simples que se traen de la India Oriental, y sirven al uso de medicina.* Madrid, 1572.

French, Peter J. *John Dee: The World of an Elizabethan Magus.* London, 1971.

Fretz, Diethelm. *Konrad Gessner als Gärtner.* Zurich, 1948.

Friedenwald, Harry. *The Jews and Medicine: Essays.* 2 vols. Baltimore, 1944.

Fuchs, Leonard. *New kreüterbuch in welchem nit allein die gantz histori das ist namen gestalt und zeit der wachsung natur krafft und würckung des meysten theyls der kreüter so in teütschen und andern landen wachsen.* Basel, 1543.

Gallesio, Giorgio. *Traité du citrus.* 3 vols. Pisa, 1917.

Ganzenmüller, Wilhelm. *Beiträge zur Geschichte der Technologie und der Alchemie.* Weinheim, 1956.

Garbe, Richard. *Die Sāmkhya-Philosophie.* 2d ed. Leipzig, 1917.

Gerard, John. *The Herball, or Generall Historie of Plantes. . . .* London, 1633.

Gesner, Konrad. *De rerum fossilum, lapidum et gemmarum maximè, figuris et similitudinibus liber. . . .* Zurich, 1565.

Gille, Bertrand. *Engineers of the Renaissance.* Cambridge, Mass., 1966.

Ginori-Conti, Piero, ed. *Lettere inedite di Charles de L'Escluse (Carolus Clusius) a Matteo Caccini floricultore fiorentino. Contributo alla storia della botanica.* Florence, 1939.

Giullén, Julio F. *Europa aprendió a navegar en libros españoles.* Madrid, 1943.

Goltz, Dietlinde. *Studien zur Geschichte der Mineralnamen in Pharmazie, Chemie und Medizin von den Anfangen bis Paracelsus.* "Sudhoffs Archiv," No. 14. Wiesbaden, 1972.

Grafton, Anthony T. "Joseph Scaliger (1540–1609) and the Humanism of the Later Renaissance." Ph.D. diss., Department of History, University of Chicago, 1975.

Greene, Edward Lee. *Landmarks of Botanical History. Part I—Prior to 1562 A.D.* Washington, D.C., 1909.

Gubernatis, Angelo de. *La mythologie des plantes.* Paris, 1878.

Guerra, Francisco. *Nicolás Bautista Monardes, su vida y su obra.* Mexico City, 1961.

Gupta, Shakti M. *Plant Myths and Traditions in India.* Leyden, 1971.

Hammond, L. D., trans. and ed. *Travelers in Disguise. . . .* Cambridge, Mass., 1963.

Harrison, Thomas P., and Hoeniger, F. David, eds. *The Fowles of Heaven or History of Birdes by Edward Topsell.* Austin, Tex., 1972.

Hart, Clive. *Kites: An Historical Survey.* London, 1967.

Hartmann, Franz. *The Life of Philippus Theophrastus Bombast of Hohenheim Known by the Name of Paracelsus and the Substance of His Teachings.* 2d rev. ed. London, 1896.

————. *Theophrastus Paracelsus als Mystiker.* Leipzig, 1894.

Hartmann, Hans. *Georg Agricola 1494–1555: Begründer dreier Wissenschaften: Mineralogie-Geologie-Bergbaukunde.* Stuttgart, 1953.

Hartwick, Carl. *Die Bedeutung der Entdeckung von Amerika für die Drogenkunde.* Berlin, 1892.

Hawks, Ellison. *Pioneers of Plant Study.* London, 1928.

Hayms, Edward S. *A History of Gardens and Gardening.* New York, 1971.

————. *Great Botanical Gardens of the World.* New York, 1969.

————. *Plants in the Service of Man: 10,000 Years of Domestication.* Philadelphia, 1972.

Hedges, Ernest S. *Tin in Social and Economic History.* New York, 1964.

Chapter Bibliographies

Hehn, Victor. *Kulturpflanzen und Hausthiere in ihrem Uebergang aus Asien nach Griechenland und Italien sowie in das übrigen Europa; historisch-linguistische Skizzen.* Berlin, 1887. Rev. ed. Hildesheim, 1963.

Heilmann, Karl Eugen. *Kräuterbücher in Bild und Geschichte.* Munich, 1966.

Henry, August. *Economic Botany of China.* Shanghai, 1893.

Henry, Blanche. *British Botanical and Horticultural Literature before 1800.* . . . Vol. I. London, 1975.

Herlitzins, Erwin. *Georgius Agricola (1494–1555): Seine Weltanschauung und seine Leistung als Wegbereiter einer materialistischen Naturauffassung.* Berlin, 1960.

Herrera, Alonso de. *Libro de agricultura.* Madrid, 1598.

Hodgen, Margaret. *Change and History: A Study of Dated Distributions of Technological Innovations in England, A.D. 1000–1899.* New York, 1952.

———. *Early Anthropology in the Sixteenth and Seventeenth Centuries.* Philadelphia, 1964.

Hofmann, Lorenz. *Thesaurus variarum rerum antiquarum exoticarum tam naturalium.* Halle, 1625.

Hogben, Lancelot. *Mathematics in the Making.* London, 1960.

Holmyard, Eric J. *Alchemy.* London, 1968.

Hoover, Herbert C., and Hoover, Lou Henry, trans. and eds. See Agricola, Georgius.

Hoppe, Brigitte, ed. *Das Kräuterbuch des Hieronymus Bock: Wissenschaft-historische Untersuchung. Mit einem Verzeichnis sämtlicher Pflanzen des Werkes, der literarischen Quellen der Heilanzeigen und der Anwendungen der Pflanzen.* Stuttgart, 1969.

Hornell, James. *Water Transport: Origins and Early Evolution.* Cambridge, 1946.

Huard, P., and Wong, M. *Evolution de la matière médicale chinoise.* Leyden, 1958.

Humboldt, Alexander von. *Examen critique de l'histoire de la géographie du Nouveau Continent, et des progrès de l'astronomie nautique au 15ᵉ et 16ᵉ siècles.* 5 vols. Paris, 1837.

Hunger, Friedrich W. T. *Charles de l'Escluse (Carolus Clusius) Nederlandsch Kruidkundige (1526–1609).* The Hague, 1927.

Hunt, Rachel M. *Catalogue of Botanical Books.* Pittsburgh, 1958.

Huth, Hans. *Lacquer of the West: The History of a Craft and an Industry.* Chicago, 1971.

Imperato, Ferrante. *Dell' historie naturale libri XXVIII.* Naples, 1599.

Jackson, B. D. *A Catalogue of Plants Cultivated in the Garden of John Gerard, in the Years 1596–1599.* London, 1876.

Jeffers, Robert H. *The Friends of John Gerard (1545–1612), Surgeon and Botanist.* Falls Village, Conn., 1967.

Jenkins, Rhys. *Links in the History of Engineering and Technology from Tudor Times.* Cambridge, 1936.

Johnson, Frances R. *Astronomical Thought in Renaissance England, 1500–1645.* Baltimore, 1937.

Jorge, Ricardo. *Amato Lusitano.* Lisbon, 1962.

Jung, Carl Gustav. *Alchemical Studies.* Princeton, 1967.

Kern, H., ed. *J. Huygen van Linschoten, Itinerario.* . . . 'S-Gravenhage, 1910.

Chapter IX

Kerner, Dieter. *Paracelsus: Leben und Werk*. Stuttgart, 1965.

Keynes, Geoffrey, ed. See Paré, Ambroise.

Klemm, Friedrich. *A History of Western Technology*. London, 1959.

Knappich, Wilhelm. *Geschichte der Astrologie*. Frankfurt-am-Main, 1967.

Koyré, Alexandre. *From the Closed World to the Infinite Universe*. New York, 1958.

———, ed. *La science au seizième siècle*. Paris, 1960.

Kuhn, Thomas S. *The Copernican Revolution: Planetary Astronomy in the Development of Western Thought*. Cambridge, Mass., 1957.

Laguna, Andrés. *Pedacio Dioscórides Anazarbeo, acerca de la materia medicinal y de los venenos mortiferos*. . . . Antwerp, 1555.

Lakshminarayana, Kodali. *A History of Medicine, Surgery, and Alchemy in India*. Tenali, 1970.

Lamb, Ursula. *A Navigator's Universe: The "Libro de Cosmographia" of 1538 by Pedro de Medina*. Chicago, 1972.

Larson, Gerald J. *Classical Sāmkhya: An Interpretation of Its Meaning*. Delhi, 1969.

Laufer, Berthold. *The Prehistory of Aviation*. Chicago, 1928.

L'écluse, Charles de. *Caroli Clusii*. . . . *Aliquot notae in Garciae aromatum historiam. Eiusdem descriptiones nonnullarum Stirpium . . . que à . . . Francisco Drake . . . observatae sunt*. Antwerp, 1582.

———. *Rariorum aliquot stirpium, per Dannoniam, Austriam, et vicinas quasdam Provincias observatarum historia*. . . . Antwerp, 1583.

———. *Rariorum plantarum historia. Accesserunt fungorum in Pannoniis observatorum historia; epistolae Belli et Roelsü et Ponae plantae Baldi*. 7 vols. Antwerp, 1601.

Le Comte, Louis. *Nouveaux mémoires sur l'état présent de la Chine*. Paris, 1701.

Leggett, William Ferguson. *The Story of Silk*. New York, 1949.

Legré, Ludovic. *La botanique en Provence au XVIe siècle: Pierre Pena et Mathias de Lobel*. Marseilles, 1899.

Lehner, Ernst, and Lehner, Johanna. *Folklore and Odysseys of Food and Medicinal Plants*. New York, 1962.

Lemos, Maximiano. *Amato Lusitano: A sua vida e a sua obra*. Porto, 1907.

———. *História da medicina em Portugal*. 2 vols. Lisbon, 1899.

Lequenne, Fernand. *La vie d'Olivier de Serres*. Paris, 1970.

Lewin, Louis. *Phantastica: Narcotic and Stimulating Drugs, Their Use and Abuse*. New York, 1964.

Libavius, Andreas. *Syntagma selectorum undignaque et perspicue traditorum alchymiae arcanorum*. Frankfurt, 1611.

Libbrecht, Ulrich. *Chinese Mathematics in the Thirteenth Century*. Cambridge, Mass., 1973.

Linocier, Geofroy. *Histoire des plantes aromatiques qui croissent dans l'Inde tant occidentale, qu'orientale*. Paris, 1584.

Lobel, Matthias de. *Plantarum, seu stirpium historia*. Antwerp, 1576.

Lonitzer, Adam (Lonicerus). *Kreuterbuch künstliche Conterfeitunae der Bäume Standen hecken kreuter Getrende Gewürsse. Mit eigentlicher Beschreibung derselben Namen in sechserlen Spraachen Nemlich Griechisch Lateinisch Italiänisch Frankösisch Deutsch und Hispanisch und dersels ben Gestalt natürlicher Krafft und Wirckung. Sampt fünflichem und artlichem Bericht dess Distilierens.* . . . Frankfurt, 1598.

Lopeteguí, Leon, S.J. *El P. José de Acosta y su influencia en la literatura científica española.* Madrid, 1942.

Loureiro, João de. *Flora Cochinchinensis.* . . . 2 vols. London, 1790.

MacMillan, H. F. *Tropical Planting and Gardening.* 5th ed. London, 1962.

Maggio, Lucio. *Discours du tremblement de terre, traduict d'Italien par Nicolas de Livre.* Paris, 1575.

Markham, Sir Clements, trans. See Orta, Garcia da.

Mattioli, Pietro Andrea. *New Kreüterbuch mit den allerschönsten und artlichsten figuren aller gewechss dergleichen vormals in keiner sprach nie an tag kommen.* Translated by Georg Handsch. Prague, 1563.

———. *Commentaires . . . sur les six livres de Ped. Dioscoride.* . . . Translated by Jean de Moulines. Lyons, 1572.

———. *Opera quae extant omnia.* Frankfurt, 1598.

Mattirolo, Oreste. *L'opera botanica di Ulisse Aldrovandi (1549–1605).* Bologna, 1897.

Menéndez Pelayo, Marcelino. *La ciencia española.* 4th ed. 3 vols. Madrid, 1915–18.

Meyer, Ernst Heinrich Friedrich. *Geschichte der Botanik.* 2 vols. Königsberg, 1854–57.

Mieli, Aldo. *La science arabe et son rôle dans l'évolution scientifique mondiale: réimpression anastatique augm. d'une bibliographie avec index analytique par A. Mazahéri.* Leyden, 1966.

Miranda, M. G. de. *La contribution de l'Espagne au progrès de la cosmographie et de ses techniques (1508–1624).* Paris, 1964.

Monroe, James T. *Islam and the Arabs in Spanish Scholarship (Sixteenth Century to the Present).* Leyden, 1970.

Moura, João Herculano de. *Inscripções indianas em Cintra. Nótulas de archeologia histórica e bibliographia acerca dos templos Hindús de Somnáth-Patane e Elephanta.* . . . Nova Goa, 1906.

Müller, Martin. *Registerband zu Sudhoffs Paracelsus Gesamtausgabe.* Einsiedeln, 1960.

Multhauf, Robert P. *The Origins of Chemistry.* New York, 1967.

Nakayama, Shigeru, and Sivin, Nathan, comps. *Chinese Science: Explorations of an Ancient Tradition.* Cambridge, Mass., 1973.

Needham, Joseph. *The Refiner's Fire: The Enigma of Alchemy in East and West.* London, 1971.

———. *Science and Civilization in China.* 6 vols. Cambridge, 1965–74.

———. *Classical Chinese Contributions to Mechanical Engineering.* Newcastle, 1961.

Neugebauer, Otto. *The Exact Sciences in Antiquity.* 2d ed. Providence, 1957.

Nichols, R. S. *Spanish and Portuguese Gardens.* New York, 1902.

Nissen, Claus. *Herbals of Five Centuries.* Munich, 1950.

———. *Kräuterbücher aus fünf Jahrhunderten. 50 Originalblätter aus deutschen, französischen, niederländischen, englischen, italienischen, und schweizerischen Kräuterbüchern.* Munich and Zurich, 1956.

————. *Die botanische Buchillustration: Ihre Geschichte und Bibliographie.* 2 vols. Stuttgart, 1951.

Oesterle, Friedrich. *Die Anthropologie des Paracelsus.* Berlin, 1937.

Olmedilla y Puig, Joaquín. *Estudio histórico de la vida y escritos del sabio español Andrés Laguna, médico de Carlo I y Felipe II.* . . . Madrid, 1887.

Olschki, Leonardo. *Geschichte der neusprachlichen wissenschaftlichen Literatur. I. Die Literatur der Technik und der angewandten Wissenschaften vom Mittelalter bis zur Renaissance.* Heidelberg, 1918.

O'Malley, C. D. *Andreas Vesalius of Brussels, 1514–1564.* Berkeley and Los Angeles, 1964.

Orbigny, Charles Dessalines d'. *Dictionnaire universel d'histoire naturelle.* 13 vols. plus 3-vol. atlas. Paris, 1847–49.

Ore, Oystein. *Cardano, the Gambling Scholar.* Princeton, 1953.

Orta, Garcia da. *Dell'historia de i semplici aromati, et altre cose che vengono portato dall' Indie Orientali pertinenti all'uso della medicina. Parte prima. Divisa in libri IIII. Di Don Garzia da l'Horto medico portughese; con alcune brevi annotationi di Carlo Clusio. Et due altri libri parimente di quelle cose che si portano dall'Indie occidentali; di Nicolò Monardes medico di Siviglia. Hora tutti tradutti dalle loro lingue nella nostra Italiana da M. Annibale Briganti.* . . . Venice, 1589.

————. *Colóquios dos simples e drogas e cousas medicinais da India.* Facsimile reproduction of the edition printed at Goa on April 10, 1563, in Commemoration of the Fourth Centennial of the Original Edition. Lisbon, 1963.

————. *Histoire des drogues, espéceries et de certains medicaments simple qui naissent en Indes (1563).* Translated by Antoine Colin. Lyons, 1619.

————. *Colloquies on the Simples and Drugs of India.* Translated by Sir Clements Markham. London, 1913.

Oviedo y Valdès, Gonzalo Fernandez de. *Historia general y natural de las Indias, islas y tierra firme del mar oceáno.* Madrid, 1851–55.

Pagel, Walter. *Das medizinische Weltbild von Paracelsus: Seine Zusammenhänge mit Neuplatonismus und Gnosis.* Wiesbaden, 1962.

————. *Paracelsus: An Introduction to Philosophical Medicine in the Era of the Renaissance.* Basel and New York, 1958.

Panciroli, Guido. *Nova reperta; sive, rerum memorabilium recens inventarum veteribus incognitarum.* 2d ed. Amberg, 1608.

Paracelsus, Theophrastus. *The Hermetic and Alchemical Writings of Paracelsus the Great.* . . . Translated by A. E. Waite. 2 vols. London, 1894.

————. *Paracelsus sämtliche Werke, nach der IV bändigen Huserschen Gesamtausgabe (1589–1591) zum erstenmal in neuzeitliches deutsch übersetzt.* Edited by Bernhard Aschner. 4 vols. Jena, 1926–32.

————. *Sämtliche Werke.* Edited by K. Sudhoff. 14 vols. Munich, 1929.

————. *Sämtliche Werke.* Edited by J. Strebel. Vol. III. St. Gall, 1947.

Paré, Ambroise. *The apologie and treatise of Ambroise Paré, containing the voyages made into divers places with many of his writings upon surgery.* Edited by Geoffrey Keynes. Chicago, 1952.

———. *Des monstres, des prodiges, des voyages. Texte établi et présenté par Patrice Boussel.* Paris, 1964.

Pariset, Ernest. *Histoire de la soie.* 2 vols. Paris, 1862.

Parkinson, John. *Theatrum botanicum: The theater of plants Or an herball of a large extent.* London, 1640.

Parry, John H. *The Age of Reconnaissance.* New York, 1963.

Parsons, William B. *Engineers and Engineering in the Renaissance.* Baltimore, 1939.

Partington, James R. *A History of Chemistry, 1500–1800.* 3 vols. London and New York, 1961–62.

———. *A History of Greek Fire and Gunpowder.* Cambridge, 1960.

Passebreme, E. de. *Le plaisant Iardin des receptes, ou sont plantez divers arbrisseaux et odorantes fleurs du creu de philosophie naturelle, cultivè par medicins experts en physique speculation.* Lyons, 1556.

Perry, Frances. *Flowers of the World.* London, 1972.

Petty, William. *An Apparatus to the History of the Common Practices of Dyeing.* London, 1667.

Philip, Alexander. *The Reform of the Calendar.* London, 1914.

Picatoste y Rodrigues, Felipe. *Apuntes para una bibliographia científica española del siglo XVI.* Madrid, 1891.

Pina, Luiz de. *Contribuição dos portugueses quinhentistas para a história da medicina do Oriente.* Lisbon, 1938.

———. *A medicina de alem-mar no século XVI.* Coimbra, 1935.

Poggendorff, J. C. *Poggendorff's Biographisch-literarisches Handwörterbuch zur Geschichte der exacten Wissenschaften.* 2 vols. Leipzig, 1864–1904.

Pons, Iaq. *Traicté des Melons, de la nature et usage d'iceux.* Lyons, 1584.

Porta, Giovanni Baptista della. *Magia naturalis* (Naples, 1589). Edited by G. Price. New York, 1957.

Powell, Thomas. *The history of most curious manual arts and inventions. . . .* 3d ed. London, 1675.

Price, G. de Solla. *Science since Babylon.* New Haven and London, 1961.

Priolkar, A. K. *The Printing Press in India.* Bombay, 1958.

Prost, Auguste. *Les sciences et les arts occultes au XVIᵉ siècle: Corneille Agrippa sa vie et ses oeuvres.* 2 vols. Paris, 1881–82. Reprint. Nieuwkoop, 1965.

Rauw, Johann. *Cosmographia.* Frankfurt, 1597.

Ray, P. C. *History of Hindu Chemistry.* 2 vols. London, 1902.

Read, John. *The Alchemist in Life, Literature, and Art.* London, 1947.

Reed, Howard Sprague. *A Short History of the Plant Sciences.* New York, 1942.

Rees, William. *Industry before the Industrial Revolution.* 2 vols. Cardiff, 1968.

Reis, Beatriz Cinatti Batalha. *Useful Plants in Portuguese Timor.* Coimbra, 1964.

Rey Pastor, João. *La ciencia y la técnica en el descobrimento de América.* 2d ed. Buenos Aires, 1945.

Riano, Juan F. *The Industrial Arts in Spain.* London, 1879.

Richmond, Broughton. *Time Measurement and Calendar Construction.* Leyden, 1953.

Risso, Antoine, and Poiteau, A. *Histoire et culture des oranges.* 2d ed. Paris, 1872.

Rogers, Francis M. *Precision Astrolabes: Portuguese Navigators and Trans-Oceanic Navigation.* Lisbon, 1971.

Rohde, Eleanour Sinclair. *The Old English Herbals.* London and New York, 1922.

Rosengarten, Frederic, Jr. *The Book of Spices.* Philadelphia, 1969.

Roze, Ernest, ed. *Charles de l'Escluse d'Arras. . . . Sa biographie et sa correspondance.* Paris, 1899.

Sachs, Julius von. *History of Botany (1530–1860).* Translated by Henry E. Garnsey. Oxford, 1890.

———. *Geschichte der Botanik.* Leipzig, 1875.

Sanchez Perez, José Augusto. *La arithmética en Roma, en India, y en Arabia.* Madrid, 1949.

Sarton, George. *Six Wings: Men of Science in the Renaissance.* Bloomington, Ind., 1957.

Scaliger, Joseph. *De emendatione temporum.* Paris, 1583.

Scheleng, Hermann. *Geschichte der Pharmazie.* Hildesheim, 1962.

Schmid, Alfred. *Über alte Kräuterbücher.* Berne, 1939.

Schulze, Franz. *Balthasar Springers Indienfahrt 1505/06. . . .* Strassburg, 1902.

Scott, Joseph F. *A History of Mathematics from Antiquity to the Beginning of the Nineteenth Century.* London, 1960.

Seguin, Jean Pierre. *Le jeu de carte.* Paris, 1968.

Serres, Olivier de. *Théâtre d'agriculture et mesnage des champs.* Paris, 1600.

———. *The perfect use of silk-wormes and their benefits. . . . Done out of the French originall by Nicholas Jifte Esquire.* London, 1607.

Sherrington, Sir Charles Scott. *The Endeavor of Jean Fernel.* Cambridge, 1946.

Singer, Charles. *A History of Biology to about the Year 1900.* London, 1959.

———. *The Earliest Chemical Industry.* London, 1948.

———, et al. *A History of Western Technology.* 5 vols. Oxford, 1954–58.

Sisco, A. G., and Smith, C. S., trans. See Ercher, Lazarus.

Sivin, Nathan. *Chinese Alchemy: Preliminary Studies.* Cambridge, Mass., 1968.

Smith, Archibald. *A Gardener's Dictionary of Plant Names: A Handbook on the Origin and Meaning of Some Plant Names.* London, 1972.

Smith, David Eugene. *History of Mathematics.* 2 vols. New York, 1923–25.

———. *Rara arithmetica: A Catalogue of the Arithmetics Written before the Year MDCI. . . .* Boston and London, 1908.

Soderini, Giovanni Vittore. *Opere.* 4 vols. Bologna, 1902–7.

Srinivasenger, C. N. *The History of Ancient Indian Mathematics.* Calcutta, 1967.

Stafleur, Frans A. *Taxonomic Literature: A Selective Guide to Botanical Publications with Dates, Commentaries and Types.* Utrecht, 1967.

Stevin, Simon; see Dijksterhuis, Eduard Jan, ed.

Stöffler, Isaac Conrad. *Neuer und alter cosmographischer Calender.* Nuremberg, 1675.

Stone, L. H. *The Chair in China.* Toronto, 1952.

Struik, Dirk J. *A Source Book of Mathematics, 1200–1800.* Cambridge, Mass., 1969.

Sudhoff, K., ed. See Paracelsus.

Targioni-Tozzetti, Antonio. *Cenni storici sulla introduzione di varie piante nell'agricoltura e orticoltura.* Florence, 1896.

Tartaglia, Nicholas. *Questi et inventioni diverse.* Venice, 1554.

Taton, René, ed. *History of Science: The Beginnings of Modern Science from 1450 to 1800.* Translated by A. J. Pomerans. 2 vols. London, 1964.

Taylor, Eva G. R. *The Mathematical Practitioners of Tudor and Stuart England.* Cambridge, 1954.

————. *The Haven-Finding Art.* New York, 1956.

Taylor, Norman. *Plant Drugs That Changed the World.* New York, 1965.

Taylor, Sherwood F. *The History of Industrial Chemistry.* London, 1957.

Theunisz, Johannes. *Carolus Clusius: Het merkwaardige Leven van een Pionier der Wetenschap.* Amsterdam, 1939.

Trease, George Edward. *Pharmacy in History.* London, 1964.

Uphof, Johannes C. Th. *Dictionary of Economic Plants.* 2d ed. Brunswick, 1968.

Usher, Abbott Payson. *A History of Mechanical Inventions.* Cambridge, Mass., 1962.

Valère, André. *Mathias de Lobel: Sa vie et ses oeuvres.* Liège, 1875.

Vallín, A. F. *Cultura científica de España en el siglo XVI.* Madrid, 1893.

Waite, A. E., trans. See Paracelsus, Theophrastus.

Waley, P. J., and Waley, D. P., eds. *Giovanni Botero, The Reason of State.* London, 1956.

Walter, Jaime, and Alves, Manuel, eds. *Aromatum et simplicium aliquot medicamentorum apud Indes nacentium historia (1567) de Carlos Clusio: Versão portuguesa do epítome latino dos Colóquios dos simples de Garcia de Orta.* Lisbon, 1964.

Waters, David W. *The Art of Navigation in England in Elizabethan and Early Stuart Times.* London, 1958.

Watkins, Harold. *Time Counts: The Story of the Calendar.* New York, 1954.

Watt, Sir George. *The Commercial Products of India.* London, 1909.

White, Lynn, Jr. *Medieval Technology and Social Change.* Oxford, 1962.

Wightman, W. P. D. *Science and the Renaissance: An Introduction to the Study of the Emergence of the Sciences in the Sixteenth Century.* 2 vols. Edinburgh and London, 1962.

Winter, Henry James Jacques. *Eastern Science: An Outline of Its Scope and Contribution.* London, 1952.

Worcester, G. R. G. *Junks and Sampans of the Yangtze.* Shanghai, 1947.

————. *Sail and Sweep in China.* London, 1960.

Wroth, Lawrence C. *The Way of a Ship: An Essay on the Literature of Navigation Science.* Portland, Me., 1937.

Wulff, Hans E. *Traditional Crafts of Persia: Their Development, Technology and Influence on Eastern and Western Civilizations.* Cambridge, Mass., 1966.

Zechlin, Egmont. *Maritime Weltgeschichte.* Hamburg, 1947.

Zekert, Otto. *Paracelsus: Europäer im 16. Jahrhundert.* Stuttgart, 1968.

Zeuthen, Hieronymous G. *Geschichte der Mathematik im XVI. und XVII. Jahrhundert.* Leipzig, 1903.

Chapter IX

Zimmer, Heinrich R. *Hindu Medicine*. Baltimore, 1948.

Zinner, Ernst. *Geschichte und Bibliographie der astronomischen Literatur in Deutschland zur Zeit der Renaissance*. Leipzig, 1941.

Zirkle, Conway. *The Beginnings of Plant Hybridization*. Philadelphia, 1935.

Zubler, Leonhard. *Kurtzer und gründlicher Bericht von Sonnenuhren mit Kupfferstücken*. Amsterdam, 1609.

ARTICLES

Adam, Paul. "Navigation primitive et navigation astronomique." In M. Mollat and P. Adam, eds., *Les aspects internationaux de la découverte océanique aux XVe et XVIe siècles*, pp. 91–105. Paris, 1966.

———, and Denoix, L. "Essai sur les raisons de l'apparition du goûvernail d'étambot." *Revue d'histoire économique et sociale*, XL (1962), 90–109.

Albuquerque, Luís de. "Contribução das navegações do século XVI para o conhecimento do magnetismo terrestre." *Revista da universidade de Coimbra*, XXIV (1971), 533–50.

Altazan, Maria A. Hayes. "Drugs Used by Paracelsus." *Journal of Chemical Education*, XXXVII (1960), 594–96.

Ball, Valentine. "On the Identification of the Animals and Plants of India Which Were Known to the Early Greek Authors." *Indian Antiquary*, XIV (1885), 274–87.

———. "A Commentary on the Colloquies of Garcia da Orta, on the Simples, Drugs, and Medicinal Substances of India." *Proceedings of the Irish Academy*, I (1889), 381–415.

Barnes, W. H. "Chinese Influence on Western Alchemy." *Nature*, CXXXV (1935), 824–25.

Beaujouan, Guy. "Science livresque et art nautique au XVIe siècle." In M. Mollat and P. Adam, eds., *Les aspects internationaux de la découverte océanique aux XVe et XVIe siècles*, pp. 61–83. Paris, 1966.

Beichner, Paul E. "The Grain of Paradise." *Speculum*, XXVI (1961), 302–7.

Biot, Edouard. "Notice sur quelques procédés industriels connus en Chine au XVIe siècle." *Journal asiatique*, 2d ser. XVI (1835), 130–54.

Bloch, Jules. "Médecine indienne et théories grecques." *Annales: économies, sociétés, civilisations*, V (1950), 466–68.

Bourdon, Léon. "Luís de Almeida, chirurgien et marchand avant son entrée dans la Compagnie de Jésus au Japon, 1525(?)–1556." In *Mélanges d'études portugaises offerts à M. Georges Le Gentil*, pp. 69–85. Lisbon, 1949.

Boxer, Charles R. "Portuguese Roteiros, 1500–1700." *Mariner's Mirror*, XX (1934), 171–86.

Bretschneider, Emilei Vasel'evich. "Early European Researches into the Flora of China." *Journal of the North China Branch of the Royal Asiatic Society*, N.S. XV (1880), 3–4.

Briggs, Marlen S. "Building Construction." In Charles Singer, ed., *A History of Western Technology*, III, 245–68. Oxford, 1956.

Bryant, P. L. "Chinese Camphor and Camphor Oil." *China Journal of Science and Arts*, III (1925), 228–34.

Cailleux, André. "Progression du nombre d'espèces de plantes décrites de 1500 à nos jours." *Revue d'histoire des sciences*, VI (1953), 42–49.

Chapter Bibliographies

Cermenati, Mario. "Un diplomatico naturalista del Rinascimento, Andrea Navagero." *Nuovo archivio veneto*, N.S. XXIV (1912), 164–205.

Chang Kuei-sheng. "The Maritime Scene in China at the Dawn of the Great European Discoveries." *Journal of the American Oriental Society*, XCIV (1974), 347–59.

Chou Yi-liang. "Notes on (Šaraf al-Zamān) al-Marvazi's Account on China." *Harvard Journal of Asiatic Studies*, IX (1945), 13–23.

Christ, H. "Die illustrierte spanische Flora des Carl Clusius vom Jahre 1576." *Österreichische botanische Zeitschrift*, LXII (1912), 132–35, 189–94, 229–38, 271–75.

Cipolla, Carlo M. "The Diffusion of Innovations in Early Modern Europe." *Comparative Studies in Society and History*, XIV (1972), 46–53.

Cohen, I. Bernard. "La découverte du nouveau monde et la transformation de l'idée de la nature." In A. Koyré, ed., *La science au seizième siècle*, pp. 191–210. Paris, 1960.

Conant, K. J. "The Pointed Arch: Orient to Occident." *Palaeologia* (Osaka), VII (1957), 33–36.

———, and Willard, H. M. "Early Examples of the Pointed Arch and Vault in Romanesque Architecture." *Viator*, II (1971), 203–9.

Cortesão, Armando. "Nautical Science and the Renaissance." In E. A. Underwood, ed., *Science, Medicine, and History*, I, 303–16. London, 1953.

Crone, Ernst. "How Did the Navigator Determine the Speed of His Ship and the Distance Run." *Revista da universidade de Coimbra*, XXIV (1971), 173–85.

Davis, Tenney L. "Dualistic Cosmography of Huai Nau Tzu and Its Relations to the Background of Chinese and of European Alchemy." *Isis*, XXV (1936), 327–40.

———, and Chao Yung-Tsung. "A Fifteenth-Century Chinese Encyclopedia of Alchemy." *Proceedings of the British Academy*, LXXIII (1939), 97.

——— and ———. "Chao Hsueh-min's Outline of Pyrotechnics: A Contribution to the History of Fireworks." *Proceedings of the American Academy of Arts and Sciences*, LXXV (1943), 95–107.

Debus, Allen G. "Mathematics and Nature in the Chemical Texts of the Renaissance." *Ambix*, XV (1968), 1–28.

———. "The Paracelsians and the Chemists: The Chemical Dilemma in Renaissance Medicine." *Clio medica*, VII (1972), 185–99.

———. "The Significance of Early Chemistry." *Journal of World History*, IX (1965–66), 39–58.

D'Elia, Pasquale. "L'Italia alle origini degli studi sulla Cina." *Nuovo antologia*, CCCCXXII (1942), 148–60.

Denoix, L. "Characteristiques des navires de l'époque des grandes découvertes." In M. Mollat and P. Adam, eds., *Les aspects internationaux de la découverte océanique au XVe et XVIe siècles*, pp. 137–47. Paris, 1966.

Dingle, Herbert. "Astronomy in the Sixteenth and Seventeenth Centuries." In E. A. Underwood, ed., *Science, Medicine, and History*, I, 455–68. London, 1953.

Doran, Edwin, Jr. "The Origin of Leeboards." *Mariner's Mirror*, LIII (1967), 39–54.

Dubs, Homer H. "The Beginnings of Alchemy." *Isis*, XXXVIII (1947), 62–86.

Duyvendak, J. J. L. "Sailing Directions of Chinese Voyages." *T'oung Pao*, XXXIV (1938), 230–37.

Chapter IX

———. "Simon Stevin's 'Sailing Chariot' [and Its Chinese Antecedents]." *T'oung Pao*, XXXVI (1942), 401–7.

Ewan, Joseph. "Traffic in Seeds and Plants between North America, England and the Continent during the Sixteenth and Seventeenth Centuries." *Actes du XIIᵉ congrès international d'histoire des sciences*, VIII (1968), 17–49.

Filliozat, Jean. "Ancient Relations between Indian and Foreign Astronomical Systems." *Journal of Oriental Research* (Madras), XXV (1957), 1–8.

———. "L'Inde et les échanges scientifiques dans l'Antiquité." *Cahiers de l'histoire mondiale*, I (1953–54), 353–67.

Flanagan, J. F. "Figured Fabrics." In Charles Singer, *et al.*, *A History of Western Technology*, III, 187–206. Oxford, 1956.

Folck Jon, Guillermo. "Los médicos, la botánica y la materia farmaceutica en España durante la decemosexta centura." *Asclepio*, XVIII–XIX (1966–67), 141–55.

Forbes, Robert J. "The Sailing Chariot." In Eduard Jan Dijksterhuis, ed., *The Principal Works of Simon Stevin*, V, 3–8. Amsterdam, 1955–66.

Gallois, L. "Les portugaises et l'astronomie nautique à l'époque des grandes découvertes." *Annales de géographie*, XXIII (1914), 289–302.

Gersão Ventura, Augusta F. "Duas pequenas notas à margem das obras de Clúsio." *Congresso do mundo português*, V (1940), 281–92.

Gibbs-Smith, C. H. "Origins of the Helicopter." *New Scientist*, XIV (1962), 229–31.

Giglioli, O. H. "Jacopo Ligozzi disegnatore e pittore di piante e di animali." *Dedalo*, IV (1923–24), 556–58.

Goeze, E. "Liste der seit dem 16. Jahrhundert bis auf die Gegenwart in Gärten und Parks Europas eingeführten Bäume und Sträucher." *Mitteilungen der deutschen dendrologischen Gesellschaft*, XXV (1916), 129–201.

Goithien, S. D. "Letters and Documents on the India Trade in Medieval Times." *Islamic Culture*, XXXVII (1963), 188–205.

Gomes, Fernando Amaral. "Contribuição para o estudo da medicina portuguesa no periodo da expansão." *Congresso internacional de história dos descobrimentos, Actas*, IV, 209–24. Lisbon, 1960.

Goodrich, L. Carrington. "Early Cannon in China." *Isis*, LV (1964), 193–95.

———, and Feng Chia-sheng. "The Early Development of Firearms in China." *Isis*, XXXVI (1946), 114–23, 250.

Graham, A. C. "China, Europe, and the Origins of Modern Science." In Shigeru Nakayama and Nathan Sivin, eds., *Chinese Science: Explorations of an Ancient Tradition*, pp. 45–69. Cambridge, Mass., 1973.

Gregory, J. C. "Chemistry and Alchemy in the Natural Philosophy of Sir Francis Bacon." *Ambix*, II (1938), 93–111.

Guerra, Francisco. "Drugs from the Indies and the Political Economy of the Sixteenth Century." In M. Florkin, ed., *Analecta medico-historica*, pp. 29–54. Oxford, 1966.

———. "La politica imperial sobre las drogas de las Indias [under Charles V]." *Revista de Indias*, XXVI (1966), 31–58.

———. "The Paradox of the Treasury of Medicines by Gregorio Lopez (1542–1596)." *Clio medica*, I (1966), 273–88.

Hale, John R. "Gunpowder and the Renaissance: An Essay in the History of Ideas." In C. H. Carter, ed., *From the Renaissance to the Counter-Reformation: Essays in Honor of Garrett Mattingly*, pp. 113–44. New York, 1965.

Hall, A. Rupert. "The Scholar and the Craftsman in the Scientific Revolution." In M. Clagett, ed., *Critical Problems in the History of Science*, pp. 3–23. Madison, Wis., 1959.

———. "The Changing Technical Act." *Technology and Culture*, III (1962), 501–15.

Hanbury, Daniel. "Notes on Chinese Materia medica." *Pharmaceutical Journal*, II (1861), 15, 109, 553; III (1862), 6, 204, 260, 315, 420.

Hill, Donald R. "Trebuchets." *Viator*, IV (1973), 99–114.

Ho Peng-yoke. "The Astronomical Bureau in Ming China." *Journal of Asian History*, III (1969), 137–57.

Ho Ping-yü, and Needham, Joseph. "Elixir Poisoning in Medieval China." *Janus*, XLVIII (1959), 221–51.

Hooykaas, R. "The Impact of the Voyages of Discovery on Portuguese Humanist Literature." *Revista da universidade de Coimbra*, XXIV (1971), 551–66.

Horne, R. A. "Atomism in Ancient Greece and India." *Ambix*, VIII (1960), 98–110.

Hughes, B. B. "The Private Library of Johann Scheubel, Sixteenth-Century Mathematician." *Viator*, III (1972), 417–32.

Johnson, Frances R. "Astronomical Text-books in the Sixteenth Century." In E. A. Underwood, ed., *Science, Medicine, and History*, I, 285–302. London, 1953.

Jordan, L. A. "Tung Oil." *Quarterly Journal of the Indian Tea Association*, 1929, pp. 163–99.

Jorge, Ricardo. "A renascença médica em Portugal (Pierre Buissot e Amato Lusitano)." *Lusitania*, I (1903), 187–92.

Joseph, L. "The Contemporary Medical Literature and the Experiences in the New World." *Revista di storia della medicina*, I (1957), 166–81.

Kamenetz, Herman L. "A Brief History of the Wheelchair." *Journal of the History of Medicine*, XXIV (1969), 205–10.

Keller, A. G. "The Scientific and Technological Sages of Ancient China." *Ambix*, XVIII (1971), 43–50.

Kobata, A. "The Productions and Uses of Gold and Silver in Sixteenth- and Seventeenth-Century Japan." *Economic History Review* (Utrecht), No. 2 (1965), pp. 245–66.

Koyré, Alexandre. "Mathematics." In René Taton, ed., *History of Science: The Beginnings of Modern Science from 1450 to 1800*, II, 12–52. London, 1964.

———. "The Copernican Revolution." *Ibid.*, pp. 52–74.

Lane, F. C. "The Economic Meaning of the Invention of the Compass." *American Historical Review*, LXVIII (1963), 605–17.

Lange, Erwin F. "Alchemy and the Sixteenth-Century Metallurgists." *Ambix*, XIII (1965), 92–95.

Leser, Paul. "Westöstliche Landwirtschaft: Kulturbeziehungen zwischen Europa, dem vorderen Orient und dem Fernen Osten." In *P. W. Schmidt, Festschrift*, pp. 416–84. Vienna, 1928.

Lopez, R. S. "The Silk Industry in the Byzantine Empire." *Speculum*, XX (1945), 1–42.

————. "Nuove luci sugli italiani in Estremo Oriente prima di Colombo." *Studi colombiani* (Genoa), III (1952), 337–98. ·

Maddison, Francis. "Medieval Instruments and the Development of Navigational Instruments in the XVth and XVIth Centuries." *Revista da universidade de Coimbra,* XXIV (1971), 115–72.

Marsak, Leonard M. "The Humanist as Scientist: Nicolas Claude Fabri de Peiresc." *Journal of World History,* VIII (1964), 93–100.

Martins Barata, Jaime. "O navio 'São Gabriel' e as Naus Manuelinas." *Revista da universidade de Coimbra,* XXIV (1971), 443–74.

Mattirolo, Oreste, ed. "Le lettere di Ulisse Aldrovandi a Francesco I e Ferdinando I, granduchi di Toscana e a Francesco Maria II, duca di Urbino. . . ." In *Memorie della Reale Accademia delle scienze di Torino.* 2d ser. LIV (1904), 305–90.

Miyashita, Saburo. "A Link in the Westward Transmission of Chinese Anatomy in the Later Middle Ages." *Isis,* LVIII (1967), 486–90.

Merrill, E. D. "Eastern Asia as a Source of Ornamental Plants." *Journal of the New York Botanical Garden,* XXXIV (1933), 238–43.

————. "Loureiro and His Botanical Work." *Proceedings of the American Philosophical Society,* LXXII (1933), 229–39.

Michel, Henri. "Astrolabistes, géographes et graveurs belges du XVIe siècle." In Alexandre Koyré, ed., *La science au seizième siècle,* pp. 15–26. Paris, 1960.

Millás Vallicrosa, José-M. "Nautique et cartographie de l'Espagne au XVIe siècle." In Alexandre Koyré, ed., *La science au seizième siècle,* pp. 31–46. Paris, 1960.

Mohan, Binj. "The Beginnings of Calculus in the East." *Bulletin of the National Institute of Sciences of India,* XXI (1963), 253–57.

Multhauf, Robert P. "Old Drugs in New Bottles." *Isis,* LXIII (1972), 408–12.

Naish, G. P. B. "Ships and Shipbuilding." In Charles Singer *et al.,* *A History of Western Technology,* III, 471–500. Oxford, 1956.

Nakamura, Hiroshi. "Les cartes du Japon qui servaient de modèle aux cartographes européens au début des communications de l'Occident avec le Japon." *Monumenta nipponica,* II (1939), 100–123.

Nambo, Heizo. "Who Invented the Explosives?" *Japanese Studies in the History of Science,* IX (1970), 49–98.

Needham, Joseph. "The Roles of Europe and China in the Evolution of Oecumenical Science." *Journal of Asian History,* I (1967), 3–32.

————. "Science and China's Influence on the World." In Raymond Dawson, ed., *The Legacy of China,* pp. 234–308. Oxford, 1964.

————. "Central Asia and the History of Science and Technology." *Journal of the Royal Central Asian Society,* XXXVI (1949), 135–45.

Neugebauer, Otto. "The Study of Wretched Subjects." *Isis,* XLII (1951), 111.

————. "Hindu Astronomy at Westminster in 1428." *Annals of Science,* VIII (1952), 221–28.

Neves Tavares, Carlos das. "A botânica nos *Colóquios* de Garcia de Orta." *Garcia de Orta* (commemorative volume), XI, No. 4 (1963), 677–93.

Neviani, Antonio. "Ferrante Imperato speziale e naturalista napoletana." *Atti e memorie* dell'Accademia di storia dell' arte sanitaria (Rome), 2d ser., II, No. 2 (1936), 57–74, 124–45, 191–210, 243–67.

Newcomb, R. M. "Botanical Source-Areas for Some Oriental Spices." *Economic Botany*, XVII (1963), 127–32.

Newell, W., Mowry, H., and Barnette, R. M. "The Tung-Oil Tree." *Bulletin of the Florida Agricultural Experiment Station*, CCLXXX (1935), 1–67.

Opsomer, Joseph E. "Note sur deux ouvrages portugais de botanique tropicale du XVIe siècle." *Bulletin des séances de l'Académie reale des sciences d'outre-mer*, 1966, pp. 478–92.

———. "Un botaniste trop peu connu: Willem Quackelbeen (1527–1561)." *Bulletin de la Société royale de botanique de Belgique*, XCIII (1961), 113–30.

Pagel, Walter. "The Eightness of Adam and Related Gnostic Ideas in the Paracelsian Corpus." *Ambix*, XVI (1969), 119–39.

———, and Winder, M. "The Higher Elements and Prime Matter in Renaissance Naturalism and in Paracelsus." *Ambix*, XXI (1974), 93–127.

Payne, Joseph Frank. "On the 'Herbarius' and 'Hortus Sanitatis.'" *Transactions of the Bibliographical Society*, VI (1900–1901), 63–126.

Pereira Júnior, Albano. "Garcia de Orta pioneiro da farmacognosia." In *Garcia de Orta* (commemorative vol.), XI, No. 4 (1963), 723–53.

Peres, Manuel. "A astronomia e os descobrimentos." *Congresso do mundo português*, V (1940), 197–211.

Pettazzoni, R. "The Pagan Origin of the Three-Headed Representation of the Christian Trinity." *Journal of the Warburg and Courtauld Institutes*, IX (1946), 136–51.

Pina, Luís de. "O método cientifico no luso-tropicalismo de Garcia de Orta." In *Garcia de Orta* (commemorative vol.), XI, No. 4 (1963), 631–62.

———. "As conquistas histórico-naturais dos portugueses nos descobrimentos." *Congresso do mundo português*, V (1940), 215–69.

———. "Na rota do Imperio: A medicina embarcada nos séculos XVI e XVII." *Arquivo histórico de Portugal*, IV (1939), 283–323.

Pingree, David Edwin. "Census of the Exact Sciences in Sanskrit." *Memoirs of the American Philosophical Society* (1970–71), ser. A, LXXXI in 2 vols., Vol. I, pp. 4–32; Vol. II, pp. 3–7.

Porterfield, William M. "What Is Bamboo?" *China Journal of Science and Arts*, III (1925), 153–58.

Pucci, A. "Dei bambù." *Bolletino della R. Società Toscana di orticultura* (Florence), XXIV (1899), 302–11; XXV (1900), 14–20.

Randles, M. W. G. L. "Sur l'idée de la découverte." In M. Mollat and P. Adam, eds., *Les aspects internationaux de la découverte océanique aux XVe et XVIe siècles*, pp. 17–21. Paris, 1966.

Reti, Ladislao. "Leonardo da Vinci and Cesare Borgia." *Viator*, IV (1973), 333–68.

———. "Helicopters and Whirligigs." *Raccolta vinciana*, fasc. 20 (1964), pp. 331–38.

Rockenbach, Klaus. "Von der alten Windmühle: Typen, Herkunft, Denkmalpflege, Volkskunde, Dichtung." *Archiv für Kulturgeschichte*, I (1968), 135–53.

Roddis, L. H. "Garcia de Orta, the First European Writer on Tropical Medicine and a Pioneer in Pharmacognosy." *Annals of Medical History*, I (1929), 198–207.

Rosenfeld, B. A., and Cernova, M. L. "Algebraic Exponents and Their Geometric Interpretations." *Organon*, IV (1967), 109–12.

Sarton, George. "Simon Stevin of Bruges: The First Explanation of Decimal Fractions and Measures [+1585]." *Isis*, XXI (1934), 241–304; XXIII (1935), 153–244.

———. "The Scientific Literature Transmitted through the Incunabula." *Osiris*, V (1938), 41–245.

Schulze, Franz. "Die geographische und ethnographische Bedeutung von Springers 'Meerfahrt' vom Jahre 1509." *Globus*, XCVI (1909), 28–32.

Seide, Jacob. "The Relationship of Garcia de Orta's and Cristóbal Acosta's Botanical Works." *Actes du XXᵉ congrès international d'histoire des sciences*, VII (1953), 564–67.

Sen, S. N. "Indian Elements in European Renaissance." *Organon* (Warsaw), IV (1967), 55–59.

———. "Transmissions of Scientific Ideas between India and Foreign Countries in Ancient and Medieval Times." *Bulletin of the National Institute of Sciences of India*, XXI (1963), 8–30.

Sheppard, H. J. "Alchemy: Origin or Origins?" *Ambix*, XVII (1970), 69–84.

———. "A Survey of Alchemical and Hermetic Symbolism." *Ambix*, VIII (1966), 35–41.

Singer, Charles. "East and West in Retrospect." In Charles Singer *et al.*, eds., *A History of Western Technology*, II, 753–76. 5 vols. Oxford, 1956.

Sivin, Nathan. "Introductory Bibliography of Traditional Chinese Science: Books and Articles in Western Languages." In Shigeru Nakayama, ed., *Chinese Science: Exploration of an Ancient Tradition*, pp. 279–314. Cambridge, Mass., 1973.

Skelton, R. A. "The Seaman and the Printer." *Revista da universidade de Coimbra*, XXIV (1971), 493–502.

Soares, A. X. "Garcia de Orta, a Little Known Owner of Bombay." *Journal of the Bombay Branch of the Royal Asiatic Society*, XXVI (1921–23), 195–229.

Soulard, Henri. "Alchimie occidentale et alchimie chinoise: Analogies et contrastes." *Bulletin de l'association Guillaume Budé*, 4th ser. XXIX (1970), 185–98.

Sousa Viterbo, Francisco M. de. "A jardinagem em Portugal." *O Instituto*, LIII (1906), 562–76, 627–37, 695–704, 738–48; LIV (1907), 173–79, 239–51, 285–97, 345–54, 420–35, 488–97, 543–51, 614–20, 700–708.

Stannard, Jerry. "The Greco-Roman Background of the Renaissance Herbal." *Organon*, IV (1967), 141–45.

———. "Dioscorides and Renaissance *Materia medica*." In M. Florkin, ed., *Analecta medico-historica*, pp. 1–21. Oxford, 1966.

———. "The Plant Called Moly." *Osiris*, XIV (1962), 254–307.

Strebel, J. "Plotin und Paracelsus über Horoskopie und Schicksal." *Acta nova Paracelsica*, III (1946), 95–109.

———. "Paracelsus, Neuplatonismus und Indische Geheimlehren." Reprinted from Introduction to *Philosophia sagax* in *Paracelsus Werke*, III, 1–59. St. Gall, 1947.

Teixeira da Mota, Avelino. "Méthodes de navigation et cartographie nautique dans l'Océan Indien avant le XVIᵉ siècle." *Studia*, No. 11 (1963), pp. 49–90.

———. "Evolução dos roteiros portugueses durante o século XVI." *Revista da universidade de Coimbra*, XXIV (1971), 5–32.

————. "A evolução da ciência náutica durante os séculos XV–XVI na cartografia portuguesa da época." *Memórias da Academia das ciências de Lisboa, Classe de letras*, VII (1962), 247–66.

Telepnef, Basilo de. "Wanderwege des Paracelsus von 1512–1525." *Jahrbuch der schweizerischen Paracelsus-Gesellschaft*, III (1946), 147–65.

Thompson, D. V., Jr. "Medieval Color Making." *Isis*, XXII (1934–35), 456–68.

Thorndike, Lynn. "Alchemy during the First Half of the Sixteenth Century." *Ambix*, II (1938), 26–39.

Tibbetts, G. R. "The Navigational Theory of the Arabs in the Fifteenth and Sixteenth Centuries." *Revista da universidade de Coimbra*, XXIV (1971), 323–43.

Torre de Assunção, Carlos Fernando. "A mineralogia nos *Colóquios*." In *Garcia de Orta* (commemorative vol.), XI, No. 4 (1963), 715–21.

Turner, Raymond. "Oviedo's *Historia general y natural de las Indias* . . . First American Encyclopedia." *Journal of Inter-American Studies*, VI (1964), 267–74.

Unger, Richard W. "Dutch Ship Designs in the Fifteenth and Sixteenth Centuries." *Viator*, IV (1973), 387–413.

Urdang, George. "How Chemicals Entered the Official Pharmacopoeias." *Archives internationales d'histoire des sciences*, N.S. VII (1954), 303–13.

Uvanovič, Daniel. "The Indian Prelude to European Mathematics." *Osiris*, I (1936), 652–57.

Verdoorn, Frans. "Botanical Gardens and Arboretums of the Past and Their Reconstruction." *Annals of Biology*, XXIX (1953), 277–82.

Vietor, O. "A Portuguese Chart of 1492 by Jorge Aguinar." *Revista da universidade de Coimbra*, XXIV (1971), 515–16.

Walter, Jaime. "Simão Alvares e o seu rol das drogas da India." *Studia* (Lisbon), X (1962), pp. 117–49.

————. "Os *Colóquios* de Garcia de Orta no *Tractado de los Drogas* de Cristóvão da Costa." In *Garcia de Orta* (commemorative vol.), XI, No. 4 (1963), 799–832.

Wang Ling. "On the Invention and Use of Gunpowder and Firearms in China." *Isis*, XXXVII (1947), 160–78.

Waters, David W. "Science and the Techniques of Navigation in the Renaissance." In C. S. Singleton, ed., *Art, Science, and History in the Renaissance*, pp. 189–237. Baltimore, 1968.

————. "The Iberian Bases of the English Art of Navigation in the Sixteenth Century." *Revista da universidade de Coimbra*, XXIV (1971), 347–63.

White, Lynn, Jr. "The Act of Invention: Causes, Contexts, Continuities and Consequences." *Technology and Culture*, III (1962), 486–97.

————. "Indic Elements in the Iconography of Petrarch's *Trionfo della Morte*." *Speculum*, XLIX (1974), 201–21.

————. "Cultural Climates and Technological Advance in the Middle Ages." *Viator*, II (1971), 171–202.

————. "Tibet, India, and Malaya as Sources of Western Medieval Technology." *American Historical Review*, LXV (1960), 515–26.

Chapter X

————. "Medieval Borrowings from Further Asia." In O. B. Hardison, ed., *Medieval and Renaissance Studies*, No. 5 (1974), pp. 3–26.

Wicki, Josef. "Os percalços das aldeias e terras de Baçaim vistos e julgados pelo P. Francisco Rodrigues, S.J., por 1570." *Boletim do Instituto Vasco da Gama*, No. 76 (1959), pp. 37–75.

Wilson, E. H. "The 'Wood Oil' Trees of China and Japan." *Bulletin of the Imperial Institute* (London), XI (1913), 441–61.

Wingfield Digby, G. F. "Some Silks Woven under Portuguese Influence in the Far East." *Burlington Magazine*, LXXVII (1940), 52–61.

Wunderly, Jürgen. "Zum Problem des feinstofflichen Leibes in der indischen Philosophie, im Neuplatonismus und in Paracelsus." *Episteme* (Milan), III (1969), 3–15.

Wussing, H. L. "European Mathematics during the Evolutionary Period of Early Capitalistic Conditions (Fifteenth and Sixteenth Centuries)." *Organon*, IV (1967), 89–93.

Yabunti, Kiyoshi. "Chinese Astronomy: Development and Limiting Factors." In S. Nakayama and N. Sivin, comps., *Chinese Science . . .*, pp. 91–103. Cambridge, Mass., 1973.

X. CARTOGRAPHY AND GEOGRAPHY

BOOKS

Abbot, George. *A Briefe Description of the Whole Worlde*. London, 1600.

Albuquerque, Luis G. M. de. *Introdução à história dos descobrimentos*. Coimbra, 1962.

Alexandrowicz, Charles Henry. *An Introduction to the History of the Law of Nations in the East Indies (16th, 17th, and 18th Centuries)*. Oxford, 1967.

Alfonce, Jean. *Les voyages aventureux du capitaine Ian Alfonce, Sainctongeois, À Poitins, au Pelican, par Ian de Marnef* [1559]. Facsimile ed. Boston, 1920.

————. *La cosmographie . . . par Jean Fonteneau de Alfonce de Saintonge*. Edited by Georges Musset. Paris, 1904.

Almagià, Roberto. *Monumenta cartographica Vaticana*. 4 vols. Vatican City, 1944–55.

Anania, Giovanni Lorenzo d'. *L'universale fabrica del mondo, overo Cosmographia . . . diviso in 4 trattati*. Venice, 1576.

Anghiera, Pietro Martire d'. *De orbe novo: The Eight Decades. . . .* Translated from the Latin by Francis A. MacNutt. 2 vols. New York and London, 1912.

Anthiaume, Albert. *Cartes marines, constructions navales: Voyages de découverte chez les normands, 1500–1650*. 2 vols. Paris, 1916.

Apian, Peter. *Cosmographicus liber Petri Apiani mathematici, studiose collectus. . . .* Landshut, 1524.

Arber, Edward, ed. *The First Three English Books on America. (1511?)–1555 A.D.; Being Chiefly Translations, Compilations, etc., by Richard Eden, from the Writings, Maps, etc. of Pietro Martire . . . Sebastian Münster . . . Sebastian Cabot . . . with Extracts, etc., from the Works of Other Spanish, Italian, and German Writers of the Time*. Birmingham, 1885.

Arciniegas, German. *Amerigo and the New World*. New York, 1955.

[707]

Averdunk, Heinrich, and Mueller-Reinhard, J. *Gerhard Mercator und die Geographen unter seinen Nachkommen.* Gotha, 1914.

Bachmann, Friedrich. *Die alten Städtebilder.* Leipzig, 1939.

Badia, Jacodo del. *Egnazio Danti cosmografo e mathematico e le sue opere in Firenze.* Florence, 1898.

Baginsky, Paul B. *German Works Relating to America, 1493–1800.* New York, 1942.

Bagrow, Leo, and Skelton, Raleigh A. *History of Cartography.* Cambridge, Mass., 1964.

Baranowski, Bohdan. *Znajomość Wschodu w dawnej Polsce do XVIII wieku* (Knowledge of the Orient in Poland before the 18th Century). Lodz, 1950.

Barthold. Wilhelm. *Die geographische und historische Erforschung des Orients, mit besonderer Berücksichtigung der russischen Arbeiten.* Leipzig, 1913.

Beck, Hanno. *Geographie: Europäische Entwicklung in Texten und Erläuterungen.* Munich, 1973.

Bell (Belus), Robert, comp. *Rerum hispanicarum scriptores aliquot, quorum nomina versa pagina indicabit.* 2 vols. Frankfurt, 1579.

Belleforest, François de, ed. and trans. *La cosmographie universelle [of Sebastian Münster] de tout le monde.* . . . 2 vols. in 3. Paris, 1575.

Bellemo, Vincenzo. *La cosmografia e le scoperte geografiche nel secolo XV. e i viaggi di Nicolò de' Conti.* Padua, 1908.

Belon, Pierre. *Les observations de plusieurs singularitez et choses memorables, trouvées en Grèce, Asie, Judée, Egypte, Arabie, e autres pays estranges.* Paris, 1553.

Berthelot, André. *L'Asie ancienne centrale et sud-Orientale d'après Ptolomée.* Paris, 1930.

Böhme, Max. *Die grossen Reisesammlungen des 16. Jahrhunderts und ihre Bedeutung.* Strassburg, 1904.

Bordone, Benedetto. *Libro . . . nel qual si ragiona de tutti l'Isole del mondo con li lor nomi antichi e moderni, historie, favole, e modi del loro vi usere, e in qual parte del mare stanno, e in qual parallelo e clima giacciono.* Venice, 1528.

Borges de Figueiredo, Antonio C. *A geographia dos Lusíadas de Luis de Camões.* Lisbon, 1883.

Botero, Giovanni. *Relations of the Most Famous Kingdoms and Common-wealths thorowout the World: discoursing of their Situations, Religions, Languages, Manners, Customes, Strengths, Greatnesse and Policies.* . . . London, 1630.

Brandão, João. *Tratado da majestade, grandeza a abastança da cidade de Lisboa, na 2ᵉ metade do século XVI.* Lisbon, 1923.

Brandmair, E. *Bibliographische Untersuchung über Entstehung und Entwicklung des Ortelianischen Kartenwerkes.* Amsterdam, 1964.

Braun, Georg, and Hogenberg, Franz. *Civitates orbis terrarum: The Towns of the World, 1572–1618.* Introduction by R. A. Skelton. 6 vols. in 3. Cleveland, 1966.

Calcagnini, Celio. *Opera aliquot.* Basel, 1544.

Castilho, Julio. *A ribeira de Lisboa.* 2d ed. 5 vols. Lisbon, 1941–48.

———. *Lisboa antiga.* 2d ed. 5 vols. Lisbon, 1902–4.

Castillo, Rafael del. *Gran diccionario geográfico, estadístico é histórico de España e sus provincias de Cuba, Puerto Rico, Filipinas y posesiones de Africa.* 2 vols. Barcelona, 1889–94.

Centellas, Joachim de. *Les voyages et conquestes des roys de Portugal es Indes d'Orient . . . le tout recueilly de fideles tesmoignages et mémoires du sieur Joachim Centellas.* Paris, 1578.

Coignet, Michael. *Abraham Ortelius: His Epitome of the Theater of the Worlde, Now latyle, since the Latine, Italian, Spanishe, and Frenche Editions, Renewed and Augmented, the Mappes all newe graven according to Geographicall measure. By Michael Coignet, Mathematician of Antwarpe. . . .* London, 1603.

———. *Epitome du Théâtre de l'Univers d'Abraham Ortelius.* Anvers, 1602.

Como, Ugo da. *Girolamo Muziano, 1528–92: Note e documenti.* Bergamo, 1930.

Cook, Arthur K. *About Winchester College.* London, 1917.

Cortesão, Armando. *Cartografia e cartografos portugueses dos séculos XV e XVI.* 2 vols. Lisbon, 1935.

———. *History of Portuguese Cartography.* 2 vols. to date. Coimbra, 1969–71.

———, and Teixeira da Mota, A. *Portugaliae monumenta cartographica.* 6 vols. Lisbon, 1960–62.

Costantini, Celso. *Filippo Sassetti geografo.* Trieste, 1897.

Crone, Gerald Rose. *Maps and Their Makers: An Introduction to the History of Cartography.* 4th rev. ed. London, 1968.

Cunningham, William. *The Cosmographical Glasse, conteinying the Pleasant Principle of Cosmographie, Geographie, Hydrographie, or Navigation.* London, 1559.

Dainville, François de. *La géographie des humanistes.* Paris, 1940.

———. *Le langage des géographes: Termes, signes, couleurs des cartes anciennes, 1500–1800.* Paris, 1964.

Davys, John. *The Worldes Hydrographical Description. Wherein is proved not onely by auctoritie of writers, but also by late experience of travellers and reasons of substantiall probabilitie, that the worlde in all his zones clymats and places, is habitable and inhabited, and the Seas likewise universally Navigable without any naturall annoyance to hinder the same whereby appeares that from England there is a short and speedie passage into the South Seas, to China, Molucca, Philipina, and India by Northerly Navigation. . . .* London, 1595.

Deacon, Richard. *John Dee: Scientist, Geographer, Astrologer, and Secret Agent to Elizabeth I.* London, 1968.

Dee, John. "Of Famous and Rich Discoveries." Unpublished manuscript, 1577, Brit. Mus. Vitellius, C. vii. Cotton Mss.

———. *The Private Diary of John Dee and the Catalogue of His Library of Manuscripts.* Edited by James O. Halliwell. London, 1842.

Denucé, Jean. *Oud Nederlandsche Kaartmakers in Betrekking met Plantin.* 2 vols. Antwerp, 1912.

———. *Les origines de la cartographie portugaise et les cartes des Reinel.* Ghent, 1908.

Deserpz, François. *Omnium fere gentium, nostraeq́; aetatis nationum, habitus, et effigies. In eosdem Ioannis Sluperij Herzelensis epigrammata. Adiecta ad singulas icones Gallica testrasticha.* Antwerp, 1572.

Destombes, M. *La mappemonde de Petrus Plancius gravée par Josua van den Ende, 1604.* Hanoi, 1944.

Dickinson, R. E., and Howarth, O. J. R. *The Making of Geography.* Oxford, 1933.

Chapter Bibliographies

Du Pinet, Antoine. *Plantz, povrtraitz et descriptions de plvsievrs villes et forteresses, tant de l'Evrope, Asie, & Afrique, que des Indes & terres neuues . . . auec plusieurs cartes generales & particulieres . . . Le tout mis par ordre, region par region, par Antoine du Pinet.* Lyons, 1564.

Durme, Maurice van, ed. *Correspondance mercatorienne.* Antwerp, 1959.

Eckert, Max. *Die Kartenwissenschaft: Forschungen und Grundlagen zu einer Kartographie als Wissenschaft.* 2 vols. Berlin, 1924–25.

Enciso, Martín Fernandez de. *Suma de geografía.* Seville, 1519.

Fauser, Alois. *Die Welt in Händen: Kurze Kulturgeschichte des Globus.* Stuttgart, 1967.

Fausto, Sebastiano da Longiano. *La discrittione de l'Asia et Europa di Papa Pio II e l'historia de le cose memorabili fatte in quelle, con s'aggionra de l'Africa, secondo diversi scrittori, con incredibile brevità e diligenza.* Venice, 1544.

Fontoura da Costa, Abel, ed. *Roteiros portugueses inéditos da carreira da India do século XVI.* Lisbon, 1940.

Foster, William, ed. See Lancaster, James.

Fowler, A. D. S., trans. and ed. See Willes, Richard.

French, Peter J. *John Dee: The World of an Elizabethan Magus.* London, 1972.

Gallois, Lucien. *De Orontio Finaeo gallico geographo.* Paris, 1890.

———. *Les géographes allemands de la Renaissance.* Paris, 1890.

Galvão, Antonio. *The Discoveries of the World. . . .* Edited by Charles R. Drinkwater Bethune. "Hakluyt Society Publications," O.S., No. 30. London, 1862.

Garimberto, Girolamo. *Problemi naturali et morali.* Venice, 1549.

Geiger, Theodor. *Conrad Celtis in seinen Beziehungen zur Geographie.* Munich, 1896.

George, Wilma B. *Animals and Maps.* Berkeley [1969].

Gerini, Gerolamo Emilie. *Researches on Ptolemy's Geography of Eastern Asia (Further India and Indo-Malay Archipelago).* London, 1909.

Girava, Hieronimo. *La cosmographia y geographia del S. Hieronimo Girava.* Milan, 1556.

Gomara, Francisco López de. *Primera y segunda parte de la historia general de las Indias con todo il descubrimiento y cosas notables que han acaecido dende que se ganaron āta il año de 1551.* Saragossa, 1553.

Gosche, Richard. *Sebastian Franck als Geograph.* Berlin, 1853.

Götz, Wilhelm. *Die Verkehrswege im Dienste des Welthandels: Eine historisch-geographische Untersuchung. . . .* Stuttgart, 1888.

Grande, Stefano. *Le relazioni geografiche fra P. Bembo, G. Fracastoro, G. B. Ramusio, G. Gastaldi.* Rome, 1906.

Guenther, Siegmund. *Peter und Philipp Apian, zwei deutsche Mathematicker und Kartographen des XVI. Jahrhunderts.* Prague, 1882.

Halliwell, James O., ed. See Dee, John.

Hantzsch, Viktor. *Deutsche Reisende des 16. Jahrhunderts.* Leipzig, 1895.

Hartshorne, Richard. *The Nature of Geography.* Lancaster, Pa., 1946.

Heidenheimer, Heinrich. *Petrus Martyr Angherius und sein Opus Epistolarum.* Berlin, 1881.

Herbermann, Charles George, ed. See Waldseemüller, Martin.

Hessels, Johannes, ed. See Ortelius, Abraham.

Chapter X

Hind, A. M. *Early Italian Engraving*. 7 vols. London, 1938–48.

Ivins, William M., Jr. *Prints and Visual Communication*. Cambridge, Mass., 1953.

Johnson, Hildegarde Binder. *Carta Marina: World Geography in Strassburg, 1525*. Minneapolis, [1963].

Julien, Charles-André. *Les voyages de découverte et les premiers établissements (XVᵉ–XVIᵉ siècles)*. Paris, 1948.

Keuning, Johannes. *Petrus Plancius, theolog en geograf, 1552–1622*. Amsterdam, 1946.

Koeman, Cornelis. *Collections of Maps and Atlases in the Netherlands: Their History and Present State*. Leyden, 1961.

——. *The History of Lucas Janszoon Waghenaer and His "Spieghel der Zeevaerdt."* New York, [1964].

——. *The History of Abraham Ortelius and His Theatrum Orbis Terrarum*. Lausanne, 1964.

——, comp. and ed. *Atlantes Neerlandica: Bibliography of Terrestrial, Maritime and Celestial Atlases and Pilot Books Published in the Netherlands up to 1880*. 5 vols. Amsterdam, 1969.

Konetzke, Richard. *Das spanische Weltreich: Grundlagen und Entstehung*. Munich, 1943.

Kraus, Hans Peter. *Sir Francis Drake*. Amsterdam, 1970.

Krause, Kurt. *Die Anfänge des geographischen Unterrichts im 16. Jahrhundert*. Gotha, 1929.

Kretschmer, Konrad. *Geschichte der Geographie*. Berlin and Leipzig, 1912.

Lacarrière, Jacques. *Hérodote et la découverte de la terre*. Paris, 1968.

Lamb, Ursula, trans. and ed. See Medina, Pedro de.

Lancaster, James. *The Voyages of Sir James Lancaster to Brazil and the East Indies, 1591–1603*. Edited by Sir William Foster. "Hakluyt Society Publications," 2d ser., No. 85. London, 1940.

Leithäuser, Joachim G. *Mappae mundi; die geistige Eroberung der Welt; eine Kulturgeschichte der alten Weltkarten*. Berlin, 1958.

Lynam, Edward. *British Maps and Map-Makers*. London, 1944.

MacNutt, F. A., trans. and ed. See Anghiera, Pietro Martire d'.

March, Andrew L. *The Ideas of China: Myth and Theory in Geographic Thought*. New York, 1974.

Marinelli, Giovanni. *Venezia nella storia della geografia, cartografica ed esploratrici*. Florence, 1907.

Medina, Pedro de. *A Navigator's Universe: The Libro de Cosmographia of 1538 by Pedro de Medina*. Edited by Ursula Lamb. Chicago, 1972.

Menendez-Pidal, Gonzalo. *Imagen del mundo hacia 1570; segun noticias del consejo de Indias y de los tratadistes españoles*. Madrid, 1944.

Mercator, Gerard. *Atlas sive Cosmographicae. . . .* Duisburg, 1595.

Mitchell, Mairin. *Elcano, the First Circumnavigator*. London, 1958.

Mollat, Michel, and Adam, Paul, eds. *Les aspects internationaux de la découverte océanique aux XVᵉ et XVIᵉ siècles*. Paris, 1966.

Morison, Samuel Eliot. *The European Discovery of America: The Southern Voyages, A.D. 1492–1616*. New York, 1974.

Münster, Sebastian; see Belleforest, François de, ed.

Chapter Bibliographies

Muris, Oswald, and Saarmann, Gert. *Der Globus im Wandel der Zeiten: Eine Geschichte der Globen*. Stuttgart, 1961.

Musset, Georges, ed. See Alfonce, Jean.

Näf, Werner. *Vadian und seine Stadt St. Gallen*. St. Gall, 1944.

Nakamura Hiroshi [中村拓]. *Sakoku zen ni Nambanjin no tsukureru Nihon chizu* [鎖国前に南蛮人の作れる日本地図] ("Maps of Japan Made by the Portuguese before the Closure of Japan"). 3 vols. Tokyo, 1966–67.

————. *East Asia in Old Maps*. Honolulu, [*ca.* 1964].

Nettesheim, H. C. Agrippa von. *The Vanity of Arts and Sciences*. London, 1684.

Nicolay, Nicolas de. *Les navigations et peregrinations orientales*. Lyons, 1567.

Nigri, Dominicus Marius. *Geographiae commentariorum, libri XI, nunc primum in lucem magno studio editi*. . . . Basel, 1557.

Nordenskiöld, Nils A. E. *Facsimile Atlas to the Early History of Cartography with Reproductions of the Most Important Maps Printed in the XV and XVI Centuries*. Translated from the Swedish. Stockholm, 1889.

Nunn, George E. *World Map of Francesco Roselli* [*sic*]. . . . Philadelphia, 1928.

O'Malley, Charles Donald, ed. See Servetus, Michael.

Ortelius, Abraham. *Abrahami Ortelii (geographi Antwerpiensis) et virorum eruditorum ad eundem et ad Jacobum Colium Ortelianum . . . Epistulae . . . (1524–1628)*. Edited by Johannes Hessels. Cambridge, 1887.

————. *Theatrum orbis terrarum*. Antwerp, 1575.

Osley, A. S. *Mercator*. New York, 1969.

Paassen, C. van. *The Classical Tradition of Geography*. Groningen, 1957.

Pannwitz, Max. *Deutsche Pfadfinder des 16. Jahrhunderts in Afrika, Asien und Südamerika*. Munich, 1928.

Parr, Charles M. *Jan van Linschoten: The Dutch Marco Polo*. New York, 1964.

Porcacchi, Thomaso. *L'Isole piv famose del mondo descritte da Thomaso Porcacchi da Castiglione, Arretino, e intagliate Girolamo Porro. Padovano. Al Sereniss. principe et sig.^{re} Il. S. Don Giovanni D'Avstria, Generale della Santiss. Lega. Con privilegio*. Venice, 1572.

Ptolemy. *Claudii Ptolemaei Alexandrini Geographicae Enarrationis libri Octo. Ex Bilibaldi Pirckheymeri translatione, sed ad Graeca & prisca exemplaria à Michaële Villanovano (Serveto) iam primum recogniti*. Lyons, 1535.

Puente y Olea, Manuel de la. *Los trabajos geográficos de la Casa de la Contratación*. Seville, 1900.

Quad, Matthias. *Geographisch Handtbuch*. Cologne, 1600.

Quinn, David Beers, ed. *The Hakluyt Handbook*. 2 vols. London, 1974.

————, ed. *The Last Voyage of Thomas Cavendish*. Chicago, 1975.

Quirino, Carlos. *Philippine Cartography, 1320–1899*. 2d rev. ed. Amsterdam, [1963].

Ringler, W. A., Jr., ed. See Sidney, Philip.

Ristow, Walter W., comp. *Guide to the History of Cartography: An Annotated List of References on the History of Maps and Mapmaking*. Washington, D.C., 1973.

Ritter, Carl. *Geschichte der Erdkunde und der Entdeckungen*. 2d ed. Berlin, 1880.

Rosaccio, Giuseppe. *Descrittione della geografia universale.* Venice, 1599.

Rossi, Mario. *Un letterato e mercanti fiorentino del seculo XVI, Filippo Sassetti.* Città di Castello, 1899.

Santarem, Visconde de. *Essai sur l'histoire de la cosmographie et de la cartographie pendant le moyen-âge.* . . . 3 vols. Paris, 1849–52.

Sanz, Carlos. *Mapas antiguos del mundo (siglos XV–XVI).* Madrid, 1962.

————. *La geographia de Ptolomeo ampliada con los primeros mapas impresos de América (desde 1507).* Madrid, 1959.

————. *Bibliotheca Americana Vetustissima; Ultimas Adiciones (en dos volumenens).* Madrid, 1960.

São Bernardino, Gaspar de. *Itinerario da India por terra à ilha de Chipre.* Edited by A. R. Machado. Lisbon, 1953.

Schmithüsen, Josef. *Geschichte der geographischen Wissenschaft von den ersten Anfängen bis zum Ende des 18. Jahrhunderts.* Mannheim, 1970.

Schultheiss, W. *Martin Behaim und die Nürnberger Kosmographen.* Nuremberg, 1957.

Servetus, Michael. *Michael Servetus: A Translation of His Geographical, Medical and Astrological Writings.* . . . Edited by Charles Donald O'Malley. Philadelphia, 1953.

Shawcross, J. T., ed. *The Complete Poetry of John Donne.* New York, 1967.

Sidney, Philip. *The Poems of Sir Philip Sidney.* Edited by W. A. Ringler, Jr. Oxford, 1962.

Signot, Jean. *La division du monde, contenant la declaration des provinces & regions d'Asie, Europe, & Aphricque. Ensemble les passages, lieux & destroitz, par lesquelz on peut & passer des Gaules es parties d'Italie.* . . . Lyons, 1555.

Sinnatamby, J. R. *Ceylon in Ptolemy's Geography.* [Colombo, 1968].

Skelton, Raleigh A. *Decorative Printed Maps of the 15ᵗʰ to 18ᵗʰ Centuries.* London, 1952. Reprinted in 1965.

————. *Explorers' Maps: The Cartographic Record of Geographical Discovery.* London, 1958.

————. *A Venetian Terrestrial Globe Represented by the Largest Surviving Printed Gores of the XVIᵗʰ Century.* Bologna, 1969.

————. *Maps: A Historical Survey of Their Study and Collecting.* Chicago, 1972.

Smet, Antoine de. *La cartographie hollandaise.* Brussels, 1971.

Smith, Ronald Bishop, ed. *The First Age of the Portuguese Embassies, Navigations, and Peregrinations to the Kingdoms and Islands of Southeast Asia (1509–21).* Bethesda, Md., 1968.

Stevens, Henry N. *Ptolemy's Geography: A Brief Account of All Printed Editions down to 1730.* London, 1908.

Strauss, Gerald. *Nuremberg in the Sixteenth Century.* Bloomington, Ind., 1967.

Taylor, E. G. R. *Tudor Geography, 1485–1583.* London, 1930.

Thevet, André. *La cosmographie universelle . . . illustree de diverses figures des choses plus remarquables vivës par l'Auteur et incogneuës de noz Anciens et Modernes.* 2 vols. Paris, 1575.

Thrower, Norman J. W. *Maps and Man.* Englewood Cliffs, N.J., 1972.

Tooley, Ronald V. *Maps and Map-Makers.* London, 1949.

Torres Lanzas, Pedro. *Relación descriptiva de los mapas planos etc. de Filipinas, existentes en el Archivo general de Indias.* Madrid, 1897.

Uzielli, Gustavo, and Amat de S. Filippo, P. *Mappamondi, carte nautiche, portolani ed altri monumenti cartografici specialmente italiani dei secoli XIII–XVII.* Amsterdam, 1967.

Vadianus, Joachim. *Epitome trium terrae partium Asiae, Africae et Europae.* . . . Zurich, 1534.

Waghenaer, Luc. Janszoon. *Spieghel der zeevaerdt.* Leyden, 1584–85. Reprinted edition. Amsterdam, 1964.

Waldseemüller, Martin. *Cosmographiae introductio.* Strassburg, 1509.

———. *The Cosmographiae introductio of Martin Waldseemüller in Facsimile.* Edited by Charles George Herbermann. New York, 1907.

Wauwermans, Henri E. *Histoire de l'école cartographique belge et anversoise du XVIᵉ siècle.* 2 vols. Reprint of the 1895 edition. Amsterdam, 1964.

Weyrauther, M. *Konrad Peutinger und Wilibald Pirckheimer in ihren Beziehungen zur Geographie: Eine geschichtliche Parallele.* "Münchener geographische Studien," Vol. XXI. Munich, 1907.

Wieder, Frederick Caspar, ed. *Monumenta cartographica.* . . . 5 vols. The Hague, 1925–33.

Willes, Richard. *"De re Poetica" by Wills [Willes].* Edited and translated by A. D. S. Fowler. Oxford, 1958.

———. *The History of Traveyle.* London, 1577.

Yusuf Kamal. *Monumenta cartographica Africae et Aegypti.* 5 vols. in 15. Cairo, 1926–51.

ARTICLES

Anon. "Old Inventories of Maps." *Imago mundi,* V (1948), 18–20.

Abendanon, E. C. "Missing Links in the Development of the Ancient Portuguese Cartography of the Netherlands East Indian Archipelago." *Geographical Journal,* LIV (1919), 347–55.

Almagià, Roberto. "The Atlas of Pietro Coppo, 1520." *Imago mundi,* VII (1950), 48–50.

———. "Un grande planisfero di Giuseppe Rosaccio." *Revista geografica italiana,* XXXI (1924), 264–69.

———. "Padova e l'Ateneo padovano nella storia della scienza geografica." *Revista geografica italiana,* XIX (1912), 467–510.

———. "On the Cartographic Work of Francesco Rosselli." *Imago mundi,* VIII (1951), 27–52.

———. "La diffusion des produits cartographiques flamand en Italie au XVIᵉ siècle." *Archives internationales d'histoire des sciences,* XXXIII (1954), 46–48.

Andrews, Michael C. "The Study of Classification of Medieval *Mappae Mundi.*" *Archaeologia,* LXXV (1926), 61–76.

Bagrow, Leo. "A Page from the History of the Distribution of Maps." *Imago mundi,* V (1948), 57–59.

———. "A. Ortelii catalogus cartographorum." *Petermanns Mitteilungen,* XLIII (1920), No. 199 (1928) and No. 210 (1930). Included respectively in *Ergänzungsband* XLIII and XLV.

Chapter X

Ballesteros Gaibrois, Manuel. "Fernandez de Ovideo, etnólogo." *Revista de Indias*, XVII (1957), 445–67.

Banfi, Florio. "The Cosmographic Loggia of the Vatican Palace." *Imago mundi*, IX (1952), 23–34.

Baratta, M. "Ricerche intorno a Giacomo Gastaldi." *Revista geografica italiana*, XXI (1914), 117–36, 373–79.

Beck, Hanno. "Entdeckungsgeschichte und geographische Disziplinhistorie." *Erdkunde*, IX (1955), 197–204.

Biermann, Benno. "Die 'Geografía y descripción universal de las Indias' des Juan López de Velasco als Quelle für die Missionsgeschichte (1570)." *Neue Zeitschrift für Missionswissenschaft*, XVII (1961), 291–302.

Bonacker, Wilhelm. "Der Erdglobus von Johann Schöner aus dem Jahre 1520." *Mitteilungen des Vereins für die Geschichte der Stadt Nürnberg*, LI (1962), 441–42.

Bonaparte, R. "Les premiers voyages des Neerlandais dans l'Insulinde, 1595–1602." *Revue de géographie*, XIV (1884), Pt. I, 440–51.

Broek, Jan O. M. "Place Names in 16th and 17th Century Borneo." *Imago mundi*, XVI (1962), 129–48.

Buczek, Karol. "Ein Beitrag zur Entstehungsgeschichte der 'Kosmographie' von Sebastian Münster." *Imago mundi*, I (1935), 35–40.

Burmeister, Karl Heinz. "Achilles Pirmin Gasser (1505–1577) as Geographer and Cartographer." *Imago mundi*, XXIV (1970), 57–62.

Campos, Viriato de, and Machado, José Pedro. "Taprobana, Ceilão e Samatra." *Revista de Portugal*, XXXI (1966), 284–92.

Chang Kuei-sheng. "Africa and the Indian Ocean in Chinese Maps of the Fourteenth and Fifteenth Centuries." *Imago mundi*, XXIV (1970), 21–30.

Cortesão, Jaime. "Influência dos descobrimentos dos Portugueses na história da civilização." In Damião Peres, ed., *História de Portugal* (Barcelos, 1932), IV, 179–240.

Crone, Gerald Roe. "Richard Hakluyt, Geographer." In D. B. Quinn, ed., *The Hakluyt Handbook*, I, 8–14. 2 vols. London, 1974.

Dainville, François de. "Les amateurs des globes." *Gazette des Beaux Arts*, 6th ser. LXXI (1968), 51–64.

———. "Les découvertes portugaises à travers des cahiers d'écoliers parisiens de la fin du XVIᵉ siècle." In M. Mollat and P. Adam, eds., *Les aspects internationaux*, pp. 39–46. Paris, 1966.

———. "Libraires d'écoliers toulousains à la fin du XVIᵉ siècle." *Bibliothèque d'humanisme et renaissance*, IX (1947), 129–40.

Destombes, Marcel. "Un Antwerp *unicum*: An Unpublished Terrestrial Globe of the 16th Century in the Bibliothèque Nationale, Paris." *Imago mundi*, XXIV (1970), 85–94.

Dindinger, Giovanni. "Il contributo dei missionari cattolici alla conscenza del Siam e dell' Indocina." In C. Costantini *et al.*, *Le missioni cattoliche e la cultura dell'Oriente*, pp. 293–338. Rome, 1943.

Ferrando, Roberto. "Fernandez de Oviedo y el conocimiento del Mar del Sur." *Revista de Indias*, XVII (1957), 469–82.

Gallo, Rodolfo. "Le mappe geografiche del Palazzo ducale di Venezia." *Archivio veneto*, 5th ser. XXXII (1943), 47–113.

Gernez, D. "Lucas Janszoon Wagenaer 1584." *Mariner's Mirror*, XXIII (1937), 190–97.

Grenacher, Franz. "Guide to the Cartographic History of the Imperial City of Augsburg." *Imago mundi*, XXII (1968), 85–106.

Grössing, H. "Johannes Stabius: Ein Oberösterreicher im Kreis der Humanisten um Kaiser Maximilian I." *Mitteilungen des oberösterreichischen Landesarchivs* (Graz), IX (1968), 239–64.

Günther, Siegmund. "Wilibald Pirckheimer, einer der Wiedererwecker der Geographie in Deutschland." *Das Bayerland*, IV (1893), 569–72, 583–85.

———. "Der Humanismus in seinem Einfluss auf die Entwicklung der Erdkunde." *Geographische Zeitschrift*, VI (1900), 65–89.

Haardt, Robert. "The Globe of Gemma Frisius." *Imago mundi*, IX (1952), 109–10.

Hamann, G. "Auswirkungen der Entdeckungsfahrten auf der südlichen Hemisphäre auf die Kartographie." *Sitzungsberichte der Österreichische Akademie der Wissenschaften, philosophische-historische Klasse* (Vienna), CCLX (1968), 62–74, 418–37.

Hantzsch, Viktor. "Deutsche Geographen der Renaissance." *Geographische Zeitschrift*, III (1897), 507–44, 557–66, 618–24.

Heawood, Edward. "The World Map before and after Magellan's Voyage." *Geographical Journal*, LVII (1921), 431–45.

Heiberg, J. L. "Théories antiques sur l'influence morale du climat." *Scientia*, XXVII (1920), 453–64.

Hervé, R. "L'oeuvre cartographique de Nicolas de Nicolay et d'Antoine de Leval, 1544–1619." *Bulletin de la section de géographie du comité des travaux historiques et scientifiques* (Paris), LXVIII (1955), 223–63.

Hoff, Door Bert van't. "De catalogus van de bibliotheek van Gerard Mercator." *Het Boek*, XXXV (1961–62), 25–27.

———. "Gerard Mercator (1512–94) en de kartografie de 16de eeuw." *Duisburger Forschungen*, VI (1962), 1–27.

Hulshoff Pol, E. "The Library." In Th. H. Lunsingh Scheurleer and G. H. M. Posthumus Meyjes, eds., *Leiden University in the Seventeenth Century*, pp. 395–459. Leyden, 1975.

Ishida Mikinosuke. "A Brief Note on the Two Old European Maps of Japan Recently Discovered." *Monumenta nipponica*, I (1938), 259–65.

Kellenbenz, Herman. "La participation des capitaux de l'Allemagne méridionale aux enterprises portugaises d'outre-mer au tournant du XVe siècle." In Mollat and Adam, eds., *Les aspects internationaux*, pp. 309–17. Paris, 1966.

Keuning, Johannes. "Sixteenth-Century Cartography in the Netherlands." *Imago mundi*, IX (1952), 35–63.

———. "The History of an Atlas: Mercator-Hondius." *Imago mundi*, IV (1947), 27–62.

———. "Overzicht van de Ontwikkeling van de Kartografie van den indischen Archipel tot het Jaar 1598." In Johannes Keuning, ed., *De tweede Schipvaart der Nederlanders naar Oost-Indië . . .*, pp. 214–318. 's-Gravenhage, 1949.

———. "Hessel Gerritz." *Imago mundi*, VI (1950), 49–66.

Kish, George. "The Life and Works of Gemma Frisius, 1508–55." *James Ford Bell Lectures* (Minneapolis), Vol IV (1967).

———. "Two Fifteenth-Century Maps of 'Zipangu': Notes on the Early Cartography of Japan." *Yale University Library Gazette*, XL (1966), 206–14.

———. "The Japan on the 'Mural Atlas' of the Palazzo Vecchio, Florence." *Imago mundi*, VIII (1951), 52–54.

———. "The Cosmographic Heart: Cordiform Maps of the XVI Century." *Imago mundi*, XIX (1965), 13–21.

———. "Some Aspects of the Missionary Cartography of Japan during the Sixteenth Century." *Imago mundi*, VI (1949), 39–46.

Lamb, Ursula. "The Spanish Cosmographic Juntas of the Sixteenth Century." *Terrae incognitae*, VI (1974), 51–62.

Lessa, William A. "Francis Drake in Mindinao?" *Journal of Pacific History*, IX (1974), 55–64.

McFarland, J. "Jesuit Geographers of India, 1600–1750." *New Review* (Calcutta), XII (1940), 496–515.

Merens, A., ed. "De reis van Jan Martenez. Merens door Frankrijk, Italie en Duitschland, anno 1600." *Mededeelingen van het Nederlandsche Historisch Instituut te Rome*, 2d ser. VII (1937), 49–157.

Millás Vallicrosa, J. M. "Nautique et cartographique de l'Espagne au XVIᵉ siècle." In A. Koyré, ed., *La science au seizième siècle*, pp. 35–47. Paris, 1960.

Nakamura Hirosi. "Les cartes du Japon qui servaient de modèle aux cartographes européens au début des relations de l'Occident avec le Japon." *Monumenta nipponica*, II (1939), 100–123.

Nordenskiöld, A. H. "Intorno alla influenza dei 'Viaggi di Marco Polo' sulle carte dell' Asia di Giacomo Gastaldo." *Revista geografica italiana*, VIII (1901), 496–507.

Po, Guido. "La collaborazione Italo-Portoghese alle grandi esplorazione geografiche ed alla cartografia nautica." In Reale Accademia d'Italia, *Relazioni storiche fra l'Italia e il Portogallo: Memorie e documenti*, pp. 261–322. Rome, 1940.

Pölnitz, Graf Freiherr von. "Martin Behaim." In K. Rüdinger, ed., *Gemeinsames Erbe: Perspektiven europäischer Geschichte*, pp. 134–36. Munich, 1959.

Quinn, David Beers. "Simão Fernandes, a Portuguese Pilot in the English Serivce, 1573–1588." *Congresso internacional de história dos descobrimentos, Actas*, III (1960), 449–65.

———, et al. "The Primary Hakluyt Bibliography." In D. B. Quinn, ed., *The Hakluyt Handbook*, II, 461–97. 2 vols. London, 1974.

Ribeiro, Luciano. "Uma geografia quinhentista." *Studia*, VII (1961), 151–318.

Rogers, Francis M. "Hakluyt as Translator." In D. B. Quinn, ed., *The Hakluyt Handbook*, I, 37–48. 2 vols. London, 1974.

———. "Valentim Fernandes, Rodrigo de Santaella, and the Recognition of the Antilles as 'Opposite-India.'" *Boletim da sociedade de geografia de Lisboa*, LXXV (1957), 279–309.

Sanz, Carlos. "The Discovery of America: The Three Maps Which Determined It, Promoted Knowledge of Its Form, and Fixed Its Name." *Terrae incognitae*, VI (1974), 75–85.

Chapter Bibliographies

Schilling, Dorothe. "Il contributo dei missionari cattolici nei secoli XVI e XVII alla conoscenza dell'isola di Ezo e degli Ainu." In C. Costantini *et al.*, *Le missioni cattoliche e la cultura dell'Oriente*, pp. 199–215. Rome, 1943.

Schütte, Joseph F. "Ignacio Moreira of Lisbon, Cartographer of Japan, 1590–92." *Imago mundi*, XVI (1962), 116–28.

Skelton, Raleigh A. "Mercator and English Cartography in the Sixteenth Century." *Duisburger Forschungen*, VI (1962), 158–70.

———. "Hakluyt's Maps." In D. B. Quinn, ed., *The Hakluyt Handbook*, I, 48–69. 2 vols. London, 1974.

———. "Les relations anglaise de Gerard Mercator." *Bulletin de la Société royale de géographie d'Anvers*, LXVI (1953), 3–10.

Smet, Antoine de. "Cartographes scientifiques neérlandais du premier tiers du XVIᵉ siècle, leurs références aux portugais." *Revista da faculdade de ciências da universidade de Coimbra*, XXXIX (1967), 363–74.

Strauss, Gerald. "A Sixteenth-Century Encyclopedia: Sebastian Münster's *Cosmography* and Its Editions." In C. H. Carter, ed., *From the Renaissance to the Counter-Reformation: Essays in Memory of Garrett Mattingly*, pp. 145–63. London, 1966.

Taylor, E. G. R. "John Dee and the Map of North-east Asia." *Imago mundi*, XII (1955), 103–6.

Teixeira da Mota, Avelino. "Influence de la cartographie portugaise sur la cartographie européenne à l'époque des découvertes." In M. Mollat and P. Adam, eds., *Les aspects internationaux*, pp. 223–48. Paris, 1966.

———. "A viagem de Bartolomeu Dias e as concepções geopoliticas de D. João II." *Boletim da sociedade de geografia de Lisboa*, LXXVI (1958), 42–48.

———. "A evolução da ciência nautica durante os séculos XV–XVI na cartografia portuguesa da época." *Memórias da Academia das ciências de Lisboa, Classe de letras*, VII (1962), 247–66.

———. "Evolução dos roteiros portugueses durante o século XVI." *Revista da universidade de Coimbra*, XXIV (1969), 5–32.

Tooley, M. J. "Bodin and the Medieval Theory of Climate." *Speculum*, XXVIII (1953), 64–83.

Tooley, Ronald V. "Maps in Italian Atlases of the Sixteenth Century, Being a Comparative List of the Italian Maps Issued by Lafreri, Forlani, Duchetti, Bertelli, and Others, Found in Atlases." *Imago mundi*, III (1939), 12–47.

Torodash, Martin. "Magellan Historiography." *Hispanic American Historical Review*, LI (1971), 313–35.

Uhden, Richard. "The Oldest Portuguese Original Chart of the Indian Ocean, A.D. 1509." *Imago mundi*, III (1939), 7–11.

Van Beylen, J. "Schepen op Kaarten ten tide van Gerard Mercator." *Duisburger Forschungen*, VI (1962), 130–33.

Voet, Léon. "Les relations commerciales entre Gerard Mercator et la maison Plantinienne." *Duisburger Forschungen*, VI (1962), 171–232.

Wallis, Helen. "Edward Wright and the 1599 World Map." In D. B. Quinn, ed., *The Hakluyt Handbook*, I, 69–73. 2 vols. London, 1974.

———. "The Use of Terrestrial and Celestial Globes in England." *Actes du XIe congrès international d'histoire des sciences*, IV (1965), 204–12.

———. "The Influence of Father Ricci in Far Eastern Cartography." *Imago mundi*, XIX (1965), 38–45.

Washburn, Wilcomb E. "The Meaning of 'Discovery' in the Fifteenth and Sixteenth Centuries." *American Historical Review*, LXVIII (1962), 1–21.

Welser, Hubert Freiherr von. "Der Globus des Lukas Rem." *Mitteilungen des Vereins für Geschichte der Stadt Nürnberg*, XLVIII (1958), 96–114.

Winter, Heinrich. "Francisco Rodrigues' Atlas of Ca. 1513." *Imago mundi*, VI (1942), 20–26.

Woodward, David. "Some Evidence for the Use of Stereotyping on Peter Apian's World Map of 1530." *Imago mundi*, XXIV (1970), 43–48.

Wroth, Laurence C. "The Early Cartography of the Pacific." *Papers of the Bibliographical Society of America*, XXXVIII (1944), 87–268.

Yoshitomo Okamoto. "Desenvolvimento cartográfico da parte Extrema Oriente da Asia pelos Jesuitas Portugueses em fim do século XVI." *Studia* (Lisbon), XIII (1964), 7–29.

XI. LANGUAGE AND LINGUISTICS

BOOKS

Adelung, Johann Christoph. *Mithridates oder allgemeine Sprachenkunde mit dem Vaterunser als Sprachprobe in beynahe fünfhundert Sprachen und Mundarten*. Berlin, 1806.

Alvar, M., *et al. Enciclopedia lingüística hispánica*. 2 vols. Madrid, 1967.

Ambrosius [Ambrogio], Theseus. *Introductio in chaldaicam linguam, syriacam, atque armenicam, et decem alias linguas*. Pavia, 1539.

Anania, Giovanni Lorenzo d'. *L'universale fabrica del mondo.* . . . Venice, 1576.

Apel, K. O. *Die Idee der Sprache in der Tradition des Humanismus von Dante bis Vico*. "Archiv für Begriffsgeschichte," Vol. VIII. Bonn, 1963.

Arens, Hans. *Sprachwissenschaft, der Gang ihrer Entwicklung von der Antike bis zur Gegenwart*. 2d ed. Freiburg, 1969.

Arthus, Gotthard. *Historia Indiae Orientalis, ex variis auctoribus collecta.* . . . Cologne, 1608.

———. *Dialogues in the English and Malaiane Languages*. Translated from Latin by Augustus Spalding. London, 1614.

Arveiller, Raymond. *Contribution à l'étude des termes de voyage en français (1505–1722)*. Paris, 1963.

Bahner, Werner. *La lingüística española del Siglo de Oro: Aportaciones a la conciencia lingüística en la España delos siglos XVI y XVII*. Madrid, 1966.

Barbosa, Jorge Morais. *A língua portuguesa no mundo*. 2d rev. ed. Lisbon, 1969.

Barnett, L. D., and Pope, G. U. *A Catalogue of the Tamil Books in the Library of the British Museum*. London, 1909.

Barros, João de. *Compilação de várias obras do insigne portuguez Joam de Barros*. Lisbon, 1785.

Chapter Bibliographies

Battisti, Carlo, and Alessio, Giovanni. *Dizionario etimologico italiano*. Florence, 1948–57.

Benfey, Theodor. *Geschichte der Sprachwissenschaft und orientalischen Philologie in Deutschland*. . . . Munich, 1869.

Bennett, Josephine W. *The Rediscovery of Sir John Mandeville*. New York, 1954.

Benzing, Joseph. *Der Buchdruck des 16. Jahrhundert im deutschen Sprachgebiet*. "Beiheft zum Zentralblatt für Bibliothekswesen," No. 68. Leipzig, 1936.

Bertola, M. *I due primi registri di prestito della Biblioteca Apostolica Vaticana*. "Codices e Vaticanis selecti," Vol. XXVII. Vatican City, 1942.

Bibliander, Theodor. *De ratione communi omnium linguarum et literarū commentarius*. . . . Zurich, 1548.

Blau, Joseph Leon. *The Christian Interpretation of the Cabala in the Renaissance*. New York, 1944.

Bloch, Oscar. *Dictionnaire étymologique de la langue française*. Paris, 1932.

Blumentritt, Ferdinand. *Vocabular einzelner Ausdrücke und Redensacten welche dem Spanischen der Philippinischen Inseln eigenthümlich sind*. Leitmeritz, 1885.

Bonacini, Claudio. *Bibliografia delle arti scrittorie e della calligrafia*. Florence, 1953.

Borst, Arno. *Der Turmbau von Babel: Geschichte der Meinungen über Ursprung und Vielfalt der Sprachen und Völker*. 4 vols. Stuttgart, 1957–63.

Bouwsma, William J. *Concordia Mundi: The Career and Thought of Guillaume Postel*. Cambridge, Mass., 1957.

Braunsberger, Otto, ed. *Beati Petri Canisii . . . epistulae et acta*. 5 vols. Freiburg, 1923.

Brerewood, Edward. *Enquiries Touching the Diversity of Languages and Religions throughout the Chief Parts of the World*. London, 1614.

British Museum. *A Catalogue of the Lansdowne Manuscripts in the British Museum with Indexes of Persons, Places, and Matters*. London, 1819.

Broek, Jan Otto Marius. *Place Names in 16th and 17th Century Borneo*. Minneapolis, 1959.

Bry, Johann Theodor de. *Characters and Diversitie of Letters Used by Divers Nations in the World*. . . . Frankfurt, 1628. Reissue of *Alphabeta et charactera*, 1596.

Burmeister, Karl Heinz. *Sebastian Münster: Versuch eines biographischen Gesamtbilder*. "Basler Beiträge zur Geschichtswissenschaft," Vol. 91. Basel, 1963.

Burnell, Arthur C., and Tiele, P. A., eds. *The Voyage of John Huyghen Van Linschoten to the East Indies*. "Hakluyt Society Publications," O.S. Nos. 70–71. 2 vols. London, 1885.

Butler, Edward H. *The Story of British Shorthand*. London, 1951.

Canini, Angelo. *Institutiones linguae Syriacae Assyriacae atque . . . Arabicae collatione*. Paris, 1554.

Carlton, William John. *Timothy Bright*. London, 1911.

Casamassima, Emanuele. *Trattati di scrittura del Cinquecento Italiano*. Milan, 1967.

Cayet, Pierre Victor Palma. *Paradigmata di quatuor linguis orientalibus praecipuis, Arabica, Armena, Syra, Aethiopica*. Paris, 1596.

Chao Yuen-ren. *Language and Symbolic Systems*. London, 1968.

Cidade, Henri. *A literatura portuguesa e a expansão ultramarina*. 2d ed. 2 vols. Coimbra, 1968.

Cobarruvias, Don Sebastian de. *Tesoro de la lengua Castellana o Española*. Madrid, 1611.

Corazzini, D. A., ed. *Diario fiorentino di Agosto Lapini*. Florence, 1900.

Cornelius, Paul. *Languages in Seventeenth- and Early Eighteenth-Century Imaginary Voyages*. Geneva, 1965.

Corominas, Juan. *Diccionario crítico etimológico de la lengua castellana*. 4 vols. Berne, 1954.

Cortez-Pinto, Américo. *Da famosa arte da imprimissão*. Lisbon, 1948.

Costantini, C., et al. *Le missioni cattoliche e la cultura dell' Oriente*. Rome, 1943.

Dahlmann, Joseph. *Die Sprachkunde und die Missionen, ein Beitrag zur Charakteristik der ältern katholischen Missionsthätigkeit, 1500–1800*. Freiburg-im-Breisgau, 1891.

———. *Missionary Pioneers and Indian Languages*. Trichinopoly, 1940.

Dainville, François de. *La géographie des Humanistes*. Paris, 1940.

Dalgado, Sebastião Rodolfo, and Soares, A. X. *Portuguese Vocables in Asiatic Languages: Translated into English with Notes, Additions and Comments by Anthony Xavier Soares*. Baroda, 1936.

———. *Glossário luso-asiático*. 2 vols. Coimbra, 1919, 1921.

Dauzaut, Albert. *Dictionnaire étymologique de la langue française*. Paris, 1949.

David, Madeleine V. *Le débat sur les écritures et l'hiéroglyphe aux XVIIᵉ et XVIIIᵉ siècles.* . . . Paris, 1965.

Dee, John. *Monas hieroglyphica*. Antwerp, 1564.

De Jongh, W. F. J. *Western Language Manuals of the Renaissance*. Albuquerque, 1949.

Delatte, Armand. *Études sur la littérature pythagoricienne*. Paris, 1915.

D'Elia, Pasquale M., ed. *Storia dell' introduzione del Cristiansimo in Cina, scritta da Matteo Ricci S.I.* 3 vols. Rome, 1942–49.

Diarium nauticum itineris Batavorum in Indiam orientalem, cursuum, tractuum, variorumque eventuum, qui ipsis contigerunt diligentur descriptum. . . . Arnheim, 1598.

Diringer, David. *The Alphabet a Key to the History of Mankind*. New York, 1948.

———. *Writing*. The Hague, 1962.

Dugat, Gustave. *Histoire des orientalistes de l'Europe du XIIᵉ au XIXᵉ siècle*. Paris, 1868.

Duret, Claude. *Thresor de l'histoire des langues de cest Univers.* . . . Cologne, 1613[?], Yverdon, 1619[?].

———. *Discours de la verité des causes et effets des decadences, mutations, changements, conversions, et ruines des monarchies, empires, royaumes, et republiques.* . . . 2d ed. Lyons, 1598.

Ebisawa Arimichi. *Christianity in Japan: A Bibliography of Japanese and Chinese Sources*. Part I. Tokyo, 1960.

Elizalde, Ignacio. *San Francisco Xavier en la literatura española*. Madrid, 1961.

Equilaz y Yanguas, Leopoldo de. *Glosario etimológico de las palabras españolas . . . de orígen oriental (árabe, hebreo, malayo, persa, y turco)*. Granada, 1886.

Esquivel, Jacinto. *Vocabulario de la lengua de los indios de Tanchui, en la isla Hermosa o Formosa*. Manila, 1630.

———. *Vocabulario de las lenguas japonesa y española*. Manila, 1630.

Fairbank, Alfred, and Wolpe, Bernard. *Renaissance Handwriting: An Anthology of Italic Scripts*. London, 1960.

Febvre, Lucien, and Martin, Henri-Jean. *L'apparition du livre.* Paris, 1958.

Ficalho, Conde de. *Flora dos Lusíadas.* Lisbon, 1880.

Figueiredo, A. C. Borges de. *A geographia dos Lusíadas de Luis de Camoës.* Lisbon, 1883.

Filliozat, Jean. *Un catéchisme tamoul du XVIe siècle en lettres latines.* Pondichéry, 1967.

Firth, John R. *The Tongues of Men.* 2d ed. London, 1964.

Florio, John. *A Worlde of Wordes.* . . . London, 1598.

Fornari, Simone. *La spositione sopra l'Orlando furioso di M. Lodovico Ariosto.* Florence, 1549.

Foucault, Michel. *Les mots et les choses.* Paris, 1966.

Frede, Carlo de. *La prima traduzione italiana del Corano sullo sfondo dei rapporti tra Christianità e Islam nel Cinquecento.* Naples, 1967.

Friedensburg, Walter, ed. *Nuntiaturberichte aus Deutschland, erste Abtheilung, 1553–1559.* Gotha, 1892.

Fueck, Johann. *Die arabischen Studien in Europa bis zu dem Anfang des 20. Jahrhunderts.* Leipzig, 1955.

Gelb, Ignace J. *A Study of Writing: The Foundations of Grammatology.* Chicago, 1952.

Gesner, Konrad. *Mithridates: De differentiis linguarum tum veterum tum quae hodie apud diversas nationes in toto orbe terrarū in sus sunt . . . observationes.* Zurich, 1555.

Giuletti, Francesco. *Storia delle scritture veloci (dall' antichità ad oggi).* Florence, 1968.

Godefroy, Frederic. *Dictionnaire de l'ancienne langue française et de tous ses dialectes du IXe au XVe siècle.* 14 vols. Paris, 1881–1902.

Gramaye, Jean-Baptiste. *Specimen litterarum et linguarum universi orbis.* Ath, 1622.

Gray, Louis H. *Foundations of Language.* New York, 1939.

Haex, David. *Dictionarivm Malaico-Latinvm et Latino-Malaicvm cum aliis qvamplvrimus quae quarta pagina edocebit.* Rome, 1621.

Hall, Robert A., Jr. *Bibliography of Italian Linguistics.* Baltimore, 1941.

Hallberg, Ivar. *L'Extrême Orient dans la littérature et la cartographie de l'Occident des XIIIe, XIVe, et XVe siècles.* Göteborg, 1906.

Hamada Kosaku [濱田耕作]. *Tenshō Ken'ō Shisetsu ki* [天正遣欧使節記] ("Chronicle of a Mission to Europe in the Tensho Period"). Tokyo, 1931.

Houtman, Frederick de. *Spraecke ende Woordboeck inde Maleysche ende Madagaskarsche Talen.* . . . Amsterdam, 1603.

Huguet, Edmond. *Mots disparus ou viellis depuis le XVIe siècle.* Geneva, 1967.

———. *Dictionnaire de la langue française du XVIe siècle.* 13 vols. Paris, 1925–47.

Hymes, Dell, ed. *Studies in the History of Linguistics: Traditions and Paradigms.* Bloomington, Ind., 1974.

Ishida Mikinosuke [石田幹之助]. *Ōjin no Shina kenkyū* [欧人の支那研究] ("Researches on China by Europeans"). Tokyo, 1932.

———. *Ō-Bei ni okeru Shina kenkyū* [欧米に於ける支那研究] ("Sinological Studies in Europe and the United States"). Tokyo, 1942.

Iversen, Erik. *The Myth of Egypt and Its Hieroglyphs.* Copenhagen, 1961.

Jal, Auguste. *Glossaire nautique: Répertoire polyglotte de termes de marine anciens et modernes.* Paris, 1850.

Johnson, Alfred Forbes. *Periods of Typography: The Italian Sixteenth Century.* London, 1926.

Joseph, Francesco de S. *Arte y reglas de la lengua Tagala.* Bataan, 1610.

Kahane, Henry, Kahane, Renée, and Tietze, Andreas. *The Lingua franca in the Levant.* Urbana, 1958.

Kahn, David. *The Codebreakers: The Story of Secret Writing.* New York, 1967.

Keynes, Geoffrey Langdon. *Dr. Timothie Bright, 1550–1615; A Survey of His Life, with a Bibliography of His Writings.* London, 1962.

Klaproth, Julius Heinrich. *Asia polyglotta.* Paris, 1823.

Knowlton, Edgar C. "Words of Chinese, Japanese, and Korean Origin in the Romance Languages." Ph.D. diss., Stanford University, 1959.

Kukenheim, Louis. *Contributions à l'histoire de la grammaire grecque, latine et hebraique à l'époque de la Renaissance.* Leyden, 1951.

Lagoa, João Antonio de Mascarenhas Judice, Visconde de. *Glossário toponímico de antiga historiografia portuguesa ultramarina . . . por nomes que divergem dos actuais.* Lisbon, 1950.

Lahovary, Nicholas. *Dravidian Origins and the West.* Bombay, 1963.

Lapesa, Rafael. *Historia de la lengua española.* 6th ed. Madrid, 1965.

Lapino, Agostino. *Diario Fiorentino di Agostino Lapino.* Edited by G. A. Corazzini. Florence, 1900.

Laures, Johannes. *Kirishitan Bunko: A Manual of Books and Documents on the Early Christian Missions in Japan.* Tokyo, 1940.

Lefevre, Renato. *L'Ethiopia nella stampa del primo Cinquecento.* Como, 1966.

Lefranc, Abel. *Les navigations de Pantagruel.* Paris, 1905.

Leitão, Humberto. *Dicionário da linguagem de marinha antiga e actual.* Lisbon, 1963.

Léon Pinelo, Antonio Rodriguez de. *Epítome de la biblioteca oriental i occidental, náutica i geográfica.* Buenos Aires, [1919]. Facsimile reprint of the Madrid edition of 1629.

Leroy, Maurice. *Main Trends in Modern Linguistics.* Berkeley and Los Angeles, 1967.

Leslau, Wolf. *An Annotated Bibliography of the Semitic Languages of Ethiopia.* New York, 1946.

Levi della Vida, Giorgio. *Ricerche sulla formazione del più antico fondo dei manoscritti orientali della Biblioteca Vaticana.* Vatican City, 1939.

———. *Studi orientalistici in onore di Giorgio Levi della Vida.* 2 vols. Rome, 1956.

Little, William, et al. *The Oxford Universal Dictionary on Historical Principles.* Revised and edited by C. T. Onions. 3d ed. Oxford, 1955.

Littmann, Enno. *Morgenländische Wörter im Deutschen, nebst einem Anhang über die amerikanischen Wörter.* Berlin, 1920. Reprint. Tübingen, 1924.

Lokotsch, Karl. *Etymologisches Wörterbuch der europäischen . . . Wörter orientalischen Ursprungs.* Heidelberg, 1927.

Lopes, David. *A expansão da lingua portuguesa no Oriente durante os séculos XVI, XVII, e XVIII.* Barcelos, 1936.

Maças, Delmira. *Os animais na linguagem portuguesa.* Lisbon, 1950–51.

Machado, José Pedro, ed. *Duarte Nunes de Leão: Origem da língua portuguesa.* Lisbon, 1945.

Machado, R. *A flora da India nos Lusíadas.* Lisbon, 1947.

Maffei, Giovanni Pietro. *Historiarum Indicarum libri XVI.* Venice, 1589.

Manuzio, Antonio, ed. *Viaggi fatti da Vinetia alla Tana, in Persia, in India et in Constantinopoli. . . .* Venice, 1545.

Marques-Rivière, Jean. *Amulettes, talismans, et pantacles dans les traditions orientales et occidentales.* Paris, 1950.

Matsuda Kiichi. *The Relations between Portugal and Japan.* Lisbon, 1965.

Medina, José Toribio. *La imprenta en Manila desde sus origenes hasta 1810.* Santiago de Chile, 1904.

Megiser, Hieronymus. *Thesaurus polyglottus: vel dictionarium multilingue: ex quadringentis circitur tam veteris, quam novi (vel potius antiquis incogniti) orbis nationum linguis, dialectis, idiomatibus et idiotismis, constans.* Frankfurt, 1603.

――――. *Chorographia Tartariae.* Leipzig, 1610.

――――. *Hodeporicon Indiae Orientalis.* Leipzig, 1608.

Meillet, Antoine, and Cohen, Marcel. *Les langues du monde.* Paris, 1924.

Menéndez Pidal, Ramón. *La lengua de Cristobal Colón.* Madrid, 1937.

Métral, Denyse. *Blaise de Vigenère, archéologue et critique d'art (1523-1596).* Paris, 1939.

Michaelis, Henriette. *A New Dictionary of the Portuguese and English Languages.* New York, 1945.

Migliorini, Bruno. *The Italian Language.* Abridged and recast by T. Gwynfor Griffith. New York, 1966.

Mollema, J. C., ed. *De eerste Schipvaart der Hollanders naar Oost-Indië, 1595-97.* The Hague, 1935.

Morais-Barbosa, Jorge. *A língua portuguêsa no mundo.* 2d rev. ed. Lisbon, 1969.

Mosto, Andrea da. *Il primo viaggio intorno al globo.* In *Raccolta di documenti e studi publicati dalla R. Commissione Colombiana.* Part V, Vol. III. Rome, 1894.

Muller, J., and Roth, E. *Aussereuropäische Druckereien im 16. Jahrhundert.* Baden-Baden, 1969.

Müller, Max. *Johann Albrecht von Widmanstetter, 1506-1557: Sein Leben und Wirken.* Bamberg, 1908.

――――. *Lectures on the Science of Language.* London, 1882.

Münster, Sebastian. *Chaldaica grammatica antehac a nemine attentata sed iam primum per Seb. Munsterum conscripta et edita no tam ad chaldaicos interpretes quam hebraeorum commentarios intelligendos, hebraicae linguae studiosis utilissima.* Basel, 1527.

Müntz, Eugène. *La bibliothèque du Vatican au XVIe siècle: Notes et documents.* Paris, 1886.

Naïs, Hélène. *Les animaux dans la poésie française de la Renaissance.* Paris, 1961.

Nève, Félix. *La Renaissance des lettres et l'essor de l'erudition ancienne en Belgique.* Louvain, 1890.

Nicot, Jean. *Thresor de la langue française. . . .* Paris, 1606.

Nimer, Miguel. *Influências Orientais na lingua Portuguesa: Os vocábulos Arabes, Arabizados, Persas e Turcos.* Vol. I. São Paulo, 1943.

Nocentini, Lodovico. *Il primo sinologico P. Matteo Ricci.* Florence, 1882.

Nunes de Leão, Duarte. *Origem da lingua portuguesa.* Lisbon, 1601.

Omont, Henri. *Alphabets grecs et hébreux publiés à Paris au XVIe siècle.* Paris, 1885.

————. *Journal autobiographique du cardinal Jérôme Aléandre (1480–1530), publié d'après les manuscrits de Paris et Udine.* Paris, 1895.

Paige, Paula Spurlin, trans. and ed. *The Voyage of Magellan: The Journal of Antonio Pigafetta. A Translation . . . from the Edition in the William L. Clements Library, University of Michigan, Ann Arbor.* Englewood Cliffs, N.J., 1969.

Palatino, Giovannibattista. *Libro . . . nel quale s'insegna à scrivere ogni sorti lettera antica et moderna, di qualunque natione. . . .* Rome, 1547.

————. *Compendio del gran volume dell'arte del bene, e leggiadramente scrivere tutte le sorti di lettere e caratteri. . . .* Venice, 1588.

Paquier, Jules. *Jérôme Aléandre et la principauté de Liège (1514–1540).* Paris, 1896.

Partridge, Eric. *Name into Words.* New York, 1950.

Pedersen, Holger. *Linguistic Science in the Nineteenth Century: Methods and Results.* Translated from Danish by J. W. Spargo. Cambridge, Mass., 1931.

Pelliot, Paul. *Notes on Marco Polo.* 3 vols. Paris, 1959–73.

————. *Inventaire sommaire des manuscrits et imprimés chinois de la Bibliothèque Vaticane.* Rome, 1922.

Pinpin, Tomas, and Magaurlua, J. *Vocabulario de Japon declarado primero en Portugues por los padres de la Compañia de Jesus de aquel reyno y agora em Castellano en el Colegio de Santo Thomas de Manila.* Manila, 1630.

Pirckheimer, Willibald. *Germaniae ex variis scriptoribus perbrevis explicatio.* Nuremberg, 1530.

Possevino, Antonio. *Biblioteca selecta qua agitur de ratione studiorum.* Rome, 1593.

Postel, Guillaume. *Des merveilles du monde.* Paris, 1552.

————. *Linguarum duodecim characteribus differentium alphabetum. . . .* Paris, 1538.

Potken, Johannes. *Psalterium in quatuor linguis hebrea, graeca, chaldea, i e aethiopica latina.* Cologne, 1518.

Pratt, I. A. *List of Grammars, Dictionaries, etc. of the Languages of Asia, Oceania, Africa, in the New York Public Library.* New York, 1909.

Predari, Francesco. *Origine e vicende dei Zingari: Con documenti. . . .* Milan, 1841.

Prilokar, A. K. *The Printing Press in India: Its Beginnings and Early Development.* Bombay, 1958.

Rajamanickam, R. P. *Doctrina Christam en lingua Malavar Tamil.* Tuticorin, 1963.

Rao, G. Subba. *Indian Words in English. . . .* Oxford, 1954.

Ravenstein, E. G., ed. *A Journal of the First Voyage of Vasco da Gama, 1497–99.* "Works Issued by the Hakluyt Society." O.S. No. 99. London, 1898.

Retana y Gamboa, Wenceslao. *La imprenta en Filipinas. . . .* Madrid, 1897.

Robin, Percy A. *Animal Lore in English Literature.* London, 1936.

Robins, Robert H. *A Short History of Linguistics.* London, 1967.

Rocca, Angelo. *Biblioteca apostolica vaticana a Sisto V in splendidiorem locum translata.* Rome, 1591.

Rodriguez, João. *Arte de lingoa de Iapam composta pello Padre Ioão Rodriguez Portugues da Côpanhia de Iesu divida em tres livros.* Nagasaki, 1604–8.

Rohlfs, Gerhard. *Manual de filología hispánica: Guía bibliográfica, crítica y metódica.* Bogotá, 1957.

Ross, Alan S. C. *Ginger: A Loan-Word Study.* Oxford, 1952.

Rossi, Paolo. *Clavis universalis.* Naples, 1960.

Ruano, Ferdinando. *Setti alphabeti di varie lettere.* . . . Rome, 1554.

Ruyl, A. C. *Spieghel van de Maleysche taal.* Amsterdam, 1612.

Sainéan, Lazar. *La langue de Rabelais.* Paris, 1923.

São Luiz, D. Francisco de (Cardinal Saraiva). *Glossário de vocábulos portuguezes derivados das linguas orientaes e africanas, excepto a Arabe.* Lisbon, 1837.

Sapir, Edward. *Language.* New York, 1921.

Saraiva, António J. *História da cultura em Portugal.* 2 vols. Lisbon, 1955.

Sassetti, Filippo. *Lettere edite e inedite di Filippo Sassetti.* Edited by E. Marcussi. Florence, 1855.

Scheil, Gustav. *Die Tierwelt in Luthers Bildersprache.* Bernburg, 1897.

Schultze, B., and Fritz, J. F. *Orientalisch- und Occidentalischer Sprachmeister, welcher nicht allein 100 Alphabete nebst ihrer Aussprache, so bey denen meisten Europäisch-Asiatisch-Afrikanisch und Amerikanischen Völkern und Nationen gebräuchlich sind.* . . . 2 parts in 1 vol. Leipzig, 1748.

Schurhammer, Georg. *Das kirchliche Sprachproblem in der japanischen Jesuitenmission des 16. und 17. Jahrhunderts.* Tokyo, 1928.

Schwab, M. *Les incunables orientaux et les impressions orientales au commencement du XVIᵉ siècle.* Paris, 1883. Reprinted. Nieuwkoop, 1965.

Secret, François. *Les kabbalistes chrétiens de la Renaissance.* Paris, 1965.

Segert, Stanislav, and Beránek, Karel. *Orientalistik an der Prager Universität.* 2 vols. Prague, 1967.

Serís, Homero. *Bibliografía de la lingüística española.* Bogotá, 1964.

Serjeantson, Mary S. *A History of Foreign Words in English.* 2d ed. London, 1961.

Silva Neto, Serafim da. *História da língua portuguêsa.* Rio de Janeiro, 1952.

Soares, João. *Cartinha para ensinar a ler e escrever.* Lisbon, 1550.

Speroni, Sperone. *Dialogo delle lingue e dialogo della rettorica: Con introduzione di Giuseppe De Robertis.* Lanciano, 1912.

Spitzer, Leo. *Linguistics and Literary History: Essays in Stylistics.* Princeton, 1948.

Staunton, G. T., ed. *The Historie of the great and mightie Kingdom of China.* . . . "Hakluyt Society Publications," O.S. Nos. 14–15. 2 vols. London, 1853–54.

Stegagno Picchio, L., ed. *João de Barros Dialogo em louvor da nossa linguagem.* . . . Modena, 1959.

Steinschneider, Moritz. *Die europäischen Übersetzungen aus dem Arabischen bis Mitte des 17. Jahrhunderts.* Graz, 1956.

Stewart, George R. *Names on the Land: A Historical Account of Place-naming in the United States.* Rev. ed. Boston, 1958.

Stoppell, Jacobus [Stoppel, Jakob]. *Repertorium in formam alphabeticam redactū.* . . . Memmingen, 1519.

Tarchagnota, Giovanni. *Delle historie del mondo.* . . . Venice, 1573.

Thani Nayagam, Xavier S. *A Reference Guide to Tamil Studies: Books.* Kuala Lumpur, 1966.

———. *Antão de Provençá's Tamil-Portuguese Dictionary, A.D. 1679.* Kuala Lumpur, 1966.

Thomsen, Vilhelm. *Geschichte der Sprachwissenschaft bis zum Ausgang des 19. Jahrhunderts.* Halle, 1927.

Thurneisser, Leonhart. *Onomasticon.* Berlin, 1572.

Tiraboschi, G. *Storia della letteratura italiana.* 9 vols. in 20. Florence, 1805–13.

Trithemius, Johannes. *Steganographia: hoc est: ars per occultam scripturam animi sui voluntatem absentibus aperiendi certa; . . . .* Frankfurt, 1606.

Ullman, Berthold L. *The Origin and Development of Humanistic Script.* Rome, 1960.

Valignano, Alessandro. *Catechismus christianae fidei. . . .* Lisbon, 1586.

Vasiliev, Alexander. *The Goths in the Crimea.* Cambridge, Mass., 1936.

Velho, Alvaro. See Ravenstein, E. G., ed. "Hakluyt Society Publications," 1st ser., No. 99. London, 1898.

Vermeer, Hans. *Das Indo-Englische Situation und linguistische Bedeutung.* Heidelberg, 1969.

Vernero, Michele. *Studi critici sopra la geografia nell' Orlando furioso.* Turin, 1913.

Vigenère, Blaise de. *Traicté des chiffres.* Paris, 1586.

Viñaza, Conde de la. *Biblioteca histórica de la filología castellana.* Madrid, 1893.

———. *Escritos de los castellanos y portugueses referentes a las lenguas de China y el Japon.* Lisbon, 1892.

Vittorio, Mariano. *Chaldeae seu Aethiopicae linguae institutiones.* Rome, 1552.

Vries de Heekelingen, Herman de, ed. *Correspondance de Bonaventura Vulcanius pendant son séjour à Cologne, Genève, et Bâle (1573–1577). . . .* The Hague, 1923.

Vulcanius, Bonaventura. *De litteris et lingua Getarum sive Gothorum. . . .* Leyden, 1597.

Wardrop, James. *The Script of Humanism: Some Aspects of Humanistic Script, 1460–1560.* Oxford, 1863.

Waser, Caspar. *Mithridates Gesneri, exprimens differentias linguarum, tum veterum, tum quae hodie, per totum terrarum orbem, in usu sunt. . . .* Zürich, 1610.

Weekley, Ernest. *Something about Words.* London, 1935.

Weinreich, Uriel. *Languages in Contact: Findings and Problems.* New York, 1953.

Whitney, William D. *Oriental and Linguistic Studies.* New York, 1873–74.

Wiest, Donald H. *The Precensorship of Books.* Washington, D.C., 1953.

Wijnman, H. F. *The Origin of Arabic Typography in Leiden.* Leyden, 1957.

Wilkins, John. *Essay toward a Real Character.* London, 1668.

Williams, Edwin B. *From Latin to Portuguese.* 2d ed. Philadelphia, 1962.

Willis, Edmond. *An Abbreviation of Writing by Character.* London, 1618.

Xavier, Francis. *Epistolae S. Francisci Xaverii aliaque eius scripta.* 2 vols. Edited by Georg Schurhammer and J. Wicki. Rome, 1945.

Zaccaria, Enrico. *L'elemento iberico nella lingua italiana.* Bologna, 1927.

———. *Contributo allo studio degl' iberismi in Italia e della Wechselbeziehung fra le lingue romanze ossia voci e frasi spagnuole e portoghesi nel Sassetti aggiuntievi quelle del Carletti e del Magalotti.* Turin, 1905.

ARTICLES

Allen, P. S. "The Trilingual College of the Early Sixteenth Century." In *Erasmus, Lectures and Wayfaring Sketches*, pp. 138–63. Oxford, 1934.

Alston, R. C., and Danielsson, B. "The Earliest Dictionary of the Known Languages of the World." *Newberry Library Bulletin*, VI (1966), 211–15.

Alvarez-Taladriz, J. L. "Cacería de refranes en el 'Vocabulario de lingoa de Japam.'" *Monumenta nipponica*, X (1954), 169–92.

Arngart, O. S., et al. "The Earliest Dictionary of the Known Languages of the World." *English Studies Presented to R. W. Zandvoort on the Occasion of His Seventieth Birthday*, supplement to *English Studies*, XLV (Amsterdam, 1964), 9–13.

Aurousseau, Leonard. "Sur le nom de Cochinchine." *Bulletin de l'École française d'Extrême-Orient* (Hanoi), XXIV (1924), 562–79.

Ballini, Ambrogio. "Il contributo delle missioni alla conoscenza delle lingue e della cultura dell' India." In C. Costantini *et al.*, ed., *Le missioni cattoliche e la cultura dell' Oriente*, pp. 233–60. Rome, 1943.

Bandmann, G. "Das Exotische in der europäischen Kunst." In *Der Mensch und die Künste: Festschrift Heinrich Lützeler*, pp. 337–54. Düsseldorf, 1962.

Barberi, Francesco. "Libri e stampatori nella Roma dei Papa." *Studi romani*, XIII (1965), 433–56.

Bausani, Alessandro. "The First Italian-Malay Vocabulary by Antonio Pigafetta," *East and West* (Rome), XI (1960), 229–48.

Bertieri, Raffaello. "Italienische Kalligraphen und Schriftkünstler im 16. Jahrhundert." *Gutenberg Jahrbuch*, IV (1929), 269–86.

———. "Un disegnatore di caratteri italiano del XVI secolo, poco noto." *Gutenberg Jahrbuch*, XV (1940), 63–70.

Biermann, Benno. "Chinesische Sprachstudien in Manila." *Neue Zeitschrift für Missionswissenschaft*, VII (1951), 18–23.

Bischoff, Bernard. "The Study of Foreign Languages in the Middle Ages." *Speculum*, XXXVI (1961), 209–24.

Blagden, C. O., ed. and trans. "Two Malay Letters from Ternate in the Moluccas, Written in 1521 and 1522." *Bulletin of the School of Oriental Studies* (London), VI (1930–32), 87–101.

Bonfante, Giuliano. "Ideas on the Kinship of the European Languages from 1200 to 1800." *Journal of World History*, I (1953–54), 679–99.

Borchardt, Frank L. "Etymology in Tradition and in the Northern Renaissance." *Journal of the History of Ideas*, XXIX (1968), 415–29.

Boxer, Charles R. "Padre João Rodriguez Tçuzu S.J. and His Japanese Grammars of 1604 and 1620." In *Miscelânea de filologia, literatura e história cultural a memória de Francisco Adolfo Coelho (1874–1919)*, II, 338–63. Lisbon, 1950.

Braga, J. M. "The Beginning of Printing at Macao." *Studia*, XII (1963), 29–138.

Briggs, Laurence P. "The Appearance and Historical Usage of the Terms Tai, Thai, Siamese and Lao." *Journal of the American Oriental Society*, LXIX (1949), 60–73.

Caland, W. "Roberto De' Nobili and the Sanskrit Language and Literature." *Acta orientalia*, III (Lund, 1904), 38–51.

Cardon, L., trans., and Hosten, H., ed. "Earliest Jesuit Printing in India. From the Spanish of the Rev. Cecelio Gomez Rodeles, S.J." *Journal of the Asiatic Society of Bengal*, IX (1913), 149–68.

Carvalho, J. G. C. Herculano de. "O vocabulário exótico na *Histoire des Indes* (1553)." *Biblos*, XXVII (1951), 397–420.

Casamassima, Emanuelle. "Ancora su Ludovico degli Arrighi Vicentino (notizie 1510–1527). Risultati di une 'recognitio.'" *Gutenberg Jahrbuch*, XL (1965), 35–42.

———. "I disegni di caratteri di Ludovico degli Arrighi Vicentino notizie (1510–1527)." *Gutenberg Jahrbuch*, XXXVIII (1963), 24–36.

Chamberlain, B. H. "Rodriguez' System of Transliteration." *Transactions of the Asiatic Society of Japan*, XVI (1889), 10–16.

Chasca, Edmundo de. "The Phonology of the Speech of the Negroes in Early Spanish Drama." *Hispanic Review*, XIV (1946), 322–39.

Chastel, André. "Notes sur le sphinx à la Renaissance." *Archivio di filosofia, umanesimo e simbolismo* (Padua), 1958, pp. 179–87.

Chavannes, Edouard. "Le cycle turc des douze animaux." *T'oung pao*, 2d ser. VII (1906), 51–122.

Cidade, Hernani. "João de Barros: O que pensa da lingua portuguesa—como a escreve." In *Miscelânea de filologia, literatura, e história cultural a memória de Francisco Adolfo Coelho (1847–1919)*, II, 282–89. Lisbon, 1950.

Colomiès, Paul. "Gallia orientalis." In *Opera theologici, critici et historici*, pp. 59–66. Hamburg, 1709.

Conrady, August. "Alte westöstlichen Kulturwörter." *Berichte über die Verhandlungen der sächsischen Akademie der Wissenschaften zu Leipzig, philologisch-historische Klasse*, III, 3–19. Leipzig, 1925.

Cortelazzo, Manlia. "Rapporti linguistici fra Mediterraneo ed oceano Indiano." In M. Cortelazzo, ed., *Mediterranée et Océan Indien*, pp. 293–306. Venice, 1970.

Dan, Robert. "The First Hebrew Printed Texts in Vienna." *Studies in Bibliography and Booklore*, IX (1970), 101–5.

Deecke, W. "Ueber das indische Alphabet in seinem Zusammenhang mit den übrigen südsemitischen Alphabeten." *Zeitschrift der deutschen morgenländischen Gesellschaft*, XXXI (1877), 598–612.

Derrett, J. D. M. "Thomas More and Joseph the Indian." *Journal of the Royal Asiatic Society*, 1962, pp. 18–34.

———. "The Utopian Alphabet." *Moreana*, XII (1966), 61–66.

Dieckmann, L. "Renaissance Hieroglyphics." *Comparative Literature*, IX (1957), 308–21.

Doi, Tadao. "Researches in the Japanese Language Made by the Jesuit Missionaries in the XVIth and XVIIth Centuries." *Proceedings of the Imperial Academy of Japan* (Tokyo), XIII (1937), 232–36.

———. "A Review of Jesuit Missionaries' Linguistic Studies of the Japanese Language in the 16th and 17th Centuries." Japanese National Commission for UNESCO, *International Symposium on History of Eastern and Western Cultural Contacts*, 1957, pp. 215–23. Tokyo, 1959.

————. "Das Sprachstudium der Gesellschaft Jesu in Japan im 16. und 17. Jahrhundert." *Monumenta nipponica*, II (1939), 437–65.

Dorez, Léon. "Le Cardinal Marcello Cervini et l'imprimerie à Rome (1539–1550)." *École française de Rome, Mélanges*, XII (1892), 289–313.

————. "Recherches sur la bibliothèque du Cardinal Girolamo Aleandro." *Revue des bibliothèques*, II (1892), 49–68; VII (1897), 293–304.

————. "Recherches et documents sur la bibliothèque du Cardinal Sirleto." *Mélanges d'archéologie et d'histoire*, XI (1891), 457–91.

Duyvendak, J. J. L. "Early Chinese Studies in Holland." *T'oung pao*, XXXII (1936), 293–344.

Edwards, E. D., and Blagden, C. O., eds. and trans. "A Chinese Vocabulary of Malacca Malay Words and Phrases Collected between A.D. 1403 and 1511 [?]." *Bulletin of the School of Oriental Studies* (London), VII (1930–32), 715–49.

Ehrle, Franz. "Zur Geschichte der Catalosierung der Vatikana." *Historisches Jahrbuch*, XI (1890), 718–29.

Ewert, A. "Dante's Theory of Language." *Modern Language Review*, XXXV (1940), 355–66.

Filliozat, Jean, ed. and trans. "Un catéchisme tamoul du XVIᵉ siècle en lettres latines." *Publications de l'Institut français d'Indologie* (Pondichery), Vol. XXXIII (1967).

Fokker, A. A. "Quelques mots espagnols et portugais d'origine orientale, dont l'étymologie ne se trouve pas ou est insuffisamment expliquée dans les dictionnaires." *Zeitschrift für romanische Philologie*, XXXIV (1910), 560–68; XXXVIII (1914), 481–85.

Freitas, Jordão A. de, and Gonçálvez Viana, A. R. "Subsídios para a bibliographia portugueza, relativa ao estudo da lingua do Japão." *O Instituto*, LI (1904), 762–68; LII (1905), 115–28, 310–20, 437–48, 499–512.

Giese, Wilhelm. "Mots malaisiens empruntés au Portugais," Congresso (Actas do IX) Internacional de Linguistica Românica. I. Lisboa Centro de Estudos Filológicos 1961. *Boletim de filologia*, Vol. XVIII (1959), 275–94.

————. "Notas sôbre a fala dos negros em Lisboa no principio do século XVI." *Revista lusitânia*, XXX (1932), 251–57.

Gonda, J. "Pigafetta's vocabularium van het Molukken-Maleisch." *Bijdragen tot de taal-, land- en volkenkunde van Nederlandsch-Indië*, XCVII (1938), 101–24.

Gutierrez, L. C. "Dos grandes bibliotecas del Extremo-Oriente para la Nacional de Madrid." *Gutenberg Jahrbuch*, XXXIV (1959), 120–26.

Hall, Robert Anderson. "Linguistic Theory in the Italian Renaissance." *Language*, XII (1936), 96–107.

Hamada Atsushi. "The Nature of the Research in the Japanese Language Carried out by the Jesuit Missionaries in the 16th and 17th centuries." Japanese National Commission for UNESCO, *International Symposium on History of Eastern and Western Cultural Contacts, 1957*, pp. 233–37. Tokyo, 1959.

Han, Yu-shan. "A Historical Survey of Some Geographical Names of China." *Sinologica*, I (1947), 152–70.

Hirth, Friedrich. "Fremdwörter aus dem Chinesischen." *Archiv für das Studium der neueren Sprachen und Litteraturen*, LXVII (1882), 197–212.

————. "Words Introduced from the Chinese into European Languages." *China Review*, II (1873), 95–103.

Hoenigswald, Henry M. "Linguistics in the Sixteenth Century." *Library Chronicle*, XX (1954), 1–4.

Holmes, Urban T. "French Words of Chinese Origin." *Language*, X (1934), 280–85.

Johnson, Alfred Forbes. "A Catalogue of Italian Writing Books of the Sixteenth Century," *Signature*, N.S. X (1950), 22–48.

Josten, C. H. "A Translation of John Dee's 'Monas Hieroglyphica' (Antwerp, 1564) with an Introduction and Annotations." *Ambix*, XII (1964), 84–221.

Kahane, Henry, and Kahane, Renée. "Two Nautical Terms of Greek Origin: *Typhoon* and *Galley*." In *Etymologica: Walther von Wartburg zum siebzigsten Geburtstag, 18. Mai 1958*, pp. 417–39. Tübingen, 1958.

Kern, W. "Waar verzamelde Pigafetta zijn Maleise woorden?" *Tijdschrift voor Indische taal-, land- en volkenkunde*, LXXVIII (1938), 271–73.

Knowlton, Edgar C., Jr. "Antão de Provença's Vocabulario Tamulico Lusitano-Indo-Portuguese Elements." *Tamil Culture*, XI (1964), 135–64.

Koda Shigetomo [幸田成友]. "Ito Mansho no ni-shokan" [伊藤満所の二書朝] ("Ito Mancio's Two Epistles"). *Shirin* [史林] (Journal of History [of the *Shigaku kenkyu kai* of Kyoto Imperial University]), XVI, No. 2 (1931), 81–91.

————. "Notes sur la presse jésuite au Japon et plus spécialement sur les livres imprimés en caractères japonais." *Monumenta nipponica*, II (1939), 42–53.

König, K. "Ueberseeische Wörter im Französischen vom 16–18. Jahrhundert." In *Beihefte zur Zeitschrift für romanische Philologie*, XCI (Halle, 1939).

Kraner, Werner. "Zur englischen Kurzschrift im Zeitalter Shakespeares: Das Jane-Seager-Manuscript [The Divine Prophecies of the Ten Sibyls]." *Shakespeare Jahrbuch*, LXVII (1931), 26–61.

Krom, N. J. "De naam Sumatra." *Bijdragen tot de taal-, land- en volkenkunde van Nederlandsch-Indië*, C (1941), 5–25.

Lasinio, F. "Di alcune voci italiane credute d'origine orientale." *Giornale società asiatica italiana*, III (1889), 140–48.

Laufer, Berthold. "The Name China." *T'oung pao*, 2d ser. XIII (1912), 710–26.

Lefevre, Renato. "Documenti pontifici sui rapporti con l'Ethiopia nei secoli XV e XVI." *Rassegna di studi ethiopici*, V (1946), 17–41.

————. "Appunti sull'ospizio di S. Stefano degli 'Indiani' nel Cinquecento." *Studi romani*, XV (1967), 16–33.

Le Roux, C. C. F. M. "Nogmaals Pigafetta's Maleische woorden." *Tijdschrift voor Indische taal-, land- en volkenkunde*, LXXIX (1939), 446–51.

Leroy, Maurice. "La classification en linguistique." In *La classification dans les sciences*, pp. 132–54. Gembloux, 1963.

Loewe, Richard. "Über einige europäische Wörter exotischer Herkunft." *Zeitschrift für vergleichende Sprachforschung*, LX (1933), 45–84; LXI (1934), 37–136.

Lubac, H. de, and Bernard-Maître, Henri. "L'humanisme européen et les civilisations d'Extrême-Asie: Le découverte du bouddhisme." *Bulletin de l'association Guillaume Budé* (Paris), 3d ser. No. 3 (1953), 97–112.

Machado, José Pedro. "Lexicologia científica de origem oriental nos *Colóquios dos Simples e Drogas*." *Garcia da Orta*, XI (1963), 755–88.

Meersman, A. "Notes on the Study of Indian Languages by the Franciscans." *Neue Zeitschrift für Missionswissenschaft*, XVI (1960), 40–54.

Metcalf, George J. "The Views of Konrad Gesner on Language." In *Studies in Germanic Languages and Literatures in Memory of Fred O. Nolte*, pp. 15–26. St. Louis, 1963.

Murakami Naojirō [村上直次郎]. "Ōtomo Ōmura Arima sanke shisetsu no kanshajō. (san-tsū)." [大友大村有馬三家使節の感謝状 (三通)] ("A Letter in Appreciation from the Envoys of the Three Clans of Ōtomo, Ōmura, and Arima. [Three Letters]), *Shigaku Zasshi*, XII (1901), 496–504.

———. "New Historical Materials concerning an Embassy to Spain and Italy." *Shigaku-Zasshi*, XIV (1903), 360–65.

Nachod, O. "Die ersten Kenntnisse chinesischen Schriftzeichen im Abendlande." *Asia Major*, I (1923), 235–73.

Nair, V. B. "A Nair Envoy to Portugal." *Indian Antiquary*, LVII (1928), 157–59.

Nestle, Eberhard. "Aus einem sprachwissenschaftlichen Werk von 1539." *Zeitschrift der deutschen morgenländischen Gesellschaft*, LVIII (1904), 601–16.

Panhuys, L. C. van. "Indian Words in the Dutch Language and in Use at Dutch Guiana." *Bijdragen tot de taal-, land- en volkenkunde van Nederlandsch-Indië*, LVI (1904), 611–14.

Parks, G. B. "More's Utopia and Geography." *Journal of English and Germanic Philology*, XXXVIII (1938), 224–36.

Paschini, Pio. "Un cardinale editore: Marcello Cervini." In *Miscellanea di scritti di bibliografia ed erudizione in memoria di Luigi Ferrari*, pp. 383–413. Florence, 1952.

Peixoto da Fonseca, Fernando Venâncio. "Vocábulos franceses de origem portuguesa vernácula." *Revista de Portugal*, XXI (1956), 348–53; XXII (1957), 26–30, 50–53, 82–86, 111–16, 166–70, 207–11, 254–57.

———. "Vocábulos franceses de origem portuguesa exotica." *Revista de Portugal*, XXXI (1966), 105–8; XXXIII (1968), 115–19, 178–82.

Pelliot, Paul. "L'origine du nom de 'China.'" *T'oung pao*, 2d ser. XIII (1912), 722–42.

Phelan, John L. "Philippine Linguistics and Spanish Missionaries, 1565–1700." *Mid-America* (Chicago), XXXVII (1955), 153–70.

Pons, Émile. "Les langues imaginaires dans le voyage utopique, un precurseur: Thomas More." *Revue de littérature comparée*, X (1930), 589–607.

Post, H. Houwens. "A terminologia portuguesa ou aportuguesada do *Itinerário, viagem ou navegação à India Oriental ou portuguesa* de João Huyghen Van Linschoten." *Revista de Portugal*, XXV (1960), 349–61, 454–72.

Radojičič, Djordje S. "Die ersten Serbischen Druckereien." *Gutenberg Jahrbuch*, XV (1940), 248–54.

Ridolfi, Roberto. "Nuovi contributi sulle 'stamperia papali' di Paolo III." *La bibliofilia*, L (1948), 183–97.

Riemens, K. J. "Het spraeck ende woord-boeck van Fr. de Houtman en de vocabulaire van Noël de Barlaimont." *Het Boek*, VII (1918), 193–96.

Rijckmans, J. "L'orientalisme à Louvain avant 1936." *Le Muséon* (Louvain), LXXIX (1966), 13–33.

Rocher, Ludo. "Les philologues classiques et les débuts de la grammaire comparée." *Revue de l'Université de Bruxelles*, X (1958), 251–86.

———. "Paulinus a Sancto Bartholomaeo on the Kinship of the Languages of India and Europe." *Adyar Library Bulletin*, XXV (1961), 321–52.

Ross, E. Denison. "New Light on the History of the Chinese Oriental College, and a 16th Century Vocabulary of the Luchuan Language." *T'oung pao*, 2d ser. IX (1908), 689–95.

Sainéan, Lazar. "Rabelaisiana—Le Montville de Rabelais." *Revue des études rabelaisiennes*, IX (1911), 265–75.

Saltini, Guglielmo Enrico. "Della stamperia orientale medicea e di Giovan Battista Raimondi." *Giornale storia degli archivi toscani*, IV (1860), 237–96.

Schilling, Dorotheus. "Christliche Druckereien in Japan (1590–1614)." *Gutenberg Jahrbuch*, XV (1940), 356–95.

Schlegel, G. "Etymologie of the Word Taifun." *T'oung pao*, VII (1896), 581–85.

Schurhammer, Georg. "Some Malayalam Words and Their Identification." *Kerala Society Papers*, I (1930), 221–24.

———. "Letters of D. João da Cruz in the National Archives of Lisbon." *Kerala Society Papers*, I (1930), 304–7. Also in *Varia. I. Anhänge*. Lisbon and Rome, 1965.

———. "Some Remarks on Series 4 of K. S. P. [Kerala Society Papers]." *Kerala Society Papers*, I (1930), 303–4. Also in *Varia. I. Anhänge*. Lisbon and Rome, 1965.

———. "Ein seltener Druck (Der erste gedruckte tamulische Katechismus)." *Die katholischen Missionen* (Bonn), LVIII (1930), 211–12.

———. "Der Marathidichter Thomas Stephens S. I., Neue Dokumente." In L. Szilas, ed., *Orientalia*, pp. 383–88. Lisbon, 1963.

———, and Cottrell, G. W. "The First Printing in Indian Characters." *Harvard Library Bulletin*, VI (1952), 147–60.

Secret, François. "Les Jésuites et la Kabbale." *Bibliothèque d'humanisme et renaissance*, XX (1958), 542–55.

Sinor, Denis. "Mongol and Turkic Words in the Latin Versions of John of Plano Carpini's Journey to the Mongols (1245–1247)." In Louis Ligeti, ed., *Mongolian Studies*. Amsterdam, 1970.

Sommerfelt, Alf. "The Origin of Language, Theories and Hypotheses." *Journal of World History*, I (1953–54), 885–902.

Sousa Viterbo, Francesco Marques de. "Noticia de alguns arabistas e interpretes de linguas Africanas e Orientaes," *O Instituto*, LII (1905), 367–74, 417–25, 491–98, 547–52, 683–93, 749–61; LIII (1906), 48–53, 107–14, 237–41; LVI (1909), 22–33, 62–72, 105–19, 168–82, 229–38, 298–308, 360–72, 452–63, 520–29, 600–610.

Szczeniak, Boleslaw. "The Origin of Chinese Language according to Athanasius Kircher's Theory." *Journal of the American Oriental Society*, LXXII (1952), 21–29.

Tervarent, Guy de. "Un humaniste: Piero Valeriano." *Journal des Savants*, 1967, pp. 162–71.

Thani Nayagam, Xavier S. "The First Printed Books in Tamil." *Tamil Culture*, VII (1958), 288–301.

Tsuboi Kumazō [坪井九馬三]. "Ōtomo Ōmura Arima sanke shisetsu Enechia seifu e teiseshi kanshajō" [大友大村有馬三家使節ゑねちあ政府

へ呈せし感謝状] ("A Letter in Appreciation Presented to the Government of Venetia [Venice] by the Envoy from the Ōtomo, Ōmura, and Arima Clans"). *Shigaku Zasshi*, XII (1901), 616–20.

Vermeer, Hans J. "Indisch *boy*." In Robert Schmitt-Brandt, ed., *Donum Indogermanicum: Festgabe für Anton Sherer*, pp. 70–81. Heidelberg, 1971.

Wardrop, James. "The Vatican Scriptors." *Signature*, N.S. V (1948), 3–28.

———. "*Civis Romanus sum*, Giovanbattista Palatino and His Circle." *Signature*, N.S. XIV (1952), 3–38.

Wijnman, H. F. "De studie van het Ethiopisch en de ontwikkeling van de Ethiopische typographie in West Europa in de 16de eeuw." *Het Boek*, XXXII (1955–57), 225–46.

Yamagiwa, Joseph K. "Revisions in the Rakuyōshū at the Time of Its Printing in 1598." *Monumenta nipponica*, XI (1955), 185–94.

Yu, Margaret W. S. "Words and Things." *Studies in Linguistics* (Buffalo), XX (1968), 7–36.

Index

[735]

Index

Index

Enkhuizen, 359

Erasmus of Rotterdam, 6, 228, 324, 355; geographical interests, 20; and Góis, 19–20; and John III of Portugal, 19–20; library of, 72; and Ptolemy, 449; and spice trade, 20

Eratosthenes, 446

Erbard, Jean, 34

Ercilla, Alonso de, 179

Erik XIV, king of Sweden: golden globe of, 486

Erizzo, Sebastiano, 212 n.

Ernst, archduke, regent of Netherlands, 63

Ernst, duke of Bavaria: library of, 58

Escalante, Bernardino, 188, 401, 494 n.; in English, 374, 537; and González de Mendoza, 189

Escorial, El, 185; Chinese books at, 47; library of, 72

Essais of Montaigne, 293, 294; on barbarism, 295; and overseas discoveries, 295; on Portugal and East, 296; sources, 295; and spice trade, 295; universality of moral precepts 297; variety in manners and morals, 297

Estaço, Aquilas (Statius), 9–10; personal library of, 10

Este, Alfonso d', 49

Este, Borso d', 49; library of, 205

Este, Ercole I d', 48, 202, 254

Este, Ippolito d', 204, 254

Este, Isabella d' (Gonzaga), 166, 168, 199; library of, 49–50; world map of, 202, 206

Este, Lionello d', 49

Este, Luigi d', 215 n.

Este family, 214, 477; and Ariosto, 205; book collections of, 48–50, 202; and map collecting, 477

Étaples, Lefèvre d', 162

Ethiopia, 90, 307, 504; Bodin on, 312; church, 23; and Góis, 18, 23; Portugal's relations with, 23

Euphuism (in English literature), 374, 387, 391; Sidney on, 384; and similes and antitheses, 384

Europe, 401; alchemy of, 421; algebra of, 409; algorism in, 399, 407; and anatomical dissection, 399; ancient ideas of India, 90–91; Arabic astronomical texts in, 411; arms of, 404; artisans of, 406–7; and Asian languages, 491, 518, 526, 532–33; Asians in, 231, 494, 497, 500; astrology of, 411; astronomy of, 410; book collections of, 42–43; books in Oriental languages in, 504, 511, 515 n., 528, 529; borrowings from Asia, 398, 400, 401, 403, 444; botanical gardens of, 441; botanical study in, 429–31; calendar reform in, 414; and Catalans, 411; Chinese in, 231, 497; Chinese books in, 504, 511, 515 n., 528; Christian writers on India, 89–90; common vocabulary of, 539; continuous screw of, 398 n.; criticisms of, 273; and Crusades, 100, 109, 330; cultivation of Asian plants, 441, 442; and energy,

399, 400; fireworks in, 404 n.; first map printed in, 450 n.; folk calendars of, 408; geographical conceptions of Japan, 484; and Hindu astronomy, 410; Hindu-Arabic mathematics in, 398, 408; and historical chronicle, 317; and Holy Roman Empire, 326; and ideographic languages, 494; images of Asia, 109–10, 216, 451, 484; imports, 233, 425; imports from Asia, 401, 405, 444; inflation in, 327; internal migrations, 404, 406; international trade of, 326; and Islam, 215; Japanese emissaries to, 53 n., 54, 61–62, 481, 494–95, 497; Jesuit "living letters" in, 32; lacquerware of, 405; language study in, 502, 507, 540; loan words of Asiatic origin (appendix), 544–54; in Macer's satire, 271; machines of, 400; and magnetism, 399; and Malay blowgun (*sumpitan*), 399; methods of basic production, 400; migration of artisans in, 406; migration of Asian inventions to, 398; migration of Indian tales to, 100–102, 108–9; "mirrors of princes" of, 105–7, 111; Mongol invasions of, 100, 109, 232, 330; moral problems of, 37; newsletters in, 54, 57, 66; oranges in, 441–42; Oriental stereotypes in, 380–81; orthography of, 538; and Ottoman Empire, 226, 557; paddle-wheel boats of, 403; and perpetual motion idea, 399; plants from Asia in, 443; playing cards in, 399; and pointed arch and vault of Indian Buddhist architecture, 398; porcelain manufacture in, 404; Portuguese in, 74; Postel's criticism of, 269; printing in Oriental languages, 527; reactions to Asia, 83–84; Sanskrit studies in, 100–102; scientific instruments of, 406; ship construction in, 417, 421; Sinophilism of, 234–35, 250; sermon books of, 110; Spain's position in, 161–63; spiritual qualities of, 268; stereotypes of, 85; superiority of, 400, 444; syphilis in, 424; Tartar slaves in, 399; technological superiority of, 397, 400; and tolerance, 252; transmission of Buddha story to, 102; transportation, 403; travel books of, 109, 111; and Turks, 228–29, 250, 254; vernacular literatures of, 83; vocabulary, 490–91; and wheelchair, 403; and zinc, 425. *See also* Asia; Language; Printing

Euthynius of Athos, 103

Évora, 32, 123, 498

Exempla: in sermon books, 110

Exoticism: in English literature, 371; and Goulart's commentaries, 283–84; in Latin verse, 371–72; in literature, 290, 330, 371, 391; in novel, 290; in Rabelais, 262, 264 n. *See also* Language

Fabrice, Arnauld, 31

Facio, Bartolomeo, 97

Index

347, 355, 387, 505, 558; and censorship, 40, 146; *Chronicle of King Manuel*, 144–45; and Erasmus, 19; collected works, 25; and historical theory, 148; and Humanism, 144, 148–49; library of, 44; at Louvain, 465; and John More, 368; and Thomas More, 17, 368; and Osório, 147–48; in Padua, 224; and pagans, 148; and Protestantism, 17, 19; sources, 144–45, 147

Gomara, Francisco López de, 46, 172–73, 175, 191, 230, 292, 295, 358; in French, 280; *Historia general de las Indias*, 174; and Thevet, 305

Gomes de Brito, Bernardo: *História trágico-maritima*, 131–35

Gongora, Luis de, 157, 184, 186

Gonsalves, Juan, 496

Gonzaga, Federico: library of, 50

Gonzaga, Francesco, 49

Gonzaga, Isabella d'Este. *See* Este, Isabella d'

González de Mendoza, Juan, 189–90, 211, 217, 235, 238, 238 n., 240, 246, 295, 297, 387, 391, 392, 401, 494 n., 532; in Arrivabene's *Il magno Vitei*, 221; and Barahona de Soto, 182–83; and Barros, 189; and Matthias Dresser, 348; in Dutch, 360; in English, 375, 537; and Escalante, 189; in French, 296, 537; in German, 347; in Latin, 538; in Spanish, 360

Gorizia: Mattioli at, 431

Goulart, Simon, 25, *282–84*, 294, 296, 321; annotations to *Sepmaine*, 282, 284; and Du Bartas, 283; *Histoire de Portugal*, 282; *Histoires admirables*, 287

Gourmont, Hieronymous, 476

Gouveia, André de, 12, 30, 31, 293

Gouveia, António de, 11, 12

Gouveia, Diogo de (the Elder), 11, 30, 31

Gracian, 163 n.

Granada, 179

Granada, Luis de, 37 n.

Granjon, Robert, 528

Granvelle, Antoine Perrenot de, cardinal: library of, 63

Grapheus, Cornelius, 16

Gravius, Henricus, 105

Gray, Richard, 232

Gray of Wilton, Lord, 373

Greece: Hellenistic age, 86; Homeric age, 85–86; Pythagoreanism in, 86, 407 n.; relations with India, 88

Greek language: manuscripts in, 512; study of in Europe, 507

Green, Thomas, 374 n.

Gregory XIII, pope, 189, 234, 414, 528; and cartography, 464

Grieninger, Johann, 335

Grolier, Jean: library of, 66–67

Grotius (Hugo de Groot), 357; on sailing chariots, 402

Groto, Luigi, 214

Grouchy, Nicolas de, 71, 274–75, 293, 294, 321, 343, 536; translation of Castanheda, 31–32, 66, 274, 275

Gruget, Claude, 286

Grüninger, Martin, 455

Grynaeus, Simon, 19, 60, 331, 339–41, 387, 416; and Thomas More, 368

Gryphius, Sebastien, 254

Gualdo, Paulo, 51

Guarino da Verona, 97

Guazzo, Steffano, 220

Gubbio, 98

Guérente, Guillaume, 31

Guicciardini, Francesco, 27, 224

Guintherius, Johannes, 424 n.

Giustiniani, Marc Antonio, 212

Gunpowder: Chinese invention of, 404

Guyon, Loys, 286

Guzman, Luis de, 44, 192; on Japanese language, 530

Gymnosophists, 90, 95, 96, 365

Habsburg: book collections, 55. *See* Germany; Holy Roman Empire

Haex, David, 357 n.

Hakluyt, Richard, 380, 382, 383, 386, 392, 467, 472, 478, 537; correspondence, 375; and geography, 474; at Oxford, 482; and travel books, 474; vocabularies, 493; world chart, 475

Hall, John Leonard, 472

Hall, Joseph, *385–86*, 388, 392

Hamburg, 326; Paracelsus in, 422

Hamel, Jacques du, 284 n.

Handsch, Georg, 432 n.

Hangchow, 406

Hanno (elephant of Rome), 124, 126, 168, 215

Harff, Arnold von, 503

Hargen, Splinter van, 21

Hartlieb, Johann, 98

Harvey, Gabriel, 71

Hautesville, Jean de, 107

Hawes, Stephen, 376 n.

Hayton, prince of Armenia, 307; in English, 362, 378

Hayyan Jabir, ibn (Geber),' 427

Hebrew language, 515, 542; characters, 510; as mother of all languages, 509, 519; study of in Europe, 507. *See also* Language; Linguistics

Hecataeus of Miletus, 86 n.

Hedio, Caspar, 19

Heidelberg, 98 n.

Heinrich, Nicolas, 343 n.

Heinsius, Daniel, 358

Heliodorus: in English, 371

Helmont, J. B. van, 423 n.

Henriques, Henrique, 496; and Tamil, 495

Index

Index

Mace, 429

Macer, Jean, *270–73*, 278, 321, 322, 357 n.; humor of, 272; "philosophe" of sixteenth century, 273; sources, 270, 271; *Les trois livres de l'histoire des Indes*, 270

Machado, Simão, 137

Machiavelli, Niccolo, 199; and Botero, 237, 240; and Possevino, 234

Madagascar: on Cantino map, 451

Madrid, 34, 185

Madruzzo, Cristoforo, 26 n., 525

Maerlant, Jacob van, 93 n., 352

Maffei, G. B., 37, 192, 217, 235, 242, 244, 245, 285, 296, 371, 372, 481, 538; on Chinese books, 530; on Chinese ideographs, 530; on Portuguese, 420; *Rerum a Societate Jesu in Oriente*, 280

Magdeburg, 346

Magellan, Ferdinand, 168, 170–71, 302; Le Roy on, 311; portrait, 305

Maggi (May Plays of Tuscany), 103

Magic. *See* Occultism

Magnabotti, Andrea de', 205; and geographical terms, 114; *Guerrino il Meschino*, 114

Magnus, Albertus, 95

Magnus, John, 18

Mahābhārata, 86, 107, 113, 205

Malabar, 127, 154; languages of, 516, 539, 541

Malacca, 58, 120, 132, 152, 167, 349; in Franck's *Weltbuch*, 337; maps of, 464; in Vespucci, 335

Malay language, 200, 229, 541; in Arabic script, 492 n.; in China, 493; as "language of Malacca," 494; letters in, 492–93; of Pigafetta, 494; universal language of East Indies, 529; vocabularies, 493

Malay peninsula: on Cantino map, 451

Malaya: De Thou on, 318; tin coinage of, 406

Malayālam language, 541; and More's alphabet, 531; script, 531; vocabularies, 493

Malayo-Polynesian group: vocabularies, 493

Mallart, Jean, 259

Mandeville, John, 42, 114, 202, 264 n., 390, 447; alphabets of, 530; and circumnavigation, 206; in Dutch, 353; in England, 381, 387; in English, 362, 368, 371; and Euphuists, 391; in German, 330; in Germanic Europe, 325; and Protestants, 331, 389; Purchas on, 386; satirized, 331, 385; in Spanish, 165; as *Volksbuch*, 331

Manicheans: and Indian and Buddhist beliefs, 89

Manila, 386

Mantua, 197, 220

Manuel I, king of Portugal, 6, 26, 121, 145, 162, 167; and Camoëns, 150; and cartography, 461; court of, 16; Javanese map, 483; letter to Pope Julius II (1508), 277; letter to Pope Leo X (1514), 56, 58; letters of, 6, 46, 72; library of,

43; tapestry of, 36, 124; and Thevet, 305. *See also* Portugal

Manuel, Don Juan, 104, 163

Mapheo, Maphei de: garden of, 432

Maps, 72; of Agnese, 58; at Ambras, 56; of Apian, 460; and Ariosto, 205; of Asia, 284, 457, 462, 464, 466, 467 n., 468, 476; atlas, 448, 475, 476–77; of Caneiro, 452; Cantino planisphere of 1502, 206, 451; *Carta marina* of 1516, 455; and censorship, 41; of China, 54, 402, 450, 464, 466, 468, 475, 483, 538; commerce in, 475–76, 487; of Contarini, 452, 457; convergence of meridians, 461; cordiform projections, 454, 455, 460; of *Cosmographiae introductio* (1507), 454; as cosmographies, 485; of Danti, 52; decorative, 477; decorative devices on, 485; double cordiform projection, 461 n., 465; of Gastaldi, 51, 200–201, 212; graduated into latitudes, 451; of *Gyogi* type, 483; historical, 469; Homem's planisphere of 1554, 463; illustrations on, 455, 457, 460, 461, 462; of Japan, 52, 464, 468, 483; Javanese, 419, 483; King-Hamy planisphere (1504?), 452; of Korea, 464, 484; legends, 455, 457, 461, 484, 485; Lisbon planisphere of 1545, 462; the loxodromic curve, 420; and Marlowe's *Tamburlaine*, 379; medieval, 447–48; Mercator projection, 466, 470; Mercator's world map of 1538, 465, 470; of mission stations, 484; of the Moluccas, 207 n.; and More's *Utopia*, 364; of Münster, 340; nautical charts, 470; and navigational. techniques, 450; oceanic, 460; of Ortelius, 468–69; *padrão* of Lisbon, 206, 462; on palm leaves, 483; as pictorial statements, 449; Plancius' world map, 470; planispheres, 206, 451, 458, 460; portolan, 450; of pre-printing era, 447; projections, 448, 455, 461 n., 465, 466, 470; as prototypes, 452, 454; Ptolemaic, 448–49; rhumb lines on, 461, 466; of Ribeiro, 458; in Shakespeare, 382; of the southern continent, 458, 461, 473; stereotypes, 485; tables of latitudes, 461; in Thevet, 304; wall, 463, 464; and woodcuts, 484, 485; of Waldseemüller, 454–55; world, 455, 460, 465, 470. *See also* Cartography; Geography

Marathi language: Stevens on, 529 n.

Marcellus II, pope. *See* Cervini, Marcello

Margaret of Austria, archduchess, 16, 423

Margaret of Navarre, 33, 253, 286; and Parmentier, 258

Mariana, Juan de: *Historia*, 191, 192

Marinix, Philips van: library of, 63–64

Marlowe, Christopher, 388, 391; anachronism in, 378–79; circle of, 380; and circumnavigation, 379; *Doctor Faustus*, 380; and religion, 380; *Tamburlaine*, 378–80

Marot, Jean, 254, 257

[753]

Index

Marshe, Thomas, 371
Martellus, Henricus: maps of, 450
Martins, Inácio, 32
Mártires, Bartolomeu dos, 10
Martyr, Peter (Pietro Martire d'Anghiera), 23, 46, 142, *169–71*, 172, 175, 200, 228, 230, 237, 458; in English, 370; and exotic plants, 435; in French, 256
Mary, queen of England, 369, 471
Mascarenhas, Pedro de, 9, 15, 127
Masius, Andreas, 64
Massys, Quentin, 486
Mateus, Pedro, 133
Mathematics: algebra, 407; algorism, 399, 407; applied, 408, 409, 410; Arabic works on, 407; in astronomy, 408; and cartography, 453; decimal fractions, 414; the decimal system, 399; and geography, 472; *ghubar* numerals, 407 n.; in India, 398, 399; intuition in, 398 n.; in navigation, 408; Pascal triangle, 408; symbols of, 409; techniques, 409; trigonometry, 408; in universities, 409
Matthias, archduke of Austria, 349
Mattioli, Pietro Andrea Gregorio, *431–33*, 435, 442; collections of plant specimens, 432; on Dioscorides, 431–32; and Lusitano, 431; portraits of Asian plants, 432. *See also* Botany
Maurice of Nassau, 402
Maximilian, duke of Bavaria, 350
Maximilian I, emperor, 55
Maximilian II, emperor, 55
Maximilian of Transylvania, 171, 272 n., 343, 459, 465, 538; and Agrippa, 423
Mayer, Johannes, 350
Medici, Catherine de': library of, 65
Medici, Cosimo I de', 52; and cartography, 463
Medici, Fernando de', 514; printing in Oriental languages, 527
Medici, Francesco I de', 52; and plants of East, 438
Medici, Giulio de', 166
Medici, Marie de', queen of France, 291
Medici family: collections, 52; and Jovius, 225
Medicine: Arabic writings on, 427; and Asian plants, 442; chemical drugs, 425; of Egypt, 439; Fracastoro on syphilis, 201; in India, 208; and Jews, 9, 430; metals as remedies, 424–25; Paracelsian and Oriental, 424–25; Salneritan, 427. *See also* Botany
Medina, Pedro de, 173, 218, *420–21*, 444
Megasthenes, 88, 90, 95
Megiser, Hieronymous, 331; and Asian languages, 517; *Thesaurus polyglottus* (1603), 516–17; as translator of travel books, 516
Mekong River, 156
Mela, Pomponius, 46, 89, 479, 481
Melanchthon, Philip, 99, 347
Mendes, António, 31

Mendoza, Juan González de. *See* González de Mendoza, Juan
Mendoza, Diego Hurtado di, 210; library of, 51, 60
Meneses, João de, 119
Mercator, Gerard, 198 n., 356, *465–66*, 470, 471, 476, 480; atlas of, 466, 467; celestial globes of, 412; and censorship, 42; correspondence, 467; library of, 64–65; and Ortelius, 468; and Ptolemy, 449, 456; and southern continent, 466; world map of, 466. *See also* Cartography; Geography; Ortelius, Abraham
Mercator, Rumoldus, 65 n.
Mesquita, Diego de, 497
Metals: "calay," 426; confusion over names, 426–27; *pai-t'ung* or "white copper," 422; properties, 426; "tutenag," 426; zinc, 425
Metempsychosis, 86, 107
Mexía, Pedro, 387; in English, 371, 378; in French, 286; *Silva de varia lección*, 173–74
Mexico: and ginger, 442
Meyerpeck, Wolfgang, 431
Michelangelo, 9
Middle Ages: bestiaries, 90; cartography of, 446, 447–48; and linguistic theory, 502; and Oriental tales, 110; popular conception of India, 96; public preaching, 110; and romance of Alexander, 94–95; sermon books, 110; technology of, 397–400. *See also* literature
Middleburg, 359
"Mien" (India), 283 n.
Milan: Ambrosian library, 52, 54; Spanish-dominated society of, 211 n.
Miltitz, Bernhard von, 329
Mineralogy: of Agricola, 426
Mirandola, Pico della, 115, 142, 279
Modena, 206; and Este library, 49 n.
Molina, Luis de, 37
Molina, Tiro de, 134
Moluccas, 151, 170, 193, 272 n., 285, 305, 310; conflict over, 33–34, 45, 169, 458; De Thou on, 318; literature on, 45; map of, 470; northern voyage to, 361, 367; placement, 458–59; Spanish in, 169
Molyneux, Emery, 474
Momos (mummeries), 122–23, 127
Monachus, Franciscus, 465
Monardes, Nicolas, 48, 179, 433 n., 435, 440
Mongols, 96; Boemus on, 336; invasions of, 232. *See also* Tartars
Montaigne, Michel, 12, 265, *292–97*, 320; on barbarism, 322; and Charron, 297–98; on China, 297; on color, 295; comparisons in, 301; curiosity of, 293; *Essais* (1580), 293; *Essais* (1588), 294; *Journal*, 293; library of, 67, 294–95; in Paris, 296; and prodigy literature, 288; on Osório, 145, 296; relativism of, 295, 301; skepticism of, 293, 301, 322; and

[754]

Index

Priuli, Lorenzo de, 171
Protestantism, 62, 395; and diversity of languages, 508 n.; of Du Bartas, 280–81; in England, 368; and history, 347; and geography, 480, 487; and Japanese mission, 347; and Jesuits, 344–45, 350; mission interests of, 347; in Netherlands, 355; opposition to Mandeville, 331; and overseas discoveries, 302, 324, 391; "reformed" *Lucidarius*, 338; of Hans Sachs, 342
"Pseudo-Callisthenes": "A" version, 92; Arabic version of, 93; and Isaac Casaubon, 91 n.; as a source, 93
Ptolemy, 43, 72, 232, 446; Asian place names, 459; and cartography, 448–49, 487; geographical ideas of, 448, 456; *Geography*, 452; in Germany, 452–53; portrait of, 460; revisions of *Geography*, 334, 335, 339, 351, 452, 454, 455, 462, 464, 465, 467, 478, 487; text of *Geography*, 454; translations of *Geography*, 456. *See also* Cartography; Geography; Ortelius, Abraham
Pulci, Luigi, 104 n., 115
Punicale (India), 496
Purchas, Samuel, 386
Puttenham, George, 372, *375–77*, 388, 391
Pynson, Richard, 362 n.
Pythagoras: and Indian ideas, 407, 407 n.

Quackelbeen, Wilhelm, 432
Quad, Matthias, 346 n., 477
Qualichius di Spoleto, 97
Quilon: printing at, 496
"Quinsay," 472

Rabelais, François, 254, *259–66*, 273, 321, 323; Abbey of Thélème, 261–62, 264; anagrams of, 261; and Asian names, 531; and censorship, 259; on education, 261; and exoticism, 264, 531 n.; geographical knowledge, 260; and hearsay, 264; on hieroglyphs, 531 n.; on history, 319; and Thomas More, 260; and occultism, 260, 262; "Pantagruelion," 262; and Portuguese "discovery" of Japan, 266; as publicist, 263; scholarship on, 260 n.; sources, 66, 260, 264. See also *Gargantua and Pantagruel*
Rada, Mârtin de, 182, 221 n., 239 n., 500
Raimondo, Giovan Battista, 528
Raleigh, Walter, Sir, 357 n., 378, 386, 388, 390, 391, 404 n., 472
Rāmāyana, 113, 265 n.
Ramusio, Giovanni Battista, 51, 171, 200, 201, 210, 211, 222, 227 n., 230, 233 n., 237, 389, 430, 536; and cartography, 462; in French, 274
Rastell, John, 366, 387, 390, 391
Rastell, William, 368 n.
Recorde, Robert, 370

Redoer, Mathurin de, 255
Reformation. *See* Protestantism
Regensburg, 326
Regiomontanus, 409, 411, 479; criticism of Ptolemy, 453
Reinel, Pedro, 452
Reisch, Gregor, 366 n., 453
Relativism: and Christianity, 299, 301; in English literature, 385; in French literature, 273, 297–99; in geographical sciences, 488–89
Rem, Lucas: painting of, 486
Renaissance: and Antiquity, 310; and Barlaam legend, 104–5; in France, 253–54; gardens, 441; scholarship of, 395
René II, duke of Lorraine, 334, 454, 478
Rescius, Rutger, 19, 25
Resende, André de, 9, 15, 19, 26, 28, 31, 135, 135 n., 192, 355
Resende, Garcia de, 118, 119, 120, 122, 125, 142, 149; *Miscellanea* of, 126–27
Reuchlin, Johann, 324
Rheanus, Beatus, 60, 339
Rheticus, Georg Joachim, 409
Rhinoceros, 16, 184, 231, 262, 288, 342, 532 n.; Dürer's woodcut of, 265
Rhubarb, 231, 337; in France, 442
Ribadeneira, Marcelo de, 192
Ribadeneira, Pedro de, 190
Ribeiro, Diogo, 478; map of, 462; translation of *Book* of Duarte Barbosa, 458
Ricci, Matteo, 188, 237, 488; and censorship, 41; and Chinese calendar, 415; and geography, 480; at Roman College, 409
Rice: cultivated in Europe, 441
Richeôme, Louis, 481
Ridolfi, Niccolò, cardinal, 53
Ringmann, Matthias, 334, 454
Rio, Martin Antoine del, 359, 391
Rivey, Pierre de la, 106
Rivers, Earl, 93
Rivière, Pierre de, 363 n.
Rocca, Angelo, 499 n., 515; and Ruggiero, 528
Rodrigues, Francisco, 483
Rodrigues, Miguel, 25 n.
Rodrigues, Simão, 11, 25
Rodriguez, João: Japanese vocabularies and grammars of, 499–500
Rogers, Daniel, 472
Rojas, Fernando de, 163
Rollenhagen, Gabriel, 347 n.; on Alexander, 99
Rollenhagen, Georg, 346–47
Román, Jerónimo: on Asia, 189–90; and censorship, 42; and Mendoza, 189
Romances, 113–15, 210–12; Arrivabene's *Il magno Vitei*, 220–23; Asia in, 163, 208; and Boiardo, 202; censorship of, 178; and Jesuit letterbooks, 212; Linschoten on, 360; Oviedo on, 172; and *Song of Roland*, 202; in Spain,